SAINTS

DAWN MARIE BEUTNER

SAINTS

Becoming an Image of Christ Every Day of the Year

IGNATIUS PRESS   SAN FRANCISCO

Cover art Duncan 1890, iStockphoto.com

Cover design by Riz Boncan Marsella

© 2020 by Ignatius Press, San Francisco
All rights reserved
ISBN 978-1-62164-341-8 (PB)
ISBN 978-1-64229-115-5 (eBook)
Library of Congress Control Number 2019947889
Printed in the United States of America ∞

CONTENTS

CHART OF CALENDARS

S: Solemnity   **F:** Feast   **M:** Memorial   **OM:** Optional Memorial

Calendar of Saints and Blesseds on the Official Calendar 35

Calendar of Marian Dates   483

PREFACE

It all started with Saint Athanasius.

I was sitting in my apartment, a relatively new convert to Catholicism from atheism, reading a book. I already loved the Mass, and I had decided to start my new life as a Catholic by reading and praying the daily and Sunday Mass readings. But then I found a book about saints. Specifically, I found *Butler's Lives of the Saints: Concise Edition, Revised and Updated*. The Reverend Alban Butler's original *Lives of the Saints* from the eighteenth century was not one book of saints' biographies, but four volumes long. The modern version I had found condensed his four books into one and added some biographies of recently canonized saints. For someone who knew absolutely nothing about Catholic saints, reading about one saint per day seemed the perfect addition to my daily prayer life.

So there I was, trying to pray, when the book introduced me to someone I had never heard of before: Saint Athanasius of Alexandria. The first part of his biography seemed unremarkable, but then I read how this bishop from the fourth century was sent into exile for refusing to capitulate about a heretical teaching. More specifically, he was sent into exile not once, but five times. A personal realization brought me to a complete stop at that moment. I realized that if I had been in Athanasius' position, unlike him, I would have given up. If the emperor considered me a criminal, public leaders ridiculed me, most people shunned me, and the government forced me to live in the wilderness, in constant danger for my life, what could possibly give me the strength to keep going? Why not become a hermit? Write books? Take up gardening? What was it that made Athanasius keep teaching the truth and not give up? How did he manage to persevere when practically everyone wanted him dead?

That's when I realized that becoming a saint wasn't the painless, ethereal experience that saints' statues and glowing hagiographies seemed to imply. While I had sometimes found it hard to relate to Jesus' world of tax collectors, Jewish holy days, and the geography of the Holy Land, I could often relate to the difficulties described in the biographies of the saints. There's a reason that practically every Catholic mother has a devotion to Saint Monica. Even if none of your children are fallen-away Catholics or living in an immoral situation, what mom can't relate with her years of suffering? Did she agonize in private with her friends over whether it was appropriate even to go visit her son Augustine because he was living in sin with his girlfriend and had abandoned the faith? Did she blame herself for not being the perfect Catholic mom when he was small? Like all saints, many of Saint Monica's daily challenges are not very different from my own, and learning about how she faced them as a Catholic not only gives me hope, but it gives me ideas.

I read my copy of *Butler's Lives of the Saints* until the spine broke and I had to buy another copy. By then I had noticed what was for me a serious problem: it's a "concise edition", which means it omits many great saints. So I found other saints' books and resources and tried to piece together a short reading about a saint each morning from multiple sources. Unfortunately, this was not a very convenient solution every morning when I was only half-awake.

Since I was working as a technical writer at this point, I eventually started writing my own collection of saints—that is, I not only added information about new saints, but I rewrote the saints' biographies so that they would help me pray. While we can read individual biographies to learn about saints in depth, we also need collections of saints to help us talk to God about our own seemingly insurmountable struggles.

The Church recognizes saints, in part, to honor them for their lives, devotion, and personal sacrifices. But the Church also recognizes saints to encourage us to become one. May the lives of the saints be for you, as they are for me, a daily reminder that God desires us all to be holy.

INTRODUCTION

There are many great books about the saints available today. However, this book is designed to be *prayed with*, rather than simply *read*. Why?

The saints are most helpful spiritually when we can imagine ourselves in *their* situations. There are many resources that list only the most basic information about the saint. There are also resources that provide information about a saint's entire life, personality, experiences, and theology. It is difficult for the former to inspire us to deep personal sacrifice, and the latter would be impossible to read before breakfast. The biographies in this book aim for the golden mean between those two extremes.

The language used to describe saints' lives also matters. Some older biographies use phrases that sound awkward to modern ears, and some modern biographies have been modernized to the point of fluffiness. Once again, this book attempts to find the mean between the two. There are many passages in which I believe *Butler's Lives of the Saints* describes the situation or person pricelessly, so those passages are included.

Another area of confusion involves the calendar itself. When the Second Vatican Council introduced changes to the liturgical calendar, these changes primarily affected our liturgical commemoration of the saints in two ways: (1) some saints' dates were changed, and (2) some saints' days were removed from the liturgical calendar entirely. Regardless of your position on the spectrum of attitudes toward the changes resulting from Vatican II, it's clear that a laudable goal of this reform was to ensure that each Mass is focused on Jesus Christ and the Gospel readings, rather than falling into an overemphasis of individual saints. However, the list of saints recognized by the Church and the saints in the liturgical calendar are two different things: the former can be used in many contexts outside Mass, and the latter is designed as an aid to worship God during the liturgy. Thousands of men and women have lived lives of such holiness that other Catholics should remember them, call upon their intercession, and try to live like them, any day of the year, any time of the day. That's one of the reasons that the Church has developed a list of saints in the first place and the reason for this book. On the other hand, it makes sense to remember certain specific saints annually *during the liturgy* because of their important contributions to the Body of Christ. The fact that certain saints are no longer on the liturgical calendar does not mean that we should forget them.

The main body of this book is a daily collection of saints and blesseds arranged by date, as given in the Church's latest official list of saints, the 2004 *Martyrologium Romanum*.[1] Those who have been proclaimed saints and blesseds by a pope since 2004 are also included.

---

[1] *Martyrologium Romanum*, Editio Altera (Libreria Editrice Vaticana, 2004).

The date listed for every saint in this book either follows the *Martyrologium Romanum* of 2004 or, when no such date is available, the date of death of that saint (his "birthday" into Heaven) or the date traditionally associated with that saint. Note that if you consult an older collection of saints that follows a previous version of the *Martyrologium Romanum*—the first version was created in 1583, and there have been many revisions since—the date given for a particular saint may differ.

Another important consideration in developing this book of saints involved the decision about which of the thousands of saints in the Church's calendar to include and (sadly) which to omit.

Our Blessed Mother, the greatest of all the saints, is celebrated by the Church somewhere in the world almost every day of the year, sometimes because of an important event in her earthly life, sometimes because of a Church-approved apparition, or sometimes because of a Church teaching or a local devotion. The main calendar in this book contains the solemnities, feasts, and memorials of the Blessed Virgin Mary that are listed in the *Martyrologium Romanum* of 2004; the supplemental calendar lists some of the other important dates for our Blessed Mother.

Sadly, our culture today would like to believe that every pope of the Catholic Church was power-hungry, weak, and unfaithful to his vow of chastity. To counter that false belief, all the men who have served the Church as pope and who are acknowledged by the Church for their holiness have been included in this collection.

Another group of holy men and women we commonly overlook come from our "elder brothers", the Jewish people. The Church has commemorated great figures from the Old Testament in the *Martyrologium Romanum* for hundreds of years. Remembering the great Jewish prophets—who predicted the coming of the Messiah—during December, for example, is spiritually helpful.

Direct quotations are also useful. For some individuals who lived during the time period of the Old and New Testaments, relevant Scripture quotes are included in this collection. Some saints, particularly the Doctors of the Church, are noted for their outstanding ability to explain our faith; short quotes from these saints or memorable prayers are included because their actual words can sometimes help us understand their holiness even better than their biographies.

Because the lives of the saints included in this book cover thousands of years and every continent, some assumptions had to be made about dates and spelling. For many saints—even up to the twentieth century—we're not always certain what year they were born or even the year that they died. The most widely accepted dates have been included to help the reader mentally situate the person in a particular time frame. Multiple names and spellings are also included where it might be difficult to identify a given saint. Because this book is written in English, English versions of names have been used, except where a saint has been become well known by his native name (e.g., Saint Pier Giorgio Frassati, rather than the anglicized version, Saint Peter George Frassati). Depending on the time period, the names shown in parentheses may be alternate spellings due to language differences or names given at birth, as opposed to names chosen in religious life.

A short statement must be made about miracles: they happen. While some of the miraculous stories included in this book may cause twenty-first-century readers to roll their eyes, we must remember that our Savior performed some amazing miracles Himself, culminating in His Resurrection from the dead. Miracles have accompanied some modern saints' lives—see, for example, Saint Pio of Pietrelcina—even with TV cameras rolling.

As much as possible, the biographies in this collection are brief so that you can read about a few saints in a day. Supplemental appendices provide additional details.

- Appendix 1: Calendar of Marian Dates. The main calendar of this book includes all of the Marian dates that are present in the *Martyrologium Romanum* of 2004. But there are memorials that are widely celebrated that have been omitted from the *Martyrologium Romanum* and they are included in this section.

- Appendix 2: Correspondence of the 1962 Roman Missal to the 2004 *Martyrologium Romanum*. For those who attend the Extraordinary Form (Latin) Mass, a chart is included that lists the saints' names as given in the Roman Missal of 1962 and the corresponding saints' names as given in the *Martyrologium Romanum*.

- Appendix 3: Frequently Asked Questions. Common questions about terms used by the Church are explained, such as the differences between a "saint" and a "blessed".

- Appendix 4: Catholic Church Terminology. Definitions are provided for less-familiar Catholic terms (e.g., solemnity).

- Appendix 5: Heresies or Theological Complexities. Brief explanations are given of heretical teachings and how they endangered the practice of the Catholic faith in individual lives.

- Appendix 6: Times of Anti-Catholic Persecution. In order to help the reader understand why there are so many groups of martyrs in particular times and places and where it was particularly dangerous to be a Catholic, a chart is provided that lists the centuries, locations, and causes of some major persecutions.

Finally, because this book is intended as a devotional aid, there's a short intercessory prayer to every saint (or group of saints) each day. Note that God is ultimately the source of all wisdom, strength, grace—everything—but we can ask the saints for help in emulating their virtues, as well as avoiding their mistakes. Feel free to ignore these short prayers and add your own petitions if you prefer. But pray. Praying daily with saints' lives helps us to want to become like them, because they are images of Jesus Christ.

Daily Calendar of Saints and Blesseds

Introduction to the Daily Calendar of Saints and Blesseds

As previously mentioned in the main introduction, the following calendar includes only those saints and blesseds found in the *Martyrologium Romanum*[1] with the addition of those holy men and women who have been named saints and blesseds by a pope since that edition was issued. The *Martyrologium Romanum*, which is currently available only in Latin, contains anywhere from a half dozen to more than a dozen entries for every day of the year. Since this book is designed to be a devotional aid used on a daily basis, this book lists only a representative sample of those saints, those that will (God willing) be most helpful in encouraging us to follow in their footsteps and also become saints.

Every day in this collection includes entries for *at least two saints*. Why? Because of the martyrs. Although starting your day with the story of someone's beheading may sound gruesome, in reality, it grounds you. When I realized that the Church celebrates the death of a martyr (or sometimes large groups of martyrs) almost every single day,[2] I realized it was a good, humbling lesson for me to remember, every single day, that many people have died for the faith that I so often take for granted. Also, we Catholics have the happy problem that multiple saints with inspirational life stories are occasionally commemorated on the same date. Why overlook Saint Christopher just because he shares July 25 with Saint James the Greater?

Note that the order of names for each day follows the *Martyrologium Romanum*. That is, solemnities, feasts, memorials, and optional memorials are listed first (in that order) on a given day, followed by all the saints commemorated that day, generally in chronological order. Also, all solemnities, feasts, memorials, and optional memorials of saints that are noted in the Daily Roman Missal[3] are included in this collection, along with a few other saints honored on that date. However, note that this book is a collection of saints, not a liturgical book. For important dates in the liturgical calendar that are not associated with a saint or group of saints, particularly moveable dates such as Easter, please consult the appropriate liturgical book or Church calendar. The memorials and optional memorials from the liturgical calendar published by the USCCB (United States

---

[1] *Martyrologium Romanum*, Editio Altera (Libreria Editrice Vaticana, 2004).

[2] According to the *Martyrologium Romanum*, there are only three days of the year where no Catholic martyrs are explicitly listed and remembered.

[3] *Daily Roman Missal: According to the Roman Missal, Third Edition*, 7th ed., ed. Rev. James Socias (Downers Grove, Ill.: Midwest Theological Forum, 2011).

Conference of Catholic Bishops) have been footnoted.[4] Other nation's conferences also have additions and changes to their liturgical calendars to emphasize their own native saints.

If you have questions about Church terminology while reading these biographies, see the detailed appendices at the end of this book.

[4] The calendar, officially published as the *Liturgical Calendar for the Dioceses of the United States of America*, is based on the General Roman Calendar and the Proper Calendar for the Dioceses of the United States of America. Links to the most recent liturgical calendars can be found on the USCCB's website.

January

January 1

The Blessed Virgin Mary, Mother of God, Solemnity

According to Ludwig Ott, "The dogma of Mary's motherhood of God contains two truths: a) Mary is truly a *mother*, that is, she contributed everything to the formation of the human nature of Christ, that every other mother contributes to the formation of the fruit of her body; b) Mary is truly the Mother of God, that is, she conceived and bore the Second Person of the Divinity, not indeed according to the Divine Nature, but according to the assumed human nature."[1]

And as stated by Saint Louis de Montfort, "It was through the most holy Virgin Mary that Jesus came into the world, and it is also through her that He has to reign in the world."[2]

Saint Odilo of Cluny

Odilo was born in 962 into a noble family in Avergne, France. When he was a child, he was miraculously cured of a serious illness by praying to the Virgin Mary, which deepened his devotion to her. He chose to become a monk at the monastery of Cluny, and he later became the abbot, an office he held for fifty years. In response to the widespread and ongoing violence of the times in Europe, he promoted the "Truce of God", a practice that suspended military hostilities for ostensibly religious reasons, allowing trade so that ordinary people could survive and guaranteeing sanctuary to those who sought refuge in churches. During a famine, he sold church property to feed the poor; to commemorate all the faithful departed, he instituted All Souls' Day. The great reformer bishop Saint Peter Damian personally pressed for the cause of Odilo's canonization after he died by natural causes in 1049.

Saint Joseph Mary Tommasi

As *Butler's Lives of the Saints* explains, "By the canonization of Cardinal Joseph Mary Tommasi, the Church may be said to have set the seal upon the principle that neither profound learning nor the critical spirit of accurate scholarship nor independence of judgment, as long as it is kept in check by regard for dogmatic truth, are inconsistent with the highest sanctity."[3] Joseph was born in 1649 and

---

[1] Ludwig Ott, *Fundamentals of Catholic Dogma* (Oil City, Pa.: Baronius Press, 2018), 212.

[2] Louis de Montfort, *True Devotion to the Blessed Virgin with Preparation for Total Consecration*, trans. Fr. Frederick Faber, D.D. (Charlotte, N.C.: TAN Books, 2010), no. 1.

[3] Michael Walsh, ed., *Butler's Lives of the Saints, Concise Edition, Revised and Updated* (San Francisco: HarperCollins Publishers, 1991), 3.

came from a devout family in Sicily; four sisters and his mother all eventually entered religious life, and his father wanted to pass on his position to Joseph and enter religious life too. But Joseph didn't want a worldly life—he wanted to enter the Theatine order. His father agreed to remain in the world instead, and Joseph pursued the priesthood. While Joseph was studying Eastern languages, he had a Jewish teacher whom he eventually brought to the Catholic faith. When he became a priest, God blessed Joseph with an abiding presence of His love, which strengthened him during his frequent bouts of bad health. He lived austerely, though he recommended moderation to those under his direction. Joseph later became confessor to Giovanni Cardinal Albani, and when Albani was chosen to be pope, Joseph told him that it would be a mortal sin to fail to accept. When Albani followed Joseph's counsel and became Pope Clement XI, he said, "What Tommasi did to us, we will do to him,"[4] and made him a cardinal. However, Joseph was able to refuse the honor for a long time, serving the Church with his intellectual gifts instead. Eventually, he was made a cardinal, but he told others, "Well! It will only be for a few months."[5] As he had predicted, he died within a year in 1713.

Blessed Marian Konopinski

Marian was born in 1907 in Kluczewo, Poland. He became a priest as well as the vicar general of the Archdiocese of Poznan and the chaplain of the Congregation of the Holy Archangels. When Germany invaded Poland in 1939, he was arrested, along with many other Polish priests, and sent to the Dachau concentration camp. There he encouraged and helped other prisoners, saying the Rosary daily. In the end, when his health deteriorated, he was used by the Nazis for medical experimentation, which killed him. He died in 1943.

> *Blessed Mother, be a mother to me.*
> *Saint Odilo, show me how to bring holiness to the problems of the world today.*
> *Saint Joseph, help me hunger to be absorbed in the love of God.*
> *Blessed Marian, help me to look to God's kingdom,*
> *not this one, for encouragement in difficulties.*

* * * * *

January 2

Saint Basil the Great, Memorial

Basil was born in 328 into a devout Christian family in the region formerly known as Caesarea, now in modern Turkey. While he was a young man studying at the University of Athens, he met a Christian man named Gregory from the city of Nazianzus (Gregory also became a saint; see below). The two men

---

[4] Ibid., 4.
[5] Ibid.

became great friends. Basil was a natural leader, a brilliant thinker, and deeply devout; Gregory later recounted how Basil's holy example and strong leadership inspired those around them. Basil eventually left the city to live an ascetic life in solitude, which in time led him to establish a monastery at Pontus. His personal experience, writings, and example shaped monastic life for centuries. He was later consecrated archbishop. He was an excellent administrator, a strong leader, and an orthodox teacher. His eloquent words and powerful writings were very influential in the discussions of theological questions of the day, particularly the widespread Arian heresy. Though he suffered from a long illness at the end of his life, he died unexpectedly in 379; many people mourned. Known to Catholic history as the father of Eastern monasticism and a Father of the Church, the Church also recognized him for his highly influential writings about Church doctrine by naming him a Doctor of the Church.

Just as when a sunbeam falls on bright and transparent bodies, they themselves become brilliant too, and shed forth a fresh brightness from themselves, so souls wherein the Spirit dwells, illuminated by the Spirit, themselves become spiritual, and send forth their grace to others.[6]

Saint Gregory of Nazianzus (Gregory Nazianzen), Memorial

Gregory was born in 330 into a devout Christian family in the region of Caesarea (modern Turkey). He studied at the University of Athens and met Saint Basil, but then he recognized God's call to return home and care for his elderly father, who was the bishop of Nazianzus. While Gregory was later convinced to accept ordination as a bishop, he hated the pomp associated with the position and was too much of a poet to enjoy handling the politics involved, so he resigned. He spent the rest of his life living quietly and bringing many people to the faith through his excellent preaching. Though Gregory didn't write long commentaries, as did some Fathers of the Church, he did write hundreds of poems, letters, and sermons, and in these short writings, he cleared up controversies so effectively that he became known as Gregory the Theologian. A symbol of orthodoxy during his own lifetime and long considered a Father of the Church, the Church also named him a Doctor of the Church.

Always be revolving, in speech and in your mind, / upon the words of God: for God gave this / to be a prize for labors, a little light for seeing, / something hidden; or else, to be a blessing, / that by the holy God's great laws you might be pierced; / or, third, that by these cares you might withdraw your mind from earthly things.[7]

Saint Telesphorus

Telesphorus (d. 139) was the eighth pope; he reigned for ten years. His liturgical decisions are still with us today: he attempted to unify the celebration of Easter in all churches to Sundays (as opposed to dates following a lunar calendar), started

[6] Basil the Great, *On the Holy Spirit* 9.23, trans. Bloomfield Jackson, in *Nicene and Post-Nicene Fathers*, 2nd series, vol. 8, ed. Philip Schaff and Henry Wace (Buffalo, N.Y.: Christian Literature Publishing, 1895). Revised and edited for New Advent by Kevin Knight, NewAdvent.org, accessed September 9, 2019, http://www.newadvent.org/fathers/3203.htm.

[7] Gregory of Nazianzus, *On God and Man: The Theological Poetry of St. Gregory of Nazianzus*, trans. Peter Gilbert (Crestwood, N.Y.: St. Vladimir's Seminary Press, 2001), 85.

the tradition of celebrating Midnight Mass on Christmas, and decided that the Gloria should be sung during Mass. Like many early popes living under the intermittent persecution of Christians during the time of the Roman Empire, he died a martyr for the faith.

> *Saints Basil and Gregory, beg the Lord to give me wisdom.*
> *Saint Telesphorus, teach me to love Christ and His Church.*

* * * * *

January 3

The Most Holy Name of Jesus, Optional Memorial

The name of Jesus has power.[8] So when we invoke our Lord's name with confidence in that power, He responds. For example, He consoles us in times of trial, He brings healing to our bodies and relationships, and He protects us against the devil. When we call on the name of Jesus, He gives us the graces we need both now and in eternity. The monogram that represents the Most Holy Name of Jesus and which is commonly found on crucifixes—IHS—is an abbreviation of IHESUS and was commonly used in medieval times.[9]

Saint Anterus

Anterus (d. 236) was born in the Calabria region of Italy and became the nineteenth pope. But nineteen days after he became pope, the Roman emperor Maximinus the Thracian ordered his execution. Anterus' death was one of many during the ensuing violent persecution of all Christians.

Saint Daniel of Padua

Daniel died during the persecution of the early Church by the Roman Empire; some traditions say this occurred in the year 168, while others say it happened in the year 304. In the eleventh century near a church in Padua, Italy, his remains were found under miraculous circumstances, and his relics were enshrined in that city on this date in the year 1064.

Saint Genevieve of Paris

Genevieve was born in 422 near Paris, France. From a very young age, she decided to give her life to God, and she became a nun when she was only fifteen years old. She was known to be a holy woman, and she was able, for

---

[8] See Phil 2:10.

[9] See Frederick Holweck, "Holy Name of Jesus", in *The Catholic Encyclopedia*, vol. 7 (New York: Robert Appleton, 1910). Edited for New Advent by Kevin Knight, NewAdvent.org, accessed September 9, 2019, http://www.newadvent.org/cathen/07421a.htm.

example, to read people's consciences and calm those who were possessed. She predicted invasions and disasters for Paris for some time, and, when those predictions came true, she led the repentant people of her city in prayer. She asked God to protect the city, but she also encouraged the people to be courageous and defend it from attackers. When food ran out in the city, she personally led an expedition to bring back food—and succeeded. She died in the year 500.

> *May the Holy Name of Jesus my Savior be my only consolation.*
> *Saint Anterus, help me to love Christ and His Church.*
> *Saint Daniel, show me how to live and die for Christ.*
> *Saint Genevieve, help me to remain close to God through prayer.*

* * * * *

January 4

Saint Angela of Foligno

Angela (1248–1309) was born outside the Catholic faith, married when she was young, and had several children. As she herself later stated, she lived an adulterous, sacrilegious life for many years. But in 1285, she received a vision from God and went through a profound conversion. After her mother, husband, and children all died, she began to live a life of penance as a Franciscan tertiary. In time, she received the gifts of visions and mystical prayer. She spent her whole life in Foligno, Italy, where she was well known for her patience and humility, and is regarded as a great spiritual writer.

> *Whoever has been able to obtain these most sweet gifts of God should know that he has reached consummation and perfection in the most sweet Lord Jesus Christ; and likewise, has become this most same sweet Lord Jesus Christ through transformation. The more one grows in these gifts, the more the being of the most sweet Jesus will grow in him.*[10]

Blessed Thomas Plumtree

Thomas was born in Lincolnshire, England. He became a priest and then became a rector in 1546. During an uprising against the repressive anti-Catholic measures of Queen Elizabeth, Thomas resigned from his office and went to serve as chaplain to the Catholic forces. When their revolt failed, he was arrested and charged with the crime of celebrating Mass. Though he was offered his freedom if he would give up his faith, he refused and was hanged, drawn, and quartered on this date in 1570 in Durham, England.

[10] Angela of Foligno, *Complete Works*, trans. Paul Lachance, O.F.M. (New York; Mahwah, N.J.: Paulist Press, 1993), 285.

Saint Elizabeth Bayley Seton, Memorial[11]

When Elizabeth (1774–1821) was young, her mother died; her father, a wealthy and respected doctor, later remarried. Elizabeth grew up in material comfort, but she also knew emotional upheaval, due to her father's absences, her father and stepmother's separation, and being sent to live with an uncle for a time. She was devout in her practice of the Protestantism in which she was raised, well educated for a young woman of her station, and part of the well-to-do New York society. She married into a wealthy family when she was twenty years old, and she and her husband had a happy marriage and five children. However, financial misfortunes struck her husband's business, and her husband died while in Italy seeking a cure for his health. There she began to learn about the Catholic faith. When she returned to America, she decided to become a Catholic, at which point her extended family completely abandoned her, leaving her poor, a widow, and alone. But with God's help, she began a school for children while caring for her own children, and female friends joined her as teachers. She eventually founded a religious community called the Daughters of Charity of Saint Joseph, a community that grew to include numerous houses and schools throughout the United States. Elizabeth died of natural causes on this date.

Saint Angela, teach me repentance.
Blessed Thomas, help me make personal sacrifices to lead others to Christ.
Saint Elizabeth, help me place the welfare of my family in God's hands.

* * * * *

January 5

Saint Deogratias of Carthage

Deogratias (d. 457) was a priest of Carthage (a city in modern Tunisia) when Genseric, king of the Vandals, controlled the city; he grudgingly allowed Deogratias to be named bishop of Carthage. When Genseric sacked Rome and brought back hundreds of captives to Carthage, Deogratias sold everything he could to ransom them, including gold and silver from the churches. The Arians of the city resented his leadership and even tried to kill him. After three years spent trying to feed and house innumerable, needy Christian families, he died.

Saint Edward the Confessor

Edward (1003–1066) was the son of the English king Ethered the Redeless, but when the Danes invaded England, he and his brother, Alfred, were sent to Normandy, France, for their safety. When Alfred returned to England in 1036, he was captured, mutilated, and killed under the orders of the English leader Earl Godwin. In 1042, English leaders asked Edward to return to his homeland and

---

[11] This saint is celebrated as a memorial in the *Liturgical Calendar for the Dioceses of the United States of America.*

become their king. So he did, and two years later, he married Edith, Godwin's daughter. It is said that they lived chastely as brother and sister, and there are many reasons for Edward to have made that decision—spiritual ones as well as concerns about his dangerous father-in-law. Edward faced continual opposition from Godwin, and at one point, he banished Godwin, his followers, and even Edith from his court. But neither side wanted a civil war, so Godwin was allowed to return to court several months later. Edward was a just and devout ruler, was kind to the poor, and supported monasteries. He loved hunting, but he was careful to make time for daily Mass even when he was away on hunting trips. After he had been king for some time, Edward explained to his council that he had made a private vow to go on a pilgrimage to Rome if God should be pleased to bring an end to the troubles of his family. The council told Edward that it would be unwise for him to leave the country—it could lead to political turmoil—so he asked the pope. The pope told Edward to give the money he would have spent on a pilgrimage to the poor and build or repair a monastery in honor of Saint Peter. Edward followed the pope's direction. He died soon after the church he had built was completed.

Blessed Jacques Ledoyen

Jacques (1761–1794) was a parish priest at Contigne, France, when the French Revolution began. On November 29, 1791, all priests were ordered to take an oath agreeing that bishops would be appointed by the local clergy rather than by the pope. Jacques escaped being ordered to take this false oath only by going into hiding. While hiding with another priest in the home of a Catholic widow, the home was raided, and the two priests fled. Jacques was captured. He was sentenced to death and guillotined on this date. Two other diocesan priests, Francis Peltier and Peter Tessier, died as martyrs with him. The woman and daughter who had sheltered him were executed three months later.

Saint John Nepomucene Neumann, Memorial[12]

Born and raised in Bohemia (now known as the Czech Republic), John (1811–1860) studied for the priesthood, but there were too many priests in that diocese already (!), so his bishop wouldn't ordain him. Since he had wanted to serve in the American missions anyway, John traveled to faraway Manhattan in America, where there was a great need for priests. He was immediately ordained and sent to serve in a rural area. He built himself a log cabin, slept little, and lived on bread and water. He walked miles from farm to farm and communicated with his flock through the twelve languages he was able to speak. He was attracted to the Redemptorist order, and he became the order's first member in the United States in 1840. He served as a home missionary throughout Maryland, Ohio, Pennsylvania, and Virginia, until he was ordained as bishop of Philadelphia in 1852. During his time as bishop, he ordered the building of fifty churches to serve his growing flock, started a cathedral, opened almost one hundred schools, and wrote numerous newspaper articles and two

---

[12] This saint is celebrated as a memorial in the *Liturgical Calendar for the Dioceses of the United States of America*.

catechisms to teach his people the faith. He was the first American man and American bishop to be canonized.

> *Saint Deogratias, show me how to spend my life for those in need.*
> *Saint Edward, teach me how to lead with humility.*
> *Blessed Jacques, show me how to live and die for Christ.*
> *Saint John, help me to think big in spreading the Gospel.*

* * * * *

January 6

The Epiphany of Our Lord, Solemnity[13]

Regarding the Epiphany, Saint Augustine wrote, "Recently we celebrated the day on which the Lord was born of the Jews; today we are celebrating the one on which he was worshipped by the Gentiles.... On that day the shepherds worshipped him, on this one the Magi. To those the message was brought by angels, to these by a star.... Thus it is that those hurrying up from nearby on the very day, and these arriving today from far away, marked two days to be celebrated by posterity, and yet both saw the one light of the world."[14]

Saints Julian and Basilissa of Antioch

During the persecution of the Church under the Roman emperor Diocletian in the early fourth century, Julian and Basilissa, husband and wife, were arrested for the crime of being Christians in the city of Antioch (now in Turkey). Many pious stories have been told over the centuries about the couple, but all we're certain about is that they chose martyrdom together, rather than unfaithfulness to Christ.

Saint Andrew Corsini

Andrew was born in 1301 into a noble Italian family but lived a wild life when he was a young man. His mother eventually brought him to repentance for his sins, and he decided to enter the Carmelites and become a priest. He rose to the position of superior general of the order in 1348 and was named bishop of Fiesole in 1349. As bishop, he served as a peacemaker between feuding Italian families, personally cared for those who were poor, and was known for gifts of miracles and prophecy. He died on this date in 1373.

Saint John de Ribera

John was born in 1532 to a noble family in Spain, and John eventually became a priest and archbishop of Valencia. He was both a zealous shepherd and a

---

[13] In the United States, this solemnity may be celebrated on the Sunday between January 2 and 8, instead of January 6.

[14] Augustine, *Sermon* 199, in *Essential Sermons* (Hyde Park, N.Y.: New City Press, 2007), 254.

scrupulously faithful one. But Spanish culture was troubled at the time with a widespread weakness in both faith and morals, and John found his position so demanding that at one point he tried to step down as archbishop. The pope refused to let him, so John obediently spent the next forty-two years of his life leading his people and trying to strengthen their faith. The dangerous political manueverings of the Moriscos (Jews who had converted to Christianity for cultural reasons and who secretly practiced the Jewish faith) were a scandal to faithful Catholics; to protect his flock, he led the effort that forced their deportation from Spain. He died soon afterward.

Saint André Bessette, Optional Memorial[15]

Andre was born in 1835 near Montreal, Canada, the son of a woodcutter and the eighth of twelve children. He was adopted by an uncle and was forced to go to work to support himself after his parents died, rather than attend school. He tried several occupations as a young man but was unsuccessful at all of them. At his first attempt to enter the Congregation of the Holy Cross, they rejected him because of his poor health. Fortunately, his bishop intervened, and Andre was allowed to enter, serving as doorkeeper, sacristan, laundry worker, and messenger in the house over the years, patiently and uncomplainingly. But he also spent most of each night in prayer, was known for his strong devotion to Saint Joseph, and had a special ministry to those who were sick. In time, so many people had received healing after asking Andre to pray for them that there was a constant stream of visitors, all asking for Andre's prayers. While his superiors became concerned about all this attention, Andre always attributed cures to the intercession of Saint Joseph. Through the help of Andre's prayers, the congregation purchased land on Mount Royal, where a great chapel to Saint Joseph was eventually built. When Andre died on this date in 1937, more than a million people came to pay their respects at his funeral.

Saints Julian and Basilissa, show me how to live and die for Christ.
Saint Andrew, show me how to bring the peace of Christ to others.
Saint John, give me the wisdom to protect those God has placed in my care.
Saint Andre, pray for me to grow in humility.

* * * * *

January 7

Saint Raymund (Raymond) of Penyafort, Optional Memorial

Raymund was born in 1175 into a noble family in Penyafort, Spain. Initially, he became a professor and taught philosophy, canon law, and civil law, but then he heard God's call to become a priest. His bishop made him archdeacon, and Raymund decided to enter the Dominican order. One of his first acts was

[15] This saint may be celebrated as an optional memorial in the *Liturgical Calendar for the Dioceses of the United States of America.*

to ask his new Dominican superiors to give him a penance for the years when (he believed) he had been too complacent as a Christian. Instead of the physical penance he probably had in mind, they gave him an intellectual one: they assigned him the task of compiling a collection of cases of conscience for the sake of confessors, which became widely known as the *Decretals*, the first document of its kind. He also created the first comprehensive compilation of canon law in the history of the Church, at the pope's request. When the Dominicans elected him master general of the order, he resisted, but he eventually accepted the position out of obedience. As master general, he was a humble, efficient leader, but he also created an option for the master general to retire. When it was possible, he took advantage of that option and retired from his position. He spent the remainder of his long life working against heresy and for the conversion of the Muslims living in his native Spain. He died in 1275.

Saint Polyeuctus of Melitene

Polyeuctus (d. 250) was a Roman officer and convert to Christianity. When he received the Roman emperor Valerian's written orders to persecute Christians, Polyeuctus tore up the orders rather than obeying them. Later, he destroyed pagan idols that were being carried in a procession through the city of Melitene (now in Armenia). For this crime, he was arrested, tortured to try to make him give up his faith, and finally martyred. His name lived on in ancient culture for many years: many churches were later built in his name, one of those churches was often used when swearing legal oaths, and an account of his life was so popular that theatrical tragedies followed its style.

Saint Canute Lavard

Canute (1096–1131) was the son of King Eric of Denmark, and his uncle was Saint Canute, also a king of Denmark. Canute grew up in the Saxon court, defended his people from Viking raids, and supported missionaries in his country. After he became king of the Western Wends, his uncle Nils, king of Denmark, saw him as a threat to the throne and had him killed. Canute was murdered by his own cousins, dying a martyr for justice.

> *Saint Raymund, help me to confess my sins.*
> *Saint Polyeuctus, show me how to stand up for Christ and Christians.*
> *Saint Canute, help me to do what is right and just.*

* * * * *

January 8

Saints Theophilus and Helladius of Libya

From the early days of the Church, these two men have been honored as martyrs and saints, but we know very little about them or even the date of their martyrdoms. According to tradition, Helladius was a layman, Theophilus was a deacon, and the two men were martyred in Libya, Africa, by being burned to death in a furnace.

Saint Severinus of Noricum

Severinus (410–482) was a Roman citizen of North Africa who left everything behind to live in the Egyptian desert as a Christian hermit. In time, he recognized God's call to go to Noricum, a city now in modern Austria, and spread the Gospel there. During his years as a missionary in Noricum, he gradually brought many people to the faith, so many that he had to establish monasteries for all those who wanted to be monks. He also brought a rich woman who had hoarded food during a plague to repentance for her lack of charity, and he successfully prayed for an end to a plague of locusts that afflicted the area. He spent himself for his people, but he also spent many hours alone with God, living in a small cell and eating only after sunset. When one of his friends became blind, he prayed for his healing, and when that healing didn't occur, it disturbed his peace with God for a time. Severinus died of pleurisy, a painful lung condition.

Saint Laurence Giustiniani (Lawrence Justinian)

Laurence was born in 1381 into a noble family in the Italian city of Venice. His father died when he was young, but his mother raised her children to be faithful Catholics. When Laurence was considering a vocation to the priesthood, he asked his uncle, a priest, for advice. The uncle told Laurence to think about the pleasures of the world and compare them against the hardships of religious life. At the same time, his mother began arranging a marriage for him. Laurence then made up his mind and went to live in his uncle's community. He was ordained a priest, led a prayerful and penitential life, experienced raptures when he prayed, and was seen to weep while celebrating Mass. In 1433, Pope Eugenius IV named him bishop of Castello. These were difficult political times, but Laurence faced them with deep peace, personal meekness, and patience. In 1451, the pope suppressed the see of Castello and made Laurence patriarch of Venice. When the senate of Venice opposed this decision, seeing it as a challenge to their own authority, Laurence personally appeared before them. He told them that he had wanted to give up his position as bishop, that he had held the office against his own wishes for eighteen years, and that he believed he was unworthy of the important position. The embarrassed senate finally recognized his humility and gave in. Laurence spent the remainder of his life serving as patriarch. In 1456, he died shortly after he had finished writing *The Degrees of Perfection*, the last of his ascetical writings.

> *Saints Theophilus and Helladius, show me how to live and die for Christ.*
> *Saint Severinus, help me hear God's voice in my prayers.*
> *Saint Laurence, help me to grow in humility.*

* * * * *

January 9

Saint Adrian of Canterbury

Adrian (d. 710) was born in Africa and was an abbot when the pope asked him to leave his country behind and serve as the archbishop of Canterbury to the newly converted English people. Not thinking he was called to the position, he humbly declined and recommended another monk—Saint Theodore—to take his place. Adrian also offered to accompany Theodore to England in his mission. Theodore agreed and made him abbot of the monastery of Canterbury, which Adrian turned into a great center of learning. Adrian taught Greek, Latin, Roman law, ecclesiastical sciences—and virtue—in his new country, living a holy life in England for thirty-nine years before his death.

Saint Honorius of Buzancais

Honorius (d. 1250) was a wealthy cattle merchant in France who was known for his love of life and generosity to those in need. One day, he returned from a trip and found that his servants had robbed him. He patiently explained to them the sinfulness of what they had done, and, in retaliation, they killed him. Since Honorius died performing a work of mercy (reproving sinners), the people considered him a martyr. Although people didn't consider him a saint while he was alive, miracles occurred at his tomb, and devotion to his intercession grew accordingly.

Saints Agatha Yi and Teresa Kim

Agatha (1824–1840) was a young, unmarried woman, and Teresa (1797–1840) was a married woman and then a widow. Both lived in Korea when they were arrested for the crime of being Christians. They were beaten, tortured, and then executed when they refused to give up their faith in Christ.

> *Saint Adrian, help me grow in humility and virtue.*
> *Saint Honorius, teach me how to correct sinners with love.*
> *Saints Agatha and Teresa, show me how to live and die for Christ.*

* * * * *

January 10

Saint Miltiades (Melchiades)

Miltiades (d. 314) was the first pope to reign after the Roman emperor Constantine had brought an end to the persecution of Christians, so he witnessed many improvements in the life and freedom of the Church; he reigned for two years. The emperor gave him the Lateran Palace as the papal residence, and he presided over the first Lateran council in 313. He responded to the widespread heresies of the time with careful explanations of Catholic truths. These false teachings included Manichaeism, a religion that synthesized various Eastern religions into one, and Donatism, a long-lived Christian heresy that taught that the sacraments were invalid when conferred by clergy who had committed a serious sin, such as apostasy under threat of persecution.

Saint Paul the Hermit

Paul was born into a well-to-do Christian family in Thebes, Egypt, around the year 230. His parents died when he was only fifteen years old and left him all their wealth. Soon afterward, he decided to leave everything behind and become a hermit, both to avoid the persecution of Christians under the Roman emperor Decius and also because he was tired by his family members' attempts to steal his property. For the rest of his long life, he lived in the desert as a hermit, living on only fruit and water, wearing clothes made of palm leaves, and praying. It's said that a raven once brought him bread to eat, just like the prophet Elijah. He met the famous monk Saint Anthony the Great late in his long life, and they became friends. We know of his life through a contemporary biography written by Saint Jerome called *The Life of Paul the First Hermit*. Paul died in the year 342.

Saint Gregory of Nyssa

Gregory was born around the year 330 into a pious Christian family, so pious that many of his family members are now canonized saints. Gregory was educated at Athens, married a woman named Theosebeia, and became a professor of rhetoric. However, he later decided to leave the world behind and become a hermit. In time, he became a priest, then he was made bishop of Nyssa in Lower Armenia, and finally he became archbishop of Sebaste. His relationship with his wife when he was made an archbishop is debated: some say he continued to live with his wife, though Saint Jerome wrote that the Eastern churches would not permit that. Although Gregory was a pillar of orthodoxy during the Church's fight with Arianism, he was an easygoing man and somewhat lax with money issues. When he had been cheated and deceived by others in a matter involving money, the governor accused him of theft and put him in prison. Gregory escaped and wandered in exile for a few years before he was able to return to his see. Gregory was a theologian at the second ecumenical council at Constantinople, and there he affirmed the decrees of the Council of Nicaea. For his many writings on Scripture, theology, and the practice of the faith, he's sometimes called the Father of the Fathers of the Church. He died around the year 395.

Saint Agatho

Agatho (d. 681) was the seventy-ninth pope; he reigned two years. Before becoming pope, he was a married man and businessman for many years, but he eventually left the world behind and became a monk, with his wife's blessing. He put his business skills to work when he became pope, handling the accounting records personally, and he resolved important disputes within the English Church and between the churches of Rome and Constantinople before his death.

Saint Peter Orseolo

Peter (928–987) was born into a distinguished family of Venice and was given the command of the city's fleet when he was only twenty years old, successfully protecting Venice against pirates. When a riot in the year 976 led to the death of the city's doge, the famous bishop Saint Peter Damian claimed that Peter was involved in the assassination. Whether or not he was is unclear, but Peter Orseolo did become an excellent leader. However, he served for only a short time; on September 1, 978, he left his wealth, power, and family behind and left the city to enter the Benedictine abbey of Cuxa. Apparently, his decision was made secretly since his wife and son didn't know where he had gone at first. Peter lived an ascetic and holy life under the direction of the abbot Guarinus and built a hermitage for himself, perhaps with the encouragement of another abbot, Saint Romuald. Miracles occurred at his tomb.

Blessed Gregory X

Gregory (d. 1276) was the 184th pope; he reigned for four years. He was born Teobaldo Visconti, and he was archdeacon of Liege when he was elected. He spent his pontificate trying to restore peace between the warring Christian nations, improve the moral life and discipline of his clergy and the people, deliver the Holy Land from Muslim control, and reunite the Greek Church with Rome. Though he reigned for only a short time, his strong actions as pope had far-reaching consequences for the Church.

> *Saints Miltiades and Agatho and Blessed Gregory,*
> *help me to love Christ and His Church.*
> *Saint Paul, help me give up everything that separates me from God.*
> *Saint Gregory, teach me how to be a pillar of faith to those around me.*
> *Saint Peter, show me how to use my abilities for God's greater glory.*

* * * * *

January 11

Saint Hyginus

Hyginus (d. 142) was the ninth pope; he was from Athens, Greece. During his four-year reign, he faced down two heretical teachings and their leaders, trying hard to bring the leaders back to the faith before they were eventually excommunicated. Hyginus is listed as a martyr since martyrdom was always close at hand for a pope at that time, but it's not certain how he died.

Saint Theodosius the Cenobiarch

Theodosius was born in 423 in Garissus (in modern Turkey); he was ordained to the position of lector in the Church. Inspired by the example of the patriarch Abraham, he decided to leave his homeland behind. In his journeys, he visited the famous hermit Saint Simeon the Stylite, went as a pilgrim to the holy places in Jerusalem, and finally placed himself under the direction of a holy man named Longinus. After a wealthy lady had built a church for Longinus, he asked Theodosius to take charge of it. He did this briefly, but then he moved to live alone in a cave at the top of a nearby mountain. News of his miracles and holiness attracted many people, and he was forced to build a monastery for all the men who came to see him and wanted to live as his disciples. Theodosius' title—Cenobiarch—comes from the word "cenobite", which means "men living in community". His monastery was "like a city of saints in the midst of a desert",[16] people said, and he had so many monks that he divided them into four churches: three for the three different languages of the monks and one for those in a state of penance. Since the Roman emperor at the time, Anastasius, was a follower of the Eutychian heresy and banished any bishops who followed the orthodox understanding of the faith, he tried to win Theodosius over to his side. First, he sent Theodosius money, which Theodosius gave to the poor. Then Anastasius sent him a heretical profession of faith, thinking he would sign it, but Theodosius replied with a letter, "full of apostolic spirit",[17] which apparently chastened the emperor for a time. However, when the emperor continued persecuting the faithful, Theodosius traveled throughout the area to encourage faithful Christians and was banished for doing so, but was soon called back when the emperor died. He spent the rest of his life in his monastery. In 529, he died at the age of 106 after suffering patiently throughout a painful illness. Miracles occurred at his funeral.

Saint Hyginus, help me to love Christ and His Church.
Saint Theodosius, show me how to help my family
and community become a "city of saints".

* * * * *

January 12

Saint Arcadius of Mauritania

During a fierce persecution of Christians in the days of the early Church, Arcadius (d. 302) hid from the authorities in the countryside around Caesarea, Mauritania (now in modern Algeria). However, when the authorities captured one of his relatives and threatened him in order to find out where Arcadius

---

[16] Walsh, *Butler's Lives of the Saints*, 10.
[17] Ibid.

was hidden, Arcadius turned himself in. The judge gave him the chance to renounce his Christian faith, threatening him with torture if he refused, but Arcadius remained faithful. They then killed him slowly, cutting off his limbs one at a time, starting with his fingers, then toes, feet, and legs. But Arcadius simply kept repeating—and died saying—the biblical phrase "Teach me wisdom in my secret heart."[18]

Saint Benedict (Benet) Biscop

Benedict was born around the year 628 into a noble family in Northumberland in England. When he was twenty-five years old, he traveled to Rome, and he returned with a desire to study his Catholic faith more deeply. After a second trip to Rome, he decided to enter the famous monastery of Lerins in France. There he became a monk, and after two years in the monastery, he returned for a third time to Rome. While there, Pope Saint Vitalian decided to send two men (now also known as saints) back to England with him: Theodore, the new archbishop of Canterbury, and Adrian, an abbot. Two years later, Benedict went for a fourth time to Rome because he wanted to learn how to practice the monastic rule more perfectly and bring that practice to his people; he returned to England with a great collection of books to do both. The king of Northumberland himself gave Benedict land on which he built the monastery of Wearmouth in the year 674. Eleven years later, Benedict built a second monastery at Jarrow, and he governed both of them, though he also appointed superiors since he traveled so often. The excellent library he established in England bore fruit later; it made possible the work of Saint Bede the Venerable, a Benedictine monk whose writings included the earliest history of the Church in England. In the year 686, Benedict became paralyzed, and he was confined to bed for three years. Each day, his monks would pray the Divine Office with him, and Benedict would pray in his heart when he was too ill to pray with his voice. He died on this date in the year 690.

> *Saint Arcadius, beg the Lord to teach me His wisdom.*
> *Saint Benedict, help me bring the teachings of the Church to others.*

* * * * *

January 13

Saint Hilary of Poitiers, Optional Memorial

Hilary (d. ca. 368) came from an important pagan family in Gaul (now called France). He married, and he and his wife had a daughter. It wasn't until late in his life that he became a Christian, and, despite his objections about his unworthiness, he was chosen to be bishop of Poitiers. As bishop, he wrote eloquently in support of the persecuted bishop Saint Athanasius and wrote against the Arian

---

[18] Ps 51:6.

heresy, which was spreading all over the empire at the time. For no crime—except for opposing a heresy supported by the emperor—Hilary was condemned without a trial and sent into exile in the area of Phrygia (modern Turkey) in the year 356. However, as often happens when men try to oppose God's plan, they soon find that their plans work to His favor. Through his personal example and writings, Hilary became such an effective witness to the Gospel to the Arians living in Phrygia that they eventually begged the emperor to send him back to Gaul. Hilary triumphantly returned to Poitiers to serve as bishop; he held councils, wrote hymns and explanations of the faith, and engaged in public debates with heretics to explain the true Catholic faith. He is considered a Father of the Church. Because of his perseverance and faithful teaching about Christ's divinity, he was named a Doctor of the Church by Pope Pius IX in 1851.

> The one gift [of the Spirit], which is in Christ, is available to everyone in its entirety, and what is present in every place is given in so far as we desire to receive it, and will remain with us in so far as we desire to merit it.[19]

Saints Hermylus and Stratonicus of Belgrade

Hermylus (d. 315) was a deacon in the region now known as Belgrade, Serbia, and Stratonicus (d. 315) was his servant. During the persecution of Christians under the Roman emperor Licinius, they were rewarded with their refusal to renounce their faith by being martyred by drowning in the Danube River.

Saint Remigius of Rheims

Remigius was born in 438 into a noble and pious family; his brother is also known as a saint (Principius of Soissons), and so is his uncle (Lupus of Soissons). Remigius was chosen to be bishop of Rheims when he was only twenty-two years old and still a layman, but he served his flock diligently for an amazing seventy-four years. He brought the Gospel to many people, including his own king, Clovis, king of the Franks. At the end of his life, he became blind, and he died of natural causes in 533.

Saint Hilary, help me lead others to the truth.
Saints Hermylus and Stratonicus, show me how to live and die for Christ.
Saint Remigius, help me use the years God gives me to speak to others about Christ.

* * * * *

January 14

Saint Felix of Nola

Felix (d. ca. 255) was the son of a soldier who had retired to live in Nola, Italy. When his father died, Felix sold most of what he had inherited, gave

[19] Hilary of Poitiers, The Trinity 2, trans. Stephen McKenna, C.Ss.R., Fathers of the Church Series, vol. 25 (Washington, D.C.: Catholic University of America Press, 1968), 63.

the money to the poor, and was ordained a priest by the bishop of Nola, Saint Maximus. During the renewed persecution of Christians under the Roman emperor Decius, Felix was arrested and beaten, but he somehow managed not only to escape death but to hide Bishop Maximus from the authorities. According to one tradition, while they were hiding in a vacant building, a spider spun its web over the door, convincing the soldiers that the building was uninhabited and saving them from detection. The persecution under Decius ended in 251, and when Bishop Maximus died, Felix was chosen to become bishop. He declined in favor of another priest, and he spent the rest of his life farming a little land and giving the proceeds to those in need. Felix is sometimes named a martyr because of the imprisonment and tortures he endured.

Martyrs of Mt. Sinai

Thirty-eight monks lived as hermits near Mount Sinai in Egypt, perhaps during the fourth century. Marauding Bedouins (Arabic tribesmen) killed all these men, who died as martyrs for their faith.

Blessed Peter Donders

Peter (1809–1887) grew up in a poor family in Holland, a region of the Netherlands; he had to work as a servant to fund his lifelong desire of someday becoming a priest. He first tried to enter different religious orders—the Franciscans, the Jesuits, and the Redemptorists—but was turned down by them all. He was finally accepted into the seminary. After he completed his studies, he was ordained a priest and was sent to the Dutch colony of Surinam, New Guinea, in 1842 as a missionary. He evangelized, cared for, and baptized the plantation slaves who lived there. His repeated complaints about their mistreatment eventually improved their conditions. When the Redemptorists arrived to take charge of the mission, he became a novice in that order and then a full member. He evangelized natives in the town of Batavia and learned their languages, but at this point he became ill with nephritis, a kidney disease. He served the sick until the very end of his life.

Saint Felix, show me how to serve the poor around me.
Holy Martyrs, help me to forgive always.
Blessed Peter, show me how to rejoice in rejection as a stepping stone in God's plan.

* * * * *

January 15

Saint Maurus

Maurus was born into a noble family in Rome in the year 512. He was sent to be educated by Saint Benedict of Nursia at the age of twelve; he became

Benedict's first disciple, later becoming a deacon and a monk under Benedict's direction. Maurus was sent by Benedict to found a new Benedictine abbey in 543; years later, it was renamed after him. Maurus' prayers worked wonders—including curing the sick and raising the dead back to life. He died on this date in 584.

Blessed Peter of Castelnau

Peter was born in France. He advanced rapidly in the Church, becoming an archdeacon in the year 1199, a Cistercian monk in 1202, and a papal legate for Pope Innocent III in 1203. He was sent to evangelize the region of France troubled by the Albigensian heresy, just like his contemporary Saint Dominic. However, in 1208, a group of Albigensians, with the support of a power-hungry count, murdered him. He was stabbed with a lance near Saint Gilles Abbey in the year 1208, making him a martyr.

Blessed Nicholas (Nikolaus) Gross

Nikolaus (1898–1945) was the father of seven children. He worked as a miner in his native Germany, becoming a member of a Christian miner's union. Later, he worked as a journalist at the newspaper of the Catholic Worker Movement. In that newspaper, he promoted nonviolent opposition to Nazism; when his newspaper was shut down in 1938, he continued the paper underground despite the risk. Although he wasn't involved in the 1944 assassination attempt on Hitler, he tried to unite Catholic workers in preparation for it and was therefore arrested and condemned for treason. He was executed in Berlin's Plötzensee Prison on this date. His body was cremated, and his ashes were scattered.

Saint Maurus, teach me how to pray with faith.
Blessed Peter, show me how to bring the truth of Christ to those around me.
Blessed Nicholas, help me to respond to evil always with the peace of Christ.

* * * * *

January 16

Saint Marcellus I

The papal chair had been vacant for three years when Marcellus (d. 309) was elected pope; he reigned for a year. Marcellus ruled during the end of the persecution under the Roman emperor Diocletian, which had been so brutal that few clergy were left, and most of the faithful were simply waiting for martyrdom. Some Christians had apostatized under threat of death and torture; although many did penance in order to be allowed back into the Church after the persecution had temporarily abated, some of these lapsed Catholics refused. Marcellus wouldn't allow those who refused to do penance to return to the Church. But some of the lapsed were offended and had political clout, and they succeeded in getting the Roman emperor Maxentius to send Marcellus into exile. He died in exile as a result of the poor treatment he received.

Saint Honoratus

Honoratus (d. 429) was born into a well-born Roman family living in Gaul (modern France). He became a Christian and converted his brother Venantius as well. The two brothers decided to go to Greece; although their father discouraged them, they eventually sailed with Caprasius, a holy hermit who is also now venerated as a saint. All three men planned to live as hermits in the desert. Venantius died on the way, however, and Honoratus was forced to return to Gaul. He decided to live as a hermit in the mountains near the city of Frejus, and later he lived in Lerins. He founded a monastery there in about the year 400, with some of his monks living in community and some living as anchorites in cells, following the rule of monks devised by Saint Pachomius. (The monastery he founded in Lerins has been there, with its ups and downs, ever since.) Honoratus was reluctantly made archbishop of Arles, France, in the year 426, and he dedicated himself to the care of his flock, while still living an ascetical life, until his death.

> *Saint Marcellus, show me how to suffer joyfully for the sake of righteousness.*
> *Saint Honoratus, help me to live a life of holiness wherever God places me.*

* * * * *

January 17

Saint Anthony the Great, Memorial

Anthony was born in 251 into a wealthy but Christian family in Egypt during the days of the early Church. He was educated at home, and his parents protected him from worldly influences by giving him a very limited knowledge of secular literature. When he was almost twenty years old, his parents died and left him their large estate. Six months later, he heard Christ's words to the rich young man preached—"Go, sell what you possess"[20]—and Anthony obediently gave his best land to neighbors, sold most of the rest, gave the money to the poor, and kept a small amount for himself and his sister to live on. But shortly afterward, he heard another homily preached, this time on the subject "Do not be anxious about tomorrow."[21] He then gave away everything else that he owned to the needy and placed his sister in a nunnery (the first known mention of a Catholic convent for women). Imitating a local hermit, he retired into the desert in the year 272. He drank only water, ate only bread with a little salt and only after sunset, and grew in humility and charity—while the devil tried to terrify him with noises and beatings.

In the year 285, he crossed the Nile River and settled on top of a mountain. There he lived for twenty years, seeing only the man who brought him bread

---

[20] Mt 19:21.
[21] See Mt 6:34.

twice a year. However, many men were attracted by his holiness and came to be his disciples; he visited them in their cells from time to time. In the year 311, the Roman emperor Maxentius renewed the persecution of Christians; Anthony traveled to Alexandria to encourage the Christians living there to remain faithful. He publicly wore his sheepskin tunic (a sign of his poverty and presumably his life as a Christian hermit) and appeared in the sight of the governor, but he was also careful not to provoke judges to act against him or others. When the persecution ended for a time, he returned to his monastery, founded another one, and settled in a cell that was hard to reach. There he grew a garden and made mats. In the year 336, the emperor Constantine wrote to him, and his disciples were amazed to receive a letter from the emperor. Anthony told them: "Do not consider it marvelous if a ruler writes to us, for he is a man. Marvel, instead, that God wrote the law for mankind, and has spoken to us through his own Son."[22] In the year 355, he returned to Alexandria to confront those following the Arian heresy who were living there. He converted many people back to the orthodox understanding of the faith, performed miracles through his prayers, and impressed even the pagans. Anthony famously taught his disciples that "the knowledge of ourselves is the necessary and only step by which we can ascend to the knowledge and love of God."[23] At the end of his life in 356, Anthony visited his monks, asked for his body to be buried secretly (to avoid people fighting over the honor of having it), gave his sheepskin tunic to Saint Athanasius of Alexandria (the bishop), and said farewell to his disciples. Then he lay down and quietly passed away. He was 105 years old. Both Saints Athanasius and Jerome wrote biographies of his life.

> Now the Greeks leave home and traverse the sea in order to gain an education, but there is no need for us to go abroad on account of the Kingdom of Heaven, nor to cross the sea for virtue. For the Lord has told us before, "the Kingdom of God is within you." All virtue needs, then is our willing, since it is in us, and arises from us.[24]

> Anyone who lives in solitude and quiet is saved from three kinds of warfare—against hearing, talking, and seeing. All he still has to fight against is his heart.[25]

Saints Leonilla, Speusippus, Eleusippus, and Meleusippus

Leonilla was the grandmother of triplet boys named Speusippus, Eleusippus, and Meleusippus. The family lived in Cappadocia (now in modern Turkey). During the reign of the Roman emperor Marcus Aurelius, they were martyred together for the crime of being Christians in the year 175.

> Saint Anthony, help me give my heart to Christ.
> Holy Martyrs, show me how to live and die for Christ.

* * * * *

[22] Athanasius, *The Life of Antony and the Letter to Marcellinus*, trans. Robert C. Gregg (Mahwah, N.J.: Paulist Press, 1980), 89.

[23] Walsh, *Butler's Lives of the Saints*, 16.

[24] Saint Anthony, quoted in Athanasius, *Life of Antony and Letter to Marcellinus*, 46.

[25] Saint Anthony, quoted in Jacobus de Voragine, *The Golden Legend*, trans. William Granger Ryan (Princeton and Oxford: Princeton University Press, 2012), 95.

January 18

Saint Prisca of Rome

During the early persecution of the Church, the martyr Prisca died in the city of Rome. Some traditions say she was a member of the nobility and supported the Church financially before her martyrdom.

Saint Deicolus (Desle)

When Deicolus (d. 625) was young, he was educated by the abbot and future saint Columban. Columban once asked him why he was always smiling. Deicolus replied, "Because no one can take God from me."[26] Deicolus eventually left his home country of Ireland with Columban to go to Luxeuil, France; when Columban later left France, Deicolus stayed behind and founded an abbey. Afterward, he became a hermit, living a joyful, peaceful life until his death.

Saint Margaret of Hungary

Margaret (1242–1270) was the daughter of the king and queen of Hungary. Her parents apparently noticed her piety, since they thought that she was called to religious life and suggested that she offer her life as a gift to God that He might protect Hungary from neighboring nations. Margaret happily consented. As a nun, she fasted and took the lowest duties in the convent despite her noble birth. When the king of Bohemia offered to marry her for political reasons, she refused. She died when she was only twenty-eight years old, and she was immediately acclaimed a saint by those who knew her.

Saint Prisca, show me how I can support the Church.
Saint Deicolus, help me to remember that no one can ever take God from me.
Saint Margaret, teach me humility.

* * * * *

January 19

Saints Maris, Martha, Audifax, and Abachum of Rome

Maris and Martha were a noble, married couple from Persia (modern Iran). When they converted to the Christian faith, they gave away their wealth to the poor. Around the year 270, they traveled to Rome with their two sons, Audifax and Abachum. Christians were being persecuted in Rome at that time, and, out of Christian charity, they buried the ashes of those martyred for their faith. The whole family was put to death for that "crime".

---

[26] Walsh, *Butler's Lives of the Saints*, 17.

Saints Liberata and Faustina of Como

Liberata and Faustina (both d. ca. 580) were sisters who grew up in Como, Italy. They jointly decided to set aside marriage and instead live only for God. At first, they lived in nearby caves as hermits, but later they became Benedictine nuns and founded the Convent of Saint Margaret in their hometown.

Holy Martyrs, help me to practice the corporal works of mercy.
Saints Liberata and Faustina, show me how to encourage
my family members to love and serve God.

* * * * *

January 20

Saint Fabian, Optional Memorial

Fabian was a layman and a farmer who came into Rome on the day in the year 236 when a new pope was to be chosen. A dove settled on his head during the ceremony, and the Christians of Rome took this as a sign from God. After he was made the twentieth pope, Fabian sent missionaries to Gaul (modern France), condemned heretical teachings, and died a martyr during the persecution of Christians under the Roman emperor Decius around the year 250.

Saint Sebastian, Optional Memorial

Sebastian (d. 288) was a soldier in the Roman army who converted to the Christian faith during the days of the underground Church. He kept his faith a secret, and although his duties as a soldier made it difficult for him to remain faithful, he did his best and used his position to comfort other Christians. Sebastian's faith was finally discovered, and he was sentenced to be shot to death by arrows. Despite being shot numerous times, he recovered through the care of a Christian widow named Irene. When Sebastian returned to publicly profess his faith, the Roman emperor Diocletian ordered him to be clubbed to death. After his death, his body was thrown into a sewer, but Christians recovered it and buried it on the Appian Way in Rome, where a church in his name still stands today.

Saint Wulfstan of Worchester

Wulfstan was born around the year 1008 and was from Warwickshire, England. He studied in Evesham and Peterborough and was educated by the bishop of Worchester while he studied for the priesthood. As a priest, Wulfstan devoted himself to prayer, instructed children in the faith, and advanced to greater responsibilities, culminating in his ordination (against his own objections) as bishop of Worchester. As bishop, he was such a zealous preacher that his listeners were often moved to tears. He also brought an end to the widespread local practice of men kidnapping other men and selling them into slavery in Ireland. People noticed that whenever Wulfstan passed a church, he always took time to enter it and pray. When people complained to him about the Normans, who were oppressing his people, he told them it was a "scourge of God for our sins, which we must bear with patience".[27] When wealthy young gentlemen were sent to him, he humbled them by giving them the chore of serving food to the poor, which he also did himself. He died at about eighty-seven years of age in the year 1095.

Saint Eustochia (Smeralda) Calafato

Smeralda was born in 1434 near Messina, Italy. Her father was a wealthy merchant, and her mother was a devout Christian. While a young woman, she received a vision that changed her life: she saw the Crucified Christ. Deeply moved, she decided to enter a Poor Clares convent, but her brothers objected, even threatening to burn the convent down if she tried. The nuns refused to admit her out of fear, but she was eventually able to change the minds of both her brothers and the sisters. She took the name Eustochia and lived an austere life, sleeping on the ground and imposing other penances on herself. Her convent included members of many rich families, and, in time, Eustochia realized that she wanted to live a simpler, more rigorous religious life than was lived in that convent. So, with the financial support and company of her mother, she entered a new convent. Unfortunately, the Franciscan priests near this convent refused to celebrate Mass for them, and Eustochia had to appeal to Rome to convince them to do it. Eustochia eventually became the nuns' spiritual director, and her holiness attracted other women to the convent. Soon they had so many vocations that the buildings had to grow in size to match. Eustochia's spiritual life reflected her vision of the Crucified Christ, and she even wrote a book on the subject. She spent many nights in adoration before the Blessed Sacrament, was known for the miracles that resulted from her prayers, and was deeply revered by the people of the city of Messina when she died in 1491.

> *Saint Fabian, help me to accept the gifts of God humbly,*
> *however surprising they may be.*
> *Saint Sebastian, give me your fortitude.*
> *Saint Wulfstan, teach me humility.*
> *Saint Eustochia, show me how to grow in faith through*
> *meditating on the sufferings of the Crucified Christ.*

* * * * *

January 21

Saint Agnes, Memorial

Agnes (d. 305) was a wealthy and beautiful Christian girl who lived in Rome during the reign of the Roman emperor Diocletian. According to the custom of

[27] Ibid.

the time, several young men asked for her hand in marriage when she was thirteen years old. She turned them all down, explaining that Jesus Christ was her bridegroom. The rejected suitors retaliated by reporting her to the authorities as a Christian. The governor threatened her with torture to make her give up her faith, and when she refused him, he sent her to a brothel. When no man would touch her there, he ordered Agnes to be executed.

Saint Meinrad (Meginrad)

Meinrad was born around the year 797 into the noble Hohenzollern family in Swabia (modern Germany). He became a priest, entered a Benedictine abbey, and taught for a time. However, he yearned for a life of solitude and, with the permission of his superiors, he became a hermit in the year 829 and lived in the forest. His reputation for holiness soon attracted visitors, so seven years later, he moved to a more remote spot. He lived in this place for twenty-five years. On this date in 861 he was killed by two bandits who came to see him, thinking he had some sort of treasure. Although he understood their intentions, he treated them kindly, gave them food, and showed them hospitality. That night, they smashed his skull and ran away when they couldn't find any valuables. A Benedictine abbey was later founded there and continues to this day.

Saint Agnes, help me live a life of purity for Christ.
Saint Meinrad, show me how to share the treasure of Christ's love through hospitality.

* * * * *

January 22

Saint Vincent of Saragossa

See January 23.[28]

Saint Anastasius (Magundat) the Persian

Magundat (d. 628) was a soldier in the army of King Khusrow II of Persia (modern Iran) during a campaign that brought the relic of the True Cross to Persia from Jerusalem. The miracles that occurred in the presence of the relic moved him so deeply that he left the army, became a Christian, and even became a monk, taking the name of Anastasius. After living for several years as a monk, he returned to Persia to evangelize his countrymen. But he was arrested almost immediately, refused to give up his faith, and was strangled and beheaded, with several dozen other Christians whose names we don't know.

---

[28] Because January 22 is commemorated as the Day of Prayer for the Legal Protection of Unborn Children in the United States, Saint Vincent, deacon and martyr, may be celebrated as an optional memorial on January 23 and is listed on that date.

Saint Vincent Pallotti

Vincent (1795–1850) was the son of a prosperous grocer in Rome. Vincent was known to all as a virtuous boy, though not a great student. However, he was ordained a priest at the age of twenty-three and became an assistant professor at the University of Rome. He eventually left that position and became a pastor, where he was an excellent confessor. Despite (or perhaps because of) his popularity with his flock, other clergy of the diocese persecuted and ridiculed him relentlessly for more than ten years. As his persecutors were later forced to admit, Vincent always responded to their cruelty in a Christlike way and treated each of them with the greatest respect. Through his pastoral work, Vincent gradually instituted the Society of Catholic Apostolate, a work that involved coordinating both clergy and laity to bring people to the Church as well as encouraging works of social justice within the community. He organized schools for tradesmen to learn their jobs, and he established a local celebration at Epiphany, utilizing different rites to encourage reunification between the different Christians in Rome. He came home half-clothed many times because he had given away his own clothes; he reconciled those separated from the Church; and he served as an exorcist. He died on this date at the age of fifty-five.

Blessed William (Joseph) Chaminade

William was born in 1761, one of fifteen children in a devout family in Perigeux, France. He and three of his brothers eventually became priests. He remained a faithful priest throughout the French Revolution, ministering to his flock secretly, narrowly escaping death several times, and refusing to swear allegiance to the anti-Catholic government. After the revolution was over, he helped fifty priests who had taken the oath of allegiance to the atheistic French government be reconciled back to the Church. He was exiled to Spain for a few years due to further political troubles; but when he returned, he founded the Sodalities of Our Lady in response to a message from Heaven that he believed he had received. He said that our Lady had asked him to be her missionary; the goal of this sodality was to unite both men and women and both laity and clergy into a community of faith, supporting one another and working under Mary's protection. Other institutes grew from this work, and its members began teaching in schools. Other orders he founded—the Society of Mary, Daughters of Mary, and Marianist Sisters—gradually spread throughout the world. William died on this date in 1850.

Blessed Laura Vicuna

Laura was born in 1891 soon after the end of a civil war in Chile. When her father died, her mother became the mistress of a man named Manuel Mora. Mora paid for Laura to attend a boarding school run by Salesian Sisters; there she was very happy and full of love for the Lord. When she came home for the Christmas holidays one year, Mora made sexual advances to her, but she was able to escape from him. She continued to pray for her mother, whom she knew was living in sin; in her prayer, Laura offered God her own life in exchange for her mother's life. Her confessor noticed her piety, saw that she had a true call to religious life, and invited her to join a Marian sodality, a group that encouraged Christian devotion among children. In late 1903, Laura became sick and was sent home to stay with her mother. When the drunken Mora became violent and began ordering Laura and her mother around, Laura tried to escape, but he beat her unconscious. She died eight days later in 1904. When her mother learned of her daughter's self-offering, she left Mora and returned to the Church.

> Saint Anastasius, show me how to live and die for Christ.
> Saint Vincent, help me to respond to hatred with love.
> Blessed William, help me to spread a love for the Mother of God wherever I go.
> Blessed Laura, show me how to sacrifice myself that others might be saved.

* * * * *

January 23

Saint Vincent of Saragossa, Optional Memorial[29]

Vincent was born in Spain. In the early fourth century, he was a deacon in the city of Saragossa when the persecution of Christians increased during the reign of the Roman governor Dacian. Dacian had Vincent arrested; when he refused to give up his faith, Vincent was tortured by being placed on a rack then stretched and torn with iron hooks. When torture didn't succeed in breaking his faith, the governor put him in prison. Though Christians cared for him there, Vincent died of his wounds. It was the year 304.

Saint Emerentiana of Rome

During the persecution of the Church under the Roman emperor Diocletian in the year 305, the martyr Emerentiana died in the city of Rome. According to tradition, she was the foster sister of the martyr-saint Agnes; while on her way to pray at her sister's grave, she was confronted by a pagan mob. The angry mob stoned her to death when she admitted that she too was a Christian.

Saint Ildephonsus of Toledo

Ildephonsus (607–667) was from a noble Spanish family and decided to become a monk over his family's objections. In time, his fellow monks recognized his wisdom and holiness and made him their abbot. Fifteen years later, he was made archbishop of Toledo. He was greatly devoted to the Blessed Mother; he recommended the practice of meditating on Jesus by looking at the Lord through her eyes. Once, while he was sitting on his bishop's throne, the Blessed Virgin

---

[29] Note that the optional memorial for Saint Vincent is moved to January 23 in the United States because of the annual commemoration of the Day of Prayer for the Legal Protection of Unborn Children.

appeared to him in a vision and presented him with a chasuble as a sign of her favor on him and his priestly leadership. He governed his flock for nine years before dying peacefully.

Saint Marianne Cope, Optional Memorial[30]

Barbara was born in 1838 in Germany into a working-class family of eight children. Her family immigrated to the United States when she was small, and she left school in the eighth grade to work and support her siblings. As a young woman, she joined the Sisters of Saint Francis, taking the name in religious life of Marianne, in the year 1863. She eventually became a teacher, superior, and director of novices. In 1883, she and six of her sister Franciscans were sent to Honolulu, Hawaii, to care for lepers. Though she planned to stay only for a few weeks, she spent the next thirty-five years in Hawaii, where she and her sisters dramatically improved the housing and care of those suffering from leprosy. Working with Saint Damien de Veuster, she and two sisters founded a home and school for girls on Molokai; she later took over the boys' home founded by Saint Damien after his death. She spent her final years in a wheelchair due to chronic kidney disease. She died on August 9, 1918, of a heart attack.

Holy Martyrs, pray for me to be always faithful to Christ.
Saint Ildephonsus, help me to see the Son of God through the eyes of His Mother.
Saint Marianne, show me how to serve the neglected people around me.

* * * * *

January 24

Saint Francis de Sales, Memorial

Francis was born in 1567 into nobility, the first child of a large family, at the Chateau de Sales in Savoy, France; he was baptized the next day. He was educated by his mother, then a tutor. He made the decision to consecrate his life to God when he was still a young man, although his father had planned a secular career for him instead. When Francis was fourteen years old, he convinced his father to let him attend a Jesuit school; there he excelled in rhetoric and theology, while also taking fencing and dancing classes to please his father. He received his doctor of law degree when he was twenty-four years old. His mother knew and supported his desire to become a priest, but it wasn't until another relative, Canon Louis de Sales, suggested that Francis might be appointed as provost in Geneva that Francis was able to convince his father. Francis put on clerical dress the same day that his father agreed. Six months later, he was ordained a priest.

---

[30] This saint may be celebrated as an optional memorial in the *Liturgical Calendar for the Dioceses of the United States of America.*

When the bishop of Geneva discussed with his priests the deplorable religious condition of Catholics living in the region of the Chablais—where Calvinism was so strong that the few Catholics there faced persecution and threats—Francis volunteered to go and serve them. Although his father refused to bless him in this dangerous mission, his cousin, Canon Louis, accompanied him. They lived simply and traveled throughout the region on foot. They preached daily in a city called Thonon, gradually going to other villages; Francis narrowly escaped death both by wolves (he slept in a tree one night) and assassins (twice he was saved by apparent miracles). While his father wrote him letters, threatening and imploring him to give up, Francis sought new ways to reach the people with the truths of the faith, including writing leaflets. He was once attacked by a mob that beat and insulted him, but he survived. His patience, perseverance, and the effects of his leaflets gradually won conversions as well as better attendance at his sermons. Four years after Francis had started, the bishop came for a visit. He was welcomed by the people, administered Confirmation to those who needed it, and presided at a Forty Hours' Devotion (forty continuous hours of public Adoration of the Blessed Sacrament), an amazing improvement in the community's devotion for such a short time.

The bishop asked Francis to become his coadjutor bishop, and, although Francis had to be persuaded first and recover from a dangerous illness next, he then was sent to Rome. There Pope Clement VIII and several cardinals (including Saint Robert Bellarmine) examined him on complicated theological questions, but his simple, modest, and learned answers impressed them, so they made him coadjutor. In 1602, Francis succeeded his predecessor and became bishop of Geneva. He ran an economical household as bishop, organized the religious education of the young throughout the diocese, and founded the Order of the Visitation nuns in 1610 with the future saint Jane de Chantal. All who knew or met him remarked on his gentle but firm manner in dealing with administrative details and the spiritual growth of those under his direction, particularly through thousands of personal letters. In 1622, he traveled with a duke to meet King Louis XIII and discuss diocesan business, but he seemed to have realized that he would not be returning home and put all his affairs in order before he left. He was struck by a paralytic seizure, and when he recovered consciousness, he patiently endured painful medical treatments that only brought him closer to his death. He received the last sacraments and serenely passed away with the name of Jesus on his lips. The Church named him both the patron of the Catholic press and a Doctor of the Church.

When your ordinary work or business is not especially engrossing, let your heart be more fixed more on God than on it; and if the work be such as to require your undivided attention, then pause from time to time and look to God, even as navigators who make for the haven they would attain, by looking up at the heavens rather than down upon the deeps on which they sail. So doing, God will work with you, in you, and for you, and your work will be blessed.[31]

---

[31] Saint Francis de Sales, *Introduction to the Devout Life*, pt. 3, chap. 10 (San Francisco: Ignatius Press; DeKalb: Lighthouse Catholic Media, 2015), 96.

Saint Sabinian of Troyes

Sabinian (d. 275) was a pagan from the Greek island of Samos who traveled to Gaul (modern France) because he was disillusioned with his native society and its low moral standards. He was converted to the faith and baptized by Patroclus, a wealthy Christian and evangelist. After Patroclus died a martyr, Sabinian became a missionary himself and brought many people to Christ. During the persecution of Christians under the Roman emperor Marcus Aurelius, he died a martyr.

Blessed Vincent Pewoniuk and Companions

During the eighteenth century, today's eastern Poland was governed by Russia, and the Catholic Church was persecuted. Bishops and priests were deported or imprisoned for refusing to join the Orthodox Church, and laypeople had to defend their faith on their own. On this date in 1874, Russian soldiers entered the village of Pratulin (also known as Podlasie) to transfer the Catholic Church building to the care of the Orthodox Church. When the Catholic faithful gathered to protect it, the soldiers tried to disperse the crowd, even offering them bribes. When that didn't work, the soldiers fired into the crowd of hymn-singing, unarmed men, and thirteen of them were killed. Those who died were mostly married men with families. Since their families were not even allowed to honor them with funerals but watched their bodies be buried by the soldiers without any religious rites, we honor them today by remembering their names: Vincent Lewoniuk, Daniel Karmasz, Lucas Bojko, Bartholomew Osypiuk, Onuphrius Wasiluk, Philip Kiryluk, Constantine Bojko, Michael Hryciuk, Ignatius Franczuk, John Andrzejuk, Constantine Lubaszuk, Maximus Hawryluk, and Michael Wawrzyszuk.

> *Saint Francis, help me remain in God's presence at all times.*
> *Saint Sabinian, show me how to bring the faith, with charity,*
> *to the immoral culture around me today.*
> *Holy Martyrs, pray for me to be a faithful defender of Mother Church.*

* * * * *

January 25

The Conversion of Saint Paul the Apostle, Feast

The Apostle Paul (born as Saul; d. ca. 67) was converted to faith in Christ while traveling to Damascus when "he fell to the ground and heard a voice saying to him, 'Saul, Saul, why do you persecute me?' And [Paul] said, 'Who are you, Lord?' And he said, 'I am Jesus, whom you are persecuting; but rise and enter the city, and you will be told what you are to do.' "[32] Obeying the voice, one of the greatest persecutors of the Church became one of her greatest defenders.

[32] Acts 9:4–6.

Saint Ananias of Damascus

Ananias was a Christian living in the first century in Damascus (in modern Syria) when our Lord told him in a vision to find the great persecutor of Christians, Saul (the Apostle Paul), and restore his sight. Ananias risked his life and obeyed; he cured Saul of his blindness, baptized him, and prepared him for his great missionary work.[33] According to tradition, Ananias evangelized Damascus and was martyred in Eleutheropolis (modern Palestine).

Blessed Henry Suso

Henry was born into a noble family in Germany around the year 1295. Unlike his warlike father, Henry had a sensitive, poetic disposition, so he was delighted when he was sent to study at a Dominican convent at the age of thirteen. Five years later, he decided he had been living a "careless life" up to that point, though he was probably more adolescent than lukewarm. He chose to devote his entire life to becoming "the Servant of the Eternal Wisdom", imposing various physical mortifications on himself and dedicating himself to God as a priest. Throughout his lifetime, he preached, served as prior at several Dominican houses, and tried to serve as a peacemaker in family feuds, including difficult situations in his own family. He also befriended and followed some of the teachings of the well-known German theologian Meister Eckhart. Since Eckhart was a controversial figure at the time, Henry spent years in prison as a result of his association with him. Even after Henry's death, notes of his sermons were sometimes confused with Eckhart's, delaying the Church's acknowledgment of his holiness. But Henry's poetry and spiritual writings helped people then and now draw close to God in prayer. He died on this date in Ulm, Germany, in the year 1365.

Saint Paul, help me to see God.
Saint Ananias, help me to trust in God, despite any danger.
Blessed Henry, pray for me that I might live in the presence of the Eternal Wisdom.

* * * * *

January 26

Saint Timothy, Memorial

Timothy (d. ca. 97) had a pagan father and a Jewish mother.[34] His mother converted to the Christian faith and brought Timothy to be baptized. He met the Apostle Paul, was ordained by him, and was sent to be bishop of Ephesus,[35] a city in modern Turkey. Paul wrote two letters to him to encourage him in

[33] Acts 9:10–19.
[34] See Acts 16:1.
[35] See 1 Tim 1:3.

his duties. In his Second Letter to Timothy, Paul wrote, "I thank God whom I serve with a clear conscience, as did my fathers, when I remember you constantly in my prayers. As I remember your tears, I long night and day to see you, that I may be filled with joy. I am reminded of your sincere faith, a faith that dwelt first in your grandmother Lois and your mother Eunice and now, I am sure, dwells in you. For this reason I remind you to rekindle the gift of God that is within you through the laying on of my hands; for God did not give us a spirit of timidity but a spirit of power and love and self-control."[36]

Saint Titus, Memorial

Titus (d. ca. 96) was a Greek pagan before he became a Christian, and the Apostle Paul himself may have converted him. Paul's letter to him, directing him in his duties as bishop of Gortyna on Crete (Greece), is part of Scripture. In his Letter to Titus, Paul wrote, "Show yourself in all respects a model of good deeds, and in your teaching show integrity, gravity, and sound speech that cannot be censured, so that an opponent may be put to shame, having nothing evil to say of us."[37]

Saint Paula of Rome

Paula (347–404) was a wealthy noblewoman of Rome, and she was a young widow with four daughters and one son when she met the famous Saint Jerome, who was the secretary of the pope at the time. Inspired by the words and Christian example of Jerome, she decided to convert her home into a church, and she devoted herself to a life of charity and mortification. She was devastated when one of her daughters died, but Jerome sternly reminded her of the importance of heavenly things in a famous letter[38] he wrote to her. She settled with another daughter to live near Jerome in Bethlehem in the Holy Land, living very simply in a cottage. She gave away so much of her money that she was sometimes in need herself. She assisted Jerome in his work as his sight deteriorated, making possible his Latin translation of the Bible.

Saint Eystein (Augustine) Erlandsson of Nidaros

Though the Norwegian government interfered in the Church's business by demanding that Eystein become the second archbishop of Nidaros in 1157, Eystein did his best as archbishop to keep the government from controlling the young Church of Norway. He intentionally went all the way to Rome to be consecrated bishop and receive the pope's blessing, not returning until 1161. He enlarged his cathedral, crowned the king's son, Magnus, and enjoyed a good relationship with the king himself, getting good laws passed for the governance of the Church. He was disappointed in his desire to require celibacy among his clergy, but Christianity was new in Norway, and the culture was not yet ready

---

[36] 2 Tim 1:3–7.

[37] Tit 2:7–8.

[38] Jerome, Letter 39; available on New Advent's website at http://www.newadvent.org/fathers/3001039.htm.

for such a radical change. When King Magnus became involved in a power struggle with another leader, Sverre, Eystein fled to England. While there he wrote a biography of the martyr-saint of Norway, King Olaf. After Magnus was killed, he returned to Norway and was reconciled with the new king, Sverre. He died on this date in 1188.

Blessed Michael Kozal

Michael was born into a peasant family in Poland in 1893 and became a priest in 1918. He became auxiliary bishop of Wloclawek in 1939 and was arrested five months later as part of the Nazi persecution of the Church in Poland. He was imprisoned and tortured first, and then he was sent to the Dachau concentration camp. There he cared for other prisoners as best he could, until he died twenty-one months later on this date in 1943.

> *Saints Timothy and Titus, help me be a good shepherd to those God has placed under my care.*
> *Saint Paula, pray for me to trust completely in God for everything.*
> *Saint Eystein, help me speak the truth, whether others listen or not.*
> *Blessed Michael, show me how to love my persecutors.*

* * * * *

January 27

Saint Angela Merici, Optional Memorial

Angela was born at Desenzano, Italy, in 1470. She and her brothers and sister worked on the family farm until their parents died. She was then sent to live with a well-to-do uncle in the city of Salo. When her sister died suddenly, Angela feared for her sister's salvation until she received a vision in which her sister encouraged her from Heaven. She later decided to become a Franciscan tertiary. She lived austerely, giving up fancy clothes, sleeping on the floor, and living on only bread, water, and some vegetables. At the age of twenty-two, her uncle died, and she returned to her hometown of Desenzano. There she recognized that many children and adults were ignorant of the truths of the faith due to a lack of religious education. So, with the help of some friends, she began a school for girls. It was so successful that she opened a similar one in the city of Brescia. In 1525, she went to Rome for the Jubilee Year, and, although Pope Clement VII asked her to stay in Rome and lead a congregation of nursing sisters, she recognized her true vocation as a teacher and declined. She returned to Brescia, but had to leave when the city was caught up in war; she stayed in Cremona until she was able to return to Brescia. In 1533, she gradually began training a few sisters in an informal novitiate, and within two years, twenty-eight women had consecrated themselves to what later became known as the Company of Saint Ursula. At this point, her company was merely an association, not a religious order. As time passed and the novel idea of a teaching order of sisters became more culturally acceptable, a congregation was approved by the pope, but not until four years after Angela died in 1540.

Saint Vitalian

Vitalian (d. 672) was the seventy-sixth pope; he reigned fourteen years. A strong leader, he worked to improve relations between the Roman Church and the Eastern emperor, opposed the Monothelite heresy (and tried to win the emperor back from it), and strengthened ties between the Church and England.

Blessed Rosalie du Verdier de la Soriniere

Rosalie (d. 1794) was a Benedictine nun in France. During the French Revolution, the government persecuted the Church; she was executed for her faithfulness, dying a martyr in Angers, France.

Saint Angela, show me how to place my life at the service of others.
Saint Vitalian, help me to love Christ and His Church.
Blessed Rosalie, show me how to live and die for Christ.

* * * * *

January 28

Saint Thomas Aquinas, Memorial

Thomas was born in 1225 into a noble family at Rocca Secca, in the central part of modern Italy. When he was five years old, he was sent to be educated at the famous Abbey of Monte Cassino, where a relative was abbot. At the age of thirteen, he was removed from Monte Cassino, probably because of the dangers of the times, but a year later he was sent to study at the University of Naples. There he became acquainted with the members and practices of the Dominicans, and he became one himself at the age of nineteen. His family was outraged that he had chosen a mendicant order, rather than a more established and wealthy one. Although the Dominicans were able to send him away on two occasions before his angry mother arrived, she then sent two of his brothers with a troop of soldiers to capture him. He was kidnapped and then imprisoned by his brothers at Rocca Secca and Monte San Giovanni; during that time, he wasn't allowed to see anyone but two of his sisters. He used his two years' imprisonment to memorize much of the Bible and study *The Four Books of Sentences* by Peter Lombard, which was a standard theology textbook of the time; he even quickly sent away a woman who was sent to seduce him. The pope himself tried to intervene in this very public family disagreement. Eventually, Thomas was released so that he could return to the Dominicans to study.

An extremely intelligent student with a demanding, inquiring mind, Thomas studied at the University of Paris under a great teacher, Saint Albert the Great. Although some underestimated Thomas' abilities due to his quiet nature, Albert did not. After completing his degree, Thomas taught, preached, and wrote. He was highly respected by the king of France, Saint Louis IX. While living in Paris, he began work on his famous *Summa Theologicae*, which was intended to be a comprehensive summary of Catholic teaching for theology students. His many writings—which are still studied today—address the philosophical and theological questions of the day with a depth and clarity that came from his deep prayer life. For example, at the university's request and after praying fervently for divine assistance, he wrote a treatise explaining the doctrine of transubstantiation to explain the Blessed Sacrament; it was *his* explanation that was later accepted by the whole Church. As a man, he was noted for his chastity and fervent prayer life; as a friar, he was noted for his obedience; as a writer and teacher, he was noted for his humility and charity toward his opponents. Late in his life, Thomas was called back to Italy, where, while celebrating Mass, he received a vision that affected him deeply. He explained to his friend Brother Reginald that he could no longer work on his *Summa* because "the end of my labours has come. All that I have written appears to be as so much straw after the things that have been revealed to me."[39] Although he was ill, he obeyed Pope Blessed Gregory X's order to attend a general council at Lyons that tried to bring about a reunion between the Eastern and Latin churches; but during the journey his health declined so seriously that he was taken to a nearby Cistercian abbey. Seeing that he was dying, the monks prayed with him. While he was explaining to them the biblical book Song of Songs, at their request, he died. It was March 7, 1274. Often called the Angelic Doctor for his writings on angels and one of the most influential theologians and philosophers in Church history, Thomas was unsurprisingly named a Doctor of the Church; his works have been praised by popes and studied by Catholic theologians ever since.

We must point out that what we are discussing here is the contemplative life as it concerns human beings. And the difference between us and the angels, as Dionysius makes clear, is that angels look at the truth with a direct grasp of it, whereas we have to start with many different things and proceed step by step from there before we reach the point where we can see truth in its simplicity.[40]

Blesseds Agatha Lin Zao, Jerome Lu Tingmei, and Laurence Wang Bing

Agatha Lin Zao was a teacher in a Christian school, and Jerome Lu Tingmei and Laurence Wang Bing were catechists; all were born in China. When the persecution of Christians by the Chinese government increased, they were arrested

---

[39] Walsh, *Butler's Lives of the Saints*, 29–30.

[40] Thomas Aquinas, "Active and Contemplative Life: Summa Theologiae II.II, Questions 179–182", in *Albert and Thomas: Selected Writings*, Classics of Western Spirituality, trans. Simon Tugwell, O.P. (New York; Mahwah, N.J.: Paulist Press, 1988), 545.

and ordered to renounce their faith in Christ. When they refused, they were beheaded and died as martyrs for the faith on this date in 1858 in Maokou, China.

Saint Thomas, help me find words to explain God's truth to others.
Holy Martyrs, show me how to teach the faith to those who do not know Christ.

* * * * *

January 29

Saints Sarbellius and Barbea of Edessa

Sarbellius was a pagan priest in Edessa, a city in modern Turkey, and Barbea was his sister; both of them converted from paganism to Christianity. When the Roman emperor Trajan began persecuting Christians, they were arrested and tortured with red-hot irons, in order to try to make them give up their faith in Christ. They died as martyrs in the year 101.

Saint Gildas the Wise

Gildas was born along the River Clyde in Scotland, around the year 500. He traveled south and lived as a monk in Britain under the direction of the abbot, Saint Illtud. In about the year 540, he wrote a treatise called *De excidio Britanniae*, in which he explained, with many scriptural references, the "miseries, the errors and the ruin of Britain".[41] This is still considered a controversial work because of the critical, argumentative way in which he wrote, but his intention was clearly to stir up his countrymen to a more perfect practice of the Christian faith. He lived for a time on an island; he directed the monks who came to learn from him and served as their abbot. He traveled to encourage other Christians in their faith until his death around the year 570.

Saints Sarbellius and Barbea, help me to remain faithful to Christ at all times.
Saint Gildas, help me speak painful truths, when needed.

* * * * *

January 30

Saint Martina of Rome

Martina (d. 228) was the child of a wealthy, Christian consul living in Rome. When her parents died, she gave her riches away to the poor and devoted her life to prayer. During the persecution of Christians under the Roman emperor Alexander Severus, she was arrested and tortured for refusing to sacrifice to pagan

---

[41] Walsh, *Butler's Lives of the Saints*, 30.

gods. According to one legend, her body bled milk when she was beheaded, which is why she's known as the patron of nursing mothers. Her relics were discovered in 1634 during a construction project in Rome.

Saint Bathildis (Bathild) of France

Bathildis was born in England and kidnapped into slavery when she was young, around the year 626. She grew up in France and eventually was made house-keeper over King Clovis II's household. In the year 649, she married the king—going from slave to servant to queen! She had three sons, all of whom later became kings. As queen, she particularly used her position to help the poor and to protect the Church. In the year 655, her husband died, and she became regent for her son, the future king. While serving as regent, she forbade the enslavement of Christians, supported the work of the bishop, Saint Eligius, and funded religious houses with endowments from the crown. She handed over the throne to her son Clotaire when he was fifteen years old and then retired to the convent of Chelles. She spent the rest of her life praying and caring for the sick, dying in the year 680 of natural causes.

Saint Hyacinth Mariscotti

Though she was named Clarice by her noble parents in Viterbo, Italy, at her birth in 1585, today we know her by her name in religious life, Hyacinth. She was educated at a Poor Clares convent and decided to enter it as a tertiary when she was a young woman. But she didn't feel called to religious life and only did so because she didn't want to give up what she considered an easy life. She lived comfortably in the convent until a priest came to bring her Holy Communion when she was ill. When he saw the frivolous way she was living, he was scan-dalized. She repented and began changing her ways, mortifying her body and doing the most menial work of the convent. She became an excellent novice mistress and example to other nuns; she eventually founded the Oblates of Mary to serve the aged poor. She died of natural causes in 1640.

Saint Mucian Mary (Aloysius) Wiaux

Aloysius was born in 1841, one of six children in a pious family in Belgium. As a boy, he attended school and helped in his father's blacksmith shop. In 1856, he entered the Brothers of the Christian Schools and took the name of an obscure martyr-saint from the early Church, Mucian. He was a gentle, kind elementary school teacher, so gentle that some complained that his classes sometimes got out of hand. He was therefore reassigned to teach music and art classes for smaller classes of younger boys. In this work he excelled and found his true vocation, bringing out the best in his students and leading them to follow his example of personal holiness. In 1917, he died greatly loved by his brothers and students.

Blessed Columba (Joseph) Marmion

Joseph was born in Ireland in 1858; he studied in Rome before becoming a priest. Though he considered becoming a missionary, he instead chose to serve God as a parish priest, and later as a seminary professor and chaplain to a convent and a women's prison. In 1886, he turned away from a promising ecclesiastical career as a priest to enter the Benedictine order instead, taking the name Columba. In time, Columba helped found an abbey in Belgium and served as its prior, spiritual director, and theology and philosophy professor. He preached retreats, edited several publications, and became widely known as a Catholic author. Many of his works are still considered spiritual classics. While his abbey physically survived World War I, many monks were forced to leave during the war—some because German lay brothers were expelled from Belgium and others for their general safety. He died on this date in 1923 of influenza.

Saint Martina, pray for me to remain faithful to Christ.
Saint Bathildis, show me how to accept my state of life with grace and graciousness.
Saint Hyacinth, help me repent of my lukewarmness and be filled with zeal for Him.
Saint Mucian, show me how to bring others to excellence through gentleness and love.
Blessed Columba, help me to live the Benedictine motto: pray and work.

* * * * *

January 31

Saint John Bosco, Memorial

John was born in 1815 into a family of peasant farmers in Piedmont, Italy, and his father died when he was only two years old. He grew up in poverty, but he had a saintly mother who taught him to love God. He was devout and zealous for Christ from an early age. As a child, he had a dream that deeply affected him; in the dream he saw a group of fighting boys whom a mysterious lady told him to win over and lead with gentleness. He later recognized Mary in the mysterious lady and recognized his vocation as leading boys to Christ. He taught himself to juggle and perform gymnastic tricks, which he used to lure other children to attend Mass and pious activities. He went away to the seminary when he was sixteen years old, though he was too poor to pay for it himself and had to be supported by friends. He initially thought he was called to become a foreign missionary, but a rector convinced him that he was called to serve the boys of his own country, whom John had already been helping while still a seminarian. He was made an assistant chaplain for a wealthy noblewoman, but his "festive oratories" (which combined Sunday school and recreational activities) were so successful and consumed so much of his time that she gave him an ultimatum: either serve her or serve his boys. He chose his boys. Don Bosco caught pneumonia soon afterward, but his mother cared for him and helped him form a new, more permanent home for boys. Gradually, his work served 500 boys, with workshops for them to learn trades. In his home, 150 boys lived together, taking classes, including Latin, and with ten priests serving as teachers. Other adults often found his techniques (and the gentleness he emulated of his patron saint, Saint Francis de Sales) hard to imitate, and it wasn't until 1854 that he found the young men he needed to form a new congregation of priests, specifically focused on the education of boys. This became the Salesians of Don Bosco, although he didn't organize it into a religious congregation until 1859, and it took fifteen more years for the constitutions to be approved. His work spread geographically, as well as branching into a female order of nuns for the education of girls. He begged throughout Italy and into France for money to build churches for his boys, and his reputation as a saint and wonder-worker grew and brought in donations. However, his health, worn out by his dedication to his vocation, finally gave out, and after several months of decreasing strength, he died on January 31, 1888. Thousands came to pay their respects at his funeral.

Saint Metranus of Alexandria

During the persecution of the Church under the Roman emperor Decius around the year 250, the martyr Metranus died in Alexandria, Egypt. He was executed and stoned to death outside the city walls for refusing to make a sacrifice to a pagan god.

> *Saint John, beg the Lord to give me the zeal and the strength to serve Him wholeheartedly.*
> *Saint Metranus, give me the courage to recognize and reject the idols of my own culture.*

February

February 1

Saint Tryphon of Campsada

During the persecution of the Church under the Roman emperor Decius around the year 222, the martyr Tryphon died in the city of Campsada (in modern Turkey). Some traditions say he was raised in a Christian family and had the gift of healing. He was a persuasive evangelist for the faith before he was arrested, tortured, and killed for his faith in Christ.

Saint Brigid of Ireland

Brigid was born in 435 in Ireland to a Christian mother who was a slave; her father was the pagan king to whom her mother belonged. Her mother was sold before she was born, and Brigid lived with her mother until she was old enough to be returned to her owner/father. She was a high-spirited, tenderhearted girl who was precociously generous in giving away her own property (and others' property) to those who were in need. Her father eventually freed her from slavery, and she returned to live with her mother. Despite Brigid's continued generous assistance to the poor, her mother's dairy business flourished, and her mother was finally freed from slavery too. Although Brigid's father tried to arrange a marriage for her, she refused. She wanted to be a nun; she took her vows from the famous bishop at the time, Saint Patrick himself. She founded her own convent, starting with seven nuns, but in time, she founded other convents and double monasteries (monks and nuns under the same rule) all over Ireland. She served as abbess for many years until her death.

Saint Henry Morse

Henry (1595–1645) was raised a Protestant, but while he was studying law in London, he decided to become a Catholic. This was illegal in England at that time, and when he later decided to become a priest, he had to travel to Douai, France, as well as Rome, to study and be ordained. In 1624, he returned to England to minister secretly to Catholics. He was soon arrested for the crime of being a priest, but his time in prison wasn't wasted; a Jesuit priest was also in prison, and he instructed Henry and admitted him to the Jesuit order. Henry was finally released from prison but banished from England. So he went to Spain to serve as a chaplain to the English soldiers serving there. In 1633, he was able to return secretly to England, living under the assumed name of Cuthbert Claxton. He ministered to plague victims, though he caught the disease himself three times; and he provided spiritual and material help to both Protestant and Catholic families. He was too zealous (and too obviously a priest), so he was arrested, but Queen Henrietta

Maria of France intervened on his behalf. He was released again, this time on a large bail, then went to Europe and cared for English troops abroad until he was able to return to England in 1643. Eighteen months later he was arrested yet again, and he almost escaped with the help of the Catholic wife of one of his captors. But when his guide got lost, Henry was caught. He was quickly condemned to death on the basis of his previous conviction as a Catholic priest. He celebrated Mass before being brought to the place of execution. The ambassadors from France, Portugal, and Spain all came to pay honor to him in his martyrdom, though not everyone attended for friendly reasons. Before his execution, he prayed aloud for himself and his persecutors, as well as the kingdom of England.

> *Saint Brigid, teach me generosity.*
> *Saints Tryphon and Henry, help me to be zealous*
> *and selfless in bringing the Gospel to others.*

* * * * *

February 2

The Presentation of the Lord, Feast

According to the Gospel of Luke, "When the time came for their purification according to the law of Moses, they brought him up to Jerusalem to present him to the Lord (as it is written in the law of the Lord, 'Every male that opens the womb shall be called holy to the Lord') and to offer a sacrifice according to what is said in the law of the Lord, 'a pair of turtledoves, or two young pigeons.' ... And when they had performed everything according to the law of the Lord, they returned into Galilee, to their own city, Nazareth."[1]

Saint Catherine dei Ricci

Catherine was born in 1522 into a noble family in Florence, Italy. Her mother died when she was an infant. She was raised by her godmother and was a devout child. After being educated at a convent school, she announced that she wanted to become a Dominican tertiary. Her father initially objected, but he eventually agreed. Catherine began receiving visions and ecstasies in the convent, but many of the sisters ridiculed her, some saying that she was merely asleep and not seeing a vision at all, while others called her stupid. Catherine also suffered from painful illnesses, which she bore with great patience. When she was twenty years old, these supernatural phenomena began to occur according to a pattern: every Thursday at noon when she meditated on the Passion of Christ, she went into an ecstasy and received the marks of Christ's wounds on her body, which were visible until Friday at 4 P.M. This amazing experience continued for twelve years. Crowds of people came to see her, skeptics and sinners were converted at the sight of her, three future popes (Marcellus II, Leo XI, and Clement VIII)

---

[1] Lk 2:22–24, 39.

asked for her prayers, and she corresponded with (and bilocated to see) the priest, Saint Philip Neri. Over time, the Lord made her wounds less visible to others. Our Heavenly Bridegroom espoused her to Himself with a ring that only she could see, and then He called her to Heaven on this date in 1590.

Saint Joan de Lestonnac

Joan was born in 1556 and came from a distinguished family in Bordeaux, France. When her mother became a Protestant, she tried to convert Joan, and when Joan refused to give up her faith, she was mistreated. At the age of seventeen, she married Gaston de Montferrant; she and her husband eventually had four children, two of whom became nuns. After many years of happy married life, her husband died; she then tried to enter a Cistercian monastery, despite her son's opposition. Her health broke down while she was there, however, and she was sent home, recovering miraculously as soon as she left. She led others to nurse the sick during a time of plague, which led two Jesuit priests to seek her out. Because of the strength of Calvinism in the area, the two men recognized the need to provide a Catholic education to girls. With the encouragement of the two priests, Mother Joan and her companions opened the first house for educating and training girls of all classes. The Sisters of the Company of Our Lady began to grow, but a director of one of the houses along with one of the nuns, Blanche Herve, invented lies about Joan, lies that were unfortunately believed. Joan was deposed from her position, insulted, and even beaten, while Blanche herself took over the order. Joan's unalterable patience even during such cruelty finally touched Blanche's heart, and she repented. By this time, Joan thought she was too old to be a superior, and another woman, Mother de Badiffe, was elected. Joan lived in retirement, preparing for death, until it came on this day in 1640.

Saint John (Jean) Theophane Venard

John was born in 1829 into a pious family at Saint Loup, France; one of his brothers became a priest and another became a bishop. He was ordained a priest in 1852 and was sent as a missionary to Southeast Asia shortly afterward. He lived first in Hong Kong, then West Tonkin (modern Vietnam). Shortly before he had arrived, the government had begun persecuting Catholics. Despite poor health, John threw himself into the work of serving his Catholic flock secretly, at night, and in great danger. In 1860, he was betrayed to the authorities and arrested. He spent several weeks imprisoned in a cage, but the letters he wrote to his family were consoling and full of joy. He was executed by beheading on this date in 1861.

Lord, help me to give myself fully to God the Father.
Saint Catherine, help me to meditate on the Passion of Christ.
Saint Joan, help me to accept opposition and rejection with humility and love.
Saint John, show me how to be joyful in my suffering.

* * * * *

February 3

Saint Blaise, Optional Memorial

Blaise was bishop of Sebastea (now in modern Armenia) when he was martyred in 316 for the faith during the persecution of Christians under the Roman emperor Licinius. Later traditions also say he was born of noble parents, became a bishop when he was young, and lived in deserted places during times of persecution, where he befriended the wild animals who lived there. When a poor woman came to him with her dying son, who had a fishbone stuck in his throat, Blaise healed the boy. This miracle led to the annual prayers for his intercession for sicknesses of the throat. Blaise is one of the Fourteen Holy Helpers, great saints who were called upon particularly for help during the bubonic plague in the fourteenth century.

Saint Ansgar, Optional Memorial

Ansgar was born in 801 into a noble family in France. He became a Benedictine monk and studied under two holy and learned abbots, Saints Adelard and Paschasius Radbert. While accompanying King Harold in exile to Jutland (a region now including Denmark and Germany), he recognized God's call to become a missionary there. He taught the Gospel to the people and founded the first Christian church in Sweden around the year 832. Pope Gregory IV ordained him archbishop of Hamburg, Germany, and he served as papal legate to Scandinavian countries as well as archbishop of Bremen, Germany. He built a Christian school in Denmark, though it was later burned down by pagans; he converted King Erik of Jutland to the faith; and he spoke out against the practice of slavery. He was known for his care for the poor and the sick, his great preaching, and his miracles. After his death in 865, paganism destroyed much of his work, but subsequent generations of missionaries restored the Christian faith to the area.

Prophet Simeon and Prophetess Anna of Jerusalem

According to the Gospel of Luke,

> Now there was a man in Jerusalem, whose name was Simeon, and this man was righteous and devout, looking for the consolation of Israel, and the Holy Spirit was upon him. And it had been revealed to him by the Holy Spirit that he should not see death before he had seen the Lord's Christ. And inspired by the Spirit he came into the temple; and when the parents brought in the child Jesus, to do for him according to the custom of the law, he took him up in his arms and blessed God and said, "Lord, now let your servant depart in peace, according to your word; for my eyes have seen your salvation which you have prepared in the presence of all peoples, a light for revelation to the Gentiles, and for glory to your people Israel." ... And there was a prophetess, Anna, the daughter of Phanuel, of the tribe of Asher; she was of a great age, having lived with her husband seven years from her virginity, and as a widow till she was eighty-four. She did not

depart from the temple, worshiping with fasting and prayer night and day. And coming up at that very hour she gave thanks to God, and spoke of [Jesus] to all who were looking for the redemption of Jerusalem.[2]

> *Saint Blaise, help me bring the healing of Jesus Christ to others.*
> *Saint Ansgar, show me how to trust in the Lord despite apparent setbacks.*
> *Prophets Simeon and Anna, show me how to proclaim the coming of Christ to others.*

* * * * *

February 4

Saint Gilbert of Sempringham

Gilbert was born in 1083 at Sempringham, England. He became a priest and teacher. When his wealthy father gave him the revenues to two parsonages, he gave the money to the poor instead of keeping it for himself. As a priest, he guided his flock like a good shepherd, and he established a house for enclosed nuns. Though the order he founded, the Gilbertines, gradually expanded to include lay brothers, lay sisters, and canons regular, it was always primarily a women's order, and houses were founded only in England. Their austere way of life was strongly influenced by the Cistercians, and the Divine Office was celebrated simply and humbly. Gilbert himself ate sparingly; for the poor, though, he always filled a plate of food with the best of what had been served, which he called "the plate of the Lord Jesus".[3] At the end of his life, Gilbert lost his sight and stepped down as master general. In 1189, he died at the age of 106. Sadly, all Gilbertine houses were destroyed during the dissolution of the Catholic Church in England under King Henry VIII.

Saint Jane Valois

Jane (1464–1505) was the daughter of King Louis XI of France. She was deformed at birth and was often sick when she was a child. She was married to a duke for political reasons when she was nine years old; she praised him to others, prayed for him, and developed great affection for him. But as soon as the duke became king, he annulled their marriage. As a former princess, she was made a duchess and given a province to govern. Not only did she bear this humiliating separation with humility and forgiveness, but she became a wise leader and founded the Order of the Annonciades, which encouraged members to imitate the virtues of the Blessed Mother.

Saint John de Britto

John was born in 1647 into a noble family from the court of Lisbon in Portugal, receiving all its privileges of wealth and power, including growing up in the

[2] Lk 2:25–32, 36–38.
[3] Michael Walsh, ed., *Butler's Lives of the Saints, Concise Edition, Revised and Updated* (San Francisco: HarperCollins Publishers, 1991), 49.

company of the future king of Portugal, a boy his own age. But John had only one vocation in mind: to become a missionary and spread the Gospel. Despite his family's objections, he entered the Jesuit order when he was fifteen years old. He was such a good student that many thought it was a shame to let him leave Portugal, but in 1673, he and sixteen other Jesuits set sail for Goa (now called India) as missionaries. He lived austerely among the native people and respected their caste laws in all ways lawful. He later became the superior of the mission in Madura, where his personal devotion was a great example to both his fellow priests and the native people. His mission was also physically dangerous; on one occasion, he and a group of devout Indians were captured and tortured. John miraculously recovered and was called back to Portugal, but there he begged to be allowed to return to India. He returned and served three more years before he was arrested by a local ruler for having "taught things subversive of the worship of the gods of the country".[4] Although the nervous ruler delayed the execution temporarily, John was finally beheaded on this date in 1693. When the news reached Portugal, King Pedro called for a Mass of thanksgiving, which John's mother attended, dressed in festive clothing to celebrate her son's entry into Heaven.

> *Saint Gilbert, help me find a way to fill "the plate of the Lord Jesus" today.*
> *Saint Jane, help me to accept rejection with peace and charity.*
> *Saint John, pray for me to think less of myself and more of the salvation of others.*

* * * * *

February 5

Saint Agatha, Memorial

Agatha (d. ca. 250) was a beautiful, wealthy young Christian from Catania, Sicily, who consecrated her life to God during the days of the early Church. When she refused to marry a Roman consul named Quintian, he tried to punish her by forcibly putting her in a brothel. When she refused to be shamed into living such a life, he turned her in to the authorities, denouncing her as a Christian. To try to make her give up her faith, they tortured her—cutting off her breasts, stretching her on a rack, and throwing her onto burning coals. During all these tortures, onlookers said she prayed deeply to Jesus Christ. Her torturers were careful not to torture her to death and threw her back into prison. After praying to be released from this world, she died. All this occurred during the persecution of Christians under the Roman emperor Decius.

Saint Adelaide of Bellich

Adelaide was born around the year 970 and was the daughter of the count of Guelder in Germany. She chose to enter the Ursuline convent of Cologne,

---

[4] Ibid., 39.

then became a Benedictine nun and ultimately was made abbess of two convents that her father had founded: the Abbey of Villich and the Abbey of Saint Mary of Cologne. She valued education; to ensure that her nuns understood and could fully participate in the Mass, they were taught Latin. The archbishop of Cologne, Saint Heribert, often consulted her for advice; she and her nuns provided for the poor who came to the convent for help. She died on this date in 1015.

Blessed Elizabeth Canori Mora

Elizabeth was born in 1774 into a devout, well-to-do family in Rome and was an intelligent girl. Her family fostered her spirit of penance and her profound interior life. She married Cristoforo Mora, a young lawyer, when she was twenty-two years old. Unfortunately, Cristoforo changed dramatically after they married and became a jealous, controlling husband. He was also unfaithful to her, and he ultimately squandered the entire family fortune on his mistress. Elizabeth bore him four children, two of whom died soon after birth. When her husband abandoned her, she was forced to raise her two daughters alone and in great poverty. She cared for her home, served the poor and the sick, and dedicated a great deal of time to prayer. Her experiences led her to a profound understanding of suffering, and she joined the Trinitarian Third Order. She also experienced prophetic visions, one of which paralleled the future Fatima vision of an attack on the pope. She died on this date in 1825, with her daughters by her side. Her husband, who had been with his mistress when she died, repented after her death, as Elizabeth had predicted, and eventually became a priest.

> *Saint Agatha, help me to accept suffering for the sake of Christ.*
> *Saint Adelaide, lead me to learn more about my faith.*
> *Blessed Elizabeth, show me how to forgive with my whole heart.*

* * * * *

February 6

Saint Paul Miki and Companions, Memorial

On this date in 1597, twenty-six Catholics were martyred for the Catholic faith in Japan. One of them, Paul Miki, was a Japanese man from a highly placed family who had converted and become a Jesuit priest. The other twenty-five men were Franciscans and Jesuits; laymen and catechists and lay brothers; and Portuguese, Spaniards, and Japanese. As part of the Japanese practice of execution, the men had parts of their ears cut off, and twenty-four of them were led through various towns as an example to others before being taken to Nagasaki. The men were allowed to receive the Sacrament of Confession before their executions, but they were then fastened to crosses with chains and iron collars. At a signal, each executioner threw a lance into the side of one of the men, and thus all twenty-six died at the same instant. Their fellow Christians treasured their garments and blood; miracles were ascribed to the intercession of these martyrs.

Saint Dorothy

Dorothy was a Christian from Caesarea, a region now in modern Turkey, who consecrated herself to Jesus Christ. During the persecution of Christians under the Roman emperor Diocletian in the year 311, she was arrested and condemned to death. According to tradition, as she was taken to her execution, a lawyer mocked her faith, but she told him she would send him flowers from Heaven. When he unexpectedly received roses after her death, he converted to the faith.

Holy Martyrs, help me be an example of Christian charity to others.

* * * * *

February 7

Saint Luke the Younger

Due to the dangers of attacks by Muslim Arabs, Luke (d. 946) and his family left the island of Aegina for Thessaly (both in modern Greece), where the family lived as peasant farmers. Luke was a good, pious boy who tended the family's fields and sheep. Even at a young age, he would often feed the hungry from his own food and give his clothes to beggars. People noticed that he scattered some of his father's seed on the land of the poor, but his father's crops still flourished. When his father died, Luke decided to live a contemplative life. However, while traveling to a monastery to become a monk, soldiers arrested him. They thought he was a runaway slave, so they treated him cruelly and locked him up. When they discovered his true identity, he was released, but when he returned home, his neighbors ridiculed him for running away. Luke's family wouldn't let him leave their home again until one day when two monks happened by and convinced his mother to let him live with them in a monastery. But soon after Luke arrived at the monastery, his superior received a vision of Luke's mother and sent him home to help her. His mother, however, now recognized his true vocation as a monk and allowed him to leave. He was eighteen years old when he left home and built a hermitage on Mount Joannitsa near the city of Corinth. It's said that he was once seen raised from the ground during prayer and that his cell was made into an oratory after his death.

Blessed Pius IX

Pius (d. 1878) was the 255th pope; he reigned thirty-one years. His reign is considered the second longest reign in papal history after Saint Peter. He opened the First Vatican Council, which was unfortunately cut short due to political instability in Italy; regions previously known as the papal states became part of the kingdom of Italy and were no longer under the temporal rule of the pope. Pius proclaimed the dogma of the Immaculate Conception of Mary and defined papal infallibility. He was also known for his charity for the poor, personal kindheartedness, and devotion to the Blessed Mother.

Blesseds Anselm (Anselmo) Polanco and Philip (Felipe) Ripoll Morata

Anselm was born in 1881 in Buenavista de Valdavia, Spain. He became an Augustinian Canon, was ordained a priest, and traveled to Peru, Colombia, China, and the United States as provincial superior of the Augustinian order. As bishop of Teruel, he stood up for his flock when the anti-Catholic Republican Army overran the city during the Spanish Civil War. Philip was born in 1878 in Teruel, Spain. He became a priest and rector, and he was Bishop Anselm's assistant when the Republican Army took control of Teruel. Both men resisted government control of the Church and their people; they were imprisoned for over a year and were finally shot on this date in 1939.

> *Saint Luke, help me to pray.*
> *Blessed Pius, strengthen my devotion to the Blessed Virgin Mary.*
> *Blesseds Anselm and Philip, show me how to live and die for Christ.*

* * * * *

February 8

Saint Jerome Emiliani, Optional Memorial

Jerome was born in 1481 into a wealthy family in Venice, Italy, and served in the army as a commander of soldiers. During a battle, he was taken prisoner. While suffering in a prison dungeon, he recognized that he had been living a lukewarm life as a Christian. He repented, prayed, and was able to escape from prison by an apparent miracle. When he was able to return home, he hung up his prison fetters at the altar of the shrine of Our Lady of Treviso, symbolically giving his life to Mary. People made him mayor of the town, but it wasn't long before he left that post to pursue ordination, simultaneously taking charge of the care and education of his orphaned nephews. In 1518, he was ordained a priest. Venice had recently suffered from both famine and plague, and Jerome threw himself into the hard work of caring for and feeding people in need, particularly abandoned orphans. He caught the plague himself, but after he recovered, he devoted all his time and remaining money to establish orphanages, a home for penitent prostitutes, and a hospital. In 1532, he and two other priests founded the Somaschi (named after the city of Somascha, where they were located), a congregation primarily devoted to the care of orphans. One of his educational innovations was to use a set order of questions and answers to teach the faith to children. In 1537, he caught an infectious disease, and he died on this date.

Saint Josephine Bakhita, Optional Memorial

Born in a wealthy family in Sudan, she (1868–1947) was kidnapped when she was nine years old by slave traders who named her Bakhita. The trauma of the experience caused her to forget her birthname. She was brutally treated when she was a slave: Bakhita was flogged to unconsciousness after committing a minor mistake; as another punishment, she was forcibly tattooed with sixty-six patterns over her body—with salt poured in. She was bought and sold several times until she was finally bought by Callisto Legnani, an Italian consul. She worked for the Legnani family as a nanny and grew to love her new home in Italy; she converted to the faith and took the name Josephine. In 1893, she entered the Institute of Canossian Daughters of Charity, serving as a Canossian sister for the next fifty years. She was gentle and amiable, was willing to help with any task, and was a comfort to those who came for help from the sisters. A biography of her life was published in 1930; she became a well-known Christian speaker, raising money for the missions through her story.

Martyrs of Constantinople

In the late fifth century, a charming, intelligent priest named Acacius became patriarch of Constantinople. Unfortunately, history strongly indicates that Acacius was a manipulative grandstander who did everything in his power to shift political control to himself. When the faithful monks of Constantinople opposed him and appealed to faraway Rome and orthodox teaching, Acacius had them imprisoned and then executed in the year 485. They all died as martyrs.

> *Saint Jerome, help me to recognize those who need my help.*
> *Saint Josephine, show me how to trust in God in my sufferings.*
> *Holy Martyrs, help me stand up for Christ.*

* * * * *

February 9

Saint Apollonia of Alexandria

Apollonia (d. 249) was a consecrated virgin and deaconess living in Alexandria, Egypt, when an anti-Christian riot broke out. A mob seized her since she was a leader in the local Christian community, and the angry crowd beat her, even beating her teeth out. When she was told to renounce Christ or die, she leapt into the fire that had been prepared to burn her to death, dying a martyr.

Saint Michael Febres Cordero

Though he was given the name Francisco in 1854 when he was born to a prominent family in Cuenca, Ecuador, he's known today by his name in religious life, Michael. He was educated at a college that had been established by the Brothers of the Christian Schools and was an excellent student. His parents wanted him to become a priest, so they resisted when he said he wanted to join the brothers and instead sent him to a seminary; but when he was sent home from the seminary because of poor health three months later, his mother changed her mind. As a brother, he taught students (languages, in particular), prepared children for First Communion, and wrote textbooks and a catechism. In 1907, he was sent to Belgium and then to Barcelona to give him more time to write and to improve his health. However, he died there on this date in 1910.

Saint Apollonia, give me your gift of fortitude.
Saint Michael, teach me humility.

* * * * *

February 10

Saint Scholastica, Memorial

Scholastica (d. 543), twin sister of Saint Benedict, was born into a good family in Nursia, Italy. Scholastica lived a holy, secluded life (whether in community or at home, it's not certain) before she founded a nunnery near Benedict's monastery. She served as abbess of that nunnery, but under Benedict's direction. She and Benedict met only once a year and only for one day. The last time they met, Benedict started to leave over Scholastica's objections. She bent her head and prayed, and a storm broke out. A brother to the end, Benedict blamed his sister for the storm and asked what she had done. Scholastica replied, "I asked a favour of you, and you refused it. I asked it of God, and He has granted it."[5] Since Benedict couldn't leave, they spent the night talking about holy things. When Scholastica died three days later, Benedict saw a vision of her soul flying up to Heaven like a dove.

Blessed Aloysius (Alojzije) Stepanic

Aloysius was born in 1898 into a large Catholic family in Croatia. During World War I, he served as a soldier for the Austrian Army, and, in 1918, he was captured, imprisoned, and released. After the war, he considered marriage but recognized a call to the priesthood. In time, he earned doctorates in philosophy and theology, but he also served the poor as a parish priest. He became archbishop of Zagreb in 1937. When Nazism gained power in Europe, Aloysius recognized another call: to defend the human rights of all people, regardless of religion, nationality, race, or social class. During World War II, Aloysius hid people in need, particularly Jews, from the Nazis using church property and monasteries. When the war ended, the oppression of Nazism was simply replaced

---

[5] Walsh, *Butler's Lives of the Saints*, 43.

by the oppression of Communism in Yugoslavia. Once again, Aloysius spoke and wrote against government infringement of human rights. The government responded by attacking the Church and arresting Aloysius, subjecting him to a show trial. When officials accused him of collaborating with the Nazis, Jewish leaders all over the world protested and pointed to Aloysius' strong voice in their defense against Nazism. He was sentenced to sixteen years of hard labor in 1946, but when his health deteriorated in 1951, his sentence was reduced to house arrest. During that time, he was able to receive visitors, write letters, and otherwise act as a priest; he never showed any resentment for the persecution he endured. When Pope Pius XII named him a cardinal in 1953 to honor his sacrifices, the government angrily broke all ties with Rome. On this date in 1960, Aloysius died. He suffered from multiple medical problems at the time, but during the examination of his body in the beatification process, arsenic was found in his bones, indicating that his death had been murder. Unsurprisingly, Pope John Paul II declared him a martyr in 1998.

Saint Scholastica, help me pray with childlike trust in God.
Blessed Aloysius, help me stand up for those who are treated unjustly.

* * * * *

February 11

Our Lady of Lourdes

In 1858, a fourteen-year-old peasant girl named Bernadette was looking for wood with friends in the area near the city dump. She saw a vision of a beautiful lady, who reappeared to her repeatedly over the next several days. The woman prayed with (the future saint) Bernadette and finally identified herself as "the Immaculate Conception". Since then, numerous miraculous healings have occurred at Lourdes, a reminder of our Lady's maternal care for all of us.

Saint Soteris of Rome

Soteris (d. 304) was from a noble family in Rome during the days of the early Church. Despite her wealth and beauty, she gave her life to God, living simply and dressing plainly. During the persecution of Christians under the Roman emperor Decius, she was arrested, tortured, and released. For a half century, she lived a prayerful life, but she was arrested again during the renewed persecution under the Roman emperor Diocletian. She refused to cry out as she was being tortured and was finally beheaded.

Saint Gregory II

Gregory (d. 731) was the eighty-ninth pope; he reigned for fifteen years. Before being made pope, he was a Roman citizen, then a subdeacon, and the first known papal librarian. When he became pope, he immediately ordered the walls of Rome to be repaired to protect the citizens from attack (a serious threat at the time); he spent the rest of his papacy concerned with the safety of Christians from the Saracens (Muslim Arabs). He sent Saints Corbinian and Boniface, the missionary priests, to bring the faith to Bavaria; he supported the monasteries, most notably, ordering the restoration of the famous Abbey of Monte Cassino. The Greek emperor Leo III followed the iconoclastic heresy; Gregory faced many complex situations with him over his persecution of those who possessed and prayed with icons, as well as other political issues that threatened the Church.

Saint Paschal I

Paschal (d. 824) studied at the Lateran Basilica before becoming a Benedictine monk; later, he was made abbot of a monastery near Rome. In the year 817, he was elected pope. During his papacy, he fought the iconoclastic heresy in two ways: he protected Christians who were persecuted by the empire for the "crime" of possessing and using Christian images, and he supported the creation of religious art. In more worldly matters, a murder that was perpetrated by members of his own household resulted in limits being placed on the judicial and law enforcement powers of the pope. (Paschal had resisted the efforts of the state to interfere and wanted to judge the responsible individuals himself.) Paschal supported the saintly monks Nicephorus and Theodore the Studite, who wrote against iconoclasm, and he enshrined relics of the martyrs in churches.

> *Our Lady of Lourdes, beg the Lord to heal me of _____.*
> *Saint Soteris, show me how to glorify God through a life of prayer.*
> *Saints Gregory and Paschal, help me to draw closer to God through sacred art.*

* * * * *

February 12

Martyrs of Carthage

During the persecution of the Church under the Roman emperor Diocletian in the year 304, soldiers were sent into the churches of Albitina in North Africa on a Sunday morning. Everyone who had come to Mass was arrested and taken to the city of Carthage for interrogation. Of that number, at least forty-six men and women refused to renounce their faith in Christ and were tortured and then executed.

Saint Meletius

Meletius (d. 381) was born into a distinguished family in the city of Melitene (in today's Armenia), and, because of his kind and gentle disposition, he was nominated to the position of bishop of Sebastea (now the city of Sivas, Turkey). There were violent divisions between Catholics and Arians at that time, and the strong opposition he faced in defending traditional Catholic teaching caused him to leave Sebastea and settle in the desert. The city of Antioch, also deeply divided by the Catholic/Arian controversy, chose Meletius to become their archbishop in the year 361. Both sides wanted to know whether he was a Catholic or an Arian, so Meletius and two others were asked to explain a passage publicly from the book of Proverbs (8:22): "The LORD created me at the beginning of his work." When Meletius explained it in the Catholic sense, showing Jesus to be both true God and true man, the Arians convinced the emperor to banish him to Lesser Armenia and put an Arian bishop in his place instead. In the year 378, the Arian persecution of Catholics was ended by the death of the emperor, but at that point there were two orthodox Catholics who had been named archbishop of Antioch: Meletius and one other. The resulting schism wasn't ended until several years after Meletius' death. But Meletius served his flock as best he could and presided over the second ecumenical council at Constantinople in the year 381. There he died. Gregory of Nyssa, bishop of Nyssa and also a saint, delivered his funeral oration.

Saint Benedict of Aniane

Benedict (d. 821) was the son of Aigulf of Maguelone, France, and served as cupbearer (a high-ranking position in a royal household) to the French king Pepin as well as to Charlemagne. During a military campaign, he jumped into the river to save his brother and almost drowned in the process. His brush with death made him decide to leave the world behind, so he lived an austere life as a monk in an abbey for a few years, even adding some practices from the Rules of Saint Pachomius and Saint Basil to the Benedictine Rule, which his abbey was already following. When his abbot died, his fellow monks asked Benedict to succeed him. Since he believed that they wouldn't accept the reforms he wanted to institute, he left the abbey. He built a hermitage for himself near the brook Aniane, "praying continually that God would teach him to do His will",[6] as *Butler's Lives of the Saints* describes it. Some other hermits gradually placed themselves under his direction, and together they worked in the fields, begged for alms to feed themselves, and lived on bread and water except on Sundays and feast days. He eventually built a monastery to house these men; his influence grew as he brought his simple way of life to other monasteries as well. Emperor Louis the Pious asked Benedict to serve him as an advisor, so Benedict obediently moved to a monastery nearby. The collection of monastic regulations that Benedict created, called the *Codex Regularum*, was eventually used throughout the empire's monasteries. Benedict, having reformed monastic life in the West, died at the age of seventy-one.

> *Holy Martyrs, help me to remember to thank God*
> *for the privilege of attending Mass without fear.*
> *Saint Meletius, teach me how to speak the truth about Jesus Christ to others.*
> *Saint Benedict, teach me how to do God's will.*

* * * * *

---

[6] Walsh, *Butler's Lives of the Saints*, 43.

February 13

Saint Benignus of Todi

During the persecution of the Church under the Roman emperor Diocletian in the year 303, the martyr-priest Benignus died in the city of Todi, Italy. Benignus' name is one of the 140 saints listed on the Doric collonnades in Saint Peter's Square in Rome.

Blessed Eustochium (Lucrezia Bellini) of Padua

Lucrezia was born in 1444 at a Benedictine convent in Padua, Italy, because her mother, a nun at the convent, had been seduced. But Lucrezia enjoyed growing up in the convent and wanted to become a nun herself. Despite opposition from some of the other nuns, who were offended by her scandalous birth, the bishop accepted her request. In 1461, Lucrezia entered the novitiate, and she took the name of Eustochium. She was noted for being gentle, humble, and pious, but she was also subject to violent fits for four years. To attempt to cure her, she was starved, exorcised repeatedly, and imprisoned. A mob accused her of poisoning her own abbess at one point. But she accepted all her crosses with patience and had won over the majority of the nuns to her side by the time she took her formal vows. She died soon afterward, on this date in 1469.

> *Saint Benignus, help me be a witness to Christ and His Church.*
> *Blessed Eustochium, help me to be scandalized only by my own sins.*

* * * * *

February 14

Saint Cyril and Saint Methodius, Apostles of the Slavs, Memorial

Two brothers were born in the city of Thessalonika, Greece, in the ninth century: Cyril (though born with the name Constantine) and Methodius. Cyril was the younger brother but was sent to study at Constantinople, where he became a deacon and teacher of philosophy before becoming a monk. Methodius had become the governor of a Slav colony when he too decided to leave the world behind and become a monk. The nearby patriarch of Constantinople, Photius, was asked to send missionaries to bring the Gospel to the faraway Slavic people; he chose to send Cyril and Methodius because they spoke the Slavic language and were educated men. So in the year 863, the two brothers and their assistants set out for the court of Rotislav, the prince of Moravia (today's Czech Republic). As they taught the Slavic people about the Christian faith, they used the Slavic language when they preached and developed a written alphabet for the Slavic language. This innovative approach of accommodating the Gospel to the culture of the people led many Slavs to become Catholics. But nearby German Catholics objected to this, even refusing to ordain their Slavic converts to be priests.

The brothers returned to Constantinople to gain Church approval of their methods, but while in Venice, they discovered that Patriarch Photius, the man who had originally sent them, had been excommunicated. (History also tells us that it was deserved and that Photius was a scheming and arrogant man.) So the brothers went to Rome instead of Constantinople, bringing relics of the late pope, Saint Clement, as gifts for the current pope. Pope Adrian II received them warmly; he ordained both men as bishops, gave them permission to use the vernacular in the liturgy, and ordained their Slavic neophytes to the priesthood. Unfortunately, Cyril died in Rome on February 14, 869, and Methodius returned without him to be the metropolitan of the large area where the Slavic people lived. However, local politics had changed in his absence, and Methodius was imprisoned and put in a leaking prison cell for two years until the new pope, John VIII, could get him released. This pope withdrew permission for him to use the Slavic language (which he called barbarous), except for preaching. Apparently, Methodius used the Slavic language anyway and was recalled to Rome, where he was able to convince the pope not only of his orthodoxy but also of the value of using the vernacular language. Methodius returned to his people and spent the last four years of his life translating the Bible into Slavonic and completing a compilation of Byzantine church and civil law. It's possible that he did so much writing at this time because the changed political climate left him unable to do much missionary work. For example, Methodius was still strongly opposed by the nearby Germans, and in particular by a priest named Wiching, who opposed Methodius so completely that he forged pontifical documents and undid much of Methodius' work after his death. Methodius died in the Czech Republic on April 6, 884.

Saint Valentine of Rome

According to an ancient tradition, Valentine of Rome (d. 269) was a Roman priest and physician who was imprisoned for the faith (perhaps for officiating at the marriages of Roman soldiers, who were forbidden to marry at the time), restored the sight of his jailer's daughter, and was beaten and beheaded for being a Christian.

> *Saints Cyril and Methodius, help me to trust in the Lord in every obstacle.*
> *Saint Valentine, show me how to bring Christ's love to those around me.*

* * * * *

February 15

Saint Onesimus

Onesimus (d. ca. 90) was a slave to Philemon and Apphia, two Christians living in Colossae (a city in modern Turkey); his name means "useful". (Historians say that this name was sometimes given to infants who had been abandoned by Romans but were saved from death by Christians.) Onesimus stole something, then ran away and later came to serve the Apostle Paul. Paul wrote a letter to Philemon, which is now part of Sacred Scripture. In the letter, Paul says that he is sending Onesimus back to Philemon, "no longer as a slave but more than a slave, as a beloved brother, especially to me but how much more to you, both in the flesh and in the Lord"[7]. Since the punishment for a runaway slave was death, Paul's forceful words must have reconciled Philemon and Onesimus. According to tradition, Onesimus later became a bishop and was martyred for the faith.

Saints Faustinus and Jovita of Brescia

Faustinus and Jovita (both d. ca. 118) were from a noble family in the city of Brescia, Italy. Faustinus was a priest, and Jovita was a deacon. Despite the persecution of Christians under the Roman emperor Hadrian, they preached the Good News to those around them; so they were arrested, tortured, and beheaded, dying as martyrs.

Saint Sigfrid of Sweden

Sigfrid was born in late tenth-century England and had become a priest of York before he was sent as a missionary bishop to serve the people of Norway and Sweden. Sigfrid set up his headquarters at the city of Vaxjo and eventually brought the Swedish king to the faith. At one point, he left his diocese in the care of his three assistants, who happened to be his nephews; while he was gone, a troop of men murdered the nephews and plundered the church. When Sigrid returned, he forgave the murderers and asked the king to spare their lives. (A colorful tradition says that the heads of the dead nephews were recovered from a pond and spoke to Sigrid.) When the king tried to give Sigfrid the heavy fine imposed on the murderers as a gift, he refused. Sigfrid was known for his simple way of life and personal honesty. He died in the year 1045.

Saint Claude de la Colombiere

Claude was born into the French nobility in 1641 and heard God's call to become a priest when he was very young. He was educated by Jesuits, became a Jesuit priest in 1659, and taught in Avignon, France. He became the spiritual director of Saint Margaret Mary Alacoque, who promoted devotion to the Sacred Heart of Jesus. He also helped to spread this devotion to oppose the dour heresy of Jansenism, which was widespread in France at the time. He was sent to England to serve as chaplain to the Catholic duchess of York. While there, he converted many Protestants to the Catholic faith. For this reason, he was imprisoned and accused of being part of a "popish plot"; only the efforts of King Louis XIV of France kept him from being executed. He was forced to leave England, but prison life had ruined his health. He died on this date in 1682

[7] Philem 16.

at Paray-le-Monial, France. Since he suffered every abuse for the faith except death, he's considered a dry martyr.

> *Saint Onesimus, pray for me to be a "useful" servant of Jesus Christ.*
> *Saints Faustinus and Jovita, help me be fearless in speaking of the Lord.*
> *Saint Sigfrid, teach me the words that will bring others to God.*
> *Saint Claude, show me how to offer my sufferings to the Sacred Heart of Jesus.*

* * * * *

February 16

Martyrs of Cilicia

During the time of the persecution of the Church under the Roman emperor Maximinus II in the early fourth century, five Christian men went to the mines of Cilicia to minister to the Christians who were imprisoned there. When it was discovered that they were Christians, the five men—Elias, Jeremiah, Isaiah, Samuel, and Daniel—were arrested, tortured, and executed. The Christians in the mines who were identified as a result were also martyred with them: Pamphylus, Paul of Jamnia, Valens of Jerusalem, Julian of Cappadocia, Porphyrius of Caesarea, Seleucis of Caesarea, and Theodulus the Servant. This happened in the year 309.

Saint Maruta of Syria

Maruta became bishop of Mayferkqat, Syria, in the late fourth century, shortly after the anti-Catholic persecution by Persian King Sapor had done great damage to the community and its churches. Maruta organized the building and repairing of churches. He also collected relics of the martyrs—so many that his city became known as the city of martyrs—and wrote hymns and biographies of them. Because of his theological writings, the Church in Syria acclaims him a Doctor of the Church. According to tradition, a later king, Yezdigerd, also persecuted Christians, and Maruta went in person to ask the king to end it. While he was there, the king was cured of his painful headaches. This caused the Zoroastrian priests in favor at court to be afraid that Yezdigerd would convert, so they created a hiding place in their temple. The next time the king came to the temple, a mysterious voice (from their hiding place) told him not to allow Christians to enter. Fortunately, Maruta was able to expose the deception by pointing out the trap door in the floor. While the king never became a Christian, he at least tolerated them in his kingdom. Maruta died around the year 415 of natural causes.

> *Holy Martyrs, give me courage to help Christians in need, regardless of the cost.*
> *Saint Maruta, help me to draw strength from the witness of the martyrs.*

* * * * *

Seven Holy Founders of the Servite Order, Optional Memorial

Seven devout men of prominent families lived in the city of Florence, Italy, during the thirteenth century: Buonfiglio Monaldi, Bartholomew degli Amidei, John Buonaguinta, Benedict dell'Antela, Geraldino Sostegni, Ricovero Uguccione, and Alexis Falconieri. As pious men, they all became members of the Confraternity of the Blessed Virgin, a voluntary association of laypeople with a devotion to Mary; living upright lives despite the immoral culture around them. In time, these men all recognized a desire to renounce worldly life; while praying together on the Solemnity of the Assumption, they all saw the Blessed Mother in a vision and were inspired to make an even greater sacrifice and live for God alone. This wasn't easy to do, however, because although three of them were celibates, two were widowers, and two were still married. After they had made arrangements for their families and received approval from the bishop, the men withdrew to live in a house outside of Florence. Because they were still close to their native city, many friends and family came to visit them, and they decided to move farther away. They settled at Monte Scenario and lived a simple and austere life. They initially refused to allow other people to join them, but after a cardinal counseled them to be cautious about that decision, they prayed for God's direction. Again the Virgin Mary appeared to them, this time holding a black habit and accompanied by an angel who held a scroll with the title "Servants of Mary" on it. They founded the Servants of Mary on April 13, 1240, followed the Rule of Saint Augustine, and wore black habits. All were ordained priests except Brother Alexis, who humbly asked to be excused. The number of followers grew rapidly, although formal recognition of the order took decades. These seven men served as priors general and founders of new houses as the order grew until they died, one by one, of old age and sickness. Brother Alexis lived to be 110 years old and was the only one who survived to see the order finally recognized.

Saint Theodore Tiro

Theodore was a Roman soldier in Anatolia, a region in modern Turkey, who was accused of being a Christian around the years 306–311. A military tribunal decided Theodore had simply made a mistake, so they let him go and gave him the chance to "reconsider". In response, Theodore burned down a pagan temple. He was then arrested and ordered to apostatize. When he refused, he was tortured by having his flesh torn off. While enduring this torture, he recited the words of the psalms until he died, sometime in the early fourth century. (His title, Theodore Tiro, simply means "Theodore the Recruit". He is also called Theodore Stratelates, the latter term meaning "general".)

Saint Flavian of Constantinople

Flavian was a Church leader in Constantinople when he was named patriarch of the city around the year 446. Despite the fact that the Arian heresy was widespread in Constantinople, Flavian remained faithful to the truth and taught that Jesus was both fully human and fully divine. When the Second Council of Ephesus in 449 was convened by the Byzantine emperor Theodosius II, Pope Saint Leo the Great wrote a letter to Flavian, now called the *Tome of Leo*, in which Leo eloquently explained that Jesus Christ was both true God and true man. However, the emperor was a follower of the Arian heresy and didn't want the council to support orthodox doctrine. Under his orders, soldiers refused to allow this letter to be read aloud at the council. They deposed Flavian as patriarch, beat him, and sent him to prison. He died soon afterward, a martyrdom that horrified the pope and all the Christian faithful.

> *Servants of Mary, show me how to be Mary's servant always and everywhere.*
> *Saint Theodore, may the power of God's Word give me strength in my difficulties.*
> *Saint Flavian, help me to speak the truth about Jesus Christ, regardless of the cost.*

* * * * *

February 18

Saint Tarasius of Constantinople

Tarasius was born in 750 to Byzantine nobility and rose to be secretary of state to the emperor Constantine IV and the empress Irene in Constantinople. In his private life, he lived like a monk, and perhaps for that reason was unanimously chosen to be patriarch of Constantinople. He refused to lead his flock, however, until his see of Constantinople had been fully reconciled to Rome. The most immediate cause of division between Rome and Constantinople had been the heresy of iconoclasm, so Tarasius convoked a council to reverse previous orders against the use of holy images in his see. Ultimately, though not until after a riot and a papal decision, iconoclasm was defeated. When a later emperor plotted to get rid of his wife for another woman, Tarasius condemned his actions. Tarasius was persecuted and spied upon, and his friends were banished, but ultimately the emperor was ousted by other political realities. (The emperor's own mother won over the court and army, had her son imprisoned, and ordered his eyes to be put out, but she too later lost power and was banished.) Tarasius' final years were spent peacefully. Before his death in 806, he appeared to fall in a trance, in which he argued and defended his past actions, until he serenely gave up his spirit.

Saint Theotonius of Coimbra

Theotonius (d. 1166) was the nephew of the bishop of Coimbra, Portugal; under his uncle's direction, Theotonius studied to become a priest. After ordination, he was sent to Viseu, where he became known for his personal holiness and preaching ability. Although he was repeatedly offered the position of bishop by the queen and her husband, he declined. Instead, he spoke out against vice (including the queen's actions on occasion), led processions that included collecting alms for the poor, and sang a solemn Mass every Friday for the poor and for the poor souls in Purgatory. After his second pilgrimage to the Holy Land, he chose to enter a monastery of Augustinian Canons in Coimbra, where he became a monk and later prior. The king and queen had the greatest respect for Theotonius, though he would never allow the queen (or any woman) to enter the monastery. He insisted on reverence in the praying of the Divine Office and was abbot for the last thirty years of his life. The king liberated Christians captured in war at Theotonius' request and attributed his recovered health to Theotonius' prayers. When the holy man died at the age of eighty, the king said, "His soul will have gone up to Heaven before his body is lowered into the tomb."[8]

Blessed John (Fra Angelico) of Fiesole

Giovanni (John) was born in 1387 in Vicchio, Italy, and was already a well-known painter when he heard God's call to become a religious. He became a Dominican friar at Fiesole and "preached" through his magnificent artwork. He painted throughout Tuscany and at the Vatican; he adamantly refused the pope's offer to make him a bishop and died in Rome in 1455.

Saint John Peter Neel

John Peter was born in 1832 in Soleymieux, France. He became a Jesuit priest and was sent as a missionary to Kuy-tsheu, China, in 1858. A few years later, he was arrested, along with some of his Chinese converts; he was tortured and martyred. He was beheaded on this date in 1862.

Saint Tarasius, pray for me to be a peacemaker.
Saint Theotonius, show me how to live a holy, penitential life.
Blessed John, pray that my work will speak of God.
Saint John Peter, show me how to live and die for Christ.

* * * * *

February 19

Blessed Boniface of Lausanne

Boniface was born in 1183 in Brussels, studied in Paris, and became a popular lecturer there. When disputes arose between the students and teachers, he decided to move to Cologne, Germany. Within two years, he had been raised to the position of bishop of Lausanne in Switzerland. He worked vigorously and zealously for his flock, but he suffered for eight years from continuous opposition from his people. For example, he was physically attacked and wounded because he opposed the policies of the emperor Frederick II, whose political

---

[8] Walsh, *Butler's Lives of the Saints*, 51.

policies caused repeated and violent disputes with the Church. So Boniface set off for Rome. There he begged the pope to be relieved of his position, claiming that he was unfit for the office; the pope accepted his resignation. He spent the remainder of his life in a Cistercian abbey in Brussels, living an austere life among the monks, whether or not he actually took the vows. He died in the year 1260.

Blessed Conrad of Piacenza

Conrad (1290–1351) was a married nobleman from northern Italy who loved hunting. One day, he ordered his servants to set fire to some brush to flush out the game he was hunting. Unfortunately, the resulting fire got out of control and destroyed fields, homes, and villages. A peasant was blamed, tortured into confessing, and sentenced to death for the crime until Conrad confessed his guilt and saved the man's life. However, Conrad was severely fined by the authorities for ordering the fire to be started, and he and his wife were left virtually penniless. But they took their change in fortune as a penance and a sign from God; Conrad became a Franciscan tertiary and hermit, while his wife entered a Poor Clares monastery. In time, his prayers resulted in miraculous healings, and when too many people came to visit him, he moved to a more deserted place so that he could live alone with God. Conrad died kneeling before a crucifix.

Blessed Joseph (Jozef) Zaplata

Joseph was born in Jerka, Poland, in 1904. He had a limited education because he was needed on the family farm. He served in the army for a time and then decided to enter the Brothers of the Sacred Heart of Jesus in 1927. He served in his archbishop's office and as a sacristan in his parish church. The Gestapo arrested him and sent him to various concentration camps. While he was at Dachau, an epidemic of typhus struck the camp. Joseph volunteered to serve those sick with the disease; he caught it himself and died of it on this date in 1945. Pope John Paul II declared him a martyr.

> *Blessed Boniface, help me understand and do God's will.*
> *Blessed Conrad, help me to repent deeply of my sins.*
> *Blessed Joseph, help me sacrifice for others.*

* * * * *

February 20

Saint Serapion of Alexandria

Serapion was tortured and killed in Alexandria, Egypt, because he allowed his fellow Christians to worship in his home. His martyrdom occurred during the persecution of Christians under the Roman emperor Decius in the year 250.

Saint Eleutherius of Tournai

Eleutherius (456–532) evangelized the Frankish people, and he became the first bishop of Tournai, France. He and Saint Medard (also a bishop) were good friends. Eleutherius was murdered by Arian heretics as he was leaving his church and died a martyr.

Saint Jacinta Marto

Jacinta (1910–1920), her brother Francisco, and their cousin Lucia cared for their parents' sheep in the fields in Aljustrel, Portugal. On May 13, 1917, they saw an apparition of a beautiful Lady; for several months following, the Lady appeared to them again on the thirteenth day of each month. Despite pressure, threats, and the burden of favorable but overwhelming attention from others, the children firmly repeated what they had seen and passed on the message of penance given them by the Virgin Mary. Jacinta lived the rest of her short life praying and offering her sufferings for others.

Saint Serapion, pray that my home may always be a domestic church at God's service.
Saint Eleutherius, show me how to live and die for Christ.
Saint Jacinta, help me to obey the Blessed Virgin's
call to live a life of prayer and penance.

* * * * *

February 21

Saint Peter Damian, Optional Memorial

Peter was born in Ravenna, Italy, in the year 1001. His parents died when he was young, and he was placed in the care of an older brother. However, his brother cruelly mistreated him, and another brother, who was the archpriest of Ravenna, took pity on the boy and took him in. Instead of caring for the family pigs as he had been doing, Peter was well educated and, in gratitude, took this brother's name (Damian) as a surname. Peter was devout from an early age, mortifying himself through fasting, prayer, wearing a hair shirt, giving alms, and caring for the poor. He was a good student, and he became a successful teacher as an adult. In his early twenties, he recognized God's call to enter monastic life through the example of Benedictine hermits. He decided to become a monk and also lived as a hermit, particularly enjoying the solitary life and the time for sacred studies. Though he never sought higher positions in the Church, he became the abbot of his monastery and eventually founded several other Benedictine monasteries. In addition to calling his fellow monks to live a more disciplined, contemplative, and holy life through his letters and writings, he also wrote openly—and scathingly—about cultural problems that were harming the Church at the time, particularly simony (the practice of clerical offices being sold to the highest bidder, rather than to worthy candidates) and clerical incontinence. Pope Stephen IX raised Peter to the position of cardinal-bishop of Ostia in 1057, but Peter constantly requested to resign. Two popes later, Pope Alexander II allowed him to do so. Peter then reduced himself to the role of a simple monk, setting aside his responsibilities as cardinal, bishop, and abbot to live an austere life, and made things with his own hands, such as wooden spoons, when he wasn't praying. His last act was to serve as papal legate to Ravenna; the archbishop there had been excommunicated and died before Peter arrived. Peter made the archbishop's accomplices acknowledge their guilt, gave them suitable penances, and returned to Rome. However, in the year 1072, he developed a fever on the way and died seven days later, with his monks praying the Divine Office around him. His eloquent preaching, voluminous writing, and willingness to speak hard truths to leaders and even popes caused him to be named a Doctor of the Church in 1828.

> *Therefore, if we seek to possess with God the glory of paradise, it is necessary that we first present ourselves to him as his dwelling, so that, while he lives in us and we in him, we so strive to celebrate the sabbath, not in ungenerous idleness but in diligent quiet, that we may deserve to pass on to the Lord's day that will have no end.*[9]

Saint Robert Southwell

Born in a pious Catholic family in England during a time of severe anti-Catholic persecution, Robert (1561–1595) had to leave the country to study for the priesthood. While in Douai, France, he became a priest and joined the Jesuit order. After ordination, he returned to England to minister to Catholics who were practicing their faith in secret. A few years later, he was arrested for the crime of being a priest. He was tortured repeatedly (in hopes of locating other priests) and was so badly treated in prison that his family petitioned for a quick trial to save him further suffering. Between episodes of torture, he was able to study the Bible and wrote poetry. He was finally convicted of treason because he admitted that he had administered the Catholic sacraments. He was condemned to be hanged, drawn, and quartered. During his hanging, he blessed the crowd by making the sign of the cross repeatedly. Onlookers felt sympathy for him and pulled on his legs to speed his death so he would not be alive during the gruesome tortures of being drawn and quartered. He is still remembered for the beautiful poetry he wrote during his lifetime, as well as his martyrdom.

> *Saint Peter, help me live in humility and simplicity.*
> *Saint Robert, help me to see God's beauty, even in suffering.*

* * * * *

---

[9] Peter Damian, Letter 49, in *Letters 31–60*, trans. Owen Blum, O.F.M. (Washington, D.C.: Catholic University of America Press, 1990), 288.

February 22

The Chair of Saint Peter, Feast

From the earliest days of the Church, a feast has been celebrated—previously on January 18—to commemorate the day when the first pope, Peter, held his first Mass in Rome. February 22 marks the date of his first Mass in Antioch. A portable chair that is believed to be the chair from which Saint Peter presided is preserved at the Vatican.

Saint Margaret of Cortona

Margaret was born in 1247 in Laviano, Italy. Her father was a farmer. Her mother died when she was seven years old; she was a pleasure-loving girl, and her new stepmother was hard and demanding. So when she was a young woman and a young cavalier from Montepulciano asked her to elope with him, she agreed. Although he repeatedly refused to marry her, he supported her well as his mistress. She bore him a son and remained faithful to him. After nine years of living with him, he failed to return from a visit to one of his properties. But his dog did return; it pulled at her dress and led her to the body of her dead lover, who had been killed and thrown into a pit. Her profound grief brought Margaret to repentance, and as soon as she was able, she gave away everything she had to the man's family and to the poor and left Montepulciano. Dressed as a penitent, she went back to her father's house with her son and asked for her father's forgiveness. When her father refused to take her back, she was tempted to despair. Fortunately, she was inspired to go to the city of Cortona and ask help from the Franciscan friars living there. When she arrived in Cortona, she couldn't find the friars, but two pious women noticed her suffering, brought her home, and introduced her to the Franciscans. The friars offered her spiritual direction while she struggled with herself and truly tried to live as a Christian for the first time in her life. Initially, she nursed ladies of the city to earn her living, but then she cared for the sick and poor and lived on alms. When she was given unbroken food, she gave that to the poor; she and her son ate only the other food they were given. After three years of inner struggles and temptations, Margaret received a deep experience of the love of Christ for her soul. Soon afterward, she was allowed to become a Franciscan tertiary. Other women followed her example and learned to help nurse the sick; this group eventually became an association supporting a hospital and the poor called the Confraternity of Our Lady of Mercy. She received many visions from God during this time, including a vision that led her to write to the bishop of Arezzo himself and warn him to change his ways and stop encouraging feuds between the cities of his diocese. Ten days after she met personally with the bishop to rebuke him, he died in battle. Later in life, she spent entire nights in prayer, slept on the bare ground, ate only bread and vegetables, wore a hair shirt, and disciplined her body. She died in the year 1297, having spent the majority of her life as a penitent.

Blessed Diego (Didacus) Carvalho

Diego was born in Coimbra, Portugal, around the year 1578. He became a Jesuit priest and went to Japan to serve as a missionary. While there, he was arrested for being a Christian. By long-term exposure to cold, he and a large number of other Christians were martyred on this date in 1624 in the city of Sendai.

> *Saint Peter, help me always trust in the authority of Christ's Vicar on earth.*
> *Saint Margaret, help me to repent of my sins truly.*
> *Blessed Diego, show me how to live and die for Christ.*

* * * * *

February 23

Saint Polycarp, Memorial

Polycarp (d. 155) was a disciple of Saint John the Evangelist and became bishop of Smyrna, a city now in Turkey. He kissed the chains of the bishop of Antioch (and future saint), Ignatius, when he passed through on his way to martyrdom around the year 107. Polycarp also met with Pope Saint Anicetus to discuss the proper date to celebrate Easter, and although they couldn't convince one another, they agreed to respect each other's customs. In the year 155, the Roman emperor Marcus Aurelius renewed the persecution of Christians, and the Christian faithful begged Polycarp to hide and avoid arrest. He did, but his location was betrayed by a slave who was threatened with torture. When the guards came to arrest him, Polycarp refused to escape, seeing his arrest as God's will. He ordered the guards to be fed and asked for some time to pray before leaving with them. He cheerfully went before the proconsul, and when he was told to say, "Away with the atheists!" as a condemnation of Christians, he turned to the pagan crowd in the stadium and said sternly, "Away with the atheists!"[10] When he was ordered by the proconsul to renounce Christ, he replied, "Fourscore and six years have I served Him and He has done me no wrong. How then can I blaspheme my King and my Saviour?"[11] He confessed to being a Christian. When the proconsul told him to try to persuade the people in the stadium to win his release, Polycarp replied, "I address myself to you; for we are taught to give due honor to princes, so far as is consistent with religion. But before these people I cannot justify myself."[12] Although the proconsul was impressed by Polycarp's words, he gave in to the crowd's demand that Polycarp be burnt alive. When the executioners started to nail him to a stake, Polycarp said, "Suffer me to be as I am. He who gives me grace to endure the fire will enable me to remain at the pile unmoved."[13] The flames encircled his body

---

[10] Walsh, *Butler's Lives of the Saints*, 56.
[11] Ibid., 57.
[12] Ibid.
[13] Ibid.

like a sail; people smelled a smell not like burning flesh, but like bread being baked. A guard was ordered to pierce his body with a spear to kill him; from his wound, a dove came forth, along with enough blood to quench the fire. His body was burned to ashes out of fears that Christians would begin worshipping him instead of Christ, but Christians, of course, knew where Christ had taken His beloved bishop. For his writings in defense of the faith, Polycarp is also considered a Father of the Church.

Blessed Rafaela Ybarra Arambarri de Vilallonga

Rafaela was born in 1843 into a pious but wealthy family living in Bilbao, Spain. Even as a young girl, she loved to pray and meditate on the sufferings of Jesus Christ. When she was eighteen years old, she married Joseph Vilallonga, who was also pious but wealthy. Together, they had seven children; they also supported the poor and sick of their community. With her husband's permission and approval, she made a personal vow to obedience, poverty, and chastity when she was still in her thirties. When her husband died, she gave away her fortune to the care of those in need, founding an institute to care for abandoned children. She died on this date in 1900.

Saint Polycarp, teach me your complete trust in God.
Blessed Rafaela, show me how to sacrifice myself for the needy.

* * * * *

February 24

Saint Evetius of Nicomedia

During the reign of the Roman emperor Diocletian in the year 303, a written order against Christians was posted in Evetius' hometown of Nicomedia (now in Turkey). A Christian himself, Evetius tore it down. He was arrested and killed.

Saint Ethelbert of England

King Ethelbert (d. 616) of Kent, England, was a pagan king, but he married a Christian. He welcomed the monk Augustine (future bishop of Canterbury and a saint) when he arrived with other monks to evangelize the English. Apparently, Ethelbert was superstitious and agreed to meet Augustine only outside the castle, so that he wouldn't be harmed by any magic he feared that Augustine might possess. But Ethelbert eventually became a Christian, establishing just laws and building a cathedral. His example led many of his countrymen to embrace the faith. He died on this date, having been a Christian for twenty-one years.

Saint Evetius, show me how to respond to injustice.
Saint Ethelbert, help me to lead others to Christ by my example.

* * * * *

February 25

Saint Nestor of Magydos

Nestor was bishop of Magydos in Asia Minor (modern Turkey) during the persecution of Christians under the Roman emperor Decius in the year 250. According to tradition, he sent the entire Christian community outside the city for protection, while he remained at prayer. When he was found, he was arrested; when he refused to renounce the faith, he was crucified.

Saint Caesarius of Nazianzus

Caesarius (329–369) was the son of two saints (Gregory the Elder and Nonna) and the brother of another one, the future Doctor of the Church Gregory of Nazianzus. Caesarius was an excellent student, and he chose to become a doctor. In time, he became known as the best doctor in Constantinople and was chosen to be the chief physician to Roman emperor Julian the Apostate. Despite the emperor's persecution of Christians, Caesarius refused to renounce his faith and was exiled; later, he returned to Bithynia (a region now in modern Turkey). There he remained a bachelor and gave his entire estate to the poor at his death.

Saint Walburga of Heidenheim

Walburga (710–779) was the daughter of an English king, and her brothers Willibald and Winebald became priests and saints as well. She was a student at the Wimborne monastery and became a nun there as an adult. In the year 748, she traveled to Germany with Saints Lioba and Boniface and her two brothers to bring the Christian faith to the people there. During their successful missionary journey, she evangelized and even healed people through her prayers. She later became the abbess of a community of men and women at Heidenheim, and although the date that her relics were translated to Eichstatt is celebrated with a pagan festival in some places today, she was a holy woman, a Christian healer, and a saint.

Blesseds Luigi Versiglia and Callisto Caravario

A Salesian priest from Italy and missionary to China, Luigi (1873–1930) became apostolic vicar at Shiuchow, China, and titular bishop of Carystus. Callisto (1903–1930) was also a Salesian missionary priest from Italy. When the two men were on board a ship, Bolshevik pirates boarded the ship and planned to abduct and enslave the girls onboard. The two men were killed trying to prevent them.

> *Saint Nestor, help me to trust in the power of prayer.*
> *Saint Caesarius, help me to witness to my faith through my vocation.*
> *Saint Walburga, pray for me to bring healing to those around me who do not know God.*
> *Blesseds Luigi and Callisto, show me how to help the helpless.*

* * * * *

February 26

Saint Alexander of Alexandria

Alexander (d. 328) was a zealous, faithful bishop of Alexandria, Egypt, and was known for his charity to the poor. He also had a mild temperament; when the priest Arius began spreading his heresy, Alexander at first tried gentleness and reason to bring Arius back to the truth. When that failed and when the heresy began to spread, he summoned Arius to a council and, when Arius refused to acknowledge his errors, Alexander excommunicated him. In the year 325, accompanied by his deacon and future successor Saint Athanasius, Alexander attended the first ecumenical council of Nicaea, where he helped expose the dangers of Arianism, which was condemned. Alexander is considered a Father of the Church.

Saint Porphyry of Gaza

Porphyry was born around the year 347 into a wealthy family in Macedonia. He left home when he was twenty-five years old to become a hermit in the Egyptian desert. After he developed a serious illness, he moved to a cave by the Jordan River and visited the holy places in Jerusalem daily. Though many people saw his sickness and tried to help him, he refused their help, saying that he undertook these daily pilgrimages to beg God's forgiveness for his sins. Later, he was (unwillingly) made bishop of Gaza (in modern Palestine). The town had many pagans, but by the time Porphyry died in the year 420, he had converted almost every pagan in Gaza.

Blessed Robert Drury

Robert was born in 1567 in Buckinghamshire, England. Because of the anti-Catholic laws of the time, he had to travel to France and Spain to study to become a priest. In 1593, he returned to England and ministered to Catholics secretly in London. Although he signed an oath in 1603, accepting Queen Elizabeth as his sovereign—in earthly matters, but not in religious ones—he was tested again when James I ascended to the throne and demanded authority over religious matters as well. When Robert refused to sign the oath, he was arrested. On this date in 1607, he was hanged, drawn, and quartered at Tyburn.

> *Saint Alexander, show me how to reprove sinners with love.*
> *Saint Porphyry, help me to accept illness in a spirit of peace and reparation.*
> *Blessed Robert, show me how to live and die for Christ.*

* * * * *

February 27

Saint Baldomer of Lyons

Baldomer (d. ca. 650) was a locksmith in Lyons, France. Not only did he make locks for the poor for free out of charity, but he was generous with his own money and lived in poverty himself. When Abbot Viventius of Saint-Just heard about this holy man, he ordained him a deacon, and Baldomer spent the last years of his life in a cell next to Viventius' monastery.

Saint Gregory of Narek

Gregory (d. 1003) came from a devout family. His father was a bishop and theologian, and an uncle was the abbot at the famous Nerak Monastery in modern Turkey. Gregory lived his life in his native Armenia as a monk, priest, and teacher. His spiritual writings include a commentary on a biblical book, the Song of Songs, and a collection of prayers called the *Book of Lamentations*. The latter has been used by the Armenian people for centuries for consolation and encouragement through times of Muslim invasion, war, and genocide. Because of the enduring power and faithfulness of these writings, Gregory was named a Doctor of the Church by Pope Francis in 2015.

Saint Anne Line

Although Anne (d. 1601) and her brother were born into a wealthy Protestant family in England, both converted to Catholicism and were disinherited as a result. When Anne was nineteen years old, she married Roger Line, who was also a Catholic convert. Soon afterward, Roger was imprisoned for returning to the Catholic Church. He was then allowed to leave the country and died in 1594. Anne suffered from many health problems, but she devoted her life and her wealth to help her fellow Catholics. She ran a house of refuge for the hidden Catholic clergy in London; each time the local authorities began to be suspicious that she was hiding priests, she moved to a new location. However, on Candlemas Day in 1601, she had invited a number of Catholics to her house for Mass. The neighbors noticed and informed the authorities, who broke in and found a room prepared for Mass. The priest had been hidden in a hiding place, so he escaped detection. She and some of the other people present were arrested. At her trial, she had to be carried in on a chair because she was so sick, and when asked if she was guilty of harboring a priest, she replied, "My lords, nothing grieves me more but that I could not receive a thousand more."[14] Although the trial produced only one witness who said he had seen a man dressed in white and the evidence of the prepared altar was weak, the judge ordered the jury to find her guilty. It did. She was sentenced to death and spent her last hours peacefully in Newgate Prison. At Tyburn, she kissed the gallows and knelt in prayer to the last moment. She was hanged with her Jesuit confessor, Blessed Roger Filcock, and Blessed Mark Barkworth, the first Benedictine to die a martyr since the suppression of the monasteries in England.

Saint Gabriel (of Our Lady of Sorrows) Possenti

Born in 1838 into a family of thirteen children in Assisi, Italy, Francis lived a worldly life and spent his time hunting animals and chasing women until he

---

[14] Ibid., 61.

became sick. He vowed to become a religious if he recovered from his sickness, but he forgot the vow when he got better. However, when he became ill a second time and his sister died, he remembered his vow. Our Lady led him to the Passionist order, where he took the name of Gabriel of Our Lady of Sorrows. He spent the remainder of his relatively short life praying and making many personal sacrifices, and he had a great devotion to the Blessed Virgin Mary and to the sufferings of Christ. He died of tuberculosis in 1862 in Abruzzi; many miracles were attributed to his intercession after his death.

Saint Baldomer, help me to do my work with charity and generosity.
Saint Gregory, help me to pray.
Saint Anne, show me how to be bold in my support of Christ and His Church.
Saint Gabriel, help me make and keep promises that please God.

* * * * *

February 28

Martyrs of Alexandria

In the year 261, a plague swept through the great city of Alexandria, Egypt. Following the command of Jesus Christ to care for those in need, a number of priests and laymen stayed in the city to minister to the sick. On this date, we commemorate those who died as martyrs of charity.

Saint Romanus

Romanus was born in the Upper Bugey region of France around the year 390. He became a monk at Lyons when he was thirty-five years old and then retired to the Jura Mountains between Switzerland and France to live as a hermit. He took only a few tools, some seeds, and a copy of Cassian's *Lives of the Fathers of the Desert* with him. He spent his time praying, reading, and farming. Initially, he saw only animals and a few huntsmen. In time, his brother, Saint Lupicinus, joined him; so many other men eventually joined them that they had to build two monasteries, which the two men ruled as joint abbots. Their sister and a few other women lived in a nearby nunnery. Although they tried to live as the Desert Fathers did, they made some adaptations due to the climate. The monks never ate meat, had milk and eggs only when they were sick, and wore wooden shoes and the skins of animals. Romanus once made a pilgrimage to what is now the Abbey of Saint Maurice in the Valais. He cured two lepers along the way, which caused the bishop of Geneva and the whole town to come out to greet him. He died around the year 460.

Holy Martyrs, show me how to care for those in need around me.
Saint Romanus, help me apply the wisdom of the saints to my life.

* * * * *

February 29

Note about leap day: Since the days of Julius Caesar in 46 B.C., people have recognized the need to fine-tune the annual calendar to reflect the true date, relative to naturally occurring events such as the equinoxes. But it took many centuries for people to determine that the actual length of a year is closer to 365¼ days and create a calendar to match. The Church, of course, desires the calendar to be accurate primarily so that we can worship God more perfectly. In the year 1582, Pope Gregory XIII, with the help of the scientists of his day, removed ten erroneous days that had crept into the calendar and refined the method of keeping the calendar. In the Gregorian calendar, named after him, only centurial years that are multiples of four (i.e., 2000, 2400) include leap days. Thirty-five centuries from now, there will still be an error of a day, but that gives mankind plenty of time to figure out how to correct this and still worship God as best we can.

Saint Hilary (Hilarus or Hilarius)

Hilary (d. 468) was born in Sardinia, an island of Italy. He became an aide to Pope Saint Leo the Great, and he was sent by Leo to a synod in the city of Ephesus in the year 449 as one of the papal legates. This "Robber Synod", however, was packed with those who not only supported the Monophysite heresy, but who ordered the beating and mistreatment of Flavian, the patriarch of Constantinople, which led to his death soon afterward. Hilary and the other papal legates barely managed to escape with their lives. Hilary returned to Rome and was later chosen to be the forty-sixth pope in the year 461. As pope, he confirmed the teaching of the Church against the Monophysite heresy, and he built churches, including one he dedicated to Saint John the Evangelist, in thanksgiving for the saint's intercession in protecting him from death at the synod at Ephesus. He died of natural causes on this date.

Saint Auguste Chapdelaine

Auguste was born in 1814 into a large family at La Rochelle, France, and had to drop out of school to help on the family farm. His parents refused when he asked to become a priest, but after two of his brothers died suddenly, they reconsidered. Because of his lack of formal education, he studied with boys half his age. But he was eventually ordained a priest; he served as a pastor for a time and then was sent as a missionary to China. Before reaching his assigned territory, he was robbed by bandits of everything he possessed and had to return to his superiors before he could continue. When he did reach his assignment in Kwang-si province, he was arrested and had to spend a few weeks in prison before being released. He served his community for two years and brought many people to the faith until he was arrested again. Because of government opposition to Christianity, he was sentenced to death, was tortured, and then beheaded on this date in 1856.

Saint Hilary, help me to thank God at all times.
Saint Auguste, help me accept setbacks with peace.

March

March 1

Saint Felix III

Felix (d. 492) was the forty-eighth pope; he reigned eight years. He had been a married man with children, then a widower, before becoming a priest and then pope. He was a strong leader who faced down the heretical patriarch of Constantinople, but his perhaps overzealous decisions led to the Acacian Schism, which lasted until 519.

Saint David (Dewi) of Wales

David (d. 589) was the son of a noble family in Ceredigion in Wales; his mother, Non, was a holy woman and also later declared a saint. David was ordained a priest and lived in a monastery, but he decided to leave the monastery and settle at Mynyw (sometimes pronounced "Menevia"). There he established a community of monks that lived a simple life. They farmed the land by hand, without cattle, and lived austerely, having only bread, vegetables, salt, and water. He taught his monks to maintain a rule of silence, speaking only when necessary, and also taught them to practice constant mental prayer. When a synod was held at Brefi to combat the dangers of the heresy of Pelagianism, which was spreading in the area, David spoke so eloquently that his fellow Church leaders unanimously elected him their primate. Although his predecessor was happy to resign in his favor, David accepted the position only on the condition that his episcopal seat would be transferred to the quiet town of Mynyw. He died there in his monastery. The Welsh have embroidered his biography with many stories showing their love for this bishop and his love for God.

Saint Agnes Cao Guiying

Agnes was born in 1821 in Wujiazhai, China, and raised in a Catholic home. When her parents died, she moved to Zingyi, married a young farmer, and then became a widow when he was executed for being a Christian. At the suggestion of Saint Auguste Chapdelaine, she moved to the Guangxi province to serve the community there. Agnes not only taught the catechism to the children; she also taught younger women how to care for their homes and families. When the government cracked down on Christians, she was arrested, tortured, and placed in a tiny cage. She refused to renounce her faith, so she was starved to death, dying on this date in 1856.

> *Saint Felix, help me to love Christ and His Church.*
> *Saint David, help me to pray to God in my heart at all times.*
> *Saint Agnes, show me how to live and die for Christ.*

* * * * *

March 2

Saint Chad (Ceadda) of Mercia

Born into a devout family in Northumbria, England, Chad (d. 672) and his three brothers heard God's call and became priests. Chad spent his life surrounded by other holy men who also are now acclaimed as saints. For example, he was educated at the monastery school governed by the holy monk (and future saint) Aidan of Lindisfarne, but returned home when his brother Bishop Cedd (also a saint) requested it. For a time, Chad served as abbot in the abbey that his brother had founded in Lastingham, then the king, Oswin, asked him to serve as the bishop of York. Another man (and future saint), Wilfrid, had already been consecrated to this position. It was a very complicated political situation, described for us by the historian Saint Bede, but Chad accepted the request to become bishop of York in good faith. As bishop, Chad promoted truth in both Church doctrine and practice; lived a humble life; and traveled on foot as he preached throughout his diocese, rather than taking advantage of the power of his position. However, when Theodore of Tarsus (yet another future saint) was made archbishop of Canterbury, he recognized the confusion caused by the ordination of two bishops to the same post. When he told Chad that he had been improperly ordained, Chad humbly offered to resign, saying that he had never thought he was worthy of the honor but had only accepted out of obedience. Theodore was impressed with his humility, and although he had Chad retire to Lastingham, "demoting" him to serve as abbot there, he also ordained Chad as bishop, supplying whatever might have been defective in his previous episcopal consecration at the hands of Bishop Wine. When the bishop of the nearby city of Mercia died, Theodore asked the king to give that position as bishop to Chad. Due to Chad's advanced age, Theodore ordered him to travel on horseback while he visited his people, rather than on foot. Chad moved his seat to the city of Lichfield, founded an abbey there, and often stayed to pray and read with a group of monks that he had established at a retreat house. He served as bishop for less than three years, but his virtue left a deep impression on his people. They named many churches after him after his death.

Blessed Charles the Good

Charles was born in 1083 and was the son of Saint Canute, the king of Denmark. When his father was murdered, he was taken to the court of Flanders and raised there. He fought in the Second Crusade to protect Christians in the Holy Land and returned to become the count of Flanders in 1119. The people acclaimed him Charles the Good because he consistently made decisions that protected the poor from the rich and powerful. However, those powerful enemies resented his goodness. He was attacked and beheaded on this date in 1127 in Bruges, Belgium.

Blessed Angela Guerrero y Gonzalez

Angela was one of fourteen children, born to pious but poor parents in Spain in 1846. Only five of the children survived to adulthood. Angela had to quit school when she was twelve years old to help support the family. She had always been a pious child, so no one was surprised when, as a young woman, she tried to enter two religious orders: the Carmelites and the Daughters of Charity. But on both occasions, she became ill after becoming a postulant and had to return home to her family. She decided to live at home and follow a simple rule of life, renewing her vows to that rule annually, with the blessing of her priest and spiritual director, Father Padilla. In 1873, she received a vision in which she recognized God's call to serve the poor. She began serving the poor, the sick, and the homeless in her area, keeping a diary of her spiritual experiences. Other women began to follow her, and together they began living on alms to support themselves and to provide food, medicine, and other needs for the poor. During her lifetime, the order she founded, the Congregation of the Cross, grew from just Angela and three sisters to twenty-three convents full of sisters. She died in 1932.

> *Saint Chad, show me how to accept all challenges with humility.*
> *Blessed Charles, help me seek justice for the poor in my own community.*
> *Blessed Angela, help me to see and serve Christ in the poor.*

* * * * *

March 3

Saints Marinus and Asterius of Caesarea

During the persecution of Christians under the Roman emperor Gallienus, Marinus (d. ca. 260) was serving as a soldier in the Roman army in Caesarea (in modern Israel) and was secretly a Christian. He was offered a promotion to the position of centurion, but a rival for the position pointed out that a centurion must offer sacrifice to the gods. Marinus was given three hours to change his mind and make a sacrifice; he prayed and read Scripture—and refused. After his execution, a Roman senator named Asterius buried his body and was executed as well. Both men died as martyrs around the same year.

Saint Cunegund

Cunegund was born around the year 978 into a noble and holy family: her father was Siegfried, the count of Luxembourg, and her mother was Hedwig, who was known for her holiness. Cunegund was a pious young woman; she was married to Henry, duke of Bavaria, who became a great leader and a saint as well. When Pope Benedict VIII crowned her husband as Holy Roman Emperor Henry II in 1013, Cunegund was crowned as empress. She encouraged Henry to establish a monastery and cathedral at Bamberg. It was said that Cunegund's "silken threads were a better defence than walls",[1] due to the privileges she obtained from the pope for the people. She and Henry never had children. When Henry died, she

---

[1] Michael Walsh, ed., *Butler's Lives of the Saints, Concise Edition, Revised and Updated* (San Francisco: HarperCollins Publishers, 1991), 65.

retired to a convent at Kaufungen that she had founded after recovering from a dangerous illness. Cunegund had a niece named Judith, whom she had educated and who was made superior at a convent. When Cunegund discovered that Judith had become lax and frivolous—she was the first to come to dinner and the last to come to pray, and she had a feast with some of the sisters instead of attending a Sunday procession—Cunegund confronted Judith; she reproved her and struck her across the face. Judith bore the marks of Cunegund's hand on her face for the rest of her life—and repented. Cunegund lived as a nun in great humility, believing herself the lowest member of the household—praying, reading, and caring for the sick. She died on this date around 1033 (or some say 1039).

Saint Teresa Eustochio (Ignazia) Verzeri

When Ignazia's mother was young, she told her sister that she felt drawn to religious life. Her sister predicted instead that she would be the mother of holy children. The prediction came true: Ignazia was the oldest of her mother's seven children, and one of her brothers eventually became a bishop. Born in 1801 at Bergamo, Italy, she was educated at home, then became a Benedictine nun, took the name of Teresa Eustochio, and founded the Institute of the Daughters of the Sacred Heart of Jesus. She and her nuns brought God's love to others through orphanages and retreat centers, as well as caring for the sick and the elderly. Teresa became a spiritual guide and teacher to many people, particularly through her letters. She died in 1852.

Saint Katharine Drexel, Optional Memorial[2]

Katharine was born in 1858 into an extremely wealthy family in Philadelphia, yet it was also a devout Catholic family who taught her to put her wealth at the service of others. For example, the Drexel family opened homes for the poor, trade schools for orphans, and schools for black Americans. During a papal audience in 1887, Katharine asked Pope Leo XII to send more missionaries to her friend, a bishop in Wyoming. The pope asked her, point-blank, to become a missionary herself, and Katharine accepted the challenge. Eventually, she spent her entire family fortune serving the missions in the American West. But it wasn't just money: she herself became a sister and founded an order of sisters to care for Native Americans. She also established schools for black Catholics, despite persecution from segregationists. After suffering a heart attack, she retired from her position and spent her remaining twenty years of life in prayer. She died in 1955.

> *Holy Martyrs, show me how to live and die for Christ.*
> *Saint Cunegund, teach me humility.*
> *Saint Teresa, show me how to guide those around me to Christ.*
> *Saint Katharine, help me to be generous in using*
> *the gifts God has given me to care for others.*

* * * * *

[2] This saint may be celebrated as an optional memorial in the *Liturgical Calendar for the Dioceses of the United States of America.*

March 4

Saint Casimir of Poland, Optional Memorial

Casimir was the third of thirteen children and was born in 1458 to King Casimir IV of Poland and his wife, Elizabeth of Austria. Casimir and his two brothers were well educated by a pious canon who was also a noted historian. Casimir was devout as a child and as an adult: he meditated on Christ's Passion, wore a hair shirt under the plain clothes he wore, slept on the ground, and was known for his pleasant temperament. He cared for the poor and reminded his father and brother, the king of Bohemia, to remember the poor in their actions as rulers. He recited the hymn "Omni die dic Mariae" (translated into English as "Daily, daily sing to Mary") so frequently that he's sometimes incorrectly considered its author. Casimir was only fifteen years old when the nobles of nearby Hungary begged his father to make Casimir their king. He obeyed his father and led a Polish army to fight in Hungary very reluctantly. When he arrived at the frontier at the head of his army, he saw that many men had deserted because they hadn't been paid. His own advisors told him to return home, which is what he did, but his father was furious. Despite the facts that the pope had discouraged this expedition, the war had been unjust, and battles between European nations helped only the Turks in their invasion of Europe, Casimir was punished by being locked up in a castle for three months. When he was released, he returned to his studies and refused to take up arms again. He lived a celibate life and turned down a proposed marriage. His father must have forgiven him because Casimir served as viceroy when his father was away from Poland for a time. He had suffered from lung trouble for years, which led to his death at the age of twenty-five in 1484.

Blesseds Christopher Bales, Alexander Blake, and Nicholas Horner

During the anti-Catholic laws of England of the sixteenth century, it was dangerous to have anything to do with a Catholic priest. Christopher Bales was condemned to death for being a Catholic priest, and Alexander Blake and Nicholas Horner, though only Catholic laymen, were condemned to death for helping a Catholic priest. All three were hanged, drawn, and quartered in London on this date in 1590. To add insult to injury, Nicholas Horner's martyrdom occurred in front of his own home.

Saint Casimir, give me a love of purity.
Holy Martyrs, show me how to help my priests.

* * * * *

March 5

Saint Cono the Gardener

Cono was a gardener. During the persecution of Christians under the Roman emperor Decius at Pamphylia (modern Turkey) around the year 250, he was arrested and executed for being a Christian.

Saint Lucius I

Lucius (d. 254) was the twenty-second pope; he reigned only 253 days. Due to the ongoing persecution of Christians by the Roman emperor Gallus, Lucius was sent into exile soon after he was consecrated pope; but not long afterward, he was able to return to Rome, presumably because Emperor Valerian had succeeded Emperor Gallus. Following the tradition of previous popes, during his reign Lucius pardoned those who had lapsed in their faith due to imperial persecution but who had then repented and sought reconciliation with the Church. Though it's not clear how he was martyred, the earliest records state that Lucius was a martyr for the faith.

Saint Phocas the Gardener

Phocas (d. 303) kept an inn and a garden in Sinope, Pontus (modern Turkey). He practiced his Christian charity by feeding the poor with his surplus crops. When Roman soldiers were sent to execute him for being a Christian, he fed them, gave them shelter, and even dug his own grave first.

Saints Adrian and Ebulus of Caesarea

In the early fourth century, Adrian and Ebulus went to Caesarea (in modern Israel) to help the Christians living there, but they were soon arrested, convicted of being Christians, and sentenced to death. Adrian was torn apart by wild beasts and then beheaded on this date, and Ebulus was martyred two days later. It was the year 308.

Saint John Joseph-of-the-Cross (Carlo Calosinto)

Carlo was born in 1654 to well-to-do, devout parents on the island of Ischia, near Naples in Italy. Although four of his brothers also entered religious life, Carlo was especially pious from a young age. Carlo was particularly inspired by the example of two Spanish Franciscan friars of the Alcantarine reform of the Franciscan order who visited his family. First, he spent nine months training in mental prayer and self-discipline under the direction of a Franciscan, and then, when he was only sixteen, he entered the Franciscan order and took the name John Joseph-of-the-Cross. By the time he was twenty-one years old, he had so impressed his superiors with his holiness and abilities that he was sent to lead the founding of a new monastery. Despite John Joseph's desire to remain a mere brother like Saint Francis, his superiors decided he should become a priest. He was particularly gifted as a confessor, in spite of his youth and personal innocence, and he became an excellent novice master and superior in the house. During a time when he was tried by great aridity in his personal prayer, he received a vision of a deceased brother. This consolation apparently marked a time of growth in his spiritual life; soon afterward, people noticed that his prayers resulted in miracles, including many healings and the miraculous multiplication of food. When John Joseph returned to visit his dying mother, he was given the unusual blessing of being acclaimed a saint in his own hometown. In his old age, John Joseph knew that his end was near; he warned others about it, but kept working. After suffering from a seizure, he lingered briefly, and died at the age of eighty on this date in 1734.

> *Holy Martyrs, help me find ways to put my abilities in God's service.*
> *Saint Lucius, help me to love Christ and His Church.*
> *Saint John Joseph, help me to grow in piety.*

* * * * *

March 6

Saint Julian of Toledo

Julian was born to Christian parents of Jewish origin in Spain around the year 642. He became a diocesan priest and then bishop of Toledo. He served his flock with such zeal, discretion, courage, and love for the poor that they acclaimed him a saint at his death in 690.

Saint Fridolin the Wanderer

Fridolin was born into the Irish nobility and lived around the eighth century. He traveled to continental Europe to bring the Catholic faith to the people there and became a Benedictine monk at Poitiers, France. After receiving a vision in which he was given the location of the relics of Saint Hilary of Tours, he built a chapel to house them. He traveled to France and Switzerland, bringing them the faith and building churches. Demonstrating that he didn't always receive a warm welcome, in one city, the people thought that he was a cattle thief and chased him away. He founded the monastery of Sackingen, Germany.

Saint Chrodegang of Metz

Born into a noble and devout family in Belgium around the year 712, Chrodegang was related to King Pepin the Short, and his sister became a saint and Benedictine abbess. Though Chrodegang held very important positions—for example, secretary to Charles Martel and chancellor of France—he wore a hair shirt as a personal penance, supported the poor, prayed, and fasted. While he was still a layman, he was chosen to become bishop of Metz in France in the year 742. As bishop, he became ambassador to the Vatican and defended the papacy against the Lombards, who were German pagans and who ruled part of the Italian peninsula. He brought about a reformation of his clergy by encouraging them to live in community and follow Saint Benedict's Rule; he restored and founded monasteries and churches. He brought Gregorian chant and the Roman liturgy to his see, liturgical changes that spread to the rest of Europe. He died at Metz on this date in the year 776.

Martyrs of Amorium

When Muslim forces invaded the city of Amorium (now in Turkey) in 838, most of the population was killed or enslaved. But forty-two senior officials of this Christian city in the Byzantine Empire were arrested and put in prison. They assumed they were being held for ransom, but all offers of ransom were rejected. Instead, the caliph sent Islamic scholars to them in prison to convert them to Islam. After seven years of imprisonment, they still refused to renounce their faith in Christ. The caliph gave up and simply had them beheaded on this date in 845.

Saint Rose of Viterbo

Rose was born in 1235 into a poor family in Viterbo, Italy. When she was eight years old, she became very ill and had a vision of the Virgin Mary. In the vision, the Blessed Virgin told Rose that she would wear the Franciscan habit of Saint Francis of Assisi but live at home. When she was twelve years old, she began to preach publicly in the streets against the emperor Frederick II, who was fighting the pope for control of the papal states. Her courageous words in support of the pope drew crowds of listeners, but this frightened her father. He ordered her to stop and threatened to beat her until the parish priest intervened. She preached publicly on behalf of the pope for two years, when supporters of the emperor tried to have her executed. The city's mayor was a just man, and he protected her from death. She and her family were, however, ordered to leave Viterbo. Rose predicted that Frederick would die soon, and when it happened as she had predicted, she returned to the city. She tried on many occasions to enter a convent and become a nun, but she was always refused. When she died at the age of eighteen in 1252, the pope gave her justice: he ordered that she be buried in the convent that had refused her.

Saint Colette Boylet of Corbie

Nicolette's parents were devout and lived in Picardy, France. They prayed to Saint Nicholas of Bari after many years of childlessness, and when God gave them a child, they named her after that saint. Nicolette was born in 1381, and both of her parents died when she was seventeen years old. She lived in a convent first, but, wanting a simpler life, she became a Franciscan tertiary and moved to a small hermitage by the church in Corbie. Many people came for her prayers and advice. She received visions, and in one of them, Saint Francis of Assisi appeared to her and called her to restore the Poor Clares to their original and stricter way of life. When she hesitated, she became blind for three days and then dumb for three more days. Recognizing this as a clear sign from God, she obediently left her cell in 1406 and went to a few convents to do as God had asked. But she soon realized that she needed the proper authority to make such changes happen. Peter de Luna was acknowledged as pope in France (though considered an anti-pope to us today), and she went to seek his help. He was so impressed with Colette's holiness that he officially professed her under the Rule of Saint Clare and essentially gave her authority to reform religious life every-where she went. So she did. Colette went throughout France, Savoy, and Flanders, though at first people responded violently to the changes she proposed. She responded with kindness and even joy when people threatened and verbally abused her, and gradually people began to listen. She eventually founded seventeen religious houses and reformed several others. In the year 1447, while staying at one of these houses in Flanders, she became ill; she predicted her own death and died after receiving the sacraments.

> *Saint Julian, give me your zeal for serving Christ.*
> *Saint Fridolin, help me to walk the paths that will lead me to Christ.*
> *Saint Chrodegang, show me how to reform my life and my heart.*
> *Holy Martyrs, help me be steadfast in the truth.*
> *Saint Rose, show me how to support Christ's Church in my words and actions.*
> *Saint Colette, help me to respond to unkindness with charity.*

* * * * *

March 7

Saint Perpetua, Felicity, and Companions, Memorial

In the year 203, six Africans from Carthage (a city in modern Tunisia) asked to be baptized. Soon after being baptized, they were arrested and condemned to death for the crime of being Christians. Four of them were men: Secundulus, Saturninus, Saturus, and Revocatus (who was a slave). Perpetua was a twenty-two-year-old wife with a prosperous husband and a small child, whom she was still nursing. Felicity was her maid and friend, and she was pregnant. For the entertainment of the crowds, they were all martyred by being thrown to wild beasts in the arena. The two women were gored by a wild cow before they were beheaded. One of the men, Saturus, wrote about the faith and bravery of Perpetua and Felicity before their martyrdom, and an unknown person completed the story after all had been killed. This deeply moving story was widely read in the days of the early Church.

Saint Simeon-Francois Berneux

Simeon was born into a poor family in France in 1814. He heard God call him to become a priest when he was only ten years old. He attended seminary but had to leave for two years when he developed health problems; he worked as a tutor until he was well enough to return. He was ordained in 1837 and became a professor at a seminary. He was first sent as a missionary to Vietnam with the Paris Foreign Missionary Society, and later he went to Korea. While serving as a missionary in Korea, he was captured, beaten, and sentenced to death for the crime of being a Christian missionary; but a French admiral interceded on his behalf, and he was released. Simeon was then sent as a missionary to the countries of Singapore and Macao, and he became apostolic vicar to Korea and titular bishop of Capsa. As bishop, he built a seminary and published Catholic books in Korean to help the people learn about the faith. But the Korean government became alarmed that so many people had converted to Christianity, and he and all the non-Korean priests were put in prison. After being brutally tortured, Simeon was executed by beheading in Seoul, Korea, on this date in 1866, along with other priests of the Paris Mission Society: Just Ranfer de Bretenieres, Louis Beaulieu, and Peter Henrici Dorie.

Holy Martyrs, help me to be strong in the faith despite opposition and pain.

* * * * *

March 8

Saint John of God, Optional Memorial

John was born in 1495 in Portugal and worked as a bailiff, soldier, and shepherd. He did not live a holy life. But at about the age of forty, he realized that and repented. He first opened a business selling Catholic items in Granada, Spain. But when the zealous Franciscan preacher and future saint John of Avila came to the city to preach, John heard his sermons and was so deeply repentant that he began to cry uncontrollably. He ran through the streets of Granada and acted so strangely that people threw stones at him. John gave away all the stock from his business and roamed the streets in misery. Friends felt sorry for him and took him to see Father John, and the priest's words comforted him. However, after Father John had left the area, John became inconsolable again, and people thought he was mentally ill. John was taken to an asylum, where he was treated brutally in an attempt to "bring him to his senses". When Father John heard of this, he visited John, told him that he had done penance for his sins for long enough, and said that now he needed to do something more helpful for his neighbor. Father John's words instantly calmed John, greatly surprising his jailors. At first, John stayed at the hospital to care for the sick, and then he began selling wood, using the proceeds to open a house to care for sick people who were too poor to pay for care. Although John never intended to found a religious order, this was the beginning of his hospital and of the order of the Brothers Hospitallers. Ten years later, John wore himself out trying to save the wood he was selling and the property of the poor during a flood. Though he knew he was ill, he carefully reviewed the accounts of his hospital and the devotional exercises used by his helpers, and he prepared himself for his own death. When people found out that he was seriously ill, a noblewoman forced him to come to her home and be cared for. John complained, saying that his Savior had been forced to drink gall at His death while he, a sinner, was being treated with such kindness. He died on his knees before the church altar on this date in 1550. He was fifty-five years old, and the entire city of Granada, Spain, mourned his death.

Saints Apollonius and Philemon of Antinopolis

During the persecution of the Church under the Roman emperor Diocletian in the late third century, a man named Apollonius was in a public place when he was ordered to offer sacrifice to pagan gods. Apollonius thought Philemon, a friend standing near him who was also an actor, was a pagan. He asked Phile-mon to exchange clothes with him so he wouldn't have to offer the sacrifice and so no one would know he wasn't a pagan. But Philemon announced, in front of witnesses, that he was a Christian too. Apollonius then admitted publicly that he was a Christian. Both men were tortured and died in 287 as martyrs in Antinopolis, Egypt.

Saint Duthac (Duthus) of Scotland

Duthac was born in Tain, Scotland, educated in Ireland, and eventually became bishop of Ross. He died on this date in 1065 of natural causes. When his tomb was opened seven years later, his body was found to be incorrupt. He's consid-ered the chief confessor of Ireland and Scotland.

Saint John, help me repent deeply of my sins.
Holy Martyrs, help me be unashamed to confess that I am a Christian.
Saint Duthac, show me how God wants me to confess my faith in Christ to others.

* * * * *

March 9

Saint Frances of Rome, Optional Memorial

Frances was born in 1384 into a noble and pious family living in Rome. She was a precocious child and asked to become a nun when she was only eleven years old. Her family refused point-blank and instead arranged for her to marry Lorenzo Ponziano when she was thirteen. Lorenzo was from a wealthy family and a good man. She initially found it very difficult to live in her new husband's family home, but she soon found a kindred spirit in her sister-in-law, Vannozza. The two young women, with the support of their husbands, spent their time caring for those who were poor, and they dressed in simple, modest clothes. Frances and her husband were blessed with three children: John Baptist, Evan-gelist, and Agnes. When Frances' mother-in-law died, she became the house-keeper for the entire household, but she treated her servants as if they were her brothers and sisters. When the city of Rome was attacked and invaded, her hus-band had to run away and barely escaped with his life. She and the other women and children of the household were forced to live in the ruined family home, facing violence and poverty. The plague broke out in Rome, and Frances per-sonally cared for the sick, though she lost her own son Evangelist to the disease. A year later, an angel appeared to her and predicted that her daughter, Agnes, would soon die, but he also comforted her by saying that he would be her guide and protector for the rest of her life and that she would even be able to see him. At this point, her husband was able to return to Rome, and the family regained its property. But Lorenzo returned home in very poor health, and Frances had to care for him. Lorenzo wanted their son to marry. Unfortunately, the wife he chose for their son, Mobilia, was bad-tempered and despised Frances. While complaining bitterly about Frances one day, Mobilia suddenly became ill. Frances cared for her with great kindness until she recovered, which moved Mobilia to repentance. A changed woman, she even began to imitate her saintly mother-in-law. By now, people all over Rome acknowledged Frances as a virtuous, devout woman and miracle worker, and she was called on not only to help with caring for the sick but also to help settle disputes. Lorenzo, seeing his wife's holiness, was willing to release her from her marriage vows and only asked her to continue to live in the family home. With the approval of her confessor, she then began a congregation called the Oblates of Tor de' Specchi, a society of women who lived in the world but devoted themselves to serving God and the poor. Though she refused to be called the foundress, Frances shared in the life of the oblates as much as she could until Lorenzo died three years later. Frances then joined the oblates formally, and the superioress resigned immediately, insisting that Frances be made the superior. Frances died on this date in 1440 after a short illness.

Forty Martyrs of Armenia

In the year 320, the Roman emperor Licinius reversed the policy of toleration toward Christianity that he and his co-emperor Constantine had established. When the governor of Armenia announced the imperial decree to his army, forty soldiers of the city of Sebaste refused to give up their Christian faith. The governor ordered them to be taken outside the city walls to a frozen lake. The soldiers were told to take off their clothes and lie on the ice, while a huge bath of hot water was placed near the edge of the lake to tempt them to give in. After some time, the temptation was too great for one of the soldiers, and he ran to the hot bath. But when he jumped in, the shock of the temperature change killed him. Another soldier, witnessing the bravery of the thirty-nine men, stripped off his clothes and joined them. The men died quickly, and the last to die was a boy named Melito.

Saint Catherine of Bologna

Catherine was born in 1413, the daughter of a diplomat in Bologna, Italy. She was well educated and even served as maid of honor to the daughter of a marquis. Yet she heard God's call and left it all behind to become a Franciscan tertiary when she was only fourteen years old. Later she became a Poor Clare nun, and eventually she became the abbess. She painted, received visions, and performed miracles through her prayers. After she died in 1463, miracles occurred near her grave, and her body was found incorrupt and placed in her cell. (It's still there.)

Saint Dominic Savio

Dominic was born in 1842 in Turin, Italy, one of ten children. His father was a blacksmith, and his mother was a seamstress. He attended school at Don (Saint John) Bosco's Oratory, and he wanted to become a priest. At the time of his

First Holy Communion, he made a personal vow to please God by leading a life of prayer, always seeking sanctity, and performing works of charity. He organized other boys into a group he called the Company of the Immaculate Conception, in order to grow spiritually, take care of their school, and help other boys in need. He died in 1857 during a cholera epidemic at the young age of fifteen.

> *Saint Frances, help me to be in the world, but not of the world.*
> *Holy Martyrs, beg the Lord to give me fortitude.*
> *Saint Catherine, show me how to entrust all my gifts to God.*
> *Saint Dominic, pray for me to be pure and holy.*

* * * * *

March 10

Saint Simplicius

Simplicius (d. 483) was the forty-seventh pope; he reigned fifteen years. During his reign, the city of Rome came under the rule of leaders who followed the Arian heresy. Despite being outnumbered and politically stymied by the Arian rulers, Simplicius courageously defended the true faith against the widespread teachings of the Monophysite and Arian heresies. He also supported the local Roman Church by rebuilding churches and caring for the poor.

Saint John Ogilvie

John was born in 1579 to a Scottish baron. He was raised a Calvinist, but when he was thirteen years old, he was sent to Europe to be educated. While there, he attended the public debates between Catholics and Calvinists; these arguments and the witness of the martyrs led him to become a Catholic when he was seventeen years old. He entered the Jesuit order and was ordained a priest in 1610. He then returned to his native Scotland to serve the Catholics living their faith in secret, pretending to be a horse trader or soldier. Unfortunately, he was disappointed to find that most Catholics were at least pretending to conform to the established Anglican church and that only a few middle-class families were willing to help a Catholic priest. When he returned to Paris to report all this to his superior, his superior rebuked him for leaving his mission and sent him back. So John returned to Edinburgh and set up his headquarters at the home of a sincere Catholic named William Sinclair, met a Franciscan priest also named John, and ministered to small groups of Catholics who gathered in private homes. John encouraged faithfulness among the Catholics, took on the dangerous task of visiting Catholics in prison, made many converts in a short period of time, and reconciled members of the gentry to the Catholic Church. But he was finally betrayed to the authorities, arrested, and brought before the Anglican archbishop and the Glasgow court. When he was asked if he had said

Mass in Scotland (which was illegal), John tried to make them follow the law, demanding that they provide proof through witnesses. The trial dragged on until he hadn't been fed for twenty-six hours and was trembling from a fever, but he refused to incriminate himself or anyone else. To weaken his resistance, he was kept awake for eight days and nights by physical and verbal abuse. He was allowed to rest only when doctors declared that he would die otherwise. After allowing him to rest for a day and a night, new charges were brought against him. Now he was accused of treason, and when he was given a questionnaire about church-state relations by the king himself, the only answers he could honestly give as a faithful Catholic led to his condemnation. He was initially treated more kindly—the whole country had heard of his heroic behavior in prison—but soon that changed. He wrote a description of his arrest and the poor treatment he had received in prison, which he passed under the door to visitors, who in turn made it public. The authorities had set up a gallows to execute him before he had even been tried; after the pretense of a trial had been completed, he was condemned and sentenced to death in 1615. A friend of John's who was with him said that John was offered his freedom if he would give up his faith just moments before the execution.

Saint Simplicius, help me to defend the truths of the faith with charity.
Saint John, show me how to encourage other Catholics to faithfulness.

* * * * *

March 11

Saint Sophronius of Jerusalem

Sophronius (d. 639) was from Damascus, Syria; he traveled extensively, living near the holy patriarch of Alexandria, Saint John the Almsgiver, for many years. He lived the simple life of a monk; his letters, poems, and writings were widely read during his lifetime. In the year 634, he was chosen to be patriarch of Jerusalem. As patriarch, he vigorously wrote against the growing Monothelite heresy, explaining in his writings the orthodox Catholic teaching that Jesus had both a divine will and a human will. He also led his flock before and after the conquest of Jerusalem in the year 638 by Muslim Arabs. Through his Christlike treatment of the caliph Omar—he personally took Omar on a tour of the holy sites of the city—Sophronius was able to convince the Muslims to be more tolerant of Christians in the city. Sophronius died soon after the conquest, a year later. He is considered a Father of the Church.

Saint Oengus (Aengus)

Oengus was born in the eighth century into a royal family in Ulster, Ireland, and was educated at the famous monastery of Clonenagh in Leix. His contemporaries said that no one in Ireland could equal him for virtue and knowledge of the faith. After a time, he decided to retire from the world and lived in a cell seven miles from a monastery at Dysartenos. There he lived an austere life; his penances included making three hundred genuflections every day and reciting the Divine Office daily in his cell or sometimes while in a tub of cold water while tied by the neck to a stake as a mortification. When he decided too many people were coming to see him, he left in secret and anonymously joined a monastery near Dublin. For seven years, he performed the humblest tasks of the house. One day a schoolboy skipped school and spent the day with Oengus—and had learned his lesson perfectly by the end of the day. The abbot, Saint Maelruain, then recognized Oengus was the missing holy man from Dysartenos. Oengus and Maelruain became great friends, and Oengus stayed there for several years until Maelruain's death. He then returned to Clonenagh, where, in time, he became abbot and bishop. Near the end of his life, he withdrew to Dysartbeagh, but the exact details of his death (though probably in the year 824) aren't certain.

Blessed John Kearney

John was born in Cashel, Ireland, in 1619. He entered the novitiate of the Franciscan Friars Minor in Kilkenny but went to Belgium to enter the seminary and become a priest. After ordination in 1642, he returned to Ireland, but he was arrested for the crime of being a priest while passing through London. He was tortured and given a death sentence but somehow managed to escape from prison. After traveling to France, he returned to Ireland, safely this time. He lived in Cashel for several years, outwardly teaching philosophy and serving as porter and novice master, but still wanted by the English police. In 1653, he was found and arrested for the outstanding charge of being a Catholic priest and was hanged on this date.

> *Saint Sophronius, help me to love those who oppose me.*
> *Saint Oengus, show me how to take the lowest place and serve others.*
> *Blessed John, help me to set aside the anxieties of life and live my vocation in joy.*

* * * * *

March 12

Saint Maximilian of Theveste

Maximilian (274–295) was the son of a Roman soldier; therefore, he was required to report for military service in the Roman Empire. However, since Maximilian and his father had become Christians, Maximilian refused to serve in the army on the grounds that his faith prohibited the acts of pagan worship expected of a soldier. During his trial, his father stood by his side, and after he was beheaded, his father thanked God that his son had remained faithful to death for Christ. All this occurred at Theveste, Numidia, in northern Africa.

Saint Innocent I

Innocent (d. 417) was the fortieth pope; he reigned for fifteen years. During his reign, he took steps against heretical groups and leaders—retaking churches in Rome from the Novatians and banishing a leader of a heretical group following the false teaching of Photinus—as well as attempting (unsuccessfully) to make peace with Alaric, king of the Goths, and keep his army from capturing Rome. He was also active in opposing the Pelagian heresy. At first, for example, he condemned attacks against convents near Saint Jerome in Bethlehem by brutal followers of Pelagius. After he received warnings about that heresy from Saint Augustine and other bishops of Africa, he formally rejected the teachings of Pelagius.

Saint Theophanes the Chronographer

Theophanes was born in the eighth century in Constantinople and educated in the Byzantine imperial court. Although he married, he and his wife later mutually agreed to separate and give their lives to the Lord. She became a nun, and he became a monk and eventually founded two monasteries. He became abbot at one of them, Mount Sigriana, and he used his education to write a *Chronography*, or history of the world. He also participated in the Second Council of Nicaea, which approved the use of sacred images, against the heresy of iconoclasm. However, the emperor at the time, Leo V, opposed the use of images and tried to win Theophanes over to his side with both flattery and threats. Theophanes, who was suffering at the time from a painful disease, wrote back to the emperor, saying, "Being now far advanced in years and much broken with pain and the weakness of my body, I have neither relish nor inclination for any of those things which I despised, for Christ's sake, in my youth. As to my monastery and my friends, I commend them to God. If you think to frighten me into compliance by your threats, as a child is awed by the rod, you are only losing your pains."[3] The emperor ordered Theophanes to be scourged with three hundred strokes; he was then imprisoned, virtually ignored for two years in a stinking dungeon, and banished to the island of Samothrace, where he died in the year 817.

Blessed Luigi Orione

As a young man, Luigi (1872–1940) was a student of the saintly priest Saint John Bosco. Like Saint John, he founded many good works to organize people to serve the poor, educate the needy, and worship God. While still a seminarian, Luigi started a boarding school for poor boys called the Little Work of Divine Providence. In time this gave birth to several orders and associations: the Sons of Divine Providence (priests, brothers, and hermits who sought to bring children, the poor, and others to the Church, taking the usual vows plus a fourth of faithfulness to the pope); the Little Missionary Sisters of Charity; the Blind Sisters; the Adorers of the Blessed Sacrament; the Contemplative Sisters of Jesus Crucified;

---

[3] Walsh, *Butler's Lives of the Saints*, 78.

and lay associations of ladies, former pupils, and friends. The works of these associations included schools, boarding houses, and charitable works—and spread all over the world. Luigi's incorrupt body has been in Tortona, Italy, since 1980.

Saint Maximilian, pray for me to speak God's truth at all times.
Saint Innocent, help me to recognize the false teachings of my culture.
Saint Theophanes, teach me how to love suffering for the sake of Christ.
Blessed Luigi, pray for my life to bear fruit for Christ.

* * * * *

March 13

Saint Sabinus of Egypt

Sabinus was a nobleman who was martyred during the persecution of Christians under the Roman emperor Diocletian. He was executed by being drowned in the Nile River in the year 287.

Saint Leander of Seville

Leander (d. ca. 600) came from a holy family in Cartagena, Spain: his brothers Isidore and Fulgentius both became bishops (and saints) and his sister Florentina became a nun. The Visigoths ruled Spain at this time, and the heresy of Arianism was widespread. After Leander converted some members of the royal family from Arianism to Catholicism—in particular, two sons of the Arian king Leovigild himself—Leander was expelled from Spain in retaliation. He took refuge in Constantinople, and there he met the man who would become Pope Saint Gregory the Great. After King Leovigild died, Leander returned to his position as bishop of Seville, and with the new Catholic king's support, he convened a council in Toledo to confirm the conversion of the kingdom to Catholicism. Leander served his people as bishop until he died.

Saint Sabinus, show me how to live and die for Christ.
Saint Leander, pray for me to be a conduit of holiness to those around me.

* * * * *

March 14

Saint Alexander of Pidnae

During the persecution of the Church under the Roman emperor Maximus Galerius in the year 305, the martyr Alexander died in the city of Pidnae (now in Greece). His crime? Refusing in public to make a sacrifice to a pagan idol.

After he was beheaded, a spring of water sprung out of the ground where he had been executed.

Saint Leobinus (Lubin)

Leobinus (d. ca. 558) was born near Poitiers, France, into a peasant family. He worked in his family's fields until he was sent to a nearby monastery as a servant. There he worked at menial tasks for the monks and continued studying late into the night. Through hard work and humility, he eventually became a monk in the monastery. Two future saints—Carilef and the hermit Avitus—became his friends. When his monastery was raided during a war between the Franks and the Burgundians, all the monks fled except Leobinus and one old man. The raiders asked the old man about the location of the monastery's treasures, and he referred them to Leobinus. When Leobinus wouldn't tell them, they tortured him by tying his head with a cord and tightening it, and then by tying his feet together and dipping him, head first, into the river. They left him for dead, but he recovered and was able to make his way to a monastery in Le Perche. When the abbot of that monastery died, he became a hermit for a time, but the bishop of Chartres decided to make him the abbot of Brou and then raised him to the priesthood. Leobinus longed for his previous life as a simple monk, so he went and asked the bishop, Saint Caesarius, for advice. Saint Caesarius told him not to leave his sheep without a shepherd and to go back to Brou. Leobinus obeyed; he was ordained soon afterward as bishop of Chartres and took part in two important councils in France. After suffering from a long illness, he died on this date.

Saint Matilda of Saxony

Matilda was born in Saxony (modern Germany) around the year 895 and was educated by nuns. She married King Henry I of Germany, and she was an exemplary Christian queen. She prayed and cared for the poor, sometimes in disguise. She had three sons and two daughters. After twenty-three years of marriage, her husband died. She supported her second son, Henry, to become king, over her first son, Otto, because she thought Henry would be better able to lead the kingdom, but Otto was elected. When Henry tried to take the throne by force and failed, Matilda intervened and made peace between the brothers. Both her sons criticized her for giving too much to the poor and treated her unkindly, but Otto's wife managed to bring Otto to repentance. He asked his mother's forgiveness, and later she was left in charge when he left the kingdom to be crowned emperor. However, Matilda preferred to spend her time away from court, and she eventually settled in one of the convents she had built. She gave away everything in the year 968 and left this world owning nothing.

Saint Alexander, give me courage to stand up for Christ
rather than appease the idols of my world.
Saint Leobinus, help me always to seek the greatest treasure, which is Jesus Christ.
Saint Matilda, help me to be generous with those in need.

* * * * *

March 15

Saint Zachary

Zachary (d. 752) was the ninety-first pope; he reigned for ten years. He was from a Greek family living in Calabria (a region of modern Italy), and he was probably a deacon when he was elected to the papacy. He was known to be gentle and conciliatory, but also shrewd. During his reign, he fought against the iconoclasm promoted by the emperor in Constantinople, specifically by writing in support of the use of sacred images. He negotiated a truce with the pagan Lombards who controlled much of Italy, freeing some cities from their control. He worked to improve Church discipline by speaking against heretical teachings, and he served as a peacemaker in disputes between nations. Zachary was generous in supporting the restoration of churches in Rome, and he provided alms for the poor people who came to the papal palace. When Venetian merchants brought slaves to Rome on their way to sell them to Muslims in Africa, Zachary bought them all to protect Christians from becoming the property of unbelievers.

Saint Leocritia of Cordoba

Leocritia was born around the early ninth century in Cordoba during a time when Muslims controlled much of Spain. Her parents were Muslim, so when she chose to become a Christian, they kicked her out of the house. The priest (and also a martyr-saint) Eologius hid her for a time among other Christian women, but eventually she was discovered to be a Christian and was scourged then beheaded on March 9 in 859.

Saint Louise de Marillac

Louise was born in 1591 in Meux, France. Her mother died when she was a child, and her father died when she was only fifteen years old. In 1611, she married Antony Le Gras, an official to the queen; the couple was happily married and had a son. But Antony became seriously ill and had to be cared for by Louise until he died in 1625. At that point, she decided she would never marry again and instead decided to devote herself to serving God. Saint Vincent de Paul was her spiritual director at this time, and although he limited her activities at first due to her poor health, she began visiting and caring for the sick in one of the homes that he had established. Eventually, other women wanted to join Louise and care for the sick, so these women lived and trained in her home. Louise had wanted to make a formal vow and give herself to the service of God for some time. Vincent, a patient man, was finally convinced that this was God's will in 1634. Louise drafted a rule of life for her spiritual daughters to follow, but it wasn't until 1642 that he thought that she and three other women were ready to take formal vows of chastity, poverty, and obedience. The sisters cared for the sick in hospitals, tended orphans in orphanages, and even taught children in schools. Many new houses of nuns were founded, and the Congregation of the

Vincentian Sisters of Charity was formally approved in 1655. Louise cared for the growing needs of her congregation, but she also continued to care about the welfare of her son, Michael, and his family. They visited her on her deathbed, and she died on this date in 1660. Her body is still incorrupt.

Saint Clement Marie (John Dvorak) Hofbauer

Though he was born in 1751 with the name John Dvorak, John's father changed his Moravian name to the Germanic "Hofbauer" when John was small. His father died when he was six years old, and although John felt called to become a priest, his family was too poor to pay for his education. So he became a baker at the Premonstratensian Monastery at Bruck and then lived as a hermit. When his hermitage was abolished by order of the emperor, John worked as a baker in Vienna, and then traveled to Italy to live as a hermit, taking the name of Clement. After his third pilgrimage to Rome, he joined the Redemptorist order and added Marie to his name in honor of our Blessed Mother. He still yearned to become a priest, and after Mass one day, he met some people who volunteered to pay for his education. He studied for the priesthood at the University of Vienna and was ordained in 1785. He was initially assigned to Vienna but was sent as a missionary priest to Warsaw from 1786 to 1808. There he worked with the poor; preached; built schools; gave spiritual direction (including the direction of Venerable Joseph Passerat, a vicar general of the Redemptorists); introduced the Redemptorist order to Poland; and sent missionaries to Germany and Switzerland. When Napoleon suppressed all religious orders, he was imprisoned and then expelled to Austria. But in Vienna, he continued his work of revitalizing the spiritual life of Catholics. He served as a preacher and spiritual director, founded a Catholic college, fought efforts to establish a German national church separate from the Catholic Church, and worked against efforts that would've allowed the government to control the Church and the clergy. He died of natural causes in 1820 at Vienna.

Saint Zachary, help me to love Christ and His Church.
Saint Leocritia, help me to forgive those who harm me.
Saint Louise, help me to be patient and wait for God's timing in all things.
Saint Clement, pray for me to see each apparent setback as a stepping stone to God.

* * * * *

March 16

Saint Heribert of Cologne

Heribert was born in 970 and was the son of the duke of Worms in Germany; he was well educated and became a chancellor and a great statesman. When he was chosen to be archbishop of Cologne in the year 998, he showed his humble, penitential acceptance of the honor by walking barefoot to the consecration ceremony, even though it was winter. When the emperor Otto died, Heribert insisted that the new emperor be properly appointed and refused to hand over the imperial insignia until that had been done, which infuriated the powerful men who were seeking to be made king. One of those men did succeed Otto as King Henry II, and he imprisoned Heribert and resented him for many years until he finally recognized Heribert's wisdom in keeping the Church apart from political intrigues. Heribert's prayers were credited with the ending of a drought and other miracles, and he was considered a saint by many people even during his lifetime. He died in 1021 of natural causes in Cologne.

Blesseds John Amias and Robert Dalby

John was a married cloth merchant in the sixteenth century in Wakefield, England. When his wife died, he divided his property among his children and traveled to Rheims, France, to study for the priesthood. He returned after his ordination in 1581 to minister to Catholics secretly. Robert was a Protestant minister who was born in Yorkshire and who converted to the Catholic faith when it was illegal to do so in England. He went to France to study for the priesthood and returned to England after he was ordained in the year 1588. Both men were arrested for the crime of being priests. They were hanged, drawn, and quartered together on this date in 1589 in York, England.

Saint Heribert, help me speak the truth without compromise.
Blesseds Robert and John, help me find the words
to encourage other Catholics to remain faithful.

* * * * *

March 17

Saint Patrick of Ireland, Optional Memorial

Patrick was born to a Roman family living in England around the year 385 when he was kidnapped, probably at the age of sixteen. He was carried off to pagan Ireland, sold as a slave, and lived the harsh life of a slave there for six years. However, his difficulties brought him closer to the Lord, and he began to pray. One day he heard a voice in his sleep and ran away from his master, traveling two hundred miles to a ship that he somehow seemed to know would take him to freedom. Although the sailors refused to take him on board at first, he prayed, and they miraculously changed their minds. The sea journey was followed by a long journey on foot until he eventually returned to his family. He was welcomed back warmly, but he felt God calling him to serve the Irish people. He then studied in several monasteries in Europe, became a priest, and was sent by Pope Celestine I to evangelize both England and Ireland as a bishop. Patrick confronted the paganism of the Irish people and faced many difficulties for thirty-three long years. He was given the title of archbishop of Armagh, and in the end, he converted all of Ireland. He died in County Down of natural causes in the year 461.

I read aloud where it began: "The Voice of the Irish." / And as I began to read these words I seemed to hear the voice of the same men / who lived beside the forest of Foclut, . . . / They seemed to shout aloud to me "as if with one and the same voice": / "Holy broth of a boy, we beg you, / come back and walk once more among us." / I was utterly "pierced to my heart's core," / so that I could read no more.[4]

Martyrs of Alexandria

In Alexandria, Egypt, the worship of the Egyptian sun god Serapis was popular among the residents. Around the year 392, a mob of pagans attacked and killed a group of Christians (number unknown) because they wouldn't worship Serapis.

Saint Jan Sarkander

Jan was born in 1576 in Skoczow of modern Poland. He married, but after his wife died, he heard God's call to the priesthood. Jan studied in Prague, was ordained in 1607, and served as a parish priest in the city of Olmutz. As a Catholic priest, he was caught in a spiritual and political battle between Catholic and Protestant leaders in the area during the tumultuous time of the Protestant revolt. In 1620, Jan visited a Polish field commander, armed only with the Blessed Sacrament in a monstrance, as Polish and German armies faced one another. When no battle ensued afterward, an anti-Catholic local leader accused Jan of being a spy and traitor. Jan was arrested and tortured to extract information about the Catholic forces, but he didn't betray them or his faith. He was executed by being burned alive on this date in 1620.

Saint Patrick, show me how to bring the Gospel to others.
Holy Martyrs, help me be courageous in leading others to the true God.

* * * * *

March 18

Saint Cyril of Jerusalem, Optional Memorial

Cyril was born in 315 and raised in Jerusalem, apparently in a Christian home. He was ordained a priest by his bishop, Saint Maximus, and was given the important task of instructing catechumens who were preparing to enter the Church. Thankfully, his gentle, pastoral lectures were written down and give us an excellent example of the catechetical teachings of the early Church. He was made bishop of Jerusalem in the year 348; he constantly battled the widespread

---

[4] Patrick, *The Confession of Saint Patrick: The Classic Text in New Translation*, trans. John Skinner (New York: Image Books, Doubleday, 1998), 45.

heresy of the time, Arianism. He was sent into exile by the government three times for a total of sixteen years. Each time, he was arrested and convicted on trumped-up charges, although it was obvious that his only "crime" was his unwillingness to capitulate on Church teaching. He died in 386 of natural causes, having served his flock as bishop for thirty-eight years. Known to the Church as the Doctor of Catechesis and a Father of the Church, on the strength of his catechetical writings and his orthodox teaching, he was also named a Doctor of the Church.

> *Let your mind be refined as by fire unto reverence; let your soul be forged as metal: let the stubbornness of unbelief be hammered out: let the superfluous scales of the iron drop off, and what is pure remain; let the rust of the iron be rubbed off, and the true metal remain.... Then may the gate of Paradise be opened to every man and every woman among you.*[5]

Saint Braulio of Saragossa

Braulio was born around the year 590 and educated at a college in Seville, Spain, which had been founded by Saint Isidore, the bishop. Braulio was such an excellent student that he eventually became Isidore's friend and disciple, even editing Isidore's writings for him. He was ordained a priest, and in the year 631, he was chosen to be bishop of Saragossa. As bishop, Braulio brought order and discipline to the Church in Spain and to his clergy, and he worked to eradicate the Arian heresy that still infected some areas. When the pope made charges of negligence against the Spanish bishops, they asked Braulio to respond for them, and his dignified response appeased the pope. Braulio lived an austere personal life, gave generously to the poor, and spent many days and nights in prayer. Near the end of his life, he lost his eyesight, which was a great trial to a man who loved reading; when his end was near, he spent his final day of life reciting the psalms. He died in the year 651 and is considered a Father of the Church.

Blesseds John Thules and Roger Wrenno

During the time of anti-Catholic persecution in England, being a priest or helping a priest was a capital offense. John Thules was a priest who minister secretly to Catholics, and Roger Wrenno was a Catholic layman. Both were executed on this date in 1616.

> Saint Cyril, help me know and speak the truth about Jesus Christ.
> Saint Braulio, show me how to use what I learn to lead others to Christ.
> Blesseds John and Roger, help me remember to give
> thanks for the gift of the priesthood every day.

* * * * *

[5] Cyril of Jerusalem, *The Protocatechesis* 15, trans. Edwin Hamilton Gifford, in *Nicene and Post-Nicene Fathers*, 2nd series, vol. 7, ed. Philip Schaff and Henry Wace (Buffalo, N.Y.: Christian Literature Publishing, 1894). Revised and edited for New Advent by Kevin Knight, accessed September 20, 2019, http://www.newadvent.org/fathers/310100.htm.

March 19

Saint Joseph, Spouse of the Blessed Virgin Mary, Solemnity

Speaking about Saint Joseph on the Feast of the Assumption, Pope Saint John Paul II said, "'When Joseph woke from sleep, he did as the angel of the Lord commanded him and took Mary as his wife' (cf. Mt 1:24). He took her in all the mystery of her motherhood. He took her together with the Son who had come into the world by the power of the Holy Spirit. In this way he showed a readiness of will like Mary's with regard to what God asked of him through the angel."[6]

Blessed Marcel Callo

Marcel was born in 1921 into a large family in Rennes, France. He was a member of the Boy Scouts and the Catholic movement Young Christian Workers. During the Nazi occupation of France, Marcel and his friends went to the train station daily to help refugees. He was engaged to a young woman but didn't marry because of the dangers of the war. He was ordered to work in a forced labor camp, where he tried to help other workers. Finally, in 1944, the Gestapo arrested him because he was "too Catholic". He was sent to various prison camps, living in horrible conditions, until he finally died in an Austrian camp on this date in 1945.

Saint Joseph, help me do God's will.
Blessed Marcel, show me how to find and serve those who are in great need around me.

* * * * *

March 20

Saint Cuthbert of Lindisfarne

Cuthbert (634–687) was apparently an orphan, for he was raised by a widow named Kenswith. When Cuthbert was fifteen years old and working as a shepherd in England, he had a vision of a dazzling beam of light and a host of angels accompanying a soul to Heaven. He later learned that the holy monk, bishop, and saint Aidan had died that night. He was deeply affected by this vision, so he later traveled to Melrose Abbey, asking to be admitted as a monk. Since he arrived on horseback and armed with a spear, it's presumed that he was a soldier at the time. In the year 660, he left the abbey with his abbot to found a new one at Ripon, but he later returned to Melrose and became the prior. When a

---

[6] John Paul II, apostolic exhortation *Redemptoris Custos* (Guardian of the Redeemer) (August 15, 1989), no. 3, http://www.vatican.va/content/john-paul-ii/en/apost_exhortations/documents/hf_jp-ii_exh_15081989_redemptoris-custos.html.

deadly plague swept the area and the people living outside the monastery began turning to superstitious practices to protect themselves, Cuthbert helped the local people remember to ask God for healing instead. The monks of Melrose later became divided over the proper date to celebrate Easter (a disagreement that took centuries for the Church to settle), and Cuthbert and some of the other monks moved to Lindisfarne Abbey. There he served as prior and abbot, and he later became bishop of Hexham. In the year 685, he was ordained bishop of Lindisfarne. He traveled throughout his diocese to serve and preach to his people, made sure the poor were cared for, and became known as a healer for the power of his prayers. At the end of his life, he lived quietly at Lindisfarne Abbey, suffered patiently during his final illness, and died peacefully. The shrine containing his relics was plundered during King Henry VIII's reign, but monks hid his relics, which were recovered in 1827.

Saint John Nepomucene

John was born in Bohemia (the modern Czech Republic) in the year 1330. When he was a young boy, he became seriously ill, and when he recovered, his parents, in thanksgiving, consecrated him to God. He later became a priest. He was a great preacher and a counselor to the king, and he spoke up for the needs of the poor. His king became suspicious of his (innocent) queen, whom he suspected of adultery. The king even demanded that John break the priestly seal of confession and reveal what she had confessed to him. When John refused to do so, he was executed by being thrown into the river. He thus died a martyr for the Sacrament of Confession in the year 1383.

Saint Cuthbert, help me to bring the light of Christ to those in darkness. Saint John, remind me to be thankful for the graces of the Sacrament of Confession.

* * * * *

March 21

Martyrs of Alexandria

This group of martyrs, whose names we do not know, died for the faith under the persecution of Christians during the reign of the Roman emperor Constantius. They died together in Alexandria, Egypt, on the Feast of Pentecost in the year 339.

Saint Enda of Ireland

Enda (d. ca. 530) was an Irish prince and soldier who left everything behind to live the monastic life. On land given him by King Oengus (his brother-in-law), he founded the first Irish monastery, which gave birth to many others. He lived a penitential, prayerful life and led his monks to do the same. He was the spiritual teacher of many great Irish saints: Ciaran of Clonmacnoise, Brendan the

Voyager, Finnian, Columba of Iona, Jarlath of Tuam, and Carthach the Elder. He died of natural causes.

Saint Nicholas of Flue

Nicholas was born in 1417 into a wealthy family in Switzerland, rose to the rank of captain while serving as a soldier, and then served as a judge and government advisor. He married Dorothy Wiss when he was thirty years old, and they had ten children. After having a vision of a harnessed draft horse eating a lily (symbolizing his worldly life versus a life of purity), he felt God calling him to withdraw from the world. With his family's approval, he became a hermit, spent his days in prayer, and attended Mass daily. For nineteen years, he lived solely on Holy Communion. In 1481, he left his hermitage to mediate peace in his native country and avert a civil war. He died on this day (as he had been born on this same day) in 1487, with his wife and children at his side.

My Lord and my God, take everything from me that separates me from Thee. My Lord and my God, give everything to me that brings me nearer to Thee. My Lord and my God, take me from myself, and give me completely to Thee.[7]

Holy Martyrs, show me how to live and die for Christ.
Saint Enda, show me how to live a prayerful, penitential life.
Saint Nicholas, help me give everything to God.

* * * * *

March 22

Saint Lea of Rome

Lea (d. 384) was a Roman woman who was left a widow at an early age. Although a high-ranking official wanted to marry her, she took the advice of Saint Jerome and joined the convent founded by Jerome's saintly female followers, Paula and Marcella, instead. Jerome wrote to Marcella[8] when Lea died, praising Lea's virtues and her dedication to prayer and charity, and telling us most of what we know about her.

Saint Nicholas Owen

Nicholas was born in the sixteenth century in England and lived a virtuous life, despite the rampant immorality of his culture. For eighteen years, he served as the faithful servant of Fathers Henry Garnet and John Gerard, two Catholic priests who served their people secretly because of the bitter persecution of

[7] Prayer widely attributed to Nicholas of Flue.
[8] See Jerome's Letter to Marcella, Letter 23; available on New Advent's website at http://www.newadvent.org/fathers/3001023.htm.

Catholics at the time. Though he was a short man, Nicholas was strong, and he was ingenious at creating hiding places for Catholic priests. He received the Holy Eucharist before he built each hiding place and prayed while he worked. In 1580, Father Garnet secretly admitted him to the Jesuits and made him a lay brother. In 1594, Nicholas and Father Gerard were captured and imprisoned in the Tower of London. Nicholas was tortured to try to make him disclose the names of other Catholics. Because of his skill in devising hiding places, a Catholic gentleman paid for his release. Soon afterward Nicholas came back to the Tower—to help Father Gerard escape. He hid from the authorities for several years. But one day, in order to protect two priests who were in a hiding place, Nicholas came out of his hiding place and was taken again to the Tower. He was tortured by being kept hanging in the air for hours a day. He refused to answer questions until finally the iron band that was holding him enlarged a wound, and he died in great pain on March 2, 1606.

Saint Lea, help me to choose holy pleasures always over the pleasures of the world.
Saint Nicholas, help me understand and follow my vocation.

* * * * *

March 23

Saint Turibius of Mogrovejo, Optional Memorial

Turibius was born in 1538 in Mayorga, Spain, and was pious even as a child. He studied law and became such a brilliant scholar that the king decided he was the perfect candidate for the vacant archbishopric of the Spanish colony of Lima, Peru. Turibius objected, pointing out that canon law forbade laymen from accepting ecclesiastical offices. However, he was overruled, ordained, and sent by boat to Lima in 1581. When Turibius arrived, he quickly saw the challenges of his position: his diocese was four hundred miles long; it included the Andes Mountains and was therefore difficult to cross; and the Spanish conquistadores mistreated the native peoples shamefully. Turibius established discipline among his clergy, corrected those who committed unjust acts, even those with high social standing, and eradicated some of the worst abuses in his diocese. He founded hospitals, churches, and religious houses; learned the Indian dialects so that he could speak to his people, staying for days to visit them even when there was no bed or food for him; and eventually visited his entire diocese, despite the danger. Turibius offered Mass every day, even when traveling, and he confessed to his chaplain every night. He encouraged the faith of four people who are also canonized saints: he confirmed Rose of Lima, Martin de Porres, and John Massias, and he knew the Franciscan missionary Francis Solano. In 1606, when he was sixty-eight years old, he became ill and realized that his end was near. He then gave his belongings to his servants and everything else for the benefit of the poor. After receiving Viaticum, he died while the following psalm passage was being recited: "I was glad when they said to me, 'Let us go to the house of the LORD!' "9

Blessed Edmund Sykes

Edmund was born in Leeds around the year 1550. During the reign of Queen Elizabeth I (r. 1558–1603), it was illegal to be a Catholic priest in England; therefore, Edmund secretly became a priest, serving his fellow Catholics covertly and in constant danger. He was arrested and died a martyr for the faith on this date in 1587.

Saint Rebecca (Boutrossieh) de Himlaya Ar-rayes

Boutrossieh was born in 1832 in Himlaya, Lebanon. Her mother died when she was six years old, and she didn't get along with her stepmother. She worked as a maid from the age of eleven until she was fifteen. She told her father she felt called to religious life even when she was a teenager, but it wasn't until she was twenty-one years old that she became a nun of the Marian Order of the Immaculate Conception. She took the name of Anissa (Agnes) and made final vows in 1856. When her order was about to merge with another in 1871, she had a dream in which Saint Anthony the Great appeared to her. She therefore chose to join the Order of Saint Anthony of the Maronites instead and took the name of Rafqa (Rebecca). In 1885, she felt called to pray that she might share Christ's sufferings, and our Lord complied; she gradually became blind, crippled, and paralyzed, and she lived her life in great pain. Despite her disabilities, she continued to pray and work at the tasks she was able to do: spinning wool and knitting. Her superior, Mother Ursula, ordered her to dictate her autobiography late in her life. Rebecca asked God to allow her to see Mother Ursula's face despite her blindness, and God granted her request for an hour before she died in 1914. Miraculous cures followed her holy death.

> Saint Turibius, beg the Lord to give me courage in charitably confronting injustice.
> Blessed Edmund, help me to follow my vocation at any cost.
> Saint Rebecca, show me how to bear my pains with peace.

* * * * *

March 24

Martyrs of Caesarea

During the persecution of the Church under the Roman emperor Diocletian in the year 303, a group of martyrs was executed for being Christians. We only know the names of six of them: Agapius, Alexander, Dionysius, Pausis,

9 Ps 122:1.

Romulus, and Timolaus. They were beheaded in Caesarea (in modern Israel) and have been remembered as martyrs on this date for centuries.

Saint Catherine of Sweden

Catherine was born in 1331 in Sweden, the fourth child of Saint Bridget and her husband, Ulf. She was married to a pious German nobleman named Eggart von Kurnen when she was thirteen years old, but the couple mutually agreed soon afterward to live chastely together. After her father died and her mother left for Rome, she was so sad that she never smiled, as she later told Saint Catherine of Siena. Her husband allowed her to go to Rome to be with her mother, and he died soon afterward, around the year 1350. Now a widow, Catherine was not only troubled by men who wanted to marry her, but was also unable to leave her home due to the dangerous environment of Rome at the time. Still, she helped her mother for the next twenty-five years, as they prayed and taught the faith to the poor, and she went on several pilgrimages. When Bridget died, Catherine returned her mother's body to Sweden and became superior and abbess at one of the houses of her mother's religious order. Through Catherine's efforts, the Bridgettine order received papal approval in 1375, and she worked for her mother's canonization. She died in 1381 of natural causes.

> *Holy Martyrs, show me how to live and die for Christ.*
> *Saint Catherine, help me to bear my crosses with trust in God.*

* * * * *

March 25

The Annunciation of the Lord, Solemnity

Nine months from now, the Church celebrates the birth of Jesus Christ; today, the Church celebrates His conception—that is, the humble Virgin Mary's acceptance of God's invitation to bear the Messiah. In his prayer on the Feast of the Annunciation, Saint Alphonsus Liguori wrote,

> O immaculate and holy Virgin! O creature the most humble and the most exalted before God! Thou wast so lowly in thine own eyes, but so great in the eyes of thy Lord, that He exalted thee to such a degree as to choose thee for His mother, and then made thee Queen of heaven and earth. I therefore thank God who so greatly has exalted thee, and rejoice in seeing thee so closely united with Him, that more cannot be granted to a pure creature. Before thee, who art so humble, though endowed with such precious gifts, I am ashamed to appear, I who am so proud in the midst of so many sins. But miserable as I am, I will also salute thee, "Hail, Mary, full of grace." Thou art already full of grace; impart a portion of it to me.[10]

---

[10] Saint Alphonsus Liguori, *The Glories of Mary* (Charlotte: TAN Books, 2012), 331.

Saint Dismas the Good Thief

According to the Gospel of Luke, "One of the criminals who were hanged railed at [Jesus], saying, 'Are you not the Christ? Save yourself and us!' But the other [the man traditionally known as Dismas] rebuked him, saying, 'Do you not fear God, since you are under the same sentence of condemnation? And we indeed justly; for we are receiving the due reward of our deeds; but this man has done nothing wrong.' And he said, 'Jesus, remember me when you come into your kingly power.' And he said to him, 'Truly, I say to you, today you will be with me in Paradise.'"[11]

Saint Margaret Clitherow

Margaret was born in 1556 and was the daughter of Thomas Middleton, who was a candlemaker and sheriff of York, England. She was raised an Anglican. In 1571, she married John Clitherow, who was a wealthy butcher and chamberlain to the city of York. In 1574, she converted to Catholicism, despite the danger. She organized clandestine Masses to be celebrated in her home, and she sheltered priests (including her husband's brother), which led to her being put in prison on several occasions. In 1586, she was put on trial at Tyburn for her "crimes", yet she refused to answer the charges against her in order to avoid incriminating her servants and children. She was pressed to death on this date in 1586 (Good Friday) while pregnant with her fourth child, the first woman to be martyred under Queen Elizabeth's persecution of Catholics. Both her sons became priests, and her daughter became a nun.

Saint Lucy Filippini

Lucy was born in 1672 in Tuscany, Italy, and she was orphaned when she was young. She was a pious, serious, gifted young woman when the bishop of her diocese, Cardinal Barbarigo, recognized her talents and encouraged her to come to a school he had established to educate teachers. There she met Saint Rose Venerini, who also later organized schools in the neighboring city of Viterbo. Lucy was modest, charitable, courageous, and full of common sense, and she founded many schools for girls, as well as educational centers. In Rome, everyone called her the "holy schoolmistress". In 1726, she became very ill, and despite excellent medical care, she never regained good health. She died on this date in 1732.

Blessed Mother, help me always say yes to God.
Saint Dismas, teach me how to repent deeply.
Saint Margaret, help me bear my sufferings for Christ.
Saint Lucy, show me how to teach the faith to those I encounter daily.

* * * * *

---

[11] Lk 23:39–43.

March 26

Saints Montanus and Maxima of Sirmium

During the persecution of the Church under the Roman emperor Diocletian in the year 304, Montanus and Maxima were executed for failure to worship the pagan gods in the city of Sirmium. Montanus was a Catholic priest, and Maxima was his wife. They were martyred by drowning and died together.

Saint Ludger of Utrecht

Ludger was born into a noble and wealthy family in the Netherlands around the year 743; he was the brother of Saints Gerburgis and Hildegrin. He was so moved by the preaching of Saint Boniface that he went to study under Saint Gregory of Utrecht and Saint Alciun in England, then became a deacon. In the year 773, he returned to the Netherlands as a missionary. For several years, he restored Christian chapels that had been destroyed, destroyed pagan idols, taught school, and was ordained a priest. He left the area in the year 784 when the pagan Saxons invaded and expelled all the priests. He then traveled to Rome, met with Pope Adrian I, and lived as a Benedictine monk (but without taking vows) until he was invited by Charlemagne to return to the Netherlands as a missionary. When he healed the blindness of a pagan bard, the man converted. Ludger refused an offer to become the bishop of Trier and instead built a monastery, although he later became the bishop of Munster. Ludger continued his heavy workload, not neglecting his time for prayer even when he suffered from poor health. It's said that his enemies could find fault with him for only two reasons: that he spent more on charity than on church decorations and that he celebrated Mass twice on the day of his death in the year 809.

Blessed Maddalena Caterina Morano

Maddalena was born in 1847 in Chieri, Italy. After her father and older sister died, she had to go to work to help her family, although she was only eight years old. She became a teacher and helped raise her brothers and sisters. When she had saved enough money to care for her mother, she left home to enter Saint John Bosco's order, the Daughters of Mary, Help of Christians. For twenty-five years, she served as superior of her community in Sicily, training teachers and catechists, organizing classes and after-school activities, and inspiring her nuns and those they served with the Salesian principles of loving, joyful service. She died on this date in 1908 of cancer.

> *Saints Montanus and Maxima, help my family members draw close to Christ.*
> *Saint Ludger, show me how to be "excessively" generous with God.*
> *Blessed Maddalena, help me make sacrifices with joy for the salvation of others.*

* * * * *

March 27

Saint Rupert of Salzburg

Rupert was born around the year 660. He was a Frank (perhaps from French nobility) and became bishop of Worms before being sent to evangelize Bavaria, Germany. His missionary work was successful, perhaps because unlike some other missionaries who knocked down pagan temples, he converted them to churches. He converted so many people in Bavaria that Christians had to be called in from neighboring areas to help the converts. His sister, Saint Erentrudis, became the first abbess at a now-famous convent called Nonnberg. He centered his missionary work around Juvavum, an ancient Roman town near salt springs. This city became Salzburg, and it was here that he died around the year 715.

Blessed Panacea de Muzzi of Quarona

Panacea was born in 1383 in Quarona, Italy; her mother died when she was a baby. She tended her family's sheep when she was old enough to do so, and her father remarried. But her stepmother hated the girl, particularly her devotion to God. One night in 1393, while the ten-year-old Panacea was praying, her stepmother stabbed her with a spindle. Panacea died and was immediately acclaimed a martyr by the townspeople.

Blessed Francis (Francesco) Faa di Bruno

Francis was born in 1825 in Alessandria, Sardinia, into a noble, large, and happy family. He served as an officer in the army before he resigned his commission and decided to study mathematics. He became a professor of mathematics at a local university, and in time, he was recognized for his research and contributions to the field. Outside of work, he personally served the poor and elderly in his community. When he discerned that God was calling him to the priesthood, he was initially turned down because he was already in his late forties. After appealing to the pope himself, Francis was admitted to the seminary and eventually ordained at age fifty-one. As a priest, he founded the Minim Sisters of Saint Zita in 1881, an order of sisters that cared for women in need, such as maids, domestic servants, unmarried mothers, and prostitutes. He died in 1888, at the age of sixty-three.

Saint Rupert, help me to convert my own
past faults into holy habits.
Blessed Panacea, help me to forgive
my family members.
Blessed Francis, show me how to serve God
with the talents He has given me.

* * * * *

March 28

Saints Priscus, Malchus, and Alexander of Caesarea

These three men were hermits living in the desert in Caesarea (in modern Israel). When they entered the city and proclaimed themselves Christians, they were arrested, tortured, and died as martyrs for the faith in the year 260, during the reign of the Roman emperor Valerian.

Saint Guntramnus of France

Born in the sixth century, Guntramnus' mother was Saint Clothildis, the queen of France, but his father was the worldly King Clotaire, and he grew up without believing in Christ. He became king of Orleans and Burgundy in the year 561, and he married Mercatrude, though he later divorced her. However, when she became ill and a doctor was unable to cure her, Guntramnus angrily had the doctor executed. After his crime, he underwent a conversion. He became a Christian, repented, and spent the rest of his life building up the Church. As king, he generously supported the sick and poor, particularly during times of plague and famine; was a tender father to his subjects; and strictly enforced the law while forgiving offenses, including two attempts on his life. After his death in the year 592, his subjects immediately proclaimed him a saint.

Saint Stephen Harding

Stephen was born around the year 1060 in Dorset, England. After traveling in Europe, he joined a group of hermits at Molesme, France. Stephen and two of his friends—Saint Robert of Molesme and Saint Alberic—later left the hermits, and in Citeaux, they established a monastery that combined the strict manner of life of the hermits with elements of community life found in monasticism. In time, Robert returned to Molesme, but Stephen remained and was eventually named abbot. He then instituted seemingly severe measures: rulers couldn't hold their courts in the abbey (which disrupted the monks' peace) and everything used in the service of God had to be simple and common. This brought simplicity to the monastery, but it also dried up sources of revenue and new postulants. Several monks died of a mysterious disease. For a time, things looked bleak, and even Stephen became concerned. But when a man named Bernard (later known as Saint Bernard of Clairvaux) showed up on the doorstep with thirty noblemen, all of whom wanted to enter and join Stephen and his monks, the tide turned. There was now no lack of novices or food; daughter houses for this new order, the Cistercians, began to spread. When Stephen was very old and nearly blind, he stepped down as abbot to prepare to meet our Lord. He died in 1134.

> *Holy Martyrs, help me be unafraid to call myself a follower of Christ.*
> *Saint Guntramnus, teach me true repentance for my sins.*
> *Saint Stephen, teach me trust in the Lord at all times.*

* * * * *

March 29

Blessed Berthold of Mount Carmel

Berthold (d. ca. 1195) was born the son of a count in Limoges, France, and served as a soldier in the Crusades. While in the Middle East, he received a vision of Jesus Christ. This moved him so profoundly that he left everything behind and traveled to Mount Carmel, the mountain where the prophet Elijah dramatically defeated the priests of Baal with his faith in God.[12] Berthold decided to live as a hermit on Mount Carmel, and, in time, other hermits began to follow his way of life and his direction. Some say this was the start of the Carmelite order; others, that this was the inspiration for the order.

Saint Ludolf of Ratzeburg

Ludolf (d. 1255) was a Premonstratensian canon and priest in Schleswig-Holstein, Germany, when he was made bishop of Ratzeburg in 1236. The duke of Lauenburg, Albert Urso, was a powerful man who demanded the financial support of the Church, at any price. When Ludolf opposed the duke and tried to stop him from confiscating church property, he was thrown in prison. He was so badly mistreated while in prison that he died soon after he was released. His martyrdom occurred on this date.

> *Blessed Berthold, help me to place my faith in God at all times.*
> *Saint Ludolf, help me stand up for justice with charity.*

* * * * *

March 30

Saint John Climacus

John was born in Syria around the year 579; he became a monk at Mount Sinai when he was sixteen years old. He later spent many years as a hermit in the Arabian Desert near his monastery. At the request of nearby monks, he composed his great work, *The Ladder*, in which he describes the steps on the ladder to Heaven—that is, the stages by which we pass on our journey to holiness and to union with God. He became abbot of Mount Sinai when he was seventy-five years old, but in the last few years of his life, he resigned and returned to life as a hermit. He died around the year 649.

> *Prayer is by nature a dialog and a union of man with God. Its effect is to hold the world together. It achieves a reconciliation with God.*[13]

---

[12] See 1 Kings 18.

[13] John Climacus, *The Ladder of Divine Ascent*, trans. Colm Luibheid and Norman Russell (Mahwah, N.J.; New York: Paulist Press, 1982), 274.

Saint Leonard Murialdo

Leonard was born into a rich but devout family in Turin, Italy, in 1828. He felt called to the priesthood, studied theology, and was ordained in 1851. He continued his theological studies rather than serving in a parish, using his family's wealth to support him. But after becoming acquainted with other devout clergy in Turin, including Saints John Bosco and Joseph Cafasso, his work as a priest changed. He preached, heard confessions, taught catechism, and took charge of one of Bosco's oratories. Leonard studied in Paris for a year, and when he returned, he was asked to take charge temporarily of a college for young working men that had been founded by another priest. Leonard's "temporary" commitment lasted thirty-seven years. He included music, gymnastics, and theater in the men's education; founded the Pious Association of Saint Joseph, to encourage devotion and to help support the college; and encouraged devotion to the Blessed Mother and the Sacred Heart of Jesus. He died on this date in 1900.

Blessed Mary Restituta (Helena) Kafka

Helena was born in 1894 in Brno, Czechoslovakia, the sixth daughter of a shoemaker, and grew up in Vienna, Austria. She worked as a sales clerk and nurse until she joined the Franciscan Sisters of Christian Charity in 1914, taking the name Mary Restituta. (The latter name is that of an early Church martyr.) She began working as a surgical nurse in 1919 and continued that work for twenty years. After the Nazis invaded Austria, she boldly and vocally opposed Nazism. When a new surgical wing was opened, she placed a crucifix in each room. However, she was ordered to remove the crucifixes, and when she refused, she was arrested and sentenced to death for treason. She cared for other prisoners and was spoken well of by them while she awaited her execution. She was offered her freedom, if she would abandon her religious community. When she refused, she was beheaded on this date in 1943 at Vienna.

> *Saint John, show me the way to Heaven.*
> *Saint Leonard, help me say yes when asked to serve others.*
> *Blessed Mary, pray for me to be courageously Christian in today's culture.*

* * * * *

March 31

Saint Benjamin the Deacon

Benjamin (d. 424) was a deacon in Persia (modern Iran) who was imprisoned for his faith. He was released on the condition that he would never speak of the faith where those of the royal court could hear. So he became a street preacher, speaking of Jesus Christ on the streets. King Varanes was not amused by the irony, and Benjamin was arrested, tortured, and impaled on a stake, dying a martyr.

Saint Guy (Guido) of Pomposa

Guy was born around the beginning of the eleventh century in Ravenna, Italy. His parents took great pride in him, and, to please them, he was very careful of his appearance. However, he repented of this habit one day and gave away his clothes to the poor, put on shabby ones, and set out for Rome, despite his parents' embarrassment. He lived under the direction of a hermit for three years until the hermit sent him to live in a monastery. There he became a devoted monk and eventually abbot. So many men came to follow him, including his own father and brother, that he had to build another monastery. However, he was careful to delegate his duties at times and to withdraw to pray in solitude. Though he was terribly hard on his own body, he was gentle with his monks. As a bishop, Saint Peter Damian came to his monastery to deliver lectures to the monks and dedicated his work *De perfectione monachorum* (On the Perfection of Monks) to Guy. At the end of his life, the emperor Henry III wanted to consult with the holy abbot; Guy reluctantly obeyed him and traveled to see him. But as Guy had predicted, he died of a sudden illness in 1046 when he arrived near Parma and never returned to his monks.

Blessed Christopher Robinson

Christopher was born at Woodside, England, around the year 1565. Because of the anti-Catholic laws in England at the time, he had to go to Douai and Rheims in France to study for the priesthood; he was ordained in 1592. He returned that same year to minister secretly to Catholics in the regions of Cumberland and Westmoreland. After he personally witnessed the martyrdom of a priest, Saint John Boste, he wrote an account of the execution. In 1597, he was detected and arrested for the crime of being a priest. When the authorities tried to execute him, the rope used to hang him broke twice. On the third attempt, they succeeded. His martyrdom occurred on this date in the year 1598.

> *Saint Benjamin, help me to have God's sense of humor over my difficulties.*
> *Saint Guy, teach me humility.*
> *Blessed Christopher, help me to give my life to Christ.*

April

April 1

Saint Venantius of Spalato and Companions

Around the year 255, the persecution of Christians in the Roman Empire was renewed in the Dalmatia region of modern-day Croatia. The bishop of Spalato, Venantius, and many other Christians from the region gave their lives for Christ during this time. Their relics were later gathered and taken to the Lateran Basilica in Rome in the year 641.

Saint Mary of Egypt

Mary (344–421) was the beautiful, spoiled child of a rich family living in Egypt. She ran away from home when she was twelve years old and worked as a dancer, singer, and prostitute for seventeen years in the great city of Alexandria before moving to Jerusalem. On the Feast of the Triumph of the Cross, still living as a prostitute, she followed the crowds to a great church. She decided to enter the church with other pilgrims, but she was mysteriously unable even to open the church door. This experience brought her to deep repentance for her sinful life. She asked the Virgin Mary for guidance, and she heard a voice tell her that if she crossed the Jordan River, she would find rest. She crossed the river the next day and spent the next fifty years living as a penitent and hermit in the desert, eating berries, herbs, or whatever she could find. One day, she met a hermit in the desert named Zosimus, now also acclaimed a saint. She told him her life story, then he gave her the Eucharist. When he returned a year later, he found her dead as she had predicted.

Saint Hugh of Grenoble

Hugh was born in Chateau-neuf, France, in 1052. Hugh's father was a soldier and leader in the local community, and he was a pious Christian who later became a Carthusian monk. His mother was known for her prayerfulness and generosity with those in need. Hugh was intelligent, but he was also bashful and tended to underrate his abilities. When he was twenty-five years old, he became an Augustinian Canon at the cathedral church. A short two years later, he was made bishop of Grenoble. For two years, he worked tirelessly and zealously to reform the spiritual state of his diocese, but he was so disheartened by the apparent (to him) lack of improvement that he left his position to live in a Benedictine monastery. However, the pope, Saint Gregory VII, disagreed that Hugh's work had been ineffective and ordered him to return to Grenoble. The results were amazing. His holiness drew people in crowds to hear his preaching, and his clergy were inspired and full of zeal for the faith. Hugh encouraged the holy monk Bruno to found the Grande Chartreuse, the motherhouse of the Carthusian order. Hugh loved to visit the monastery, so much so that Bruno, who became the abbot and is acclaimed a saint as well, sometimes had to remind Hugh to return to his flock rather than remain at the monastery. Hugh's personal care for the poor led many others, including those who were wealthy, to follow his example. He spent his final years suffering patiently from a painful illness. He died on this date in 1132, two months shy of eighty years old and having served as bishop for fifty-two years.

Holy Martyrs, show me how to be a witness for Christ today.
Saint Mary, help me to repent deeply.
Saint Hugh, help me to be joyful in obedience.

* * * * *

April 2

Saint Francis of Paola, Optional Memorial

Francis was born in 1416 in Paolo, Italy. His parents were childless for years until, after praying for the intercession of Saint Francis of Assisi, they were blessed with three children. Francis was the eldest. As a teenager, Francis went on a pilgrimage to Rome and Assisi, and when he returned, he began living as a hermit. Many people were struck by his holiness, and other men began to follow him and his way of life before he was even twenty years old. By the time he was in his forties, Francis had so many followers that he founded a religious order, the Hermits of Saint Francis of Assisi. (The order was approved in 1474 and renamed the Franciscan Order of Minim Friars in 1492.) This order focused on the virtues and penitential practices that Francis taught his friars: the importance of practicing charity, humility, and penance, which included sleeping on the ground and observing a perpetual Lent (i.e., never eating meat, eggs, or milk). When the king of France, Louis IX, was dying, he sent a personal request to Francis, begging him to come heal him. Francis ignored this request until Pope Sixtus IV ordered him to go to the king and prepare him for his impending death. When Francis entered the king's presence, the king fell on his knees, begging for healing. Francis gently explained that the lives of kings are in the hands of God and that prayers should be addressed to Him instead. After a series of meetings with Francis, the king's heart was gradually changed, and he died in resignation to God's will. Though Francis was not an educated man, his personal holiness and the events with the king later gave him the opportunity to defend the poor from the power of the rich and even to negotiate peace between feuding nations. He died on Good Friday, 1507, at ninety-one years of age.

Saint Appian of Caesarea

Appian was born around the year 287. He and his brother, Aedesius (also a future saint), were born to wealthy, pagan parents in Asia Minor (modern Turkey) during the time when the early Church was underground and when membership was illegal. He received a good education, and, as an adult, he became a Christian. He and his friend Eusebius, the bishop of Caesarea, made a pilgrimage together to Palestine. Afterward, Appian studied under Saint Pamphilus, a great scholar now considered a Father of the Church. When the Roman emperor Maximinus ordered that everyone participate in public pagan sacrifices at the time of his coronation in the year 305, Appian tried to convince the official in his city (Caesarea in modern Israel) to stop. His attempts to explain about the true God resulted in him being beaten, put in prison, and tortured. When he refused again to sacrifice to the Roman gods, he was executed by being tied up, weighed down with stones, and thrown into the sea.

Saint Pedro (Peter) Calungsod and Blessed Diego (James) Luis de San Vitoris

Pedro was born in 1654 in the city of Ginatilan of the Philippines and was educated by Jesuits. He learned to speak three languages; he could paint, sing, and draw; and he worked as a carpenter. While still a teenager, he decided to become a catechist, accompanying a Jesuit missionary to bring the faith to natives in the islands of Guam. While at Tomhom, Guam, evil rumors were circulated among the native people that Pedro and the priest he served, Blessed Diego Luis de San Vitores, were using poisoned water to kill children, rather than to baptize them. One day in 1672, after Father Diego and Pedro had baptized a mother and infant, an apostate Christian became angry and attacked them both. Though Pedro could have escaped, he chose to try to protect Father Diego. Pedro was hacked to death with Father Diego, who was named a martyr soon afterward; but it wasn't until 2012 that Pedro was declared a saint by Pope Benedict XVI.

Saint Francis Coll Guitart

Francis was born in 1812 in Spain into a family of ten children. His father died when he was only four years old. As a boy, he was a good student and even taught grammar and the catechism to other children. He joined the Dominican order at the age of eighteen and, when monastic orders were suppressed by the Spanish government, he went to France to continue his studies for the priesthood in secret. He served as parish priest in Arles, France, and then cared for those who had been displaced by war. Later, he helped another priest, Saint Anthony Claret, found a religious group called the Apostolic Fraternity. He directed Dominican tertiaries in the area, reopened a closed Dominican monastery, preached the Gospel through the Catalan region, cared for cholera victims during an epidemic, and founded the congregation of La Annunciata, a teaching branch of Dominican tertiaries. When the Dominicans were later allowed to return to the area, they simply reclaimed the houses that Francis had established. Francis was struck blind during a homily in 1869, but he continued to be active until his death by natural causes several years later in 1875.

Saint Francis of Paola, help me to bring the peace
of Christ to others through self-sacrifice.
Saint Appian, show me how to be courageous in choosing Christ over the world's gods.
Saint Pedro and Blessed Diego, help me return evil with good.
Saint Francis Coll Guitart, teach me how to spread the Good News wherever I go.

* * * * *

April 3

Saint Sixtus I

Sixtus (d. 125) was the seventh pope; he reigned about ten years. He was born into a family of shepherds living in Rome. His ordinances as pope show his concern for proper celebration of the liturgy and proper order in the Church. As often happened to popes during the days of the early Church, he was martyred during the persecution of Christians, specifically under the Roman emperor Hadrian.

Saint Richard of Wyche

Richard was born the second son of a well-to-do family in England around the year 1197; he was by nature a great lover of learning. His parents died and left the family's money in the care of a guardian. When Richard realized that the lazy guardian had allowed the family to go into debt, he humbly devoted himself to simple manual labor to recover the debt. After Richard had successfully saved the family, his elder brother recognized Richard's hard work and half-heartedly offered to give him the family title, deeds, and a comfortable marriage. But Richard refused and instead left for the University of Oxford. Though he was almost penniless, Richard studied hard and became widely respected. He refused the offer of yet another wife at this point and became chancellor of the university. Later, after he became a priest, his name was proposed as a candidate as bishop of Chichester. This led to a nasty political battle with King Henry III, who wanted this important position and its funds under his control. Eventually, Richard was ordained to the post, but the king was so angry that people initially refused even to give Richard a place to live out of fear of reprisals. Fortunately, one good priest ignored the king's threats and invited Richard to stay with him. Richard lived for years like a missionary bishop; he traveled on foot, visited ordinary people, and held synods to deal with abuses within the diocese. After Pope Innocent IV threatened the king with excommunication, Henry relaxed his threats, and Richard was better able to serve his people as their true bishop. He won their affection through his tenderness for those in need, but he was stern with clergymen guilty of avarice, heresy, or immorality. He died at a house for poor priests and pilgrims in the year 1253, while preaching for a crusade against the Saracens (Muslim Arabs) to protect the Holy Land for Christians.

Saint Luigi Scrosoppi

When Luigi (1804–1884) was about eleven years old, drought, famine, typhus, and smallpox struck his hometown of Udine, Italy; the misery that he saw, particularly among the orphans, made a strong impression on him. When he grew up, he became a priest, then a Franciscan tertiary, and then the director of an orphanage. In his work to help orphans, he himself went begging for funds when hard times struck. He supervised the construction of new buildings, encouraged and organized women to serve God as religious sisters through his Congregation of the Sisters of Providence, and opened homes and schools for abandoned girls and deaf-mute girls. As a member of the Oratory founded by Saint Philip Neri, he helped in their works of charity and learning until anti-clerical movements in Italy forced the works of the Oratory to close.

> Saint Sixtus, help me worship the Lord worthily.
> Saint Richard, help me to bear suffering with patience,
> particularly at the hands of those above me.
> Saint Luigi, beg the Lord to give me a heart to love and serve the needy.

* * * * *

April 4

Saint Isidore of Seville, Optional Memorial

Isidore was born around the year 560 into a family in Seville, Spain, that was not only noble but also saintly. He struggled as a student when young, perhaps because he was educated by his elder brother, Leander, who was a demanding and strict teacher. But eventually Isidore came to love learning and spent his life trying to learn more about God and His creation. Leander became bishop of Seville (and is acclaimed a saint). After his death, Isidore succeeded him, leading his flock for thirty-seven years. His knowledge of many subjects could be accurately called encyclopedic—after all, he wrote the first encyclopedia—and people were astonished by his detailed explanations of subjects ranging from Church doctrine to medicine to music. Serving his people as their bishop, Isidore reconciled many Arians to the Catholic faith, founded schools, and developed a rule of life for monks. When Isidore realized his end was near, he gave away his possessions to the poor, had himself taken to church to pray, and begged aloud for forgiveness from God and the people for his past sins. He died a few days later, in the year 636. Pope Benedict XIV named him a Doctor of the Church in 1722.

> Prayer purifies us, reading instructs us. Both are good when both are possible. Otherwise, prayer is better than reading.... Learning unsupported by grace may get into our ears; it never reaches the heart. It makes a great noise outside but serves no inner purpose. But when

God's grace touches our innermost minds to bring understanding, his word which has been received by the ear sinks deep into the heart.[1]

Saint Agathopedes (Agathopus) the Deacon

Agathopedes (d. 303) was a deacon of the Church in Thessalonica in Greece. When ordered to give up the Church's books (Scriptures and other holy writings) to the authorities to be destroyed, he refused. During the persecution of the Church under the Roman emperor Diocletian, Agathopedes was martyred by drowning.

Saint Francisco Marto

Francisco (1908–1919), his sister Jacinta, and their cousin Lucia cared for their parents' sheep in the fields in Aljustrel, Portugal. On May 13, 1917, they saw an apparition of a beautiful Lady; for several months following, the Lady appeared to them again on the thirteenth day of each month. Despite pressure, threats, and the burden of favorable but overwhelming attention from others, the children firmly repeated what they had seen and passed on the message of penance given them by the Virgin Mary. Francisco died young of influenza, but he lived as the Blessed Mother had told him to do, making sacrifices every day for sinners.

Saint Gaetano Catanoso

Gaetano was born into a wealthy but devout family of landowners in Italy in the year 1879. He was ordained a priest in 1902. As a priest, he fostered Christian practices, particularly through devotion to the Holy Face of Jesus, Eucharistic Adoration, and the Blessed Mother. He inspired young people who were in need of role models and served the elderly who were suffering from isolation. He created "flying squads" of priests who would come to a parish, give homilies, and hear confessions. He founded the Congregation of the Daughters of Saint Veronica, Missionaries of the Holy Face, an order focused on offering service in worship and catechesis, prayers of reparation, and acts of service for youth, the elderly, and priests. Near the end of his life, he became blind and suffered from ill health, though he patiently accepted these limitations. By the time he died in 1963, the constitutions for his order had received diocesan approval.

Saint Isidore, beg the Lord to open my heart to understand His wisdom.
Saint Agathopedes, help me to appreciate the treasure of God's Word in the Bible.
Saint Francisco, help me to obey the Blessed Virgin's
call to live a life of prayer and penance.
Saint Gaetano, stir up my devotion to Christ in the Blessed Sacrament.

* * * * *

[1] Quoted by Saint Isidore in *The Liturgy of the Hours*, vol. 2, from the Book of Maxims by Saint Isidore, bishop (New York: Catholic Book Publishing, 1976), 1760–61.

April 5

Saint Vincent Ferrer, Optional Memorial

Vincent was born around the year 1350 in Spain, and both his English father and Spanish mother were devout Catholics. After he became a Dominican priest, he began preaching the Gospel, which he did so powerfully that both conversions and miracles occurred, eventually making him one of the greatest preachers in the history of the Church. For example, his vocal disapproval of outrageous women's fashions in one region caused women to dress more appropriately (not a small miracle), and during a famine, he predicted that food would arrive—and it did. Vincent also brought unity to the Church during a time when three men claimed the title of pope, one of whom was Vincent's friend. Despite Vincent's attempts—both political and personal—that friend would not seek reconciliation with the Church, and he was ultimately deposed, ending a dangerous public scandal. Vincent played an important role in this peaceful solution. He died in 1419.

Saint Irene of Thessalonica

Irene was born in Macedonia (Greece) and had two sisters, Agape and Chionia, who also are remembered as martyr-saints. During the persecution of Christians under the Roman emperor Diocletian in the year 304, Irene was arrested and convicted for two crimes: for possessing a copy of the Scriptures and for refusing to eat food that had been offered to the gods. When she refused to deny her faith in Christ, she was forcibly sent to a house of prostitution and left naked and chained. However, when no one molested her, she was executed.

Saint Juliana of Mont Cornillon

Juliana (1193–1258) became an orphan when she was five years old, and she and her sister were placed in the care of Augustinian nuns at a convent in Belgium. Intelligent and well educated, she was also devout. She chose religious life and served the sick in the convent hospital. She was only sixteen years old when she had her first vision, which encouraged her to promote a special feast in honor of the Blessed Sacrament. In 1230, she became superior of her convent at Mont Cornillon, and in time, she encountered a few other holy souls who had the same intention that she did: to adore the Eucharist so that she might increase in faith and virtue and make reparation for offenses against Jesus' Real Presence in the Most Holy Sacrament. Her bishop and others eventually supported this effort, but she also faced bitter persecution, most notably from a dishonest male superior who was able to force her out of her convent (though she left obediently) on two occasions. Although Juliana died several years before the Solemnity of Corpus Christi was formally instituted by

Pope Urban IV in 1264, her prayers and writings in support of this day helped pave the way for it.

Saint Vincent, show me how to reconcile sinners to God.
Saint Irene, help me to love the Scriptures.
Saint Juliana, show me how to adore our Lord in the
Blessed Sacrament more fervently every day.

* * * * *

April 6

Saint Irenaeus of Sirmium

Irenaeus (d. 304) was a husband and father before he became bishop of Sirmium, a city in modern Serbia. He was brought before the governor during the persecution of Christians under the Roman emperor Diocletian and ordered to give up his faith. With his wife, children, and friends surrounding him, crying and begging him to save his life, he refused to renounce his faith even under torture. He was condemned to death by drowning, but he begged to be allowed to show that a Christian could face great pain for the sake of Christ. He was therefore beheaded, and his body was thrown into the river.

Blessed Notkar (Notker the Stammerer) Balbulus

Notker was born around the year 840 in Switzerland into a distinguished family. He became a Benedictine monk and priest and lived at the Abbey of Saint Gall. There Notker wrote poetry and music, specifically many liturgical sequences for the celebration of Mass. He was also a gifted writer, teacher, and Church historian. From his nickname, it's clear that he had a stutter, but his written and musical works inspired and educated Christians for centuries. He died on April 6, 912.

Saint William of Eskilsoe

William was born around the year 1125. As a young Augustinian Canon living in Paris, his fellow clergy persecuted and ridiculed him for his desire to live a more austere life. Later, he was sent to Denmark to establish better discipline in a religious house there, and his past experience of dealing with ridicule served him well. He eventually became abbot at the monastery at Eskilsoe, and he died surrounded by his devoted monks in 1203.

Saint Peter of Verona

Peter was born in 1202 in Verona, Italy. He entered the Dominican order at the hands of Saint Dominic himself and became a Dominican priest. Peter served as an inquisitor to protect the Church from heretics and was widely known for the miracles that occurred through his prayers. Heretics attacked him with a cleaver, and he died a martyr for the faith in 1252.

Saint Irenaeus, teach me how to love Christ above all others.
Blessed Notkar, show me how to appreciate God's beauty in music.
Saint William, help me to live a more austere life than is comfortable to me.
Saint Peter, help me lead others to true faith in Christ.

* * * * *

April 7

Saint John Baptist de la Salle, Memorial

John was born into a noble family in Rheims, France, in 1651 and had a very devout mother. At the age of twenty-seven, John became a priest and decided to serve God by educating poor boys. However, he found it hard to find other men who were willing to dedicate their entire lives to this vocation and who would also follow his teaching methods. He eventually gave up his position and income as a canon—in part because the other teachers resented it—and founded a religious order of brothers specifically devoted to education: the Brothers of the Christian Schools. His work revolutionized theories of elementary education, as, for example, he controversially taught the students in French and not in Latin. He eventually founded many schools and colleges throughout Europe and died in 1719.

Blessed Edward Oldcorne

Edward was born at York in 1561, was ordained a priest at Rome, and was received into the Jesuit order. He returned to England quietly to serve Catholics in secret due to the anti-Catholic laws, living in Worcestershire for sixteen years. He was particularly helpful to his flock through his preaching, despite the fact that he had throat cancer. That cancer was miraculously healed after he went on a pilgrimage to Saint Winifred's Shrine in England. But after the Gunpowder Plot (a failed assassination attempt against the king by a group of Catholics), there was a widespread crackdown against Catholics by the government. Edward was arrested for the "crime" of being a priest in England, falsely accused, and tortured and interrogated for five days in the rack. He was hanged, drawn, and quartered on this date in 1606.

Blessed Mary Assunta Pallotta

Born in 1878 in Italy, Mary Assunta attended school only long enough to learn how to read and write. She entered the Franciscan Missionaries of Mary, and she was sent to China to work at a leper colony, at her request. She arrived in the city of Tong-Eul-Keou in 1904, and she spent several months working as a cook in the orphanage. In 1905, when typhus, which was fatal at the time, swept through the house and it looked like one of the sisters was about to die, Sister Mary Assunta begged God to take her instead. Her prayer was granted, and she died. At her death, a mysterious perfume filled the house for three days. Her body was found to be incorrupt eight years later.

Saint John, help me bring Christ to others through humility.
Blessed Edward, teach me fortitude.
Blessed Mary Assunta, show me how to be willing to suffer for others.

* * * * *

April 8

Saint Agabus the Prophet

In Acts 11:27–30, a Christian prophet named Agabus predicted that a great famine would affect many people. His prophecy allowed the Christian community to prepare in advance for the needy. According to an ancient tradition, Agabus was one of the seventy-two disciples that Jesus sent out to preach during His lifetime, and he is most probably the same prophet who predicted that the Apostle Paul would be imprisoned if he went to Jerusalem.[2]

Martyrs of Antioch

During the persecution of the Church in the days of the Roman Empire, a group of men were martyred together in the city of Antioch, Syria. We only know their names: Timothy, Diogene, Macario, and Maximo.

Blessed Julian of Saint Augustine

Julian was born around the year 1550 in Segovia, Spain, served as an apprentice to a tailor in his youth, and briefly joined a Franciscan monastery. He was not thought to be suited to monastic life, so he was dismissed; he worked as a tailor for a time, and then tried again at another Franciscan monastery. Once again, he was dismissed—because they thought he was mentally unstable—so he began to live as a hermit. But life as a hermit helped Julian grow in holiness, and later the monks at the second monastery allowed him to join them. Julian became an effective preacher, lived an austere life among his brothers, and died on this date in 1606.

Saint Julie Billiart

Julie was born in 1751 into a family of well-to-do peasant farmers in France. When a shot was fired at her father, the shock disturbed her so profoundly

---

[2] Acts 21:10–11.

that she became paralyzed. This suffering, however, drew her closer to God and strengthened her faith. When the Reign of Terror enveloped France and the Church was bitterly persecuted, she opposed the constitutional (apostate) priest who was sent to her village, and she led others in her village to reject him as well. She helped fugitive priests escape the authorities, so eventually the police began hunting her from place to place too. After the French Revolution finally ended, she became involved in efforts to restore the practice of the faith in France, specifically by providing spiritual encouragement and education to children and to the poor. In 1804, her priest, Father Joseph Varin, asked her to pray and sacrifice for an unspecified special intention, which she obediently did. After she had prayed for this intention for a time, Father Varin then called on her to walk in honor of the Sacred Heart of Jesus—and she discovered that she was miraculously and completely healed of her paralysis. The religious teaching order she founded, the Institute of Notre Dame de Namur, continued to grow rapidly before and after her death, despite one painful period in which a priest with poor judgment managed to create a situation that alienated her from her bishop. In 1816, she died at the age of sixty-five.

> *Saint Agabus, beg the Holy Spirit to give me the*
> *gifts that will help me grow in holiness.*
> *Holy Martyrs, show me how to live and die for Christ.*
> *Blessed Julian, help me to accept setbacks as steps on the path of holiness.*
> *Saint Julie, help me to accept my powerlessness and trust in God's power.*

* * * * *

April 9

Saint Aedesius of Caesarea

Aedesius, like his brother Saint Appian (a martyr), was born in the third century into a wealthy, pagan family in a city in modern Israel, but he became a Christian during the days of the early Church. When Aedesius publicly spoke out against a judge who had forced nuns to live in brothels to destroy their faith, he was arrested, tortured, and then martyred by drowning. It was the year 306.

Saint Waldetrudis (Waudru or Waltrude)

Waudru's parents, sister, husband, and four children are all saints as well! Sometime after the birth of their last child in the seventh century, Waudru's noble husband withdrew into a monastery. Waudru herself left the world behind a few years later, living in simplicity and poverty in a small house in Mons, Belgium, renowned for her works of mercy and the miracles of healing resulting from her prayers. She died in 688.

Saint Casilda of Toledo

Casilda was born in the tenth century. Since her father was an emir in Toledo, Spain, she was raised as a Muslim. She secretly brought food to Christians in prison out of pity. After being healed by God of an incurable illness at the shrine of San Vincenzo, she converted to the faith and lived the remainder of her life as a hermit, dying at about one hundred years of age in the year 1050.

Blessed Thomas of Tolentino

A group of Franciscan missionaries, led by Thomas of Tolentino, traveled together in the year 1322, leaving from Italy to evangelize Ceylon (modern Sri Lanka) and China. However, while they were on their way, they were captured by Muslims and beheaded for the faith in Thama, Hindustan (India).

> *Saint Aedesius, help me to speak for those who cannot speak for themselves.*
> *Saint Waldetrudis, help me bring a hunger for holiness to my family.*
> *Saint Casilda, pray for me to spend my days in thanksgiving*
> *to the Lord for all that He has done for me.*
> *Blessed Thomas, show me how to bring the good news to those I encounter today.*

* * * * *

April 10

Saint Terence and Companions of Africa

Terence and thirty-nine companions were martyred in the third century during the persecution of Christians under the Roman emperor Decius in the city of Carthage (modern Tunisia) for refusing to worship pagan gods. During interrogation, Terence repeated words from the Gospels. His companions—Africanus, Maximus, Pompeii, Alexander, and Theodorus—were tortured and beheaded one by one in front of him, until he too was finally executed.

Saint Fulbert of Chartres

Despite his humble birth around the year 960 in Italy, Fulbert rose to high positions within the Church, first serving as assistant to Pope Sylvester II, Fulbert's former teacher, then as chancellor at the Chartres Cathedral, and finally as bishop of Chartres, France. He called himself "the very tiny bishop of a very great Church".[3] He rebuilt his cathedral after a fire, but the current famous cathedral is not the one built under his direction. He died in the year 1029.

Saint Magdalen of Canossa

Magdalen was born in 1774 in Verona, Italy, to a prominent and noble family. Her father died when she was six years old, and her mother remarried a few

---

[3] James Bentley, *A Calendar of Saints: The Lives of the Principal Saints of the Christian Year* (London: Time Warner Books, 2005), 70.

years later. She and her siblings were taken to live with other relatives. Though the children were treated kindly by their family members, they suffered from a harsh governess. As a young woman, Magdalen became ill (perhaps as a result of the governess' mistreatment), and she decided after she had recovered that she would become a nun. She lived in a Carmelite monastery for a short time as a postulant, but she soon returned home. During the chaos resulting from the Napoleonic Wars, her family left the city of Verona. At about this time, she had a dream that affected her greatly. In the dream, the Virgin Mary appeared to her, along with six women religious dressed in brown; Mary led them to three groups of people: girls and women in a church, people in a hospital, and children dressed in rags. The Blessed Virgin told Magdalen and the other women to care for all three groups of people, but particularly the third group. Later, Magdalen's family was visited by the emperor Napoleon himself. She used that opportunity to ask for—and was granted—permission to have an empty convent to care for poor people. Gradually, Magdalen made her dream a reality, and her sisters' work of teaching the faith, caring for the sick, and helping needy children spread and became a religious congregation called the Canossian Daughters of Charity. Despite her active vocation, Magdalen was also a woman of deep prayer and contemplation; on several occasions she was seen caught up in ecstasy during prayer and once was lifted off the ground. At the end of her life, she was bent almost double and could only sleep sitting up. Though those around her didn't recognize that her end was near, she did. In 1835, she asked for the last sacraments and died soon afterward.

Holy Martyrs, pray that the words of Christ will be always on my lips and in my heart.
Saint Fulbert, teach me humility and love for the Church.
Saint Magdalen, help me to see Christ in the poor and needy around me.

* * * * *

April 11

Saint Stanislaus of Cracow, Memorial

Stanislaus' noble parents prayed for years to have a child. When Stanislaus was born in 1030, they encouraged his natural piety and his vocation to the priesthood. His preaching and example greatly improved the morals of his flock, and eventually he was named bishop of Cracow. The king of Poland at the time, Boleslaus II, was a cruel and lustful ruler, and Stanislaus stood up to him on several occasions, even though other leaders were afraid to do so. When the king kidnapped a beautiful, married woman, Stanislaus corrected him publicly and excommunicated him. In 1079, the angry king had Stanislaus killed by his guards; some say they failed three times and Boleslaus himself did the evil deed. Stanislaus' body was cut into pieces and scattered, but the relics were saved and later privately buried. Indignation over Boleslaus' act didn't end his reign immediately, but it did hasten the end.

Saint Gemma Galgani

Gemma was born in 1878 in Lucca, Italy. Her mother died when she was seven years old, and her father died when she was eighteen years old. Gemma spent the remainder of her short life in Lucca, caring for her seven brothers and sisters. She was miraculously cured of spinal tuberculosis and attributed her cure to prayers to Saint Gabriel of Our Lady of Sorrows. Religious orders didn't believe that she had been cured or her claims of a miracle and refused to admit her, so she became a tertiary instead. Living at home, she received the stigmata on her hands and feet every Thursday evening through Friday afternoon starting in June 1899 through 1901. She saw her guardian angel daily, but she was also tempted by the devil, who tried to convince her to spit on a cross and break a rosary. After her death, her canonization was delayed by those who disbelieved her or were embarrassed by her visions and stigmata.

> *Saint Stanislaus, help me to correct sinners with love and patience.*
> *Saint Gemma, help me never to be ashamed of my love for Christ.*

* * * * *

April 12

Saint Julius I

Julius was the thirty-fifth pope (d. 352); he reigned fifteen years. He was a strong defender of the faith against the Arian heresy, he established the date of the Solemnity of the Nativity as December 25, and when he ordered that all official papal acts be preserved, he founded what is now the Vatican Apostolic Archive.

Saint Alferius of La Cava

While serving as ambassador to the French court for the duke of Salerno, Italy, Alferius (d. 1050) became seriously ill and vowed to enter religious life if he recovered. When he did recover, he kept his vow and entered the Abbey of Cluny. His duke later asked him to return and reform the monasteries in his territory, but Alferius declined, thinking that it was beyond his abilities. Instead, he settled in a remote but lovely spot outside Salerno. Men sought him out and became his disciples, forming the well-known abbey of the Holy Trinity of La Cava. He died alone in his cell at the age of 120 on Holy Thursday, after celebrating Mass with his monks and washing the feet of his brothers.

Saint Teresa of the Andes

Juanita (Teresa) was born in 1900 into a devout and well-to-do family and with five siblings in Santiago, Chile. When she was six years old, she felt Jesus lay claim to her heart. Wanting to prepare herself to receive Holy Communion worthily for the first time at the age of ten, she made serious efforts to defeat the human pride and stubbornness that she saw in herself. From a young age, she knew that God wanted her to become a Carmelite nun, but she was also granted the knowledge that she would die young. Despite her spiritual depth, to others she seemed a cheerful, happy, and sympathetic teenager, and she spoke about God to her friends and helped those in need. She privately consecrated herself to God when she was only fourteen. At the age of eighteen, she entered the Discalced Carmelite nuns at Los Andes and took the name Teresa of Jesus. She inspired those around her with her deep, Christlike faith, but she was still only a novice when she died of typhus in 1920.

> *Saint Julius, help me to love Christ and His Church.*
> *Saint Alferius, teach me to love solitude.*
> *Saint Teresa, help my heart hear our Lord.*

* * * * *

April 13

Saint Martin I, Optional Memorial

Martin (d. 656) was from the Italian town of Todi and was papal nuncio to Constantinople when he became pope. Because of his opposition to heresy, he was imprisoned, unlawfully tried, and banished by the Roman emperor Constans II. He died of sickness as a result of his banishment and cruel treatment.

Saint Hermenegild of Spain

Hermenegild (d. 586), a prince of Spain, was converted from the Arianism of his father, the king, through the prayers and example of his fervent Catholic wife, Indegundis, and through the encouragement of Saint Leander, archbishop of Seville. When his father demanded that Hermenegild give up his position because he had become Catholic, he refused and led a revolt. His wife and son were held hostage, and his friends betrayed him; but he was finally reconciled with his father. However, the king's second wife resented him and reignited family resentments until Hermenegild was imprisoned on the charge of heresy. While in prison, Hermenegild began to pray more deeply and added extra mortifications, such as wearing sackcloth. His father offered him his freedom if he would simply receive Communion from an Arian bishop, but Hermenegild refused. His father angrily had him executed immediately. Pope Saint Gregory the Great attributed the conversion of Hermenegild's brother Reccared and all of Visigothic Spain back to the true faith as a result of his martyrdom.

Saint Caradoc of Wales

Caradoc (d. 1124) was a musician and keeper of greyhounds for the prince of Wales in England. When the dogs escaped (through no fault of his own), the prince was furious with him and threatened him with violence. Caradoc said that he preferred to serve a king who rewarded faithful service, so he left, became a monk, and later became a hermit. This wasn't an easy life: he was once carried off by pirates, and another time his livestock were stolen. But he lived in faith and peace, with a great love for animals.

> *Saint Martin, help me to love Christ and His Church.*
> *Saint Hermenegild, show me how to seek out and learn from holy people.*
> *Saint Caradoc, help me to see God in all His creatures.*

* * * * *

April 14

Saints Tiburtius, Valerian, and Maximus of Rome

In third-century Rome, during the time when Christianity was officially illegal, Valerian married a lovely young woman named Cecilia. Cecilia, now known to us as a saint and martyr, explained her faith in Christ to her new husband and brought both Valerian and his brother Tiburtius to the Catholic faith. The two brothers began performing acts of charity, particularly in burying the dead, which led to them being publicly known as Christians. They were arrested and executed for that crime, along with a prefect named Maximus.

Saint Benezet (Benedict) of Hermillon

Benezet (d. 1184) was a shepherd in France. During a solar eclipse, he heard a voice tell him three times to build a bridge across a rapid river near Avignon. At the time, the difficulty of building a bridge and its value to the community made bridge-building a work of mercy. Benezet obeyed the heavenly voice, although he was young, had no money, and was disbelieved when he told the bishop his amazing story. Through miracles and faith, Benezet led the building of a stone bridge for seven years. The main challenges with the bridge construction had been resolved when he died.

Saint Peter (Telmo) Gonzalez

Peter was born in Astorga, Spain, in 1190 and led a comfortable life as a deacon. When he fell from a horse, bystanders mocked him, and the humiliation caused him to recognize the emptiness of his worldly life. He became a Dominican friar, and he served as a peacemaker and preacher. He was particularly known for preaching to sailors, who invoke him as a patron. He died in 1246.

Saint Lidwina of Schiedam

Lidwina was born in Holland in 1380. Her father was from the nobility, but her family was poor. When she was fifteen years old, she fell while ice skating and broke a rib. For the rest of her life, she was in pain from various medical problems that treatment seemed unable to cure, which led to rumors about a possible evil cause for her pains. But God rewarded her with visions, miracles, and many gifts in prayer. At the end of her life, she received a vision of her impending death, and pilgrimages to her grave started immediately after her death in 1433. She was declared a saint by Pope Leo XIII in 1890. A relatively recent scientific study of her medical symptoms has suggested that she may have been the first person recorded to suffer from multiple sclerosis.

> *Holy Martyrs, help me to practice corporal works of mercy.*
> *Saint Benezet, help me hear and answer God's call.*
> *Saint Peter, show me how to be purified through my humiliations.*
> *Saint Lidwina, teach me patience in suffering.*

* * * * *

April 15

Saints Theodore and Pausilopo of Thrace

During the persecution of the Church under the Roman emperor Hadrian, Theodore and Pausilopo were martyred for their faith in Christ. This happened in Thrace (probably in modern Greece) in the early second century.

Saint Paternus of Wales

Paternus was born to pious parents in France in 482. His father left, with his wife's consent, to become a monk in Ireland, and Paternus grew up to be a godly man who cherished his father's memory. He traveled to Wales to become a hermit himself and met the great Welsh saints. He was known to be so obedient that when his abbot, Saint Samson, commanded him to come to him while he was getting dressed, Paternus obeyed even before putting on his second boot. Paternus later founded a monastery at Llanabarn Fawr, and 120 monks eventually joined him there. He opposed the pagan kings who lived around him, and it's said that on one occasion he proved to an evil king that he was innocent of theft by plunging his hand in boiling water and taking it out unharmed. He died in 565.

Blessed Cesar de Bus

Cesar was born in 1544 in Cavillon, France, into a big family of thirteen children. He served as a soldier and fought the anti-Catholic Huguenots for a time, then lived a wild life in Paris writing poetry and painting. He accepted a position as a canon in his hometown purely for the steady income. One evening, while walking to a party, he passed an image of the Blessed Virgin Mary and was overwhelmed with the memory of a deceased friend who had prayed for his salvation. In that moment, he was converted. He was ordained a priest, particularly tried to imitate the virtues of Saint Charles Borromeo, and taught people about the faith. He founded two religious orders: the Fathers of Christian Doctrine and the Ursulines of Provence. He died on Easter Sunday on this date in 1607.

> *Saints Theodore and Pausilopo, show me how to live and die for Christ.*
> *Saint Paternus, teach me your humble obedience and trust in God.*
> *Blessed Cesar, help me take my salvation seriously.*

* * * * *

April 16

Martyrs of Saragossa

Seventeen men died in Saragossa, Spain, during the persecution of Christians under the Roman emperor Diocletian in the year 304. The names of these holy men were Apodemus, Caecilianus, Evodius, Felix, Fronto, Julia, Lupercus, Martialus, Primitivus, Publius, Quintilianus, Saturnius (four men with this same name), Successus, and Urbanus.

Saint Benedict Labre

Benedict (1748–1783) was the oldest of fifteen children in a middle-class French family and was known for his piety, cheerfulness, and spirit of mortification from a young age. He was well educated by his uncle, who was the parish priest, but interest in worldly studies disappeared for him as his desire for intimacy with Christ grew. He tried to join the Trappists, Carthusians, and Cistercians, but he was refused by them all. In a moment of divine inspiration, he recognized his vocation: to live as a pilgrim. For the rest of his life, he traveled all over Europe, living in extreme poverty as he went to Catholic holy sites and prayed and adored our Lord in the Eucharist. Those who knew him spoke of amazing miracles they had seen; for example, people reported seeing Benedict deaf to the world while caught up in ecstasies, floating in the air while in prayer, and in two places at the same time. Homeless people, for he was homeless too, were cured by him, and his prayers miraculously multiplied bread to feed the hungry. In Rome, people of all stations of life sought him out for his advice. He died in a hospice, and, within three months, 136 miraculous cures had been attributed to his intercession.

Saint Bernadette Soubirous

Bernadette was born in 1844 to a poor family in Lourdes, France, the oldest of six children. Because of her bad health and her family's poverty, she attended school only infrequently. Friends noticed, however, that she was patient and charitable despite her difficult life. While gathering wood with young companions one day near a grotto in Massabielle, she saw a "beautiful Lady". During this and other visions, she prayed with the "Lady" and reported the content of her visions. For some time, she was both persecuted by those who disbelieved her and pestered by the endless curiosity of those who did believe her. After the apparitions of the Lady of Lourdes had ended, Bernadette's family was lifted out of poverty, and Bernadette herself entered the Sisters of Notre Dame of Nevers. She was allowed to take her first vows as a sister earlier than expected, but only because it was thought she was dying. She recovered, however, by a seeming miracle, and she spent the remainder of her short life suffering from many physical maladies, patiently enduring questioners about the apparitions, and living a simple and saintly life as a sister. She died in 1879.

> *Holy Martyrs, show me how to live and die for Christ.*
> *Saint Benedict, help me to spend every moment in God's presence.*
> *Saint Bernadette, show me how to live a prayerful, penitential life.*

* * * * *

April 17

Saint Simeon Bar Sabas and Companions

Simeon was born in Persia in the third century, and his father was a fuller. He became the bishop of Seleucia-Ctesiphon, making him the head of the Church in Persia (in modern Iran) at the time. In the year 345, King Shapur II ordered Christians to convert to Zoroastrianism, a dualistic religion with components from multiple beliefs, including Catholicism. Those who refused were executed. Simeon, along with several thousand bishops, priests, and laymen, died as martyrs during this time. Simeon himself died on Good Friday.

Saint Robert of Molesme

Robert was born in 1027 into the French nobility and became a Benedictine monk when he was seventeen years old. He eventually became abbot, but he wanted a more strict form of life than existed at his monastery. So he and some other hermits worked together to found a monastery at Molesme. This monastery grew in size and in financial support, but some of the brothers began to resent the strict demands of their way of life. Robert left them twice to live on his own, but both times the pope ordered him to return and govern them. In 1098, Robert, along with Saint Stephen Harding, Saint Alberic of Citeaux, and eighteen other monks, left Molesme to found a monastery of Citeaux near Dijon, France. This house became the founding house of the Cistercian order. The new community lived a strict life of poverty and frequent spiritual retreats, otherwise following the Benedictine Rule, and Robert was the first abbot. He later returned to Molesme to bring about the same reforms there and serve as abbot. He died in 1111.

> *Saint Simeon, show me how to suffer like Christ.*
> *Saint Robert, help me simplify and mortify my life.*

* * * * *

April 18

Saint Galdinus of Milan

Galdinus (1096–1176) was from a well-known family of Milan, Italy, and he rose in the ranks of the Church. When the people of Milan supported a papal claimant against the true pope, the pope was angry with Milan, and Galdinus (then a deacon) and his bishop, as representatives of the Church, had to leave the city. When he was able to return, Galdinus helped restore the war-torn Milan, later becoming its archbishop. He was known for his personal learning and eloquence, as well as his work in restoring discipline among his clergy and his opposition to the Cathari heresy. At the end of his life, though in poor health, he delivered a strong homily during Mass against false doctrine and died before the Mass ended.

Blessed Joseph Moreau

Joseph was born in 1763 in Saint Laurent de la Plaine, France. He served as a priest in Angers, France, until the time of the French Revolution. During the anti-Catholic violence of this revolution, he was arrested and executed by the guillotine on this date, Good Friday, of 1794 in Angers.

> *Saint Galdinus, show me how to accept apparent setbacks with patience.*
> *Blessed Joseph, show me how to live and die for Christ.*

* * * * *

April 19

Saint Alphege of Canterbury

Alphege (d. 1012) entered a monastery as a young man, became a hermit, and later became the abbot of Bath, England. He eventually became bishop of Winchester, and he governed his flock wisely for twenty-two years. He was widely known for his long fasts; people said he was so thin that they could see through his hands during his prayers at Mass. He was also known for his care for the poor—it was said that there were no beggars in his diocese while he was bishop. Alphege later became archbishop of Canterbury; when the Danes invaded the city, Alphege came in person to appeal to them to stop their destruction. The Danes imprisoned him, and he was brutally killed. He was thus a martyr both for justice and for his people.

Saint Leo IX

Bruno was born in Alsace, Germany, in 1002 and was the son of a count and the cousin of an emperor. He became a canon, deacon, and bishop of Toul, France, by the time he was twenty-four years old. In 1049, he was elected pope and took the name of Leo. During his pontificate, he worked to reform his clergy along the ideals of the great reforming abbot of Cluny, Saint Odo, and opposed the practice of simony. He was known as the "pilgrim pope" due to his many travels, as well as the "warrior pope" since he led his own army in defense of new territories that he had acquired—a decision that earned him the criticism of the monk-saint Peter Damian. The Normans defeated him in battle and imprisoned him. During his imprisonment, tensions between the Eastern and Latin churches increased, and Leo could do little about it. When it was clear he was close to death, the Normans allowed him to return to Rome. Leo could no longer retain food and had to be carried into Rome on a litter. He had himself taken to Saint Peter's Basilica, and he lay next to his own coffin, daily speaking to the crowds and praying with and for the Church. He died on April 19, 1054, just after Mass, having reigned for only five years.

> *Saint Alphege, teach me how to make sacrifices for Christ.*
> *Saint Leo, help me to reform myself into the image of Christ.*

* * * * *

April 20

Saint Anicetus

Anicetus (d. ca. 168) was the eleventh pope; he reigned for eleven years. He was pope during a difficult period in the early Church. He worked to defend the faith against those who taught that Jesus' physical life was an illusion (Manichaeism) and against those who rejected the Jewish background of the faith (Marcionism) completely. He also tried to settle disagreements among different groups of Christians over the correct date to celebrate Easter. Some traditions say he died as a martyr.

Saint Agnes of Montepulciano

Agnes was born around the year 1268 and convinced her noble parents to place her in a convent at Montepulciano, Italy, when she was only nine years old. She was devout and wise beyond her years, and at the age of fourteen she was made housekeeper. When the convent decided to found a daughter house in Procena, she became the abbess of the new convent, although it required a special dispensation from the pope since she was only fifteen years old. For fifteen years more, she slept on the ground, used a stone for a pillow, and lived only on bread and water. Her personal holiness attracted many women to religious life. She received two well-known visions: one in which angels brought her Holy Communion and another in which she was given the blessing of holding the Infant Jesus in her arms. Montepulciano's residents wanted this holy woman to live in their town again, and so they built a convent for her. She returned to the city to serve as prioress there for the rest of her life, dying at the age of forty-nine in the year 1317.

Blessed Anastasius (Anastazy) Pankiewicz

Anastasius (1882–1942) joined the Franciscans at the age of eighteen and was ordained a priest six years later. He led the building of a seminary in Lotz, Poland, and founded an order of nuns, the Antonian Sisters of Christ the King. During the Nazi persecutions of the Church, he was arrested because he was a Catholic priest and sentenced to the Dachau concentration camp. He died on the way to the camp. His body was burned, and his ashes were scattered.

> *Saint Anicetus, help me to be a true peacemaker.*
> *Saint Agnes, help me make sacrifices to grow in holiness.*
> *Blessed Anastasius, show me how to forgive my persecutors.*

* * * * *

April 21

Saint Anselm of Canterbury, Optional Memorial

Anselm was born into a noble family in Italy around the year 1033. Although his mother was devout, his father wasn't, refusing to let the young Anselm consider entering religious life. Anselm lived a worldly, dissipated life at school—focused on sports and current events—until his mother died. At the age of twenty-three, in part because of his difficult relationship with his father, he decided to travel around France. After three years, he reached the Benedictine abbey of Bec in France, where the celebrated scholar-turned-monk Lanfranc lived. At the time, Anselm didn't know whether God was calling him to be a hermit, a monk, or a layman. At Bec, Anselm heard God's call to be a monk, and there he settled down. After a short three years, he became the prior at Bec. In 1078, the monks chose him to be their abbot, though they found it difficult to convince the humble Anselm to accept the position. In 1093, he traveled to England to comfort King William Rufus, who believed (wrongly, it turned out) that he was dying. While there, the bishops of England begged Anselm into accepting the position of archbishop of Canterbury. For the next fifteen years, Anselm served as archbishop and fought—charitably but firmly—with King William Rufus to protect the people and property of the Church from being forced to serve the political needs of the English government. When Anselm was forced into exile by the king, he lived in Italy under the protection of the pope and participated in Church councils. He was able to return to England when Rufus died. Rufus' successor, King Henry I, demanded the right to appoint Church officials so that he could control both the Church leadership and revenue; he had to be threatened with excommunication before Henry and Anselm could reach a compromise. Gradually, Anselm and the king established a relationship of mutual respect. Throughout all his service of others as abbot and archbishop, Anselm had become widely known for his theological writings, his defense of the Church and the pope, his personal humility, and his profound and tender spirituality. Anselm died when he was an old man, living among his monks in Canterbury, in the year 1109. He's widely considered the greatest theologian since Saint Augustine of Hippo and was the founder of the philosophical system known as Scholasticism. He was named a Doctor of the Church in 1720.

> Come now, insignificant mortal. Leave behind your concerns for a little while, and retreat for a short time from your restless thoughts. Cast off your burdens and cares; set aside your labor and toil. Just for a little while make room for God and rest a while in him. "Enter into the chamber" (Matthew 6:6) of your mind, shut out everything but God and whatever helps you to seek him, and seek him "behind closed doors" (Matthew 6:6). Speak now, my whole heart: say to God, "I seek your face; your face, Lord, do I seek" (Psalm 27:8).[4]

Saint Apollonius of Rome

Apollonius lived during the second century and was a pagan and a Roman senator. After he began studying both pagan philosophy and the Scriptures, he made the decision to become a Christian. Unfortunately, being a Christian was still illegal, and a slave betrayed him to the authorities. Apollonius was told to abandon his faith or be executed, but instead he gave an eloquent speech defending his Christian beliefs in the senate itself. The authorities condemned him anyway. He was tortured by having his legs crushed, and he was then beheaded. It was the year 185.

> Saint Anselm, teach me how to seek the Lord in silence.
> Saint Apollonius, help me to explain my faith to others.

* * * * *

April 22

Saint Soter

Soter (d. 174) was the twelfth pope and succeeded Pope Anicetus; he reigned for eleven years. The Christian faithful loved him for his personal kindness, charity for the needy, and care for the persecuted faithful. He also condemned the early heresy of Montanism, whose proponents claimed that the Church was too lax. Some traditions say that he died a martyr.

Saints Epipodius and Alexander of Lyons

These two unmarried men of Lyons, France, were arrested by the authorities of the Roman Empire for being Christians. The judge mocked both them and

---

[4] Anselm of Canterbury, *Proslogion with the Replies of Gaunilo and Anselm*, chap. 1, trans. Thomas Williams (Indianapolis: Hackett Publishing, 2001), 4.

Christ, and when Epipodius didn't reply, he was killed by the sword immediately. Alexander was flogged and crucified two days later. Other details and the exact date are unknown.

Saint Caius

During Pope Caius' (d. 296) reign of twelve years, the Church experienced the beginnings of the persecution of Christians under the Roman emperor Diocletian. But although Caius, the Church's twenty-eighth pope, was imprisoned for the faith, he was probably not martyred since early Church documents call him a "Confessor". One of his other acts as pope was to confirm the orders of the hierarchy with the early Church.

Saint Agapetus I

Agapetus (d. 536) was the fifty-seventh pope; he reigned almost one year. He was the archdeacon of the priests of Rome when he was elected pope at an advanced age and was widely known for his personal holiness. Agapetus spent his brief reign caught up in political battles between the Roman emperor Justinian and Theodoric, king of the Goths. He wasn't successful in his attempts to prevent Italy from being invaded, but he was successful in replacing an unorthodox patriarch of Constantinople with a faithful one; he surprised his powerful enemies with his constancy under great pressure.

Saint Theodore of Sykeon

Theodore (d. 613) was born in the sixth century in the village of Sykeon, now in modern Turkey. His mother ran an inn that was situated on a public highway. Some traditions say that his mother was a prostitute and never married; others say she later became devout. However, Theodore himself was a devout Christian and charitable to the poor from the time he was a boy, even sometimes shutting himself in his mother's cellar or an unused chapel in order to pray in solitude. While on a pilgrimage from his native Sykeon (now in modern Turkey) to Jerusalem, he began wearing the habit of a monk. He also lived austerely, eating only vegetables and wearing an iron belt as a penance. His prayers resulted in miracles, and his words, people noticed, were prophetic. He later founded several monasteries and ruled them as their abbot, but even then he lived in solitude, apart from his monks. He was eventually ordained bishop of Anastasiopolis, but he felt himself unworthy of the position and was able to resign after serving for ten years. He was called out of retirement once to bless the emperor; on the same trip, he miraculously cured the emperor's son of leprosy. Theodore also had a great devotion to the intercession of the martyr Saint George (the saint celebrated tomorrow). He died on this date.

> Saints Soter, Caius, and Agapetus, help me to love Christ and His Church.
> Saints Epipodius and Alexander, show me how to live and die for Christ.
> Saint Theodore, give me your love of prayer and solitude.

* * * * *

April 23

Saint George, Optional Memorial

George was a martyr for the faith, probably during a persecution of Christians in the year 303 in Diaspolis (Palestine). For centuries, Christians have told the story of the Christian knight George killing a dragon to save a city and a princess from destruction. George is one of the Fourteen Holy Helpers, great saints who were called upon particularly for help during the bubonic plague in fourteenth-century Europe.

Saint Adalbert (Vojtech) of Prague, Optional Memorial

Vojtech was born into a noble family in Bohemia (the modern Czech Republic) around the year 957. He took the name of Adalbert from the archbishop who healed, taught, and converted him to the faith. He was even made the bishop of Prague. But his attempts to evangelize his own people seemed unsuccessful to him and made him very unpopular, so he withdrew to a monastery to live as a Benedictine monk. The pope disagreed and sent him back to evangelize and serve his people. In time, Adalbert brought the Catholic faith to many people living in Pomerania, Poland, Hungary, Prussia, and Russia. However, paganism was still very strong in the area, and Adalbert and his companions were betrayed by a pagan priest. They died as martyrs in 997.

Blessed Maria Gabriella Sagheddu

Maria's father was a shepherd in Dorgali, Sardinia (Italy), and she was born the fifth of eight children in 1914. As a child, she wasn't a very promising future saint: her family found her to be obstinate, critical, rebellious, and bad-tempered. But she was also dutiful, intelligent, and pure of heart. When Maria was eighteen years old, her younger sister died. In her grief, she started to think about the importance of eternal things rather than worldly life, and she gradually became more gentle, sweet-tempered, and prayerful in her behavior. She joined a Catholic youth movement and made the decision to become a nun in a Trappist monastery when she was twenty-one years old. As a postulant, Maria still struggled with impatience, but she also felt at home living in the monastery. When one of the leaders of her community asked the nuns to pray and make personal sacrifices for the cause of Christian unity, Maria felt God calling her to make this her personal vocation. With her superior's permission, she made a vow to offer her life for the sake of unity between all Christians. Though she had been a healthy young woman, she contracted tuberculosis soon afterward and spent the final fifteen months of her life praying and suffering for unity among Christians. After her death in 1939, it was found that chapters 12 through 20 of the Gospel of John, particularly chapter 17,[5] in her Bible had been yellowed by her repeated reading of this passage.

---

[5] In chapter 17 of the Gospel of John, Jesus prays for the unity of the Church. See the explanation of Blessed Maria's prayer in Pope John Paul II's encyclical *Ut Unum Sint*, no. 27.

Saint George, by your prayers, protect me from the evils of this world.
Saint Adalbert, help me to love God's peace, not worldly popularity.
Blessed Maria Gabriella, remind me to pray daily for unity among Christians.

* * * * *

April 24

Saint Wilfrid of York

Wilfrid was born in 634 and was the son of a chief in Northumbria, England. His mother died when he was young, and he left his father's home when he was thirteen years old because of an unkind stepmother. He then lived in the court of the king of Northumbria and was educated in a monastery school. When he realized that some Celtic religious practices were somewhat less than perfect, he decided to find out how to devote his life to God better. He traveled and found good, saintly teachers: Saint Honorius of Canterbury and Saint Annemund of Lyons, who were both bishops, and the archdeacon Boniface, who was the pope's secretary. When Wilfrid returned to England, he was made abbot of Ripon and a priest, and the king asked him to teach the English clergy how to follow Roman practices. By winning over the clergy to the Roman practice, he gradually ended the most obvious problem—the Roman versus the Celtic calculation of Easter, which had resulted in terrible disunity and the king and queen of Northumbria each celebrating Easter at different times. After Wilfrid was ordained bishop of York, he became a beloved and respected bishop to his people and traveled throughout his large diocese on foot. When Princess (and future saint) Etheldreda refused to consummate her marriage to Prince Egfrith for ten years, telling Wilfrid that she wanted to be a nun, he encouraged her. To get even, Prince Egfrith stirred up complaints against Wilfrid to his archbishop, Theodore. Archbishop Theodore unfortunately believed the complaints, divided the diocese, and consecrated three bishops to replace Wilfrid. Wilfrid then traveled to Rome to plead his case to the pope, and he returned home with papal decrees in his favor. Prince Egfrith simply declared that the documents were forgeries and put Wilfrid in prison for nine months. Ultimately, Wilfrid was released, but he was forced to live among the pagan South Saxons. There he brought many people to the Christian faith, freed 250 slaves, and established a monastery. Archbishop Theodore, however, regretted that he had acted against an innocent man. When Egfrith died and Prince Aldfrith succeeded him, Theodore allowed Wilfrid to return to his diocese and to the monastery of Ripon. But Wilfrid was later banished due to another disagreement, this time with Prince Aldfrith, and he again appealed to the pope. Wilfrid was vindicated of these charges against him too, and although Aldfrith still caused him trouble from time to time, he was able to return to the Diocese of Wexham, giving the bishopric of the Diocese of York to Saint John of Beverly as a compromise solution. He later died in 709 while he was staying in one of the monasteries that he directed.

Saint Fidelis (Mark Rey) of Sigmaringen, Optional Memorial

Mark Rey was born in 1578 to well-to-do parents in Sigmaringen (modern Germany) and studied law. His willingness to take on the cases of the needy earned him the nickname of "the poor man's lawyer". But in time he became disgusted by the lack of honesty of his fellow lawyers, specifically their willingness to take bribes, so he left his profession. He then decided to become a Capuchin monk and took the name Fidelis. His excellent preaching, insight as a confessor, and personal care for the sick earned him a reputation for holiness, and he was sent to preach to fallen-away Catholics who were now Zwinglian Protestants in Switzerland. Many people converted to Catholicism as a result of Fidelis' preaching and example. But his success also earned him enemies among the Protestants. Although he knew his life was in danger, he continued to preach. On April 24, 1622, two attempts were made on his life while he was in the city of Seewis, Switzerland; the second attempt was successful.

> *Saint Wilfrid, pray for my faith in God to grow each time I face difficulties.*
> *Saint Fidelis, help me to bring the love of Christ to everyone I meet.*

* * * * *

April 25

Saint Mark the Evangelist, Feast

Some say that the naked boy who fled from the guards in the Garden of Gethsemane[6] was the young Saint Mark the Evangelist. According to tradition, Mark the Evangelist is also thought to be the John Mark whom Saints Barnabas and Paul quarreled about taking with them on their evangelical journey,[7] although Paul later referred to him positively, telling those concerned to receive Mark,[8] and later saying, "Get Mark and bring him with you; for he is very useful in serving me."[9] Saint Peter called him "son",[10] and Mark is traditionally believed to have been Peter's assistant. Tradition also says that Mark was a priest, that he became bishop of Alexandria, and that he died a martyr for the faith in the year 74. Venice has claimed the happy privilege of possessing his relics for many centuries.

> *And [Jesus] said to them, "Go into all the world and preach the gospel to the whole creation."*[11]

Saint Peter of Saint Joseph Betancur

Peter was born in 1619 in Guatemala and lived as a shepherd until he was thirty-one years old. He tried to become a priest, but since he had very little education, studies for the priesthood were too difficult for him. He withdrew from the

[6] Mk 14:51–52.
[7] Acts 15:37–39.
[8] Col 4:10.
[9] 2 Tim 4:11.
[10] 1 Pet 5:13.
[11] Mk 16:15.

seminary and later became a Franciscan tertiary. As a Franciscan, Peter's work gradually grew: he opened hospitals, schools, and chapels, as well as helped the poor and encouraged the practice of intercessory prayer. He's the first canonized Guatemalan native, and he's often credited with developing the tradition of Los Posadas processions at Christmas. He died in 1667.

Saint Mark, show me how to preach the Good News.
Saint Peter, remind me to pray for all those who have asked for my prayers.

* * * * *

April 26

Saint Anacletus (Cletus)

Anacletus (d. ca. 91) was the third pope; he reigned for around fifteen years. As pope, he divided Rome into twenty-five parishes and ordained priests. He also died a martyr during the persecution of Christians ordered by the Roman emperor Domitian.

Saint Stephen of Perm

Though Stephen (1345–1396) was born to Russian parents, he grew up among the Zyriane people, an ethnic group in northeastern Russia. He became a monk at Rostov and then later went back to preach the Gospel to his native people. Following the example of Saints Cyril and Methodius, he taught them the faith by first developing a written language of their spoken language, using the designs in their embroidery and carvings. He also translated the Mass into the vernacular so that they could understand it. He was careful to make his celebrations of the Mass both beautiful and solemn, which eventually turned many unbelievers into Catholics. As the first bishop of Perm, he also faced down opposition from groups of Christians who followed controversial teachings popular at the time.

Saint Anacletus, help me to love and serve the Church.
Saint Stephen, teach me how to bring the beauty of Christ to our culture.

* * * * *

April 27

Saint Simeon of Jerusalem

Simeon was a relative of Jesus,[12] and tradition says that he was one of the seventy disciples sent out to preach the Gospel[13] and was present at the Ascension[14]

---

[12] See Mt 13:55, where he is referred to as Simon.
[13] See Lk 10:1. Note that some ancient manuscripts refer to seventy-two disciples instead.
[14] See Acts 1:9.

and Pentecost.[15] Also according to tradition, he was present at the martyrdom of Saint James and succeeded him as bishop of Jerusalem. In A.D. 66, persecution of the Church by Jews in Jerusalem led Simeon to withdraw from the city with many other Christians and settle in the city of Pella. Simeon was arrested during a later persecution of Christians under the Roman emperor Trajan. He was tortured and crucified, dying in the year 106.

Saint Zita of Lucca

Zita (1218–1278) was raised by poor but pious parents who sent her to work as a servant in a rich household in Lucca, Italy, when she was twelve years old. She practiced her faith by sharing her food with the poor, attending daily Mass, rising in the night to pray, and once she even gave up her bed for a beggar. The other servants ridiculed her devotion and acts of charity for some time, but gradually the entire household came to rely upon and trust her. She was the only one who would face the master of the household when he became violently angry, and she was eventually placed in charge of the entire house. By the end of her life, people treated her with such veneration that she was embarrassed, but she was also relieved of many of her duties and was therefore left free to care for people who were poor, ill, or in prison. She died at the age of sixty, having served her family for more than forty years.

Saint Peter Armengol

Peter was born in 1238 into a noble family of Tarragona in the eastern Spanish Pyrenees. He lived a dissolute life and became a thief, but when his band attempted to hijack his own father's entourage, the shock of what he was doing brought him to his senses. He repented, joined the Mercedarian order in 1258, and worked tirelessly to ransom Christian hostages. He willingly took the place of eighteen captured Christian children and endured tortures for each one of them, including being hanged until his torturers thought he was dead. He survived the torture but was in great pain. He died in 1304 as a result of the torture and is, for this reason, considered a martyr.

> *Saint Simeon, show me how to face trials with the peace of Christ.*
> *Saint Zita, help me to take the lowest place joyfully.*
> *Blessed Peter, help me be willing to suffer for the sake of others.*

* * * * *

April 28

Saint Peter Mary Chanel, Optional Memorial

Peter (1803–1841) came from a poor but pious family in France, and he worked as a shepherd before he became a priest. His zeal as a country priest rekindled his

---

[15] Acts 1:14.

parishioners' devotion, and he was later sent as a missionary to Futuna, an island in the New Hebrides (now Vanuatu, an island group in the South Pacific). He and his companions won the respect of the native people through their care for the sick, which brought many people to the Christian faith. However, when the local chief learned that his own son had been baptized, he became angry and ordered Peter to be clubbed to death. His death completed his work of evangelization; within a few months, the whole island population had converted.

Saint Louis Marie Grignon de Montfort, Optional Memorial

Louis was born in 1673 to a poor family in Montfort-sur-Meu, France. He spent his priestly life living humbly and preaching zealously, particularly emphasizing the importance of praying the Rosary and developing a devotion to Mary. He founded two religious institutes to care for the poor—the Daughters of Divine Wisdom and the Brothers of Saint Gabriel—as well as the Company of Mary, now known as the Montfort Missionaries, to evangelize people with the truths of the faith. He preached often against the heresy of Jansenism, which was widespread in France, but his greatest legacy to the Church is perhaps found in his writings, particularly those about our Blessed Mother. These writings were lost for many years until they were rediscovered seemingly by accident. He died in 1716.

> *I avow, with all the Church, that Mary, being a mere creature that has come from the hands of the Most High, is in comparison with His Infinite Majesty less than an atom; or rather, she is nothing at all, because only He is "He who is" (Exod. 3:14); consequently that grand Lord, always independent and sufficient to Himself, never had, and has not now, any absolute need of the holy Virgin for the accomplishment of His will and for the manifestation of His glory. He has but to will in order to do everything. Nevertheless, I say that, things being as they are now—that is, God having willed to commence and to complete His greatest works by the most holy Virgin ever since He created her—we may well think He will not change His conduct in the eternal ages; for He is God, and He changes not, either in His sentiments or in His conduct.*[16]

Saint Vitalis of Milan

According to tradition, Vitalis was a rich man who lived in Milan in the third century. He became a Christian and was arrested during the persecution of Christians in the reign of the Roman emperor Marcus Aurelius. When he refused to give up his faith, he was tortured to death. Vitalis' wife (Valleria) and twin sons (Gervase and Protase) are also canonized saints.

Saint Gianna Molla

Gianna (1922–1962) came from a large, pious family in Milan, Italy. Both before and after she earned her medical degree, she cared for the poor and elderly and was active in Catholic associations. She considered entering religious life, but

---

[16] Louis de Montfort, *True Devotion to the Blessed Virgin with Preparation for Total Consecration*, trans. Fr. Frederick Faber, D.D. (Charlotte, N.C.: TAN Books, 2010), nos. 14–15.

she decided God was calling her to marriage and family. She married Pietro Molla when she was thirty-three years old, had three children, and continued to serve others as a medical doctor. During her fourth pregnancy, she was found to have a large ovarian cyst and absolutely refused to abort the child, though she understood that it would cost her her life. She died that her child might live, and that child (also named Gianna) grew up to become a physician and pro-life worker.

> Saint Peter, give me your zeal for bringing others to Christ.
> Saint Louis, teach me how to be a slave of Mary.
> Saint Vitalis, show me how to live and die for Christ.
> Saint Gianna, show me how to sacrifice myself for my family
> and those whom God has placed in my life.

* * * * *

April 29

Saint Catherine of Siena, Memorial

Catherine was born in 1347, the youngest of twenty-five children in a middle-class Catholic family in Siena, Italy. She was a pious child even from a young age but received no formal education. While a young girl, she decided to give herself wholeheartedly to Christ, choosing to fast, pray, and do penance out of her great love for Him, despite constant persecution from family, friends, and the community. God blessed her for her profound charity with visions and mystical phenomena, such as receiving the stigmata (though invisibly) and being spiritually espoused to Christ Himself. She underwent heroic fasts and penances to save sinners from the horrors of Hell, and she personally served the poor, the sick, and the imprisoned. She converted so many sinners through both gentle and confrontational words that confessors were assigned specifically to take care of those who sought the Sacrament of Confession after speaking with her. In her simplicity, she obeyed God when He called her to speak and write to both the rich and the poor. She rebuked two popes and told them to move their courts from Avignon, France, back to Rome, and against all odds, Pope Urban VI did return to Rome. She served as a peacemaker, healing feuds between families and entire cities. Her profound love for Christ in the Eucharist and willingness to mortify herself in penance for herself and others led to another gift: in the final years of her life, she consumed only the Eucharist and couldn't retain ordinary food. At the end of her life as she saw the Church torn by violence, particularly due to fighting over an anti-pope, she offered herself as a sacrifice to God, for the sake of the Church. She died in 1380 at the age of thirty-three. Though her writings were limited, they were deeply mystical, and her influence on the Church—from the pope down to the poor—is still felt today. She was named a Doctor of the Church in 1970.

[Jesus said to Catherine,] "Each of you has your own vineyard, your soul, in which your free will is the appointed worker during this life. Once the time of your life has passed, your will can work neither for good nor for evil; but while you live it can till the vineyard of your soul where I have placed it." [17]

Saint Hugh of Cluny

Hugh (1024–1109) was born into the French nobility. Though his father wanted him to become a knight, he eventually recognized Hugh's religious devotion and sent him to be educated by his great-uncle, also named Hugh, who was the bishop of Auxerre. Hugh became a monk when he was only fourteen years old, deacon at the age of eighteen, and priest by the time he was twenty. After some time as a monk, he became abbot; his leadership eventually transformed not only his own monastery, but almost every monastery in Europe. In addition to emphasizing prayer and devotion in the liturgy to his monks, he spoke out against corruption among the clergy and even confronted powerful secular leaders about the widespread practices of simony and lay investiture, which put worldly men in positions of authority in the Church. In time, he founded almost two thousand new religious houses, and he served as a peacemaker between the Church and the nobility.

Saint Antonius Kim Song-u

Antonius was born in 1795 in the city of Gusan (modern South Korea). He became a Christian, despite the danger at the time, married, and taught Christians about the faith in his own home. He was arrested for the crime of being a Christian, imprisoned, and executed by being strangled on this date in 1841.

Saint Catherine, give me your zeal for souls.
Saint Hugh, give me courage in speaking against injustice and for holiness.
Saint Antonius, show me how to live and die for Christ.

* * * * *

April 30

Saint Pius V, Optional Memorial

Pius V was born Antonio Ghislieri in 1504 in Lombardy, Italy. He became a Dominican priest, took the name of Michael, and gradually rose in rank within the Church. He became a lector in philosophy and theology, a novice master, the bishop of Nepi and Sutri, an inquisitor general, and then a cardinal. When he was made a cardinal, he ruefully said that it was so that "irons should be riveted to his feet to prevent him from creeping back into the peace of the cloister." [18]

---

[17] Catherine of Siena, *The Dialogue*, trans. Suzanne Noffke, O.P. (New York; Mahwah, N.J.: Paulist Press, 1980), 60.

[18] Michael Walsh, ed., *Butler's Lives of the Saints, Concise Edition, Revised and Updated* (San Francisco: HarperCollins Publishers, 1991), 127–28.

After Pope Pius IV died, Michael was elected pope, and he chose the name Pius V. Immediately, he began enforcing the recent decrees of the Council of Trent. For example, at his coronation, instead of having money scattered among the crowds and spent on banquets, he sent the money to hospitals, the poor, and the poorer convents of the city. He commanded all bishops and priests to reside in their dioceses and parishes or risk severe penalties. He purged his own curia, legislated against bullfighting, bearbaiting, and prostitution, and provided food for the poor during a famine at his own expense. He reluctantly followed tradition and made one of his nephews a cardinal, but he gave him and the rest of his family no influence or power. Pius revised the Divine Office and catechism and recognized Thomas Aquinas as a Doctor of the Church. Although he was unsuccessful in his attempts to win over Queen Elizabeth of England (his bull of excommunication against her only increased the persecution of Catholics), his efforts to unite Catholic nations against the Muslims was pivotal in the saving of Europe. He prayed, particularly the Rosary, throughout the Battle of Lepanto, and after its success, gave the title of Mary, Help of Christians to our Blessed Mother. All this, in a reign of only six years. He died in 1572.

Saints Amator, Peter, and Louis of Cordoba

When Muslims controlled Spain in the eighth and ninth centuries, they imposed Islamic law over the land. Acts of apostasy and blasphemy against Islam were punishable by death. Amator was a Catholic priest living in Cordoba, Peter was a monk, and Louis was a layman. On this date in 855, all three were executed for proclaiming their faith in Christ and blaspheming Islam, which were considered one and the same thing.

Saint Marie of the Incarnation Guyart Martin

Marie was a pious child born in 1599 in Tours, France. She wanted to become a nun, but against her wishes, she was married to Claude Martin at the age of seventeen. When she became a widow with a small son two years later, she returned to her family, refused to remarry, and worked as an embroiderer. After a profound vision of her failings and of herself covered in Christ's blood, she rededicated herself to prayer and acts of charity. She left her family and worked for her brother-in-law for a time, but then decided to join the Ursulines, leaving her son in the care of her sister. Her son, Claude, unsurprisingly prayed vigorously for his mother to return, and she herself couldn't explain her decision to leave her son—except obedience to the Lord's call. (When Claude grew up, he became a Benedictine priest and wrote a biography of his mother's life.) She took her vows under the name of Marie of the Incarnation, and she later became the novice mistress of the house. When she received a vision in which she was commanded to go to Canada to build a house for Christ, she gathered the money and goods she needed and obeyed. As the first superior of the Ursulines in Canada, she worked as a missionary to the natives and became so proficient with the tribal languages that she was able to write dictionaries and a catechism for them. She was strong-willed, however, and it's said that she sometimes had differences of opinions with Blessed Francis Laval, her bishop, about the work of her nuns. In 1672, she died of hepatitis at the age of seventy-two.

> *Saint Pius, give me your trust in the love of our Blessed Mother.*
> *Holy Martyrs, help me be unafraid of the cost of*
> *publicly confessing my faith in Jesus Christ.*
> *Saint Marie, help me always to obey God first.*

May

May 1

Saint Joseph the Worker, Optional Memorial

While Communist Russia was celebrating Communism and their emphasis on the "rights" of workers each year on May Day, Pope Pius XII instituted this day in 1955 in honor of Saint Joseph. It reminds us of the value of work in the light of Catholic teaching, as Pope Saint John Paul II explained: "If the Family of Nazareth is an example and model for human families, in the order of salvation and holiness, so too, by analogy, is Jesus' work at the side of Joseph the carpenter.... What is crucially important here is the sanctification of daily life, a sanctification which each person must acquire according to his or her own state."[1]

Prophet Jeremiah

From about the year 627 to the year 585 B.C., Jeremiah prophesied to the Jewish people, calling on them to reject war as a solution to their oppression by the Babylonian Empire and telling them to turn to the Lord for guidance instead. His prediction of the destruction of Israel and of the Babylonian Exile was fulfilled in 586 B.C. Jeremiah was forcibly taken to Egypt, where it's said that he died. It's also said that Jeremiah removed the Ark of the Covenant and hid it after the destruction of Jerusalem. It has never been found.

> *Thus says the LORD:... "I the LORD search the mind and test the heart, to give to every man according to his ways, according to the fruit of his doings."*[2]

Saint Sigismund of France

Sigismund (d. 539) was the first Christian king of Burgundy (modern France). Unfortunately, he listened to the lies of his second wife and had his own son killed out of jealousy. Sigismund later repented of his crime and spent the rest of his life trying to atone for it. For example, he rebuilt monasteries (that God might be continually praised) and served the poor. He believed a great calamity was necessary for him to atone for this sin, and when an enemy of his father overran the country and beat him in battle, he thought the time had come. His enemy hunted him down and killed him, making him a martyr.

Saint Peregrine Laziosi

Peregrine was born in 1260 into a wealthy family in Forli, Italy. Feuds split most of Italy into two major factions at the time, and the people of Forli, including

---

[1] John Paul II, apostolic exhortation *Redemptoris Custos* (Guardian of the Redeemer) (August 15, 1989), nos. 22, 24, http://www.vatican.va/content/john-paul-ii/en/apost_exhortations/documents/hf_jp-ii_exh_15081989_redemptoris-custos.html.

[2] Jer 17:5, 10.

Peregrine himself as a young man, belonged to the faction that opposed the pope. Forli's opposition was so violent that the pope had placed the town under an interdict, which prevented the townspeople from receiving any of the sacraments. In 1283, the prior general of the Servants of Mary, Saint Philip Benizi, came to Forli to attempt a reconciliation between the pope and the town. Father Benizi was heckled, struck by the eighteen-year-old Peregrine, and violently driven from the town. But Benizi had literally turned the other cheek to Peregrine's attack, and his kindness moved the young man to repentance. In time, he even entered the same order as Father Benizi and became a Servite priest. To atone for his past sins, Peregrine served the poor and sick; he was known for his personal penances, such as remaining standing whenever it wasn't necessary to sit. When he was about sixty years old, he developed a cancerous growth on his leg, which progressed to the point that the doctor decided it was necessary to amputate it. But on the night before the surgery was scheduled to occur, Peregrine prayed and received a vision of Jesus Christ, in which our Lord healed his leg. When he woke up, the cancer was miraculously healed. Peregrine died decades later in 1345 at the age of eighty-five.

Saint Richard (Erminio) Pampuri

Erminio was born in 1897 in Pavia, Italy. His mother died when he was three years old, and his father died when he was ten. He was a devout Catholic; he wanted to become a missionary but his health wasn't strong enough, so he decided to become a medical doctor. He first became a Franciscan tertiary, but then he chose to enter the Hospitallers of Saint John of God as a brother. He was thirty years old. As Brother Richard, he gave his life to the care of the sick, and he gradually became known and loved by many. When he contracted a lung illness, in part as a result of his military service in World War I, his health declined rapidly, and in 1930 he died. His body was taken back to his hometown, where he's still venerated.

> *Saint Joseph, teach me how to sanctify my daily work.*
> *Prophet Jeremiah, help me hear God's hard truths.*
> *Saint Sigismund, help me to become holy, that God might continually be praised in me.*
> *Saint Peregrine, intercede for those people I know who have cancer.*
> *Saint Richard, show me how to care for the sick with the Heart of Jesus Himself.*

* * * * *

May 2

Saint Athanasius of Alexandria, Memorial

Athanasius came from a Christian family of Alexandria, Egypt, and was born around the year 297. He was very well educated and learned theology from those who had been confessors to the faith during the persecution of Christians in the reign of the Roman emperor Maximian. Athanasius became secretary to Bishop Alexander of Alexandria while the priest Arius was spreading his heresy that Christ wasn't really the Son of God. Athanasius succeeded Alexander as the bishop, though he wasn't even thirty years old, and he spent the rest of his life fighting Arius' heresy. He wrote works explaining the true faith (the reason he was named a Doctor of the Church) and endured constant opposition from civil leaders (including the emperor), Church leaders (including many bishops), and even some of the laypeople. As almost the only bishop of a major see to remain faithful to Church teaching at the time, the Latin expression "Athanasius contra mundum" later arose to describe the situation of one man holding to the truth despite opposition from the entire world. Although he was exiled from his see five times, totaling seventeen years spent in hiding and banishment, his people rejoiced each time he returned. Athanasius spent the last seven years of his life at home and in peace in Alexandria, writing his biography of Saint Anthony, the Desert Father he had learned about while in exile among the monks of the desert. He died in 373. Because of his unswerving faith to the truth and strong leadership despite powerful opposition, he's not only considered a Father of the Church, but he has also been named a Doctor of the Church.

> He who takes up this book—the Psalter—goes through the prophecies about the Savior, as is customary in the other Scriptures, with admiration and adoration, but the other psalms he recognizes as being his own words.[3]

Saints Exsuperius, Zoe, Cyriacus, and Theodolus of Attalia

Exsuperius and Zoe were husband and wife, and Cyriacus and Theodolus were their children. All of them were slaves in Attalia, Pamphylia (modern Turkey), were owned by a rich pagan, and were Christians. On a pagan feast day, they were given meat to sacrifice to an idol. When they refused to do so, the entire family was tortured and killed. This happened in the year 127.

Saint Antoninus of Florence

Anthony was born in 1389 in Florence, Italy. He was small for his size, so his family gave him the nickname Antoninus ("little Anthony"). As a young man, he tried to enter the Dominican order, but the abbot tried to discourage him, telling him to go study a particular Latin document first. When Antoninus returned a year later and had memorized the entire document, the abbot quickly said yes. Antoninus became known as a great scholar and eventually held the positions of prior and superior at various Dominican houses. Since he had been a novice with a Dominican friar named John (now known to the Church as Blessed John, and to the world of art as Fra Angelico), Antoninus asked him to decorate one of the convents he directed. When Antoninus became archbishop of Florence, he lived a simple monastic life as much as possible and focused on

---

[3] Athanasius, *The Life of Antony and the Letter to Marcellinus*, trans. Robert C. Gregg (Mahwah, N.J.: Paulist Press, 1980), 109.

helping the poor. Both secular and religious leaders turned to him for his wisdom and diplomacy. He died in 1459.

> *Saint Athanasius, teach me perseverance.*
> *Holy Martyrs, pray for my family to be always united in our Christian faith.*
> *Saint Antoninus, help me to seek God's wisdom at all times.*

* * * * *

May 3

Saint Philip the Apostle, Feast

Philip, according to the Gospel of John, was from Bethsaida, the city of Peter and Andrew. The day after Jesus called Peter and Andrew to be his disciples, he also called Philip, who then found Nathaniel and brought him to see Jesus.[4] Although Philip was one of the Twelve Apostles, John's Gospel records his words only a few times: at the multiplication of the loaves[5] and at the Last Supper.[6] Although he's often confused with Philip the deacon who's described in Acts, tradition says that this Philip was a missionary to Greece and Asia Minor and that he died a martyr in Phrygia, a region now in Turkey.

Saint James the Lesser, Apostle, Feast

This James is the son of Alphaeus,[7] not the son of Zebedee[8] who's mentioned so often in the Gospels; he's often called James the Lesser. He may have been a relative of Jesus or was the James who became the bishop of Jerusalem.[9] He may also be the author of the New Testament Letter of James. According to tradition, he died by being beaten to death with clubs in Jerusalem.

Saints Eventius, Alexander, and Theodolus of Rome

Eventius, Alexander, and Theodolus were all priests serving the Church in Rome when they were arrested for being Christians in about the year 113, apparently during the persecution of the Roman emperor Trajan. They were imprisoned, tortured, and died as martyrs together.

Saint Juvenal of Narni

The earliest information we have about Juvenal was his ordination to the priesthood at the hands of Pope Saint Damasus I. In the year 368, he became the first

---

[4] Jn 1:43–48.
[5] Jn 6:5–7.
[6] Jn 14:8–9.
[7] Mt 10:3; Mk 3:18; Lk 6:15.
[8] Mk 1:19; 3:17.
[9] See Acts 15:13.

bishop of the city of Narni in Italy, where he survived an assassination attempt. He successfully prayed for the city to be saved from invasion because of a great thunderstorm that scared away the superstitious army. He may have died as a martyr around the year 373.

Saint Theodosius of Kiev

Theodosius (d. eleventh century) was from a well-to-do family, but he was a humble man who would sometimes work in the fields with the peasants, and he was persecuted by others for his piety. He became an apprentice baker so that he could make the hosts for Mass (the Holy Mysteries, as the East calls it), and then he became a monk in the caves near Saint Anthony Pechersky in Kiev, Ukraine. After Anthony's death, he became the abbot and reorganized religious life at the monastery. For example, he emphasized the corporal works of mercy by giving food to the nearby jails and supporting a nearby hospital. He sent his monks outside the monastery to preach the Gospel to the people in the community, and he defended the rights of the poor when they were threatened by the rich and powerful. His work laid the foundation for the Russian tradition of "staretz", monastic elders who were widely respected and provided spiritual direction and advice to others. He was particularly fond of a married couple named John and Mary because of their love of God and for one another. Despite his heavy duties as abbot, he did his share of the daily work in the fields and the house. He died soon after Easter, and he was originally buried in a cave. When his body was later moved to the principal church in the area, it was found to be incorrupt. He was the second Russian to be canonized by the Church, and he's known as the first of the "'very-like ones', that is, Christlike monks".[10]

> *Saints Philip and James, show me how to bring the Gospel to others today.*
> *Holy Martyrs, show me how to live and die for Christ.*
> *Saint Juvenal, help me trust God with my safety and the safety of others.*
> *Saint Theodosius, help me to become Christlike.*

See also Saint Alexander I in the Supplemental Calendar.

* * * * *

May 4

Saint Florian

Florian (d. ca. 304) was a veteran of the Roman army, and he lived in what is now Austria. He was a brave man, and it's said that he once saved his town by putting out a fire (some even say miraculously, by throwing a single bucket of water on the flames). During the persecution of Christians under the Roman

---

[10] Michael Walsh, ed., *Butler's Lives of the Saints, Concise Edition, Revised and Updated* (San Francisco: HarperCollins Publishers, 1991), 211.

emperor Diocletian in the early years of the fourth century, he was arrested for being a Christian and was executed by being thrown into the river with a millstone around his neck. A devout woman recovered his body and buried it. Centuries later, some of his relics were brought to Poland, and many miracles were attributed to Florian's intercession.

Blessed John Martin Moye

John was born in 1730 into a large family in Cutting, France, and became a priest in 1754. He founded the Sisters of the Congregation of Divine Providence, in order to care for the needy as well as to provide schools for poor children. He joined the Paris Foreign Mission Society in 1769 and was sent to China in 1773. Despite being repeatedly imprisoned, he organized a group of local women to care for the sick and teach the faith to families. When his health deteriorated, he was sent back to France in 1784 to recover. He preached missions throughout the countryside until he was forced to leave France with his sisters due to the violence of the French Revolution. When French soldiers invaded the city of Trier, where they were living, there was an epidemic of typhoid fever. John and his sisters worked tirelessly to care for the sick, and he died on February 8, 1793.

Saint Florian, show me how to face opposition with peace.
Blessed John, help me to find and serve the needy around me.

* * * * *

May 5

Saint Hilary of Arles

Hilary was born in 400 and came from a noble family of Lorraine, France; he was related to Saint Honoratus, the monk who had founded the Abbey of Lerins. Honoratus left the abbey to beg his relative Hilary to enter religious life, but initially Hilary refused. Finally, after Hilary fought an internal struggle over whether to continue following his worldly dreams or give his life to God, Christ won out. Hilary sold his patrimony, gave the money to the poor, and never looked back at the life he left behind. After Hilary had served the Lord as a monk under Honoratus for some time, Honoratus died and Hilary succeeded him as bishop of Arles. Although Hilary was a zealous leader and deeply devout, his autocratic temper led him to make a few bad decisions that caused him to be censured by the pope. In 449, he died when he was forty-nine years old.

Saint Godehard (Gothard) of Hildesheim

Godehard was born in the ninth century in Reichersdorf, Germany, and his father worked for the canons who lived near the village church. Godehard was educated by those canons, grew up to become a priest among them, and eventually became their abbot. Because of his well-known holiness, the emperor

Henry II recommended Godehard for the position of bishop of Hildesheim. As bishop, Godehard built a hospice for the sick and poor, encouraged better education among the people, built and restored churches, and brought order and discipline to the priests of his diocese. He died in 1038.

Blessed Gregory (Grzegorz) Boleslaw Frackowiak

Gregory was born in 1911 into a poor family in Lowecice, Poland. He wasn't able to afford an advanced education, so he decided to become a brother in the Society of the Divine Word. In 1938, he was ordained a friar. In 1940, the Nazis invaded and sent the friars to concentration camps. Gregory was able to escape, and for the sake of his Polish countrymen, he helped organize an underground religious ministry. The Nazis ultimately found him, arrested him, tortured him, and imprisoned him. In 1943, he was executed on this date by being guillotined.

> *Saint Hilary, help me control my temper.*
> *Saint Godehard, help me to bring order and discipline to my own life and family.*
> *Blessed Gregory, show me how to live and die for Christ.*

* * * * *

May 6

Saint Lucius of Cyrene

According to Scripture, Lucius of Cyrene was one of the early Church leaders who prayed over Saints Paul and Barnabas before sending them out on their first missionary journey.[11] Though this event occurred in Antioch, tradition says that Lucius was the first bishop of Cyrene.

Saints James and Martin of Numidia

James was a deacon and Martin was a lector (both d. 259) when both men were arrested and imprisoned in Cirta (modern-day Constantine, Algeria) during the persecution of Christians under the Roman emperor Valerian. Despite being tortured for several days, James refused to renounce his Christian faith, and he was encouraged by a dream in which he saw himself in Heaven. They were martyred by beheading with hundreds of others on this date. We know about their suffering because a fellow prisoner who was not martyred wrote an account of the events.

Saint Peter Nolasco

Peter was probably born in Barcelona, Spain, around the year 1180. As a priest, he dedicated himself to helping Christian slaves held by Muslims, who controlled most of Spain at the time. He founded the order of Our Lady of Ransom, which

[11] Acts 13:1–3.

was based on the Rule of Saint Augustine and which worked to free Christians who had been captured and enslaved by Muslims. He died in 1256.

Saint Francis de Montmorency-Laval

Francis (1623–1708) was from a distinguished and devout family in Normandy, France, and his father died when Francis was thirteen years old. He felt God calling him to the priesthood from the time he was young, and when he became a priest, his family connections led him to be given various clerical positions in the Church. In 1658, he was named apostolic vicar of New France and was later consecrated as bishop of the new and huge territory now known as Canada. From this new country, he supported missionaries who came to spread the Gospel in the area, restored and built new churches, founded a seminary for priests to be educated, and started the Catholic school system in Canada. He also strongly opposed the trade of alcohol to natives. His actions protected the native peoples from exploitation, but it also made him powerful enemies who resented the loss in profits. He retired from his position and began living as a hermit in 1684, but he came out of retirement on one occasion to help rebuild church buildings after a destructive fire.

Blessed Henryk Kaczorowski

Henryk (1888–1942) was a priest and rector of a major seminary in Wloclawek, Poland, when he was arrested in 1939 by the Nazis, who imprisoned many Catholic priests, particularly Polish ones, in concentration camps. Henryk ministered to other prisoners while he was imprisoned and remained faithful despite the horrific conditions. He was executed by being gassed to death on this date at the Dachau concentration camp.

Saint Lucius, show me how to pray with faith.
Holy Martyrs, help me look to Heaven for my comfort.
Saint Peter, show me how to rescue those in slavery to sin.
Saint Francis, teach me how to shepherd my family as you shepherded your flock.
Blessed Henryk, help me to trust God at all times, particularly in my suffering.

See also Saint Petronax of Monte Cassino in the Supplemental Calendar.

* * * * *

May 7

Saint Flavia Domitilla

Flavia Domitilla was a Roman noblewoman who lived in the second century and was related to emperors. When she converted to the Christian faith, despite the fact that it was illegal, she then brought others to faith in Christ. When the persecution of Christians was renewed, her political connections protected her for a while, but she was finally sentenced to exile on the island of Ponza, where she died a martyr.

Saint John of Beverly

John (d. 721) was a monk who became the bishop of York. Bede the Venerable (the English historian and saint) wrote about John, saying that he was an intelligent and holy man whose prayers led to several miraculous healings. For example, his prayers cured a boy of dumbness and healed a woman who had been in so much pain that she hadn't been able to move for weeks.

Saint Anthony of Kiev

Anthony was born in 983 near the city of Chernigov (in modern Ukraine). When he was a young man, he tried to live on his own like one of the great Egyptian anchorites, but "he soon realized that one must be trained for that life as for any other",[12] as described in *Butler's Lives of the Saints*. He traveled to the famous monastery at Mount Athos in Greece and lived there as a monk for several years, but eventually his abbot told him it was time to return to his homeland. Anthony obediently returned home, but he found that the monasteries in his native land, which had been founded by princes, didn't give him the peace and solitude to which he had become accustomed on Mount Athos. So he moved and settled in a cave near the river Dnieper near the city of Kiev (Ukraine). In time, many people began to come and seek out the advice of this holy man. Because Anthony would accept any man as a disciple if he had the right disposition, many men began to join him, digging caves for themselves and following his example and spiritual direction. For a time, he returned to Chernigov due to political strife in the area, and he founded another monastery. However, he was later able to return to his previous monastery, Pecherskaya Laura, and died there at the age of ninety in the year 1073.

Saint Agostino Roscelli

After living a peaceful life as a mountain shepherd, Agostino (1818–1902) recognized that God was calling him to the priesthood when he was still a young man. He was too poor to pay for his priestly education, so he asked God for help. When several people came forward and donated money to pay the seminary costs for him, he was able to study and eventually became a priest. He became a chaplain of an orphanage and a prison. He later started a religious order of sisters called the Institute of Sisters of the Immaculata, and his nuns ran residential schools to support young women who were so poor that they were susceptible to starvation or turning to prostitution. Agostino was a great example to other Christians, in that he lived a very active life while remaining a man of deep prayer.

> *Saint Flavia, help me live only for Christ.*
> *Saint John, pray for my healing from _____.*
> *Saint Anthony, teach me how to live in peace while living in the world.*
> *Saint Agostino, show me those who need my help.*

* * * * *

---

[12] Walsh, *Butler's Lives of the Saints*, 209.

May 8

Saint Acacius (Agathius) of Constantinople

Acacius was a Roman soldier who was executed for the crime of being a Christian during the persecution ordered by the Roman emperor Diocletian in the early fourth century. Some traditions say he died by crucifixion; others by being impaled. Acacius is one of the Fourteen Holy Helpers, great saints who were called upon particularly for help during the bubonic plague in the fourteenth century.

Saint Arsenius

Arsenius (d. 449) was rich with servants and possessions and served the Church as a deacon in Rome. A widely respected teacher, he was recommended by Pope Damasus himself when the emperor's children needed a tutor. But Arsenius heard God's voice calling him to abandon everything for the sake of his soul. So he obediently left the world and all his wealth behind and moved to live with the desert monks near the Wadi Natrun in Egypt. Arsenius loved silence, and he remarked that he had frequently been sorry for what he had said, but never for saying nothing. When invasions made the region dangerous and he was forced to leave, he found an even more austere site, living on a rock called Petra near Memphis. When he received the news that a relative had left him his large estate, Arsenius simply tore the will in two and said that he had died to the world, long before the relative. Although he feared for many years that his previous life of luxury would keep him from Heaven, he finally found peace with God when he died. He left his only possessions—a skin coat, palm-leaf sandals, and a goat-skin shirt—to another monk.

Saint Boniface IV

Boniface (d. 615) was the sixty-seventh pope; he reigned six years. Before becoming pope, he was a Benedictine monk, prior, and deacon under Pope Saint Gregory the Great. He converted the Pantheon in Rome into a church, the first instance of a pagan temple being turned into a church. Late in his life, he turned his home into a monastery, and he lived the life of a simple, prayerful monk as much as possible while simultaneously performing his duties.

Saint Benedict II

Benedict (d. 685) was the eighty-first pope; he reigned less than a year. Personally, he was known for his knowledge of Scripture and for his care for the poor. His ascension to the papacy was delayed because the practice had developed of waiting for the emperor to confirm a papal election; after Benedict became pope, he abolished that practice to separate the papal office from influence by the emperor. Benedict also opposed a common heresy of the time: Monothelitism, which taught that Christ had only a divine will, denying Christ's free and human will and making his human nature just an instrument.

> Saint Acacius, show me how to live and die for Christ.
> Saint Arsenius, help me guard my tongue.
> Saints Boniface and Benedict, show me how to love Christ and His Church.

* * * * *

May 9

Prophet Isaiah

Isaiah, the son of Amos, preached God's words to the people of Judah during the reigns of kings Uzziah, Jotham, Ahaz, and Hezekiah in the eighth century B.C. He told the people of the need for repentance and predicted that the nation would be destroyed by the Babylonians and sent out of their land into exile. Isaiah's powerful predictions of the Messiah, the Suffering Servant, and future events reveal Jesus Christ to us centuries before His birth.

> Surely he has borne our griefs and carried our sorrows; yet we esteemed him stricken, struck down by God, and afflicted. But he was wounded for our transgressions, he was bruised for our iniquities; upon him was the chastisement that made us whole, and with his stripes we are healed.[13]

Saint Hermas of Rome

Hermas was a first-century Christian who lived in Rome and was mentioned by Saint Paul in his Letter to the Romans.[14] Hermas became bishop of Philippi and was a martyr for his faith in Jesus Christ.

Saint Pachomius the Great

Raised in a pagan family in Thebes of Egypt, Pachomius (292–348) was forcibly conscripted (a euphemism for kidnapping) into the Theban army when he was twenty years old. As he and his fellow soldiers passed through the city of Lato-polis, the Christians living there noticed the miserable way that the soldiers were treated and did their best to feed and comfort them. This genuine and disinter-ested charity to strangers both impressed and mystified Pachomius; therefore, when he was later taken prisoner in a battle, he made a vow to himself that he would become a Christian if he was released. When he got out of prison, he kept his vow. He became an anchorite and learned how to live this way of life from a Desert Father who directed his penitential practices. For example, Pachomius ate very simply, not using wine or oil, and he walked barefoot as

[13] Is 53:4–5.
[14] Rom 16:14.

he collected briars to draw closer to Christ's suffering. Eventually, he founded the very first Christian monastic community, and his rule of monastic life has been followed by Christians of the East and West ever since. Pachomius ensured that all his monks worked at a trade, were gathered together daily for prayer, and memorized the Bible. Pachomius was visited by the exiled bishop, Saint Athanasius—though he refused to indulge himself in a visit to his own sister, who lived in a nunnery—and he was an outspoken opponent of the heresy of Arianism. He died during an epidemic and is considered a Father of the Church.

> *Prophet Isaiah, help me see the Messiah in my own sufferings.*
> *Saint Hermas, give me your zeal for Christ.*
> *Saint Pachomius, help me to draw others to Christ by sharing in their sufferings.*

* * * * *

May 10

Patriarch Job

The patriarch Job is said to have lived in the land of Uz (an unknown area in the region of the Holy Land) around 1500 B.C. As described in the biblical book that bears his name, Job suffered greatly: he lost his wealth, material possessions, all his many children, and his health. Even his friends opposed him, telling him that his sufferings were a result of his sins. Job questioned God, but he remained faithful, humble, obedient, and accepted what he didn't understand.

> Then Job answered the LORD: "I know that you can do all things, and that no purpose of yours can be thwarted. 'Who is this that hides counsel without knowledge?' Therefore I have uttered what I did not understand, things too wonderful for me, which I did not know. 'Hear, and I will speak; I will question you, and you declare to me.' I had heard of you by the hearing of the ear, but now my eye sees you; therefore I despise myself, and repent in dust and ashes."[15]

Saints Gordian and Epimachus of Rome

Both these men died as martyrs in Rome and are buried together in a crypt, but they died at different times. Epimachus was burned at the stake, under the persecutions of the Roman emperor Decius around the year 250, and Gordian was a judge who was tortured and beheaded, under the persecutions of the Roman emperor Julian the Apostate in the year 362.

Saint John of Avila

John was born in 1499 in Castilian Spain into a Catholic family of Jewish ancestry. His pious parents ensured that he was well educated, and he became a

---

[15] Job 42:1–6.

lawyer. After a time, he discerned that God was calling him to be a priest. While he was still studying in the seminary, his parents died. After his ordination, rather than celebrating with a banquet for his friends, he invited a dozen poor men to join him for a celebratory dinner and gave away his parents' fortune to the poor. The rest of his life was marked by this humble, austere way of life and dedication to serving those in need. He was initially determined to serve God as a missionary in the New World, but his archbishop convinced him that it was God's will for him to stay and renew the faith of Catholics in his native Spain instead. For forty years, John reevangelized the region of Andulasia, which had been previously ruled by the Moors (Spanish Muslims) and was only gradually returning to the practice of the Catholic faith. His eloquent preaching drew large crowds. But not all his listeners appreciated his strong words in support of the poor and against the materialism of the rich. He made powerful enemies, who had him imprisoned by the Spanish Inquisition for a year. However, the false charges were eventually disproved, and he returned to preaching all over Spain. Several saints—Teresa of Avila, Francis Borgia, John of God, John of the Cross, Peter of Alcantara, and Louis of Granada—turned to John for advice and spiritual direction, and John encouraged many priestly vocations to the Jesuit order. He was a man of prayer to the very end, dying of poor health at the age of seventy in 1569. His forceful, faithful writings caused him to be named a Doctor of the Church by Pope Benedict XVI in 2012.

Just as plowing and sowing are the means to harvest wheat, so prayer is the means to obtain spiritual fruits. For this reason we ought not to marvel if we harvest so little, since we sow so little prayer.[16]

Saint Damien Joseph de Veuster of Molokai, Optional Memorial[17]

Damien was born on a small farm in Belgium in 1840. He joined the Fathers of the Sacred Hearts of Jesus and Mary, became a priest, and asked to be sent out as a missionary. He was sent to Hawaii, where his parish was the size of his entire native Belgium. For years he worked alone on an island leper colony, ministering to the spiritual and medical needs of these abandoned people, bringing love, respect, order, and the best medical treatment possible to a community that had previously been living in chaos and despair. He contracted leprosy himself in 1885, but he continued serving those around him until his death in 1889.

Patriarch Job, help me seek God in my suffering.
Saints Gordian and Epimachus, show me how to live and die for Christ.
Saint John, teach me to pray with great faith.
Saint Damien, show me how to serve abandoned people in my own community.

* * * * *

[16] John of Avila, *Audi, filia—Listen, O Daughter*, trans. Joan Frances Gurmley (New York; Mahwah, N.J.: Paulist Press, 2006), 209.

[17] This saint may be celebrated as an optional memorial in the *Liturgical Calendar for the Dioceses of the United States of America*.

May 11

Saint Anthimus of Rome

Anthimus (d. 303) was a parish priest of Rome who converted many people to the Christian faith. When he converted a Roman prefect, Roman officials condemned him to death by drowning. According to tradition, he was rescued by an angel, continued his work, but was later recaptured and martyred by beheading.

Saint Walter (Gauthier) of l'Esterp

Walter was born in 990 in Conflans, France, was educated at an Augustinian monastery at Dorat, and later became a monk there. A difficult superior forced him to leave the monastery, so he entered the abbey of l'Esterp. Over time, he became the abbot, and he was greatly loved by his monks, who refused to let him give up his office even when he became blind. He was wise and gentle with them; for example, when every monk forgot that it was a Friday and meat was cooked for the meal, Walter told them that they would be forgiven and simply sat down to eat with them. He spent the last seven years of his life in blindness, faithfully observing the rules and duties of his abbey. He died in 1070.

Saint Francis di Girolama

Francis was born in 1642 in Apulia, Italy, one of eleven children. He taught catechism to other children, received the monastic tonsure when he was only sixteen years old, was ordained a priest (which required a dispensation due to his young age) at the age of twenty-four, and entered the Jesuits (after overcoming his parents' opposition) by the time he was twenty-eight years old. He and another priest, who was well known as a preacher, were sent by their superiors to preach missions to the peasants of the province, and Francis eventually became widely known as a great preacher. He attracted huge crowds, trained other missionaries, and brought many people to conversion and to the confessional. His most well-known penitent was a woman who had murdered her father and served in the army disguised as a man. Francis brought her to repentance, and, under his direction, she lived a holy life. Some claimed Francis was a wonder-worker as well, but he always gave the credit for his miracles to the intercession of Saint Cyrus, an early Church martyr and physician. He died in 1716.

Saint Ignatius (Vincenzo Peis) of Laconi

Born in Sardinia, Italy, in 1701, Vincenzo was eighteen years old when he vowed to enter the Franciscan order if he recovered from a serious illness. He recovered, but then ignored the vow for two years until he suffered a serious fall from a horse. He then presented himself at a convent in Cagliari and lived as an obedient and humble lay brother for the rest of his long life. At his death in 1781, he was loved and known as a saint by all around him.

Saint Anthimus, help me to remember to seek the help of my guardian angel.
Saint Walter, show me how to be wise and gentle with those around me.
Saint Francis, help me to repent of my sins.
Saint Ignatius, remind me to keep my promises to God.

* * * * *

May 12

Saints Nereus and Achilleus of Terracina, Optional Memorial

Nereus and Achilleus were first-century soldiers who became Christians. They decided that, as Christians, it was wrong for them to fight for the pagan Roman Empire. So they ran away to the island of Terracina (located southeast of Rome); when they were found, they were beheaded. This occurred during the persecution of Christians under the Roman emperor Trajan. Pope Saint Damasus honored them with a tombstone years later, at a church dedicated at the site of their deaths.

Saint Pancras of Rome, Optional Memorial

Pancras was a fourteen-year-old orphan who was brought to Rome by an uncle and who then converted to the faith. He was martyred with the other martyrsaints Nereus, Achilleus, and Flavia Domitilla in the first century. His relics were sent to England by Pope Saint Vitalian during its early evangelization; devotion to Pancras' intercession spread there.

Saint Germanus of Constantinople

Germanus (d. 732) was born in Constantinople, where his father was a senator. Germanus became a priest, then bishop of Cyzicus, and then patriarch of Constantinople. When Germanus crowned Leo the Isaurian as emperor in the year 717, Leo solemnly swore to preserve the Catholic faith. When Leo became a follower of the heresy of iconoclasm ten years later and passed laws against the veneration of images—forbidding outward displays of reverence to statues and pictures and having them raised to a height that prevented them from being kissed by the faithful—Germanus reminded the emperor of his vow. Leo repeatedly tried to win over Germanus to iconoclasm, but when he failed to do so, Leo practically forced him to give up his office. Germanus spent the rest of his life in monastic seclusion and died when he was over ninety years old.

Saint Dominic of the Causeway

Dominic (1019–1109) tried to become a Benedictine monk several times but was refused by the monks, so he decided to become a monk on his own. At first, he lived as a hermit near Rioja, Spain. Later he moved to a spot along the pilgrimage route that led to the shrine of Saint James at Compostela. Out of compassion for pilgrims, he built a bridge, hospice, and road for them.

> *Holy Martyrs, show me how to be a strong witness to my faith in God.*
> *Saint Germanus, help me speak the truth at any cost.*
> *Saint Dominic, help me to grow in compassion and love of solitude.*

* * * * *

May 13

Our Lady of Fatima, Optional Memorial

On May 13, 1917, near the end of World War I and before the Communist Revolution in Russia, the Virgin Mary appeared to three shepherd children in the little village of Fatima, Portugal. Lucia, Jacinta, and Francisco saw the Lady on the thirteenth day of each month for seven months, except once when they were prevented by the authorities. They passed on the powerful messages that she gave them about the importance of prayer, doing penance for others, the seriousness of Hell, and the need to pray for the conversion of Russia. At the final vision, believers and unbelievers alike saw an inexplicable and miraculous vision of the sun.

> *My God, I believe, I adore, I trust, and I love You! I beg pardon for all those that do not believe, do not adore, do not trust, and do not love You.*[18]

Saint Andrew Hubert Fournet

Andrew was born in 1752 in Maille, France, to a devout mother who wanted him to become a priest. But he was a lazy student who preferred enjoying himself to studying. His mother sent him to stay with an uncle who was the priest of a very poor parish, and there Andrew recognized his true vocation and eventually became a priest. During the French Revolution, he initially ran away to Spain for safety. But he became ashamed that he had escaped and returned in secret to minister to Catholics during the time of persecution. Many times he narrowly escaped capture and death for the crime of being a priest. For example, on one occasion, he put a sheet over himself and pretended that he was a dead body when officials arrived, and another time a parishioner pretended that he was a lazy servant and beat him over the head to distract the authorities. After the revolution, he continued to serve his flock, and he founded the Daughters of the Holy Cross with Jeanne-Elizabeth Bicher des Ages, a nun and

---

[18] Prayer taught to the three children of Fatima by an angel.

future saint. The order was devoted to the education of poor girls. He died in 1834.

> *Our Lady of Fatima, teach me to pray.*
> *Saint Andrew, show me how to bear humiliations for love of Christ.*

* * * * *

May 14

Saint Matthias the Apostle, Feast

Matthias was chosen by lot to replace Judas among the Twelve Apostles after Judas' suicide. Saint Peter spoke highly of Matthias, pointing out that both he and the other candidate, Joseph called Barsabbas, had been faithful followers of the Lord from the beginning of Jesus' ministry and witnesses to His Resurrection.[19] Matthias is traditionally believed to be a martyr, but the details of his death are uncertain.

Saint Theodore (Anne-Therese) Guerin

Anne-Therese Guerin was born in France in 1798. She joined the Sisters of Providence in 1823, took the name Sister Saint Theodore, and made her final vows in 1831. After serving as a teacher for some time, she was sent with five other sisters to Vincennes, Indiana, in the year 1840. The sisters established the Academy of Saint Mary-of-the-Woods in Terre Haute, the first Catholic women's liberal arts college in America. She later established ten other schools in Indiana and one in Illinois. She also founded an orphanage for boys and another for girls, opened pharmacies that served the poor for free, and supervised the construction of the order's motherhouse. She died of natural causes in 1856.

Saint Michael Garicoits

Michael was born in the year 1797; his parents were poor peasants in Ibarre, France, who remained faithful and had hidden priests during the French Revolution. They repeatedly refused Michael's requests to become a priest because, as they told him, they simply couldn't afford it. But Michael's grandmother reminded the parish priest how the family had protected priests during the French Revolution, so he arranged for Michael to work for the clergy and in the bishop's kitchen to pay for his seminary education. As a young vicar, Michael revitalized his parish; encouraged devotion to the Sacred Heart to combat the common heresy in that time and place, Jansenism; and eventually became the superior at a seminary. When the bishop decided to merge two seminaries,

---

[19] Acts 1:21–26.

Michael and two other priests weren't assigned to serve at the new one. But Michael had a new plan for his life: founding an order of priests who would live in community and do mission work among the people, in many ways following the rule of the Jesuit order. This order became the Priests of the Sacred Heart of Betharram. But a new bishop came along who wasn't as supportive, so the order faced many delays for years. Michael accepted these limitations on his new order peacefully and without complaint. He died in 1863.

Saint Mary Domenica Mazzarello

Mary (1837–1881) was a pious girl from Mornese, Italy, who joined a Marian association when she was fifteen years old. At the age of twenty-three, she became seriously ill with typhoid; her experience of suffering and powerlessness taught her to trust even more in God when she recovered. She opened a dressmaking workshop to teach girls how to sew, but she also taught them about the love of God. In 1872, Saint John Bosco (commonly called Don Bosco) chose her to be the superior (and co-founder) of his new order, the Institute of the Daughters of Mary, Help of Christians. She spent the rest of her life in humble, loving service of her teaching sisters and the girls they served.

Saint Matthias, help me spread the Gospel today.
Saint Theodore, help me find ways to serve those who are most vulnerable.
Saint Michael, show me how to accept delays without complaint.
Saint Mary Domenica, help me to trust God.

* * * * *

May 15

Saints Cassius and Victorinus of Clermont

Cassius was a senator living in Clermont, France, and Victorinus was a pagan priest. Both converted to Christianity through the evangelization of a bishop, Saint Astromonius. Around the year 264, a leader named Chrocas led an invasion of Germanic tribes into France. According to tradition, Chrocas slaughtered thousands of Christians when he invaded; the martyrdoms of the leaders Cassius and Victorinus are counted among them.

Saint Isidore the Farmer, Optional Memorial[20]

Isidore was born to poor parents in Madrid, Spain, around the year 1080 and worked his entire life as a peasant farmer for John de Vergas, a wealthy resident of the city. Isidore and his wife were good and devout; after the death of their only child, a son, they agreed to live the remainder of their lives as brother and

---

[20] This saint may be celebrated as an optional memorial in the *Liturgical Calendar for the Dioceses of the United States of America.*

sister. Isidore's neighbors noticed his generosity with the poor and the time he spent in prayer and at Mass; they initially accused him of shirking his work. Later, they began to attribute his successful crops to the help of angels. He died in 1130. His incorrupt body remains in a shrine in Spain.

> *Saints Cassius and Victorinus, help me remain faithful to Christ.*
> *Saint Isidore, help me to work for the glory of God, regardless of criticism.*

* * * * *

May 16

Saint Brendan

Born in Ireland in 484, Brendan was educated by Saint Ita, the mother superior at one of the convents that she directed. He made several trips in skin-covered coracles on voyages to Scotland, England, Wales, and Newfoundland to evangelize the people there, as he described in his work *The Navigatio*. He also founded several monasteries, including a large one at Clonfert that became the home of three thousand monks. Tradition is unclear whether he died in 577 or in 583.

Saint Ubaldus (Ubaldo) Baldassini

Ubaldus was born around 1084 into a noble family near Ancona in Italy. His father died when he was young, and his mother suffered from a disorder that left her an invalid. Ubaldus was raised by an uncle, became an Augustinian Canon Regular and monk, and was ordained a priest in 1115. A few years later, he convinced his fellow canons to live a common life under a rule, in order to protect them from becoming too drawn into the worldly ways of life that surrounded them. Although Ubaldus wanted to become a hermit, he accepted the call to become bishop of Gubbio. He was a brave protector of his flock, as when he faced down the emperor Frederick Barbarossa during a military campaign and convinced him not to sack the city. But his people particularly reverenced him as a model of Christian virtues: modest, humble, gentle, and generous with the poor. Ubaldus died on this date in 1160 of natural causes.

Saint Simon Stock

Simon (d. 1265) was from Kent, England, and he joined the Carmelite order after returning from a pilgrimage to the Holy Land. At this point in history, the Carmelite order had only been an order of hermits, but seeing the blessings of the new Dominican and Franciscan orders, Simon and other Carmelites debated whether to turn their order into an order of mendicant friars as well. Simon became prior general of the Carmelites in London, and, after a great deal of prayer, the Carmelites became a begging order, but still focused on the contemplative life. He's usually represented in art with the brown scapular, a garment that symbolized the order's devotion to our Blessed Mother, a symbol Mary showed him in a vision. He's also often depicted with a flame due to the emphasis on Purgatory in his preaching.

Saint Andrew Bobola

Andrew (1591–1657) came from an aristocratic Polish family, and he became a Jesuit priest. Later, he served as a Jesuit superior. He eventually served as a missionary, bringing the faith to a region plagued by Cossack raids, in what is now Lithuania. The Cossacks were a Slavic ethnic group known for producing tough soldiers, and they used violence to drive the Jesuits out of their churches and colleges. Despite the danger, Andrew and other Jesuit priests hid in the wilderness and swamps to bring the sacraments to the Catholic faithful in secret. Andrew accepted an invitation to stay with a leader in the city of Pinsk, and when the city was attacked by Cossacks, he was arrested. The Cossacks tortured him brutally, and the fact that he continued to pray while they tortured him infuriated his captors even more. He finally died from the tortures. Decades later, his casket was rediscovered and opened. His body—still mutilated by the tortures—was found to be incorrupt. And it still is.

> *Saint Brendan, show me how to speak of Christ to others.*
> *Saint Ubaldus, help me to keep from being drawn into worldly ways.*
> *Saint Simon, help me to contemplate the love of God*
> *shown to us through our Blessed Mother.*
> *Saint Andrew, give me your courage.*

* * * * *

May 17

Saint Restituta of Carthage

During the persecution of the Church under the Roman emperor Diocletian in the year 304, the virgin Restituta was arrested for being a Christian in the city of Carthage in modern Tunisia. She was tortured to try to make her give up her faith; when that failed, she was burned to death in a boat off the coast of Carthage.

Saint Paschal Baylon

Paschal was born in 1540 to pious parents in Torre Hermosa, Spain; he worked as a shepherd until he was twenty-four years old. When he decided to become a monk, he traveled two hundred miles to ask a fervent community of Franciscan Friars Minor living at Loreto if he could enter their order. They refused. But he persisted, and they eventually allowed him to enter, though they quickly realized that their new postulant was a very holy young man. Paschal became a brother in the Franciscan order and was deeply devoted to the Blessed Sacrament. His brother friars saw him kneel for hours before the tabernacle without any support and with his hands clasped and held in front of his face. He was once sent as a messenger to France to deliver an important message, and although he completed his mission, he barely escaped with his life. He was treated roughly and stoned, and he suffered a shoulder injury that caused him trouble for the rest of his life. At the moment he died in 1592, the church bells tolled for the Consecration at Mass, and he died speaking the Holy Name of Jesus.

Blessed Antonia Mesina

Antonia was born in 1919, the second of ten children in a peasant family in Sardinia, Italy. She went to school for four years, but she had to stop and care for the household instead when her mother became bedridden with a heart condition. Antonia became a member of Catholic Action, a group of lay Catholics that encouraged a Catholic influence on the culture. She was an active and lively young girl. One day in 1935, when she was sixteen years old, she was out gathering wood. A teenaged would-be rapist attacked her, and she fought him to her last breath. The Church acknowledges her as a martyr for purity.

> *Saint Restituta, show me how to live and die for Christ.*
> *Saint Paschal, beg the Lord to give me a heart full of love*
> *for His Real Presence in the Blessed Sacrament.*
> *Blessed Antonia, help me to seek purity in my life.*

* * * * *

May 18

Saint John I, Optional Memorial

John was the fifty-third pope (d. 526); he reigned for three years. Italy's ruler, King Theodoric, was a follower of the Arian heresy, but he initially left Christians alone. Theodoric later became paranoid and saw conspiracies against him everywhere. When Pope John decided to go to Constantinople—the first pope to travel to that city—to crown Justin as the Eastern Roman emperor, Theodoric interpreted this as a political threat. He had John put in prison when he returned to Rome, and then he ordered John to be starved to death. John died of thirst and starvation in custody, a martyr for the Church.

Saint Eric of Sweden

When Eric became king of Sweden in the year 1150, he wanted to bring Christianity to his people. So he ordered the building of many Christian churches and invited at least one bishop to come evangelize the Swedish people. Though many people followed the king's example, some of his nobles objected and conspired with the king of Denmark to assassinate him. While King Eric was at Mass on the day after the Solemnity of the Ascension of the Lord, a messenger falsely brought him the news that an army was approaching. He replied calmly, "Let us at least finish the sacrifice; the rest of the feast I shall keep elsewhere."[21] He waited to the end of the Mass, then prayed and commended his soul to God, leaving the church marching in front of his guards. The conspirators surprised him, killed him, and cut off his head, making him a martyr in the year 1161.

Saint Felix of Catalice

Felix (1515–1587) was a farmer from Cantalice, Italy, who had wanted to become a Capuchin Franciscan friar for many years. At the age of thirty, he was finally able to leave his home and join the order as a lay brother. People began to call him Brother Deo Gratias because, whether people gave him anything or not when he was out begging for his community, he always replied, "Deo gratias," which means, "Thanks be to God." He was particularly attentive to young people, and he loved to speak of the value of praising God. His contemporary Saint Philip Neri thought highly of Felix.

Saint John, help me to love those who turn against me.
Saint Eric, help me to live as a Christian, regardless of opposition from others.
Saint Felix, show me how to praise and thank God unceasingly.

* * * * *

May 19

Saint Urban I

Urban was the seventeenth pope (d. 230); he reigned seven years. There was relative peace for the Church during part of his reign because the Roman emperor Alexander Severus and his mother were friendly to Christians, although the official laws against the Catholic faith remained unchanged. The Church grew accordingly during Urban's reign. Little else is known for certain about him, except that he died a martyr.

Saint Dunstan of Canterbury

Dunstan was from a noble English family, born around the year 910; his teachers were great Irish scholars. His uncle was Alphege, the bishop of Winchester and also a future saint. Alphege encouraged Dunstan to consider the religious life, but at first Dunstan said no. However, after Dunstan became ill with a skin problem that appeared to be leprosy and then recovered, he changed his mind. Dunstan became a hermit, built a cell to live in, prayed, studied, and supported himself with manual tasks, such as making bells and copying and illuminating

[21] Walsh, *Butler's Lives of the Saints*, 147–48.

books. Dunstan was also musically gifted and played the harp. Many years later, Dunstan was made the abbot of Glastonbury. As abbot, Dunstan encouraged education and made his abbey a great center of learning. When a young English prince's immoral behavior was causing a public scandal, Dunstan didn't hesitate to rebuke him, but he was forced into exile as a result and had to escape to Flanders. After a rebellion in England brought a new king to the throne, Dunstan was able to return home. He was eventually named archbishop of Canterbury; as the archbishop, he restored monasteries that had been destroyed by Danish invasions, reformed his clergy, and served as an advisor to successive kings. When Ethered became king of England, Dunstan predicted a reign full of calamities and retired from the court. At the end of his life, Dunstan spoke of his own death while preaching at Mass, chose a spot in which to be buried, and then died peacefully as he had predicted in the year 988.

Saint (Pietro) Celestine V

Born in 1215 in Sicily, Pietro Angelerio became a hermit and gradually formed a new monastic order from those who followed him. When the pope died and a conclave of cardinals in Rome failed to elect a new pope for two years, Pietro wrote a stern letter to them, telling them that God was displeased at their delay. They promptly chose him to be the new pope. He took the name Celestine V, but he reigned for only five months because, although he was a truly holy man, the challenges of being pope were too much for him. Some say he decided to resign because he could not say no to anyone, which caused confusion. Some say he resigned because he saw that he was being used by others for political gain. Whatever his reasons for resigning, he first tried to escape and live in solitude, but, at the order of Pope Boniface VIII, he was placed in a cell-like room in a palace, dying less than a year afterward in 1296.

Saint Crispino of Viterbo

Crispino (1668–1705) was consecrated to the Blessed Virgin by his mother when he was five years old. Even his neighbors in Viterbo, Italy, noticed his devotion from an early age and spoke of him as a little saint. One day, Crispino saw a procession of Capuchin friars in the street, and he recognized that God was calling him to religious life. He became a Capuchin lay brother, and he served the monastery as a cook. But his personal holiness eventually attracted visitors who wanted his spiritual advice and prayers too. These visitors included future priests, bishops, cardinals, and even a pope, although he treated all his guests with equal charity. It was said that he could predict the future and that miracles occurred when he touched the sick. He died of pneumonia. Centuries later, in 1959, his body was found to be incorrupt.

Saint Urban, help me to love Christ and His Church.
Saint Dunstan, show me how to speak the truth at all times.
Saint Celestine, help me know what God is asking of me.
Saint Crispino, teach me humility.

* * * * *

May 20

Saint Bernardine of Siena, Optional Memorial

Bernardine was born at Massa di Carrara, Italy, into a noble family in 1380. His parents died when he was only seven years old, but he was raised by an aunt and her daughter who loved him dearly and taught him of the love of God as well. As an adult, he took charge of a hospital when a plague struck the town, and he worked tirelessly to care for the sick and the dying. After the plague had ended and he himself had recovered, he cared for his aunt. When she died, he no longer had any earthly responsibilities, so he decided to enter the Franciscan Friars of the Strict Observance. He was so well loved, however, that many friends came to see him, and he was moved to another friary so that he could enjoy greater solitude. After he was ordained a priest, he lived quietly for about a dozen years, preaching only occasionally. The topic of his preaching, however, was often to encourage people to have a devotion to the Holy Name of Jesus and to call upon His name for help. Bernardine's zeal for Christ and eloquent preaching gradually began to attract large crowds and bring many people to conversion and repentance. Unfortunately, his success also provoked jealousy and even false rumors that he was encouraging superstition, so he was ordered by the pope to keep silence for a time. After he had been investigated by the authorities, he was completely exonerated of the false charges and was given full permission to preach wherever he liked. He was offered the position of bishop three times, but he always declined. The Franciscans eventually made him vicar general, and one of his more controversial decisions was to insist that that all the friars be educated in theology and canon law. This was contrary to Saint Francis' original rule but was clearly designed to help the friars in their vocations. After he retired from this position, he traveled all over Italy as a missionary. He died when he was sixty-four years old in the year 1444.

Saint Lydia of Thyatira

Lydia was a wealthy merchant—a "seller of purple goods"[22]—who heard the preaching of Saint Paul while he was in the city of Philippi (Greece). She was converted and baptized along with her family members.[23] She invited Paul and his companions to stay with her, and he did. After he had been imprisoned and released, he stayed in her home before leaving the area.

Saint Protasius Chong Kuk-bo

Chong was born in 1799 in Songdo of modern South Korea. He married and became a Christian. Due to the anti-Catholic persecution at the time, he left the faith at one point, but then he returned. He was imprisoned for being a Christian and was tortured before being martyred on this date in prison in 1839.

[22] Acts 16:14.
[23] Acts 16:15.

Saint Bernardine, show me how to rely on the Holy Name of Jesus at all times.
Saint Lydia, help me to be open to strangers, that they might lead me to Christ.
Saint Protasius, help me to pick myself up when I have fallen and return to God.

* * * * *

May 21

Saint Christopher (Cristobal) Magallanes Jara and Companions, Optional Memorial

During the Mexican Revolution (1910–1920), there was a brutal persecution of the Catholic Church. Of the many men and women martyred for the faith during this time, twenty-two priests and three lay companions of the Cristeros movement, which opposed the government's persecution of the Church, are acknowledged as saints on this date. All were martyred between the years 1915 and 1937. One of those priests was Christopher Magallanes. He was a parish priest with a strong devotion to the Virgin Mary and who had helped establish schools, carpentry shops, catechism centers, a mill, and agricultural cooperatives for the indigenous people of his area before the revolution. When the government closed seminaries, he opened his own. The government successively shut them down, until he finally had seminarians studying in private homes. He opposed armed rebellion against the government, but he was falsely accused of promoting revolution anyway. He was arrested while he was on his way to celebrate Mass secretly at a farm. Before he was executed, witnesses heard Father Christopher shout from his cell that he was innocent, that he forgave all those responsible, and that he asked God to bring peace to Mexico through his death. He gave away his possessions to his executioners, gave them absolution, and was shot to death on May 25, 1927.

Saint Eugene de Mazenod

Eugene (1782–1861) was the son of an arranged marriage between his aristocratic but poor father and his wealthy but middle-class mother. Their marriage was intended to improve the finances and positions of both families, which it did, but his parents had a stormy relationship with continual and bitter fighting. During the French Revolution, young Eugene and his family fled from France for their safety. They traveled in Italy, and there he was influenced by the pious example of Father Bartolo Zinelli, a local priest. Unfortunately, he was also exposed to the immoral life of rich nobles and grew up in an unsupervised, angry home. His parents ultimately divorced, which was highly unusual at the time. Surrounded by all this turmoil, Eugene was torn between choosing a life of secular success or the simplicity of religious life. One day, however, while he was praying at the foot of a cross on Good Friday, he felt himself touched by the power of God. Soon afterward, he entered the seminary and was later ordained. He gave up his family's wealth and accepted the humble, simple life of a parish priest. For example, in his service among the poor and through his preaching, he spoke in the local dialect, not the upper-class French he had been taught. He reached out to men in prisons, though he almost died from a case of typhus that he contracted there. He organized a group of priests to preach missions in the area, which eventually became a religious congregation known as the Oblates of Mary Immaculate. He eventually became the archbishop of Marseille, and there he built and restored churches, developed catechetical instruction for young people, and, by his personal example and good leadership, doubled the number of priests in his diocese. As archbishop, he received civil honors from the state, and even during his lifetime, his Oblates began traveling the world as missionaries, bringing Christ to others all over the world.

Holy Martyrs, show me how to forgive everyone
and everything out of love for Jesus Christ.
Saint Eugene, help me to find God's peace during times of conflict.

* * * * *

May 22

Saint Rita of Cascia, Optional Memorial

Rita was born in 1381 in Roccaparena, Italy. She was devout from childhood, and she unsurprisingly asked her parents' permission to become a nun. They refused, however, and chose a husband for her instead. Unfortunately, her husband turned out to be a brutal, unfaithful, and bad-tempered man. Rita not only bore his insults with Christian charity and patience for eighteen years, but she bore him twin sons. Eventually, her husband was moved to repentance for his cruelty, but shortly after his conversion, he was murdered. Her sons were angry and planned revenge on their father's murderer. Rita, horrified that her children would commit a mortal sin, prayed to God for them to be saved. Before they could carry out their plans, her sons became seriously ill. While she cared for them, they repented of their anger and died in her arms. Now that she was freed from family commitments, Rita tried to enter a convent and realize her lifelong desire to give her life completely to Christ. However, the convent refused her repeatedly because, contrary to their rules, she was a widow and not a virgin. Finally, because of her persistence, they allowed her to enter, and she lived a humble, obedient life as a nun. She often meditated on the sufferings of Christ, and while meditating one day, she became aware of a great wound in her forehead. To her, it felt as if a thorn from Jesus' crown of thorns had embedded itself in her head. The wound also became so foul-smelling that she was forced to live apart from the other sisters until her death. Yet after her death on this date in 1457, her body was found to be incorrupt.

Saint Julia of Corsica

Julia was from a noble Christian family living in the city of Carthage in northern Africa. When the Vandals invaded in 616, she was captured and sold into slavery to a pagan Syrian merchant and sent away on a slave ship. When the ship arrived in Corsica, a pagan festival was going on. Her new owner ordered her to participate in the pagan ceremonies, and when she refused, despite promises that she would be freed if she did, she was beaten. First, they tore her hair out of her head, and when she still refused, she was killed. It was the year 620.

Saint Humility (Rosanna) of Florence

Born to wealthy parents in 1226 in Faenza, Italy, Rosanna had wanted to enter a convent from the time she was young, but her parents insisted that she get married. Her husband, Ugoletto, turned out to be a frivolous and uncaring husband who mocked her Christian devotion. She bore her husband two sons, but they both died soon after being baptized. However, when Ugoletto became so ill that he almost died from a serious illness, he repented. After he recovered, he decided to enter religious life as a brother at a nearby monastery, while Rosanna chose to enter a convent, taking the name in religious life of Humility. After living for a time at the convent, she realized that she wanted to live a life of greater discipline than was practiced there. She chose to live as a penitent in a cell that was located against the wall of a church. She was bricked into her cell, lived on only bread, water, and herbs, and slept on her knees. After some years of this solitary life, the master general of the Vallumbrosan order begged her to become the abbess of their first nunnery. She agreed, founded that convent as well as a second one, and lived an austere and holy life until her death at the age of eighty-four in 1310.

> Saint Rita, help me to trust that God's grace can do the impossible.
> Saint Julia, give me the courage to do what is right, for the sake of Jesus Christ.
> Saint Humility, show me how to live simply out of love for Christ.

* * * * *

May 23

Saint Desiderius of Vienna

When Desiderius (d. 608) became the bishop of Vienna, Austria, his first task was to try to improve the immoral behavior of both his clergy and local leaders. After he made a point of publicly condemning the shameful actions of one of Queen Brunhildis' courtiers, she made up charges against him and complained to Pope Saint Gregory the Great. The queen then had Desiderius banished from the kingdom. This lasted for several years until the pope intervened and Desiderius' innocence was established. Years later when Desiderius corrected the immoral behavior of that queen's grandson, King Thierry of Burgundy, more false accusations were made. This time it was said that Desiderius was involved in an immoral relationship with a woman. While he was being arrested, men hired by the queen killed him, making him a martyr.

Saint John Baptist Rossi

John was born in 1698 near Genoa, Italy. When he was ten years old, his pious but poor parents allowed him to be taken away and trained in a nobleman's house. John's devotion and intelligence impressed others so much that his cousin, a canon, invited him to come to Rome to study at the Roman College when he was only thirteen years old. Later, John imposed such demanding mortifications on his body that his health broke down. But he recovered and was eventually able to complete his studies for the priesthood by the age of twenty-three. In addition to serving his parish, John served the needy: the sick, the dying, the homeless, and laborers. An excellent confessor, he brought many people back to the Church through that sacrament. When the position—and money—associated with his cousin's position as a canon was given to John, he gave the money to buy an organ for a church and pay the stipend for an organist to play it. Pope Benedict IV selected John to be the priest to give catechetical instruction to prison officials and state servants, and John also preached and gave many missions. At the end of his life, he suffered from a stroke. He recovered enough to say Mass afterward but then died of an apoplectic seizure in 1764. He was sixty-six years old.

> *Saint Desiderius, help me to correct the errors of others with charity. Saint John, teach me how to spend my life serving God and His people.*

* * * * *

May 24

Saint Manean

According to Scripture, Manean was a friend of Herod Antipas—and a friend of Jesus Christ. He was also one of those early Church leaders who prayed over Saints Paul and Barnabas before sending them out on their first missionary journey.[24] Tradition says that he may have been the source of information for King Herod's words and actions in the Gospel of Luke and that he was a founder of the Church in Antioch.

Saint Joanna

According to Scripture, Joanna was married to Chuza, King Herod Antipas' steward, and she supported Jesus and His disciples.[25] She was also one of the women at the tomb of Christ on Easter Sunday.[26]

---

[24] Acts 13:1–3.
[25] Lk 8:3.
[26] Lk 24:10.

Saint Vincent of Lerins

Vincent (d. 445) was a soldier when he arrived at the Abbey of Lérins in France and asked to become a monk. He later also became a priest and an eloquent ecclesiastical writer. His major work was *The Commonitorium against Heresies*, in which he explains the principles he had gathered from the Fathers of the Church for distinguishing truth from falsehood. Part of the document has been lost to us, but the forty-two chapters we do have contain the important axiom that a dogma is to be regarded as a Catholic truth if it is held always, everywhere, and by all the faithful. Vincent's work has been controversial since it was written; some say that Vincent wrote it in opposition to the extreme Augustinian view of predestination that was being debated at the time, and they propose that many of the monks in Lerins (including Vincent) at that time were followers of some tenets of the Pelagian heresy. As *Butler's Lives of the Saints* says, "If St. Vincent erred in that direction he erred in company with many other holy men."[27] Vincent is considered a Father of the Church.

Saint John del Prado

John was born around the year 1563 in Morgobresio, Spain; he became a priest and then entered a Franciscan order. He was sent to Morocco in 1630, and there he cared for the needs of the small Christian community living there. On this date in 1631, the local Muslim ruler had him arrested and imprisoned because he was a Christian. John was scourged before being executed.

> *Saint Manean, help me find friends who will help me to eternal life.*
> *Saint Joanna, help me find ways to care for Christ's disciples today.*
> *Saint Vincent, teach me the truths of our faith.*
> *Saint John, show me how to live and die for Christ.*

* * * * *

May 25

Saint Bede the Venerable, Optional Memorial

Bede was born around the year 672 into an England that had recently become Christian. He was educated at the Abbey of Saint Peter and Saint Paul at Wearmouth-Jarrow, and he studied under the direction of a great abbot, Saint Benedict Biscop. As a monk and a priest, he spent his whole life at this abbey, teaching and writing on many subjects and eventually becoming the most learned man of his day. He's known as the Father of English History because his *Ecclesiastical History* provides almost all we know about early England, but most of his writings were Scripture commentaries. He lived a holy life until his death in the year 735. An old breviary summarized his life by saying that "[h]e

---

27 Walsh, *Butler's Lives of the Saints*, 154.

always read, he always wrote, he always taught, and he always prayed."[28] For his faithful, scholarly contributions to the teachings of the Church, he was declared a Doctor of the Church in 1899 by Pope Leo XIII.

Figuratively speaking, the fact that both before and after [Jesus] gave his opinion he bent and wrote on the ground admonishes us that both before we rebuke a sinning neighbor and after we have rendered to him the ministry of due correction, we should subject ourselves to a suitably humble examination, lest perhaps we be entangled in the same things that we censure in [our neighbors], or in any other sort of misdeeds.[29]

Saint Gregory VII, Optional Memorial

Gregory's birthname was Hildebrand, and he was born around the year 1020, educated in Rome, and became a Benedictine monk. He declined the papacy on one occasion and served as an advisor to several popes. When he was later elected pope, he only accepted because of his desire to confront the serious problems in the Church at that time which were caused by simony and a corrupt clergy. Though he took the name of Gregory when he became pope, the reform that he instituted became known as the Hildebrandine reform and was followed by many good and holy Church leaders. However, despite the fact that the emperor Henry IV had promised to help Gregory with these changes, the emperor sided with his enemies when Gregory tried to force the clergymen who had literally bought their way into their positions to step down. Gregory was driven into exile, and Henry supported an anti-pope who tried to take Gregory's place. In the ensuing political battles between Gregory and Henry, Gregory lost support and was driven into exile in Salerno, Italy. Pope Gregory, one of the greatest reformers in the history of the Church, died of natural causes in the year 1073.

Saint Mary Magdalene de Pazzi, Optional Memorial

Mary (1566–1607) was raised in a devout family in Florence, Italy, and she was sent to a convent to be educated when she was fourteen years old. Although her family initially wanted her to marry, they eventually agreed to her desire to become a Carmelite nun. Mary became a great mystic, and she spent her life in prayer and self-denial. She particularly focused on prayer for renewal in the Church and experienced many graces in prayer.

Saint Madeline Sophie Barat

Madeline was born in 1779 in France, and her father was a cooper and owner of a small vineyard. Her brother Louis, who was eleven years older and had become a priest, was convinced that God had destined her for some great work in God's service. During the French Revolution, Louis lived in great danger

---

[28] Christopher Rengers, O.F.M. Cap., and Matthew E. Bunson, K.H.S., *The 35 Doctors of the Church*, rev. ed. (Charlotte, N.C.: TAN Books, 2014), 223.

[29] Bede the Venerable, *Homilies on the Gospels, Book One, Advent to Lent*, trans. Lawrence T. Martin and David Hurst, O.S.B., Cistercian Study Series 101 (Athens, Ohio: Cistercian Publications, 1991), 248.

while serving Catholics in secret and spent two years in prison. After the revolution, he brought Madeline to Paris with him. Since the revolution had literally destroyed Catholic schools in France, Louis' Jesuit superior wanted to found an institute of consecrated women to educate young girls. Although Madeline was only twenty-one years old, she and three other female postulants agreed, and two years later, she became the superior of the new order, the Society of the Sacred Heart. Over the following decades, her order expanded, and she and her nuns eventually taught children in twelve countries and on two continents. In 1865, she died at the age of eighty-six after a short illness.

Blessed Nicholas (Mykola) Tsehelsky

Nicholas was born in 1896 in the Ukraine and was a Greek Catholic. He married, had four children, was ordained, and served as a parish priest. After World War II, the Soviets tried to intimidate him and had him beaten and arrested. Simply because he was Catholic, he was sentenced to ten years of hard labor in Modovia, Russia. He died while in prison on this date in 1951, a martyr for the faith.

> *Saint Bede, show me how to seek and find God's truth.*
> *Saint Gregory, teach me how to afflict the comfortable and comfort the afflicted.*
> *Saint Mary Magdalene, help me to pray.*
> *Saint Madeline, show me how to serve the needs of those around me.*
> *Blessed Nicholas, help me to face persecution with trust in God.*

* * * * *

May 26

Saint Philip Neri, Memorial

Philip was born in 1515 in Florence, Italy. Although his mother died when he was a young boy, his father remarried, and Philip was raised by a loving, pious stepmother. Philip was a good, happy child. When he became a young man, his family sent him to the city of San Germano to live with a childless relative, who (it was hoped) would make him his heir. Soon after he arrived in the city, though, Philip underwent what he referred to as his "conversion". This experience caused him to be no longer interested in any worldly plans or goals; he only wanted to serve Jesus Christ. He traveled to Rome, trusting solely in divine providence to get him there, and he happened upon Galeotto Caccia, a man who gave him room and board in exchange for becoming a tutor to Caccia's two young sons. Philip lived like a recluse for two years, spending his days and nights in prayer except when he served as a tutor, and he began to study philosophy and theology on his own. Suddenly he was moved by God to stop all his studies. Instead, he simply stood on city streets, talked with people as they passed by, and invited them to join him as he helped the sick in hospitals and visited the Seven Pilgrim Churches in Rome. Gradually, the laymen who followed him became a confraternity, and they met for spiritual exercises and cared for pilgrims who came to Rome. Philip's confessor was convinced he could do more to help people if he became a priest, so Philip was ordained to the priesthood. By God's grace, Philip could read the souls of those who came to him for confession, and many people later attested to Philip's mystical gifts, which included levitation during prayer. He also led spiritual conferences and brought many people to conversion. Several other priests joined him, and they began to live in community together, becoming known as Oratorians because they used a bell to summon their members to prayer (since the Latin word *orare* means "to pray"). When the pope gave Philip an ancient church to use, Philip had it torn down and built a new one (the Chiesa Nuova) in its place. On May 25, 1595, on the Solemnity of Corpus Christi, everyone thought Philip looked radiantly happy, and his doctor said he hadn't looked so well for a decade. He spent the day as usual, meeting visitors and hearing confessions, but at the end of the day, he told those around him, "Last of all, we must die."[30] Later that night, he developed a hemorrhage, and it was clear he was dying. The other priests of his community were called, and his successor, Father Baronius, asked him to bless his sons. Philip died while bestowing his blessing upon them. He was eighty years old.

Saint Eleuterus (Eleutherius)

Eleuterus was the thirteenth pope (d. 189); he reigned for fifteen years. He was born in Nicopolis, Greece, and he was a deacon before he became pope. The Montanist heresy, which was founded by a man who claimed that he was the incarnation of the Holy Spirit, spread to Rome during Eleuterus' reign. Eleuterus attempted to preserve the unity of the Church by responding to the claims of Montanus without alienating Christians who had been misled into his false teachings. Eleuterus was martyred in Rome and is buried near Saint Peter in the Vatican.

> Saint Philip, pray for me to be converted to a deeper love of God.
> Saint Eleuterus, help me lead people from falsehood to truth.

* * * * *

May 27

Saint Augustine of Canterbury, Optional Memorial

Augustine (d. 705) was a Benedictine monk living in Rome when Pope Saint Gregory the Great decided to send him and thirty other monks to bring the Christian faith to England. On the way to England, they heard rumors about

---

[30] Walsh, *Butler's Lives of the Saints*, 158.

the ferocity of the pagan English people along the way. This scared his companions, so Augustine wrote to the pope. Pope Gregory encouraged them, saying he was convinced that this was the proper time for the evangelization of the Anglo-Saxons, so Augustine and his monks continued on their way to England. As the pope had predicted, the English were open to the Gospel, and many people were baptized. Augustine purified and consecrated pagan temples before making them into Christian churches, he rebuilt ancient churches that had fallen into ruin since the first evangelization of the English centuries before, and he tried to conform the new English Church's practices to follow Roman practices as much as he could. After serving as archbishop of Canterbury for only seven years, Augustine passed away.

Saint Julius of Dorostorum

Julius (255–302) had been a soldier in the Roman army for twenty-seven years when he became a follower of Christ. He continued to serve in the army for some time until one of his fellow soldiers reported him as a Christian. He was stationed at Dorostorum (modern-day Bulgaria) at the time. The prefect offered Julius bribes to renounce his faith in Christ, but when he refused, he was beheaded and died a martyr.

> *Saint Augustine, teach me how to evangelize in today's world.*
> *Saint Julius, show me how to be a soldier for Christ.*

* * * * *

May 28

Saint Germanus

Germanus (496–576) was a priest and abbot from Autun in France. He happened to be in Paris at a time when the office of bishop was vacant, and the king chose him to become the new bishop. As bishop, Germanus set a holy example for his people by dressing and eating simply and caring for the poor; his fervor and good works brought many people to repentance. A truly holy man, he wasn't afraid to speak up, even to the king when necessary, to oppose immoral behavior and the wars of the nobility.

Blessed Margaret Pole

Margaret was born in 1471 of the royal Plantaganet family in Somerset, England, and was the niece of King Edward IV and King Richard III of England. She married Sir Richard Pole in 1491. Together, they had five children, and when she became a widow, she became the unofficial ward of King Henry VIII, who made her the countess of Salisbury and governess to his daughter, Princess Mary. However, when she opposed the king's marriage to Anne Boleyn, she was sent away from the court. When her son Reginald Cardinal Pole wrote against the king's attempt to claim spiritual supremacy over the Church in England, the king sought revenge against the entire family. Two of Margaret's other sons were executed simply because they were Reginald's brothers, and Margaret herself was arrested and sent to the Tower of London under the obviously false charge of plotting a revolution. When there was an actual uprising against the king two years later, she was summarily executed without a trial and died a martyr in 1541.

Saint Germanus, show me how to care for the poor today.
Blessed Margaret, help me to bear injustice with love and forgiveness.

* * * * *

May 29

Saints Sisinnius, Alexander, and Martyrius of Trentino

Sisinnius was a deacon, and Alexander and Martyrius were lectors in the Church in the fourth century. The three men were sent by their bishop, Saint Ambrose of Milan, to spread the Gospel to the people living in the Alps Mountains in Austria. In Trentino, they built a small church. Some of the pagans living there opposed the Christian faith and attacked them. The three men were killed by being burned alive using wood from the church they had built. They died in 397.

Blessed William Arnaud and Companions

In the thirteenth century, eleven men, led by Dominican priest William Arnaud, were sent to Toulouse, France, as part of a Church Inquisition. Their assignment was to investigate those following the heresy of Albigensianism in that area and help Christians return to a true understanding of the Catholic faith. The heresy was so widespread in the region of Toulouse that when they arrived in any town, angry mobs would gather and threaten them. However, the men—who were variously Dominicans, Benedictines, Franciscans, clergymen, and lay brothers—simply preached the truth of the Gospel, leaving each town while peacefully chanting the Salve Regina and the Apostles' Creed. When they arrived at Avignonet in 1242, they stayed in a castle with what they thought was a friendly host. However, their host betrayed them and sent a band of soldiers into their room in the middle of the night to kill them all. The men died praising God and singing the Latin hymn Te Deum. After their deaths as martyrs, God showed his favor through miraculous cures that occurred at their graves.

Saint Ursula Ledochowska

Ursula was born in Austria in 1865, one of five children, and was given the name Julie by her parents. Her father was a Polish count, and her mother was a Swiss noblewoman. Her family was pious, so pious that it included an uncle who became a Polish cardinal and an older sister who (like her) later founded an order of religious sisters. Unfortunately, the family finances failed, the family moved to Poland, and her father died soon afterward. As a young woman, she felt God calling her to religious life, so she became an Ursuline nun, taking the name in religious life of Ursula as well. She and her nuns went to Russia to serve the Catholic immigrants living there until she was expelled during the Communist Revolution because she was Austrian. A woman of deep faith, Ursula founded her own religious order of Ursulines to educate and serve the poor and needy, now known as the Ursulines of the Sacred Heart (or Gray Ursulines). She lived in Scandinavia, where she wrote a Catholic catechism in Finnish, but she eventually moved to Rome to direct her order more effectively. The congregation she founded expanded to serve in eleven different countries. She died in 1939.

Saint Paul VI

Giovanni Montini was born in 1897 in Italy, the son of influential parents and with two brothers. He served in the Vatican's Secretariat of State soon after entering the priesthood and was noted for his administrative and pastoral abilities. He became archbishop of Milan in 1954, and he succeeded Pope Saint John XXIII in 1963. When he became pope, he chose the name Paul to emphasize his desire to continue dialogue between the Church and the modern world, in the tradition of the famous Apostle Paul. He continued the Second Vatican Council and saw it to completion in 1965. He instituted its reforms, including making changes to the Curia, reducing the trappings of the papacy, and traveling on many pilgrimages. Great crowds met him in his travels—but so did an assassination attempt. His writings on many topics, most notably contraception, were controversial at the time, but his predictions regarding the negative repercussions of widespread access to birth control, for example, came true. As a deeply spiritual man living during turbulent times, he faced great opposition, but his life of heroic virtue led him to be declared a saint after his death. He died in 1978.

> Holy Martyrs, help me to live for Christ and His Bride, the Church.
> Saint Ursula, show me how to serve the needy.
> Saint Paul, help me face opposition with the peace of Christ.

* * * * *

May 30

Saint Dymphna of Ireland

Damon was a pagan Irish chief who lived between the seventh and ninth centuries. When his wife died and he was unable to find a woman beautiful enough to replace her, the grief-stricken man decided to marry his teenage daughter, Dymphna, who was a devout Christian. In horror, she ran away from her father with Gerebernus, an elderly Catholic priest who was also a family friend. Dymphna's enraged father found her, and he killed both the priest and his daughter. Both are considered martyrs, though we don't know the date of their deaths.

Saint Hubert of Liege

Hubert (d. 727), like the martyr-saint of the early Church Eustace, experienced a deep conversion on Good Friday. He was out hunting—not a very pious activity for such a holy day—and he saw a stag with a crucifix in its antlers when he heard a voice tell him that he was destined to go to Hell unless he gave his life over to Christ. Hubert, who was a widowed courtier at the time, obeyed the voice. He left the life of the court, became a priest, and served his bishop, Lambert. Later, Hubert lived as a hermit, at his bishop's direction. When Bishop Lambert was executed for daring to criticize King Pepin for committing adultery, Hubert was made his successor. Hubert made Liege, Belgium, the seat of his diocese, and one of his primary works was to bring the Gospel to people in the area who still followed paganism.

Saint Ferdinand III of Castile

Ferdinand was born in 1198 to Spanish nobility; his father was the king of Leon, and his mother was a princess of Castile. When Ferdinand grew up, he became king not only of Castile and Leon, but also the Spanish kingdom of Galicia. He married, and he and his wife had ten children. After that wife's death, he and his second wife had five more children. A strong leader, Ferdinand not only unified Spanish kingdoms, but he was the mastermind behind the reconquest of large parts of Spain, returning them from Muslim control to native control. In his acts as king, Ferdinand always used his power justly rather than for personal gain. In his private life, he became a Third Order Franciscan, was very forgiving, and had a great devotion to the Blessed Mother.

Saint Joan of Arc

Joan was born in 1412 in a small town of France. When Joan was only fourteen years old, she had a vision in which she saw a blaze of light and heard a voice speak to her from Heaven. Later, she heard several voices, which she gradually identified as Saints Michael, Catherine, Margaret, and others. These voices explained that God had a mission for her to help her troubled nation, which had been fighting a losing battle with England for several decades. After some time, the voices told her to present herself to the commander of the king's forces in a nearby town. When she obeyed, the commander laughed at her and sent her away. But she had made a prediction to him about an imminent defeat in a battle, and when that prediction came true, the commander decided to take Joan, dressed as a man, to see the dauphin, the heir apparent to the French crown. Even though the dauphin disguised himself, Joan was able to recognize him among the crowd of people and, after she spoke privately to him, he was convinced of her truthfulness. A group of theologians examined her, and when they agreed about her orthodoxy, she was given white armor and permission to lead the king's forces personally against the English. Her humility, simple faith, personal presence, and strong leadership revitalized the demoralized French troops and towns—and brought many military successes for the French. She was wounded in battle, but she recovered, and she happily saw what she had been longing for: the dauphin crowned as king of France at the cathedral in Rheims. But when she was captured in battle by the English soon afterward, the weak king did nothing to help her. The English imprisoned her and tried her on many charges, but her humble, insightful, and spirited answers to the complicated questions of a roomful of learned men mystified them, as they unsuccessfully attempted to trick her into some error to justify their opposition. Despite her holiness, deep faith, and innocence, she was condemned to death in 1431 by burning at the stake, dying a martyr.

Saint Dymphna, teach me how to bring healing to those
who are wounded in their hearts and minds.
Saint Hubert, help me repent deeply.
Saint Ferdinand, show me how to become a Christlike leader.
Saint Joan, help me become so small that God can do great things through me.

* * * * *

May 31

The Visitation of the Blessed Virgin Mary, Feast

According to the Gospel of Luke,

> In those days Mary arose and went with haste into the hill country, to a city of Judah, and she entered the house of Zechariah and greeted Elizabeth. And when Elizabeth heard the greeting of Mary, the child leaped in her womb; and Elizabeth was filled with the Holy Spirit and she exclaimed with a loud cry, "Blessed are you among women, and blessed is the fruit of your womb! And why is this granted me, that the mother of my Lord should come to me? For behold, when the voice of your greeting came to my ears, the child in my womb leaped for joy. And blessed is she who believed that there would be a fulfilment of what was spoken to her from the Lord."[31]

Saint Petronilla of Rome

Petronilla was a first-century Roman citizen who became a Christian and was martyred for the faith. There are many legends about Petronilla's life—that she was related to Saint Peter (the apostle), that she was one of his converts, or that she worked with him. Regardless, it's clear that she gave her life for Christ.

[31] Lk 1:39–45.

Saints Cantius, Cantianus, and Cantianella of Rome

Cantius and Cantianus (brothers) and Cantianella (their sister) were born into a noble Roman in the late third century. When their parents died, they were placed in the care of a guardian named Protus, who raised them in the Catholic faith. During the persecution of Christians under the Roman emperor Diocletian, they sold their possessions, gave the proceeds to the poor, and fled from Rome. They only got as far as the Italian city of Aquilea before they were caught. When they refused to renounce their faith in Christ, they were beheaded and died as martyrs together in the year 304.

> *Blessed Mother, may my soul proclaim the greatness of the Lord.*
> *Holy Martyrs, help me to be rich only in what matters to God.*

June

June 1

Saint Justin Martyr, Memorial

Justin was born to Greek parents living in Nablus, Palestine, around the year 100. The Catholic Church was illegal and underground at the time, but when Justin learned about the Christian faith while studying Greek philosophy, he decided to become a Christian. He even publicly opened a school of Christian philosophy in Rome, debated the faith using philosophical arguments, and wrote explanations of the faith. Because of his public witness, he was finally arrested during the reign of the Roman emperor Marcus Aurelius. He defended the Christian faith during his trial but was ultimately condemned, dying a martyr in 165. His final writings defending the faith have been an inspiration to apologists for centuries, and he's considered a Father of the Church.

> *[When asked by the Roman prefect Rusticus about the teachings he believed, Justin replied,]* "That according to which we worship the God of the Christians, whom we reckon to be one from the beginning, the maker and fashioner of the whole creation, visible and invisible; and the Lord Jesus Christ, the Son of God, who had also been preached beforehand by the prophets as about to be present with the race of men, the herald of salvation and teacher of good disciples. And I, being a man, think that what I can say is insignificant in comparison with His boundless divinity, acknowledging a certain prophetic power. since it was prophesied concerning Him of whom now I say that He is the Son of God. For I know that of old the prophets foretold His appearance among men." ... Rusticus said, "Are you not, then, a Christian?" Justin said, "Yes, I am a Christian."* [1]

Saints Ammon, Zeno, Ptolomy, Ingen, and Theophilus of Alexandria

Ammon, Ingen, Ptolomy, and Theophilus were arrested in Alexandria, Egypt, for the crime of being Christians during the reign of the Roman emperor Decius in 249. During the trial, the Roman soldier Zeno encouraged them not to apostatize, so he too was arrested. They were all martyred together.

Saint Eneco (Inigo)

When King Sancho the Great of Spain sought to reform a lax religious house at Oña in the eleventh century, his first choice as abbot died soon after taking

---

[1] Justin Martyr, *The Martyrdom of Justin* 1–2, trans. Marcus Dods, in *Ante-Nicene Fathers*, vol. 1, ed. Alexander Roberts, James Donaldson, and A. Cleveland Coxe (Buffalo, N.Y.: Christian Literature Publishing, 1885). Revised and edited for New Advent by Kevin Knight, NewAdvent.org, accessed October 1, 2019, http://www.newadvent.org/fathers/0133.htm.

over. So the king then visited a saintly hermit named Eneco in person and convinced him to accept the position. Under Eneco's leadership, the monastery grew in holiness and attracted many new monks, which led other monasteries to follow its example. Eneco negotiated peace between feuding communities, prayed successfully for rain during a drought, and is said to have fed a large, hungry crowd with only three loaves of bread. At the end of his life, he had to be carried home to his monastery on a stretcher. When he and his companions reached the abbey, Eneco asked for the boys with torches who had accompanied them to be given food. Since no one else had seen these boys, it was presumed that the holy man saw angels lighting the way. He died around the year 1060.

Holy Martyrs, help me explain my faith in Christ to others.
Saint Eneco, help me trust that angels are always at my side to help me follow Christ.

* * * * *

June 2

Saints Marcellinus and Peter of Rome, Optional Memorial

Marcellinus was a priest of Rome, and Peter was a deacon and exorcist of Rome. Both were known for their piety. During the persecution of Christians under the Roman emperor Diocletian in 304, the two men were martyred in the woods just outside Rome. The Roman emperor Constantine built a basilica over their tomb, and their names are mentioned in the first Eucharistic Prayer at Mass.

Saint Erasmus (Elmo)

Erasmus (d. ca. 303) was the bishop of Formiae, Italy. He escaped the persecution of Christians ordered by the Roman emperor Diocletian by living in the mountains. He was finally discovered, arrested, tortured, and martyred. According to one tradition, his tortures included having his intestines wound around a windlass, which later caused him to become known as the patron of intestinal problems and childbirth. Erasmus is one of the Fourteen Holy Helpers, great saints who were called upon particularly for help during the bubonic plague in the fourteenth century.

Saint Eugene I

Eugene was the seventy-fifth pope (d. 657); he reigned for more than two years. As pope, he was known to be a gentle, kind man who was generous with the poor. Despite the emperor's threats that he would roast Eugene alive for his opposition to the Monothelite heresy that the emperor supported, Eugene spoke and wrote strongly in favor of the orthodox Catholic understanding of

Jesus having two wills (human and divine) as well as two natures (human and divine). Eugene died of natural causes.

> *Saints Marcellinus and Peter, show me how to live the Mass every moment.*
> *Saint Erasmus, help me face physical infirmities with the peace of Christ.*
> *Saint Eugene, help me love Christ and His Church.*

* * * * *

June 3

Saints Charles Lwanga, Joseph Mkasa, and Companions, Memorial

When the faith came to Uganda through missionary priests known as the White Fathers in the nineteenth century, the local ruler wasn't unfriendly to Christians. However, this leader was succeeded by Mwanga, a man who was strongly opposed to Christianity. When Mwanga executed a Protestant missionary, one of his courtiers, Joseph Mkasa, reproached Mwanga both for the murder and for demanding sexual favors, particularly from the boys serving in Mwanga's court as pages. In retaliation, Mwanga had Mkasa executed for a trivial offense. Later, Mwanga learned that one of his pages had been receiving instruction in the Catholic faith. In a rage, Mwanga thrust a spear through the throat of the page's Christian teacher and that night set guards around his palace to prevent anyone from escaping. One of the young Christians, Charles Lwanga, anticipated the danger and secretly baptized some of the pages who had been learning about the Catholic faith, to strengthen them to face what he knew was coming. The next morning, the king ordered all the Christians in his palace to separate themselves from the others. Seventeen men under the age of twenty-five and two soldiers complied. Mwanga asked these men and boys if they intended to remain Christians, and they said yes. For seven days, they were mistreated while they were forcibly marched to a site thirty-seven miles away. They were then brought before a huge pyre, were bound, and were laid on the fire to be burned to death. The chief executioner killed one of the boys before he was placed on the fire: it was his own son. In the years following this initial persecution in 1886, many Catholics and Protestants were cruelly tortured and executed for the faith in Uganda.

Saint Clotilda of France

Clotilda was born a princess of Burgundy (a region of modern France) around the year 474. Raised a Catholic, she married King Clovis of the Franks, though he was a pagan at the time. With his consent, her children were baptized, and with the help of a saintly bishop, she eventually converted her husband to the faith. After Clovis' death, she served as a peacemaker and reconciled her sons when they fought one another over the succession to the throne. When she died in Tours in 545, all who knew her acclaimed her a saint.

Holy Martyrs, help me to speak out against grave sin to protect others, at any cost.
Saint Clotilda, show me how to bring Christ's peace to my family.

* * * * *

June 4

Saint Quirinus of Siscia

Quirinus was bishop of Siscia (now in Croatia) in the fourth century when he was arrested, interrogated, whipped, and put in prison for his refusal to sacrifice to pagan gods. Even in prison, he converted people to faith in Christ. Finally, he was executed by being thrown into a river with a stone around his neck, dying a martyr.

Saint Francis Caracciolo

Francis was born into a powerful, noble family that was related to Italian princes and Saint Thomas Aquinas at Abruzzi, Italy, in 1563 and given the birthname of Ascanio. When he was twenty-two years old, he developed a skin disease. His condition was considered so hopeless that he promised God that he would become a priest if he recovered. When he did recover—miraculously—he kept his vow, eventually being ordained a priest. He particularly cared for those who were in prison. When a priest named John Adorno sent a letter to an identically named relative of his and asked him to join a community of saints, he mistakenly received the letter but happily accepted the offer. The two men founded the order of Minor Clerks Regular, and he took the name in religious life of Francis.

Saint Quirinus, help me to think more of Christ's love than of my sufferings.
Saint Francis, help me keep my promises to God.

* * * * *

June 5

Saint Boniface of Germany, Memorial

Winfrid was born around the year 680 in Devonshire, England. He decided to become a monk when he was only five years old after listening to the conversation of some monks who visited his home. He was educated at a monastery and eventually did become a monk, a popular and talented teacher, and a priest.

When he heard of the missionary work of the bishop Saint Willibrord in bringing the faith to Friesland (modern Germany), he begged his abbot's permission to leave as a missionary. He and two companions were given permission to go, but when he reached Friesland, he recognized that it was not yet time for the faith to be accepted by the people there. So he returned to his monastery and lived quietly as a monk. When it was time to elect a new abbot for his monastery, Winfrid's brothers wanted him to be their abbot, but Winfrid knew God was calling him to serve elsewhere. He traveled to see the pope and discussed the evangelization of the Germanic peoples with him. The pope gave him a commission to preach the Word of God in Friesland and changed his name to Boniface. As Boniface, he returned to Friesland, where he assisted Bishop Willibrord and worked energetically to spread the Catholic faith. When a pagan ruler in the area died, he realized that the time was finally right and personally cut down a sacred oak tree that was venerated by the local people. When no pagan gods punished Boniface for his "sacrilege", the people were forced to admit the powerlessness of their gods. Over the next decades, Boniface invited monks and nuns to come help him evangelize; he was named a bishop, worked to correct abuses in his newly created diocese, was named primate of Germany, and survived various political changes that threatened the growth of the faith in his adopted land. When he was in his seventies, he began a missionary trip with thirty companions down the Rhine River, preaching and baptizing in areas that had not yet been evangelized. A hostile group of pagans suddenly attacked them, and Boniface refused to let his companions defend him. He was killed first, followed by his companions. It was the year 754.

Saint Sanctius of Cordoba

Sanctius was born in Albi, France. He was captured by Muslims and, like many Christians, was treated as a prisoner of war. He was educated in the Muslim court in Cordoba, Spain, and became a guard there. When he refused to abandon his Catholic faith and become a Muslim, he was sentenced to death by being impaled on a stake. He died in the year 851.

> *Saint Boniface, help me recognize God's timing.*
> *Saint Sanctius, help me to remain faithful to Christ.*

* * * * *

June 6

Saint Norbert of Magdeburg, Optional Memorial

Norbert was born into a noble family at Xanten, Germany, in 1080. He lived a frivolous and worldly life, and he received minor orders and became a canon only because it gave him a stable income. One day, he was thrown from his horse during a violent thunderstorm, and he was left unconscious. When he woke up, his first words were those of Saint Paul: "What shall I do, Lord?"[2] He heard a voice inside him tell him to do good, not evil, and to pursue peace. So he did. Like Saint Paul, Norbert's conversion was instantaneous, complete, and deep. At first, people were suspicious, but he sold everything except the most essential possessions. He lived as a monk for three years, was ordained a priest, and then traveled barefoot to see the pope. After hearing Norbert's general confession, the pope gave him permission to preach the Gospel wherever he chose. Norbert's preaching particularly deepened the faith of the laity through his emphasis on the importance of the Mass and the Eucharist. A later pope didn't give him the same freedom to preach, but a bishop asked Norbert to come to his diocese to reform a group of Augustinian Canons Regular living there. When the canons rejected Norbert, the bishop gave him some land in a valley instead. On this land, Norbert formed his own religious order, which eventually reformed monastic life elsewhere through their example. His monks wore a white habit and lived a rule mostly following the Rule of Saint Augustine. His order, called the Norbertines or Premonstratensians (because his first house was built in a valley called Prémontré), grew and eventually included an order for nuns as well as tertiaries, the first Third Order in the history of the Church. When he was made a bishop, Norbert continued to live like a monk; it's said that he dressed so simply that the porter at his new bishop's residence initially refused to let him enter the house. Norbert was a humble man, but he was a fearless shepherd. He corrected abuses among his clergy, worked to restore church property that had been taken by laymen, and continued to direct his Premonstratensian houses while serving as bishop of Magdeburg in Germany. When an anti-pope arose, causing schism and confusion, Norbert supported the true pope and worked with civil leaders to restore the pope to Rome. He died at the age of fifty-three in the year 1134.

Blessed William Greenwood

When King Henry VIII of England made himself the head of the Church in England in the sixteenth century, he tolerated opposition from no one. William Greenwood was a lay brother in the Carthusian monastery in London. Because he refused to accede to Henry's policies, he was arrested, sent to Newgate Prison, and starved to death in 1537, dying a martyr for his faithfulness to Christ's Church.

Saint Norbert, help me to be converted daily.
Blessed William, show me how to live and die for Christ.

* * * * *

[2] Acts 22:10.

June 7

Saints Peter, Wallabonsus, Sabinian, Wistremundus, Habentius, and Jeremiah of Cordoba

These six men were monks living in Cordoba, Spain, during a time when Muslims controlled the region. In 851, Muslim leaders renewed the persecution of Catholics; when these six men were confronted and publicly professed their faith in Christ, they were beheaded and their bodies were publicly displayed, mistreated, and burned before the ashes were dumped in a river.

Blessed Anne of Saint Bartholomew

Anne Garcia was born in 1549 in Almeneral, Spain; she tended sheep when she was young. She became a lay Carmelite under the great Carmelite Saint Teresa of Avila's direction when she was twenty years old. Later, she became Teresa's secretary and friend, as well as a nun, and Teresa died in her arms. After Teresa's death, Anne was sent to France to implement the Carmelite reform there. She became prioress at Tours and Pontoise, and she founded a Carmelite house at Antwerp in 1612. She also wrote poetry. She died on this date in 1626.

Saint Antony Gianelli

Antony was born in 1789 in Genoa, Italy, to a middle-class family. As a young man, everyone knew him to be gentle, industrious, and intelligent. While studying for the priesthood and still only a subdeacon, he was granted permission to preach because of the power of his preaching to attract crowds. He served as an ordinary parish priest, but he also preached missions, taught about the faith, was widely sought out as a confessor, and eventually founded two religious congregations: for priests, the Missioners of Saint Alphonsus; for women who taught poor children and nursed the sick, the Sisters of Saint Mary Dell'Orto. As bishop of Bobbio, Italy, he impressed his flock with his prudence, virtuous life, and good administration skills. He died in 1846.

> *Holy Martyrs, help me face down opposition with Christ's peace.*
> *Blessed Anne, help me to live a life of silence and prayer.*
> *Saint Antony, show me how to reach out to those in need.*

* * * * *

June 8

Saint William of York

William (d. 1154) was born into the powerful, noble FitzHerbert family in England. After becoming a priest, he was raised to important positions in the

Church due to his family's prominence. William was a likeable and popular man, but he was also lazy. When he was controversially elected to be the archbishop of York in England, it was widely believed that he had been given the position only because he had promised the king that he would serve the king's interests first and the Church's second. But William was eventually able to convince the pope that he would serve the Church fairly, so he was ordained to the position and began an ecclesiastical reform of his diocese. However, William failed to receive the pallium (official vestments of his office) from the papal legate—apparently because he was such a procrastinator. Then the pope died, and Eugene III, a Cistercian who had opposed William because of the appearance of simony, was elected as pope. Tensions escalated when William's hotheaded and noble relatives attacked Fountains Abbey simply because the abbot happened to be a friend of the new pope. In the attack, an archdeacon who had also been proposed for William's position as archbishop was mutilated (to prevent him from ever holding the office), and the abbey's farms were burned. As a result, the angry Pope Eugene had William deposed, and a new archbishop was chosen to replace him. During these events, William had gone personally to the pope to plead his case (unsuccessfully), and now he returned to England and lived quietly with an uncle. The violence and personal humiliation he had suffered left William chastened and penitent. After William had spent six years in this self-imposed penance, the pope died, Saint Bernard of Clairvaux (who had also opposed William) died, and the man who had succeeded William as archbishop died—all within a few months. William was able to convince the new pope, Anastasius IV, to restore him to his position as archbishop; when he entered York again, the entire city rejoiced. William visited Fountains Abbey almost immediately, and he promised restitution for the damage done by his relatives, showing no resentment toward those who had opposed him. However, he died a month later in the year 1154. After his death, miracles were reported at his tomb, which led to his canonization by the Church.

Saint Jacques Berthieu

Jacques was born in 1838 in Monlogis, France, to a family of farmers. He was ordained a priest in 1864 and joined the Jesuits in 1873. He was sent as a missionary to Madagascar a few years later, and he became the superior of their mission, bringing many people to the faith. Political troubles in the area forced him to move around the area several times. On this date in 1896, Menalamba rebels, angry that their local practice of the worship of ancestors had been replaced by Christianity, shot and killed him.

> *Saint William, help me to accept humiliations without complaint.*
> *Saint Jacques, show me how to bring Christ to others.*

* * * * *

June 9

Saint Ephraem (Ephrem) the Syrian, Optional Memorial

Ephraem was born at Nisibis (modern Syria) around the year 306. His Christian parents had been faithful to the Church and confessed, rather than denied, their faith in Christ during times of persecution under the Roman Empire. Ephraem was baptized into the faith when he was eighteen years old. He served under four bishops of the city of Nisibis and lived through three sieges of the city. Out of humility, he refused to be ordained for a long time, and it's debated whether he ever became a deacon (which is likely) or a priest (some say it's possible). When Nisibis was conquered by the Persian army, he left and went to live alone in a cave that overlooked the city. Living on barley bread and vegetables, wearing a patched tunic, and looking like an ascetic, people said that he never laughed, but that he did weep frequently. When a local leader began popularizing Gnostic teachings by writing hymns with Gnostic lyrics, Ephraem responded by organizing choirs of young women and teaching them to sing, and then writing hymns of his own with Catholic theology. The beauty and truth of the Gospel in his hymns spread the Good News and eventually defeated Gnosticism in the area. Late in his life, he traveled to spend time with a holy bishop, Saint Basil the Great. After his return, there was a severe famine, so Ephraem helped in the distribution of goods to the poor and died soon afterward. It was the year 373. The Syrians call him the Harp of the Holy Ghost, and the beauty, truth, and faithfulness of his writings (poems, hymns, and homilies) led him to become known not only as a Father of the Church, but also as a Doctor of the Church.

> Blessed are you if you will be a daughter to Mary / whose eye scorned all persons. / She turned her face away from everything / to gaze on one beauty alone.[3]

Saints Primus and Felicianus

These two men were brothers and Christians living in Rome during the days of the Roman Empire. They were arrested for the crime of being Christians, tortured, and beheaded together in the year 286 on the Roman road called the Via Nomentana.

Saint Columba of Iona

Columba (521–597) was a son of Irish royalty, but he left it all behind to become a monk and then a priest. He was a great lover of learning, a poet, and a scholar, and it's said he transcribed more than three hundred books in his lifetime. Many of his pupils later became great Irish saints. His life was not without controversy, however. It's not clear whether he left Ireland with many of his monks because he was forced into exile over a disagreement with local leaders or whether he left to bring the Gospel to the pagan peoples of the area. Either way, he and his

---

[3] Ephrem the Syrian, *Hymns*, trans. Kathleen E. McVey (New York; Mahwah, N.J.: Paulist Press, 1989), 367.

monks lived a holy monastic life on the island of Iona and converted the northern Picts (of modern Scotland), including their king, to Christianity.

Saint Joseph de Anchieta

Joseph (1534–1597) was from a wealthy family and was born in the Canary Islands of Spain. His spine became dislocated when he was young, causing him great pain. He became a Jesuit when he was seventeen years old, and the order sent him as a missionary to Brazil, partially in hope that the climate would improve his physical condition. It didn't, and his back condition caused him constant pain all his life. However, Joseph was good at languages. He soon learned the language of the Tupi natives with whom he worked, and he developed a book of grammar and a dictionary for them, which was used by Portuguese missionaries and settlers for many years. At one point, he was held hostage by another tribe of natives for five months. During this time, he composed a long poem (over four thousand lines) about the Blessed Virgin Mary, which he was only able to write in the sand. When he was released, he was able to write down the poem that he had written and memorized. He was outspoken in his opposition to the widespread enslavement of the native peoples, he converted the Maramomis tribe to the Catholic faith, and, because he also wrote plays, he's considered the father of Brazilian national literature.

Blessed Anna Maria Taigi

Anna Maria Gianetti was born in Siena, Italy, in 1769, but her family moved to Rome when she was five years old due to financial troubles. She worked as a servant until, in 1789, she married Dominico Taigi, who was a butler for a noble family. Together, they had seven children, though two of them died while young. At first, their family could hardly be called holy; her husband could be bad-tempered, and Anna Maria was overly concerned with her appearance and apparently had (or came close to having) an adulterous affair. However, after a powerful experience of God during prayer, she repented deeply of her past behavior. She began to live a more austere life and to listen more attentively to the voice of the Holy Spirit in her heart. She decided to become a Trinitarian tertiary, visited the sick, and regularly gathered her family to pray together in a small personal chapel. Through her good and holy example, her husband's attitude gradually improved. She began to experience mystical gifts: prophecy, clairvoyance, visions, and ecstasies. Though she was a simple woman, popes, cardinals, and royalty eventually came to her humble home to seek her advice. Unfortunately, she was also frequently the subject of gossip and slander during her lifetime. But after her death on this date in 1837, the entire city mourned.

Saint Ephraem, help me to weep for my sins.
Holy Martyrs, show me how to live and die for Christ.
Saint Columba, give me your love of learning.
Saint Joseph, show me how to accept the crosses I am given and to use them for God's glory.
Blessed Anna Maria, help me to lead my family to Christ.

* * * * *

June 10

Saint Landry of Paris

Landry (d. ca. 656) was the bishop of Paris, and he founded the first hospital. This became, over the centuries, the famous Hotel-Dieu de Paris, the oldest hospital in the world still in operation. Landry personally cared for the poor, and he also encouraged the founding of Benedictine monasteries in his diocese.

Blesseds Thomas Green and Walter Pierson

During the reign of King Henry VIII (r. 1509–1547), the king made himself head of the Church in England and demanded that people publicly accept his authority. In the Carthusian monastery in London, Thomas Green was a choir monk and Walter Pierson was a lay brother. When these men refused Henry's demands, they were arrested and put in Newgate Prison. They died of starvation on this date in 1537.

> *Saint Landry, show me how to reach out to those who are sick.*
> *Holy Martyrs, help me be thankful for my daily bread.*

* * * * *

June 11

Saint Barnabas, Memorial

Joseph was a Levite from Cyprus. The apostles gave him the surname "Barnabas (which means, Son of encouragement)".[4] He was the first Christian to sell his property and give the proceeds to the Church,[5] he was the one who introduced Saint Paul to the Christians in Damascus,[6] and he was a missionary partner with Paul until they had a disagreement over their assistant, Mark.[7] A letter attributed to him has come down to us, and some conjecture that the biblical book of Hebrews was written by him as well. According to tradition, Barnabas died a martyr by being stoned to death on Cyprus around the year 60 and is considered a Father of the Church.

Saint John de Sahagun (John of San Facundo)

John Gonzalez de Castrillo was born in 1419 into a devout and noble family in Sahagun, Spain, the oldest child of seven. He was educated at a Benedictine abbey and ordained a priest in 1445. His father obtained several benefices for

---

[4] Acts 4:36.
[5] Acts 4:37.
[6] Acts 9:27.
[7] Acts 15:39.

him, essentially as financial investments, but John only kept one, which he administered carefully and devoutly, giving the proceeds of the others to the poor. He continued his studies as a priest, survived a major illness and surgery, and then decided to become an Augustinian Canon. He rose to become prior of the order in Salamanca in 1471. But it was his devotion that stirred the hearts of those around him to call him a saint. John often received visions during Mass; for example, the Host appeared surrounded by light or Christ Himself appeared in bodily form at the Consecration of the Host. Some saw John levitate when he was praying, and he could read the hearts of his penitents in confession. His preaching was powerful, but not always well received: when he preached against the wastefulness of spending money on extravagant clothing, women threw stones at him; when he preached on the dignity of workers, a duke hired assassins to kill him. But the assassins realized that John was a holy man, so they refused to hurt him and asked his forgiveness. Some say John died of natural causes on this date in 1479, while others say he was poisoned by a woman whose lover left her after listening to John preach.

Saint Paula Frassinetti

Paula (1809–1882) was only nine years old when her mother died. She developed health problems when she was twenty-one, so she was sent to live with her brother, who was a parish priest on the outskirts of Genoa, Italy. Paula felt herself drawn to teaching children whose parents couldn't afford their education. With her brother's support, she started an institute to educate children, but when she met Don Passi (who had already founded the Sisters of Saint Dorothy), she joined her work to his. The work of their sisters spread throughout Italy and into other countries, and the order received papal approval. Paula was a devout, tactful, self-sacrificing, and practical woman. For example, when a sister told her that she wanted to die to be with Christ, Paula replied that God hadn't asked her advice over the date of her birth, and He wouldn't want it for the date of her death. She was said to have a great insight into people's characters and to understand the secrets of their hearts. Worn out by her untiring work, she died peacefully after a series of strokes.

Blessed Ignazio Maloyan

Choukrallah was born at Mardin, Turkey, in 1869. He became a priest in 1896 and took the name of Ignazio. He served as a parish priest in the cities of Alexandria and Cairo, was the assistant to the Armenian Catholic patriarch until health problems interfered, and then became archbishop of Mardin in 1911. Christians in Turkey had been victims of persecution since the beginning of World War I; in 1915, Turkish soldiers began to threaten Christians again, under the false claim that they were hiding weapons. On June 3, 1915, Ignazio was arrested along with many other Catholic priests and laymen. When brought into court, the local police chief ordered Ignazio to convert to Islam, and when he refused, he was beaten, tortured, chained, and imprisoned. On today's date in 1915, Ignazio and four hundred other condemned Christians were forcibly marched into the desert. When they stopped, Bishop Ignazio celebrated an impromptu liturgy with scraps of bread for all of them. All four hundred were then murdered and died as martyrs. Ignazio was shot last, after refusing one more time to renounce Christ and convert to Islam.

> *Saint Barnabas, show me how to encourage those who lack faith.*
> *Saint John, teach me how to pray with fervor.*
> *Saint Paula, help me to be both practical and pious.*
> *Blessed Ignazio, show me how to do all things with and for Christ.*

* * * * *

June 12

Saint Basilides of Rome

Basilides died a martyr for Christ in the early days of the Church; he was later buried on the Appian Way in Rome. He is mentioned in a list of saints collected by Saint Bede in conjunction with three other saints: Cyrinus, Nabor, and Nazarius. Although other details are lacking, Christians have been remembering Basilides' faithfulness to Christ for many centuries.

Saint Leo III

Leo was born in 750 in Rome; he was ordained a priest, was raised to the rank of cardinal, and became papal treasurer under Pope Hadrian. In the year 795, the pope died. To avoid the likely danger of political interference in a prolonged papal election, Leo was named pope immediately after the late pope's burial. However, two of Hadrian's nephews were furious that they hadn't been elected pope, so they gathered a group of nobles and attacked Leo as he was riding in a procession. Their intention was to blind him and cut out his tongue, making him unable to serve as pope; but Leo was able to escape to a monastery and recover from his injuries. His attackers then raised false charges against Leo, and Charlemagne, the king of the Franks and the most powerful layman of the time, placed guards around him to protect him while he investigated the allegations. Leo was exonerated of the charges—he even swore to accept trial by ordeal to demonstrate his innocence; ultimately, his opponents were condemned and sent into exile. Soon after this dramatic beginning to his papacy, Leo crowned Charlemagne as the Holy Roman Emperor. The two men worked together to halt the spread of Islam into Europe, restore destroyed churches, and resolve quarrels between European nations. Leo died on this date in the year 816.

> *Saint Basilides, show us how to live and die for Christ.*
> *Saint Leo, teach me how to serve Christ and His Church at all times.*

* * * * *

June 13

Saint Anthony of Padua, Memorial

Anthony was born to noble parents in Lisbon, Portugal, and given the birth-name of Ferdinand. As a young man, he joined the Augustinian Canons and took the name in religious life of Anthony. Unfortunately, so many friends came to visit him that the order had to move him to a different priory. Anthony was gifted with an excellent memory, and through prayer and personal study, he developed deep, personal knowledge of Scripture. When relics of Franciscan friars who had died for the Catholic faith in Morocco were brought to the community where he lived, he was so deeply moved that he entered the Franciscan order so that he could follow the friars in martyrdom. Soon after becoming a friar, the Franciscans sent him to Morocco, but he became sick on the journey and had to return to Europe almost immediately. He traveled to Assisi, attending the last chapter meeting of the Franciscans that was open to all members of the order; he personally saw the humble Saint Francis sitting at the feet of Brother Elias, the order's vicar general, during the meetings. Next, Anthony was sent to a hermitage where he lived in solitude for a time. But, during a ceremony attended by many vowed religious, it was discovered that none of the Dominicans or Franciscans present had prepared a speech. They decided that one of the many newly ordained priests should speak, perhaps as a test. Anthony was randomly chosen, and his address moved his listeners so deeply that the Franciscans immediately sent him out to preach the Gospel. Anthony had a voice that carried well over a crowd; he was well educated and knowledgeable and had a charismatic personality. Not surprisingly, his preaching drew great crowds of people, and he brought hardened criminals, heretics, and careless Christians to conversion and the sacraments, particularly the Sacrament of Confession. His logical, Scripture-based, and effective sermons against the Cathari heresy in particular caused him to be nicknamed the Hammer of Heretics. The Franciscans appointed him to various positions, but he primarily worked as a missionary and lived in the city of Padua, Italy. In 1231, he was preaching a course of sermons when he became ill. He was given the last rites and died; he was only thirty-six years old. He was canonized within a year of his death because of the many miracles that occurred due to his intercession afterward. Today, he's often invoked as a patron saint for lost items because, according to one story, a fellow friar "borrowed" his personal breviary and returned it, years later and after having left and returned to the Church—all because of Anthony's prayers. Anthony was later declared a Doctor of the Church.

For the faithful need be adorned with the linen of chastity, the blue of contemplation, the purple of the Lord's passion, and the twice dyed scarlet of the twin love of God and neighbor.[8]

---

[8] Anthony of Padua, *Sermones for the Easter Cycle*, ed. George Marcil, O.F.M. (Ashland, Ohio: Franciscan Institute Publications, 1994), 86.

Blessed Marianna Biernacka

Marianna was born in 1888 in Lipsk, Poland; she was raised in the Orthodox Church but became a Catholic when she was seventeen years old. She married when she was twenty and gave birth to six children, but only two survived, a daughter and a son. When her husband died, she moved in with her son and helped to care for her grandchildren. She particularly set an example to her grandchildren through her personal piety. During World War II, her town was under the control of Nazi forces, but local groups would secretly resist the Nazis and constantly cause trouble. The Nazis would retaliate by entering the town and killing random citizens. On June 1, 1943, soldiers arrested Marianna's son and pregnant daughter-in-law, Anna, for execution. Marianna begged the soldiers to take her in place of Anna, and they finally agreed. Marianna asked only to take her rosary with her. After being held in prison for a short time, she and her son were executed by firing squad on this date in 1943.

> *Saint Anthony, help me to study and love Sacred Scripture.*
> *Blessed Marianna, help me be ready to lay down my life for others today.*

* * * * *

June 14

Prophet Elisha

Elisha or his father must have been a wealthy man in Israel in about the eighth century B.C. because Elisha was plowing with twelve yokes of oxen when the prophet Elijah called him to be his disciple. Elisha served Elijah faithfully until Elijah's death, took over Elijah's mantle of authority (spiritually and literally), and led his people during a time of persecution.[9] He was also known for the miracles that resulted from his prayers.

> *When Elisha came into the house, he saw the child lying dead on his bed. So he went in and shut the door upon the two of them, and prayed to the LORD. Then he went up and lay upon the child, putting his mouth upon his mouth, his eyes upon his eyes, and his hands upon his hands; and as he stretched himself upon him, the flesh of the child became warm. Then he got up again, and walked back and forth in the house, and went up, and stretched himself upon him; the child sneezed seven times, and the child opened his eyes. Then he summoned Gehazi and said, "Call this Shunammite." So he called her. And when she came to him, he said, "Take up your son."[10]*

Saint Methodius I of Constantinople

Methodius was born in Sicily (Italy) around the year 800. Although he traveled to Constantinople with the goal of receiving a post in the imperial court, he changed his mind and decided to follow the example of a holy monk he met, embracing the religious life instead. He became a monk himself, and, in time,

[9] See 1 Kings 19:19—2 Kings 13:21.
[10] 2 Kings 4:32–36.

he built an entire monastery for the monks on the island of Chios. But later the patriarch of Constantinople, Saint Nicephorus, called Methodius to join him in Constantinople. There, both Nicephorus and Methodius were outspoken in their opposition to Byzantine emperor Leo's iconoclastic persecution of those who venerated images. The patriarch was eventually sent into exile as a result, and Methodius left the city to report the situation to the pope in Rome. When Emperor Leo died, Methodius returned to Constantinople with a letter from the pope asking for the reinstatement of the exiled patriarch. However, the new emperor, Michael the Stammerer, was even worse than his predecessor; he replied by having Methodius scourged, deported from Constantinople, and imprisoned. Methodius spent the next seven years in prison next to two thieves, one of whom died but was left to rot in his cell. When Methodius was finally released, he was physically emaciated as a result of his imprisonment, but he was still unbowed in spirit and faithfulness. The next emperor, Theophilus, continued the iconoclastic persecution, but when he died, his wife, Theodora, became regent for her infant son. She, on the other hand, supported the use of sacred images, so she allowed the exiled clergy to return and restored images to churches. Methodius became the patriarch of Constantinople in place of John the Grammarian, the supporter of iconoclasm who had been forced into the position by the emperor Leo. As patriarch, Methodius held a synod of bishops, which formally supported the use of icons, and he also held a festival (which is still celebrated in the Eastern Church) to celebrate the restoration of icons to their proper place. His time as patriarch was not completely peaceful; he unfortunately had a quarrel with some monks over the orthodoxy of some writings of the monk and saint Theodore the Studite. Methodius died in 847 of dropsy (a swelling in the extremities now called edema and sometimes related to congestive heart disease) after serving as patriarch for only four years.

Saints Anastasius, Digna, and Felix of Cordoba

A double monastery of monks and nuns had been established in Cordoba, Spain, by the ninth century. Digna was a nun there, and Felix and Anastasius were monks. By order of the Muslim caliph who ruled the area in the year 853, these three religious were executed for their Catholic faith, making them the first to die as martyrs in Cordoba.

> *Prophet Elisha, help me serve God faithfully all my life.*
> *Saint Methodius, show me how to persevere in times of persecution.*
> *Holy Martyrs, show me how to live and die for Christ.*

* * * * *

June 15

Prophet Amos

Amos was a shepherd who answered God's call to preach to His people in the kingdom of Israel during King Jeroboam II's reign and who lived in the eighth century B.C. Amos preached against the people's tendency to worship idols and to live without truly caring for God and those in need.

> Seek good, and not evil, that you may live; and so the LORD, the God of hosts, will be with you, as you have said.[11]

Saint Vitus of Rome

This young Christian from fourth-century Rome was apparently devout (he had two angels) and well-to-do (he had a tutor named Modestus and a nurse named Crescentia). He was also known for the miracles that resulted from his prayers, and his most famous miracle was the healing of the Roman emperor Diocletian's son from epilepsy. He was arrested along with his tutor and nurse for being Christians, but all three were eventually released. They escaped to the city of Lucania, but when they were told to worship pagan gods and refused, all three were condemned and were martyred by being boiled to death in oil. Vitus is one of the Fourteen Holy Helpers, great saints who were called upon particularly for help during the bubonic plague in the fourteenth century.

Saint Germaine of Pibrac

When Germaine was born on a small farm in Pibrac, France, around the year 1579, she was sickly, hairy, and had a deformed hand. Her father was a farm worker who didn't care for her, and her mother died when she was very small. When her father took a second wife, the woman actively disliked and mistreated her stepdaughter. Germaine was forced to sleep under the stairs or in the stable with the animals, was fed only scraps, was kept away from her healthy step-siblings, and was sent to work in the fields as soon as possible. There she took care of the sheep. But in her loneliness, God spoke to her through the natural world around her. She was very devoted to the celebration of Mass. When she heard the bell calling people to Mass in her town, she would plant her shepherd's staff in the ground, ask her guardian angel to guard her flock, and run to attend and receive her Lord. Despite the fact that there were wolves in the woods that commonly threatened other domesticated animals, her sheep always remained safe. Her neighbors noticed her deep devotion, as well as the way she shared even the scraps she was given with beggars. One day in winter, her stepmother chased her with a stick and accused her of having stolen bread. Her pitying neighbors would have protected her, but when Germaine's apron fell away, she was found to have summer flowers, not bread. This miracle amazed everyone, including her family, who now recognized her holiness and offered to let her live in the house again. She preferred to stay in her stable, and there she died and was found one morning when she was only twenty-two years old in the year 1601. Her incorrupt body remains in Pibrac.

> Prophet Amos, help me speak God's words to others.
> Saint Vitus, teach me perseverance.
> Saint Germaine, help me see beauty in all that God has created.

* * * * *

[11] Amos 5:14.

June 16

Saint Cyricus and Julitta

Julitta was a wealthy Christian widow who left the city of Iconium (modern Turkey) in the year 304 with her three-year-old son, Cyricus, and her two maids in order to escape Christian persecution under the Roman emperor Diocletian. However, they were recognized as Christian fugitives along the way, were arrested, and were put on trial by the governor, Alexander. When Julitta admitted that she was a Christian, Alexander ordered her to be taken away and tortured, and Cyricus started to cry. Alexander took the small child on his knee, but the boy scratched Alexander's face. In anger, Alexander threw the child down the nearby steps, which killed him instantly. Julitta thanked God aloud that her child had died a martyr, which angered Alexander even more. Julitta was ordered to be tortured with hooks before being beheaded. The maids recovered the two martyrs' bodies and buried them.

Saint Lutgardis of Aywieres

Lutgardis was born in 1182 at Tongres, Belgium. She was placed in a convent when she was twelve years old for the practical reason that the money her parents had intended for her dowry had been lost in a business venture and they assumed she wouldn't be marriageable without it. Lutgardis was attractive and fond of entertainment and clothes. At first, she lived like a boarder at the convent, without any apparent vocation to religious life. However, our Lord appeared to her one day while she was entertaining a friend. He showed her His wounds and asked her to love Him only. She obeyed. Some scoffed and said it wouldn't last, but instead her devotion grew. Lutgardis seemed to be able to see our Lord with her eyes, for when she was called away to perform a task, for example, she would politely ask the Lord to wait for her to come back until she returned. In time, when she meditated on our Lord's Passion, drops of blood appeared on her forehead and hair. After twelve years at the convent, she decided to live under the stricter Rule of the Cistercians. Following the advice of the nun known to us as Saint Christina the Astonishing, she entered the Cistercian convent of Aywieres. At that convent, however, only French was spoken, a language Lutgardis never learned very well. But that provided her with a useful excuse to be unable to hold an office in the monastery in her later years. Lutgardis was gifted with prophecy, healing, and an infused (God-given) knowledge of the Scriptures. She was also able to provide spiritual consolation to others. She was blind for the last eleven years of her life, a trial that she accepted with joy as a means of being detached from the visible world. Our Lord warned her when her end was near, and he told her three things: to praise God for all that she had received, to pray without ceasing for the conversion of sinners, and to rely on God alone—until He came to bring her to Heaven. She died on this date in 1246.

Saints Cyricus and Julitta, show me how to accept all things out of love of God. Saint Lutgardis, help me praise God for what I've received, pray without ceasing for the conversion of sinners, and rely in all things on God alone.

* * * * *

June 17

Saint Ranieri of Pisa

Ranieri was born around the year 1115 and was raised in Pisa, Italy. He lived an immoral life until his aunt convinced him to speak with a holy monk. With the monk's help, Ranieri realized that there was more to life than self-indulgence. At first, he was so deeply converted and full of sorrow for his past sins that Ranieri's parents were afraid for his sanity. He then traveled to places connected with Jesus' earthly life, and he began making other personal sacrifices. He struggled with his addiction to alcohol for a time, until he had a dream in which he carried a purse full of burning tar, which could be extinguished only by water. This dream finally enabled him to give up alcohol entirely for the rest of his life. He ate only two days a week, went barefoot, and lived a humble life in a monastery in his hometown of Pisa, although he never became a priest or deacon. He died around the year 1160.

Saint Peter (Phero) Da

During the persecution of Christians under the emperor Tu Dac, Vietnamese Christians were arrested, imprisoned, and killed. Peter (1802–1862) worked as a carpenter, but he was also a Catholic and served his Catholic parish as a sacristan. The authorities arrested and tortured him before his execution. He was burned at the stake on this date in Nam Dinh.

Saint Ranieri, help me be truly repentant for my sins and to live a penitential life. Saint Peter, show me how to serve Christ in my parish.

* * * * *

June 18

Saints Mark and Marcellian of Rome

Mark and Marcellian were twins born of pagan parents living in third-century Rome. According to tradition, they converted to the Christian faith and became deacons. During the persecution of Christians under the Roman emperor Maximian Herculeus in the year 286, they were arrested and imprisoned; one of the Christians who visited them in prison was the future martyr-saint Sebastian.

Mark and Marcellian were tortured and executed for being Christians by being nailed to a post and then run through with a lance. The two men were buried near the Catacomb of Saint Domitilla, and their relics were rediscovered in 1902.

Blessed Oseanna Andreasi

Oseanna was born in the city of Mantua in 1449 into a noble Italian family. She was devout even as a child, receiving a mystical vision of angels, paradise, and the Trinity that affected her deeply. When she grew up, her father wanted her to marry, but she instead chose to become a Dominican tertiary when she was seventeen years old. She spent the next thirty-seven years of her life living with her family, caring for her brothers and sisters after their parents died, personally serving the poor and sick, donating from the family's considerable fortune to help those in need, and correcting even her rich and powerful friends and family members when they lacked charity or morality in their behavior. She also received other mystical gifts from God; she would sometimes fall into ecstasies when speaking about Him, received visions of Christ, received the pain and red marks of the stigmata on her body, and encouraged others in their spiritual growth. She died of natural causes at the age of fifty-six in 1505.

Saint Gregory Barbarigo

Gregory was born in 1625 in Venice, Italy, and his father was a devout and learned nobleman who ensured that his son was well educated in his Catholic faith. Gregory studied law and became friends with the papal nuncio Fabio Chigi, becoming a priest when he was thirty years old. When Chigi was elected Pope Alexander VII, Gregory moved to Rome to support his friend, and he brought his library with him, studying science as well as Church history. (Pope Alexander was a pious man who lived a moral life. But he gave power to his relatives later in his reign, and those men abused their positions for personal profit, which has marred history's verdict of his papacy.) During a plague, Gregory personally helped with relief work, and when he was made a bishop, he was quick to implement the reforms ordered by the Council of Trent in his own diocese. He required his clergy to be tested for competency before they were allowed to hear confessions, banned the clergy from attending the theater and thereby giving scandal, distributed devotional books, and improved his seminary. When he became a cardinal, he reformed his new diocese, particularly by encouraging better education. When he visited parishes, he would specifically test parishioners' knowledge of the faith. Although he was a candidate for pope in three papal elections, he was never elected. While his heavy duties left him less time for study, he still encouraged others to continue to learn. In 1697, he died of natural causes in Padua and was buried there.

> *Saints Mark and Marcellian, show me how to live and die for Christ.*
> *Blessed Oseanna, help me live every day in Christ's presence.*
> *Saint Gregory, help me to understand my faith more fully every day.*

* * * * *

June 19

Saint Romuald, Optional Memorial

Romuald was born into a noble family at Ravenna, Italy, around the year 950; he lived a wild life as a young man. When he was about twenty years old, his father killed a man during a quarrel. Romuald was horrified that his father had become a murderer, so he ran to a nearby monastery. He lived there as a monk for the next three years and then became a hermit under the direction of another hermit named Marinus. In time, he was asked to return to the monastery and later became the abbot. After serving two years as abbot, he returned to his life as a hermit, though he was called upon to found more monasteries and hermitages. He wasn't afraid to rebuke leaders who used violence to get their way, and one of the men he moved to repentance was the future saint Peter Orseolo, the Doge of Venice who had (according to some) murdered his predecessor to take his position. Romuald died in 1027.

Saints Gervase and Protase of Milan

During the early persecution of the Church, Gervase and Protase were brothers and Christians living in Milan. They died as martyrs in an unknown year, but their relics were discovered by Saint Ambrose of Milan in the year 386.

Saint Juliana Falconieri

Juliana was born in 1270 into the nobility in Florence, Italy. Her father died when she was young, so her mother and her uncle, Alexis, who was one of the founders of the Servite order, directed her upbringing. She never liked the typical amusements of girls her age, and when she found out that a marriage was being arranged for her, she announced that she wanted to consecrate herself to God instead. She was only fifteen years old, so her mother initially opposed her decision, but eventually Juliana became a Servite tertiary and lived at home. Her mother changed her mind so completely that she later placed herself under her own daughter's spiritual direction. When her mother died, Juliana led a community of women who performed works of mercy and focused their lives on prayer. The short sleeves that the women wore led them to be called Mantellate, a term later applied to all female tertiaries. Juliana was reluctantly made their superior, and because she drew up the Rule for the Servite Nuns, she's also called its founder. At the end of her life, digestive problems kept her from receiving Holy Communion, which was a great trial for her since she had been accustomed to the unusual privilege of receiving our Lord three times a week. She died in 1341 at the age of seventy-one.

Blesseds Sebastian Newdigate, Humphrey Middlemore, and William Exmew of England

Sebastian (d. 1535) came from a pious and wealthy Catholic family, and his sister became a nun. He married, and after being widowed, he became a priest.

He served as a counselor to King Henry VIII. He was a Carthusian monk in the London Charterhouse when he was ordered to sign Henry's Oath of Succession, which was one of Henry's early acts against the Catholic Church when it opposed his invalid marriage to Anne Boleyn. Sebastian signed the document, but only after adding the words "in as far as the law of God permits"[12] to it. Two of his fellow Carthusian monks—the priest Humphrey Middlemore and the vicar and noted classical scholar William Exmew—were arrested with Sebastian in 1535 on the charge of loyalty to the pope. They were chained for several days in prison, transferred to the Tower of London, and condemned to death on the same day with the bishop-martyr John Fisher. These three men were hanged, drawn, and quartered for their Catholic faith on this date at Tyburn.

Blessed Thomas Woodhouse

Thomas (d. 1573) was ordained a Catholic priest in England in the reign of Queen Mary Tudor, during the brief period of time when Catholicism was not illegal. He served as a rector for a year, but when anti-Catholic persecution resumed, he went to Wales and lived as a tutor. In 1561, he was arrested for the crime of celebrating Mass. While in prison, he met priests of the Jesuit order and became a Jesuit himself. In 1572, after years in prison, he began writing. At first, he sent letters directly to Queen Elizabeth's chief advisor, William Cecil, encouraging him to reconcile with the Catholic Church, and when he was locked up further, he wrote other letters on the same theme and merely tied them to rocks and threw them from his window. He was sentenced to death and then was hanged, drawn, and quartered on the same day as Blesseds Sebastian, Humphrey, and William above—but thirty-eight years later.

> *Saint Romuald, show me how to live a penitential life while remaining in the world.*
> *Saint Juliana, help me balance prayer and works of mercy in my life.*
> *Holy Martyrs, help me to be always loyal to Christ's Church.*

* * * * *

June 20

Saint Methodius of Olympus

During the persecution of the Church under the Roman emperor Diocletian, Methodius was the bishop of the city of Tyre (modern Lebanon). He was arrested for being a Christian and died a martyr around the year 311. His many theological works were collected and studied by later generations of Christians; Saint Jerome was one of his admirers. He's considered a Father of the Church.

---

[12] "Blessed Sebastian Newdigate", CatholicSaints.Info, accessed October 1, 2019, https://catholicsaints.info/blessed-sebastian-newdigate.

Blessed Dermot O'Hurley

Dermot was born into a wealthy family in Emly, Ireland, around the year 1530. He studied in Belgium and became a lawyer and teacher of the law. He was still a layman when Pope Gregory XIII chose him to be the archbishop of Cashel, Ireland, in 1581. Because of the anti-Catholic laws of Queen Elizabeth, Dermot returned to Ireland clandestinely and constantly changed his location to avoid detection. But when one of the men who had been hiding him was suspected by the authorities, he turned himself in. He was imprisoned, tortured, and executed by hanging on this date in 1584 in Dublin.

Holy Martyrs, help me remain faithful to Christ in my daily challenges.

* * * * *

June 21

Saint Aloysius Gonzaga, Memorial

Aloysius was born in 1568 into a noble family that served the royal family of Italy. Although his father wanted him to pursue a military career, the only thing Aloysius wanted to pursue was holiness. However, he obediently studied secular subjects, appeared in public when required (although a painful kidney disease gave him an excuse to limit his social activities), traveled with his family according to his father's responsibilities, and fulfilled his duties by waiting on and studying with a young Italian prince, Don Diego. Aloysius was determined to become a Jesuit missionary, so he "practiced" by teaching the catechism to poor boys around him and living an ascetic life. He also fasted three days a week on bread and water, refused to have a fire lit in his room even in cold weather, and scourged himself as a physical mortification. When Aloysius' father learned that Aloysius wanted to become a Jesuit, he was furious with his son, and most of his relatives argued with and even threatened him. However, his father finally gave in and allowed Aloysius to give over the rite of succession to his younger brother. Aloysius then entered the Jesuit novitiate. There, he was forced to live under regular discipline (less strict than what he had chosen for himself) and take better care of his health. However, when he volunteered to help with plague victims, he caught the disease himself and never fully recovered. While on his deathbed in 1591, Aloysius asked his spiritual director, Cardinal Robert Bellarmine, if it was possible to go to Heaven without entering Purgatory. Saint Bellarmine, who knew Aloysius well, told him that it was possible and that Aloysius could hope for such a grace. Aloysius fell into an ecstasy of prayer that lasted all night; he seemed to recover, but then he died, with Bellarmine nearby, at the age of twenty-three.

Saint John Rigby

John (1570–1600) was a Protestant gentleman from Lancashire, England, who had been a servant and decided to become a Catholic. After his conversion, he brought many others to the Catholic faith, including his own father, and was imprisoned for this. When he refused to acknowledge Queen Elizabeth as head of the Church and refused to attend Protestant services, he was tortured and ordered to be executed. When he was asked his marital status on a questionnaire before his execution, he was able to joke, "I am a bachelor [because he was unmarried], and more than that, I am a maid [because he was a servant]."[13] He was executed by hanging at Saint Thomas, Watering. His body was chopped into pieces and scattered around Southwark.

Saint Aloysius, give me your hunger for holiness.
Saint John, give me God's sense of humor about the sufferings of life.

* * * * *

June 22

Saint Paulinus of Nola, Optional Memorial

Paulinus was born around the year 354 and became a lawyer and public official. However, he later decided to retire from public life and move to Bordeaux (modern France) with his wife. After both had been baptized as Christians, they moved to Spain. They had an infant son, but he died; the couple then decided to devote their lives more completely to God. They gave away most of their property, Paulinus became a priest, and then they gave away the rest of their property and served the poor. Paulinus was made bishop of Nola, Italy, by popular demand. He served as bishop for twenty-one years, living the simple life of a monk in his home. He was a friend to two great bishops and future saints, Augustine of Hippo and Nicetas of Remesiana. Other Fathers of the Church refer to his outstanding holiness in their writings. Paulinus died of natural causes on this date in the year 431 and is considered a Father of the Church.

Saint John Fisher, Optional Memorial

John (1469–1535) was a learned teacher, a friend of the Dutch humanist and priest Erasmus, the chancellor of Cambridge, and bishop of Rochester in England. When he steadfastly refused to accept King Henry VIII's claim to be head of the Church of England, the only Catholic bishop in the entire country to oppose the king's takeover of the Church, he was imprisoned and executed, dying a martyr.

Saint Thomas More, Optional Memorial

Thomas (1478–1535) was born in London, England; his father was a judge. Thomas received a good education, became a lawyer, and was a popular and brilliant member of Parliament. He seriously considered a calling to the monastic life or the priesthood, but in 1505, he decided his vocation lay elsewhere,

---

[13] John Wainewright, "Saint John Rigby", in *The Catholic Encyclopedia*, vol. 13 (New York: Robert Appleton, 1912). Edited for New Advent by Kevin Knight, accessed October 1, 2019, http://www.new advent.org/cathen/13055a.htm.

and he married. He and his wife had four children, and he made sure both his daughters and his sons were well educated. He became part of both the religious and learned culture around him, and his position rose when Henry VIII ascended to the throne of England. His wife died suddenly, but he remarried soon afterward; he wrote his great work, *Utopia*, during this period. He was named lord chancellor when the previous chancellor, Cardinal Wolsey, was forced to step down due to scandal. Although Thomas supported the validity of Henry's marriage when he tried to divorce his wife for another woman, the king allowed Thomas to stand apart from this controversy and continue to serve him as chancellor. However, when Henry began taking control of the Church, Thomas resigned. His family quickly became poor, and Thomas lived quietly for a time. But when he was asked to swear the oath of loyalty supporting Henry's new "marriage" and position as head of the Church, he refused. He was taken to the Tower of London, and when his sorrowing family came to comfort him, he comforted them instead. During this time, he wrote his last work, *Dialogue of Comfort against Tribulations*. He was finally put on trial and was found guilty by perjured testimony. Thomas walked serenely to the scaffold and said before his execution that he was "the King's good servant, but God's first".[14] He recited Psalm 51, then kissed and encouraged the executioner, and was beheaded.

Saint Nicetas of Remesiana

Nicetas was born around the year 335. He served as bishop of Remesiana, a city in modern-day Serbia. Saint Paulinus, also honored on this day, was a contemporary and wrote about Nicetas' zeal for souls. Nicetas is said to have written a catechesis for those preparing for Baptism and a moral tale about a fallen virgin, as well as Christian poetry. His best-known work is the Te Deum, a great hymn of thanksgiving still recited as part of the Divine Office. He died in 414 and is considered a Father of the Church.

Blessed Innocent V

Innocent was the 185th pope (d. 1276); he reigned for less than a year. Born around the year 1225, he entered the Dominican order at the age of sixteen and graduated with distinction as a master in sacred theology from the University of Paris. His short reign as pope was spent promoting peace between the warring Italian families of the Guelfs and Ghibellines and other feuding nations. The first Dominican pope, he was also noted for his writings on philosophy, theology, and canon law.

> *Saint Paulinus, show me how to give everything to God.*
> *Saint John, help me fulfill my vocation regardless of what others do or fail to do.*
> *Saint Thomas, show me how to seek comfort from Christ at all times.*
> *Saint Nicetas, help me to give thanks to God today, all day.*
> *Blessed Innocent, help me to be a peacemaker.*

* * * * *

[14] Matthew Bunson and Margaret Bunson, *Our Sunday Visitor's Encyclopedia of Saints*, 2nd ed. (Huntington, Ind.: Our Sunday Visitor Publishing Division, 2014), 810.

June 23

Saint Thomas Garnet

Thomas (1574–1608) was born in Southwark, England. His uncle was a Catholic priest named Father Henry Garnet, and his father was a distinguished fellow at Balliol College in Oxford and a faithful Catholic. At about the age of sixteen, Thomas was sent to the College of Saint Omer across the Channel to receive a Catholic education, and later he and several other students set sail for the English Jesuit College in Valladolid, Spain. It took more than a year (including some time he spent in prison in England), but Thomas reached the college and was eventually ordained a priest. He returned to England to spend six years secretly wandering the countryside to bring souls back to the Catholic faith. When his uncle was unjustly executed for involvement in the Gunpowder Plot (a failed assassination attempt against the king by a group of Catholics), Thomas was arrested too. He was cross-examined, threatened, and given a small, damp cell with no bed for nine months, but finally deported to Flanders with some other Catholic priests. Thomas had been admitted to the Jesuit order secretly, and now he went to Louvain to complete his Jesuit novitiate. He returned to England again in secret in 1608 and was arrested only six weeks later, having been betrayed by an apostate Catholic priest. He was charged with treason, but when interrogated, he refused to affirm or deny that he was a priest, but also refused to take the Oath of Supremacy, which claimed the English monarch to be the head of the Church of England. There were three witnesses who accused him of being a priest, and, on the strength of their testimony, not any evidence, he was condemned to death. While on the scaffold before his execution, he confessed that he was a priest but had refused to answer because he didn't want his accusers or judges to condemn him against their consciences. Some of the more friendly people present at the execution made sure that he was dead before he was cut down from the scaffold and the brutal practice of drawing and quartering was begun.

Saint Joseph Cafasso

Joseph (1811–1860) was born into a wealthy peasant family but with a deformed spine. Despite his health problems, he became a priest of the city of Turin, Italy. He served as a pastor, professor of moral theology, and retreat house director; he taught the young (future priest and saint) John Bosco about serving God wholeheartedly. He had a great devotion to the Blessed Sacrament and the Sacrament of Confession, and in his lifetime, he brought fifty-seven death-row inmates to repentance for their sins. Bringing hope in God's love to those who had no hope, Joseph died of pneumonia and complications from his congenital health conditions.

Saint Thomas, teach me how to recover souls that
have gone astray from Christ's Church.
Saint Joseph, show me how to bring hope to the hopeless.

* * * * *

June 24

The Nativity of Saint John the Baptist, Solemnity

According to the Gospel of Luke, before the birth of John the Baptist, his father "was filled with the Holy Spirit, and prophesied, saying, 'Blessed be the Lord God of Israel, for he has visited and redeemed his people, and has raised up a horn of salvation for us in the house of his servant David, as he spoke by the mouth of his holy prophets from of old, that we should be saved from our enemies, and from the hand of all who hate us.'"[15]

Saint Gohardus of Nantes

Gohardus (d. 843) was the bishop of Nantes in France. While he and a large group of monks and priests were celebrating Mass, Viking raiders broke in and attacked them. They died as martyrs for Christ.

Saint Joseph Yuen Zaide

Joseph (1765–1817) was a Catholic priest who lived in Tonkin, Vietnam. Because of the Vietnamese government's persecution of Catholicism, he was imprisoned for a year before he was finally executed by strangulation, dying a martyr for his faith in Christ.

> Saint John the Baptist, show me how to prepare the way for the Lord.
> Saints Gohardus and Joseph, help me trust in God at all times.

* * * * *

June 25

Saint Solomon III of Bretagne

Solomon (d. 874) was the king of Brittany (France) and was a great military leader. Though he was more sinner than saint when he was a young man, he deeply repented of his faults by the time of his death. He was murdered and proclaimed a martyr by his people after his death on this date.

Saint William of Vercelli

William was born in 1085 into a noble family in Vercelli, Italy. His parents died when he was young, and relatives raised him. When he was fourteen years old, he decided to go on a pilgrimage to Compostela, Spain; in addition to the mortification of the journey itself, he had two iron bands placed around his body. After completing his pilgrimage, he traveled the countryside and lived as a

---

[15] Luke 1:67–71.

hermit for a few years. On one occasion, his prayers miraculously healed a blind man, so he left the area to avoid becoming known as a wonder-worker. He stayed with a kindred spirit, Saint John of Matera, but when William decided to go on a pilgrimage to Jerusalem, his friend discouraged him. When William was attacked by robbers on the way, he took that as a sign that his friend was right and traveled to Monte Virgiliano instead. He lived as a hermit at first, but so many men wanted to be his disciples that he eventually founded a religious community named after the Blessed Virgin Mary, Monte Vergine. The community was initially zealous and lived an austere life, eating only vegetables and bread three days a week with no wine, meat, or dairy products. But after a time, the monks began to complain and ask for more lenient rules. William left them with a prior to govern them, and he and a small group of companions, including John of Matera, traveled to Monte Laceno. After they discovered that the barren soil and high altitude made this a very difficult place to survive and after a fire destroyed the huts in which they were living, they moved into a nearby valley. John left this community to found a monastery on his own, while William founded the monastery of Monte Cognato. He died of natural causes on this date in 1142.

> Saint Solomon, help me to repent deeply and do penance for my past sins.
> Saint William, teach me how to accept mortifications for the love of Christ.

* * * * *

June 26

Saints John and Paul of Rome

John and Paul were brothers who served in the Roman army and in the personal service of the Roman emperor Constantine's daughter in the fourth century. When the emperor sent them to fight in a battle against the Scythian army, they encouraged the general leading the Roman army to become a Christian; he did, and the battle was won. When Julian became the Roman emperor, however, toleration of Christianity ended. Julian began a violent persecution of the Church, and the two men had to leave the imperial court. They ignored an imperial summons to appear before Julian, so he sent soldiers to execute them in their home. The bodies of these two martyrs were discovered thirty-five years later when a wealthy senator decided to build a church on the site.

Saint Anthelm of Belley

Anthelm (1107–1178) was a moral but somewhat worldly Catholic priest from Savoy, France, until he went on a visit to some relatives who lived among the Carthusian monks. The holy example of Carthusian life was so powerful that he decided to become a Carthusian himself. In time, he became prior of the Grande Chartreuse, the motherhouse of the order. As prior, he updated the monastery's buildings and enforced the Carthusian Rule of life according to its original practice. His father, a brother, and a count were among the many men who decided to follow his example and enter the order as well. After twelve years, he happily retired from his responsibilities as prior, but he was then sent to serve as prior at a Carthusian monastery in Portes. This monastery was so financially blessed that Anthelm, who considered the possession of riches contrary to the Carthusian Rule, quickly distributed their overflowing produce and even some of their church treasures to support the needy. After a few years, he again tried to retire and live as a simple monk, but this time he was appointed by Pope Alexander III to serve as bishop of Belley. This was surely the pope's way of thanking him because Anthelm had encouraged other monasteries to support Alexander III against an anti-pope. Anthelm resisted the pope's efforts to make him a bishop at first, but once he had been installed, he became a zealous shepherd of his people. When he discovered that some of his clergy were openly living with women, he used persuasion and warnings for a few years to encourage clerical celibacy. When some priests still disobeyed, he deprived them of their benefices. Anthelm's limited leisure time was spent visiting Carthusian monasteries and serving lepers at a home for lepers.

Saint Josemaria Escriva, Optional Memorial

Josemaria was born in 1902 in Barbastro, Spain, one of six children (three of whom died in infancy). He first heard God's call to religious life while a young man when he saw the bare footprints of a monk left in the snow. When Josemaria's father died, he was twenty-two years old, and he helped support his family financially while he studied for the priesthood. When he became a priest, he was assigned to a rural parish at first, and then he studied law. After a spiritual retreat in 1928, he decided to found Opus Dei, an organization focused on helping the faithful to sanctify themselves in the midst of their work and ordinary duties. He continued to study, support his mother and siblings, and care for the poor. During the Spanish Civil War, he was forced into hiding due to anti-Catholic religious persecution but cared for his parishioners covertly. He escaped across the Pyrenees Mountains into France, and, after the war, he returned to his studies, received a doctor of law degree, and became a retreat master. In 1943, he founded the Priestly Society of the Holy Cross, an order of priests that worked with Opus Dei to promote holiness among secular priests. After moving to Rome in 1946, he received a doctorate in theology, became a consultor for two Vatican congregations, and was named a prelate of honor by Pope Pius XII. Opus Dei was approved as a personal prelature (a canonical structure directly linked to the pope) by the Holy See in 1950, and he traveled all over the world spreading its message. At his death in 1975, Opus Dei had over sixty thousand members on five continents.

Saints John and Paul, help me to serve the Lord of Hosts faithfully.
Saint Anthelm, teach me how to bring the simplicity
of Carthusian life into my own life.
Saint Josemaria, show me how to be holy while living in this busy world.

* * * * *

June 27

Saint Cyril of Alexandria, Optional Memorial

Cyril was born in Alexandria, Egypt, around the year 370. He lived as a hermit for a time until an uncle convinced him to serve the Gospel out in the world instead. His uncle happened to be a well-educated archbishop, but he was also a ruthless leader who strongly opposed the holy patriarch of Constantinople, Saint John Chrysostom. Like his uncle, Cyril was involved in many controversies in his life and was not always on the side later vindicated by history. Cyril was made patriarch of Alexandria in the year 312, and he was firm in opposing heretics and closed churches that followed the Novatian heresy. Unfortunately, the way in which he exerted his authority sometimes led to dangerous confrontations. For example, when he ordered Jews to leave the city (with the emperor's approval, because the Jewish community in Alexandria was causing civil unrest), it led to a disagreement with the local governor. An angry mob took revenge on the governor by attacking and killing a woman named Hypatia who was also a respected pagan philosopher. Cyril was (and sometimes still is) blamed for her death. Cyril supported the faulty condemnation of John Chrysostom (which led to John's martyrdom), but he faithfully and strongly opposed the heretical teachings of the priest Nestorius. He served the pope during the attempts to bring Nestorius back into the Church, but he was then arrested by the emperor, along with Nestorius, as a result of trumped-up charges. He unwaveringly supported the truths that Jesus was begotten by God the Father outside of time and that Jesus was also begotten in the flesh of the Virgin Mary, particularly through his repeated support of her title as Theotokos. His explanations ultimately made it possible for many who had mistakenly followed Nestorius' heresies to recognize their mistake and return to the Church. After serving as bishop for thirty-two years to the largest diocese in the world at the time next to Rome itself, Cyril died in 444. For his effectiveness in explaining the truths of the Catholic faith, Cyril is considered not only a Father of the Church but also a Doctor of the Church. After explaining the Nicene Creed against Nestorius' errors, he writes:

> This was the sentiment of the holy Fathers; therefore they ventured to call the Holy Virgin the Mother of God, not as if the nature of the Word or his divinity had its beginning from the Holy Virgin, but because of her was born that holy body with a rational soul, to which the Word being personally united is said to be born according to the flesh.[16]

Saint Arialdus of Milan

Arialdus (d. 1066) was well educated and became a deacon and teacher in Milan, Italy. At the time, some clerics had purchased their titles—a scandalous practice known as simony—in order to profit from the power and money that came

---

[16] Council of Ephesus (A.D. 431), *Epistle of Cyril to Nestorius*, trans. Henry Percival, in Nicene and Post-Nicene Fathers, 2nd ser., vol. 14, ed. Philip Schaff and Henry Wace (Buffalo, N.Y.: Christian Literature Publishing, 1900). Revised and edited for New Advent by Kevin Knight, NewAdvent.org, accessed February 11, 2020, http://www.newadvent.org/fathers/3810.htm.

with those positions in medieval Europe. The archbishop of Milan was one of those unscrupulous leaders, and when Arialdus publicly supported a program to get rid of simoniacal leaders, he had to go into hiding to avoid the archbishop's wrath. When Pope Alexander II excommunicated the archbishop, he had Arialdus arrested, put in prison, and then executed.

Saint Cyril of Alexandria, help me seek and follow after truth.
Saint Arialdus, show me how to stand up for what is right and just, at any cost.

See also Our Lady of Perpetual Help in the Calendar of Marian Dates.

* * * * *

June 28

Saint Irenaeus of Lyons, Memorial

Irenaeus was born around the year 125 and raised in Smyrna in Asia Minor (modern Turkey), an area that had a large Christian population at the time. He was taught his Christian faith by the bishop and future martyr-saint Polycarp; he was well educated in the Scriptures, as well as in Greek philosophy and literature. As a young priest, he went to Lyons, France, to serve under Bishop Pothinus. Unfortunately, Pothinus was martyred during a brief persecution while Irenaeus was away on church business in Rome. When Irenaeus returned, he was made bishop instead and eventually served the Church in Lyons for about twenty years. He successfully fought the heresy of Gnosticism by writing a long treatise that exposed the secret teachings of various Gnostic sects and compared them to Christian teachings. Exposing the secrets of Gnosticism effectively killed it as a threat to the Catholic faith. His writings are the oldest ones we have that declare that the four canonical Gospels (Matthew, Mark, Luke, and John) are the only trustworthy ones; he's considered a Father of the Church. He emphasized the importance of apostolic succession, in part through his own personal memories of the teaching of Polycarp. Irenaeus successfully served as mediator between the pope and a group of Christians who were threatening a schism over the proper date to celebrate Easter. He died in the year 203, and some traditions say he died a martyr.

Saints Plutarch, Serenus (two individuals with this name), Heraclides, Heron, Heraidis, Potamioena, and Marcella of Alexandria

These Christians were mostly students of the Catholic scholar and theologian Origen (184–253) at his famous catechetical school in Alexandria, Egypt. In the year 202, they were condemned together during the persecution of Christians under the Roman emperor Septimus Severus. One of the martyrs, Potamioena, was a young and beautiful virgin who faced great tortures with great peace. Her peaceful acceptance of suffering led to the conversion of her guard, Basilides, who saw her in dreams praying for him and for his conversion for three nights after her martyrdom. Basilides converted and died a martyr.

Saint Paul I

Paul (d. 767) was the ninety-third pope; he reigned for ten years. His brother, also a priest, was Pope Stephen II, and Paul was elected at his brother's death. Paul spent considerable effort trying to bring peace to Rome and the Roman province through complicated and tumultuous negotiations with King Pepin of the Franks, Byzantine emperor Desiderius, and the Lombard king of central Italy. He also defended Church teaching on the doctrine of the Trinity and the veneration of images. Paul encouraged religious devotion in Rome, particularly by transferring relics from the catacombs into churches.

> *Saint Irenaeus, help me always stay close to Christ, His truth, and His Church.*
> *Holy Martyrs, teach me how to suffer for God with peace.*
> *Saint Paul, help me to love Christ and His Church.*

See also Blessed Teresa Maria Pia Mastena in the Supplemental Calendar.

* * * * *

June 29

Saints Peter and Paul, Solemnity

Peter was an ordinary Jewish fisherman, and Saul was a well-educated Jewish Pharisee. But Christ called both men, and both men served him to the death. According to tradition, they were imprisoned in the Mamertine Prison and executed on the same day by the order of the Roman emperor Nero. Peter was crucified head-down because he felt himself unworthy of dying in the same way as Christ. Paul, because he was a Roman citizen, was beheaded with a sword. It was the year 67. This date has been celebrated as a joint feast since the time of the Roman emperor Constantine in the fourth century.

Blessed Raymond (Ramon) Llull

Raymond was born into a wealthy family in Palma, Spain, around the year 1232. He married, had two children, and served as a courtier to the king. But one day he experienced a vision of the crucified Christ, and it changed his life. He recognized God's call to leave his family and position behind to serve God, and Him only. So he did. He became a Franciscan tertiary, evangelized Muslims, and learned Arabic so he could do that more effectively. He wrote hundreds of works in multiple languages on various topics, such as philosophy, theology, and science. Some of his followers later pursued his studies of alchemy into the occult, which tarnished Raymond's reputation in later generations. But he was also a great poet, mystic, and Catholic thinker. Some traditions say he died a martyr, but certain evidence of that is lacking.

Saints Peter and Paul, help me be an apostle to Jesus Christ.
Blessed Raymond, help me be open to God's call, whatever that might be.

* * * * *

June 30

First Martyrs of the Church of Rome, Optional Memorial

In July of the year 64, a fire devastated the city of Rome. Although the fire was probably an accident, the story that the Roman emperor Nero had "fiddled" (recited poetry and sang while in costume) while Rome burned fanned the rumor that Nero himself had started the fire. To shift the blame away from himself, Nero blamed the Christians. Though no one believed the charges, Nero arrested and executed Christians in gruesome ways. For example, he held an evening feast in his own gardens with chariot races and "entertainment". Some of the entertainment included watching Christians who had been sewn into the skins of wild animals being thrown to hungry dogs, who tore them to pieces. Other Christians were smeared with wax or pitch and impaled on sharp spikes and ignited as human torches. Even the hardened Romans were horrified at the sight of the deaths of these unnamed and unnumbered men and women who became the first martyrs of the city of Rome.

Saint Martial of Limoges

Martial was one of seven missionaries sent from Rome to Gaul (France) in the third century. He established his see at the city of Limoges. Though some traditions confuse him with one of the seventy-two original disciples that Jesus sent out to preach, Martial was probably sent to Gaul around the middle of the third century. There are many stories told about his holiness. For example, it's said that he struck a pagan priest blind by striking him with Saint Peter's staff and that he raised the son of a Roman proconsul from death. He also brought many people to the Christian faith.

Saint Otto of Bamberg

Otto was born in 1060 into the nobility of Swabia (modern Germany). He became a priest, served the emperor Henry IV, and even became his chancellor. When Henry got into a political disagreement with the pope and even propped up an anti-pope to sway the people in favor of his position, Otto did his best to serve both the Church and his king. Specifically, he refused to approve Henry's schismatic acts, but he supported his lawful ones. Although Henry nominated him as bishop of Bamberg, Otto refused to accept the position until he was able (years later) to personally go to Rome and receive episcopal orders from the pope himself. Otto did his best to reconcile the pope and the next emperor, Henry V, and enjoyed the trust of both sides. Later, the pope sent Otto to evangelize the newly conquered land of Pomerania (now a region of Germany and Poland). He took priests and catechists with him, and as a result of their efforts, twenty thousand people were baptized into the Catholic faith. He returned to the city of Bamberg, but when he discovered that the people of some Pomeranian towns had left the faith, he went back to encourage them, although he knew it was dangerous. He finally returned to Bamberg and died there in the year 1139.

Holy Martyrs, give me your perseverance.
Saint Martial, help me lead others to Jesus.
Saint Otto, show me how to reconcile others to Christ and to one another.

July

July 1

High Priest Aaron

Aaron, the elder brother of Moses and his spokesman to Pharaoh, was the first High Priest of God's Chosen People. His lifetime is generally dated to the thirteenth century B.C. One of his descendants was John the Baptist.

> *[The LORD said,] "Then bring near to you Aaron your brother, and his sons with him, from among the sons of Israel, to serve me as priests—Aaron and Aaron's sons, Nadab and Abihu, Eleazar and Ithamar. And you shall make holy garments for Aaron your brother, for glory and for beauty.... So Aaron shall bear the names of the sons of Israel in the breastpiece of judgment upon his heart, when he goes into the holy place, to bring them to continual remembrance before the LORD."*[1]

Saint Oliver Plunket

Oliver's parents were well-born Catholics in Ireland, and Oliver (1629–1681) grew up in the tumultuous times of an Irish rebellion against the Protestant English. He studied to become a priest in Ireland and then went to Rome to complete his studies. He was an excellent student and learned in Rome under the Jesuits. When the archbishop of Armagh and primate of All Ireland died in exile in 1669, Oliver was chosen by the pope to replace him, so Oliver courageously returned to his oppressed homeland, despite the danger. He held a synod of bishops to discuss the condition of the Catholic faith in Ireland; he ordained new priests, confirmed ten thousand persons into the Catholic faith, and lived a generally peaceful life for a few years, despite one disagreement with the archbishop of Dublin over which of them had jurisdiction in Ireland. He personally lived in great poverty. The burdens of his office were great: there was an ongoing need for Catholic education of children, better discipline among his own clergy, and support for the struggling Irish people. Due to the civil penalties in Ireland associated with his obedience to the pope, he kept a low profile as much as possible. When political unrest led to persecution of Catholics in Ireland, one bishop was banished, another fled to Spain, and Oliver, though initially untouched, eventually was forced to go into hiding. After the Oates Plot (a fictitious plot against the English king that sparked anti-Catholic hysteria), all Catholic priests and bishops were expelled from the country. Two men—one who had been expelled from the Franciscan order and the other who was an excommunicated priest—betrayed Oliver to the authorities, and he was arrested

---

[1] Ex 28:1–2, 29.

and imprisoned in Dublin Castle. Ridiculous charges were made up against him, but when no witnesses came forward to testify in Ireland, it was decided to have him tried in England. There he spent a year and a half in prison, and a jury eventually found him guilty. He protested his innocence even while on the scaffold and prayed for his enemies. He died from hanging before he was cut down for the brutal practices of disembowelment and quartering.

Saint Junipero Serra, Optional Memorial[2]

Miguel was born on Majorca, an island of Spain, in 1713. He became a Franciscan friar when he was seventeen years old, took the name in religious life of Junipero, was ordained in 1737, and taught philosophy and theology for many years. At his request, he was finally sent to be a missionary in North America to the native peoples. Although he suffered from asthma and from a permanently swollen leg as a result of a mosquito bite in the New World, he covered huge distances along the West Coast (painfully on foot), and he eventually founded twenty-one missions. He converted thousands of Native Americans, trained them in European agriculture, and lived a penitential and austere life in the service of Christ. He died in 1784.

> *High Priest Aaron, help me be holy in God's sight.*
> *Saint Oliver, help me trust in God.*
> *Saint Junipero, show me how to suffer for Christ.*

* * * * *

July 2

Saints Processus and Martinian of Rome

According to an ancient Church tradition, while Saint Peter was in prison, he struck a rock that miraculously brought forth water, just as Moses had done.[3] This brought his two Roman guards, Processus and Martinian, to faith in Christ. They were even baptized with that water. Later, the two men were arrested by the authorities because they were Christians. They were tortured first and then executed by the sword when they refused to give up their faith.

Saint Swithin of Winchester

Swithin was born in Wessex, England, around the year 800; he was educated in an abbey and became a priest. He was appointed to serve as chaplain to the

---

[2] This saint may be celebrated as an optional memorial in the *Liturgical Calendar for the Dioceses of the United States of America*.

[3] Ex 17:6.

king and tutor to the young English prince, became bishop of Winchester, and, after serving God and his flock faithfully for many years, he died of natural causes in 862. Afterward, many British churches were named after him, although his shrine was destroyed during the anti-Catholic persecution that began in the sixteenth century. Tradition says that forty days of rain followed after his relics were translated from one church to another, showing his displeasure with the move, so he's invoked as a patron of weather.

> *Saints Processus and Martinian, help me to recognize God's miraculous*
> *actions in the world around me.*
> *Saint Swithin, teach me how to serve God faithfully.*

* * * * *

July 3

Saint Thomas the Apostle, Feast

Thomas was one of Jesus' apostles; he was a Jew and probably a Galilean. He's best known for doubting Jesus' Resurrection and for his faith-filled response to Jesus after his lack of belief.[4] According to an ancient Church tradition, he evangelized the people of India, going to the "ends of the earth" as he was commanded to do by Christ, and there he died a martyr.

> *Now Jesus had spoken of [Lazarus'] death, but they thought that he meant taking rest in sleep. Then Jesus told them plainly, "Lazarus is dead; and for your sake I am glad that I was not there, so that you may believe. But let us go to him." Thomas, called the Twin, said to his fellow disciples, "Let us also go, that we may die with him."[5]*

Saint Hyacinth of Cappadocia

Hyacinth (d. 120) lived in Cappadocia (modern Turkey), and he was chamberlain to the Roman emperor Trajan. When he was found to be a Christian, he was put in prison. The only food he was given while in prison was meat that had been offered to idols, so he starved to death rather than eat it. The Church reveres him as a martyr.

Saint Leo II

Leo was the eightieth pope (d. 683); he reigned less than a year. He was known for his eloquent preaching, his charity for the poor, and his strong condemnation of the heresy of Monothelitism. He also was not afraid to speak publicly against the failure of a previous pope, Honorius, to oppose this heresy.

---

[4] Jn 20:24–29.
[5] Jn 11:13–16.

Saint Thomas, beg God to increase my faith.
Saint Hyacinth, show me how to recognize and reject my own culture's idols.
Saint Leo, help me to love Christ and serve His truth.

* * * * *

July 4

Saint Elizabeth of Portugal

See July 5.[6]

Blessed Pier Giorgio Frassati

Pier was born in 1901 into a rich and powerful family in Turin, Italy, and he had one sister. He was a pious young man, an excellent athlete, a popular student, and a practical joker; he practiced his Catholic faith in unassuming but generous ways. He was active in local Catholic groups and opposed Fascism as it grew as a political power in Italy; he chose the career of mining engineer because he thought it would allow him to improve the lives of others. He quietly became a Dominican tertiary; he secretly performed many acts of charity for the poor of Turin, not even telling his own family and friends. In 1925, when he was only twenty-four years old, he contracted poliomyelitis while helping the poor, and he became ill and died suddenly. His parents, who had an unhappy marriage and little faith, were shocked by the flood of friends (rich and poor, known and unknown) who came to express their sorrow after Pier's death. His parents reconciled with one another, and Pier's agnostic father repented. When Pier's body was moved to the Cathedral of Turin in 1981, it was found to be incorrupt.

Blessed Joseph Kowalski

Joseph was born in Poland in 1911 and was educated at a Salesian school. He entered the Salesian order in 1927, was ordained a priest in 1938, and became the personal secretary to the Salesian provincial. He formed a youth choir, conducted spiritual conferences, led a youth ministry, and taught students. On May 23, 1941, he was arrested by the Nazis with eleven other Salesians for the crime of holding unapproved (that is, Catholic) youth programs. He was scheduled for shipment to the Dachau concentration camp, but when a Nazi officer disliked his attitude and ordered him to stomp on his rosary (which Joseph refused to do), Joseph was instead sent to hard labor in the Auschwitz concentration camp. For a few weeks in Auschwitz, he worked and ministered

---

[6] Because July 4 is Independence Day in the United States, Saint Elizabeth of Portugal may be celebrated as an optional memorial on July 5 and is listed on that date.

to his fellow prisoners. One day in 1942, however, the guards beat, tortured, and drowned him, for no particular reason.

Blessed Pier, show me how to bring reconciliation to families.
Blessed Joseph, help me to forgive.

* * * * *

July 5

Saint Elizabeth of Portugal, Optional Memorial[7]

Elizabeth's great-aunt was also a saint of the Church—Elizabeth, queen of Hungary. But this Elizabeth (1271–1336) was a princess of Aragon (modern Spain), and she was married to Denis, king of Portugal, when she was twelve years old. Elizabeth was careful to perform all her duties as queen, yet she also supported the poor, the sick, and orphans and lived a deep prayer life. Although her husband permitted her piety and acts of charity, he was not a devout man and was, unfortunately, repeatedly unfaithful to her and fathered illegitimate children. Elizabeth and Denis had two children, Alfonso and Constance. Alfonso resented his father's illegitimate sons, and he eventually led two rebellions against his father's rule. Both times Elizabeth literally rode out between the opposing armies of her husband and her son to keep them from going into battle and was able to reconcile the two men with one another. When Denis became ill in 1324, Elizabeth nursed him through his long illness, and her patient care for him brought Denis to some measure of repentance for his past sins. After Denis' death, she became a Franciscan tertiary and lived in a small house near a convent. Her last act before her death was again to serve as a peacemaker; she made peace between her son and her grandson-in-law, who had been facing each other in battle. She died after she returned.

Saint Anthony Zaccaria, Optional Memorial

Anthony was born in 1502 in Cremona, Italy. His father died when he was two years old, and he was raised by his widowed mother. He studied and became a medical doctor, but over time, he became aware of the need to care for his patients' souls, as well as their bodies. He therefore studied for the priesthood, became a priest, and moved to Milan. There he formed a society with the goal of reviving "the love of divine worship and a true Christian way of life by continual preaching and faithfully administering the sacraments".[8] This congregation eventually became known as the Barnabites, since the church Anthony bought for his new congregation was the Church of Saint Barnabas. He died of natural causes in 1539, and his body was found to be incorrupt in 1566.

---

[7] This saint may be celebrated as an optional memorial in the *Liturgical Calendar for the Dioceses of the United States of America* on this date.

[8] James Bentley, *A Calendar of Saints: The Lives of the Principal Saints of the Christian Year* (London: Time Warner Books, 2005), 128.

Saint Stephen of Reggio

Stephen was ordained by Saint Paul to be the first bishop of Reggio, Italy. He was martyred for the crime of being a Christian during the persecution ordered by the Roman emperor Nero in the first century.

Saint Athanasius the Athonite

Abraham was born around the year 920, studied in Constantinople, became a professor, and then entered a monastery in Bithynia (modern Turkey). He took the name in religious life of Athanasius. When the abbot died, the other monks wanted Athanasius to replace him, but he ran away instead. He took a false name and lived as a monk in a cell near Karyes (Greece) for a time, until Nicophorus Phocas—who was not only a good friend but the future Byzantine emperor—happened to find him. Nicophorus asked Athanasius to help him organize an expedition against the invading Muslim Arabs and to bless it with his prayers. Athanasius complied with his friend's request unwillingly, but the mission was a success. Nicophorus, who was a powerful and wealthy man, let Athanasius return to Mount Athos of Greece, but he forced Athanasius to take a large sum of money to build a monastery there. (This monastery is still called the Monastery of Saint Athanasius, or simply "The Laura".) When Nicophorus became emperor, Athanasius was afraid his friend would make him leave his solitude for a place at court, so he ran away (again) to hide on the island of Cyprus. Nicophorus wrote to reassure his friend that he could remain at Mount Athos, and he even gave him more money to build a harbor there. Although Athanasius' approach—isolating the monks as much as possible from the outside world—was generally accepted by the monks on Athos, there were hermits on the island who resented the order, rules, and money that Athanasius brought with him, and on two occasions someone tried to kill him. However, the blessings brought by his order and rules eventually led to him becoming superior general of all the monks on Mount Athos, and he governed fifty-eight communities of hermits and monks. He died with five other monks during construction of a church around the year 1000.

Saint Elizabeth, show me how to be a peacemaker.
Saint Anthony, help me to love and live the liturgy all day long.
Saint Stephen, show me how to live and die for Christ.
Saint Athanasius, help me to find Christ in solitude.

* * * * *

July 6

Saint Maria Goretti

Maria was born in 1890 into a poor Italian family and was one of six children. After her father died, she was often put in charge of household chores while the rest of the family worked in the fields. A man and his son also lived with her family; the son, Alexander, began to make advances on Maria, probably fueled by his attachment to pornography. One day in 1902, he grabbed her while everyone else was gone and tried to pull her into a bedroom. She resisted, saying she would rather be killed than submit to such an evil deed. Alexander almost strangled her, but stabbed her with a dagger and then ran away. When the family returned and found her, they took her to a hospital, though it was clear to everyone that she was not going to survive her injuries. In her final hours, she forgave her murderer, was quaintly worried about where her mother would sleep, and received Viaticum. She was only twelve years old. After her death, Alexander was arrested for the crime and sentenced to thirty years in prison. He was unrepentant for many years. However, one night he had a dream in which he saw Maria come to him and offer him flowers. From that day on, he was a changed man. He was released after twenty-seven years in prison, and his first act was to go to Maria's mother to beg her forgiveness for the murder. When Maria was declared a blessed in 1947, the pope appeared on the balcony of Saint Peter's Basilica with Maria's mother, two sisters, and a brother. When she was declared a saint in 1950, her repentant murderer was still alive.

Saint Sisoes the Great

Sisoes (d. 430) was born in Egypt and went into the desert to become a monk at a monastery at Scetis. After a time, he decided the monastery was too crowded, so he became a hermit on Mount Colzim, where the famous Saint Anthony the Great had lived. For the next seventy years, Sisoes lived as a hermit and grew in holiness. His prayers were so powerful that he was called a wonder-worker and surnamed "the Great" after his death.

> *Saint Maria, show me how to forgive.*
> *Saint Sisoes, help me learn to love solitude and prayer.*

* * * * *

July 7

Saint Willibald of Eichstatt

Willibald was born into a devout Catholic family in England around the year 700. He and his brother Winebald (also a future saint) decided to go to the Holy Land together on pilgrimage, but they stopped in Rome on the way and met the pope. The pope was apparently so impressed with Willibald that he asked him to go to the late Saint Benedict's run-down monastery at Monte Cassino, which had been destroyed by the Lombards in the year 577, and revive monastic life there. After Willibald spent ten years restoring the monastery with the help of its abbot, Saint Petronax, Pope Gregory III then sent him to Germany to bring the Catholic faith to the pagans living there. Willibald was ordained a priest first, and he served as a missionary to the German people alongside Saint Boniface. He was so successful at bringing people to the faith that eventually the city of Eichstatt became a diocese, and he became their bishop. He died around the year 787.

Blessed Benedict XI

Benedict was born with the name Nicholas Bocasini, in Treviso, Italy, in 1240; he became a Dominican priest and was known for his wisdom and preaching. He served the Church as a papal nuncio, cardinal, bishop, college dean, and papal legate before being chosen as the 194th pope, taking the name Benedict. He was very serious about living a penitential life and remaining humble even while he was the pope; on one occasion, his mother came to see him dressed too elegantly (he thought), and he refused to see her until she returned in more typical clothing. His example of moderation and prudence helped restore peace not only to Rome but to other cities and countries. Unfortunately, he reigned for less than a year, dying in 1304, and some said his sudden death was due to poisoning.

Blessed Peter To Rot

Peter was born in 1912 in Rakunai, a city on an island in modern Papua New Guinea, and his parents were first-generation converts to the Catholic faith. He was known for his piety even when he was a child, and he became a teacher and lay catechist as an adult. He was an excellent educator, and everyone in his village knew him as the man who was always carrying a Bible. He married Paula la Varpit in 1936, and together they had three children, although two of them died at a young age. During World War II, the Japanese invaded the country and arrested Christian missionaries and all their staff. But Peter, who hadn't been arrested, continued baptizing new Christians, teaching people, and caring for the poor and sick. When the Japanese authorities forbade Christianity and encouraged the people to practice their pre-Christian traditions (including polygamy), Peter spoke out against it. So they arrested him in 1945 and imprisoned him in a cave. When the Japanese leaders saw that his courageous example was only strengthening his people, who visited him repeatedly in prison, he was executed by being poisoned and then suffocated on this date in 1945.

> *Saint Willibald, show me how to bring people to Christ.*
> *Blessed Benedict, help me be an example of humility and prudence to others.*
> *Blessed Peter, teach me how to speak the truth in charity at all times.*

* * * * *

July 8

Saints Aquila and Priscilla the Tentmakers

Aquila and Priscilla were husband and wife; they lived during the time of the New Testament in the city of Corinth in Greece. They were Jewish converts to the Catholic faith, and they worked as tentmakers. When Saint Paul came to Corinth on one of his missionary journeys, they invited him to live with them.[9] Apparently, they later accompanied Paul when he traveled to Ephesus. When they met Apollos, a Christian disciple who preached the faith but who was ignorant of some parts of the Christian teaching on Baptism, they were the ones who explained to him the full teaching of the Gospel.[10] Paul later stayed again with them in Ephesus,[11] and he praised their faith.[12]

Saint Procopius of Caesarea

During the persecution of the Church under the Roman emperor Diocletian in the year 303, the martyr Procopius died in the city of Caesarea (in modern Israel). According to tradition, he was a soldier in the army, and he was arrested and executed by beheading when he admitted that he was a Christian in public.

Saint Adrian III

Adrian (d. 885) was the 109th pope; he reigned for only one year. During his brief reign, he tried to protect Christians from Muslims who were invading Spain and threatening the safety of the rest of Europe. He died on the way to a meeting with King Charles III to discuss the succession of the title of Holy Roman Emperor. The people acclaimed him a saint after his death.

Blessed Eugene III

Eugene (d. 1151) was the 167th pope; he reigned for eight years. Born in Pisa, Italy, he was a Cistercian monk, abbot of the monastery of Tre Fontane, and a disciple of the great reformer-monk Saint Bernard of Clairvaux when he was elected. Eugene initially dealt mercifully with Arnold of Brescia, an Augustinian Canon whose attempts at "reform" in the clergy led to violence in Rome. The political chaos that resulted from this violence caused Eugene to spend considerable effort trying to restore order there, and he was eventually forced to move to France because of the ongoing violence. While in France, he made use of the opportunity to correct errors and abuses that were going on in the Church in France. He also improved Church discipline and served as a peacemaker between political leaders. He eventually was able to return to Italy, but more unrest in Rome prevented the papal court from staying there for very long. He was beloved by the Christian people for his personal affability and generosity, still living the life of a monk while being pope.

Saints Aquila and Priscilla, teach me how to be hospitable and welcoming to strangers.
Saint Procopius, show me how to live and die for Christ.
Saint Adrian and Blessed Eugene, help me to be a peacemaker.

* * * * *

[9] Acts 18:1-4.
[10] Acts 18:24-26.
[11] 1 Cor 16:19.
[12] Rom 16:3-4.

July 9

Saint Augustine Zhao Rong and Companions, Optional Memorial

China was first evangelized in the fifth century, and missionaries continued, slowly, to reach parts of China over the centuries. In 1815, Augustine Zhao Rong, a Chinese diocesan priest, was martyred with his companions. Among those companions was an eighteen-year-old boy, Chi Zhuzi. The boy bravely cried out to those who had just cut off his right arm and were preparing to flay him alive: "Every piece of my flesh, every drop of my blood will tell you that I am Christian."[13] The persecution against Christians in China continued, and lay catechists, laymen, seminarians, and priests (both missionary and Chinese) were executed, frequently by strangulation, until the year 1846. At this point, France replaced Portugal as the power protecting the Christian missions, following a war with Britain over the opium trade. The Church was then free of persecution until the time of the Boxer Rebellion around 1900. At this point, many more missionary bishops and priests (often Franciscans, but also Jesuits), Chinese laymen, and seminarians were executed. Today we remember all these Christians who have died for their faith in Christ in China.

Saint Nicholas Pieck and Companions

In 1572, Calvinists seized the city of Gorkum in the Netherlands and captured several Catholic priests. They only mistreated them at first because they hoped to find valuable church vessels that had been hidden for protection. Eleven of the men who were ultimately martyred were Franciscan friars from the Gorkum convent, including Nicholas Pieck (guardian) and Jerome Weerden (vicar). Leonard Vechel, Nicholas Janssen, and Godfrey van Duynen were secular priests, and John van Oosterwyk was an elderly member of the Augustinian Canons Regular. John van Hoornaer was a Dominican who came to help the friars, Adrian van Hilvarenbeek and James Lacops (who had been very lax in his observance of religious life) were Premonstratensian priests, and Andrew Wouters was a secular priest who had not been living a devout life. When the Calvinists were unable to get what they wanted from these men, they marched them to the city marketplace and forced them to sing the "Litany of the Saints", as a humiliation, though the men did so happily. The Calvinists then interrogated the men and promised them their freedom if they would abandon Church teaching on the Blessed Sacrament. When the men refused, an apostate priest led them to a deserted monastery. Father Pieck was hanged first, and he encouraged the others until he died. Some of the remaining men lost their courage at this point, but all were hanged and died as martyrs for their Catholic faith. Their bodies were thrown into a ditch, and there they remained until they were removed during a truce in the fighting.

---

[13] Pope John Paul II, "Cappella Papale for the Canonization of 123 New Saints" (homily, October 1, 2000), no. 2, accessed October 4, 2019, http://w2.vatican.va/content/john-paul-ii/en/homilies/200/documents/hf_jp-ii_hom_20001001_canonization.html.

Saint Veronica (Ursula) Giuliani

Ursula was born in 1660 in Urbino, Italy. She distressed her father when she told him she wanted to become a nun, but she had already distressed almost everyone else in her life by her devout but arrogant behavior, expecting everyone to follow her own high ideals of the spiritual life. God granted her a vision of her own heart one day, which she saw as made of steel. That vision changed her life. She became much gentler, particularly with others, but she didn't lose her steely resolve to lead a holy life. At the age of seventeen, she entered a convent of Capuchin nuns and took the name Veronica. She received mystical experiences: she felt strange pains in her heart, particularly when meditating on the sufferings of Jesus, and she received the marks of the Crown of Thorns in 1694 and the stigmata on Good Friday of 1697. Veronica was a deep mystic, and she wrote down the numerous revelations that she received in her diary for thirty years, under the orders of her superior. This diary was published later as *A Diary of the Passion*. She died in 1727.

Holy Martyrs, pray for me never to lack courage in defending Christ and His truth. Saint Veronica, show me how to be gentle of heart but strong in faith.

* * * * *

July 10

Saints Rufina and Secunda of Rome

Secunda and Rufina were the Christian daughters of a senator in third-century Rome. Their father arranged for them to be engaged to two young Christian men. But during the persecution of Christians under the Roman emperor Valerian, the two men renounced their faith in Christ to avoid arrest. Secunda and Rufina refused to give up their faith, however, and ran away from Rome. They were caught, arrested, interrogated, and scourged. When they still refused to renounce their faith, they were executed.

Saints Anatolia and Victoria of Rome

Anatolia and her sister Victoria were from a noble Christian family living in Rome during the time of the persecution of Christians under the Roman emperor Decius in 250. Their parents promised them in marriage to pagans from noble families. At first, the two sisters weren't sure whether God was calling them to marriage or not, but Anatolia eventually convinced her sister that they should remain single and give their lives to God in order to be as holy as they possibly could. They told their family and the suitors, but their suitors insisted on getting married, despite the girls' refusals. Rejected, the men then turned them in to the authorities as Christians. The authorities merely imprisoned the sisters at home at first, hoping that they would change their minds, but instead the sisters converted their servants and the guards assigned to watch them. Anatolia's suitor gave up quickly and sent her to the authorities to be executed. She was locked up with a poisonous snake and then stabbed to death with a sword when the snake wouldn't bite her. Victoria's suitor tried to make her change her mind but finally gave up. She was executed by being stabbed through the heart.

Holy Martyrs, help me to be faithful to Christ, regardless of others' actions.

* * * * *

July 11

Saint Benedict of Nursia, Memorial

Benedict was born into a well-to-do, Christian family in Nursia, Italy, around the year 480 and was sent to Rome to be educated when he was a teenager. He was revolted by the immoral behavior he saw there, so he quickly left Rome with his nurse (a caregiver-turned-housekeeper) to live a life of solitude in the mountains. Soon he realized that God was calling him to an even greater abandonment of the world. While he was searching for a place to live in complete solitude, he settled on the city of Subiaco, where he met a monk named Romanus. Romanus brought bread to Benedict every day (disobeying the monastery's rules), while he lived in a nearby cave for three years. When other men found out about Benedict's holiness and simple way of life, they wanted to follow him. Benedict settled the men who wanted to be his disciples into twelve separate monasteries, with twelve monks in each. Unfortunately, the monks began to resent him, and they even tried to poison him. (Benedict later decided that he had been too severe with them.) When the cup they tried to poison him with broke after he had blessed it, he recognized what they'd tried to do. He repented of his past severity with them and left them suddenly. He moved to Monte Cassino, the site of a former pagan temple, and around the year 530, he and those who followed him began to build a monastery. This ultimately became one of the greatest monasteries that the world has ever known. Learning from his experiences at Subiaco, Benedict gathered all his monks into one monastery, developed his famous rule for monastic life, and established the practice of *ora et labora* among his monks, in which they lived a structured life of both prayer and work. He cared for the sick people who lived outside the monastery and the poor who came to the monastery for alms and food. He predicted many future events, including his own death. Benedict died in the year 547 as he stood in the monastery's chapel, with his arms supported by his brothers and his hands lifted up to Heaven.

Listen, my son, and with your heart hear the principles of your Master. Readily accept and faithfully follow the advice of a loving Father, so that through the labor of obedience you may return to Him from whom you have withdrawn because of the laziness of disobedience. My words are meant for you, whoever you are, who laying aside your own will, take up the all-powerful and righteous arms of obedience to fight under the true King, the Lord Jesus Christ.[14]

Saint Pius I

Pius (d. 155) was the tenth pope; he reigned fifteen years. During his reign, he dealt with multiple Christian heresies and their leaders, and it's clear that there was an active Christian community in Rome at that time, despite ongoing persecution. He was executed by the sword, dying a martyr.

Saint Benedict, show me how to pray and work for Christ.
Saint Pius, help me to respond to persecution with charity and perseverance.

* * * * *

July 12

Saints Nabor and Felix of Milan

Nabor and Felix were African soldiers who were sent to serve in Milan, Italy, at the end of the third century. While they were stationed there, they became Christians. During the persecution of Christians under the Roman emperor Diocletian, these two men were executed for their faith in Christ, and their memory and relics were venerated by Saint Ambrose of Milan (the bishop) and other early Christians.

Saint John Gualbert

John (d. 1073) was the son of a nobleman from Florence, Italy. When his elder brother was murdered, John thought it was his duty to avenge his brother's death. One day, he happened to meet the murderer in a narrow passageway, and he drew his sword. The frightened man fell to his knees and crossed his arms over his chest, expecting John to kill him. John, however, remembered the example of Christ, forgave the man, and walked away. Deeply affected, John then went to a monastery, and as he prayed before the crucifix, it seemed to bow before him and accept his repentance. John immediately decided to give up his former way of life and asked to be allowed to enter a nearby monastery. At first, the abbot was afraid that John's father would be angry, so he put him off. But John went home, cut his own hair, put on a borrowed habit, and showed up to enter the monastery anyway. After living in the monastery for a time, he and a companion left, apparently because of a scandal over the election of the next abbot. When more men began to follow John, together they built a small monastery out of wood and mud near Vallombrosa. The men lived an austere life following the Rule of Saint Benedict, and they became known as the Vallombrosan Benedictines. Out of humility, John refused even

---

[14] Benedict, *The Rule of Saint Benedict*, trans. Anthony C. Meisel and M. L. del Mastro (New York: Image Books, Doubleday, 1975), 43.

to receive minor orders, and he refused to let his monasteries be too fancy or costly. John was well known for giving away the goods of his monastery to the poor when people needed them. Though he lived a quiet, contemplative life, John was outspoken in his opposition to the widespread problem of simony in the Church at the time. He died around the age of eighty.

Saint Louis Martin

Louis Martin was born in 1823 in Bordeaux, France, and was the son of an army officer. He considered a religious vocation but decided to remain a layman and took up the profession of watchmaker. He met and married Zelie Guerin, and the two had nine children, five of whom survived childhood. After Zelie's death, he raised their children, encouraged their Christian devotion, and supported them in their religious vocations. He suffered two strokes and was hospitalized for three years before his death in 1894, suffering like a saint, according to his saintly daughter Therese of Lisieux.

Saint Zelie (Marie-Azelie) Guerin Martin

Zelie Guerin was an intelligent, pious, sensitive child, born in 1831 at Saint-Denis-sur-Sarthon, France. She decided to become a nun, but she was sent home from the convent, apparently because of her health. She then decided (under inspiration) to become a lacemaker. She was very successful in her work, and after a time she met and married Louis Martin. The couple had nine children, four of whom died during childhood, and Zelie's lacemaking business supported their middle-class family. Zelie developed and died of breast cancer in 1877, when she was only forty-six years old, but not before she had instilled devotion in the children God had given her—most obviously in the incomparable future saint Therese of Lisieux.

> *Saints Nabor and Felix, strengthen my faith in Christ.*
> *Saint John, help me let go of my desire for the things of this world.*
> *Saints Louis and Zelie, teach me to be a holy example to my family.*

* * * * *

July 13

Saint Henry II

Henry (973–1024) was the son of the duke of Bavaria and was educated by the bishop of Ratisbon, Saint Wolfgang. He became duke of Bavaria, then king of Germany and king of Italy; in 1014, he was crowned Holy Roman Emperor by the pope. He was a pious man even when he was at war; he asked his soldiers to receive Holy Communion before going into battle, and he publicly thanked God afterward when he won. He encouraged monasticism in his lands, called synods together to make sure priests followed canon law, and restored dioceses that had suffered from invading armies. Henry wanted to become a monk himself, so he went to an abbot, told him of his desire for monastic life, and offered to take a vow of obedience. The abbot wisely accepted Henry's vow—but then he ordered him to serve God as Holy Roman Emperor.

Prophet Ezra

Ezra was a priest and scribe from the tribe of Levi who led thousands of Jews back to Israel after the Babylonian Exile in the fifth century B.C. He encouraged people to return to the practice of their faith and grieved over their past unfaithfulness, leading many to repentance.

> *And at the evening sacrifice I rose from my fasting, with my garments and my mantle torn, and fell upon my knees and spread out my hands to the LORD my God, saying: "O my God, I am ashamed and blush to lift my face to you, my God, for our iniquities have risen higher than our heads, and our guilt has mounted up to the heavens."*[15]

Saint Myrope of Chios

Myrope (d. 251) was a Christian woman living in Chios, Greece. She made pilgrimages to the graves of martyrs and, due to the ongoing persecution of Christians in the Roman Empire, hid the relics of the martyr-saint Isidore from the authorities. When the authorities found out that she was responsible for taking the relics, she was imprisoned and scourged. She died a martyr from the effects of her torture.

Saint Clelia Barbieri

Clelia (1847–1870) was born to pious parents in Persiceto, Italy. Her father died when she was only eight years old, and Clelia had to work to support her family. She was intelligent, devout, and preferred a life of prayer and mortification, and she eventually became a catechist, teaching the faith to the children in her parish. With the help of a few other like-minded women and the encouragement of her parish priest, Clelia founded the Little Sisters of Our Lady of Sorrows to educate poor girls in the parish. At the time she founded the order, she was only twenty-one years old, making her the youngest founder of a religious congregation in the history of the Church. She had a great love for our Lord in the Eucharist, lived a life of deep prayer, and was occasionally seen in ecstasy while praying. She recovered from an illness in a seemingly miraculous way, but then she died, having done amazing things, all by the age of twenty-three.

> *Saint Henry, help me live my vocation according to God's will.*
> *Prophet Ezra, show me how to repent deeply.*
> *Saint Myrope, teach me to love the corporal works of mercy.*
> *Saint Clelia, teach me your love of prayer and mortification.*

* * * * *

[15] Ezra 9:5–6.

July 14

Saint Camillus de Lellis, Memorial

See July 18.[16]

Blessed Hroznata of Bohemia

Hroznata was born into the nobility of Bohemia (now the Czech Republic) in 1160. He married, but after his wife and only child died suddenly, he decided to leave the world behind and live only for Christ. He founded a Premonstratensian abbey at Tapi in Bavaria and became a monk himself there. At the orders of the abbot, he worked vigorously to protect his abbey from greedy nobles who wanted its wealth and property. In the year 1217, a band of knights captured him, presumably to stop his interference. They threw him into a dungeon and then left him to die. He starved to death, dying a martyr.

Saint Kateri Tekakwitha, Memorial[17]

Kateri's father was a non-Christian Mohawk chief, and her mother was a Christian Algonquin woman who had been captured by the Iroquois. Kateri was born in 1656 in modern New York State but became an orphan after a smallpox epidemic passed through her village. The disease left her with impaired eyesight and a scarred face. After she was baptized into the Christian faith by a Jesuit missionary, her family shunned her, abused her, and tried to marry her off. Instead, she ran away to a Christian village for the Native Americans in Canada, and there she lived a life of holiness and devotion until her death in 1680, at the age of twenty-four.

Blessed Michael Ghebre

Michael was from Ethiopia. He joined the Vincentian order in 1844 and was ordained a priest in 1851. During the persecution of Christians under Negus Theodore II of Ethiopia, he and four companions were arrested for the crime of being Christians. He was tortured by being dragged from place to place before he died a martyr in prison in 1855.

Blessed Hroznata, help me to remember that my sacrifices are never hidden from God.
Saint Kateri, pray that my sufferings will always draw me closer to Christ.
Blessed Michael, help me to forgive.

* * * * *

[16] Because Saint Kateri Tekakwitha is celebrated as a memorial on July 14 in the *Liturgical Calendar for the Dioceses of the United States of America*, Saint Camillus de Lellis is celebrated as an optional memorial on July 18.

[17] This saint is celebrated as a memorial in the *Liturgical Calendar for the Dioceses of the United States of America*.

July 15

Saint Bonaventure, Memorial

Bonaventure was born in Bagnorea, Italy, in 1221. As a young man, he entered the Franciscan order and studied under a famous teacher, Alexander of Hales, while at the University of Paris. He lived a life of Franciscan poverty while he was a student, but he also preached, wrote, and lectured. The Christlike example of the new orders of mendicant friars enkindled love in some hearts in Paris—but jealousy in others. Bonaventure and Thomas Aquinas were among the students who were forced to stop lecturing for a time until a special commission of scholars, ordered by Pope Alexander IV, vindicated the orthodoxy of the friars. After receiving his degree as a doctor of theology in 1257, Bonaventure began writing about spiritual matters. More a theologian than a philosopher, his many spiritual works do emphasize reason, but his primary goal was always to lead the Christian to draw closer to God. In the same year that he received his degree, Bonaventure was named minister general of the young Franciscan order. During the seventeen years he served as minister general, he was so successful in ending factions inside the order—enforcing discipline among those who had become too lax in their observance of the order's rules, while refusing to accept the disobedience of those who had become too harsh and rigorous—that he's considered the second founder of the Franciscans. Pope Clement IV nominated him to be an archbishop in 1265, but he accepted Bonaventure's request to refuse. He wasn't so lucky with Pope Gregory X, who ordered him to be made cardinal bishop of Albano in 1273. Bonaventure was also ordered by the same pope to prepare for an important general council in hopes of bringing about a reunion with the Greek Church. Thomas Aquinas died on the way to attend this council. Bonaventure's leadership was pivotal at that meeting, and he preached at the closing Mass. He died shortly afterward, in the year 1274. Because of the beauty and brilliance of his writings, he's called the Seraphic Doctor, and he was named a Doctor of the Church.

> *Since happiness is nothing other than / the enjoyment of the highest good / and since the highest good is above, / no one can be made happy unless he rise above himself, / not by an ascent of the body, / but of the heart. / But we cannot rise above ourselves / unless a higher power lift us up.*[18]

Martyrs of Alexandria

In the early fourth century in Alexandria, Egypt, thirteen Christians were executed for the crime of being Christians. One of them was named Philip, and there were two other adults in the group. The other ten martyrs were children.

> *Saint Bonaventure, show me how to follow Christ in the footsteps of Saint Francis.*
> *Holy Martyrs, help me to protect children from harm today.*

* * * * *

[18] Bonaventure, *The Soul's Journey into God, the Tree of Life, the Life of Saint Francis*, trans. Ewert Cousins (Mahwah, N.J.: Paulist Press, 1978), 59.

July 16

Our Lady of Mount Carmel, Optional Memorial

In the twelfth century, a group of men from Western Europe traveled to the Holy Land during the time of the Crusades. They lived as hermits on Mount Carmel in Israel, where the prophet Elijah had lived and prayed, and they built a chapel there in honor of the Virgin Mary. When Muslim Arabs destroyed the Latin kingdom (killing many Christians) in the Holy Land, the hermits returned to Europe, calling themselves the Brothers of the Blessed Virgin Mary of Mount Carmel. But religious life in Europe had changed greatly since the original hermits had left, particularly through the development of mendicant friars. One of the brothers, Simon Stock, was uncertain about whether the brothers should remain hermits or become begging friars like the mendicant orders. While he was praying, he received a vision of the Blessed Mother, who promised to give those who wore the Carmelite habit the gift of final perseverance. The charism of the Carmelites has been contemplative prayer, following in the footsteps of the Blessed Mother, ever since.

Blessed Marguerite Rose de Gordon and Companions

During the anti-Catholic French Revolution, faithful Catholics were routinely executed simply for being Catholics. Marguerite Rose de Gordon was born in Mondragon, France, in 1733 and was a nun during the time of the French Revolution. She and several other nuns were guillotined on this date in 1794 in the city of Orange.

Saint Mary Magdalen Postel

Julie (1756–1846) was a young woman running a girls' school in France when the French Revolution erupted in 1789. She remained faithful to the Church despite the ongoing persecution of Catholics, and she created a secret chapel under the stairs in her home so that Mass could be celebrated in secret. Due to the turbulent political situation, she couldn't return to her work as a teacher until 1801. At that time, despite great obstacles and little support from others, she founded a religious order called the Poor Daughters of Mercy, and she took the name in religious life of Mary Magdalen. She and her sisters taught poor girls, and they lived in poverty with them. Her work and the order had spread far and wide by the time she died at the age of ninety.

Our Lady of Mount Carmel, help me to persevere in prayer.
Blessed Marguerite, help me to love my Catholic faith.
Saint Mary Magdalen, show me how to trust in
God despite apparent "delays" in my plans.

* * * * *

Saint Alexis (Alexius) of Rome

Alexis was from a wealthy, respected family living in fifth-century Rome. According to tradition, he reluctantly agreed to his family's plans for him to marry, but immediately after the wedding, without consummating the marriage, he left his wife and the rest of the world behind for the sake of God. He lived in Syria for many years, living a holy life and supporting himself by begging. He then decided to return to Rome, and he became a servant in his own father's home without revealing his true identity. As their servant, he slept under the stairs and begged for his food. After Alexis' death, Pope Innocent I learned the truth about Alexis through a vision, and they found Alexis' name written on a piece of paper that the deceased man held in his fist.

Saint Leo IV

Leo (d. 855) was the 103rd pope; he reigned eight years. He was a subdeacon and cardinal priest before he became pope. His first act was to order the rebuilding of fifteen towers and the building of a new wall around the city of Rome to protect it in case of (another) attack by Muslim Arabs; the Romans named the newly fortified portion the "Leonine City" after him. After that was completed, he ordered the rebuilding of churches that had been destroyed by Muslim attacks, including Saint Peter's Basilica. He personally anointed and confirmed Alfred as king of England, improved decrees concerning ecclesiastical discipline, and settled disputes with disobedient bishops. Because of his energetic leadership after a time of destruction and the power of his prayers to work miracles, the people acclaimed him a saint after his death.

Saint Colman of Stockerau

Colman (d. 1012) was an English monk who was on his way to the Holy Land on a pilgrimage when he was stopped in Austria. The people living there thought he was a spy; though they had no evidence, they convicted, tortured, and hanged him along with two thieves. For eighteen months, his body hung where his executioners had left it, but it remained incorrupt. Even animals didn't touch it. After miracles were reported at the site, the nearby bishop transferred Colman's relics to an abbey in Melk in the year 1015.

Blessed Teresa of Saint Augustine and Companions, or the Sixteen Blessed Martyred Nuns of Compiegne

During the French Revolution, Catholic religious were routinely executed, and religious orders were suppressed. Sixteen nuns were living at Compiegne, France, in 1794, led by their prioress, Teresa of Saint Augustine (Marie Magdalene Claudine), when they were arrested and condemned to be guillotined because of their Christian faith. Before their public execution, each nun knelt and sang the "Veni Creator" (as if they were at a religious profession) and renewed her baptismal and religious vows. The sight caused even the onlookers, jaded by the terrors of the French Revolution, to watch in silence. As if God accepted their humble offering of their own lives for the sake of the French people, these nuns were the last to be executed, and the Reign of Terror soon ended.

Saint Alexis, help me learn humility by serving my family.
Saint Leo, help me to build up the Body of Christ today.
Saint Colman, help me witness to Jesus Christ to others.
Holy Martyrs, show me how to offer my life, each day, for others.

* * * * *

July 18

Saint Camillus de Lellis, Optional Memorial[19]

Camillus' mother was nearly sixty when he was born in Abruzzi, Italy, in 1550, and he grew up to be a very tall man—six feet and six inches tall. When he was seventeen years old, he left home with his father to become a soldier and to fight in the army against the Turks. However, he contracted a painful disease in his leg during his time of service and was admitted to a hospital in 1571. He was a patient and then a servant in the hospital until he was dismissed from his job for fighting, among other offenses, so he went off to fight in the Turkish war again. Camillus' worst vice was gambling, and it was at this point that he gambled away everything that he had down to his proverbial shirt. Out of remorse for his addiction, he went to a Franciscan monastery and served the friars as a laborer. When he was twenty-five years old, the guardian of the friars gave such a moving sermon that Camillus was brought to tears and repentance. He tried to enter the Capuchin order and became a novice, but he wasn't allowed to be professed into the order because of his diseased leg. So he returned to the hospital, devoted himself to the care of the sick, and eventually became the superintendent of the hospital. The unscrupulous and lazy behavior of the hired servants who were supposed to care for the sick saddened him, and he recognized that those who cared for the sick should be motivated by Christian devotion, not money. Gradually, some people followed his example in caring for those who were sick, although others treated him with the "jealousy and suspicion that are so often provoked by disinterested reformers",[20] as described by *Butler's Lives of the Saints*.

Saint Philip Neri, the famous and holy priest who revitalized the practice of the faith in Rome, was Camillus' confessor; he encouraged Camillus to become

---

[19] Because Saint Kateri Tekakwitha is celebrated as a memorial in the United States on July 14, Saint Camillus de Lellis is transferred as an optional memorial in the *Liturgical Calendar for the Dioceses of the United States of America* to July 18.

[20] Michael Walsh, ed., *Butler's Lives of the Saints, Concise Edition, Revised and Updated* (San Francisco: HarperCollins Publishers, 1991), 215.

a priest so that he might be able to help the sick spiritually as well. After he was ordained a priest, Camillus decided to separate from the hospital, against Father Neri's advice, and he and two companions followed a simple rule of life and daily served the sick at the Hospital of the Holy Spirit. As more men followed his example, this became a religious order, the Ministers of the Sick. The men cared for prisoners, plague victims, soldiers (forming the first recorded military field ambulance), and those who were dying. In 1591, Camillus himself was suffering from many physical problems: his diseased leg had troubled him for forty-six years, he had painful sores on his feet, and he was unable to retain his food. He wouldn't let anyone wait upon him, however. In 1607, he stepped down as leader of the order, visited the order's houses, and encouraged all his followers to care for the sick out of love for Jesus Christ. In 1614 he died, after giving a moving sermon to his brothers.

Saint Symphorosa and Sons of Rome

During the persecution of the Church, under the Roman emperor Hadrian in the year 138, Symphorosa was martyred with her seven sons: Crescentius, Julian, Nemesius, Primitivus, Justin, Stacteus, and Eugenius. According to tradition, Symphorosa was a wealthy widow, and she and her sons practiced their faith, particularly through service of the poor. When Emperor Hadrian was touring the region, he demanded that Symphorosa offer sacrifice to the pagan gods, and, when she refused, had her executed. The next day, Hadrian returned to threaten the seven sons with death as well. All seven men were tortured brutally and in a different manner, but all remained faithful to the death.

Saint Bruno of Segni

Born into a noble family in Piedmont, Italy, Bruno (1049–1123) was educated at the University of Bologna. When in Rome, he publicly defended Church teaching on the Blessed Sacrament against the heretical teachings of Berengarius of Tours and eventually became bishop of Segni. (Archdeacon Berengarius was a scholar who denied the teaching of transubstantiation and whose other teachings about the Eucharist were later condemned by the Church.) Pope Gregory VII respected Bruno and became a personal friend. Ongoing fighting between the pope and civil leaders of Italy led to Bruno being put in prison for three months by Count Ainulf. After Bruno was released, he returned to his diocese and served the new pope, Urban II. However, as Ainulf continued to persecute him and as Bruno's personal desire for a more solitary way of life increased, he decided to withdraw to the Benedictine Abbey of Monte Cassino. The abbot of Monte Cassino convinced the pope to allow Bruno to remain in the abbey, but the pope wouldn't relieve him of his office as bishop of Segni. In 1107, Bruno himself became the abbot of Monte Cassino. However, although Bruno lived as a monk, he spoke out against corrupt practices he saw going on within the Church. For example, he advocated improved clerical discipline and condemned the widespread practice of simony. He also rebuked Pope Paschal II for making concessions with King Henry V over ecclesiastical privileges in Germany. The angry pope replied by ordering Bruno to leave Monte

Cassino and return to serve his flock in Segni. Bruno obeyed immediately and fulfilled his duties as bishop for the remainder of his life. He was known as the greatest biblical commentator of his time, but he did hold one erroneous position: he taught that sacraments administered by simoniacal bishops and priests (there were many in his day) were invalid.

Saint Camillus, help me to learn God's will for my life through repentance. Holy Martyrs, pray for my family, that we will encourage one another in our difficulties. Saint Bruno, teach me how to speak the truth for the sake of Christ.

* * * * *

July 19

Saint Macrina the Younger

Macrina (ca. 327–379) was the eldest of the ten children born to two early Christian saints—Basil the Elder and Emmelia—and was the namesake of her grandmother Saint Macrina the Elder. The family lived in Cappadocia (modern Turkey). Although she was promised in marriage when she was twelve years old, her suitor died, and she then refused to marry at all. She was a great help to her mother and was a teacher to her younger sisters and brothers (three of whom are saints—Basil the Great, Peter of Sebastea, and Gregory of Nyssa). She taught humility to Basil, who came home from school a bit conceited (in her opinion), and she was both father and mother to her brother Peter, since their father died just as he was born. Macrina later lived with her mother, her brother Basil, and other women in an ascetical community. After their mother died, Macrina gave away their estate to the poor and lived on what she was able to earn for herself. When her brother Gregory came to visit her shortly before she died, he found that she slept on two boards as a penance and was cheerful despite her sickness. He reported that a large crowd and loudly weeping women accompanied her to her grave.

Saint Symmachus

Symmachus (d. 514) was the fifty-first pope; he reigned for fifteen years. He was born in Sardinia, Italy, and was a deacon when he was elected. On the same day as his election, a minority of clergy gathered for a false synod and claimed to elect a Byzantine candidate named Laurentius as pope, rather than the already elected Symmachus. The anti-pope Laurentius and his supporters tried to gain control of the situation by making false accusations that Symmachus had squandered church property and then demanding the right to judge him for these "crimes". During the resulting chaos, Symmachus was attacked and physically forced out of Saint Peter's Basilica. Finally, a council of bishops was able to meet and clear his name of the charges, pronouncing him as the true pope. King Theodoric had supported Laurentius throughout the controversy, but, probably for political reasons, supported Symmachus as pope at this point. During the remainder of his pontificate, Symmachus zealously defended the teachings of the Church against the schismatic teachings proposed by the patriarch of Constantinople, Acacius, as well as the heresies of Manichaeism. He also ordered the rebuilding and improving of churches in Rome that had been destroyed and damaged during the times of unrest.

Saint Aurea of Cordoba

During the Muslim occupation of Spain, the practice of Catholicism was sometimes tolerated, but discouraged and penalized in many ways. Aurea (d. 856) was born in Cordoba, Spain, raised to be a Muslim, married, and became a widow. At that point, she heard God's call to become a Christian, and she lived as a nun for twenty years. Eventually, however, her family turned her in to the authorities for the crime of converting to Catholicism. She died a martyr by beheading.

Blessed Peter (Pietro) Cresci of Foligno

Peter was born in Foligno, Italy, around the year 1243. When he was thirty years old, he decided to give everything he had to the poor and live a penitential life. As a penance, he even sold himself into slavery, but his new owner quickly freed him and asked Peter to pray for him instead. Peter then decided on a different penance: a life of complete poverty. He dressed in sackcloth and wouldn't wear shoes, and he spent his days in the cathedral, performing any service he was asked to do. Some people thought he was crazy, and he was interrogated by the Inquisition several times to verify his orthodoxy. But each time, it became clear that he wasn't crazy or a heretic, so he was always released. He died in 1323.

> *Saint Macrina, show me how to be a spiritual mother/father*
> *to those God has placed around me.*
> *Saint Symmachus, teach me to love Christ and His Church.*
> *Saint Aurea, help me be faithful to Christ, at any cost.*
> *Blessed Peter, teach me how to be a fool for Christ through penance.*

* * * * *

July 20

Prophet Elijah (Elias)

Elijah was a Jewish prophet living in the ninth century B.C. who left Israel during a time of famine and survived on food that ravens brought him. When he lived with a widow in the town of Zarepeth, God blessed the unnamed widow for her compassion on Elijah. Despite a famine in the area, their food never ran out. Elijah healed the pagan general Naaman of leprosy and single-handedly confronted five hundred prophets of Baal. His servant, Elisha, became his successor and watched Elijah go up to heaven in a flaming chariot.

[Elijah] said, "I have been very jealous for the LORD, the God of hosts; for the sons of Israel have forsaken your covenant, thrown down your altars, and slain your prophets with the sword; and I, even I only, am left; and they seek my life, to take it away." And [the LORD] said, "Go forth, and stand upon the mount before the LORD." And behold, the LORD passed by, and a great and strong wind tore the mountains, and broke in pieces the rocks before the LORD, but the LORD was not in the wind; and after the wind an earthquake, but the LORD was not in the earthquake; and after the earthquake a fire, but the LORD was not in the fire; and after the fire a still small voice. And when Elijah heard it, he wrapped his face in his mantle and went out and stood at the entrance of the cave.[21]

Saint Apollinaris of Ravenna, Optional Memorial

Apollinaris was the first bishop of Ravenna, Italy, though he was apparently originally from the city of Antioch. Some traditions say that he was ordained by Saint Peter, while others say that he died during the third century. All traditions say that he was imprisoned for his faith in Christ and died a martyr.

Saint Margaret of Antioch

Margaret's father was a pagan priest of Antioch (a city in modern Syria) who threw her out of the house when she became a Christian. Her old nurse took Margaret in, but later a pagan prefect asked her to marry him. When she refused, he reported her to the authorities as a Christian, and she was arrested and tortured to try to make her give up her faith. While she was in prison, she's said to have fought a dragon (perhaps in a dream?) who tried to swallow her, but her cross got stuck in his throat and saved her. After being tortured again and still refusing to give up her faith, she was beheaded. She was one of the saints who appeared to Joan of Arc and is one of the Fourteen Holy Helpers, great saints who were called upon particularly for help during the bubonic plague in the fourteenth century.

Saint Frumentius of Ethiopia

Around the year 330, Frumentius and his brother Aedesius were young Christian men from the city of Tyre (in modern Lebanon). They decided to travel with their teacher, to the coasts of Arabia. While their ship was moored at a port in Ethiopia, the sailors from their ship fought with the local people, and the sailors were all killed. Frumentius and his brother were studying under a tree when the native people found them after the fight. They were taken as prisoners and led to their king. The king of the Akusm Kingdom was impressed with the two young men, and he gave them important positions in his court, though they were treated as captive slaves. Aedesius became his cupbearer, and Frumentius became his secretary. When the king died, the two men were set free, but they decided to stay and serve the queen, who was regent for her son. As the secretary to the queen, Frumentius encouraged Christian merchants to come to Akusm and encouraged Christian worship. When the prince became king, the two brothers decided to leave the kingdom. Aedesius went back to Tyre and became a priest, telling what had happened to them to Rufinus, a

---

[21] 1 Kings 19:10–13.

Christian monk and historian who included the story in his well-known *Ecclesiastical History*. Frumentius, on the other hand, went to the bishop of Alexandria, Saint Athanasius, and asked him to send a pastor to Akusm to teach the people and lead them in the Christian faith. Athanasius recognized the value of Frumentius' experiences and abilities, ordained him bishop, and sent him back to Akusm sometime between the years 340 and 356. Many people converted to the Christian faith because of his preaching and the miracles that resulted from his prayers. He died in the year 380. To this day, the title that Frumentius was given by the people, "Abuna" (which means "our father"), is still the title of the primate of the Church of Ethiopia.

> *Prophet Elijah, help me to see God in all things and at all times.*
> *Saint Apollinaris, show me how to live and die for Christ.*
> *Saint Margaret, pray for me to persevere through the power of the Cross.*
> *Saint Frumentius, teach me to see God's blessings in all the sufferings of my life.*

* * * * *

July 21

Saint Praxedes of Rome

During the persecution of the Church in the second century, the martyr Praxedes died in the city of Rome. According to tradition, she was the daughter of a Roman senator and the sister of Saint Pudentiana. She was known for her generosity to the poor, and a very ancient church in Rome has been dedicated in her name for many centuries.

Saint Simeon Salus

Simeon lived as a monk for twenty-nine years in the Sinai Desert of Egypt in the sixth century. When he returned to his homeland in Syria, he spent much of his time caring for those who were outcasts of society. "Salus" means "stupid" in Syriac, which was the nickname he was given by the townspeople because he acted like he was stupid as an act of humility. Those he cared for loved him deeply for his great kindness to them. Simeon died when he was about seventy years old.

Saint Lawrence (Cesare de Rossi) of Brindisi, Optional Memorial

Lawrence was born Cesare de Rossi in 1559 in Naples, Italy, to noble parents and was educated first at a Conventual Franciscan friary and later, after the death of both his parents, by his own uncle. A pious child, he decided to enter the Capuchin order and took the name of Lawrence. He excelled in his studies and became a priest. Throughout his life, he was known for the power of his preaching, and because of his extraordinary knowledge of languages, including Latin, Greek, Hebrew, German, Bohemian, French, and Spanish, and his native Italian, he was an immensely popular and effective preacher wherever he traveled. His knowledge of Scripture gave depth to his words and writings and helped him to bring Jews to the Catholic faith. His writings include hundreds of sermons—written in Latin but delivered in the vernacular—with thousands of Scripture quotes, as well as an apologetic work answering the Lutheran arguments of the day. In his positions of authority within the Capuchin order, he traveled all over Europe to ensure fidelity to Catholic teaching within various monasteries, and while he was loved by his followers, he was vehement in demanding that they follow the ideals of their founder. His personal holiness and willingness to stand up for truth and the poor made him an excellent diplomat. When armed forces were sent to fight the Muslim Turks, he was appointed chaplain general of the European armies, gave a rousing address at a critical battle, and personally marched into the fight armed only with his crucifix. (Afterward, the Christians attributed their success on the battlefield to him.) He loved the Eucharist so deeply that each Mass would last several hours; one of his greatest works was a collection of eighty-four sermons on the role of the Virgin Mary. He died as he returned from a diplomatic mission, on his birthday, July 22, 1619. He was named a Doctor of the Church by Pope Saint John XXIII in 1959.

> *For the word of God is a light to the mind and a fire to the will. It enables man to know God and to love him. And for the interior man who lives by the Spirit of God through grace, it is bread and water, but a bread sweeter than honey and the honeycomb, a water better than wine and milk. For the soul it is a spiritual treasure of merits yielding an abundance of gold and precious stones. Against hardness of heart that persists in wrongdoing, it acts as a hammer. Against the world, the flesh, and the devil it serves as a sword that destroys all sin.*[22]

> *Saint Praxedes, show me how to live and die for Christ.*
> *Saint Simeon, teach me humility.*
> *Saint Lawrence, teach me how to love Scripture more every day.*

* * * * *

July 22

Saint Mary Magdalene, Feast

Jesus cast seven demons out of Mary Magdalene,[23] and she was one of the few people, mostly women, who stayed by Him at the foot of the Cross[24] during

---

[22] *The Liturgy of the Hours*, vol. 3, from a sermon by Saint Lawrence of Brindisi, priest (New York: Catholic Book Publishing, 1975), 1542.

[23] Lk 8:2.

[24] Mk 15:40.

His Crucifixion. She was among the women who went to anoint Jesus' body on Easter Sunday[25] and she was the first to see the risen Christ.[26]

> Now when he rose early on the first day of the week, he appeared first to Mary Magdalene, from whom he had cast out seven demons. She went and told those who had been with him, as they mourned and wept. But when they heard that he was alive and had been seen by her, they would not believe it.[27]

Saints Philip Evans and John Lloyd

Both Philip and John were Englishmen in the seventeenth century who traveled to Europe to become priests during the time of severe anti-Catholic laws in England. Philip became a Jesuit priest, and John became a secular priest. After the failed Oates Plot against the English government, a fictitious plot against the king that resulted in anti-Catholic hysteria, they were arrested and spent five months in prison. They were finally charged, not for involvement with the plot, but for the crime of being Catholic priests and for having entered England illegally. Two poor women were paid to say that they had seen Father Evans say Mass, and although there was no other real evidence, the two priests were condemned to death. They were treated better after the verdict, and Father Evans was playing tennis when the news came that their execution was the following day. They were executed on this date in 1679.

> Saint Mary Magdalene, pray for me to love Jesus Christ with my whole heart. Saints Philip and John, help me to appreciate the privilege of being able to attend Mass.

* * * * *

July 23

Prophet Ezekiel

Ezekiel lived in the sixth century B.C. and was exiled to Babylon (modern Iraq) after King Nebuchadnezzar defeated the Jewish people in battle. Following a vision, Ezekiel predicted that the deportation would lead to further disaster. This prediction was fulfilled when Jerusalem was destroyed in 586 B.C. Ezekiel also prophesied hope for the Jews to return in the future, which was fulfilled in 538 B.C., when King Cyrus allowed the Jews to go back to their homeland.

> In the thirtieth year, in the fourth month, on the fifth day of the month, as I was among the exiles by the river Chebar, the heavens were opened, and I saw visions of God.[28]

---

[25] Mk 16:1; cf. Mt 28:1; Lk 23:55—24:1; Jn 20:1.
[26] Mk 16:9; Jn 20:14; cf. Mt 28:9; Lk 24:15–18.
[27] Mk 16:9–11.
[28] Ezek 1:1.

Saint John Cassian

John was born into a wealthy family of southern Gaul (modern France) around the year 360. He and his friend, Germanus, lived as monks in various sites for several years, and he became a priest. Eventually, he founded monasteries, bringing the Eastern monastic practice of cenobites (monks living together with an emphasis on community life) to Europe. His two major writings explain how to deal with the challenges of the outer life and inner life of cenobites, particularly the deadly sins. Despite his tendency in a few of his writings to exaggerate the role of free will in the moral life (a teaching later condemned by the Church as Semi-Pelagianism), his major works on theology and monasticism have benefited saints and those in monastic life for centuries. He died around the year 435.

Saint Bridget of Sweden, Optional Memorial

Bridget was born in 1303 into a wealthy family in Uppsala, Sweden, and she was married to a nobleman, Ulf Gudmarsson, when she was fourteen years old. During their twenty-eight happy years of marriage, the couple had eight children. She became a lady-in-waiting to Queen Blanche, and Bridget's holy example (and direct rebukes, when necessary) greatly improved the behavior of both the pleasure-loving queen and her husband, King Magnus, who was weak and even sometimes wicked in his behavior. Bridget's dreams—on subjects as diverse as the importance of personal cleanliness and peace terms between feuding nations—became a common topic of conversation for even the worldly members of the court. When Bridget's husband became ill, she nursed him back to health, and after his recovery, the two agreed to live chastely as brother and sister, though Ulf died soon afterward. As a widow, Bridget lived a penitential life as a Franciscan tertiary. When she began to receive frequent and powerful personal revelations, she spoke about them to a priest, who eventually decided that they were a gift from God, not dangerous. Encouraged, Bridget then warned King Magnus of the need to reform his life, and he followed her advice (briefly) and gave her money to establish a monastery. With this monastery, she founded the Order of the Holy Savior, the order now known as the Bridgettines. Bridget traveled several times on pilgrimages to holy places. She continued to receive mystical revelations, and she wasn't afraid to confront anyone, including the pope, to direct them toward a holier way of life. On one of her last trips, Bridget's son Charles fell in love with Queen Joanna of Sweden, and although both were married, they decided to leave their spouses and marry one another. Bridget was horror-stricken and prayed constantly for her son. Soon, Charles became ill and repented of his sins, dying in his mother's arms. Bridget grieved her son's death deeply. She continued to travel and almost drowned during a shipwreck, but survived the trip and died in Rome a few months later in 1373. She was seventy years old.

Blessed Basil Hopko

Basil was born in 1904 in Hrabske, Slovakia, into a peasant family, and his father died when he was a baby. His mother was forced to leave the country and move to the United States to find work. Basil graduated with honors and hoped to rejoin his mother in the United States but was troubled by multiple health problems. When he made the decision to stay in his native country and serve people there, his medical problems were miraculously cured, and Basil saw this as a sign from God. He was ordained a priest in 1929 and particularly cared for students and the poor, though he also received a doctorate in theology. He was named auxiliary bishop in 1947, but the Communists arrested him in 1950 in their attempt to suppress the Church through her leaders. Basil was starved and tortured for weeks, was sentenced to fifteen years in prison for remaining loyal to the Church and Rome, and was transferred between prisons repeatedly for years. His health and emotional condition failed from all the mistreatment, and he was moved to a home for the elderly. In time, he was able to recover from the depression caused by his intense suffering and to minister to the nuns who were also imprisoned in the home, but his health was permanently damaged. He died as a martyr for his faith on this date in 1976, as a direct result of decades of abuse.

Prophet Ezekiel, help me to see what God wants me to see.
Saint John, help me give my inner life and my outer life to God.
Saint Bridget, help me to listen to God's voice.
Blessed Basil, help me to forgive and accept the crosses I am given.

* * * * *

July 24

Saint Sharbel (Charbel) Makhlouf, Optional Memorial

Sharbel was born in 1828 in Beka-Kafra, Lebanon, and given the name Joseph. Though his father died when he was young, his mother raised him in a pious home. *The Imitation of Christ* was his favorite book when he was a young man, and he snuck away from home when he was twenty-three years old to join a monastery in the city of Annaya. There he took the name of an early martyr, Sharbel. He took solemn vows in 1853, was ordained in 1859, and lived a model life as a monk. From 1875 until his death, he lived as a hermit, having only the barest necessities. He was known for his devotion to the Blessed Sacrament and the Blessed Mother; he spoke very little and spent hours preparing each time before he celebrated Mass. People sometimes saw him levitating while praying, and many people came to him for spiritual advice. Shortly before his death in 1898, he became paralyzed, and after his death (most particularly in the years 1927 and 1950), bloody sweat flowed from his corpse. He is still greatly venerated by the Lebanese people.

Saint Christina of Bolsena

Christina was discovered to be a Christian during the persecution under the Roman emperor Diocletian in the third century. She was tortured before being killed by a lance near Lake Bolsena in Italy and died a martyr for Christ.

Saint Euphrasia (Eupraxia) of Thebes

Euphrasia (380–420) was born into the noble family of Roman emperor The-odosius I; when her father died, Euphrasia and her mother were placed under the emperor's protection. According to the custom of the time, Euphrasia was betrothed to the son of a wealthy senator when she was only five years old. When her mother decided to withdraw from the world (and endless proposals of marriage because of her wealth), she took her daughter with her to live near a convent in Egypt. Euphrasia begged her mother to let her live with the nuns too, and her mother agreed, though she expected her daughter to tire of convent life quickly. But Euphrasia remained and eventually became a nun herself. When Euphrasia turned twelve, the emperor sent a letter to her, telling her it was time for her to marry and inherit her father's wealth. But Euphrasia asked the emperor to let her follow her religious vocation, to free her slaves, and to give her property to the poor. The emperor did as she asked, but afterward Euphrasia was tempted by thoughts about all that she had given up. Her abbess gave her hard and humbling tasks, for example, moving a pile of stones from one place to another and back again—thirty times. Euphrasia obeyed this ridiculous order promptly and cheerfully, overcoming the temp-tation and learning humility. When Euphrasia died, a nun named Julia and the abbess died soon after her; they had prayed to be her companions in Heaven.

Saint Christina the Astonishing

Christina was born in Belgium in 1150, and her parents died when she was fifteen years old, leaving her and her two sisters orphans. When Christina was twenty-two years old, she had some sort of seizure, and everyone thought she had died. During the funeral Mass, however, Christina rose up from her coffin, flew to the ceiling, and perched on the beams of the church. Everyone except one of her sisters ran away, and at the end of Mass, the priest told Chris-tina to come down to the floor. Christina obeyed, and she then explained to the priest that she had really been dead; had been to Hell and seen many friends; had been to Purgatory where she had seen even more friends; and then been to Heaven. God Himself had spoken to her, she said, and offered her two options: come to Heaven now or return to earthly life and do penance first to rescue the poor souls she had seen in purgatory. Christina chose the latter. For the rest of her life, she behaved in strange and amazing ways, both as a personal and public penance and because of what she had seen. She lived in remote places, climbed trees, and crawled into ovens. She prayed in strange positions, balanced on one leg or curled up like a ball. People saw her handle fire, jump into the river in winter, and be carried into a mill race and under the wheel, all without injury. Obviously, some thought she was possessed and tried to lock her up, but she always escaped, even from chains and once when it was thought her leg was broken. She lived by begging and dressed in rags. Despite her strange behavior, she later moved to the Convent of Saint Catherine at Saint-Trond and was treated with great respect by many people. In addition to Christina's prioress, two other holy nuns, (Blessed) Mary of Oignies and (Saint) Lutgardis, were convinced of her holiness. She died in 1224.

Saint Sharbel, teach me a love of silence.
Saint Christina the Martyr, show me how to live and die for Christ.
Saint Euphrasia, help me to be cheerful when performing humbling tasks.
Saint Christina, convict me of the truth about death, judgment, Heaven, and Hell.

* * * * *

July 25

Saint James the Greater, Apostle, Feast

James the son of Zebedee was the one of the first disciples to be called by Christ[29] and was, along with the apostles Peter and John, invited by Jesus to be present at His Transfiguration[30] and during His final night in the Garden of Gethsemane.[31] Around the years 42–44, James was also the first apostle to be martyred[32] when he was beheaded by King Herod Agrippa, as a means of pleasing the Jewish persecutors of Christians. When his relics were discovered in the ninth century in Compostela, a great devotion to James spread among the Spanish people. The Spanish church given his name has been a beloved pilgrimage site for centuries.

Saint Christopher

Christopher, according to tradition, was a giant who wanted to serve the greatest king of the world. And so he did, becoming a martyr for his faith in Jesus Christ, during the persecution of Christians under the Roman emperor Decius in the year 250. Christopher is one of the Fourteen Holy Helpers, great saints who were called upon particularly for help during the bubonic plague in the fourteenth century.

Blessed John Soreth

John was born in Normandy, France, around the year 1405, and entered the Carmelites when he was sixteen years old. Later, he became a priest and earned a doctorate. When he became prior general of the Carmelites, he reformed the order, founded the first female Carmelite communities, and instituted the Third Order of the Carmelites. The pope even offered to make him a bishop, but John felt he was unworthy of the honor. On one occasion, in 1468, he courageously risked his life to remove the Blessed Sacrament from a church that a mob of soldiers intended to loot. Faithful to the Carmelite order's rule and detached from the world, John was a model example to his fellow Carmelites. He died in 1471.

[29] Mt 4:21.
[30] Mt 17:1–8.
[31] Mk 14:33.
[32] Acts 12:2.

Saint James, give me your zeal for serving Jesus Christ.
Saint Christopher, teach me how to serve Christ wholeheartedly.
Blessed John, show me how to reform myself in Christ's image.

* * * * *

July 26

Saints Joachim and Anne, Memorial

Joachim and Anne, according to pious tradition and extrabiblical writings, are the names of the parents of the Blessed Virgin Mary. Tradition also says that they were old and childless when they separately received visions explaining that they would have a child who would be praised all over the world. And so they did.

Saint William Ward (Webster)

William Webster was born in 1560 and raised a Protestant during a time when it was illegal and dangerous to be a Catholic in England, and he became a teacher. While traveling to Spain with a Catholic friend, he converted, entered the Catholic Church, returned home, and converted his mother. At the age of forty, he traveled to Belgium to study for the priesthood, and, after ordination, he went to live in Scotland under the name of William Ward. He was imprisoned for being a priest for three years, but after his release, he took up residence in London. There he secretly served as a Catholic priest for thirty years more. In London, he cared for the poor and was repeatedly put in jail or banished until a priest-hunter finally found and betrayed him to the authorities. He was thrown into Newgate Prison and condemned for being a priest. He was hanged, drawn, and quartered on July 15, 1641, and he prayed to Jesus to the very end.

Saint Bartholomea Capitainio

Bartholomea was born in 1807 in the Brescian Alps in Bergamo, Italy. Her father was a gruff farmer who drank heavily, but her mother (and the sisters at school) taught her about the love of God. Although her parents wouldn't let her become a sister, she made a personal vow of chastity and decided to devote her life to education. She first worked as a teacher and organized a youth group. But she later chose to join Saint Vincentia Gerosa in founding a female religious order that served the needy, both through education and nursing. It was called the Sisters of Charity of Lovere. Bartholomea worked tirelessly for the growing order until illness and a doctor forced her to rest. In 1833, she died when she was only twenty-six years old, but her congregation spread all over the world.

Blessed Titus (Anno Sjoera) Brandsma

Anno Sjoera Brandsma was born in 1881 into a pious Catholic family in the Netherlands. His brother eventually became a Franciscan priest, and three of his sisters became nuns. Anno felt called to the priesthood from an early age, and he studied at a Franciscan minor seminary. He had to leave the seminary when he was seventeen years old due to health problems, but at the age of eighteen, he joined the Carmelites and took the name Titus. He learned to speak or read several languages, was ordained a priest in 1905, received a doctorate in philosophy from Rome in 1909, and taught at a seminary. He was the editor of a local daily newspaper and traveled widely as an orator, journalist, and lobbyist for the Catholic University at Nijmegen, Netherlands. He became university president in 1932 and conducted a speaking tour in the United States in 1935. Also in 1935, he wrote against the Nazi anti-Jewish marriage laws, and his opposition to Nazi propaganda led him to be continually followed by the Gestapo until he was finally arrested in April 1942. Titus was put in jail, was punished when he cared for other prisoners, and was sent to the Dachau concentration camp. At Dachau, he was beaten daily and overworked like all the other prisoners, yet he encouraged them to pray for the salvation of their guards. When he was no longer able to work, the Nazis used him for medical experimentation and killed him when he was no longer useful for their experiments. He died by lethal injection on this date in 1942.

> Saints Joachim and Anne, help me to love the Blessed Mother as you do.
> Saint William, show me how to persevere in my difficulties.
> Saint Bartholomea, help me to show the love of God to others through service.
> Blessed Titus, show me how to accept my sufferings with love for the sake of Christ.

* * * * *

July 27

Seven Sleepers of Ephesus

Seven Christian men—Constantius, Dionysius, John, Malchus, Martinianus, Maximianus, and Serapion—were arrested during the early persecution of the Church in Ephesus (in modern Turkey) around the year 250. Because they refused to give up their faith, they were executed and died as martyrs. Their bodies were placed in a cave, but they were rediscovered in the year 479 and were taken to Marseilles, France, in a large coffin for veneration. A legend later arose that they were walled up in the cave to die by suffocation in 250 and woke up when the cave was opened in 479. This is probably due to the expression "sleep in the Lord"[33] being used to describe their two hundred years of hiddenness in the cave and why they are commonly (but somewhat confusingly) known as the Seven Sleepers.

Saint Pantaleon

Pantaleon was a widely respected doctor who lived in the third century and who converted to the Christian faith. As a Christian, he continued to care for the sick, but now some of his patients were healed because of his prayers in the

---

[33] See Rom 13:11; Eph 5:14.

name of Jesus Christ. (Another tradition says that he was raised in the Christian faith, gave it up for political expedience, and was brought back to it by another Christian.) In the end, he was turned in to the Roman emperor Maximinus for the crime of being a Christian, and he was arrested and cruelly tortured. When he refused to give up his faith, he was beheaded. Pantaleon is one of the Fourteen Holy Helpers, great saints who were called upon particularly for help during the bubonic plague in the fourteenth century.

Saint Celestine I

Celestine was the forty-third pope (d. 432); he reigned for nine years. He worked energetically against the heresies spread by Nestorius and Pelagius, he defended the teachings of the bishop of Hippo, Saint Augustine, and he helped develop early canon law through his writing called *The Decretals*.

Saint Simeon the Stylite

Simeon (390–459) was a shepherd and the son of a shepherd in Cilicia, a city now in modern Turkey. He went to live among monks when he was sixteen years old and imposed very harsh penances upon himself. The other monks criticized him for this and, recognizing that his way was not meant for their community, asked him to leave. At first, he lived in a hut, then a narrow cave, and finally on top of a small pillar, called a stylite. He fasted often, so much so that people said he looked like a skeleton. He prayed in various postures for long periods of time—sometimes standing erect, sometimes bowing thousands of times, sometimes with his arms out in the form of a cross. Though his goal was to live alone with God, crowds of people came to see him, and he occasionally preached to them about subjects such as temperance, compassion, and avoiding vice. Many people were impressed with his holiness, and other men followed his example and lived lives of penance on stylites as well.

Saints Clement of Okhrida and Companions

The ruler of the Bulgars, Khan Boris, converted to the Catholic faith in the year 865, but converting the rest of the Bulgar people was difficult. Khan Boris had converted only so he could create a national church that he could control, and the churches of Rome and Constantinople disagreed repeatedly over which of them had jurisdiction over the area for evangelization. When seven men, including Clement, Gorazd, Nahum, Sabas, and Angelarius, traveled to bring Christ to the Bulgar people, they were persecuted and treated with cruelty and violence. Yet these men persevered; they brought the teachings of Christ to the region now known as Bulgaria during the ninth and tenth centuries and are now considered its apostles.

> *Holy Martyrs, pray that I too may "sleep in the Lord" after my death.*
> *Saint Pantaleon, show me God's power to heal.*
> *Saint Celestine, help me to discern the false teachings of today's world.*
> *Saint Simeon, help me to grow in humility through self-mortification.*
> *Holy apostles of Bulgaria, show me how to bring Christ to other people.*

* * * * *

July 28

Saints Prochorus, Nicanor, Timon, Parmenas, and Nicolaus

The apostles chose seven men to be the first deacons to serve the Church in the first century. Two of them—Stephen and Philip—are celebrated on other days in the Church's calendar. The other five deacons are celebrated today.

> And the Twelve summoned the body of the disciples and said, "It is not right that we should give up preaching the word of God to serve tables. Therefore, brethren, pick out from among you seven men of good repute, full of the Spirit and of wisdom, whom we may appoint to this duty. But we will devote ourselves to prayer and to the ministry of the word." And what they said pleased the whole multitude, and they chose Stephen, a man full of faith and of the Holy Spirit, and Philip, and Prochorus, and Nicanor, and Timon, and Parmenas, and Nicolaus, a proselyte of Antioch.[34]

Saints Nazarius and Celsus of Milan

During the persecution of the Church under the Roman emperor Nero around the year 60, Nazarius became a Christian. Some traditions say that his father was a pagan but that his mother was a Christian and was converted to the faith by Saint Peter. Nazarius left Rome because of the persecution, accompanied by his young friend Celsus. In Milan, however, they were arrested for being Christians, and both died as martyrs.

Saint Victor I

Victor was the fourteenth pope (d. ca. 199); he reigned ten years. He was born in Africa. At the beginning of his papacy, the Church enjoyed relative peace because the Roman emperors were friendly to Christians, despite the laws officially against the faith. Emperor Commodus' Christian mistress, for example, was able to beg for the freedom of some Christians in the Sardinian salt mines, and the list of names that Pope Victor gave her included the name of Callistus, who later became the pope and a saint. The most serious dispute that Victor faced as pope was in resolving differences among Christians over the date of the celebration of Easter. Some followed the ancient tradition of celebrating Easter on a Sunday, while others followed the tradition (just as ancient) of celebrating it on the fourteenth day of Nisan, according to the Jewish calendar. When Victor insisted that all follow the former tradition, a schism occurred. He was known for his writings about the faith, which later earned him the respect of Saint Jerome. He has always been called a martyr in Church records, but the details of his martyrdom are unknown.

Saint Samson of York

Samson's Welsh parents had been childless for many years before God answered their prayers with a son. When he was born around the year 485,

---

[34] Acts 6:2–5.

they gratefully dedicated Samson to God and took him to a monastery in Llantwit to be educated. Samson was a quick student, was virtuous and austere in his observance of monastic life, and in time became a deacon and then a priest. With the abbot's permission, Samson traveled to an island and lived in a community governed by a man named Piro. When Samson learned that his father was near death, he didn't want to leave, but Piro rebuked him and sent him to see his dying father, accompanied by a deacon. When Samson administered the last sacraments to his father, his father amazingly recovered. Both his father and uncle then decided to leave the world as Samson had done, so they returned to the island with him. Soon afterward, Piro died and Samson was made abbot. Though Samson continued to live like a hermit, he also established greater discipline in the community than his predecessor, though he was a gentle leader. Against his wishes, he was chosen bishop of Dol. He traveled by sea to bring the Gospel to Trigg, Brittany, and Normandy and to found monasteries. He died a peaceful death among his monks around the year 565.

> *Holy Deacons, show me how to devote myself to prayer and ministering to others.*
> *Holy Martyrs, show me how to live and die for Christ.*
> *Saint Victor, help me love Christ and His Church.*
> *Saint Samson, help me to hear and obey God's direction, wherever it may lead.*

* * * * *

July 29

Saint Martha, Memorial

Martha; her sister, Mary; and her brother, Lazarus, were devoted friends of our Lord. They invited Him to their home, and they served dinner to Him and His disciples. Martha's impatience with her sister, who chose to listen to Jesus rather than be busy, is legendary.[35] But so is Martha's faith in Jesus.

> *Jesus said to her, "I am the resurrection and the life; he who believes in me, though he die, yet shall he live, and whoever lives and believes in me shall never die. Do you believe this?" [Martha] said to him, "Yes, Lord; I believe that you are the Christ, the Son of God, he who is coming into the world."*[36]

Saint Lazarus

Martha's brother, Lazarus, was raised from the dead by Jesus Christ,[37] and he was so inconvenient to the Pharisees that they plotted to kill him.[38] According

[35] Lk 10:38–42.
[36] Jn 11:25–27.
[37] See Jn 11:1–44; 12:9.
[38] Jn 12:9–11.

to tradition, Lazarus did die a second time—but he died as a follower of Christ and a saint.

Saints Simplicius, Faustinus, Beatrice, and Rufo of Rome

During the persecution of the Church under the Roman emperor Diocletian in the year 303, these four martyrs died in Rome. According to tradition, Simplicius, Faustinus, and Beatrice were siblings.

Saint Olaf of Norway

Olaf (d. 1030) had to fight to succeed his deceased father and become king of Norway. At the time, he was only twenty years old, but he was successful in battle—and he was a baptized Christian. The evangelization of his people into the Christian faith had only begun recently and proceeded very slowly, in part because of the wicked and ridiculous methods used by at least one previous missionary to make conversions. Since Olaf had helped the king of England fight off the Danes a few years before he became king, he now asked the English king to send him priests and monks to bring the Gospel to his people—in the right way. One of these priests, Grimkel, became the bishop at Olaf's capital, and he helped Olaf develop good laws and remove laws that were contrary to the Gospel. However, Olaf, like many Christian kings of the time, had no problems using force to get his way, and he treated his enemies without mercy. Because of this and as the result of other political pressures, some of Olaf's men rose up against him, and with the help of King Canute of England and Denmark, he was defeated. Olaf returned to fight later with the support of some Swedish troops, but he was killed in a battle at Stiklestad on this date. A spring rose in the spot where he was buried, and when miraculous healings occurred with this water, Bishop Grimkel named him a martyr and built a chapel on the site.

Blessed Urban II

Urban (d. 1099) was the 159th pope; he reigned for eleven years. He was born with the name Otho around the year 1042 and was the son of a French knight. He studied under Saint Bruno, the future founder of the Carthusians; he became a canon, then a monk at the Abbey of Cluny. He was a cardinal when he was elected to the papacy. At the time of his election, Europe was embroiled in feuds, violence, and confusion over an anti-pope; at first, Urban wasn't even able to enter Rome and Saint Peter's Basilica as pope. Though conditions stabilized and he was able to live in Rome for a time, he was eventually forced out of Rome and had to travel throughout southern Italy, in exile and in debt. However, he continued to hold councils and attempted to improve ecclesiastical discipline. Urban eloquently called for a Crusade to protect Christians in the Holy Land, particularly Jerusalem, from Muslims, and many Christians obeyed. When political winds changed, he was able to return to Rome and enjoy a short period of calm, also attempting to reconcile with the Eastern churches. He died before news of the success of the Crusade was able to reach him.

Saint Martha, show me how to trust the Son of God with the desires of my heart.
Saint Lazarus, help me not to be afraid of bodily death.
Holy Martyrs, show me how to live and die for Christ.
Saint Olaf, help me rid my soul of all habits that are contrary to the Gospel.
Blessed Urban, help me to love Christ and His Church.

* * * * *

July 30

Saint Peter Chrysologus, Optional Memorial

Peter was born around the year 380 in Imola, Italy, and became a deacon. When the archbishop of Ravenna died in the year 433, Peter went to Rome with his bishop and the candidate selected by the people of the city. But Pope Sixtus III had received visions from God supporting another candidate, whom he recognized to be Peter when he saw him, and Peter was ordained the archbishop instead. As archbishop, Peter was trusted and respected by the emperor Valentinian III and the subsequent pope, Saint Leo the Great. Peter was known for giving short sermons—he was afraid of tiring his listeners, he said—but they were concise, expressive, down-to-earth, and comprehensible to everyone. He wrote in a reverent, Christ-centered style, with many examples and words of encouragement to live a virtuous life. For his "golden words", he's now commonly surnamed Chrysologus. Peter died on December 2, probably in the year 450. Though many of his writings have been lost to us over time, enough of his writings survived for Pope Benedict XIII to decide to name him a Doctor of the Church in 1729.

> *That is, when there is hope of mercy, when it is the time of pardon, when there is the opportunity of repentance, let us confess to him as Father, so that we do not experience him as Judge.*[39]

Saints Abdon and Sennen of Rome

These two men were from third-century Persia (modern Iran) but were living in Rome when they were accused of being Christians during the persecutions by either the Roman emperor Decius or Diocletian. Wild animals were set loose upon them in the amphitheater to kill them, but the animals refused to attack the two men. A Roman soldier was finally sent to do what the animals would not, and Abdon and Sennen were beheaded, dying as martyrs.

Saint Godelva of Gistel

Godelva (d. ca. 1070) was a kind, prayerful, and charitable girl and a daughter of Flemish nobility when she married a Flemish nobleman named Bertulf. She

---

[39] Peter Chrysologus, *Selected Sermons, Volume 2*, Sermon 46, trans. William B. Palardy, Fathers of the Church Series (Washington, D.C.: Catholic University of America Press, 2004), 179.

was eighteen years old. Her mother-in-law was furious over the marriage and convinced Bertulf to leave Godelva even before the wedding feast was over. Godelva was locked in a tiny room and given only scraps of food to eat. When Godelva escaped from her "prison", the bishop of Tournai and the count of Flanders intervened and publicly insisted that Bertulf take back his wife and treat her kindly. At first, he did. But then he became violent toward her. One day when he was out of town, he had two of his servants lure Godelva to the back door of their castle. The men grabbed her, tied a rope around her neck, and drowned her in a pond. While it was obvious that Bertulf had ordered the murder, his guilt was never proven. God proved Godelva's sanctity, however, for many miracles occurred at the site of her murder in Gistel, Belgium, including the healing of the blindness of Bertulf's daughter by his second marriage.

Saint Leopold (Adeodato) Mandic

Adeodato (1866–1942) was his parents' twelfth child, and he was born with delicate health and physical problems. He decided to leave his homeland (modern Croatia) when he was sixteen years old to become a student at a Capuchin school in Udine, Italy. After he completed his studies, he entered the Capuchin order, took the name of Leopold, and became a priest in 1890. Although he had a great desire to serve as a missionary in Eastern Europe, his superiors sent him to various friaries in Italy and Dalmatia (a region of Croatia) due to his poor health. For a year during World War I, he was sent to a prison camp because he refused to renounce his Croatian nationality. Except for that period, the last forty years of his life were spent entirely at a friary in Padua. Leopold was only four feet, four inches tall; he had a stammer, suffered abdominal pains, and had chronic arthritis, which stooped his back and painfully gnarled his hands. His health problems increased as he grew older, but he was a spiritual giant. Serving as a confessor and spiritual director for twelve hours a day, he communicated his deep faith in God and personal humility to thousands of penitents. He died at age seventy-six of cancer.

> *Saint Peter Chrysologus, help me speak the truth succinctly.*
> *Saints Abdon and Sennen, give me your courage in serving Christ.*
> *Saint Godelva, show me how to forgive.*
> *Saint Leopold, teach me how to confess my sins deeply, humbly, and immediately.*

* * * * *

July 31

Saint Ignatius of Loyola, Memorial

Ignatius was born in a castle at Loyola, Spain, around the year 1491 and was the youngest of eleven children in a noble family. He wanted to have a military career, but in a battle in 1521, a cannon ball injured his legs, giving him a permanent limp. During Ignatius' recuperation at home, he asked for a book of fiction to pass the time. When fiction books couldn't be found, he was given books about Jesus and the saints. Although he read them at first only to pass the time, he grew to love them. He went through a deep conversion; he began to pray and wept for his past sins. He went on pilgrimages and lived as a hermit for about a year. While a hermit, he began to write his *Spiritual Exercises*, his own guide to the spiritual life. Ignatius traveled to the Holy Land, but the Franciscan guardian there ordered him to leave due to the danger that he would be captured and held for ransom. In 1524, he returned to Spain and began studying Latin, logic, physics, and theology. Though living in poverty, he was able to reach many people and bring them to conversion. There were many strange teachings at this time in Spain, and Ignatius was imprisoned twice out of concerns that he was introducing dangerous teachings, but he was also safely released both times. He traveled and studied in various places throughout Europe, and he finally graduated as a master of arts. Six divinity students he had befriended decided to follow him: Diego Laynez, Alphonus Salmeron, Simon Rodriguez, Nicholas Bobadilla, Peter Faber, and Francis Xavier. (The last two are now known as saints.) Together, these seven men privately took vows of poverty and chastity, and they promised to preach the Gospel in Palestine or wherever the pope would send them. They received Holy Communion at the hands of Peter Faber, who had recently been ordained a priest, and later met Pope Paul III. The pope recognized their fervor and orthodoxy, gave them permission to preach, and ordained them. This group of men gradually grew in number and began calling themselves the Company of Jesus. Over time, this became a religious order that Ignatius led until his death, though he would only agree to be the order's superior general when ordered to do so by his confessor. At the end of his life, Ignatius was ill several times. In 1556, he died suddenly and unexpectedly, without receiving the last sacraments. Ignatius is patron of spiritual exercises and retreats.

> *First Week, Principle and Foundation: Man is created to praise, reverence, and serve God our Lord, and by this means to save his soul. And the other things on the face of the earth are created for man and that they may help him prosecuting the end for which he is created. From this it follows that man is to use them as much as they help him on to his end, and ought to rid himself of them so far as they hinder him as to it. For this it is necessary to make ourselves indifferent to all created things in all that is allowed to the choice of our free will and is not prohibited to it; so that, on our part, we want not health rather than sickness, riches rather than poverty, honor rather than dishonor, a long life rather than short life, and so in all the rest; desiring and choosing only what is more conducive for us to the end for which we are created.*[40]

Saint Helen of Skofde

Helen was born around the early twelfth century into a noble Swedish family, married young, and had one daughter. She financially supported the building of

---

[40] Ignatius of Loyola, *The Spiritual Exercises of Saint Ignatius of Loyola*, trans. Father Elder Mullan, S.J. (San Francisco: Ignatius Press, 2017), EPUB.

the church in her town of Skofde, and when she was widowed at an early age, she gave away most of her fortune to the poor. While she was away on a pilgrimage, her servants killed her cruel son-in-law and blamed Helen for his death. When she returned, her in-laws believed the servants and executed her. It was the year 1160. However, miracles were reported at her tomb, and her holiness and innocence of the crime became known. She is now known as a martyr.

Saint Ignatius, help me examine my life daily in the light of the Gospel.
Saint Helen, help me forgive from the heart.

August

August 1

Saint Alphonsus Liguori, Memorial

Alphonsus was born near Naples, Italy, in 1696 to noble parents, the first of eight children. His mother was a saintly woman, and two of his brothers eventually became priests, while two sisters became nuns. He was a brilliant student and had become a doctor of canon and civil law by the time he was sixteen years old. He was devout and never attended court without attending Mass first. He loved music, but when he attended the opera, he took off his glasses so he could ignore the overdone staging. He became a very successful lawyer, but that changed after an unfortunate court case. He had misread his papers and began a strong defense of his case. When the other side pointed out his error, Alphonsus recognized his mistake and also recognized that others thought he had been dishonest. As a result, Alphonsus humbly vowed never to enter a courtroom again. For a time, he prayed, served others by visiting the sick, and then recognized (through a vision) that God was calling him to the priesthood. Despite his father's initial opposition, he studied for the priesthood and was ordained at the age of twenty-nine. In 1730, he was called in to help determine the nature of some revelations that a community of sisters claimed to receive. Alphonsus decided that the revelations and the rule of life based on them were from God; he won over others to his side and thereby ended a bitter controversy. With his cautious, thorough leadership, the order of Redemptorist nuns was founded, and he was also able to establish an order of Redemptorist priests. Despite political opposition to his orders throughout his lifetime—particularly from those who thought there were too many religious orders in Italy at the time—his order grew and served the faithful, particularly the poor, through preaching and parish missions. He tried to avoid the honor of being named a bishop, but the pope insisted that Alphonsus become bishop of Saint Agata dei Gotti in 1762. His tireless efforts and clear, direct preaching, despite declining health, brought about a reformation within his clergy and revitalized the faith among the laity. He wrote short devotional leaflets (still read all over the world today), was always available to ordinary people, and established the practice of a daily Holy Hour at his cathedral. But by 1775, rheumatism had made it very difficult for him to move or even raise his chin from his chest, so he resigned. Later in life, the anti-clerical government tried to completely outlaw his order, and it took all of Alphonsus' many skills to keep that from happening. By this time, he had become almost blind, and he had to rely on some "friends", who tricked him into approving a revised rule for the order that would be supported by the government. When the pope saw the changes, he condemned them and removed Alphonsus as leader of the order.

This caused the scrupulous, obedient Alphonsus to suffer a crisis of confidence and faith for several years. But by the time he died at the age of ninety in 1787, he had recovered his peace with God. Though some Church leaders thought he was too lenient in his writings and his work as a confessor during his lifetime, after his death his innumerable writings, particularly on moral theology, caused him to be named a Doctor of the Church.

> *When devotion towards Mary begins in a soul, it produces the same effect that the birth of this most Holy Virgin produced in the world. It puts an end to the night of sin, and leads the soul into the path of virtue.*[1]

The Holy Maccabees

Around the year 168 B.C., King Antiochus IV enforced his control over his territories by ordering all his subjects to embrace paganism. When Jewish subjects resisted, they were brutally killed. A Jewish man named Mattathias and his sons—Judas Maccabeus, Jonathan, and Simon—led a violent and ultimately successful rebellion. On this day, we remember the bravery and faithfulness of many of these Jewish men and women, including a mother and her seven adult sons[2] and the elderly man Eleazar,[3] who chose death rather than unfaithfulness to God.

Saint Peter Faber

Peter was born in Villaret, France, into a family of farmers in 1506. As a child, he cared for the sheep, and he taught the catechism to other children. When he entered college in Paris, he became friends with Saint Ignatius of Loyola and was part of Ignatius' first band of Jesuits. He preached all over—in France, Spain, Portugal, and Germany—bringing laypeople and the clergy to greater faith in Christ while opposing Lutheranism. He was known for his great devotion to the angels. He died in 1546.

Martyrs of Nowogrodek

During World War II, 120 citizens of the city of Nowogrodek (now in Belarus) were condemned to death by the Nazis. Eleven nuns offered their lives to the Nazis in exchange for the villagers' lives. The nuns were Maria Stella (superior), Mary Imelda, Mary Rajmunda, Maria Daniela, Maria Kanuta, Maria Gwidona, Maria Sergia, Maria Kanizja, Maria Felicyta, Maria Heliodora, and Maria Boromea. The Gestapo accepted their offer and executed the women on this date in 1943.

> *Saint Alphonsus, help me to make good moral decisions every day.*
> *Holy Martyrs, show me how to give my life daily for others.*
> *Saint Peter, give me zeal for spreading the truth about Jesus.*

* * * * *

[1] Saint Alphonsus Liguori, *The Glories of Mary* (Charlotte: TAN Books, 2012), 59.
[2] 2 Mac 7:1–42.
[3] 2 Mac 6:18–31.

August 2

Saint Eusebius of Vercelli, Optional Memorial

Eusebius (d. 371) was a Sardinian whose father died for the Christian faith while in prison. Eusebius' widowed mother returned to Rome with her son and daughter; when Eusebius grew up, he became a lector in the Church. He served the church of Vercelli so well that he became the first bishop of the city, and he was the first Westerner to bring his clergy to live together in communal life. When Arians tried to force him to support the condemnation of the bishop, Saint Athanasius of Alexandria, at a public meeting, Eusebius refused and instead demanded that everyone present sign the Nicene Creed before the case of Athanasius could be debated. This caused chaos and effectively ended the meeting. As a result, the emperor Constantius (who supported the Arian heresy) ordered him and other faithful bishops to be banished. While Eusebius was in exile in Palestine, the Arians continued to threaten and persecute him. When his only powerful supporter, Count Joseph, died, Eusebius was dragged through the streets and his property was stolen. After Constantius died, the emperor Julian allowed the banished bishops to return. Eusebius traveled throughout the East, encouraged the Christian faithful to remain faithful, and was finally allowed to return to his see in Vercelli. He is considered a Father of the Church.

Saint Peter Julian Eymard, Optional Memorial

Peter (1811–1868) grew up in Grenoble, France, and worked as a cutler, making knives with his father. As a young man, he studied Latin and other subjects from a priest and then went to study at the seminary at Grenoble. He was ordained three years later. For five years, he served in various parishes, where he inspired his parishioners with his devotion and charity. Although he joined the Society of Mary, the idea that there was no religious institute that glorified Christ's mystery of love in the Blessed Sacrament saddened him. So he eventually founded the Congregations of the Priests of the Blessed Sacrament (for priests) and the Servants of the Blessed Sacrament (for nuns). Founding a religious order is never easy, but some of the criticism he endured came from those who were offended that he had chosen to leave the Marist order. However, his religious congregations grew and were approved during his lifetime, and he also wrote many books about devotion to the Blessed Sacrament. At the end of his life, he suffered from rheumatic gout and insomnia and died after a short illness.

Saint Stephen I

Stephen (d. 257) became pope after Lucius I; he reigned only three years. During that short time, however, he led the Church wisely through a difficult period. Specifically, he was faced with the challenge of how to deal with Christians who had renounced their faith under threat of persecution but who wanted to return to the Church after the persecution had ended. Persecutions resumed shortly after his death, which is why he's sometimes named a martyr.

Blessed Zephyrinus (Ceferino) Jimenez Malla

Ceferino was born in 1861 in Benavent de Segria, Spain. He wasn't an educated man, but he was intelligent and became a successful businessman. He entered the Catholic Church as an adult and married when he was fifty-one years old, though his wife died after ten years of marriage. He was a strong leader of his community, became a Dominican tertiary, and had a reputation for personal holiness. When anti-Catholicism swept Spain during the Spanish Civil War, he was arrested for hiding priests. When he was offered freedom for renouncing his faith, he refused. He was executed by firing squad on August 8 in 1936.

Saint Eusebius, show me how to face opposition with the truth lovingly.
Saint Peter, teach me how to love our Lord in the Blessed Sacrament more every day.
Saint Stephen, help me always balance God's justice with His mercy.
Blessed Zephyrinus, help me to grow in holiness.

* * * * *

August 3

Blessed Augustine Gazotich

Augustine was born in 1262 in Dalmatia (modern Croatia) and joined the Dominican order when he was twenty-nine years old. He was sent as a missionary to the Slavic and Hungarian tribes and became bishop of Zagreb. A highly educated man, he was also generous with the poor and dedicated to providing free education to needy students. The pope later sent him to serve as the bishop of Lucera in Italy to resolve troubles in that diocese. He died on this date in 1323, some say by natural causes, while others say he died a martyr.

Blessed Salvador Ferrandis Segui

Salvador was born in L'Orxa, Spain, in 1880 and became a priest in Valencia, Spain, in 1904. While serving as a parish priest, he used his personal funds to help the needy and rebuild the parish church. During the anti-Catholic violence of the Spanish Civil War, he was arrested and shot for the crime of being a priest on this date in 1936.

Blessed Augustine, help me to be a peacemaker.
Blessed Salvador, show me how to live and die for Christ.

* * * * *

August 4

Saint John Vianney, Memorial

When John (1786–1859) was three years old, the French Revolution began, with its violent persecution of the Catholic Church. John's family remained faithful Catholics despite the persecution, and they practiced their faith in secret and hid fugitive priests in their hometown of Dardilly, France. After the revolution ended and John grew up, he herded cattle and sheep until he finally received permission from his father to leave home and become a priest. John was twenty years old when he went to the seminary, but soon afterward he was conscripted to serve in the army. He became ill, so he was sent to the hospital. When he recovered enough to leave, he arrived late, missed his group of soldiers, became lost as he searched for them, and then realized he would be counted as a deserter. He hid in the village of Les Noes with the help of the sympathetic villagers there; he was almost captured several times and felt the point of a sword as it searched the hayloft he was hiding in more than once. But in celebration of the emperor Napoleon's marriage, the emperor proclaimed an amnesty, and John and other army deserters were allowed to return home. His brother volunteered to take his place in the army, and John returned to his studies for the priesthood. Despite his piety, he was a slow learner, but he did his best with the help of a good priest. After ordination, John was sent to Ars-en-Dombes, a remote village with only 230 people, and there he lived for the rest of his life. John fought for the souls of his flock by demanding that they lead lives of virtue; he told them to bring an end to their dancing, unnecessary work on Sunday, and immodest clothes, and he invited them to attend Mass and Vespers. He started a free school for girls and an orphanage. But it was the time he spent in the confessional—eleven hours a day in the winter and sixteen hours a day in the summer—that drew one hundred thousand pilgrims to Ars annually by the end of his life. His success in bringing people to repentance led to nightly visits from devils who tried to scare him and take away the little sleep John allowed himself; but John recognized that greater disturbances always preceded the arrival of more sinful penitents. Despite his success in teaching people to seek holiness, John became convinced that he was inadequate to his task as parish priest and longed for greater solitude and time for prayer. Three times he ran away from Ars, and three times his devoted villagers and the bishop himself convinced him to return. When John, whose holiness was acknowledged by secular leaders all over France, was awarded the imperial cross, he refused to let them even pin it to his cassock out of humility. When he knew the end was at hand, John lay down on his bed, surrounded by the prayers of his villagers and pilgrims, and passed away during a thunderstorm.

Saint Ia of Persia

Ia was born a Greek slave. She was so successful in converting Persian women to the Christian faith that King Shapur II of Persia (modern Iran) had her arrested. She was tortured, flogged, and beheaded in the year 360, dying a martyr for Christ.

> *Saint John, help me to draw closer to God in each confession.*
> *Saint Ia, show me how to bring others to Christ.*

* * * * *

August 5

Dedication of Saint Mary Major and Our Lady of the Snows, Optional Memorial

After the Council of Ephesus, which declared Mary to be Theotokos, or Mother of God, it's said that Pope Liberius (r. 352–366) and a pair of wealthy Romans received a vision of the Virgin Mary. In the vision, she told them to build a church on the site where they would find snow the next morning. Amazingly, they did find snow on a morning in August in Rome, so they built a church. Santa Maria Maggiore is the oldest Marian church in the West, and the foundations of the current church date to the year 432.

> *Mary, Mother of God, we salute you. Precious vessel, worthy of the whole world's reverence, you are an ever-shining light, the crown of virginity, the symbol of orthodoxy, an indestructible temple, the place that held him whom no place can contain, mother and virgin. Because of you the holy Gospels could say:* Blessed is he who comes in the name of the Lord.[4]

Saint Oswald of Northumbria

When Oswald (604–642) was a teenager, his father, the king of Northumbria (England), was killed. He and his two brothers then fled to Scotland; all three were later baptized into the Catholic faith. Although his brothers abandoned their faith, Oswald remained a fervent Christian. In the year 634, he led an army to try to regain his right to the title of king of Northumbria, and on the night before the battle, he had a dream. In it, he saw Columba, the famous deceased abbot and saint from Iona, covering his men with his cloak. Oswald encouraged his soldiers (though only a few of them were Christians) by leading them in prayer to ask for God's help before the impending battle. Oswald and his army won the battle, and he became the king. Afterward he invited monks to come from Scotland and teach the English people about the faith, led by the monk-turned-bishop Saint Aidan. Until Aidan was able to speak the language himself, Oswald personally translated Saint Aidan's sermons to the people. Oswald married Cyneburga, the daughter of the first Christian king of Wessex, and they had a son. Several years later, the pagan King Penda attacked Oswald in battle, and Oswald was killed. His dying words became a proverb: "O God, be merciful to their souls, as said Oswald when he fell."[5]

> *Blessed Mother, pray for me to be a pure temple of the Holy Spirit.*
> *Saint Oswald, beg the Lord to be merciful with me.*

* * * * *

---

[4] *The Liturgy of the Hours*, vol. 4, from a homily delivered at the Council of Ephesus by Saint Cyril of Alexandria, bishop (New York: Catholic Book Publishing, 1975), 1272.

[5] Michael Walsh, ed., *Butler's Lives of the Saints, Concise Edition, Revised and Updated* (San Francisco: Harper-Collins Publishers, 1991), 245.

August 6

The Transfiguration of the Lord, Feast

The Gospels of Matthew, Mark, and Luke[6] all describe this important event in the life of our Lord, which, according to tradition, occurred at Mount Tabor.

And after six days Jesus took with him Peter and James and John, and led them up a high mountain apart by themselves; and he was transfigured before them, and his garments became glistening, intensely white, as no fuller on earth could bleach them. And there appeared to them Elijah with Moses; and they were talking to Jesus. And Peter said to Jesus, "Master, it is well that we are here; let us make three booths, one for you and one for Moses and one for Elijah." For he did not know what to say, for they were exceedingly afraid. And a cloud overshadowed them, and a voice came out of the cloud, "This is my beloved Son; listen to him." And suddenly looking around they no longer saw any one with them but Jesus only.[7]

Saints Justus and Pastor of Alcala

Justus, age thirteen, and Pastor, age nine, were schoolboys and were also Christians. In the year 304, a man named Dacian entered their town of Alcala, Spain, to persecute Christians under the orders of the Roman emperor Diocletian. When the two boys learned that all Christians were ordered to renounce their faith or be executed, the boys decided to show that their faith was as strong as an adult's. After they presented themselves to the authorities, they were savagely flogged, but the boys encouraged one another to face their tortures without flinching. The bravery of these young boys shamed Dacian, who had them beheaded secretly. Their fellow Christians recovered the boys' bodies and buried them where they had died. Justus and Pastor are the patron saints of Alcala and Madrid, and their bodies lie under the high altar at a church in Alcala.

Saint Hormisdas

Hormisdas was a widower and deacon in Rome when he succeeded Saint Symmachus as pope in the year 514. His pontificate was spent delicately reconciling the Church from the Acacian schism, which he did in part through the creation of a confession of faith that is now called the "Formula of Hormisdas". He was an able man, a wise man, and a man of peace. His son, Silverius, later became a pope and also a saint. He died in 523.

Lord, give me the grace to see You in this life and the next.
Saints Justus and Pastor, pray for my faith to be as pure as a child's.
Saint Hormisdas, pray for me to be a means of reconciliation to all those I meet today.

* * * * *

---

[6] Mt 17:1–8; Mk 9:2–8; Lk 9:28–36.
[7] Mk 9:2–8.

August 7

Saint Sixtus II and Companions, Optional Memorial

Pope Sixtus II only reigned about a year. He personally held the erroneous view that those who held heretical beliefs could not perform valid Baptisms, but, as pope, he didn't excommunicate or punish those who disagreed with him about this theological issue. During the Roman emperor Valerian's persecution of Christians in the year 258, soldiers were sent to the catacombs where he was celebrating Mass. When he refused to renounce his faith in Christ, he was beheaded—while he was still seated on his papal chair. Four deacons, including Saints Agapitus and Felicissimus, were martyred with him.

Saint Cajetan the Theatine, Optional Memorial

Cajetan (Gaetano) dei Conti di Tiene was born in 1480 to a noble family in Vicenza, Italy; his father died in battle when he was only two years old. Cajetan became a doctor in civil and canon law and then a senator. Because of his noble birth, he could have chosen an easy life. Instead, Cajetan chose to turn his life over to God as a priest, and he was ordained in 1516. While he was in Rome, he founded the Confraternity of Divine Love, an association of clergy that encouraged devotion to God. When he returned to his hometown of Vicenza, he founded a similar group for laypeople, although his noble friends were greatly offended that Cajetan would associate with the lower classes. Cajetan ignored them and served the poor and the sick; he also encouraged people to receive Holy Communion frequently and introduced the practice of Exposition of the Blessed Sacrament while he was in Venice and Verona. In 1523, all of Christendom was in turmoil over the Protestant movements, and Cajetan's response was to establish the Theatine Clerks Regular, an order of religious clergy based on the model of the apostles. With only four members—himself, a future pope, and two others—the first men took their vows in Saint Peter's Basilica in the presence of a papal delegate. The group grew slowly at first, but his example, preaching, and works gradually brought about a reformation of discipline among the clergy and greater devotion among the laity. He also established benevolent pawnshops to benefit the poor with Blessed John Marinoni, a priest. After serving as a peacemaker in Naples, which was suffering from civil unrest, Cajetan died. Many miracles occurred after his death in 1547, which led to his canonization in 1671.

Saint Afra of Augsburg

Afra had been a prostitute in Augsburg, Germany, and when she became a Christian, she spent the rest of her life doing penance for her sins. She was arrested during the persecution of Christians under the Roman emperor Diocletian and bravely stood up to the judge and confessed her faith in Christ. She was therefore condemned to be burned to death, dying a martyr in the year

304. Her mother and three other women recovered her body and buried it. As punishment, they were then burned to death in the family tomb.

> *Holy Martyrs, give me your perseverance.*
> *Saint Cajetan, help me bring the peace of Christ*
> *to others despite the turmoil of the world.*
> *Saint Afra, show me how to do penance for my sins.*

* * * * *

August 8

Saint Dominic de Guzman, Memorial

Dominic was born in Calaruega in Spain around the year 1170, but little is known about his family life except that his mother was the devout Blessed Joan of Aza. He was educated in Palencia and became an Augustinian Canon while he was still a student. After he was ordained to the priesthood, he continued to live in his Augustinian community. He lived this quiet, contemplative life for several years until, at the age of thirty-one, his bishop asked him to accompany him on a diplomatic mission. During their travels, Dominic and his bishop passed through Languedoc, an area of France where the heresy of Albigensianism was widely practiced. They stayed in the house of a local leader, and their host believed in this heresy too—until Dominic spent the night talking with him and leading him to the truth. When the mission was over, Dominic and his bishop asked to be sent to preach the Gospel in Russia. The pope refused and told them to fight this heretical distortion of the Christian faith in Europe instead. The bishop obeyed and appointed preachers to preach in the areas affected by Albigensianism. Preachers were instructed to live and travel simply (like their opponents did) and to discuss the issues peacefully, rather than with threats. These efforts brought some of the laity back to the Catholic faith but not the leaders, so the bishop returned to his home. Dominic, however, on the feast of Saint Mary Magdalen in 1206, had a vision from Heaven. According to tradition, Dominic was visited by the Blessed Mother, who called on him to pray the Rosary and encourage others to do so. Dominic obeyed. He also founded a shelter for women who returned to the faith and for the education of girls; started a monastery for Albigensian nuns who came back to Catholicism; and spent the next ten years preaching and developing a special group of preachers who would follow his example. With the pope's verbal approval of his plan, he began selecting men to be preachers in his new order, which was generally based on the Rule of Saint Augustine, but with the unusual change of making it a mendicant (begging) order. He sent out his men in pairs to preach the Gospel and established friaries for them to live in. Over time, he drew up the final constitutions for his new order, which became known as the Order of Preachers, popularly called the

Dominicans. During his lifetime, his order increased to sixty friaries living in eight provinces. He died with his brothers around him after they had recited the "Subvenite", a chant often used in funerals, in 1221.

Saint Cyriacus and Companions

Cyriacus was a member of the Roman nobility. When he converted to the Christian faith, he gave his wealth to the poor, became a deacon in the Church, and ministered to Christian slaves who worked in the Roman emperor Diocletian's baths. According to tradition, he also exorcised devils from Diocletian's daughter, Artemisia, which led to the conversion of Artemisia and her mother, Saint Serena. Later, he was turned in to the authorities for being a Christian, was tortured, and was beheaded on the Salarian Way in Rome in the year 303. Saints Largus and Smaragdus, as well as twenty other Christians whose names we don't know, also died with him. Cyriacus is one of the Fourteen Holy Helpers, great saints who were called upon particularly for help during the bubonic plague in the fourteenth century.

Saint Mary MacKillop

Mary was born in 1842 into a large Catholic family in Australia. Her father, while loving and devout, was unable to make a success of his farm, and the family generally had to survive on the wages earned by the children. Mary worked as a clerk, governess, and teacher before she joined Father Julian Woods in opening a Catholic school. This one school eventually developed into a religious congregation called the Sisters of Saint Joseph of the Sacred Heart, and Mary took the religious name of Sister Mary of the Cross. Unique features of the order were their brown habits, which led to them being called "Brown Joeys", and the fact that the sisters lived in the community rather than in convents. Many women joined the congregation to educate the children of the poor. However, Mary suffered many trials as the founder of this new order, particularly through cruel gossip. For example, she had been ordered to drink alcohol by her doctor to relieve medical problems, but gossip distorted this into a claim that she had a drinking problem. Later, when she learned that a priest serving with her sisters had been sexually abusing children, she reported him to Church authorities. The priest was sent back to Ireland, but the priest's crime was not made public. Another priest—not knowing the truth of the matter—retaliated against Mary by pressuring her bishop to demand changes to her congregation's constitutions. When Mary did not give in immediately to the changes, she was swiftly excommunicated. The only place she could live was with a Jewish family, and most of the order's schools were closed. A year later, the bishop, as he was dying, lifted the excommunication against her. Yet another trial occurred for Mary during the approval process of the order's rule; Mary and her co-founder, Father Woods, disagreed over the Vatican's changes to the rule, and Father Woods separated himself from the order. At one point, a bishop removed Mary as superior general of the order and replaced her with another sister. Despite these repeated difficulties with the Church and suffering partial paralysis after a stroke (requiring her to learn to write with her left hand), Mary served her order and the children of the poor for many years, until her death at the age of sixty-seven in 1909.

> *Saint Dominic, beg the Lord to give me the words*
> *that will lead those around me to Christ.*
> *Holy Martyrs, help me die to myself for the sake of Jesus Christ.*
> *Saint Mary, give me your tenacity in carrying the cross of opposition.*

* * * * *

August 9

Saint Teresa Benedicta (Edith Stein) of the Cross, Memorial

Born into a Jewish German family in Breslau in 1891, Edith Stein abandoned her faith in God when she was a teenager. She was a brilliant student and studied philosophy under the famous philosopher Husserl when she was at college. But her personal reading, particularly a book by the Carmelite nun Saint Teresa of Avila, led her to Christian conversion, and she asked to receive instruction in the Catholic faith and enter the Church. Out of compassion for her mother, who was deeply hurt by her conversion, she didn't enter the Carmelite order immediately after she had become a Catholic. Instead, she attended the synagogue with her mother and worked as a teacher. But in 1934, she entered the Carmelite order and took the name Teresa Benedicta of the Cross, and she became a well-known teacher, lecturer, and writer until anti-Semitic laws in Germany forced her to stop. She was a deep thinker, and her profound words—integrating feminism, philosophy, Catholicism, and Carmelite wisdom—were widely read. One of her sisters had followed her into religious life, and when anti-Semitism increased in Germany, the Carmelites smuggled them out to live in a Carmelite convent in Holland. In 1942, however, they were arrested with other Jewish Catholics and sent to the Auschwitz concentration camp. There they died, martyrs for their faith in Christ.

Saint Romanus Ostiarius of Rome

During the persecution of the Church under the Roman emperor Valerian around the year 258, the martyr Romanus died in the city of Rome. Some traditions say he was a soldier whom Saint Lawrence of Rome had converted to the faith. He served as ostiarus, or doorkeeper, to the church before his martyrdom.

Blessed Richard Bere

Richard was born in Glastonbury, England, was the nephew of an abbot, was well educated, and studied law. He refused an arranged marriage and later decided to abandon the practice of law, becoming a Carthusian monk in 1532. When he and several of his fellow monks refused to sign King Henry VIII's Oath of Supremacy, which stated that the king, not the pope, was the head of the Church, those monks were put in prison. Richard was starved to death and died on August 9, 1537, at Newgate Prison in London.

> *Saint Teresa, pray for me that I might live a life of profound union with God.*
> *Saint Romanus, show me how to serve God in humble ways.*
> *Blessed Richard, give me your love for God's truth.*

* * * * *

August 10

Saint Lawrence (Laurence) the Deacon, Feast

Before Pope Saint Sixtus II was taken away to be executed during the persecution of Christians under the Roman emperor Valerian in the year 258, the deacon Lawrence came to him, weeping. According to tradition, Lawrence asked the pope not to go without his deacon, but the pope predicted that Lawrence would follow him three days later. After executing the pope, Roman officials ordered Lawrence to bring them the treasures of the Church. Lawrence obediently spent the next three days gathering together the poor people who were supported by the Church. When he presented these poor people to the prefect, explaining that they were the true treasures of the Church, the prefect was not amused by the irony. He had Lawrence slowly burned to death over a great gridiron. During this torture, Lawrence made the famous reply that he was done on that side and could be turned over. After having prayed for the conversion of the city of Rome in order that the Christian faith might spread throughout the world, Lawrence died. The example of his life and death made a great impact on the people of Rome, and many became followers of Christ soon afterward.

Saint Blane

Saint Blane was born in the sixth century in Scotland and studied in Ireland under the future Irish monk-saints Comgall, Kenneth, and Canice. Blane became a monk in Ireland, but then he returned to Scotland (miraculously, it's said), where he became a monk under his uncle, Saint Cathan (an abbot). He was ordained a priest, evangelized the pagan Scottish Picts, and became a bishop. It's said that he traveled across Europe to Rome entirely on foot to ask for a papal blessing on his office as bishop; it's also said that he miraculously brought the son of a British chief back to life, that he cured the blind through his prayers, and that he lit fire by making small lightning bolts jump between his fingers. He died at Kingarth of natural causes around the year 590.

> *Saint Lawrence, show me how to love and serve the poor today.*
> *Saint Blane, help me expect miracles in my life, through the grace of God.*

* * * * *

August 11

Saint Clare of Assisi, Memorial

Clare was born into a wealthy and noble family of Assisi, Italy, around the year 1193. In 1212, she heard Saint Francis of Assisi speak, and she went in secret to speak to him. Afterward, she decided to leave her home and follow his way of life, the first woman to do so; so she met Francis and his little community at the chapel of Our Lady of the Angels. Before the altar at this church, she took off her fine clothes, replaced them with a sackcloth tunic, and had her hair cut off by Francis himself. He sent her to a Benedictine convent, since he didn't have a convent for women at the time, but her family and friends came to see her continually and tried to change her mind about her vocation. They argued with her even more when her sister Agnes decided to join her. But she remained steadfast in her decision and became the first superior of the community of women following Francis' way of life, and eventually her mother and other noble women joined her. Her Poor Clare nuns, as they were later known, slept on the ground, never ate meat, didn't wear shoes or sandals, and only spoke when necessity and charity required it. Clare herself never went outside the walls of San Damiano, and she patiently bore her own health problems for many years. Although she was strict with herself, she was gentle with her sisters and the poor—for example, going through the sisters' rooms at night to make sure that they were covered warmly while they slept. The Franciscan Rule prohibiting them from possessing anything in common was challenged by popes and many others who thought it was impossible, but Clare refused to relax their way of life and their poverty. She personally drew up the rule to be followed specifically by her nuns, but it wasn't approved by the Church until two days before she died in 1253.

Saint Tiburtius of Rome

During the persecution of the Church under the Roman emperor Diocletian in the year 286, the martyr Tiburtius died in the city of Rome by beheading. According to tradition, his father was Saint Chromatius the Prefect.

Saint Susanna of Rome

During the persecution of the Church under the Roman emperor Diocletian in the year 295, the martyr Susanna died in the city of Rome. Some traditions say that she was from a noble Roman family that was secretly Christian, that members of her family were martyred for the faith, and that when she refused to marry Maximian, the emperor's son-in-law, she was arrested and martyred.

Saint Clare, help me give up anything that separates me from God.
Holy Martyrs, pray for me and my family to help one another draw closer to Christ.

* * * * *

Saint Jane Frances de Chantal, Optional Memorial

Jane was born in 1572 in Burgundy, France. Her mother died when she was a young girl, and her father arranged Jane's marriage to the baron de Chantal when she was twenty years old. Jane became a good administrator of her new husband's household, and although their first three children died soon after birth, they were later blessed with a son and three daughters. After nine years of marriage, her husband was accidentally shot while on a hunting trip with a friend, and he died nine days later. It wasn't easy for Jane to forgive the friend who shot her husband, but a holy bishop, Saint Francis de Sales, became her spiritual director and helped her to forgive and grow in the spiritual life. With his encouragement, she became a nun and founded an order of unenclosed nuns called the Order of the Visitation. Under her direction, the convents spread, although she continued to care for the needs of her children and grandchildren. In 1641, she died when she was sixty-nine years old.

Saint Euplius of Catania

Euplius was a deacon living in Catania, Spain, in the fourth century when he was brought before the governor Calvisian, during the persecution of Christians under the Roman emperor Diocletian. He carried a copy of the Gospels with him, which the governor reminded him was a crime. Euplius replied by reading the words of Jesus in the Gospel of Matthew: "Blessed are those who are persecuted for righteousness' sake, for theirs is the kingdom of heaven" (5:10), and, "If any man would come after me, let him deny himself and take up his cross and follow me" (16:24). In response, Calvisian had him tortured on the rack to try to make him give up his faith in Christ, and although Euplius was in great pain, he continued to pray to Jesus Christ and reiterate his faith. Finally, the book of the Gospels was hung around his neck, and he was beheaded, dying a martyr.

Blessed Innocent XI

Innocent (d. 1689) was the 240th pope; he reigned for twelve years. He was born with the name Benedetto in Como, Italy, in 1611, studied law, and served in various positions in the Church before becoming a cardinal and then bishop of Novara. When he became pope, he immediately reduced expenses in the Curia, passed ordinances against nepotism, and personally lived a very frugal life, with the result that the Curia's finances soon rose from an annual deficit to a balanced budget. His whole pontificate was spent in constant battles with King Louis XIV of France, who wanted absolute control over the French Church. Innocent similarly opposed the Catholic King James II of England, who tried to impose Catholicism on his subjects forcefully. Innocent also worked to improve the faith and morals of his clergy and the faithful through better clerical education, the reformation of monasteries, ordinances against immodest dress among

Roman women, and the suppression of gambling houses. He condemned the heretical teachings of Miguel de Molinos called Quietism, an exaggerated mysticism that promoted self-annihilation and extreme passivity in prayer. Innocent was more tolerant toward the heresy of Jansenism, which later delayed his beatification, but he wasn't a follower of its teachings. He died of natural causes on this date.

> *Saint Jane, help me to trust always in God's care for me during times of trials.*
> *Saint Euplius, pray that the words of the Incarnate Word will be always on my lips.*
> *Blessed Innocent, help me reform my life.*

* * * * *

August 13

Saints Pontian (Pontianus) and Hippolytus, Optional Memorial

Hippolytus was a priest of Rome in the third century who was offended that Pope Saint Callistus allowed those who had renounced their faith under persecution to return to the Church. His criticism of the pope increased until he had declared himself the pope. Later, however, anti-pope Hippolytus and the subsequent Pope Pontian (our eighteenth pope, who reigned for five years) were arrested at the same time for being Christians and were sentenced to slave labor together. Before being sent into exile to a certain death, Pontian named a successor, Anterus, to be the pope. While in captivity, Pontian helped Hippolytus be reconciled to the Church, and the two men died in prison and as martyrs for the faith together in the year 235.

Saint Cassian of Imola

During the persecution of the Church under the Roman emperor Diocletian around the year 300, the martyr Cassian died in the city of Imola, Italy. Tradition says that he was a schoolteacher, and when he was asked to offer sacrifice to the pagan gods, he refused. He was bound to a stake, and his pagan students tortured and killed him by stabbing him with the iron styles with which they wrote.

Saint Maximus the Confessor

Maximus was born around the year 580. He left his important position in the imperial court in Constantinople to become a monk, and he became the champion of orthodoxy against the Monothelite heresy that was prevalent at the time. Despite persecution from the emperor, Maximus wrote and spoke repeatedly against this heresy. He was finally seized, banished, and beaten by the authorities, though he was more than seventy years old. After six years in captivity, he and two faithful friends were condemned to be scourged, to have their tongues and right hands cut off, and to spend the rest of their lives in prison.

Maximus didn't live long after this cruel treatment, and he died around the age of seventy-eight in the year 662 in modern Georgia. He's considered a Father of the Church.

> The Word of God, born once in the flesh (such is his kindness and goodness), is always willing to be born spiritually in those who desire him. In them he is born as an infant as he fashions himself in them by means of their virtues. He reveals himself to the extent that he knows someone is capable of receiving him.[8]

Saint John Berchmans

John was born in 1599 in Driest, Belgium, into a pious family, in which three of the five children entered religious life. John was a devout altar boy, and he was also a devout caretaker when his mother became sick with a protracted illness. He became a Jesuit novice in 1616, despite his father's opposition. Since he intended to become a Jesuit priest, he studied philosophy and languages in order to serve as a missionary. Those around him noted his kindness, faithfulness, and clear thinking. In 1621, after participating in a public discussion of philosophy one evening, he died suddenly after a brief illness.

> Saints Pontian and Hippolytus, show me how to help others
> be reconciled with the Church.
> Saint Cassian, help me to forgive.
> Saint Maximus, help me to be willing to die for Christ and His truth.
> Saint John, show me how to get to Heaven through simple devotion and faith.

* * * * *

August 14

Saint Maximilian Mary Kolbe, Memorial

Raymond (Maximilian) was born in 1894 in Poland. When he was young, he had a vision of the Blessed Mother. In the vision, she offered him two crowns, one red and one white, which symbolized a choice between martyrdom and purity. He asked for both. He joined the Conventual Franciscans when he was thirteen years old, made his vows when he was seventeen years old, taking the name Maximilian, and was ordained a priest in Rome when he was twenty-four years old. While still a young priest, he established the Militia of Mary Immaculate, which encouraged faith in God and trust in Mary with the help of the materials he and his priests printed. So many men chose to follow him that he founded cities of friars, and he traveled all over the world establishing religious houses, including in Japan, despite numerous physical ailments. He was

---

[8] *The Liturgy of the Hours*, vol. 1, from the Five Hundred Chapters by Saint Maximus the Confessor, abbot (New York: Catholic Book Publishing, 1975), 519.

captured at the beginning of World War II but was released. In 1941, he was rearrested and sent to the Auschwitz concentration camp. A few months later, a prisoner escaped from the camp, and ten other prisoners were selected by the Nazis to be executed as a punishment. Maximilian offered to take the place of a married man who had been chosen to die, and since he was both a Pole and a priest (and therefore despised by the Nazis), his offer was accepted. Maximilian brought the comfort of Christ to these nine men while they died slowly in a starvation bunker. He was executed by lethal injection by the guards when they found him alive, the only one left.

Saint Eusebius of Rome

Eusebius (d. ca. 357) was a priest and member of the patrician class in Rome. When Pope Liberius gave in to threats and political pressure and briefly accepted an Arian profession of faith, Eusebius publicly denounced him. He was put in prison, where he prayed and died several months later of maltreatment.

Saint Anthony Primaldo and the Martyrs of Otranto

Anthony was an elderly layman living in Otranto, Italy, when the city was invaded by Muslim Turks in 1480. The Turks gave the city's inhabitants a choice: convert to Islam or die. Anthony was chosen as spokesman for the town, and he told the Turks that the people chose to die rather than abandon their faith in Christ. Anthony was hacked to pieces, and 812 other men were martyred with him. The incorrupt bodies of these martyrs were translated to the city's cathedral in 1481, and their relics were later placed in a nearby chapel, while some were given to other churches over the centuries.

Holy Martyrs, help me stand up for God's truth.

* * * * *

August 15

The Assumption of the Blessed Virgin Mary, Solemnity

Before 1950, belief that our Blessed Mother was assumed body and soul into Heaven at the end of her life had been a "probable opinion the denial of which would be impious and blasphemous",[9] according to Pope Benedict XIV. But Pope Pius XII made the decision to declare this solemnity in honor of Mary's Assumption into Heaven in 1950, confirming the faithful's long-held belief that the Blessed Virgin Mary reigns body and soul, beside her Son.

---

[9] Walsh, *Butler's Lives of the Saints*, 250.

O most sweet Lady and our Mother, thou hast already left the earth and reached thy kingdom, where, as Queen, thou art enthroned above all the choirs of angels, as the Church sings: "She is exalted above the choirs of angels in the celestial kingdom." ... By the merits of thy happy death obtain [for] us holy perseverance in the Divine friendship, that we may finally quit this life in God's grace, and thus we also shall one day come to kiss thy feet in Paradise, and unite with the blessed spirits in praising thee and singing thy glories as thou deservest.[10]

Saint Tarcisius

Tarcisius was taking Holy Communion to Christian prisoners in the third or fourth century when he was attacked by pagans in the street. They demanded to have what he was carrying, and when he refused to give the Blessed Sacrament to them, they killed him. It's said that the Blessed Sacrament he was carrying disappeared at his death.

Saint Hyacinth of Poland

Hyacinth (1185–1257) joined the Dominican order in the year 1218 and became a priest in the city of Rome. He was sent three years later to be a missionary in Cracow, Poland, which at that time was a very immoral city. His preaching brought many people to conversion—including members of the Polish nobility—and though he downplayed his miracles, there were some of those too. Hyacinth traveled to Denmark, Norway, Sweden, Ukraine, Ruthenia, and Russia to bring the Christian faith to the people living there. Toward the end of his life, Hyacinth was staying in the house of a noblewoman when the servant accompanying him fell into the water and drowned. When the young man was pulled from the water, Hyacinth prayed over the man, and he recovered. That same year, Hyacinth became ill and received the last sacraments before his death.

Queen of Heaven, accept me as your own child.
Saint Tarcisius, help me to love Jesus' Real Presence in the Blessed Sacrament.
Saint Hyacinth, teach me how to bring the love of Christ to all those I meet.

* * * * *

August 16

Saint Stephen of Hungary, Optional Memorial

Stephen's father was the duke of the Magyars, and, like most of the early leaders of Hungary, he became a Christian for political reasons. But Stephen himself, who was born around the year 970, was a devoted Christian, and when he became king, he encouraged the practice of the Catholic faith among his people.

---

[10] Liguori, *Glories of Mary*, 377–78.

For example, he supported churches and monasteries, repressed the practices of the people's former pagan religion, ordered all people to marry except churchmen and religious, and forbade marriage between Christians and pagans. When the pope sent ambassadors to confer the title of king on him, Stephen treated the ambassadors with great respect. His son Emeric was a good leader, but he died in a hunting accident before Stephen's death, and the king spent his final years dealing with family disputes over the succession. He died in 1038.

Saint Rock (Roch or Rocco)

Rock (1295–1327) was the son of a French governor. Both his parents had died by the time he was twenty years old, but rather than assume the family's power and position, he gave everything away and became a hermit. After a time, Rock went on a pilgrimage to Rome, where he found many people suffering from the plague. Because he cared for plague victims—an act of great charity considering the tremendous fear people had of the disease—and because the people he cared for got better, people called him a saint. Rock finally caught the plague himself, and he went to the woods to die alone. A dog came to him, licked his wounds, and brought him food, and eventually Rock recovered. When he returned to his hometown of Montpellier in France, the people there didn't recognize him, and he was put in jail because they thought he was a spy. However, after his death, they recognized him by a cross-shaped birthmark on his chest. The power of his intercession during times of plague led to his canonization.

Blessed John of Saint Martha

John was born in Prados, Spain, in 1578 and became a Franciscan. He was ordained to the priesthood in 1606 and traveled as a missionary to bring the Gospel to Japan. He quickly learned the Japanese language, but he was arrested in 1615 for the crime of being a Christian. The authorities imprisoned him for three years before he was finally beheaded in 1618, dying a martyr for Christ.

> *Saint Stephen, help me to encourage the faith of others.*
> *Saint Rock, help me to care for those in need and see Christ in them.*
> *Blessed John, show me how to give my life completely to Christ.*

* * * * *

August 17

Saint Mamas (Mammes)

Mamas' parents, Saints Theodotus and Rufina, were put in prison for the crime of being Christians around the time he was born in the middle of the third century in Cappadocia (modern Turkey). His parents died as martyrs for their faith soon afterward. Mamas was then taken in by a Christian named Ammi, now also known as a saint, and raised by him. Mamas worked as a shepherd and had a great love for animals. It's said that he preached the Gospel to them while they were in the fields, that the sheep gathered around him to listen, and that a lion even protected him from harm. During the persecution of Christians under the Roman emperor Aurelian, the lion is even said to have stood beside him during his trial. Mamas was martyred for his faith in Christ in about the year 275 and was perhaps only sixteen years old at the time.

Saint Eusebius

Eusebius was the thirty-first pope (d. 308); he reigned only four months. During his brief reign, he confirmed the teaching of previous popes, which allowed those who had denied the Christian faith under threat of persecution to return to the Church after doing proper penance. Eusebius was banished to Sicily by the Roman emperor Maxentius—it was still illegal to be a Christian at the time—and he died a martyr soon afterward.

Saint Clare of Montefalco

Clare was born in 1268 in a well-to-do family of Montefalco, Italy; she repeatedly meditated on the Passion of Christ, even from the time she was small. When she was fifteen years old, she decided to leave everything behind and live alone in a hermitage. In 1291, she became abbess of the nuns living in Montefalco. Her nuns were inspired by her extraordinary visions and the penitential way she lived throughout her life. She died in 1308.

Saint Joan Delanoue

Joan (1660–1736) was the youngest of twelve children in a French family, and she inherited the family business after her mother's death. Her goal was profit, not piety, and she scandalized her neighbors when she decided to open her shop for business on Sundays. But she also provided rooms for pilgrims, and when a devout Christian woman named Francoise Souchet stopped to stay in one of her rooms in 1693, Joan's life was changed forever. Under Francoise's gentle encouragement, Joan began caring for orphans, and this grew into not only a home for orphans, but an entire religious order of nuns dedicated to caring for them. The religious order that Joan eventually founded became the Sisters of Saint Anne of the Providence of Saumur, and Joan herself spent the rest of her life caring for those who were poor.

> *Saint Mamas, help me to love and see God in His creation.*
> *Saint Eusebius, show me how to do penance for my sins.*
> *Saint Clare, give me a passion for the Passion of Christ.*
> *Saint Joan, help me be patient with those who behave scandalously.*

* * * * *

August 18

Saint Agapitus of Palestrina

Agapitus was a fifteen-year-old boy from Palestrina, Italy. When the persecution of Christians in the Roman Empire was renewed, he proudly proclaimed his faith in Jesus Christ and died for it as a result. His martyrdom occurred around the year 274.

Saint Helen of Constantinople

Helen was the daughter of an innkeeper and born in Bithynia (modern Turkey) around the year 250. Her husband, Constantius, was also humbly born, but he had become a Roman general by the time he married her. When Constantius became Caesar, he divorced Helen so he could marry into the emperor's family for political reasons. But when their son Constantine succeeded Constantius and then became emperor, Helen was welcomed back into the palace and into society. She became a Christian when she was sixty-three years old, and she lived out her faith by giving generously to the poor and building many churches. She went on a pilgrimage to the Holy Land to direct the removal of a pagan temple and to have a church built on the site of Golgotha and the Holy Sepulchre instead. While she was in Jerusalem, she located pieces of the True Cross, which were verified through a miraculous healing and which have been revered by Christians ever since. After her death in the year 330, her body was returned to Rome.

> *Saint Agapitus, show me how to witness to my faith in Christ through my life.*
> *Saint Helen, help me to find proofs of God's love for me everywhere I go.*

* * * * *

August 19

Saint John Eudes, Optional Memorial

When the farmer Isaac Eudes and his wife were still childless after two years of marriage, they went on a pilgrimage to a shrine of the Virgin Mary. God soon blessed them with John (1601–1680), and later with five more children. John grew up in Normandy, France. His parents expected John to marry and take over their estate, but John had already privately vowed to himself to remain celibate and became a priest instead. He became a well-known preacher, speaking against Jansenist teachings, the depressing and widespread heresy in France at the time. Later, he founded the Congregation of Jesus and Mary (also called the Eudists), a religious society that gave missions and educated priests. With the assistance of Madeleine Lamy, he also founded a home for women and girls who had repented of living immoral lives. Over time, this home developed into an order of nuns who cared for these needy women, and Father Eudes founded his own order of priests to assist in the formation of virtuous and zealous clergymen. He was strongly opposed by Jansenists, and his congregation was twice rejected by Rome. (As *Butler's Lives of the Saints* says: "[E]ven saints do not do everything properly and herein Father Eudes failed, in part through his own disregard for prudence and tact."[11]) Finally, the congregation was approved. Father Eudes wrote books about the hearts of Jesus and Mary, writing about Jesus' Sacred Heart even before Saint Margaret Mary's visions had occurred. He established seminaries, with papal approval, and after completing an exhausting nine-week mission of preaching, he died at the age of seventy-nine.

Saint Sixtus III

Sixtus was the forty-fourth pope (d. 440); he reigned eight years. He is honored as a saint for his strength and wisdom in opposing the heresies of Nestorianism and Pelagianism, as well as his courage in asserting the primacy of the pope over bishops, against the desires of the Byzantine emperor.

Saint Louis of Anjou

Louis was born in 1274 into a noble family at Nocera, Italy, and was the son of Charles II of Anjou, king of Naples, and the heir to the throne of Naples. But when he became a young man, he renounced all his wealth and titles to his younger brother and instead became a priest. He was ordained to the priesthood when he was twenty-two years old, and he later became bishop of Toulouse. While a bishop, people particularly noted his care for the poor and the needy. He died in 1297.

Martyred Carmelite Sisters of Charity

During the anti-Catholic violence in Spain during the Spanish Civil War in 1936, more than six thousand Spanish clergymen and vowed religious were martyred. On this date in 1936 in El Saler, Spain, nine religious sisters, members of the Carmelite Sisters of Charity, were killed and are now considered blesseds by the Church. Their names are Elvira Torrentalle Paraire, Agueda Hernandez Amoros, Francisca de Amezua Ibaibarriaga, Maria Calaf Miracle, Maria de las Nieves Crespo Lopez, Maria Desamparados Giner, Maria Dolores Vidal Cervera, Rosa Pedret Rull, and Teresa Chambo Palet.

> *Saint John, teach me how to trust completely in the Sacred Heart of Jesus and the Immaculate Heart of Mary.*
> *Saint Sixtus, help me to love Christ and His Church.*
> *Saint Louis, show me how to renounce worldly things for heavenly ones.*
> *Holy Martyrs, help me remain faithful to Christ.*

* * * * *

[11] Walsh, *Butler's Lives of the Saints*, 255.

August 20

Saint Bernard of Clairvaux, Memorial

Bernard (1090–1153) was born to noble French parents; he was one of seven children, five of whom are recognized for their holy lives by the Church: Blessed Guy, Blessed Gerard, Saint Bernard, Blessed Humbeline, Andrew, Bartholomew, and Blessed Nivard. Bernard apparently left his pious home for college with secular goals for his life, but he soon began to consider life as a Cistercian monk. Though his friends tried to discourage him, he not only decided on religious life for himself, but he took four brothers, an uncle, and twenty-six other men with him to join the order at the Abbey of Citeaux. Abbot Stephen was delighted at their arrival, since they hadn't had a novice for several years; he soon recognized Bernard's talents and holiness. Three years later, he sent Bernard (who was not even a priest yet) to lead a group of monks to establish a new monastery at the Valley of Wormwood, which was later renamed Clairvaux, because it was right in the "eye of the sun". There were many hardships in this new monastery, including hard work, poor land, and limited food. Initially, Bernard was very severe with his monks. When he recognized that he had been too harsh, he lived in silence for a time in penance, but then he returned to preach to his monks, making sure their meals were more regular, even if still very simple. He had a charming personality, loving disposition, personal humility, and great intelligence. But he was also willing to confront absolutely anyone for any reason and with great clarity (and sometimes humor) to protect and strengthen the Catholic faith. Secular leaders came to seek his advice, he wrote and preached innumerable sermons to help his monks grow in holiness, and he preached publicly on occasion. One of the postulants in Bernard's house, originally put to work feeding the fire, eventually became Pope Blessed Eugene III. Though Bernard was often very ill and physically weak, he went out to preach repeatedly against the Albigensian heresy throughout the area of Languedoc and was successful in restoring the region to the orthodox practice of the faith. (Unfortunately, the heresy later returned and required Saint Dominic's efforts to bring it to an end.) At Pope Eugene's request, Bernard preached and convinced many men to join the Crusade of 1146 to help the Christians of the Holy Land, although the expedition itself was not successful. In later life, Bernard responded to a request to travel personally to Metz to reconcile feuding parties, despite his poor health. He was successful in convincing both sides to stop their fighting and died soon afterward. He was sixty-three years old, having been abbot for thirty-eight years and having founded sixty-eight monasteries after Clairvaux. He was declared a Doctor of the Church by Pope Pius VIII in 1830.

Nothing shows more clearly the almighty power of the Word than that he makes all-powerful all those who put their hope in him.[12]

---

[12] Bernard of Clairvaux, *On the Song of Songs*, vol. 4, Sermon 85, trans. Irene Edmonds, Cistercian Fathers Series: Number Forty (Kalamazoo: Cistercian Publications, 1980), 201.

Prophet Samuel

Hannah dedicated the son that God gave her to His service when he was three years old. Living more than a thousand years before the birth of Christ, Samuel became the last judge of Israel, and, following God's direction, he anointed both Saul and David to be kings of the Jews.

> And the LORD came and stood forth, calling as at other times, "Samuel! Samuel!" And Samuel said, "Speak, for your servant hears."[13]

Blessed Maria Climent Mateu

Maria was born in 1887 in Valencia, Spain. As was often done at the time, she was baptized the day she was born, and she was educated by Dominican nuns. She was a musician and singer, enjoyed embroidery, and never married. She was also a faithful Catholic, a member of the community's Saint Vincent de Paul Society, and the secretary of the Catholic Women's Trade Union. During the Spanish Civil War in 1936, she was arrested and executed for the crime of being a faithful Catholic. As she was being stabbed to death, her last words were "Vivo Christo Rey!"

> Saint Bernard, teach me the words that will lead others to Christ.
> Prophet Samuel, help me to hear God's voice.
> Blessed Maria, give me your courage.

* * * * *

August 21

Saint Pius X, Memorial

Pius was born in 1835, the son of a postman in Riese, Italy, and was given the name of Giuseppe Sarto. He was the second of ten children. Though he grew up in poverty, he became a priest and was ordained when he was twenty-three years old. In 1884, he became a bishop, in 1892, he was chosen patriarch of Venice, and in 1903, he was elected pope. He took the name of Pius X, and he lived his papal motto: to renew all things in Christ. One of his first acts was to issue a constitution forbidding secular leaders from interfering in papal elections (which had just occurred in Pius' election, in which a secular leader's interference caused a cardinal to withdraw his candidacy for pope). Pius worked against the separation of church and state that had been established by the French government; this bankrupted the Church in France, but it prevented it from being controlled by the government. He also reformed the liturgy and liturgical music,

---

[13] 1 Sam 3:10.

set up a commission for a revised Bible translation, and fought several popular heresies that he grouped together under the title of Modernism. He encouraged frequent reception of the Eucharist, and he allowed children who had reached the age of reason to receive their First Holy Communion. It's generally said that the outbreak of World War I killed him; he died a few months after it began. Although he had many enemies during his lifetime, everyone agreed that he was a holy man after his death in 1914, and he was canonized a saint in 1954.

Saint Privatus of Mende

In the third century, pagan Germanic tribes invaded France, killing many people as they plundered towns. Privatus was bishop of Mende, France, when the barbarians attacked. He was captured and told that he would be freed if he offered a sacrifice to their gods or if he told them where his Christian flock was hiding. He refused to do either. He was beaten to death in the year 260.

Blessed Victoire Rasoamanarivo

Rasoamanarivo was born in 1848 in Madagascar and raised in the native animist faith of her people, but after she started to study at a Catholic school at the age of thirteen, she converted and took the name Victoire. When national politics changed, her family placed her in a Protestant school and insisted that she convert from Catholicism, but she refused. Although she felt drawn to religious life, her family arranged a marriage for her in 1864. Her husband was a military man, and he was violent, a drinker, and a womanizer. Although her friends encouraged her to divorce him, she replied that marriage was a sacrament and couldn't be broken. Instead, she continued to pray for her husband's conversion. In 1883, politics turned against the French government and against the Catholic faith. Catholic missionaries were expelled, Catholic schools and churches were closed, and Catholics were ordered to renounce the Church or be considered traitors. Victoire helped lead the effort to keep schools open, in which the laity catechized new converts, held prayer services, and peacefully ignored the government orders, doing what they could without priests. She shamed the guards into allowing Christians to enter the church building, for example, and was often the first to enter it. When missionaries were able to return in 1886, they found the Catholic faith alive and growing in Madagascar because of strong Christians like Victoire. Before Victoire's husband died in 1888, he asked for her forgiveness and was baptized into the faith. She devoted the rest of her life to praying and caring for the poor, the sick, and the imprisoned. She died in 1894.

Saint Pius, through your prayers, may my heart be renewed in Christ.
Saint Privatus, help me protect those under my care.
Blessed Victoire, show me how to forgive those who persecute me.

See also Our Lady of Knock in the Calendar of Marian Dates.

* * * * *

August 22

The Queenship of the Blessed Virgin Mary, Memorial

In 1955, Pope Pius XII instituted this memorial to honor Mary as Queen of Heaven and Earth. During the reformation of the Church's General Roman Calendar at Vatican Council II, the memorial was moved to end the octave after the Assumption.

> *Hail, Holy Queen, Mother of mercy, our life, our sweetness and our hope. To you do we cry, poor banished children of Eve. To you do we send up our sighs, mourning and weeping in this valley of tears. Turn then, O most gracious advocate, your eyes of mercy towards us. And after this our exile, show unto us the blessed fruit of your womb, Jesus. O clement, O loving, O sweet Virgin Mary. Pray for us, O Holy Mother of God, that we may be made worthy of the promises of Christ. Amen.*[14]

Saint Symphorianus of Autun

Symphorianus was the son of a senator and a Christian mother; he lived in Autun, Gaul (modern France), during the time of the Roman Empire. When a statue of the pagan goddess Cybele was paraded through the city streets and everyone was asked to bow down and worship it, Symphorianus refused. The governor gave him another chance to recant his Christian faith because he was from the nobility. When he refused to do that, even after he had been flogged, he was beheaded and died a martyr. The date of his death is unknown.

Saint Timothy of Rome

During the persecution of the Church under the Roman emperor Diocletian in the year 303, the martyr Timothy died in the city of Rome on the Ostian Road. Some traditions point out his endurance under the most brutal tortures and say that other Christian martyrs died with him.

Saint Philip Benizi

Philip (1233–1285) received a degree in medicine from the University of Paris, but when he returned to his hometown of Florence to be a doctor, he felt himself drawn to sacred studies. At first, he began to study the Bible and the Church Fathers. In 1254, he recognized that God was calling him to join the mendicant order of the Servants of Mary (also known as Servites). But Philip was a humble man, so rather than asking to be admitted to the order, he decided to serve as a gardener and laborer for the brothers, living in a cave behind the church. In 1258, they sent him on an errand to Siena, and, on the way, he unwittingly revealed his education and experience as a medical doctor to his traveling companions. When the head of the Servites learned of his abilities, he insisted that Philip be made prior general of the order. As prior general, Philip established

---

[14] Hail, Holy Queen, traditional Catholic prayer.

the female order of the Servants of Mary, he codified the rules of the order, and he sent missionaries to bring the Gospel to others. On one occasion, he avoided being nominated for pope only by going into hiding. His last act was an attempt to bring peace in northern Italy, which was suffering bloody wars because of the feuds between two powerful Italian families, the Guelfs and Ghibellines.

> Queen of Heaven, intercede for me.
> Holy Martyrs, help me to renounce the false gods of my heart.
> Saint Philip, show me how to be a humble servant of Mary.

* * * * *

August 23

Saint Rose of Lima, Optional Memorial

The child born in 1586 in Lima, Peru, to Caspar de Flores and Maria de Oliva was christened Isabel, but she soon became known to everyone as Rose. Rose was a devout child, so devout that her family and friends ridiculed her for her piety. But she was not deterred. After people complimented her on her physical beauty, she disfigured her face by smearing it with pepper on one occasion and covering her hands with lime on another. When an unsuccessful mining venture caused her family's fortunes to suffer, Rose helped the family make ends meet by sewing and by selling flowers from her garden. Her family tried for ten years to convince Rose to get married, but she resisted and was eventually allowed to become a Dominican tertiary. She asked to live as a recluse in a little hut in the family's garden, and she even wore a circle of silver with sharp prickles on it as a penance. Rose lived a deep spiritual life, received visions and invisible stigmata, and repeatedly suffered both physically and mentally in her short life. Rose offered up all the trials that she suffered for sinners, particularly the trials of persecution by her own family and the desolation she suffered in her prayer. She spent the last three years of her life living in the home of a wealthy friend, Don Gonzalo de Massa. She died there in 1617 of a long and painful illness, and one of her last prayers was, "Lord, increase my sufferings, and with them increase thy love in my heart."[15] The people of Lima, who had recognized her as a living saint, now recognized her as a saint in Heaven. She was canonized in 1671, the first saint of the New World.

Blesseds Rosaria Quintana Argos, Seraphina Fernandez Ibaro, and Companions

During the persecution of Catholics during the Spanish Civil War, religious orders were particularly targeted. Rosaria (Peter Maria Victoria) Quintana Argos was the superior general of the Capuchin tertiary Sisters of the Holy Family, and

---

[15] Walsh, *Butler's Lives of the Saints*, 261.

Seraphina (Manuela Justa) Fernandez Ibaro was the general councilor. Both had been sisters in the order for decades. On August 22 in 1936, they, among others, were executed by anti-Catholic forces in La Vall d'Uixo and died as martyrs.

Saint Rose, teach me how to pray.
Holy Martyrs, help me remain faithful to Christ.

* * * * *

August 24

Saint Nathaniel Bartholomew the Apostle, Feast

The Apostle Nathaniel was also known by the name of Bartholomew, meaning "Son of Tolomei". When Christ said that He had seen Bartholomew sitting "under a fig tree", Bartholomew immediately called Him the "Son of God"[16] and spent the rest of his life following Him. According to tradition, he preached in India and Armenia, was tortured, and died a martyr by beheading.

Saint Audoenus (or Ouen or Dado) of Rouen

Ouen was born at Sancy, France, around the year 600, and his father was Saint Authaire, a courtier to the king who was known for his charity to the poor. Ouen and his brother Ado were well educated, and they served in the court of King Clotaire II and his son, King Dagobert. Ouen was eventually made chancellor of the kingdom, and he used his position to oppose the practice of simony and ensure that holy men were placed in positions of authority in the Church instead. With King Dagobert's permission, he established a monastery at Rebais and found a holy disciple of the abbot Saint Columban to serve the monks as abbot. Ouen wanted to leave the world behind and become a monk at Rebais, but the king and his nobles found his wisdom too valuable to let him go. Years later, Dagobert's son, Clovis II, did permit Ouen to be ordained bishop of Rouen instead. To prepare for his ordination, Ouen and his friend Eligius (also a future bishop and saint) prayed and fasted together. While serving as bishop, Ouen lived a humble and simple life. He cared for the poor, curbed abuses within the Church, founded monasteries to encourage learning, and sent missionaries to parts of his diocese where pagans still lived. He also served as an advisor to kings and was a supporter of Ebroin, the mayor of the palace. Ouen died after returning from a political mission in the year 684.

Saint Bartholomew, show me how to recognize Christ wherever I am.
Saint Ouen, help me to seek perfection for myself and my friends.

* * * * *

[16] Jn 1:48–49.

August 25

Saint Louis IX of France, Optional Memorial

Louis (1214–1270) became king of France at the age of twelve when his father died. His mother, Blanche, was a devout woman who served as regent until Louis was old enough to take the throne, and she was a courageous and astute leader who forced ambitious barons to stop rebelling against her rightful authority. Louis married Margaret, a daughter of the count of Provence, and their marriage was blessed with five sons and six daughters. Louis was always respectful to his mother, though she tended to be jealous of her daughter-in-law; he forgave his enemies, even those who fought against him in battle. He venerated the ministers of the Church, although he was not blind to unjust ones, and he established such just laws that succeeding generations always held their leaders to the standards that Louis had set. Louis had blasphemers branded, and when people complained about it, he said he would undergo the punishment himself if it would put a stop to the crime. When a count had three children hanged for hunting rabbits in his woods, Louis had the count tried by ordinary judges, not by his peers as he had wanted. The count was condemned to death, but Louis spared his life. Instead, the count received heavy fines, and the money was given to charity. Louis defeated King Henry III in battle, arbitrated between Henry and his English barons, and went on two Crusades. He was captured and held for ransom during the First Crusade, but he acted like a Christian and a king even while he was in captivity. During the Second Crusade, he became ill with typhus, and he died after receiving the last sacraments. Before he died, he urged Greek ambassadors who were present to reunite with the Catholic Church, and he died reciting the psalms.

Saint Joseph Calasanz (Calasanctius), Optional Memorial

Joseph was born to a noble Spanish family in 1556, and he was a good student who obtained degrees in both canon law and theology. Although his father wanted him to pursue a secular career, a near-fatal illness led him to recognize God's call to religious life. He became a parish priest, and his example inspired greater zeal in the laity and better discipline among the clergy. At his father's death, he gave away most of his inheritance, renounced the rest, and traveled to Rome. There he worked in a cardinal's residence and also cared for the poor during a plague. Seeing a need for education of the poor, he and two other priests opened a free school in 1597. This community increased in size and became a religious order known as Le Sciole Pie (The Religious Schools). Joseph's life wasn't without challenges: some people objected to the idea of educating the poor because they said it would cause social unrest, and others were offended by Joseph's friendship with Galileo Galilei. When Joseph was an old man, the new superior of his order accused him of incompetence, and the superior who succeeded that man did the same. The scandal caused by these accusations almost destroyed the order, but a papal commission investigated the allegations and cleared Joseph's name. However, later there was more trouble within the order. This time it was dissolved, and its priests were placed under the control of their local bishops. Eight years after Joseph's death in 1648, the order was reorganized, and it continues its good work to this day.

Saint Genesius of Arles

Genesius was a soldier and a secretary to the magistrate of Arles, France, in the year 305. He was also a catechumen, studying to become a Christian. When the Roman emperor Maximian issued an order persecuting Christians, Genesius threw his writing table on the floor and angrily protested the decree. Having publicly proclaimed the fact that he was a Christian, he was immediately arrested and executed.

Saint Thomas Cantalupe

Thomas was born around the year 1218, and he had four brothers and three sisters. Thomas' father served as steward to the king of England, and his mother was a countess. He was well educated, lived in wealth, and became a priest, a lawyer, and later chancellor of Oxford. He was known as a kindly, gentle scholar who was charitable to poor students, but he was also a strict disciplinarian. During a time of civil war in England, Thomas was one of the English leaders who went to France to plead their case to the king, Saint Louis IX, against their own king, Henry. After King Henry was defeated in battle, Thomas briefly served as chancellor of the kingdom. He was forty-seven years old when he was forced to leave England for France for a time due to the political unrest. When he returned, he was appointed to pastor several churches simultaneously. Though many men at the time used such positions for personal profit, Thomas directed each position carefully, appointing vicars to handle day-to-day administration and making surprise visits from time to time to check on them. When he was ordained bishop of Hereford, he used that position to confront the secular lords who had been taking away the rights and possessions of the Church, one by one facing them down and protecting the Church and the poor. He wasn't afraid to correct or excommunicate those who had committed serious sins, when necessary, and he had the practice of giving the Sacrament of Confirmation to any child he met while he was traveling who had not yet received it. He was generous with the poor, and everyone acknowledged his blameless private life. At the end of his life, he and the archbishop of Canterbury disagreed over several matters, and the archbishop excommunicated him. Thomas traveled to Rome to appeal this decision with the pope, but the tiring journey was too much for him. He died on this date in 1282 while still awaiting a decision, and his remains were returned to Hereford.

> *Saint Louis, show me how to be a Christlike leader in the secular world.*
> *Saint Joseph, when I'm criticized, help me to see it as a gift from God.*
> *Saint Genesius, give me the courage to stand up for my faith.*
> *Saint Thomas, help me to serve God wherever He places me.*

* * * * *

August 26

Patriarch Melchizedek

When the patriarch Abraham celebrated his victory over pagan kings, a previously unknown figure, Melchizedek, king and priest of Salem, came to greet him. Melchizedek offered bread and wine to God in thanksgiving for Abraham's success.[17] Since the Last Supper, when our Lord offered bread and wine and offered it to His disciples, Christians have drawn spiritual fruit from the parallels between the two.

> *[Melchizedek] is without father or mother or genealogy, and has neither beginning of days nor end of life, but resembling the Son of God he continues a priest for ever.*[18]

Saint Elizabeth Bichier des Ages

Elizabeth was born in 1773 in a noble family at the Chateau des Ages, France. She was educated at a convent, and one of her favorite childhood pastimes was a peaceful one: building sandcastles. Her father died when she was nineteen years old. Her older brother had fled France during the anti-Catholic French Revolution, and his property had been confiscated, so she decided to defend him in his absence. Although she found it difficult to learn law and accounting, she was successful in her court case, and her education in business came in handy later. In 1796, she and her mother left the Chateau des Ages and went to live on the outskirts of Bethines in Poitou. Since the French Revolution had destroyed parish life, Elizabeth herself organized meetings with prayers and hymns every evening. After she met Saint Andrew Fournet, a priest who had opened a church in a barn, the two began working together. Both of them visited the sick and poor and taught young children. When Saint Fournet asked Elizabeth to be the superior of a community of nuns who would teach girls and care for the sick, Elizabeth pointed out that she had never been a novice, much less a superior. So he sent her for a year's novitiate with Carmelite nuns and the Society of Providence. Eventually, Elizabeth led a small group of nuns who served God by teaching children and caring for the elderly and the sick, as well as making spiritual reparation for all the outrages committed against our Lord in the Blessed Sacrament during the French Revolution. This small community became the Daughters of the Cross, also known as the Sisters of Saint Andrew, and it grew dramatically. By 1830, there were sixty convents of sisters in the new order. Elizabeth traveled frequently to these convents, just like the great Saint Teresa of Avila. In 1836, her health began to fail, and by 1838, she was in such constant pain that she sometimes became delirious. She bore the ten agonizing days of her final illness with great patience, and she died peacefully in the evening on this date in 1838.

---

[17] Gen 14:17–20.
[18] Heb 7:3.

Saint Mary Baouardy

Mary was born into a Greek Melchite Catholic family in Palestine in 1846. Her parents had thirteen sons, but tragically twelve of them died in infancy. Finally, Mary was born in answer to their prayers to the Virgin Mary. Her parents then died when she was only two years old, and she was raised by an uncle. She recognized that God was calling her to religious life and refused to marry, but her uncle hired her out as a menial servant as a punishment. When another servant unsuccessfully attempted to convert her to Islam, he decided to kill her. On September 8, 1858, he cut her throat and left her in an alley to die, but, amazingly, Mary recovered from her injuries. She attributed this miracle to the Blessed Virgin Mary, whom she said appeared to her. She then worked as a domestic servant for a time, unsuccessfully tried to enter the Sisters of Saint Joseph, and entered the Carmelite monastery in Pau in 1867 as a lay sister. She took the name Mary of Jesus Crucified when she was professed as a nun. Mary had many spiritual gifts, some of which were extraordinary. For example, she fought off demonic possession for forty days, was seen to levitate, received the stigmata, and could read the consciences of others. During the building of a monastery in Bethlehem, she was injured, contracted gangrene, and died as a result in 1878.

Blessed Leucadia (Levkadia) Harasymiv

Leucadia was born in Rudnykj, Ukraine, in 1911 and was a Greek Catholic. She entered the Sisters of Saint Joseph in 1931. In 1951, she was arrested by the NKVD (Russian secret police) for being a Catholic and exiled to Siberia. There she died on August 28, 1952, of tuberculosis and exhaustion.

> *Patriarch Melchizedek, help me worship the true God worthily.*
> *Saint Elizabeth, show me how to make reparations for the sins committed*
> *against our Lord's Real Presence in the Blessed Sacrament.*
> *Saint Mary, show me how to love suffering.*
> *Blessed Leucadia, show me how to live and die for Christ.*

* * * * *

August 27

Saint Monica, Memorial

Monica was born into a Christian family in Tagaste (modern Algeria) around the year 332. She married a pagan named Patricius, whom she eventually converted to the Catholic faith, but not until he was on his deathbed in 371. She and her husband had three children that we know of, and she tried to instill the Christian faith in all of them, particularly her eldest son, Augustine, who led an immoral life for many years. Monica shed many tears for her son's immoral way of life until he finally repented and entered the Church in the year 387. She died only a few years later, but she died in peace over the state of her son's soul.

Christian mothers of wayward children have been invoking her intercession ever since.

Saint Caesarius of Arles

Caesarius was born in Burgundy, France, in 470. At the age of eighteen, he joined a monastery, and he served his fellow monks by managing the house repairs and buying supplies. (His careful attention to consumption of the house wines caused resentment among monks who were a bit too interested in alcohol.) Two years later, he withdrew from the world so that he could live a life of solitary prayer and penance, but he returned to Arles when he developed health problems. While in Arles, he publicly expressed his reservations about Christian clergymen indiscriminately studying pagan authors. His bishop, Eonus, noticed Caesarius' careful faith, made him a deacon, and then ordained him a priest. Bishop Eonus later sent him to reform a lax monastery, and Caesarius did so by simply enforcing better discipline and being a good example to the monks. When Caesarius became Eonus' successor as bishop of Arles, he continued to reform the life of religious in his diocese. For example, he drew up rules for both religious men and women to follow, regulated the singing of the Divine Office (modifying it in ways designed to encourage the laity to attend), and guided several suffragan sees as their metropolitan. When he was falsely accused of a crime to the king, Caesarius not only proved his innocence, but he convinced the king to pardon his accuser, who had been sentenced to death by stoning. When King Theodoric of the Ostrogoths invaded the area, Caesarius was captured and brought under guard to him, but Theodoric treated him respectfully. Later, Caesarius went to Rome and became the first bishop in Western Europe to receive the pallium (official vestments of his office). After an invasion by the Franks, he retired from public life and made out his will to benefit a community of nuns. He had led his flock for forty years before his death in 543. He is considered a Father of the Church.

Saint David Lewis

David was the youngest of nine children, and he was born to a Protestant father and a Catholic mother in Wales in 1616. Although he was raised Protestant, he became a Catholic when he was sixteen years old and living in Paris. There he was ordained a priest in 1642 and became a Jesuit in 1645. In 1648, he returned to Wales and secretly ministered to the Catholics for thirty years. After the Oates Plot (a fictitious conspiracy against the king that fueled anti-Catholic persecution for a time), a servant betrayed him to the authorities as a Catholic priest. David was arrested and condemned for the crime of being a priest and for saying Mass. He was hanged, drawn, and quartered on August 22, 1679, in Usk, Wales.

Saint Monica, show me how to persevere in prayer for the lost.
Saint Caesarius, help me to show others how to reform their lives and imitate Christ.
Saint David, help me grow in thankfulness for the gift of the Mass.

* * * * *

August 28

Saint Augustine of Hippo, Memorial

Augustine was born in Tagaste, Africa, in 354 and raised in the truths of the Catholic faith by his mother, Saint Monica. On one occasion when he was a young man, he became so ill that he asked to be baptized, but he recovered from his illness before the Baptism could occur. In the year 370, Augustine went to Carthage to study, and there he became involved with a woman, lived with her, and fathered a son by her. He also became interested in the popular heresy known as Manichaeism, although his sharp mind eventually saw the holes in this philosophy. He moved to Milan, where he worked as a master of rhetoric. Through the prayers and tears of his mother, the excellent talks of the bishop of Milan, Saint Ambrose, and a dramatic conversion experience he described in his autobiography, *Confessions*, he was converted and baptized in the year 387 along with his friend Alipius and his son Adeodatus. He lived a life of prayer, fasting, and study with a small community of like-minded friends in Tagaste. In the year 391, he was ordained to be an assistant to the bishop of Hippo (modern Algeria), and there he established a sort of monastery along the lines of his previous community in Tagaste. In the year 395, he was named bishop of Hippo, and for the next thirty-five years, he defended the faith against heresies and endured the political turmoil of the final years of the Roman Empire. He wrote voluminously, brilliantly, and with humility, and near the end of his life, he even wrote a book in which he listed all of the errors he found in his own writings. He died as Hippo was suffering at the hands of Vandal invaders in 430, but he calmly resigned his spirit to the Lord. The Church has poured titles over him ever since: Father of the Church, Doctor of Grace (for his teachings on the subject), and one of the four great Doctors of the Western Church.

> Great are You, O Lord, and greatly to be praised; great is Your power, and of Your wisdom there is no end. And man, being a part of Your creation, desires to praise You—man, who bears about with him his mortality, the witness of his sin, even the witness that You "resist the proud,"—yet man, this part of Your creation, desires to praise You. You move us to delight in praising You; for You have made us for Yourself, and our hearts are restless until they rest in You.[19]

Saint Hermes of Rome

During the persecution of the Church under the Roman emperor Hadrian around the year 125, the martyr Hermes, a wealthy, freed slave, died in the city of Rome. One of the Roman catacombs is named after him.

Saint Moses the Black

Moses was born a slave in Africa in 330. He was of Ethiopian descent, and he was a violent young man, as well as a thief. While trying to escape punishment

---

[19] Augustine, *Confessions* 1.1, trans. J. G. Pilkington, in *Nicene and Post-Nicene Fathers*, 1st series, vol. 1, ed. Philip Schaff (Buffalo, N.Y.: Christian Literature Publishing, 1887). Revised and edited for New Advent by Kevin Knight, NewAdvent.org, accessed October 4, 2019, http://www.newadvent.org/fathers/110101.htm.

for his crimes, he hid with some hermits at the monastery of Petra in Egypt. But during his time with the monks, he repented. He gave up his past way of life and became a monk himself. Unfortunately, his zeal for Christ was greater than his ability to change his sinful behavior, which discouraged him at first. With the encouragement of his abbot, he gradually developed virtuous habits, and he eventually became a priest. However, having rejected his former life of violence and vowed himself to a life of peace, he refused to defend himself when the monastery was attacked in the year 405. He was murdered during the attack, and his relics remain at the Church of the Holy Virgin at the Parameos Monastery in Egypt.

Saint Augustine, teach me how to confess my sins humbly.
Saint Hermes, show me how to be free of the slavery of sin.
Saint Moses, help me to cast out my past sins
and make room for God in my heart.

* * * * *

August 29

The Passion of John the Baptist, Memorial

The death of John the Baptist at the hands of King Herod completed his mission as precursor to the Word of God.

And John bore witness, "I saw the Spirit descend as a dove from heaven and remain on him. I myself did not know him; but he who sent me to baptize with water said to me, 'He on whom you see the Spirit descend and remain, this is he who baptizes with the Holy Spirit.' And I have seen and have borne witness that this is the Son of God." The next day again John was standing with two of his disciples; and he looked at Jesus as he walked, and said, "Behold, the Lamb of God!"[20]

Saint Sabina of Rome

During the persecution of the Church under the Roman emperor Hadrian around the year 125, the martyr Sabina died in the city of Rome. Tradition says that she was a wealthy widow who was converted to Christianity by her servant; the servant, Serapia, died a martyr a month before her.

Blessed Teresa Bracco

Teresa was born in 1924 to a family of humble, devout peasants in Santa Giulia, Italy. She was a pious child, was deeply devoted to the Eucharist and the Blessed Mother, and would sometimes seem to be lost in a trance while she prayed before the Blessed Sacrament. She went to Mass daily and prayed the Rosary

[20] Jn 1:32–36.

while doing her chores. On this date in 1944, a Nazi officer attacked her, and when she resisted being raped, he shot and killed her.

Saint John the Baptist, help me live my vocation.
Saint Sabina, help me to listen to those who speak of Christ.
Blessed Teresa, show me how to resist evil for God's sake.

* * * * *

August 30

Saints Felix and Adauctus of Rome

During the persecution of Christians under the Roman emperor Diocletian in the year 304, a priest of Rome named Felix was arrested, tortured, and led off to be executed. Along the way, a bystander was moved by Felix's lack of concern that he was being taken to his own death, and the man proclaimed himself a Christian and said he was also willing to die for his faith in Jesus Christ. This unnamed bystander was seized and beheaded along with Felix, and he was post-humously given the name Adauctus, which means "the additional one".

Saint Margaret Ward and Companions

Margaret (d. 1588), a lady's companion for the Whittle family of London, England, and her servant, Blessed John Roche, were arrested for smuggling a rope into Bridewell Prison to help Father Richard Watson escape. She was put in prison herself, flogged, and tortured, but she refused to give the location of Father Watson or to convert to the Church of England before she was executed. Several men, all now considered blesseds, were hanged with her on the same day: Richard Leigh (a priest), Edward Shelley (a layman condemned for hiding priests), Richard Martin (a gentleman condemned for hiding priests), John Roche (a servant to Margaret Ward who helped Father Watson escape prison), and Richard Lloyd (a layman condemned for giving wine to a priest).

Saint Jeanne Jugan

Jeanne was born in Brittany, France, in 1792. Her father was a fisherman who was frequently away at sea until his death when Jeanne was four years old. Her mother supported the family through farm work and raised her children in the Catholic faith, despite the violent persecution of the Church during the French Revolution. When Jeanne was sixteen years old, she became a maid for a Christian woman who often visited the poor and sick, and Jeanne accompanied the woman to help with these visits. Seeing and helping those in need deeply affected Jeanne, and she decided to decline proposals of marriage and give her life to God. At the age of twenty-five, she gave away her few possessions and started to work in a hospital. She gave herself over to the care of the sick and poor so completely that it brought her to exhaustion. So she stopped for a time and worked as a domestic servant for several years. Then, at the age of forty-five, she started working as a spinner and gave the extra money she made to the poor. Two years later, she started collecting money door-to-door for the poor and caring for poor widows as well. Gradually, others began to follow her example, and this became the order known as the Little Sisters of the Poor. Jeanne served as superior until she was unfortunately removed from her position by the order's spiritual moderator. She spent her remaining years as a humble sister in the motherhouse, serving the poor as best she could, dying in 1879.

Saints Felix and Adauctus, help me be at peace when suffering for Christ's sake.
Holy Martyrs, help me find ways to serve my priests.
Saint Jeanne, show me how to serve the needy with all my heart.

* * * * *

August 31

Saint Joseph of Arimathea

Joseph was a wealthy man, and as the Gospels of Mark[21] and Matthew[22] tell us, he provided his own tomb for our Lord's body after His Crucifixion. According to tradition, he also owned mines in Cornwall, England, and he brought the Catholic faith and the Holy Grail to England.

Saint Nicodemus

Nicodemus was a member of the Sanhedrin. He sought out Jesus to speak with Him privately,[23] and he helped Joseph of Arimathea bury Christ's body after His death.[24] According to tradition, he was baptized by Saints Peter and John and was martyred with Saint Stephen.

Jesus answered [Nicodemus], "Truly, truly, I say to you, unless one is born anew, he cannot see the kingdom of God." Nicodemus said to him, "How can a man be born when he is old? Can he enter a second time into his mother's womb and be born?" Jesus answered, "Truly, truly, I say to you, unless one is born of water and the Spirit, he cannot enter the kingdom of God."[25]

Saint Aidan of Lindisfarne

Aidan (d. 651) was a native of Ireland and a disciple of the abbot Saint Senan before he became a monk on the island of Iona in Scotland. When he was ordained a bishop, he continued to live as simply as a monk. For example, when

---

[21] Mk 15:43–46.
[22] Mt 27:57–59.
[23] Jn 3:1–15.
[24] Jn 19:39.
[25] Jn 3:3–5.

the king and other wealthy people gave him presents, he gave them to the poor, and he rarely attended the lavish meals of the king's table. He established a monastery on an island, now called Holy Isle or Lindisfarne, which became a great center of Celtic Christianity. He cared for children and slaves, often by buying them their freedom through the alms people gave to him. He died at the church at Bamburgh, England.

Saint Raymond Nonnatus

In 1204, Raymond's mother died giving birth to him, and he was born by caesarian section (hence his surname, Nonnatus, which means "not born"). He was well educated and from a noble family, and his father intended for him to have a career in the royal court of Aragon, Spain. But instead Raymond joined the Mercedarians, a society devoted to ransoming Christians who had been captured by the Muslims. Raymond succeeded the founder, Saint Peter Nolasco, and became its chief almoner. He traveled to Algiers in Africa, and there he ransomed many Christians from slavery. However, his money ran out, and he realized that he would leave several slaves behind if he left. So he gave himself up in exchange for them. Because he had converted some Muslims to the Christian faith, public sentiment among the Muslims rose against him. The Muslim governor at first wanted to put him to death by impaling him on a stake, but he then decided to ransom him at a high price. Raymond was publicly whipped and tortured for eight months until Peter Nolasco arrived to ransom him. Even then Raymond was willing to stay in prison in the hopes of winning more souls to Christ. Peter refused to let him, however, and brought him home. The pope made him a cardinal and would have had him live in Rome, but Raymond died on his way back in 1240.

Saint Joseph, show me how to be generous with my gifts.
Saint Nicodemus, help my weak faith.
Saint Aidan, help me be detached from the pleasures of this world.
Saint Raymond, show me how to sacrifice myself for others.

September

September 1

Prophet Joshua

After leaving Egypt around the twelfth century B.C. and wandering in the wilderness for forty years, the Jewish people finally sent scouts to investigate and determine whether it was time to enter the land that God had promised them. Of the group of men sent from each tribe, only Joshua and Caleb were willing to fight the native peoples and obtain the land.[1] God remembered Joshua's trust, and Moses later chose him as his successor as leader of the Chosen People.[2] Considered a prophet by the Jewish people for his strong leadership and trust in God, Joshua led them into many battles until they finally took possession of the Promised Land.[3]

> [Joshua said to the people], "Now therefore fear the LORD, and serve him in sincerity and in faithfulness; put away the gods which your fathers served beyond the River, and in Egypt, and serve the LORD. And if you be unwilling to serve the LORD, choose this day whom you will serve, whether the gods your fathers served in the region beyond the River, or the gods of the Amorites in whose land you dwell; but as for me and my house, we will serve the LORD."[4]

Saint Priscus of Capua

During the persecution of the Church in the time of the Roman Empire, Priscus died a martyr in the city of Capua, Italy. Some traditions say that he was the first bishop of Capua, appointed by Saint Peter himself; other traditions say that he was bishop of Capua but martyred in the fourth century.

Saint Giles

Giles (d. 710) was from a wealthy family in Athens, Greece, but he went to Provence in France to become a monk. For a time, he lived as a hermit in a cave. According to a legend, Giles befriended a deer, who gave him her milk to drink, and when the king and his hunters were chasing the deer one day, she led them to Giles' cave. The hunters, while trying to kill the deer, accidentally shot Giles, and in reparation, the king offered him land to live on. Later, Giles founded a monastery on this land and became abbot of the monks who wanted to be his

---

[1] Num 13–14.
[2] Deut 31:1–8.
[3] Josh 1–12.
[4] Josh 24:14–15.

disciples. Giles is one of the Fourteen Holy Helpers, great saints who were called upon particularly for help during the bubonic plague in the fourteenth century.

Prophet Joshua, show me how to serve God wholeheartedly.
Saint Priscus, help me to remain faithful to Christ.
Saint Giles, help me to see God in His creation.

* * * * *

September 2

Saint Habib (Abibus) of Edessa

During the persecution of the Church under the Roman emperor Licinius in the year 322, the deacon Habib was living in Edessa, Syria. He was arrested for being a Christian and executed by being burned at the stake.

Blesseds John-Marie du Lau d'Alleman, Francis-Joseph de la Rochefoucauld, Peter-Louis de la Rochefoucauld, and Companions, also known as the Martyrs of September

During the French Revolution, 191 men, mostly Catholic clergy and vowed religious, were imprisoned in a Carmelite house in Paris for refusing to take an oath supporting the civil constitution of the clergy. This oath had been condemned by the Vatican because it gave control of the Church to the revolutionary, anti-Catholic French government. The imprisoned men included Bishop John-Marie du Lau d'Alleman, bishop of Arles and member of Parliament; Francis-Joseph de la Rochefoucauld, bishop of Beauvais; and Peter-Louis de la Rochefoucauld, bishop of Saintes. Late on the night of September 2, 1792, an anti-Catholic mob broke into the house and brutally massacred all these men.

Holy Martyrs, show me how to live and die for Christ.

* * * * *

September 3

Saint Gregory the Great (Gregory I), Memorial

Gregory was born around the year 540 into an aristocratic Roman family that included two previous popes—Agapitus I and Felix III. He served in the powerful position of urban prefect until he was about thirty years old. At that point, in the year 574, he decided to leave his wealth behind him. He turned his house into a monastery, then he asked a monk named Valentius to be the abbot in charge and became a monk under his direction. However, after Gregory had happily enjoyed the peace of the life of a monk for a time, the pope sent

Gregory to represent him in the Byzantine court on an important mission in Constantinople. While he was there, Gregory continued to live like a monk but also learned about court life in Constantinople. Most importantly, he learned that the Byzantine court was uninterested in protecting the Italians from barbarians (which were a great danger to Christians in Europe at the time) and that the patriarch of Constantinople was leading a very worldly life. When Gregory returned to Rome after the mission was over, he was ordained a deacon. In the year 590, Gregory was unanimously elected pope. Though he had wanted to be a missionary himself, it was his decision as pope to send Saint Augustine, the future bishop of Canterbury, and a group of other missionaries to England to evangelize the English people. His past experience in the Byzantine court and his personal tact helped him find diplomatic solutions to protect the Italian people from invaders during violent times. The clarity and strength of his writings, his sense of justice for fair treatment of the poor and of Jews, and his encouragement of sacred music in what is now called Gregorian chant are all shown in the title he preferred for himself as pope: Servant of the Servants of God. The people called him Gregory the Great, after his death in the year 604, and tradition calls him a Father of the Church. The Church also named him one of the four great Doctors of the Western Church.

Every act of our Redeemer, performed through His human nature, was meant to be a pattern for our actions, so that in following His footsteps according to the measure of our ability we might walk unfalteringly along the path of our present lifework.[5]

Blessed Bartholomew Gutierrez and Companions

Bartholomew was an Augustinian priest born in Mexico, one of many priests sent to bring the Good News to the people of Japan in the seventeenth century. When the Japanese government renewed the persecution of Christians, priests were arrested and executed. A group of Catholic clergymen, including one from Spain, one from Portugal, and two Japanese men who had converted to the faith and become priests, died on this date in 1632. They were killed by being scalded in boiling water and then burned alive in Nagasaki, Japan.

Saint Gregory, help me serve God with all my heart.
Holy Martyrs, help me to face suffering with peace.

* * * * *

September 4

Prophet Moses

As is well known and described in the book of Exodus, Moses was born into a Jewish family in Egypt, narrowly escaped death as an infant, and ran away from

[5] Gregory the Great, *Dialogues*, trans. Odo John Zimmerman, O.S.B., Fathers of the Church Series, vol. 39 (Washington, D.C.: Catholic University of America Press, 1959), 36.

Egypt to avoid arrest for protecting a Jew from an Egyptian.[6] Moses returned when God called him to lead His people into freedom, after having revealed to Moses His divine and mysterious name: "I AM WHO I AM."[7] Moses, through God's grace and his own faith, humility, perseverance, prayer, and willingness to confront sin, led God's people to the border of the Promised Land. We commemorate Moses today for his faithfulness, but also for the way he was a precursor of Jesus Christ.

> Then Moses said to God, "If I come to the sons of Israel and say to them, 'The God of your fathers has sent me to you,' and they ask me, 'What is his name?' what shall I say to them?" God said to Moses, "I AM WHO I AM."[8]

Saint Boniface I

Boniface was born around the year 350. The day before he was elected as the forty-second and lawful pope, a small faction of the Roman clergy claimed to select another man as pope. The schism caused by this anti-pope caused violence and loss of life, lasted almost four months, and required the intervention of the Western Roman emperor Honorius. Finally, Boniface was accepted as the true pope. As pope, he was a strong leader who tightened papal control over his bishops, and he supported Saint Augustine of Hippo (the bishop) in the disputes over the heresy of Pelagianism. He died in 422.

Saint Rosalia of Palermo

Rosalia (1130–1160) was the daughter of a noble family in Palermo, Sicily, but she left it all behind when she was only a teenager to become a hermit in a cave, living alone with God. She took only a wooden crucifix, a silver Greek cross, a terracotta crucifix, and a string of beads (an early form of the rosary) with her. So many people came to her cave to get her advice that she finally moved to another cave to enjoy greater solitude. The people of the city are still very devoted to her intercession, particularly since they believe prayers for her intercession during the seventeenth century miraculously saved the city from the plague.

Blessed Scipion Jerome Brigeat Lambert

Scipion was born into a noble family in Ligny, France, in 1733 and became a priest and later vicar general of the Diocese of Avranches. When the persecution of Catholics began at the start of the French Revolution, Scipion fled to his hometown. Revolutionary officials found him there and demanded that he take an oath promising to support the new government, which was bitterly anti-Catholic. When he refused, he was arrested and imprisoned, with many other Catholic clergy and laymen, in the prison ships in Rochefort. He died on this date in 1794 of starvation and mistreatment.

[6] Ex 2:1–25.
[7] Ex 3:14.
[8] Ex 3:13–14.

Prophet Moses, teach me how to listen to God's voice.
Saint Boniface, help me to love Christ and His Church.
Saint Rosalia, teach me how to live simply for Christ.
Blessed Scipion, show me how to suffer for the sake of Christ.

* * * * *

September 5

Saints Peter Nguyen Van Tu and Joseph Hoang Luong Canh

Peter Nguyen Van Tu was born in Ninh Cuong, Vietnam, around the year 1796 and became a Dominican priest. Joseph was born in Lang Van, Vietnam, around the year 1763 and became a physician; after becoming a Christian, he became a catechist and a Dominican tertiary. Because of the brutal persecution of Catholicism in Vietnam at the time, both men were arrested and died as martyrs by beheading on this date in the year 1838.

Saint Teresa of Calcutta

Teresa was born in 1910 in Albania and was given the birthname Agnes; her father was a businessman who died when she was only nine years old. She became a sister with the Sisters of Loreto and was sent to Calcutta to serve as a teacher in 1928; but when the Lord called her to leave her convent behind and work among the poor in 1948, she obeyed. In 1950, she founded the Congregation of the Missionaries of Charity, an order of sisters serving the poorest of the poor. After decades of serving the poor in obscurity and poverty, Mother Teresa received numerous awards and worldwide praise. Yet she also suffered from an agonizing absence of the presence of God for decades and criticism from those who were mystified by her deep faith in Christ. Her humility and complete dedication to serving God and those who suffer lives on in her sisters. She died in 1997.

Saints Peter and Joseph, help me remain faithful to Christ.
Saint Teresa, teach me how to draw close to God,
that I too might be a "pencil" in His hand.

* * * * *

September 6

Prophet Zechariah

Zechariah was from the Jewish tribe of Levi and lived in the sixth century B.C. After the Jews had returned to Israel from the Babylonian Exile, God told

Zechariah to tell the people to rebuild the Temple.[9] Zechariah's prophecies and remarkable visions testify to his close relationship with God. He was buried beside the prophet Haggai.

> *[The* LORD *said,] "And I will pour out on the house of David and the inhabitants of Jerusalem a spirit of compassion and supplication, so that, when they look on him whom they have pierced, they shall mourn for him, as one mourns for an only child, and weep bitterly over him, as one weeps over a first-born."*[10]

Saint Onesiphorus

When the Apostle Paul was imprisoned, he commended Onesiphorus[11] for his personal kindness and support of the Church. According to tradition, Onesiphorus was a missionary to Spain and died a martyr during the late first century under the reign of the Roman emperor Domitian. While evangelizing a region of modern Turkey, he was killed by being tied to wild horses, which tore him apart.

Saint Cagnoald

When the abbot Saint Columban rebuked King Theodoric of France for his immoral behavior, the king responded by banishing Columban from France. Cagnoald (d. 635) was the bishop of Laon at the time, and he chose to leave the country with his friend. The two men served as missionaries around Lake Constance, near modern Germany.

Saint Bega (Bee)

Bee was born into a noble Irish family and lived in the seventh century. She refused to marry—even when she was offered marriage to a prince—and instead decided to give her life to Christ. She fled to Cumberland, England, and lived there as a hermit for many years. The king of Northumbria (Saint Oswald) eventually convinced her to enter a convent so that she would be safe from marauders. She entered a convent that was governed by the abbot of Lindesfarne, Saint Aidan, and she later founded a monastery and became its abbess. She was known for her generosity to the poor and compassion to those in need.

> *Prophet Zechariah, help me hear and obey God's words.*
> *Saint Onesiphorus, show me how to live and die for Christ.*
> *Saint Cagnoald, help me draw near to those who suffer injustice.*
> *Saint Bega, teach me how to serve God in silence and generosity.*

* * * * *

[9] Zech 6:9–15.
[10] Zech 12:10.
[11] See 2 Tim 1:16; 4:19.

September 7

Saint Sozon (Sozonte)

Tarasius was a shepherd who became a Christian during a time of persecution in the fourth century. To show his thankfulness to Christ after his conversion, he even changed his name to Sozon, which roughly means "saved". Inspired by a dream, he entered the nearby town of Pompeiopolis (now in Turkey) and used his shepherd's crook to smash the pagan idols in the town, giving the gold of the idols to the poor. When other people were falsely arrested for the crime, he turned himself in. He was forced to walk with nails driven through his feet as a torture before his trial in the amphitheater. The magistrate was impressed with Sozon's bravery, and he promised him he would release him if he would play his pipe to entertain the listening crowd. Sozon refused, saying that he once played for his sheep, but now he played only for God. He was then martyred by being burned to death.

Saint Clodoald (Cloud) of France

Cloud was born in 522, one of three sons of Clodomir, who was a son of King Clovis of the Franks. After Cloud's father was killed in battle, Cloud and his two brothers were raised in the Catholic faith by their grandmother Clotilda, who loved them very much. The boys' uncles, Childebert and Clotaire, decided to kill the boys and take over the kingdom for themselves. The two men met with Clotilda and brutally asked her whether she would prefer to have the three boys killed or have them shut up in monasteries. They then killed the two older boys in front of the shocked queen, but Cloud escaped. Cloud, having seen enough of the evils of the world, voluntarily chose a hermit's life and didn't try to take his rightful place as king away from his wicked uncles. Cloud lived a holy life, and he taught people about the Christian faith. He died at the age of thirty-eight in the year 560.

> Saint Sozon, teach me how to serve God first, last, and always.
> Saint Cloud, teach me how to forgive those who have wronged me.

* * * * *

September 8

The Nativity of the Blessed Virgin Mary, Feast

The birth of our Blessed Mother is not recorded in the Gospels, but it was instituted as a memorial for the whole Church in the seventh century by Pope Sergius I, following a previous practice of Eastern Catholics.

[The LORD said,] "Therefore the Lord himself will give you a sign. Behold, a virgin shall conceive and bear a son, and shall call his name Immanuel."[12]

Saint Adrian of Nicomedia

During the persecution of the Church under the Roman emperor Galerius Maximian in the year 306, the martyr Adrian died in the city of Nicomedia (now in Turkey). Some traditions say that he was an imperial guard and was converted to the faith by his wife, Natalia.

Saint Sergius I

Sergius (d. 701) was the eighty-fourth pope; he reigned for thirteen years. He was born the son of Syrian immigrants in Rome; he became an Augustinian Canon Regular and then a cardinal priest. When he became pope, Sergius strongly opposed efforts by the emperor Justinian II to control the Church. When the emperor sent soldiers to arrest Sergius, the people of Rome protected him, and even many of the soldiers sided with him and against the emperor instead. During his long reign, Sergius sent missionaries to Germany, ordered the celebration of processions on certain feast days, and introduced the Agnus Dei prayer to Latin liturgies.

Saint Corbinian

Waldegiso was born around the year 680 in France; when he was young, his mother changed his name to Corbinian. After he grew up, Corbinian lived alone with God as a recluse for many years, and he developed a reputation for being a miracle worker. Other men wanted to follow his holy way of life, so they formed a religious community under his guidance. He found that being a leader distracted him from prayer, however, so he went to Rome to ask the pope for advice. Pope Saint Gregory II's answer didn't make his life easier, however: he sent Corbinian to preach the Gospel to the pagans of Bavaria. Corbinian's preaching was very successful, and many people converted to the Christian faith. However, while Corbinian was traveling through one area of Bavaria, he stayed with a duke named Grimoald, at the request of the pope. When he learned that Grimoald had married his brother's widow, he distanced himself from the man and refused to associate with him until he left the lady, who was named Biltrudis. Biltrudis was so angry that she tried to have Corbinian murdered, so Corbinian had to leave the area and take refuge at Meran, Italy, for a time. Later, Grimoald was killed in battle and Biltrudis was taken away after the battle by the Franks, so Corbinian was able to return to his missionary work in Bavaria. In a popular story about Corbinian, a bear killed the bishop's pack horse, so Corbinian told the bear to carry his load, which the bear did until they reached Rome. The bear then returned to the forest. The symbolism of the story—God's grace (the bishop) taming paganism (the bear) and the load indicating the weight of the bishop's office—have made Corbinian's bear a popular

[12] Is 7:14.

Christian symbol, including on the papal coat of arms of Pope Benedict XVI. Corbinian served as a missionary until his death in 730.

Saint Thomas of Villanova

Thomas was born in 1488; his father was a miller in Castile, Spain. Thomas was sent as a young man to study at the university in Alcala, and he eventually became a professor of philosophy. He was intelligent, but he was also absentminded. Thomas became an Augustinian friar, then the prior of the house; later (despite his humble request to be excused), he became the archbishop of Valencia. As archbishop, Thomas first visited all of his clergy—and then he passed ordinances to abolish the abuses that he had observed among them. He made sure that several hundred poor people were fed every day, and he founded colleges that educated poor students. At that time in Spain, many Muslims and Jews had converted to Christianity, and while some did so in good faith, others did so for personal benefit. If they later apostatized from the Catholic faith, they were considered a threat to the safety of the country, which had only been recently freed from Muslim control, so they were brought before the Inquisition. Thomas tried, in vain many times, to protect faithful converts from persecution. Although he was unable to attend the Council of Trent for an unknown reason, he encouraged those who did attend to support changes that would respond to criticisms of the Church made by Lutherans. For example, he suggested that bishops not be moved from one diocese to another and that they should be chosen from the natives of the area if possible. He developed heart disease in August 1555. Knowing that his end was near, he gave away all his possessions, which he asked permission to keep temporarily until he no longer needed them. He died in the same year, saying the words "Father, into your hands I commit my spirit!"[13]

Blessed Antoine-Frederic Ozanam

Frederic was born in 1813 in Milan, Italy, into a family of fourteen children, though only he and two siblings survived to adulthood. He became a married man, teacher, scholar, and author, and he lived in Marseilles and Paris, France. In addition to writing about the benefits of Christianity to individuals and society, he put his faith in action to care personally for the poor. He founded an organization to serve the poor of Paris that was first known as the Conference of Charity. It later became the Society of Saint Vincent de Paul, which has spread all over the world in bringing God's love to the poor. He died in 1853.

> *Blessed Mother, on your birthday, help me make my life a gift to Jesus.*
> *Saint Adrian, show me how to live and die for Christ.*
> *Saint Sergius, help me to worship the Lamb of God worthily.*
> *Saint Corbinian, teach me how to bring God's grace to those who do not know Him.*
> *Saint Thomas and Blessed Frederic, show me where to serve the poor today.*

* * * * *

---

[13] Lk 23:46, the last words of Jesus on the Cross.

September 9

Saint Gorgonio (Gorgonius) of Rome

During the early persecution of the Church in an unknown year, the martyr Gorgonio died in the city of Rome. He was buried in the Two Laurels Cemetery on the Via Lubicana.

Blessed Maria de la Cabeza

Maria (d. 1140) married a farmer named Isidore (who is popularly known as Saint Isidore the Farmer), and the two of them lived a poor but devout life together in Torrelaguna, Spain. After the death of their only son, they decided to live as brother and sister for the rest of their lives; they were known to their neighbors for their good works and faithfulness to their duties. Maria died ten years after Isidore. Because the relic of her head has been carried in procession at times of drought to invoke her intercession, she's known to the Spanish people as Mary of the Head.

Saint Peter Claver, Memorial[14]

Peter was born in 1581 in Verdu, Catalonia, in Spain; he graduated with distinction from the University of Barcelona before he entered the Jesuit order. There he met Alphonsus Rodriguez, the holy porter and future saint, who predicted that Peter would be a missionary. Peter asked to be sent to serve in the West Indies, but instead he received additional education in theology before being sent to the city of Cartagena in Colombia. There he was ordained a Jesuit priest. Peter was assigned to help another Jesuit missionary who had been serving, for decades, the African slaves who were brought to work in the New World; Peter threw himself into this same mission. With assistants and translators, he entered the yards where slaves were kept after being taken off the boats. He anointed the dying, baptized the babies, cared for the sick, and brought food, medicine, lemons, brandy, tobacco, and, most importantly, comfort to them. His gentle care moved them, and gradually he taught them about God and the Christian faith. Many slaves later entered the Church. He fought endless battles with civil authorities and others—for example, some white women would complain that they couldn't bear to enter the church after slaves had been there. But his mission work eventually spread to the slave plantations as well as to Protestant slave traders, hospitals, and even the streets. After preaching many, many times during the Jubilee Year of 1650, he was so weak that it was thought he would die during an epidemic that swept the city. But he survived the illness, recovered slowly, and was generally forgotten during the aftermath of the epidemic. When the priest who was sent to replace him arrived in 1654, Peter dragged himself from his bed to help him. But his

---

[14] This saint is celebrated as a memorial, rather than an optional memorial, in the *Liturgical Calendar for the Dioceses of the United States of America*.

illness quickly returned, and he predicted his own death to an associate. During his final months, people remembered the holy priest, and many came to ask for his blessing. Although many people had opposed Peter's work while he lived, in 1654, the whole city turned out at his funeral.

Blessed Jacques-Desire Laval

Jacques (1803–1864) was raised in a pious family of French farmers; his mother died when he was only seven years old. As a young man, he considered becoming a priest, but he decided to become a doctor instead. He established a medical practice and ignored his spiritual life. But after a fall from a horse that could have killed him, he reexamined his life; he closed his practice within a few months and entered the seminary. He became a parish priest and then a missionary in what is now the Society of the Holy Heart of Mary. The order sent him to Maritius, an island off the coast of Africa, where he spent the rest of his life. He arrived soon after slavery had been outlawed; he lived among the freed slaves, who were poor, uneducated, and unemployed. He gave them medical treatment and learned to speak their language, but, more importantly, he treated them as human beings. He gave them positions of responsibility and worked to improve their agricultural, medical, and sanitary conditions. His work bore fruit; in his area, sixty-seven thousand people converted to the Christian faith. He was respected by the Muslim, Buddhist, and Hindu leaders in the area, and his funeral was attended by mourners of all faiths.

> *Saint Gorgonio, show me how to live and die for Christ.*
> *Blessed Maria, teach me to love self-sacrifice.*
> *Saint Peter, beg the Lord to give me the perseverance*
> *to spend myself for those who are abandoned.*
> *Blessed Jacques, show me how to bring healing to the suffering.*

* * * * *

September 10

Saint Nicholas of Tolentino

When Nicholas' parents had been married for several years and still hadn't had a child, they made a pilgrimage to the shrine of Saint Nicholas of Bari. They were blessed with a son afterward in 1245 and named him after the great saint. Young Nicholas grew up in Fermo, Italy, and he was so talented that his friends were certain that he would advance to a high position in the Church. But when Nicholas heard an Augustinian friar named Reginald preach the Gospel message "Do not love the world or the things in the world",[15] Nicholas decided to enter that friar's order; he was professed in the Augustinian Canons when he

---

[15] 1 Jn 2:15.

was seventeen years old. At San Ginesio, where he was sent to learn theology, he was so generous in giving away food to the poor that his superiors complained about it. Still, Nicholas was ordained a priest in 1270, and he became locally famous when he prayed for a blind woman, who then recovered her sight. Nicholas' religious order moved him repeatedly from one community to another, but he finally settled in the city of Tolentino, where a voice seemed to be directing him to stay. For thirty years, he served God in Tolentino, which had suffered a great deal due to fighting between the Guelf and Ghibelline families. Nicholas' street-preaching, care for the sick and the poor, outreach to children, and work in reconciling families—and the miraculous power of his prayers—brought peace to this troubled city. For example, at Nicholas' canonization process, a woman testified that Nicholas had brought about a reformation of her husband, who had treated her cruelly for many years. In 1305, Nicholas died after a year-long illness, during which he got up from bed on one occasion: to absolve a penitent whom he knew would conceal a serious sin from any other priest.

Blesseds Sebastian Kimura, Francis Morales, and Companions

In 1615, the Japanese Tokugawa government prohibited Christianity and demanded that all missionaries leave the country. While some left, others went into hiding and ministered to the Christians of Japan in secret. By 1622, the government had arrested more than fifty missionaries and lay Catholics. Of those number, Sebastian Kimura was a Jesuit priest, and Francis Morales was a Dominican priest. All were martyred for the crime of being Christians on this date in 1622 at Nagasaki, Japan, by being burned alive.

> *Saint Nicholas, help me to ask for and expect God's miracles.*
> *Holy Martyrs, teach me your heroic faith in Christ.*

* * * * *

September 11

Saints Protus and Hyacinth of Rome

In second-century Rome, Protus and Hyacinth were faithful servants to Eugenia, who was the daughter of the prefect of Egypt. All three were Christians, so when the Roman emperor Valerian renewed the persecution of Christians, all three tried to flee the city. They were arrested and died as martyrs for the faith. In 1845, a priest found the bones and ashes of Protus and Hyacinth in a wall tomb in Rome.

Saint Paphnutius of Egypt

Paphnutius (d. 350) was an Egyptian who lived in the desert under the direction of the great desert saint and monk Anthony. Later, he was made bishop of the Upper Thebaid, a region of Egypt. During the persecution of Christians under the Roman emperor Maximinus, he was blinded in his right eye, hamstrung in one leg, and then sent to work in the mines for the crime of being a Christian. After the persecution of Christians ended, he returned to his diocese and became a well-known and zealous defender of the faith against the heresy of Arianism. When he attended the Council of Tyre in the year 335 as a bishop, most of the churchmen present were followers of the Arian heresy. He saw that Maximus—the bishop of Jerusalem who had suffered the same disfigurement and punishments as he had—had chosen to sit among the Arians, rather than among the faithful bishops. Paphnutius went over to Maximus, led him outside, and talked to him. He told Maximus that he couldn't bear to see anyone with the same marks of suffering that he bore seated with those who opposed the teachings of the Church. Maximus returned to orthodoxy, publicly supported the great bishop of Alexandria, Saint Athanasius, who was persecuted for opposing Arianism, and never left the side of truth again, also becoming a saint of the Church.

Saints Protus and Hyacinth, teach me how to be a servant of God.
Saint Paphnutius, show me how to lead others to the truth about Jesus Christ.

* * * * *

September 12

Most Holy Name of Mary, Optional Memorial

This memorial in honor of the name of Mary was first celebrated in 1513, but it was added to the General Roman Calendar in 1683 after a great victory in battle, which was attributed to our Blessed Mother.

In dangers, in doubts, in difficulties, think of Mary, call upon Mary. Let not her name leave thy lips, never suffer it to leave thy heart.[16]

Blessed Pierre (Roger) Sulpice Christopher Faverge

Pierre was born in 1745 in Orleans, France. He entered the Brothers of the Christian Schools and became a teacher, taking the name Brother Roger. During the French Revolution, all French priests and religious were ordered to swear allegiance to the anti-Catholic government; of the many who refused, 827 priests and religious were imprisoned in the hulks (ships that were no longer seaworthy and were used to house slaves and prisoners) in Rochefort to await deportation. There was almost no food, water, sanitation, or medical treatment

---

[16] Bernard of Clairvaux, *Hom. II* super "Missus est", 17, quoted by Pope Pius XII, in his encyclical *Doctor Mellifluus* (May 24, 1953), no. 31, http://w2.vatican.va/content/pius-xii/en/encyclicals/documents/hf_p-xii_enc_24051953_doctor-mellifluus.html.

on the ships, and 542 of the men died. The survivors who were released in 1795 later wrote about the faithfulness of those who had been martyred. Roger, who died on this date in 1794, was one of those great witnesses to Christ in the inhuman conditions of the hulks, serving those in need around him until he too died of an illness.

> *Blessed Virgin Mary, may your name bring me God's comfort.*
> *Blessed Pierre, help me to remain faithful during times of difficulty.*

* * * * *

September 13

Saint John Chrysostom, Memorial

John was born at Antioch (Turkey) around the year 347 and was the son of the commander of the Roman imperial troops. When his father died, his mother returned to Rome to raise her two children. John was well educated and raised as a Christian, but he wasn't baptized until he was twenty years old, a typical age at the time. He then decided to live the penitential life of a hermit for several years, first in a community of monks, then under the direction of a holy monk, and finally alone in a cave. However, he overdid his penances a bit, suffered from health problems, and had to return to the city of Antioch. There he was made a deacon, then a priest, and then preacher for the bishop himself. When Nectarius, the patriarch of Constantinople, realized that he was dying, he decided to make John his successor. However, the people of Antioch loved John so much that Nectarius had to arrange for John to leave the city and be installed in Constantinople secretly, so secretly that John himself didn't know what was happening at first. Another archbishop, Theophilus, the patriarch of Alexandria, had wanted his own candidate to become patriarch of Constantinople, and although he was very angry, he waited to take his revenge. As a preacher, John's homilies frequently (and vividly) reminded the rich to remember the poor, encouraged all Christians to seek perfection, and warned about the dangers of the cruel and scandalous entertainments popular at the time. As a bishop, he was full of Christlike zeal: he reduced his own salary and bishops' furnishings to help the poor, spoke out publicly against the immodest manner of dress of some of the women of the city, and personally and emphatically corrected his own clergy. Although the faithful people loved him, this also made him many enemies, particularly Arians and the clergymen that he had reprimanded. On two occasions, his forthright speaking in defense of the faith led the empress Eudoxia to have him banished from the city, although an earthquake soon afterward led the superstitious empress to allow him to return. Through a complex political intrigue involving false charges made against John, orchestrated by the vengeful Patriarch Theophilus—and despite the best efforts of the pope—John was condemned and banished from the city and sent away into exile. John suffered for more than three years from the cruel treatment of his guards and the harsh conditions in which he was forced to live. Though his guards didn't kill him directly, they finally wore out the sick man through hard marches without rest. He died at the Chapel of Saint Basilicus on September 14, 407. After his death, he was given the surname Chrysostom, meaning "golden-mouthed", for the enduring beauty, faithfulness, and volume of his writings. Long considered a Father of the Church, the Church also named him a Doctor of the Church.

These are the two purposes for which marriage was instituted: to make us chaste, and to make us parents.[17]

Saint Marcellinus of Carthage

Marcellinus was a tribune (an important elected official) in North Africa during the late fourth and early fifth centuries. He was married, had children, and corresponded with Saints Jerome and Augustine of Hippo over theological matters, and Augustine even dedicated one of his greatest works, *The City of God*, to Marcellinus. In 411, a council was convened to settle a theological dispute between two positions: one position was what we now think of as Catholic teaching and the other was the position held by followers of the Donatist heresy, a long-lived Christian heresy that taught that the sacraments were invalid when conferred by clergy who had committed a serious sin. Marcellinus was the chairman of the council, and, after debate between bishops on both sides, Marcellinus ruled in favor of the Catholics. In retaliation, the Donatists accused him of supporting an enemy of the Roman emperor Honorius, and Marcellinus and his brother were executed on a charge of treason in 413 in the city of Carthage. A year later, the emperor publicly admitted it had been a mistake and that the two men were guiltless. Since Marcellinus died as a direct result of publicly defending orthodox Catholic teaching, he has always been considered a martyr for truth.

Saint John, help me speak with golden words to those God sends my way today. Saint Marcellinus, help me to stand on the side of truth, at any cost to myself.

* * * * *

September 14

The Exaltation of the Cross, Feast

This feast has been celebrated since the fourth century to commemorate both the building of the first church over the site of Jesus' Crucifixion and the finding of pieces of the True Cross by Helen, mother of the Roman emperor Constantine and a saint in her own right.

---

[17] Saint John Chrysostom, *On Marriage and Family Life*, Sermon on Marriage, trans. Catherine P. Roth and David Anderson, Popular Patristics Series (Crestwood, N.Y.: St. Vladimir's Seminary Press, 1986), 85.

Saint Peter of Tarentaise

Peter (1102–1174) not only entered a Cistercian monastery himself when he was twenty years old, but he persuaded his own parents, brothers, and a sister to enter religious life as well. He loved his life as a monk in the desolate Tarentaise hills of France. With the financial support of Count Amadeo III of Savoy, he built a hospital nearby and personally cared for the sick and for travelers who passed the monastery. In the year 1142, he was elected archbishop of Tarentaise to replace an unfit and incompetent bishop. Although he hadn't sought the honor of becoming an archbishop, Peter worked zealously to bring order to the diocese. After thirteen years, however, he missed monastic life so much that he ran away, joined another Cistercian monastery anonymously, and lived as a mere lay member. Within a year, however, people had discovered the truth, and he had to return to serve his flock. When an anti-pope claimed power in the Church, Peter supported the true pope. In addition to serving the poor, he served as a peacemaker; his last act was to try to make peace between two warring kings.

Saint Albert of Jerusalem

Albert (1149–1214) was a well-born, well-educated monk of the Augustinian Canons Regular when he was made bishop of Vercelli in Italy. While serving as bishop, he demonstrated wisdom and skills in diplomacy, so the Catholic leaders of Jerusalem petitioned Pope Innocent III to raise him to the position of patriarch of Jerusalem. It was a tumultuous time in Jerusalem, since both Christians and Muslims were trying to rule the city. When Albert arrived in Jerusalem as the new patriarch, he first worked to gain the respect of both the Muslims and Christians living there, something that previous Catholic patriarchs had completely failed to do. He served as peacemaker in other disputes in the region as well. Albert wrote the first description of the religious life of the hermits living on Mount Carmel, making him the first legislator of the Carmelite order. In 1214, he deposed a man as head of the Hospital of the Holy Ghost. While Albert was leading a public procession on the Feast of the Triumph of the Cross, the disgruntled man attacked and stabbed Albert, killing him.

Saint Notburga of Eben

Notburga was born around the year 1265 into a poor peasant family in Tyrol, Austria, and became a kitchen maid for Count Henry of Rattenberg. She saw that the pigs at the castle ate better than the poor people around her, and she began to give the leftover food from the castle to the poor, also giving them food from her own meals. The count's mother approved of this generosity, but when she died, the count's wife, Ottila, did not. Notburga obeyed her new mistress' order to stop feeding the poor for a time, but when she secretly began feeding those in need again, she was dismissed. Shortly afterward, Count Henry's fortunes changed, and he attributed his problems to the meanness of Ottila, who had recently died. When the count remarried, he called Notburga back and made her his housekeeper. She spent the rest of her happy and holy life serving in that position. Shortly before her death in 1313, she asked the count always to remember the poor and to choose her burial place by simply placing her body on a wagon and burying it wherever the oxen pulling it stopped. The oxen stopped at the door of the Church of Saint Rubert at Eben, where she was buried.

Saint Jean Gabriel Taurin Dufresse

Gabriel was born in France in 1750 and entered the seminary of the Society of Foreign Missions of Paris. As a new priest, he was sent as a missionary to bring the Catholic faith to China in 1775. There he was imprisoned for six months during a government persecution. When he was released, he was reassigned to Macao, but he returned to China in 1788 and became bishop of Tabraca in 1800. As a foreigner and a priest, he lived in secret and in constant danger of arrest for the fifteen years he served his flock. He was finally betrayed to the authorities by a fearful native Christian. He was beheaded on this date in 1815, and although his head and body were left on a pole to warn others, Christians later buried his remains.

Save us, Savior of the world, for by your Cross and Resurrection, you have set us free.
Saint Peter, help me to bring order and peace to my family.
Saint Albert, help me to earn the respect of others through Christlike compassion.
Saint Notburga, show me how to make sacrifices for those who are poor today.
Saint Gabriel, help me to trust in God always.

* * * * *

September 15

Our Lady of Sorrows, Memorial

The Church remembers the many sorrows that our Blessed Mother suffered for the love of God on this day.

Who are you and what is the source of your wisdom that you are more surprised at the compassion of Mary than at the passion of Mary's Son? For if he could die in body, could she not die with him in spirit? He died in body through a love greater than anyone had known. She died in spirit through a love unlike any other since his.[18]

Saint Nicomedes of Rome

Nicomedes was a priest in Rome during the time of the persecution of Christians in the Roman Empire. He was caught burying the bones of a Christian martyr, and so he too was arrested as a Christian and condemned. He died a martyr in the year 71 after being beaten with leaden whips. In the year 817,

---

[18] *The Liturgy of the Hours*, vol. 4, from a sermon by Saint Bernard of Clairvaux, abbot (New York: Catholic Book Publishing, 1975), 1402.

Pope Paschal I brought his remains and the remains of other martyrs to the Church of Santa Prassede in Rome.

Saint Catherine Fieschi of Genoa

Catherine (1675–1737) came from a noble family of Genoa, Italy, and although she felt God calling her to religious life, she married when she was sixteen years old, shortly after her father's death. Her husband Julian turned out to be both cruel and unfaithful to her. After years of moping about her unhappy situation, one day she was overcome by a realization of God's greatness and her own unworthiness. She became a daily communicant for the rest of her life and a Franciscan tertiary. Catherine's prayers and example eventually led to her husband's conversion—though not until he had become bankrupt through his own carelessness. The couple never had children, and they mutually decided to live chastely and simply for the rest of their lives. Catherine received visions and was a mystic and writer, yet she was also practical: her service as a nurse led her to become the administrator of a hospital, and she carefully kept the accounts down to the smallest amount and made four wills with multiple codicils to ensure the proper disposition of property at her death.

> *Our Lady of Sorrows, give me your spirit of compassion for the suffering.*
> *Saint Nicomedes, help me live the corporal works of mercy today.*
> *Saint Catherine, show me how to turn suffering into zeal for God.*

* * * * *

September 16

Saint Cornelius, Memorial

Cornelius (d. 253) was the twenty-first pope; he reigned for two years. At the time when he became pope, being elected to the papacy was generally a quick death sentence. During his reign, Cornelius dealt wisely with an anti-pope, as well as Christians who had apostatized during a time of persecution and who then repented and asked to return to the Church. During a plague, the authorities blamed Christians for the sickness and sent Cornelius out of the city of Rome into exile, which led to his martyrdom.

Saint Cyprian of Carthage, Memorial

Cyprian was born around the year 200 and became a public orator and a teacher in the great city of Carthage (modern Tunisia). He later became a Christian, but before he was even baptized as an adult, he took a personal vow of chastity. This was a shockingly new idea that astounded his pagan friends. An elderly Catholic priest named Caecilian had brought Cyprian to faith in Christ, and, when Caecilian died, he left his wife and children in Cyprian's care. Cyprian became a priest and bishop of Carthage. When the Roman emperor Decius renewed his persecution of the Catholic Church, a pagan mob sought Cyprian out in hopes of feeding him to the lions, but he had already escaped from the city. While in hiding, he defended his decision to flee the city: Who would direct the Church if he was gone? After the persecution had abated—and it was a particularly devastating persecution of Catholics in Carthage—Cyprian returned to the city. His first act was to settle the problem of how to respond to those Christians who had renounced their faith during the time of persecution and then wanted to return to the Church. Some Christians argued that nothing was required for them to return to the faith, while others said it wasn't even possible for them to return. Cyprian pronounced in favor of a balance between the two extremes. During a terrible plague that affected the city from the year 252 to 254, it was the Christians—encouraged by their bishop, Cyprian—who cared for those who were sick. Cyprian's writings about Christian controversies of the day and Church teachings were influential at the time and still provide us with a great deal of information about the early Church. Cyprian strongly supported the teachings of Pope Saint Cornelius, but he opposed a teaching of the later Pope Saint Stephen I, who taught that Baptism by heretics could be valid. Augustine (the bishop of Hippo and a future saint) later wrote that Cyprian atoned for the "considerable warmth"[19] that he used in his writings on this subject through his martyrdom. During the persecution of Christians under the Roman emperor Valerian, soldiers came to his house to arrest Cyprian. He confessed his faith in Christ and, according to an ancient tradition, was beheaded soon afterward in his own home in the year 258.

Saint Euphemia of Chalcedon

During the persecution of the Church under the Roman emperor Diocletian around the year 305, the martyr Euphemia died in the city of Chalcedon, now in modern Turkey. Her parents were wealthy and noble, but they were also Christians. Euphemia consecrated her life to Christ and used her wealth to serve the poor. But when she refused to offer sacrifice to pagan gods, she was arrested, heroically bore her tortures, and died a martyr when only a teenage girl.

Blessed Victor III

Victor (d. 1087) was the 158th pope; he reigned only for a year. He was born with the name Dauferius in 1027 and came from a line of dukes in Benevento, Italy, taking the name Desiderius when he became a Benedictine monk. The Church calls him the greatest of the abbots of the monastery of Monte Cassino, with the exception of its founder, Saint Benedict, because of the strict monastic discipline and excellent schools of art that he established while he was abbot. He wholeheartedly encouraged the Church's reformation of the clergy, and he was a very effective intermediary between political powers and the Church. When Pope Gregory VII died, he became the most obvious candidate for pope, but he resisted the political forces that wanted him to be pope and even ran away

---

[19] Michael Walsh, ed., *Butler's Lives of the Saints, Concise Edition, Revised and Updated* (San Francisco: HarperCollins Publishers, 1991), 291.

from Rome, going back to his monastery at Monte Cassino. He was eventually physically forced to accept the papacy, but he returned to Monte Cassino frequently and only went to Rome to deal with an anti-pope who sought power for himself. It appears that he was right in refusing to become the pope: he was much better at mediating between leaders than being one, and he also recognized that his health was failing. Before he died, he recommended a successor (Odo, who took the name Urban II when he became pope) to the cardinals and bishops of the Church.

Blessed John Massias of Lima

John was born into a poor but pious family in Ribera, Spain, in 1585. He was orphaned when he was small and worked as a shepherd for his uncle until he was a young man. He was very devout; he prayed the Rosary and received visions of the Blessed Mother and Saint John the Evangelist. When Saint John appeared to him and told him to go to the Indies, John obediently got on board a ship and traveled to Lima, Peru. There he cared for the cattle of a wealthy landowner until he was accepted at a Dominican convent. He became a lay brother, served the house as a porter, and lived a penitential life, sleeping only an hour a night; he also cared for the poor people who came to the Dominicans for help. Through his prayers, begging, and compassion, he served the needy daily and brought many people to conversion. The entire city mourned when he died in 1645.

> *Saint Cornelius, when all seems hopeless, help me hope in Christ.*
> *Saint Cyprian, beg the Lord to give me the wisdom*
> *and prudence I need to make good judgments.*
> *Saint Euphemia, show me how to live and die for Christ.*
> *Blessed Victor, help me know myself and my weaknesses.*
> *Blessed John, show me how to serve the poor today.*

* * * * *

September 17

Saint Robert Bellarmine, Memorial

Robert was the third of ten children and was born in Tuscany, Italy, in 1542. His parents were from a noble family, but they were very poor. His mother also happened to be the niece of a pope (Marcellus II) and was a very pious and generous woman. He thought about becoming a medical doctor, but he instead chose to become a Jesuit priest, despite his father's objections; he first studied at various universities and Jesuit centers. Though Robert suffered from poor health throughout his life, he didn't let his illnesses keep him from serving God and even offered up personal penances, such as fasting and limiting his sleep. Robert was a great thinker, yet also a lovable man. As a priest, he became a popular and gentle spiritual director, teacher, and confessor; for example, the young Saint Aloysius Gonzaga came to Father Robert for confession until Aloysius' death. Robert had a photographic memory, and his many writings on Catholic teaching were read widely during his lifetime. His catechisms and defenses of the Catholic faith were so popular that it was illegal to buy his most famous work, *The Controversies*, in England under anti-Catholic Queen Elizabeth. He was named a theologian at the service of the pope, as well as provincial for the Jesuit order. After Pope Clement VIII gave him the position of cardinal priest, he still lived an austere life and gave most of his money to the poor. His courtesy and generosity to the poor was known to everyone; he even gave away the tapestries on his walls to clothe those in need at one point, for as he said, "The walls won't catch cold."[20] He was involved in many controversies of the day. For example, he was on friendly terms with Galileo Galilei, yet he was given the task of delivering the order compelling Galileo to submit to the Church in his teaching. Robert served as prefect of two different Vatican congregations when he was in Rome and narrowly escaped being named pope at two conclaves. He died in 1621. For his skills as an apologist for the Catholic faith as well as for his writings and his personal holiness, he was named a Doctor of the Church in 1931.

If men realized that their souls need to breathe no less than their bodies, many people who are now perishing would be saved.... True prudence implies that we who are always in need of God's help should always be asking for it.[21]

Saint Columba of Cordoba

Columba (d. 852) was born into a pious family in Cordoba, Spain. Her brother became an abbot, and a sister and brother-in-law founded a double monastery. Although her father died while she was living with her parents and her mother wanted her to marry, she felt drawn to religious life and entered her sister's monastery instead. During a Muslim persecution of Christians in Spain, most of the nuns fled, but she refused to leave. When she was captured, she professed her faith in Christ to a Muslim magistrate, who ordered her to be martyred by beheading.

Saint Hildegard of Bingen

Hildegard was born in 1098, the tenth child of a noble family at the city of Bockelheim, Germany. Though Hildegard was chronically ill as a child, she was also very intelligent and spiritually precocious. According to a pious custom of the time, Hildegard was given by her parents into the service of God when she was only eight years old, a "tithe" of the ten children God had given them. Hildegard was first placed in the care of Blessed Jutta, a hermit of noble birth

---

[20] Quoted in Christopher Rengers, O.F.M. Cap., and Matthew E. Bunson, K.H.S., *The 35 Doctors of the Church*, rev. ed. (Charlotte, N.C.: TAN Books, 2014), 533.

[21] Robert Bellarmine, "The Mind's Ascent to God, Step Five", chap. 1 in *Spiritual Writings*, trans. John Patrick Donnelly, S.J. and Roland J. Teske, S.J. (New York; Mahwah, N.J.: Paulist Press, 1989), 98–99.

who lived next to a church. Jutta taught her to read, to sing Latin chants, and how to live the life of a vowed religious. Eventually, Hildegard became a nun in Jutta's religious community of Benedictine nuns, and when Jutta died in 1136, Hildegard succeeded her as prioress. She became the first in a long line of great, prophetic female leaders in the medieval Church, and her influence spread far beyond her German community. Hildegard had experienced visions since she was a girl, but she didn't speak about them to others until she was a teenager. As the spiritual revelations and visions she experienced became more powerful, she became concerned about them and wrote them down in Latin, at her confessor's request, for them to be investigated by the Church. Hildegard never received a formal education and was diffident about her abilities, but her abbot, her bishop, and her bishop's theologians ultimately judged her writings favorably. A monk named Volmar was sent to be her secretary, and for ten years she dictated to him the revelations she received, full of apocalyptic imagery, warnings, and praises of God. When Pope Blessed Eugenius III approved her writings and encouraged her, Hildegard replied in a long letter, full of allusions to the troubles of the time and warnings about the ambitions of people in his own household. The pope also gave her permission to speak publicly about the faith to others, and Hildegard made four preaching tours across Germany, encouraging religious and laypeople in their understanding of the Catholic faith. But she did more than write about the visions she received. During her lifetime, Hildegard wrote hundreds of letters to people at all levels of society; compiled an encyclopedia of natural science and medicine; authored a massive trilogy of ethics, doctrine, and cosmology; and wrote exquisite music, including liturgical songs. But she faced opposition as well. Nearby monks objected when Hildegard wanted to move her community to a broken-down church, but she not only was able to restore the church building but added the technological innovation of plumbing for running water. At one point, she and her nuns were placed under an interdict (prohibiting the nuns from receiving the sacraments) because she had allowed a man to be buried at her convent who had once been excommunicated. Hildegard pointed out that the man had received the last sacraments and that she had also received a vision encouraging her to permit the burial. The interdict was removed only six months before her death. She had struggled with poor health throughout her life, willingly chose many physical mortifications, and had to be carried around at the end of her life. But, as her friend and chaplain Martin Guibert wrote, "the broken instrument ... still gave out melody"[22] until she died peacefully in 1179. Pope Benedict XVI spoke of her "rare human gifts, keen intelligence and an ability to penetrate heavenly realities",[23] when he named her a Doctor of the Church in 2012.

Then I saw the lucent sky, in which I heard different kinds of music, marvelously embodying all the meanings I had heard before. I heard the praises of the joyous citizens of Heaven, steadfastly persevering in the ways of Truth; and laments calling people back to those praises

---

[22] Walsh, *Butler's Lives of the Saints*, 293.

[23] Pope Benedict XVI, Apostolic Letter Proclaiming Saint Hildegard of Bingen, Professed Nun of the Order of Saint Benedict, a Doctor of the Universal Church (October 7, 2012), no. 1, https://w2.vatican.va/content/benedict-xvi/en/apost_letters/documents/hf_ben-xvi_apl_20121007_ildegarda-bingen.html.

and joys; and the exhortations of the virtues, spurring one another on to secure the salvation of the peoples ensnared by the Devil. And the virtues destroyed his snares, so that the faithful at last through repentance passed out of their sins and into Heaven.[24]

Saint Robert, help me develop a deep understanding of my faith.
Saint Columba, help me to profess my faith, through my words and actions, at all times.
Saint Hildegard, show me how to praise God with my life.

* * * * *

September 18

Saint Joseph of Cupertino

Joseph Desa was born in 1603 to poor parents in Cupertino, Italy; his father died when he was small. As a child, Joseph was absentminded and had a bad temper, but he was also very devout. As a young man, he tried out various vocations: as a shoemaker, a Conventual Franciscan brother, and a Capuchin brother. But he was eventually rejected at all three and sent home. His mother considered him a nuisance and didn't want him back in her care, so she convinced her brother, a Conventual Franciscan, to have his friary accept Joseph as a servant. Joseph seemed to mature at this point in his life; he grew in humility and was better able to handle the simple duties he was given. In 1625, the friars allowed him to be admitted to the order. As a novice, he was clearly virtuous, but he was always a poor student. In 1628, against all the odds, he passed his exams and was ordained a priest. He fasted rigorously and fulfilled the lowly duties he was assigned. Yet from the time he became a priest, his life was "one long succession of ecstasies, miracles of healing and supernatural happenings on a scale not paralleled in the reasonably authenticated life of any other saint".[25] Because of his levitations—in one case he singlehandedly moved a cross thirty-five feet high that ten men had been unable to lift—and other disturbing phenomena, he wasn't allowed to celebrate Mass in public, take meals with his brothers, or attend public functions. Not surprisingly, he was reported to the Inquisition as a danger and was ultimately brought before the minister general of his order and the pope himself. But Joseph's sweetness and humility won them all over to his side. Joseph fell into an ecstasy at the sight of Pope Urban VIII, and the pope (convinced that he was in the presence of a saint) said that he would bear witness to the sight at Joseph's canonization if Joseph died before him. Joseph was sent to live in Assisi for thirteen years, and although he was treated with severity by his superiors initially and suffered great spiritual dryness there (suffering so much sadness that he could hardly look up from the ground), his consolations returned

---

[24] Hildegard of Bingen, *Scivias*, trans. Mother Columba Hart and Jane Bishop (New York; Mahwah, N.J.: Paulist Press, 1990), 525.

[25] Walsh, *Butler's Lives of the Saints*, 294.

as soon as he left Assisi. For the rest of his life, he was sent from one friary to another and lived in seclusion. He wasn't allowed to write, receive letters, or speak to anyone but the brothers, although laypeople recognized him as a holy man and continued to seek him out. Although he was truly deserted by men at the end of his life in 1663, he was even more clearly close to God, who surrounded this poor friar with supernatural manifestations of His love.

Blesseds Daudi (David) Okelo and Jildo (Gildo) Irwa

Jildo converted to the faith at age eleven (1916), and Daudi converted at age fifteen (1917). Both were from the Acholi tribe in Uganda and became catechists, teaching the Christian faith to children. When local chiefs demanded that they stop teaching the Gospel, they refused. These two teenagers were martyred by being speared and knifed to death on this date in 1918 in Palamuku, Uganda.

Blessed Carlos Eraña Guruceta

Carlos was a layman and a member of the Society of Mary in Spain. During the Spanish Civil War, he refused to give up his faith in Christ and died a martyr on this date in 1936.

Saint Joseph, teach me humility.
Holy Martyrs, help me speak of Jesus in all that I do.

* * * * *

September 19

Saint Januarius of Benevento, Optional Memorial

Januarius (d. 304) was the bishop of Benevento, Italy, when he went to visit some Christians in prison during the persecution of Christians under the Roman emperor Diocletian. Jailers informed the authorities about the bishop's visit, and Januarius and his two Christian companions were sought out and arrested. The three men were placed in heavy chains and forced to walk in front of the governor's chariot as a humiliation before being imprisoned. They were executed in the same year, and Januarius' blood was preserved in a vial by the Christian faithful as a relic. Since the year 1389, his blood has testified to his holiness by miraculously liquefying in public on this date and other dates of the year.

Saint (Marie Guillemette) Emily de Rodat

Emily was born at Rodez in the south of France in 1787, and, when she was eighteen months old, she was taken by her grandmother to live in the Chateau of Ginals. When she was eighteen years old, she returned to Villefranche to assist some nuns who were teaching children. Her tasks included preparing children for First Communion, teaching geography, and leading the students during recreation time. While she visited a sick woman one day, she found out how hard it was for most Christians in France to educate their children due to a lack of money and the lack of schools as a result of the French Revolution. So a few weeks later, she decided to change that: she started teaching forty children for free in her own small room. With the encouragement of the spiritual director of the nuns' school, she gradually rented more rooms and started an entire school, teaching children for free. She then made public vows as a teaching sister along with eight other sisters, and together they taught one hundred pupils. Within two years, she was able to buy better buildings for her school, but a series of mysterious deaths in the school caused Emily to reconsider the whole idea. She seriously considered uniting her community with another new order called the Daughters of Mary, but her sisters refused to have any mother superior but her. Emily's sisters first took perpetual vows in 1820. Over the years, Emily and her sisters continued to teach, but they also visited prisoners. The order eventually became known as the Congregation of the Holy Family of Villefranche. She and her nuns opened a rescue home for women, a retirement home for religious, a novitiate house, a home for orphans, and cloistered convents. In 1852, cancer appeared in her left eye. She resigned her position, accepted her suffering patiently, and died on the evening of September 18, 1852.

Saint Januarius, show me how to accept humiliations and sufferings for love of Christ. Saint Emily, help me to be both Martha and Mary, as God wills, in my daily life.

See also Our Lady of La Salette in the Calendar of Marian Dates.

* * * * *

September 20

Saints Andrew Kim Tae-gon, Paul Chong Hasang, and Companions, Memorial

One hundred and three missionaries, priests, and laypeople were canonized as martyrs of Korea from the multiple waves of anti-Catholic persecution that occurred in the years 1839, 1846, and 1867. One of those martyrs, Andrew Kim Tae-gon, was from the Korean nobility. He was the child of Christian converts (his father was also a martyr), and he became the first native-born Korean priest and the first priest to die for the faith in Korea. He was tortured and beheaded in 1846. Catherine Chong Ch'or-yom was a Christian maidservant to a pagan man. When she refused to participate in pagan rites, her master had her bound, thrown on a pile of firewood, weighed down with a millstone until the end of the pagan festival, and then beaten into unconsciousness. She was punished again in the same way at the time of the next festival and was permanently scarred. Eventually she escaped and married, but later she was arrested for being a Christian. She was tortured repeatedly with "bone-bending" torture, but never apostatized and was beaten to death on this date in 1846.

Saint Eustace of Rome

Placidus (d. 188) was given the name Eustace at birth and became a Roman general. One day while he was out hunting, he saw a stag with a luminous crucifix between its antlers. The stag even spoke to him and called his name. This vision caused Placidus to become a Christian, and he brought his wife Theopista and his sons, Agapetus and Thoepestus, to faith in Christ. When the family was ordered to make a sacrifice to pagan gods, each member refused. When they continued to refuse even after being tortured, they were martyred by being roasted alive inside a bronze bull in the Colosseum as "entertainment" for the crowds in Rome. Eustace is one of the Fourteen Holy Helpers, great saints who were called upon particularly for help during the bubonic plague in the fourteenth century.

Holy Martyrs, help me to lead my family and those around me to Christ.

* * * * *

September 21

Saint Matthew the Apostle and Evangelist, Feast

Matthew (called Levi by Saints Mark and Luke) was a tax collector who left everything behind and obeyed Jesus' call to follow Him. In addition to becoming an apostle and writing one of the Gospels of the New Testament, Matthew is said to have evangelized Syria and to have been martyred for his faith in Christ while spreading the Gospel in Ethiopia.

As Jesus passed on from there, he saw a man called Matthew sitting at the tax office; and he said to him, "Follow me." And he rose and followed him.[26]

Prophet Jonah

Jonah is one of the twelve minor prophets of the Old Testament and apparently lived in the eighth century B.C. The story of his initial refusal to follow God's command, his dramatic survival after being swallowed by a whale, his successful attempt at bringing a pagan city to repentance, and his own irritation at God's refusal to destroy them is so typical of human nature and God's mercy that it resonates with both adults and children. Christ himself quoted the example of Jonah and applied it to Himself.[27]

Then Jonah prayed to the LORD his God from the belly of the fish, saying, "I called to the LORD, out of my distress, and he answered me."[28]

[26] Mt 9:9.
[27] Mt 12:40–41; Lk 11:29–32.
[28] Jon 2:1–2.

Saints Eusebius, Nestulus, and Zeno of Gaza

After the Roman emperor Constantine permitted the practice of Christianity in the Roman Empire in the fourth century, many men and women entered the Church. However, persecution of faithful Catholics was periodically renewed for various reasons for decades. One such period occurred when Julian became the Roman emperor, a man now commonly called Julian the Apostate because he outlawed Christianity and wanted to return the empire to the worship of pagan gods. In the year 362 in the city of Gaza in Palestine, pagans held a public celebration of the rejection of Christianity in the empire. Three brothers— Eusebius, Nestulus, and Zeno—were seized by the mob because they were Christians; they were beaten and then burned to death.

Saint Matthew, show me how to follow Christ today.
Prophet Jonah, help me trust in God at all times.
Holy Martyrs, give me courage when my faith is publicly ridiculed.

* * * * *

September 22

Saint Maurice and Companions

When a Roman general commanded the Theban Legion, a group of sixty-six hundred soldiers, in the year 287 to offer sacrifice to pagan gods before they went into battle, the entire legion refused. Why? Because they were Christians. The general first ordered every tenth man to be killed, "decimating" them and to make them give in. But the soldiers, encouraged by their leaders Maurice, Exuperius, and Candidus, remained steadfast and refused to give up their faith in Christ. When all the men refused to offer sacrifice, the entire legion was killed and died as martyrs in Agaunum, Switzerland.

Saint Ignatius (Laurence Maurice Belvisotti) of Santhia

Laurence was born in 1686 in Santhia, Italy. He became a priest and served his diocese faithfully. He was offered an important position in the diocese but instead decided to enter the Capuchin order, taking the name in religious life of Ignatius. There he served as sacristan and novice master, but when he developed a problem with his eyes, he had to resign for a time. When his condition improved, he was appointed chaplain of the king of Piedmont's army, where he cared for the sick and injured during a war. Afterward, he returned to the Capuchin monastery in Turin, where he served as an instructor to his fellow friars, cared for the poor, and encouraged the many people who came daily to receive his blessing and prayers. He died in 1770.

Holy Martyrs, give me your fortitude.
Saint Ignatius, help me to accept setbacks humbly and take the lowest place.

* * * * *

September 23

Saint Pio (Francis Forgione) of Pietrelcina, Memorial

Francis was born in 1887 into a poor Italian farming family; he suffered from numerous health problems all his life. He was ordained a Capuchin priest when he was twenty-two years old, he took the religious name Pio, and in 1918, he received the stigmata, the first priest ever so blessed. His long life as a priest was filled with miracles inexplicable to the modern world: he was able to read people's consciences, heard confessions for hours a day, was physically attacked by the devil, and was reportedly able to bilocate, heal the sick, and levitate when in prayer. He founded a hospital and prayer groups that continue today. He died in 1968.

Saints Elizabeth and Zechariah

According to the Gospel of Luke, "In the days of Herod, king of Judea, there was a priest named Zechariah, of the division of Abijah; and he had a wife of the daughters of Aaron, and her name was Elizabeth. And they were both righteous before God, walking in all the commandments and ordinances of the Lord blameless. But they had no child, because Elizabeth was barren, and both were advanced in years."[29] Yet, God blessed them with a son, Saint John the Baptist.

Saint Linus

Linus (d. 76) was the second pope, but we know very little about his reign. Some say he reigned nine years; others say twelve. Some say he died a martyr, but there's no explicit mention of Church persecution in historical sources during that time period. However, he was chosen to be Saint Peter's first successor, and he was buried beside him at his death.

Saint Adamnan (Eunan) of Iona

Adamnan was born in Donegal County, Ireland, around the year 624, but he moved to the Scottish island of Iona and became the ninth abbot of the monastic community there. He was sent to England at one point to negotiate for the Northumbrian people, and while he was there, the young Saint Bede met him. Adamnan also met Saint Ceolfrith, the abbot who convinced him to conform to the Roman practice for celebrating the date of Easter, rather than the prevalent Celtic practice. Adamnan wasn't able to convince his monks at Iona to follow his example when he returned, however. He later traveled to Ireland and encouraged the passage of laws that prohibited women from fighting in warfare and from children being taken as prisoners or being killed. Adamnan was Iona's most accomplished scholar after Saint Columba, and he wrote a *Life of Saint Columba* in Latin at the request of his brothers. He died in 704.

---

[29] Lk 1:5–7.

Saint Pio, show me how to pray.
Saints Elizabeth and Zechariah, help me to be righteous in God's eyes.
Saint Linus, help me to accept a hidden life in Christ's sight.
Saint Adamnan, show me how to bring God's mercy to the world today.

* * * * *

September 24

Saint Gerard Sagredo

Gerard was born in 980 in Venice and given the birthname of George. When he became a Benedictine monk, he took the name Gerard in memory of his recently deceased father. After several years of monastic life, he left to go on a pilgrimage to the Holy Land, but on the way there, he decided to become a hermit at Csanad, Hungary, which was still largely pagan. Through his preaching of the Gospel and with the encouragement of Saint Stephen I (the king), many people were converted to the Christian faith. Gerard became bishop of Csanad, but several years later he was killed and died a martyr for the faith in 1046.

Saint Pacificus (Charles Antony Divini) of San Severino

Pacificus was born in 1653 under the name Charles Antony Divini, was orphaned when he was three years old, and was raised by an uncle (though not a very kind one) in San Severino, Italy. When he grew up, he decided to become a Franciscan friar, and he took the name Pacificus. He was a bright student and was ordained a priest when he was twenty-five years old. He taught philosophy, and, with the permission of his superiors, he preached and visited those who were sick in the nearby countryside. When he was only thirty-five years old, Pacificus suffered a great loss: he lost both his sight and his hearing. Later, another illness made it almost impossible for him to walk. Now unable to serve God through an active life, Pacificus served God by being a contemplative. He prayed, made personal sacrifices, accepted his sufferings with great patience—and multiple miracles resulted from his prayers. He spent the rest of his life in San Severino and died on this date in 1721.

Saint Gerard, show me how to share the Gospel with those around me.
Saint Pacificus, show me how to be thankful for the gifts and abilities
that God has given me.

See also Our Lady of Ransom in the Calendar of Marian Dates.

* * * * *

September 25

Saint Cleophas

After Jesus' Crucifixion, two of his disciples left Jerusalem in discouragement and walked to Emmaus.[30] Along the way, they were joined by a third person, who restored their courage by explaining how Jesus' suffering and death had been predicted by the Jewish prophets. When the man broke bread with them at supper, "their eyes were opened and they recognized"[31] the man as Jesus and said, in words that have inspired Christians to study the Bible for millennia, "Did not our hearts burn within us while he talked to us on the road, while he opened to us the Scriptures?"[32] According to tradition, one of those two men, Cleophas, continued to be a disciple of Christ for the rest of his life and died a martyr.

Saint Finbar (Lochan) of Cork

Lochan was born at Connaught, Ireland, around the year 550; his father was an artisan and his mother was a lady of the Irish court. He was educated at a monastery, and there he was given the nickname Finbar (meaning "white hair") because of his light-colored hair. As a young man, he went on several pilgrimages to Rome and preached the Gospel in his native Ireland. Then he became a hermit, and he later founded a school and a monastery and became the first bishop of Cork. He died in 623.

Saint Sergius (Bartholomew) of Radonezh

Bartholomew was born in 1314; his high-ranking family was forced to flee and leave everything behind when their native city of Rostov, Russia, was invaded in 1315. The family settled in the city of Radonezh and lived in poverty as peasants. When Bartholomew grew up, he and his older brother Stephen moved into the forest to live as hermits, building a small church and cabin to live in. The winter, the limited food, and the wild animals made it a difficult life, so Stephen eventually returned to their family in Radonezh. But Bartholomew remained. He followed a monastic way of life and took the name in religious life of Sergius. Although his goal was to live alone, people recognized his holiness and came to him to ask his advice. Gradually, men came who wanted to be his disciples, so Sergius established a monastic community. By his efforts, monasticism was reborn in Russia. A prince of Moscow came to Sergius on the night before a great battle with the Tartars in 1380 to ask his advice. After establishing that the prince had exhausted all peaceful means of resolving the conflict, Sergius blessed and encouraged him. The Russians fought and won the battle. Sergius refused to accept the position of patriarch of Moscow when

---

[30] See Lk 24:13–35.
[31] Lk 24:31.
[32] Lk 24:32.

it was offered to him. Instead, he worked to bring reconciliation to his divided countrymen and cared for the monks at the forty monasteries that he eventually founded. After he had retired as abbot, he died in peace in 1382.

Saint Cleophas, help me keep my eyes open and my heart ready to see and hear God.
Saint Finbar, help me to lead others to Christ.
Saint Sergius, teach me how to build the city of God here on earth.

* * * * *

September 26

Saints Cosmas and Damian, Optional Memorial

These twin brothers were born into a Christian family in the late third century. They lived in Cilicia (modern Turkey) and used their skills as physicians to serve the sick for free out of Christian charity. During the persecution of the Roman emperor Diocletian, they were arrested for the crime of being Christians. They were executed by being crucified. The mob of onlookers first shot arrows and threw stones at them, then cut down and beheaded the two martyrs. It was the year 303.

Prophet Gideon

Gideon (eleventh century B.C.) was chosen by God to lead the Chosen People against the Midianites, a nearby pagan tribe that was regularly attacking and stealing from the Israelites. Before a famous battle, Gideon left behind a large number of men, choosing only a band of three hundred soldiers to fight the much larger Midianite army. He surprised his enemies, and his small army won the day.

Then Gideon perceived that he was the angel of the LORD; and Gideon said, "Alas, O Lord GOD! For now I have seen the angel of the LORD face to face."[33]

Saint Teresa (Maria Victoria) Couderc

Maria Victoria (1805–1885) was from a French middle-class farming family; she took the name of Teresa when she entered a community of teaching sisters in Aps, France. This community had been founded by Father J. P. E. Terme, and when Father Terme decided to establish a new community of nuns devoted to giving retreats to women, he made Teresa their superior. Allowing nuns to organize retreats was an innovative idea at the time, but it protected pilgrims from staying in public inns where both men and women were often lodged in

---

[33] Judg 6:22.

the same room. Teresa and her nuns lived in a difficult environment at high altitudes, and after Father Terme's death, her nuns became separate from the teaching sisters. When the sources of funding they had been receiving suddenly failed, Teresa blamed herself for the community's debts. The bishop apparently agreed with her because he replaced her with a wealthy widow who had been in the community for less than a month. Mother Teresa spent most of her remaining years of her life serving the community from the background. She made a new foundation of sisters at one point, and she was later acknowledged as a founder of the Congregation of Our Lady of the Retreat in the Cenacle along with Father Terme. But generally she was left alone. After years of prayers, penances, humiliations, and nine months of poor health, Mother Teresa died. She was more than eighty years old.

> *Saints Cosmas and Damian, show me how to live and die for Christ.*
> *Prophet Gideon, give me courage to stand up and fight,*
> *when necessary, for the good of my people.*
> *Saint Teresa, help me to learn to bear humiliations with peace.*

* * * * *

September 27

Saint Vincent de Paul, Memorial

Vincent was born on a very small farm in Pouy, France, in 1581 and had three brothers and two sisters. He was educated at a Franciscan school, attended the university, and was ordained a priest when he was twenty years old. Although his initial intention as a priest was simply to be well off and he was given the comfortable assignment of chaplain to Queen Margaret of Valois, two events deeply affected him as a young man. First, a friend accused him of stealing four hundred crowns. Vincent calmly denied the theft for six months until finally the true thief confessed. Second, while he was staying in a rural area, he was called in to hear the confession of a peasant who was dangerously ill. Vincent discovered (as the man himself later stated) that all the man's former confessions had been sacrilegious, and his soul would've been in jeopardy if Vincent hadn't come to hear his confession. Soon afterward, he was asked to preach about repentance to the peasants of the area, which he was very happy to do. From that point on, Vincent gave his life to serving the spiritual needs of others, particularly the poor. He worked among galley-slaves, converted members of the nobility and others who had been leading scandalous lives, and, with the financial support and encouragement of the countess and count of Joigny, he founded a congregation of secular priests, the Congregation of the Mission, who took vows of poverty, chastity, obedience, and stability. With the assistance of Saint Louise de Marillac, Vincent also founded a religious order of nuns to serve those who were poor and sick, and this became the order of the Sisters of Charity. Wealthy women also wanted to support his work financially, so he formed them into an association called the Ladies of Charity. With their donations, Vincent founded hospitals, ransomed twelve hundred Christian slaves from slavery, and helped people who had been displaced and impoverished by wars in the Lorraine region of France. Vincent suffered from poor health at the end of his life, and he died calmly, sitting in his chair, near the age of eighty in the year 1660.

Saints Adolph and John of Cordoba

During the period when Muslims ruled much of Spain, Catholics were tolerated as second-class citizens, and Islamic law was enforced. The persecution of Catholics was intensified in the 850s. Adolph and John were brothers whose father was Muslim and whose mother was a Christian. They were martyred for refusing to renounce their faith in Christ in the city of Cordoba.

Saint Vincent, help me never to be comfortable
when there are people in need around me.
Saints Adolph and John, help me to profess my faith with courage.

* * * * *

September 28

Saint Wenceslaus of Bohemia, Optional Memorial

Wenceslaus (d. 929) and his brother Boleslaus were princes of Bohemia (modern Czech Republic) and were baptized Christians. But when their father died, their mother, Drahomira, took over the country and began to persecute Christians. The boys' grandmother Ludmilla raised them in the faith, however, and encouraged Wenceslaus to take his rightful place as ruler. Two men strangled Ludmilla to try to stop him, but other parties forced Drahomira out of control, and Wenceslaus finally took his place as the duke of Bohemia. From the beginning of his reign, Wenceslaus showed that he was a truly Christian ruler. He punished murder severely, but he also balanced his justice with mercy. He forgave his mother and allowed her to return to court, and she apparently didn't cause him any more political trouble. However, the facts that he established friendly relations with the neighboring country of Germany (a former rival), his willingness to correct members of the nobility publicly, and the birth of his son, a potential heir to the throne, led some of his nobles to encourage Wenceslaus' jealous brother to conspire against him. Boleslaus invited Wenceslaus to a feast in honor of Saints Cosmas and Damian, and the next day, Boleslaus stopped Wenceslaus while he was on his way to Mass. He struck his brother; the two men struggled, and Boleslaus' friends ran up and killed Wenceslaus.

Saint Lawrence Ruiz and Companions, Optional Memorial

Lawrence (d. 1637) was the son of Christian parents in Manila in the Philippines. His father was Chinese, and his mother was Filipino. He became a professional transcriptionist and calligrapher, a married man, and the father of three children. When he was unjustly accused of murder, he sought asylum on board a ship. Three Dominican priests (Antonio Gonzalez, Guillermo Courtet, and Miguel de Aozaraza), a Japanese priest (Vicente Shiwozuka de la Cruz), and a Christian layman (Lazaro of Kyoto, a leper) were also on board this ship. The ship sailed for Japan, although the Japanese were also persecuting Christians at the time. Lawrence could've escaped to Formosa (modern Taiwan) along the way, but he was afraid that the Spaniards there would execute him over the false murder charge. When these six men arrived in Japan, they were found to be Christians and immediately taken to the city of Nagasaki. They were tortured for several days to make them give up their Christian faith. Lawrence and the Japanese priest broke down under torture and were willing to renounce their faith at one point, but they recovered their courage and again professed their faith in Christ. When all six men were executed, Lawrence became the first Filipino martyr.

Saint Eustochium of Rome

Eustochium (d. 419) and her mother, Paula, were wealthy, pious women who left the city of Rome to move to Antioch (modern Turkey) and support the great scholar-saint Jerome. They established religious communities near Bethlehem, and Eustochium cared for the cooking and material needs of her community. She and her mother were also invaluable assistants to Jerome while he was working on his Latin translation of the Bible and began to lose his eyesight. Jerome said that the help of these two women was better than most men's and that without it he wouldn't have been able to finish his work. After Paula's death, Eustochium succeeded her mother and became abbess of their community. She died fifteen years later.

> *Saint Wenceslaus, teach me how to forgive like Christ.*
> *Holy Martyrs, pray for me, that the sufferings of life*
> *will never break my faith in our good God.*
> *Saint Eustochium, show me how to serve those in need.*

* * * * *

September 29

Saints Michael, Gabriel, and Raphael, Archangels, Feast

The names of these three great archangels reflect the tasks that God assigned to them. Raphael ("God has healed") brought healing to the pious Jew Tobit and freed his future daughter-in-law from a demon.[34] Gabriel ("God is my strength") brought God's invitation to become the Mother of God to Mary of

---

[34] Tob 5:4—12:22, esp. 12:14.

Nazareth[35] and foretold John the Baptist's birth to Zechariah,[36] as well as spoke of the coming of the Messiah to Daniel centuries before it actually happened.[37] Michael ("Who is like God?") led angelic forces against Satan and his demons, throwing them out of Heaven and down to earth.[38] Besides the book of Revelation, he's described in the books of Daniel and Jude.[39]

Saints Rhipsime, Gaiana, and Companions

This group of maidens from Armenia died in the early fourth century during the reign of King Tiridates, apparently during a persecution of Christians that occurred before the king was baptized. Legends say that Rhipsime was a noble and beautiful young woman who went to Alexandria to escape the unwanted attentions of the Roman emperor Diocletian and that she repelled the advances of King Tiridates himself when he too fell in love with her. Although she initially escaped from the king, she and the thirty-five other maidens living with her were brutally killed on October 5, around the year 312, dying as martyrs for their faith in Christ.

> *Archangels Gabriel, Michael, and Raphael, help me to hear and obey the*
> *messages that God sends me.*
> *Holy Virgin Martyrs, show me how to live a pure life for Christ.*

* * * * *

September 30

Saint Jerome of Stridon, Memorial

Jerome was born at Stridon in modern-day Hungary around the year 342; his Christian family gave him a good education. Although Jerome was baptized when he was studying in Rome and became proficient in Greek and Latin there, he didn't have a Christian teacher and instead became a great fan of pagan writers, particularly Cicero. When he traveled to the city of Trier with a friend named Bonosus, he underwent a deeper conversion, and he left to live in the city of Aquileia under the direction of a good bishop named Valerian. While he was there, Jerome's strong temperament and stronger tongue provoked opposition among both friends and enemies. He and two of his friends decided to go to the city of Antioch, but while he was there, his friends died, and Jerome became sick himself. While he was delirious in his illness, he had a vision in which an angel accused him of being more a follower of the writer Cicero than a follower of Christ. This vision affected him deeply, and he withdrew to the wilderness of Chalcis to pray in solitude. There he lived as

[35] Lk 1:26–35.
[36] Lk 1:8–23.
[37] Dan 8–9.
[38] Rev 12:7–9.
[39] Dan 12:1; Jude 9.

a hermit, suffering deeply from temptations of the flesh as well as health problems, which he combatted through prayer, fasting, and long vigils. Although Jerome was convinced to be ordained a priest, out of humility he never celebrated Mass, and he accepted ordination only under the promise that he would not be required to serve any particular church. He studied Scripture under the bishop of Nazianzen, Saint Gregory, went to Rome to attend a council that was intended to resolve a schism within the Church, and was asked to stay in Rome by Pope Damasus himself, who made Jerome his secretary. While he was living in Rome, Jerome brought about a flowering of interest in the ascetical life, particularly among the noble ladies of Rome. Unfortunately, his harsh wit also brought him enemies as well as friends within only a few years.

When Damasus died, Jerome left Rome to live in the Holy Land; some say this was because he was disappointed that he was not chosen pope, but others say that he wanted to escape the worldliness of Rome. He was deeply affected by living in the sites where Jesus had lived, founded a monastery in Bethlehem, and was supported financially by Saints Paula and Eustochium, and other noble ladies who had left Rome to live in poverty as women religious at his encouragement. Jerome opened a free school to educate the poor and a hospice for the sick and dying. He also wrote many famous defenses of the faith against contemporary arguments while living in Bethlehem, often through public letters to other Christian leaders: to Helvidius to rebut his arguments against Mary's perpetual virginity, to Jovinian regarding the value of virginity, to Pammachius about matrimony, and to Vigilantius over the question of celibacy. Jerome's exacting scholarship and sensitive nature led to an argument with his longtime friend Rufinus over the misuse of the writings of the controversial Christian writer Origen, and the bishop of Hippo, Saint Augustine, also found that he had to soothe Jerome's feelings and harsh words. At Pope Damasus' request many years before, Jerome had begun a translation of the Bible in Latin, and now, with the help of friends, he finished this task despite his failing eyesight. Though controversial at the time, his Latin translation of the Bible was used by the Church for over a thousand years, affecting the liturgy and Christian culture all over the world. In the year 404, when Rome was attacked and sacked by Alaric, Pelagian heretics sent a mob to attack the nuns and monks in Jerome's community. He died peacefully in the year 420. Not surprisingly because of his extensive and faithful writings and lifelong holiness, he's considered a Father of the Church and a Doctor of the Church, and he's considered one of the four great Doctors of the Western Church.

Read much and learn as much as possible. Let sleep creep upon you with a book in your hand, and let the sacred page catch your head as you nod.[40]

Saint Antoninus of Piacenza

Antoninus was a soldier in the Theban Legion during the days of the early Church persecutions. He died a martyr for his faith in Christ near Piacenza,

---

[40] Jerome, *The Letters of Saint Jerome*, vol. 1, Letter 22, trans. Charles Christopher Mierow, Ph.D., Ancient Christian Writers Series (New York: Newman Press, 1963), 148.

Italy, in the third century. Since his death, a vial of his blood is known to liquefy miraculously, giving future Christians courage in the face of persecution and trust in the power of his intercession.

Saint Francis de Borgia

Francis was born in 1510 into the powerful, noble Spanish family of Borgia; he was the great-grandson of both a pope and a king, and he was a cousin to the emperor Charles V. While serving at the imperial court, Francis saw Saint Ignatius Loyola, the founder of the Jesuit order, who was being taken to the prison of the Inquisition, and was impressed by him. A year later, he married Eleanor de Castro, and, in time, the couple had eight children. Though he was raised to a series of important positions—marquis of Lombay, viceroy of Catalonia, duke of Gandia—when King John of Portugal refused to recognize him as master of the household for Prince Philip of Spain, it was a serious setback to his career. He retired to his home and spent his time on family business, such as fortifying his home against attack by Muslims and pirates. When his wife died suddenly, he asked Ignatius for permission to enter the Jesuits, which he had been thinking about for a long time. Ignatius told him to settle his family and business, study theology, and keep his plans secret for the moment since his youngest child was only eight years old at the time. Three years later, Francis had settled his business and completed his studies, and at age forty, he left for Rome. After four months there, he returned to Spain, made over all his titles to his oldest son, shaved his head and beard, took up the dress of a priest, and was ordained. This news caused a sensation, and so many people came to his first Mass (for which the pope had granted a plenary indulgence) that it had to be celebrated outside. Francis had been overweight before, but he mortified his flesh (later he said too severely at first) and lost considerable weight. He preached with great success, was one of the first people to encourage the Carmelite nun Saint Teresa of Avila, and was made commissary general of the Jesuits. (Some people complained that he performed his duties with the air of a nobleman, but that's hardly surprising.) His relationship to the nobility often gave him the opportunity to comfort them in their difficulties, help them grow in their faith, and explain the then-controversial Jesuit order to them. He was called to Rome, apparently to escape persecution of Jesuits from the Inquisition in Spain, and while he was there, he essentially founded the Gregorian University, which still exists as a pontifical university in Rome. With the support of Pope Saint Pius V, he expanded the work of the Jesuits into other countries, published rules and regulations for the Jesuit order, and even directed his priests as they cared for the sick during a pestilence in Rome. He returned to Spain with a cardinal on a political journey, and many people came to hear him preach. However, his bad health and the weight of his duties had worn him out. He died only two days after he arrived. His last prayers were for his children and grandchildren.

Saint Jerome, teach me how to study God's Word.
Saint Antoninus, beg the Lord to cover my sins with His Precious Blood.
Saint Francis, show me how to use the abilities God has given me for His greater glory.

October

October 1

Saint Therese (of the Child Jesus) Martin of Lisieux, Memorial

Therese Martin was born in 1873 and was blessed with devout, loving parents, four sisters, and a comfortable, middle-class household in France. However, her mother died when she was four years old, and although her older sister Pauline cared for her as a substitute mother, Therese was quick to tears and emotional for several years. On Christmas Eve when Therese was thirteen years old, however, she experienced what she called her "conversion" and, by God's grace, ended this emotional phase of her life. She soon realized that she was called to become a Carmelite nun, and although her father agreed, the bishop and the authorities at the nearby Carmel monastery initially refused to let her because she was so young. While on a pilgrimage to Rome that was intended to distract her from her desire to be a nun, Therese broke the customary rule of silence when she knelt to receive the pope's blessing and asked him, point-blank, to be allowed to enter the Carmelite monastery at the age of fifteen. The pope gently told her to obey her bishop, and the bishop did give her permission to enter the monastery early and at that age. Two of Therese's sisters were already nuns at the Lisieux monastery, which was both a blessing and a trial, since, as nuns living the Carmelite Rule, they weren't free to chat frequently as before. As a nun, Therese prayed fervently for priests; obeyed the rules of the Carmel (as far as she was able—she wasn't allowed to fast because of her age); and wrote her autobiography, in three parts at the request of her superiors, one of whom was her sister. She essentially served as novice mistress, and when her father died in 1894, her sister Celine joined the other three sisters at Carmel. However, Therese became ill from tuberculosis, and she spent the last eighteen months of her life suffering greatly both exteriorly and interiorly. She died on September 30, 1897, seemingly an insignificant nun from a little corner of France, but her spiritual autobiography—and its "Little Way" of holiness that could be followed by anyone—touched millions of souls. Her relics have traveled the globe, making her a missionary after her death, since her canonization in 1925. On the basis of her autobiography, letters, other writings, and holiness of life, she was named a Doctor of the Church.

> *It's impossible for one bound by human affection to have intimate union with God. I've seen so many souls, dazzled by this deluding light, fly into it and burn their wings like silly moths. Then they turn again to the true unfading light of love and, with new and more splendid wings, fly to Jesus, that divine Fire which burns yet does not destroy.*[1]

---

[1] Thérèse of Lisieux, *The Autobiography of Saint Thérèse of Lisieux: The Story of a Soul*, trans. John Beevers (New York: Image Books, Doubleday, 2001), 45.

Saints Julia, Maxima, and Verissimus of Lisbon

Sisters Julia and Maxima and their brother Verissimus were Christians living in Lisbon, Portugal, during the days of the early Church. In the year 304, they were martyred for the crime of being Christians during the persecution under the Roman emperor Diocletian.

Saint Bavo of Ghent

Bavo (589–659) was a wealthy landowner in Brabant, Belgium. He lived only for himself and his pleasures, even selling his own servants into serfdom just to make more money. When his wife died, however, he underwent a deep conversion. Out of repentance for his past sins, he gave away all his money. Then he gave a large portion of land to a monk, Saint Amand, so that a monastery could be built. When the monastery had been built, Bavo joined it as a simple monk under Amand's direction and lived a penitential life. One day, he came across a man that he had sold into slavery many years before. He begged the man to lead him by a chain to the city jail as an act of public humiliation, which the man did. In time, Bavo recognized the desire to practice even greater physical mortifications than were practiced at the monastery; he was eventually permitted to leave and live as a hermit in the forest. For the rest of his life, Bavo lived only on vegetables and water and saw no one but Amand and a saintly abbot. In art, Bavo is generally shown with a falcon on his wrist, looking like the rich man he used to be.

Saint Therese, show me your little way to Jesus.
Holy Martyrs, pray for my family to be a holy family.
Saint Bavo, help me learn how to accept humiliations in penance for my sins.

* * * * *

October 2

The Holy Guardian Angels, Memorial

God spoke to Moses about the duties of the angels when He said, "Behold, I send an angel before you, to guard you on the way and to bring you to the place which I have prepared."[2]

And Jesus further explained the guardian angels when He said, "See that you do not despise one of these little ones; for I tell you that in heaven their angels always behold the face of my Father who is in heaven."[3]

---

[2] Ex 23:20.
[3] Mt 18:10.

Saints Leger (Leodegardis) and Gerinus of France

Gerinus and Leger were brothers from a noble French family living in the seventh century. Leger became a deacon, then a priest and monk, abbot, and a zealous bishop who reformed his clergy and religious houses. Leger's support of one political leader over another led to his exile in 675. In 677, Gerinus was stoned to death in Arras, France, because of his opposition to Ebroin, mayor of the palace and the real ruler of France at the time. When Ebroin had the chance, he had Leger mutilated, imprisoned, tortured, and then executed in 678.

Guardian Angel, show me how to love, hear, and follow you.
Saints Leger and Gerinus, help me suffer patiently for the sake of justice for others.

* * * * *

October 3

Saint Dionysius the Areopagite

When Saint Paul preached the Gospel in the Aeropagus in Greece to all who would listen,[4] few were converted. But one man (Dionysius) was, and he became a Christian and the first bishop of Athens. Dionysius was persecuted for his Christian faith under the Roman emperor Hadrian, and he died a martyr around the year 95.

Saint Ewald the Black and Saint Ewald the Fair

Both men were named Ewald, both studied in Ireland, and both went as missionaries to Saxony around the year 690. In the year 695, while they were at Aplerbeck, Westphalia (modern Germany), they were attacked by pagan Saxons. The Saxons killed Ewald the Fair (so-called because of his hair color) with a sword, but they tortured Ewald the Black before killing him and throwing both men's bodies into the Rhine River. Their bodies were miraculously recovered forty miles upstream where friends were camping.

Saint Ambrosio Francisco Ferro and Companions

In 1597, Portuguese colonists, accompanied by two Jesuit priests and two Franciscan priests, settled in Brazil. A group of European Calvinists later invaded the region and began persecuting the Catholic settlers living there. On October 3, 1645, a group of soldiers attacked the city of Uruacu, Brazil, killing Father Ambrosio Ferro and many other Catholics, making them all martyrs for the faith.

Saint Dionysius, help me to recognize the truth when I hear it.
Holy Martyrs, show me how to live and die for Christ.

* * * * *

---

[4] Acts 17:34.

October 4

Saint Francis of Assisi, Memorial

Francis was born around the year 1181 into a life of wealth in Assisi, Italy. His noble and ignoble pursuits later led him to found a religious order called the Friars Minor. But what made him so much like our Lord that people flocked to follow him and his message? Francis, once fully converted, gave his life completely to Christ, His Church, and God's Word. He gave up all his possessions, and he relied completely on charity for his food, clothing, housing, and companions, living in Christlike poverty and chastity. Francis was completely obedient to the Church, though he didn't refrain from correcting Her weaker members, letting God's Word guide him. One day, Francis heard the following words from a crucifix: "Repair my house, which is virtually ruined."[5] At first, this led him to devote his time to rebuilding a church building; later, the whole Church by his example. Another time, a Gospel reading during Mass led him to give up all his earthly possessions: "You received without pay, give without pay."[6] Christ's command to preach the Gospel to all nations led him to preach to the Muslims. When his followers began to stray away from his path of complete poverty, he went to the pope to be granted permission for his order to remain completely poor. Francis knew suffering intimately—he was the first person to receive the stigmata—but he also knew great joy because he suffered it all for Christ. He died in 1226.

> *Nothing should upset the servant of God except sin. And no matter how another person may sin, if the servant of God lets himself become angry and disturbed because of this, [and] not because of love, he stores up the guilt for himself (cf. Rm 2:5). That servant of God who does not become angry or upset at anything lives justly and without anything of his own. And he is blessed who does not keep anything for himself,* rendering to Caesar what is Caesar's and to God what is God's *(Mt 22:21).*[7]

Blessed Henry (Enrique) Morant Pellicer

Henry was born into a deeply devout family in Bellreguard, Spain, in 1908. He initially studied architecture, but then he heard God's call to become a priest and was ordained to the Archdiocese of Valencia in 1933. He started a choir, worked with the youth, and brought new life to his parish. But when anti-Catholic persecution became serious during the Spanish Civil War, he was forced to work quietly in diocesan administration and then to move in with his family. On October 3, 1936, at 11 A.M., officials came to arrest him, simply for being a priest. By the evening of that date, he had been shot and executed.

> *Saint Francis, help me listen to the Word of God.*
> *Blessed Henry, show me how to live and die for Christ.*

* * * * *

[5] Christopher Rengers, O.F.M. Cap., and Matthew E. Bunson, K.H.S., *The 35 Doctors of the Church*, rev. ed. (Charlotte, N.C.: TAN Books and Publishers, 2014), 340.

[6] Mt 10:8.

[7] Matthew Bunson and Margaret Bunson, *Our Sunday Visitor's Encyclopedia of Saints*, 2nd ed. (Huntington, Ind.: Our Sunday Visitor Publishing Division, 2014), 340.

October 5

Saint Placid

Placid was the son of a senator and was sent to be educated by Saint Benedict of Nursia and his monks in Subiaco. In time, Placid became a disciple of Benedict and a monk. The most well-known event of his life is that he was miraculously saved from drowning by another monk (Maurus) through the supernatural insight of Saint Benedict.

Saint Flora of Beaulieu

Flora (1309–1347) was a devout child from a good family in Auvergne, France. She decided to give her life to Christ and refused to get married, entering the nuns of the Order of Saint John of Jerusalem in 1324. She suffered so many spiritual trials that she became depressed, which annoyed the other nuns. Fortunately, a visiting confessor understood and encouraged her, and in time she not only received back her joy in life from God but also received many mystical favors. On one occasion, she fell into an ecstasy while praying and couldn't eat food afterward for three weeks. Several times, by God's grace, she made accurate predictions about events that were beyond her natural ability to know. She died at the age of thirty-eight.

Blessed Raymond de Vineis of Capua

Raymond was born in 1330 in Capua, Italy, and became a Dominican priest. As a priest, he was assigned to serve the great mystic-saint Catherine of Siena and became her spiritual director, advisor, correspondent, and biographer. He cared for plague victims until he himself caught the disease and recovered; he then became the master general of the Dominican order in 1380. Since the work he did restored discipline to the order so soon after its initial founding, he's generally considered its second founder. He died in the city of Nuremberg of natural causes in 1399.

Blesseds William Hartley, John Hewitt, and Robert Sutton

During the anti-Catholic persecution in England under Queen Elizabeth (r. 1558–1603), it was illegal to be a priest or help a priest. William became an Anglican priest, but secretly converted to Catholicism and was ordained a Catholic priest in France. He returned to England to serve Catholics in secret; however, he was arrested and deported. He later returned to England again and ministered to Catholics until he was captured. John was born in Yorkshire, England, and also studied for the priesthood in France and returned to England, quietly living under assumed names until he was arrested. Robert was a layman and a teacher when he was arrested for being a Catholic. All three men were hanged on this date in 1588.

Blessed Francis Xavier Seelos, Optional Memorial[8]

Francis was born in 1819, one of twelve children in Fuessen (Germany). He wanted to become a priest and studied philosophy and theology before entering the seminary in 1842. When he learned about the work of the Redemptorist order in evangelizing the immigrants of North America, he decided to enter the congregation and received permission to travel to America in 1843. He completed his studies in 1844 and was ordained a Redemptorist priest, serving as assistant pastor for several years under Saint John Neumann, who was serving as a priest in Pittsburgh; he also served as superior and master of novices in his Redemptorist community. He became well known for his simple, yet biblically rich, preaching; his innate kindness in understanding the needs of the faithful, particularly in the confessional (helping both whites and blacks and speaking in three languages); and his smiling presence. He served in various Redemptorist churches and positions; he met with President Lincoln himself to request that the Redemptorist seminarians be exempted from military service during the Civil War (and they were). When a zealous colleague complained that Francis was not strict enough with the seminarians, Francis was relieved of his office and spent three years as an itinerant missionary, traveling through many states. After being reassigned as a pastor in New Orleans, he contracted yellow fever while visiting and caring for the sick. In 1867, he died after several weeks' illness.

Blessed Bartholomew (Bartolo) Longo

Bartolo was born in 1841 and was raised in a pious family in southern Italy that prayed the Rosary daily. He became an excellent student, but he was restless. While he was studying law in Naples, he began to live an immoral way of life, became openly hostile with Christian faith through the lectures of a fallen-away priest, and dabbled in occultism, eventually becoming a Satanic priest. But his family and friends didn't give up on him and continued to pray. Finally, with the help of a professor and a Dominican friar, Bartolo was "deprogrammed" from his evil way of life and returned to the practice of the Christian faith. He chose to become a Dominican tertiary, specifically to make amends for his past deeds; when he saw the spiritual poverty in which so many people lived, he built a shrine to Our Lady of Pompeii, in order to encourage them spiritually. So many pilgrims came and so many miracles occurred that his first church had to be rebuilt into a bigger one, and that church was later made into a basilica. Bartolo wrote articles, founded a trade school for boys whose fathers were in jail, and then founded a similar school for daughters of prisoners. He worked closely with the widowed Countess Marianna in these good deeds, and because their association caused so much unkind gossip, the two were married in 1885, though they lived together chastely. Other lies about him became so widespread—that he was guilty of adultery and profiteering and that he was insane—that he accepted Pope Saint Pius IX's request that he retire

[8] This saint may be celebrated as an optional memorial in the *Liturgical Calendar for the Dioceses of the United States of America.*

as administrator; he became a regular employee in the works he had founded. Bartolo died of pneumonia in 1926.

Saint Faustina (Helena) Kowalska

Helena Kowalska was born in 1905, the third of ten children in a poor Polish family. She attended school for only three years, and when her parents refused to allow her to become a nun, she worked as a domestic servant. But one day at a dance, our Lord appeared to her, covered with wounds, and said to her, "How long shall I put up with you and how long will you keep putting Me off?"[9] She went at once to Warsaw, and after being refused by several other religious orders, she became a nun in the Congregation of the Sisters of Our Lady of Mercy in 1925, an order that cared for troubled young women. She took the name Sister Maria Faustina of the Most Blessed Sacrament and served as cook, gardener, and porter in various houses of her order. At the instruction of her confessor, she began to write down the visions and revelations that she received, though she wrote phonetically due to her lack of education. This later caused her writings to be labeled heretical until Bishop Karol Wojtyla, the future Pope Saint John Paul II, had them retranslated. She received hidden stigmata and suffered greatly as a sensitive soul. But the powerful, central message that our Lord gave her—His message of His Divine Mercy, which He yearns to offer to the whole world—was at the heart of her diary. Faustina lived and died like her Lord—hidden and misunderstood. Although she wished to found a new order and was unable to do so, a movement of priests, religious, and laypeople called the Apostles of Divine Mercy spread over the world after its approval in Cracow in 1996.

> Saint Placid, help me find teachers and friends who will rescue me when needed.
> Saint Flora, teach me to hope in God at all times.
> Blessed Raymond, pray that my love for Christ might ignite the same love in others.
> Holy Martyrs, show me how to support my priests.
> Blessed Francis, help me bring Christ to others.
> Blessed Bartolo, help me to love our Blessed Mother.
> Saint Faustina, teach me to trust in God's mercy in every moment.

* * * * *

October 6

Saint Bruno the Carthusian, Optional Memorial

Bruno was born in Cologne, Germany, around the year 1030; he was educated at Rheims, returned to be ordained a priest in Cologne, and became a canon

---

[9] Maria Faustina Kowalska, *Diary of Saint Maria Faustina Kowalska: Divine Mercy in My Soul* (Stockbridge, Mass.: Marian Press, 2016), 7.

in the collegiate church. A brilliant man, Bruno had become a professor of grammar and theology by the time he was only twenty-six years old, and he taught many great scholars, including the future Pope Blessed Urban II. However, when he was made chancellor of the diocese under Bishop Manasses, he quickly became aware that Manasses was unfit for the position of bishop, particularly because of simony. Bruno and two other canons left the diocese to attend a council in Autun, and there they explained the seriousness of the situation to the secular authorities. When the council listened to their testimony and decided against Manasses, the angry bishop retaliated violently. He had the three canons' homes looted, and he managed (temporarily) to deceive Pope Saint Gregory VII into believing that he was innocent of the charges against him. Bruno had been considering leaving his worldly duties and retiring from the world for some time, and these events convinced him of the emptiness of living in the secular world. Although other people understood the reasons behind the persecution against Bruno and although he was still widely respected, he chose to leave the world behind, only accompanied by a few friends. The men lived in solitude and eventually settled at what is now called the Grande Chartreuse, the motherhouse of his new order in France. Bruno had a separate cell built for each monk, prohibited women from entering their land, and led them in a simple life of solitude. The monks ate meager food and farmed their poor land just enough to feed themselves, but he made sure that they had a rich library and a rich spiritual life. It was a great trial to Bruno when Pope Blessed Urban II ordered him to come to Rome and serve as his advisor, but Bruno obediently left his monks and lived near the pope in a hermitage among the ancient ruins of the Baths of Diocletian. He refused to accept the pope's offer to make him an archbishop, however, and later he was given the pope's permission to retire from Rome and go back to his monks. At the end of his life, Bruno gathered his monks about him, made a public confession of his whole life, made a profession of faith, and laid down his life to God. He died in 1101. Bruno has never been formally canonized by the Church, but only because of the Carthusian order's predilection against publicity.

Blessed Marie-Rose (Eulalia) Durocher, Optional Memorial[10]

Eulalia was born in 1811, the tenth of eleven children in a family living near Montreal, Canada. She wanted to enter religious life, but the nuns refused to admit her because she had such poor health. So instead she became the housekeeper for her brother Theophile, who was a priest. Because of the lack of European religious orders in Canada at the time, the local bishop (his diocese was the entire country of Canada) decided to found a new order: the Sisters of the Holy Name of Jesus and Mary. He also decided to make Eulalia the mother superior of this new teaching order of nuns, and she took the name of Mother Marie-Rose. There was a great need for education, so the order grew rapidly. In 1849, she died of natural causes when she was only thirty-eight years old.

---

[10] This saint may be celebrated as an optional memorial in the *Liturgical Calendar for the Dioceses of the United States of America*.

Saint Francis Tran Van Trung

Francis was born around the year 1825 and was a Vietnamese layman who converted to the Christian faith. While serving as a corporal in the Vietnamese army, he was arrested for being a Christian, which was illegal at that time in Vietnam. When he refused to renounce his faith, he was beheaded on this date in 1858.

> *Saint Bruno, help me to live a life of Gospel simplicity and humility.*
> *Saint Marie-Rose, show me how to trust in God's providence at all times.*
> *Saint Francis, help me remain faithful to Christ.*

* * * * *

October 7

Our Lady of the Rosary, Memorial

On this date in 1571, Christian forces, despite the odds against them, miraculously defeated the Muslim Turks in the Battle of Lepanto, off the coast of western Greece. Pope Saint Pius V, who had encouraged the Catholic world to pray to Mary, Help of Christians, during the fight, instituted this memorial after the great victory, which saved Europe from invasion by the Muslims.

Saint Mark (Marcus)

Mark (d. 336) was the thirty-fourth pope; he reigned less than a year. He was born in Rome and was a priest when he became pope. He built two basilicas in Rome, died of natural causes, and was buried in the Catacomb of Balbina. Though he didn't die a martyr, the people acclaimed him a saint.

Blessed Joseph Llosa Balaguer

During the anti-Catholic persecution of the Spanish Civil War, many Catholic religious were killed. Joseph was born in 1901 near Valencia, Spain, and entered the order of the Capuchin Tertiary Fathers and Brothers of Our Lady of Sorrows. A humble man, it's said that he declined to be ordained a priest because he felt himself unworthy. When the violence against priests intensified, he took refuge from the violence in different locations. But after he was arrested, on October 1, he was prepared for death by a priest who was also in prison. He accepted his martyrdom, forgave his murderers, and was killed on this date in 1936 in Valencia.

> *Our Lady of the Rosary, defeat everything in me that opposes God's will.*
> *Saint Mark, help me to love Christ and His Church.*
> *Blessed Joseph, help me to forgive others with all my heart.*

* * * * *

October 8

Saint Reparata

During the persecution of the Church under the Roman Empire in the third century, the martyr Reparata died in Caesarea (in modern Israel). Tradition says that she was a young maiden, perhaps only twelve years old, and that she died rather than abandon her faith in Christ.

Blessed Hugh Canefro of Genoa

Hugh was born into a noble family of Italy in 1148. He became a soldier and fought in the Third Crusade to protect the rights of Christians living in the Holy Land. When he returned home, he went to serve at a hospital in Genoa. Finding his calling in life, he sold his armor to pay for clothes for the hospital's nurses and cared for those who were sick and too poor to pay for assistance—for the next fifty years. He died in 1233.

> Saint Reparata, may your love for Christ inspire me to a greater love for Him.
> Blessed Hugh, show me how to sacrifice myself to serve others.

* * * * *

October 9

Saint Denis and Companions, Optional Memorial

Denis was an Italian bishop who was sent to preach the Gospel in pagan Gaul (France) around the year 250. He had six companions, including Rusticus, a priest, and Eleutherius, a deacon. Because of their success in converting others to the faith, Denis, Rusticus, and Eleutherius were arrested by the Roman authorities, imprisoned for a long time, and finally beheaded around the year 275. Denis is one of the Fourteen Holy Helpers, great saints who were called upon particularly for help during the bubonic plague in the fourteenth century.

Saint John Leonardi, Optional Memorial

John was born in Lucca, Italy, in 1541 and worked as a pharmacist's apprentice while he studied for the priesthood. As a priest, he served prisoners and the sick, and many men were inspired by his example to follow him, some of whom became priests. During this turbulent time of the Protestant Revolt, John and his followers, who became known as the Clerks Regular of the Mother of God, suffered from a great deal of opposition. John also formed the Confraternity of Christian Doctrine around this time, and he published a compendium of Catholic doctrine that was used for centuries by the Church. The Clerks Regular has always been intentionally a small congregation of scholars and writers and was confirmed by Pope Clement VIII. John was exiled from Lucca for the last fourteen years of his life, but he was given quarters (and a pet cat) by Saint Philip Neri. John died while tending plague victims in 1609.

Patriarch Abraham

The faith of millions of Jews and Christians is rooted in the faith of Abraham (who lived perhaps in 1700 B.C.), the man who left everything behind in obedience to God's call[11] and who trusted in God's promise that his wife would bear him a son in their old age.[12]

Saint Louis Bertrand

Louis was born in Valencia, Spain, in 1526. His father was related to the famous priest Saint Vincent Ferrer. Louis took the Dominican habit, was ordained a priest, and served as a Dominican master of novices for thirty years. He was known to be strict and severe, but he was also a holy man and saintly example to those around him. During this period, he met the Carmelite nun Saint Teresa of Avila and corresponded with her over her plans to reform the Carmelite order. In 1555, pestilence struck the area, and he gave himself over completely to serving the poor in their need. In 1562, he left Spain to preach the Gospel to Native Americans in Cartagena (today's Colombia). He spoke only Spanish and had to use an interpreter, but the Holy Spirit clearly supplied what he lacked. Through his gifts of tongues, prophecies, and miracles and through his powerful preaching, thousands of people gave their lives over to Christ in Cartagena, Tubera, Cipacoa, Paluato, Leeward Islands, the Virgin Islands, and other places to which he traveled. Louis was offended and angered by the greedy and cruel behavior of many of the Spanish conquistadores toward the native peoples, and when he was recalled to Spain, he did all he could to ensure that these crimes were punished and stopped. He also trained the preachers who succeeded him as missionaries, telling them that they must be humble, fervent, and prayerful if they wanted to change hearts. He died in 1581 after two years of enduring a painful illness.

Saint John Henry Newman

John was born in 1801 in London, England, the son of a banker, and he had two brothers and three sisters. He underwent a personal conversion to a deep love of Christ at the age of fifteen, becoming an evangelical Christian. An extremely intelligent man, John later became an Anglican priest and a professor at Oxford University, where his leadership led to the development of the Oxford Movement, a group of Anglicans who sought a renewal of Catholic thought in England. His later decision to become a Catholic caused considerable talk—and cost him relationships within his own family and friends. During the rest of his long life, he wrote many works in defense of the Catholic faith, led many people in English society back to the Catholic Church, and served God as a bishop and then cardinal. He died in 1890.

[11] Gen 12:1–9.
[12] Gen 17:15–19.

Saint Denis, show me how to bring others to Christ.
Saint John, help me to grow in my understanding of the teachings of the Church.
Father Abraham, teach me to trust in God and His promises.
Saint Louis, beg the Lord to give me the words and the works that will change hearts.
Saint John, teach me how to speak the words that
will bring others to Christ and His Church.

* * * * *

October 10

Saints Eulampius and Eulampia of Nicomedia

The persecution of Christians under the Roman emperor Maximian wasn't limited to adult followers of Jesus Christ. Eulampius and Eulampia were brother and sister and were just children in the year 302. When they were arrested, they admitted that they were Christians, refused to give up their faith, and were executed by beheading. Some traditions say that they were thrown into boiling oil first, but when that failed to kill them, they were executed by beheading.

Blessed Angela (Sophia Camille) Truszkowska

Sophia was born in 1825 in Kalisz, Poland, to a noble family. She was a pious child but had poor health, so she was sent to Switzerland to be educated in a better climate. When she was twenty-three years old, God blessed her with a conversion experience that led her to join the Society of Saint Vincent de Paul to help the poor. In 1854, she and a cousin rented a small apartment, where they daily invited homeless children to come learn, attend Mass, and be cared for. This evolved into a religious order known as the Sisters of Saint Felix, and Sophia took the name of Sister Angela. Later in life, she had to step down from her position because of deafness. But she spent her life caring for the poor, the elderly, and the sick, dying on this date in 1899.

Saints Eulampius and Eulampia, teach me your childlike trust in God's providence.
Blessed Angela, help me to find ways to serve the needy around me.

* * * * *

October 11

Saint Philip the Deacon

Philip was probably Jewish and living in Palestine when he became a Christian. He was one of the first seven deacons in the Church,[13] preached the Gospel

---

[13] Acts 6:5.

in Samaria, performed miracles, and brought many people to the faith,[14] most notably the magician Simon Magus and the eunuch of Queen Candace from Ethiopia.[15] It's generally assumed he was the Philip who met with Saint Paul on his last journey to Jerusalem.[16] According to tradition, he became the bishop of Tralles (in modern Turkey) and died around the year 58.

Saint Bruno the Great of Cologne

Bruno (925–965) was the youngest son of Emperor Henry the Fowler and his queen, Saint Matilda of Saxony (modern Germany). He was sent to be educated at the cathedral school when he was four years old, but when he was fourteen, he was called to serve at the court of his brother, Emperor Otto I. When he was only twenty-four, he was made archbishop of Cologne and given secular titles, such as duke of Lorraine. But no one could claim that he had been given his positions in the Church without good reason: he lived a pious, holy life and was a zealous bishop for his people. He improved the education of his clergy, watched over the moral life of his diocese, lavishly supported monasteries, and built churches, including the abbey church of Saint Pantaleon in Cologne, which survives to this day. His prudence, tact, and skills as a mediator, and his family connections, helped him resolve countless disputes, making him a true Christian peacemaker.

Saint Peter (Phero) Le Tuy

Peter was born around the year 1773 in Bang Son, Vietnam. He became a Catholic priest and served in three different parishes. When the Vietnamese government began its persecution of Catholics, he was arrested while on a home visit to a sick parishioner. When his parishioners, who loved him, tried repeatedly to free him from prison, the authorities sent him away to Hanoi. After months in a prison cell, he refused to give up his faith. He was finally beheaded on this date in 1833.

Saint Mary Soledad (Emmanuala) Torres Acosta

Emmanuala was born in 1826 to pious parents in Madrid, Spain, and was one of five children. She considered a vocation as a Dominican nun, but she wasn't certain that it was God's will, so she waited. In time, a priest from her area decided to gather women to care for the sick of the parish; Emmanuala was one of the seven women he chose. When the informal group became a religious community, she took the name Sister Mary Soledad, a name emphasizing her commitment to the Blessed Virgin and to solitude. When the vicar who had founded the group and half of the members of the community left five years later to go make another foundation, Mary Soledad became the leader of the original group, with the help of an Augustinian friar named Father Gabino Sanchez. Their community, which became known as the Handmaids of Mary

---

[14] Acts 8:4–40.
[15] Acts 8:26–40.
[16] Acts 21:8.

Serving the Sick, grew and began to serve young delinquents as well as people who were sick. At this point, as *Butler's Lives of the Saints* descriptively puts it, "there was a secession of some members to another congregation, with the usual complaints and accusations from which mother-foundresses have to suffer."[17] Mary's work and the congregation itself grew despite the complaints, however, and she spent the last ten years of her life in peace, dying in 1887.

Saint John XXIII

John was born Angelo Roncalli in 1881 near Bergamo, Italy, and was one of thirteen children in a family of sharecroppers. He was ordained when he was twenty-two years old and then served in a number of important positions: secretary to the bishop of Bergamo, seminary professor, apostolic visitor to Bulgaria, apostolic delegate to Turkey and Greece, papal nuncio in Paris at the end of World War II, and patriarch of Venice. In 1958, he was elected pope and took the name Pope John XXIII. John was a warm, endearing man. As pope, he doubled the number of cardinals in the Church to establish the largest College of Cardinals in history, and he surprised many people when he called for the Second Vatican Council, to bring the Gospel to the modern world more effectively. He died in 1963 before the council was over. Because of the importance of the council, his memorial is celebrated not on the date of his death but on the date of the opening session of Vatican II.

> *Saint Philip, help me learn how to be obedient to the voice of the Holy Spirit.*
> *Saint Bruno, show me how to be a peacemaker.*
> *Saint Peter, help me remain faithful to God.*
> *Saint Mary, help me reach out to those who are farthest from God.*
> *Saint John, beg the Holy Spirit to give me the wisdom to make good decisions.*

* * * * *

October 12

Martyrs of North Africa

In the year 477, Hunseric became king of the Vandals, a group of Germanic peoples that ruled regions around the Mediterranean Sea. He was a follower of the Arian heresy, but he initially didn't persecute faithful Catholics. However, that changed around the year 483. On today's date, we commemorate almost five thousand Christians who were killed during the Vandal persecution in North Africa. In addition to many bishops and priests, the majority of those killed were laypeople whose major crime was refusing to accept the false teaching that Jesus Christ was not true God.

---

[17] Michael Walsh, ed., *Butler's Lives of the Saints, Concise Edition, Revised and Updated* (San Francisco: HarperCollins Publishers, 1991), 328.

Saint Felix IV

Felix (d. 530) was the fifty-fourth pope; he reigned four years, having been a cardinal priest before his election. Felix was chosen pope at the insistence of the king of the Goths, and he used his good reputation with that king to bring peace between the Church and civil power. When the kingship passed to a child, the boy's mother (who was friendly to Catholics) became regent. She donated some ancient Roman buildings to the Church, which Felix converted into the Church of Saints Cosmas and Damian. Parts of those ancient buildings are still incorporated in that church today. His writings show his opposition to the heresy of Semi-Pelagianism found in southern Gaul (modern France), particularly his explanation of Church teaching on grace and free will. When Felix became ill, he was concerned about dangers to the peace of the Church after his death, and he publicly named a successor.

Blessed Roman Sitko

Roman was born in Czarna Sedziszowska, Poland, in 1880. He was a priest of the Diocese of Tarnow when the Nazis invaded Poland. He was sent to the dreaded Auschwitz concentration camp and died there on this date in 1942.

> *Holy Martyrs, help me to stand up for the truth.*
> *Saint Felix, help me to love Christ and His Church.*
> *Blessed Roman, show me how to live and die for Christ.*

See also Our Lady of the Pillar in the Calendar of Marian Dates.

* * * * *

October 13

Saint Theophilus of Antioch

Theophilus lived in the second century, and, like most Christians of the time, was an adult convert to the faith. Reading the Scriptures brought him to the faith, and he was a zealous defender of Church teaching against heretical teachers. He became bishop of Antioch, and we still have one of his writings today. He died around the year 184.

Saints Faustus, Januarius, and Martial of Cordoba

During the persecution of the Church under the Roman emperor Diocletian in the year 304, the martyrs Faustus, Januarius, and Martial died in Cordoba, Spain. They were burned to death because of their refusal to give up their faith.

Blessed Alexandrina Maria da Costa

Alexandrina was born in 1904 in Balasar, Portugal, and was a pious child. When she was fourteen years old, she was attacked by a would-be rapist, but she jumped from a window to get away. She was badly injured and ultimately became bedridden. But she spent her time fruitfully: she prayed. Alexandrina became a mystic and prayed constantly for the salvation of souls. She was also granted a gift from God; she overcame her paralysis each Friday for three hours, when she rose from her bed and relived the Passion of Christ. This happened from 1938 to 1942. Though a simple lay Catholic, she wrote repeatedly to the pope to ask him to consecrate the entire world to the Immaculate Heart of Mary. Pope Pius XII did, on October 31 in 1942. Deeply in love with the presence of Christ in the Blessed Sacrament, she received daily Communion and no other food for the last thirteen years of her life.

> *Saint Theophilus, teach me your love of Sacred Scripture.*
> *Holy Martyrs, show me how to live and die for Christ.*
> *Blessed Alexandrina, help me pray for the salvation of souls.*

* * * * *

October 14

Saint Callistus I (Calixtus), Optional Memorial

All we know about Callistus (d. 222) before he became pope comes from Hippolytus, a priest who made himself an anti-pope before finally repenting and reconciling with the Church near the end of his life. According to Hippolytus' unfriendly account, Callistus was a Christian slave who was put in charge of a bank by his master. He lost the money that other Christians had deposited with him, ran away, was caught, and was sentenced to a life of slavery. When his creditors allowed him to go free, he tried to recover his debt, but a riot broke out in the synagogue, apparently because he was trying to regain the money from Jews present there. Callistus was then sentenced to the horrible punishment of working in mines in Sardinia, an island in the Mediterranean. Fortunately, he and some other Christians were later freed at the request of the Roman emperor Commodus' Christian mistress. In the year 199, Pope Saint Zephyrinus made Callistus the superintendent of the Christian cemetery, which is (apparently) the first land owned by the Church. He was ordained a deacon, became the pope's friend and counselor, and then succeeded Zephyrinus as pope. He was a forgiving pope—too forgiving for some. Hippolytus, among others, objected to the fact that Callistus allowed murderers, adulterers, and fornicators to return to the Church when they expressed repentance over their sins. According to tradition, he died a martyr during a riot.

Blessed Roman Lysko

Roman was born in Horoduk, Ukraine, in 1914 and was a Greek Catholic. He married and was ordained a priest in 1941. In 1949, the Soviets controlled Ukraine, and the NKVD (Russian secret police) arrested and tortured him for the crime of being a Catholic priest. His jailors thought that he had lost his mind while he was in prison because he sang the psalms loudly from his cell. On this date, just a month after his arrest, he died by starvation.

Saint Callistus, help me to see worldly failures as stepping stones in God's plan for me. Blessed Roman, help me draw close to the Lord through the psalms.

* * * * *

October 15

Saint Teresa of Jesus, Memorial

Teresa was born near the city of Avila in the Castile region of Spain in 1515. She was pious even when she was a child; she once conspired with her brother Rodrigo to run away from home, with the unusual goal of hoping to be martyred by the Muslims and thus go to Heaven quickly. Fortunately, they were soon found by a relative. When she was fourteen years old, her mother died, and her father sent her to a convent school to be educated. But after she had been there for a year and a half, she became so sick that they sent her home. When she recovered, she asked her father's permission to become a nun. He refused, so she snuck away in secret to join the Carmelite nuns living in Avila. Her father gave in. She was professed a nun a year later, but she became very ill (some say with malignant malaria), and she was sent home again. At one point, everyone thought that she had died and even planned her funeral, but she miraculously recovered and was allowed to return to her life in the convent. During the three years of her recovery, Teresa began to practice mental prayer, but since she lacked a good spiritual director and since the religious life of her convent was so relaxed (i.e., not strict), she eventually gave up trying. Instead, she enjoyed her life as a nun, entertaining visitors in the convent parlor, leaving the convent frequently, and becoming, by her own admission, spiritually dull. When her father died, a Dominican friar confronted her with her spiritual lukewarmness, and Teresa returned to the practice of mental prayer for the rest of her life. When she began withdrawing from social life and other pleasures of the convent, God blessed her with what she called the "prayer of quiet". But those around her were offended by the resulting change in her behavior and even said that her prayer was from the devil instead. One day, while Teresa was praying the prayer Veni Creator Spiritus, as a Jesuit priest had directed her to do, God spoke deeply to her heart, saying, "No longer do I want you to converse with men but with angels."[18] The Franciscan priest Saint Peter of Alcantara and other holy people encouraged her in her spiritual life, and she received many spiritual gifts: spiritual espousal, mystical marriage, and, in one vision, she saw and felt her heart be pierced by an arrow from an angel. Another nun suggested that Teresa should found a

---

[18] Teresa of Avila, *Teresa of Avila: The Book of Her Life*, trans. Kieran Kavanaugh, O.C.D., and Otilio Rodriguez, O.C.D. (Indianapolis, Cambridge: Hackett Publishing Company, 2008), 159.

convent of her own, so, taking only a dozen other nuns (unlike the 140 nuns living at her convent in Avila), Teresa left her convent. She and her nuns lived a life of poverty, in almost perpetual silence, in perpetual abstinence, and in strict enclosure. Unfortunately, these changes seemed innovative to the people of the time, and Teresa was persecuted and slandered by many people in Avila. But she trusted in God and eventually charmed many people into accepting her simple way of life through her God-given wisdom. In time, Teresa founded and reformed other Carmelite convents and began a reformation of the Carmelite friars with the help of the priests Saint John of the Cross and Jerome Gracian. By the end of her life, Teresa had founded seventeen convents and the Discalced Carmelite order, and she had written several works that have since become masterpieces of the spiritual life. Teresa died on the evening of October 4, 1582, in the arms of her friend Blessed Anne of Saint Bartholomew. Since the Gregorian calendar reform fell into effect on the following day, that date was counted as October 15. A true "Doctor of Prayer" for the universal Church, she was named a Doctor of the Church in 1970 by Pope Saint Paul VI.

> It happened to me at other times that I was suffering great tribulations and criticism, on account of a certain matter I shall speak of afterward, from almost the entire city where I live and from my order, and afflicted by the many occasions there were for becoming disturbed, when the Lord said to me, "Why are you afraid? Do you not know that I am all-powerful? I will fulfill what I have promised."[19]

Saint Magdalena of Nagasaki

Magdalena was born around the year 1610 in Nagasaki, Japan, into a Catholic home. Her parents died as martyrs for the faith when she was only nine years old. She became an Augustinian tertiary and served as an interpreter for two Augustinian priests. On this date in 1634, when she was still a young woman, she was executed by the government for being a Christian and died a martyr for Christ.

> Saint Teresa, teach me to pray with my whole heart.
> Saint Magdalena, help me to remain faithful to Christ during my trials.

* * * * *

October 16

Saint Hedwig of Silesia, Optional Memorial[20]

Hedwig (1174–1243) was the daughter of the duke of Carinthia (modern Austria and Slovenia); she married Henry I, the duke of Silesia (modern Poland), when

---

[19] Ibid., 172.

[20] "Hedwig" and "Jadwiga" are different versions of the same name. Note that this Hedwig is not the same person as Saint Jadwiga of Poland; see the dates.

she was twelve years old and he was eighteen years old. Hedwig asked her husband to use her large dowry to build a convent for nuns, and he did, building the first women's convent in the region. Though Hedwig and Henry were both very devout, their seven children quarreled constantly as adults. In 1209, with her husband's permission, Hedwig retired to a Cistercian abbey that she had founded to live a simple life. Her husband became known as Henry the Bearded at that time because he stopped shaving and wearing fancy clothes. When he died in 1238, Hedwig officially took the habit of religious life. Though formerly a duchess, she lived the humble life of a poor nun, walked to church in bare feet, and taught the poor about the faith.

Saint Margaret Mary Alacoque, Optional Memorial

Margaret Mary (1647–1690) was the fifth of seven children, and she grew up in L'Hautecour in Burgundy, France. Her father died when she was eight years old, and she was sent to be educated by Poor Clare nuns. When she became very ill, she was sent home to recover and discovered that her mother had essentially become a servant to other members of the family, and Margaret was treated the same way when she recovered from her illness. She was pressured to marry when she was twenty years old, but she resisted, wanting to become a nun; finally, her brother provided the dowry so she could enter the Visitation convent at Paray-le-Monial in 1671. From that time, Margaret felt our Lord calling her to ask for humiliations, and she certainly received them. She was made assistant infirmarian, but since she was quiet, slow, and clumsy—very unlike the efficient and active sister in charge of the infirmary—it was a great trial for both of them. On December 27, 1673, she felt our Lord's presence and experienced a revelation from Him concerning His desire to be adored in His Sacred Heart. She told her superior about this revelation, but her superior refused to allow her to do any of the things that Jesus had asked of her. Margaret became so upset over her inability to obey the Lord that she became dangerously ill. Her superior was looking for a sign to understand how to deal with Margaret and told her that she would follow the instructions from the revelation if Margaret recovered. Margaret recovered immediately. Although she faced persecution from other sisters and various priests for her devotion, she was encouraged too, most notably by Saint Claude de la Colombiere, who stayed for a short time with the sisters. Over the years, Margaret suffered ongoing opposition for encouraging devotion to the Sacred Heart of Jesus, although she received interior consolations from God as well. She was able to keep her identity as the actual recipient of the revelation about the Sacred Heart secret for years, and it became known only when a book by Father de la Colombiere was accidentally read aloud to the sisters. Later in life, Margaret became the mistress of novices and encouraged the novices to pray to the Sacred Heart of Jesus. At one point, the family of a dismissed novice made scandalous claims about Margaret, that she was unorthodox and an imposter; but eventually the claims were seen to be false and that trial passed. At the end of her life, Margaret became ill. While receiving Viaticum, she said, "I need nothing but God, and to lose myself in the heart of Jesus."[21] And then she died.

---

[21] Walsh, *Butler's Lives of the Saints*, 341.

Saint Longinus the Centurion

Longinus is the traditional name of the unnamed centurion who was present at Jesus' Crucifixion and said, "Truly this was the Son of God!"[22]—showing his belief that the man he had just crucified was no ordinary man, but also divine. According to tradition, he was martyred in Cappadocia (modern Turkey) for his faith in Christ.

Saint Gerard Majella

Gerard (1725–1755) lost his father, who was a tailor, when he only was twelve years old, and the family had to live in poverty in Muro, Italy, afterward. Gerard tried to join the Capuchins as a young man, but they refused him because of his poor health. Eventually, he was accepted by the Redemptorists and became a lay brother with them, serving as a sacristan, gardener, porter, infirmarian, and tailor. Despite the fact that he served in such lowly positions as a mere brother, he was also a wonder-worker, was able to bilocate, and could read other people's consciences. When a pregnant woman falsely accused him of being the father of her child, he remained charitably silent. The woman later admitted that she had lied. This incident caused him to become known as a patron of pregnant women. He died of tuberculosis at the age of thirty.

Blesseds Anicet Koplinski and Joseph Jankowski

Anicet was born in 1875 and was a Polish friar and priest. Joseph was born in 1910 and was also born in Poland, joined the Pallottines (a society serving the poor that was founded by Saint Vincent Pallotti) before becoming a priest, and was known for his ministry to youth and his devotion to Saint Teresa of Avila. Along with many Polish Catholic priests during World War II, they were arrested and taken by the Nazis to the Auschwitz concentration camp. On this date in 1941, Anicet died in the gas chambers of the camp, and Joseph was beaten to death by guards.

> *Saint Hedwig, help me to be holy and draw those around me to holiness.*
> *Saint Margaret Mary, teach me to love the Sacred Heart of Jesus.*
> *Saint Longinus, show me how to bear witness to Christ.*
> *Saint Gerard, show me how to trust in God at all times.*
> *Holy Martyrs, pray for me to be faithful to Christ in my sufferings.*

* * * * *

October 17

Saint Ignatius of Antioch, Memorial

According to tradition, Ignatius Theophorus (his surname means "God-bearer") learned about the Christian faith from Saint John the Evangelist and was one of

---

[22] Mt 27:54.

his disciples. He was born in Syria, he became bishop of Antioch, Syria, around the year 69, and he was condemned to death when the Roman emperor Trajan renewed his persecution of Christians around the year 107. Since Ignatius was a prominent Christian, he was taken by soldiers to Rome so that his death could be personally enjoyed as "entertainment" in the bloody games offered there. Ignatius joyfully submitted to this journey, for he believed that through his death he could show his faith in Christ. He encouraged the Christians who came to meet him as he traveled to Rome to remain faithful during the persecution, and he sent letters to seven churches along his journey. Ignatius was brought before the Roman city prefect on December 20, 107, the last day of the games, and when he was put in the amphitheater, two lions killed and devoured him immediately. Because of the enduring power of the spirit-filled letters he wrote while on his way to martyrdom, he's considered a Father of the Church.

> *I am writing to all the churches to declare to them all that I am glad to die for God, provided you do not hinder me. I beg you not to show me a misplaced kindness. Let me be the food of beasts that I may come to God. I am his wheat, and I shall be ground by the teeth of beasts, that I may become Christ's pure bread.*[23]

Prophet Hosea

Hosea was one of the twelve men named as minor prophets of the Old Testament, and he spoke God's words to the Jews during the reign of King Jeroboam II of Israel. The book that bears his name makes a vivid comparison between adultery and idolatry: Hosea wedded and forgave his wife, Gomer, despite her repeated infidelities, just as the Jewish people were repeatedly unfaithful to God through idolatrous practices. He died around the year 750 B.C.

> *Let us know, let us press on to know the LORD; his going forth is sure as the dawn; he will come to us as the showers, as the spring rains that water the earth.*[24]

Saint John of Egypt

John was born in the early fourth century at Lycopolis (modern-day Egypt) and was trained to be a carpenter. When he was twenty-five years old, he withdrew from the world and placed himself under the direction of a hermit. For about ten years, John obeyed his spiritual father unquestioningly, even watering a dry stick daily for a year when he was told to do so. When the hermit died, John traveled to different monasteries for several years, finally living in a cave at the top of a steep hill near Lycopolis. He walled himself into the cave, leaving only a small window through which he could receive the necessities of life. On Saturdays and Sundays, men came to him to receive spiritual advice. He ate only dried fruit and vegetables and only after sunset, and although he initially had trouble with this diet, he was eventually able to live on it for fifty years. Other men living similar ascetic lives came to visit him, and he had so many visitors

---

[23] *The Liturgy of the Hours*, vol. 3, from a letter to the Romans by Saint Ignatius of Antioch, bishop and martyr (New York: Catholic Book Publishing, 1975), 324.

[24] Hos 6:3.

that they ended up building a home to house them all. God gave John the gift of being able to read the thoughts of those who came to see him, and his prayers worked many miracles and cures. For example, he predicted to a visitor that the man would become a bishop, which he did, and he recognized that another visitor was a deacon simply by looking at him, though there was no way for him to have known. When he was ninety years old, God revealed to him that his end was near, and he shut his window, refused visitors for three days, and died peacefully on his knees while he was praying. It was the year 394.

Saint Jadwiga of Poland[25]

Hedwig was born the youngest daughter of King Louis I of Hungary in 1371; she became queen of Poland when her father died in 1382. She was engaged to William, duke of Austria, whom she loved, but she had to break off the engagement for political reasons and instead marry Jagiello, the non-Christian prince of Lithuania, when she was thirteen years old. She offered this sacrifice to Christ and eventually converted her husband to the faith. She was noted for her charity to the sick and poor and for revising laws to help the poor. She died in childbirth when she was still a young woman on July 17, 1399.

> *Saint Ignatius, show me how my sufferings can serve Christ.*
> *Prophet Hosea, teach me how to be faithful to God.*
> *Saint John, show me how to live a life of self-denial and solitude.*
> *Saint Hedwig, help me to see God's will in all the difficulties of life.*

* * * * *

October 18

Saint Luke the Evangelist, Feast

Saint Paul writes that Luke was a physician and was one of his personal traveling companions.[26] In Luke's own writings—his Gospel and the Acts of the Apostles—we learn about Luke only indirectly. Due to his detailed account of Jesus' birth,[27] he probably knew and spoke with Jesus' Mother about it. Luke also pays careful attention to Gentiles, the poor, and women in his writings. Although he may or may not have met Jesus himself, he was clearly an eyewitness to some of the events of the early Church that are recounted in Acts. Tradition says that Luke was an artist, a native of Antioch in Syria (according to the saintly historian Bede), and that he died a martyr in Greece when he was over eighty years old.

---

[25] "Hedwig" and "Jadwiga" are different versions of the same name. Note that this Jadwiga is not the same person as Saint Hedwig of Silesia; see the dates.

[26] Col 4:14.

[27] Lk 2:1–20.

Saint Peter of Alcantara

Peter was born in Spain in 1499, studied in the city of Salamanca, and became a Franciscan priest. He lived a very austere life and founded a reform branch of the Franciscans called the Alcantarines, to bring them back to Saint Francis' original poverty and simplicity. Peter was a friend and supporter of the Carmelite nun and foundress Saint Teresa of Avila in her work to reform the Carmelite order. A deep mystic, Peter experienced the gifts of ecstasy in prayer, levitation, and miracles. The Alcantarine order was approved by the pope in 1562, the same year that Peter died in the city of Las Arenas.

> *Saint Luke, help me to bring the Good News to those around me.*
> *Saint Peter, show me how to reform my life daily to the model of Jesus Christ.*

* * * * *

October 19

Saint Paul of the Cross, Optional Memorial

See October 20.[28]

Saints John de Brebeuf and Isaac Jogues and Companions, Memorial[29]

French Jesuit priests and lay members of the Jesuits traveled to the French colonies in North America (now Canada and northern America) in the seventeenth century to bring the Gospel to the native peoples living there. These Jesuits lived in poverty and danger among the Hurons and other tribes, who often responded with violence and acts of brutality unheard of for centuries. Rene Goupil, a layman whose health prevented him from becoming a Jesuit but who served the Jesuits as a surgeon, was killed simply because he made the sign of the cross on a child's forehead. Isaac Jogues, a Jesuit priest, was enslaved and brutally tortured by a tribe but was able to escape and return to France. Since his hands had been mutilated by the torture, he had to be given permission to celebrate Mass by the pope himself, yet Jogues returned to North America in 1644 to continue serving the people there. After returning, he was attacked without warning and beheaded. John Lalande, a layman who served the Jesuits, and Father Anthony Daniel were killed on July 4, 1648, when the Iroquois attacked the Huron village in which they were living. Fathers Gabriel Lalemant and John de Brebeuf were captured during an Iroquois raid and tortured in horrific ways.

---

[28] Because the North American Martyrs are celebrated on October 19 in the *Liturgical Calendar for the Dioceses of the United States of America*, Saint Paul of the Cross is transferred as an optional memorial to October 20.

[29] These saints are celebrated as a memorial in the *Liturgical Calendar for the Dioceses of the United States of America*, rather than an optional memorial.

In 1649, when the Iroquois attacked a mission where Father Charles Garnier lived, he went about baptizing children and giving absolution to Christians until he was killed. Father Noel Chabanel, Father Garnier's missionary companion, was recalled from his mission because of the attack, but he was killed by an apostate Christian while he was trying to escape. All were named martyrs.

Prophet Joel

Joel was one of the twelve men known to us as minor prophets of the Old Testament, and he was apparently a priest who lived in the nation of Judah sometime between the eighth and sixth centuries B.C. He warned the people of the coming judgment of the Lord, as well as the salvation of the just.

> For the day of the LORD is great and very awesome; who can endure it? "Yet even now," says the LORD, "return to me with all your heart, with fasting, with weeping, and with mourning; and tear your hearts and not your garments."[30]

Saint Frideswide

Frideswide was born around the year 650 and was the daughter of a prince in Mercia (modern England). According to tradition, she made a vow of perpetual virginity so that she could give her life to Christ, and she refused to marry Algar, a local prince. A story says that when Algar tried to pursue her, he was struck blind, but when he gave up, his sight returned. Frideswide lived in hiding at first, but she eventually founded a nunnery and became its first abbess. She died around the year 735, and her relics were venerated for centuries until anti-Catholicism swept England in the sixteenth century.

> Holy Martyrs, give me your Christlike courage in facing
> the evils that enslave the people of my own culture.
> Prophet Joel, show me how to repent deeply.
> Saint Frideswide, help me to remain always faithful to my vocation.

* * * * *

October 20

Saint Paul of the Cross, Optional Memorial[31]

Paul (1694–1775) was the son of a merchant in northern Italy. Pious even as a child, he attended daily Mass, was a faithful student and virtuous young man, and had a deep devotion to the Blessed Sacrament. In response to a vision he

---

[30] Joel 2:11–13.

[31] Because the North American Martyrs are celebrated as a memorial on October 19 in the United States, Saint Paul of the Cross is transferred as an optional memorial to October 20.

received, he began the founding of the Congregation of Discalced Clerks of the Most Holy Cross and Passion while he was still only a layman. The Passionists, as they're now known, have the primary mission of preaching about the Passion of Jesus Christ. Paul became a great preacher, and many hardened sinners were moved to tears by his sermons. Though all the brothers in his order left him at one point, the order began to grow again after his Passionist Rule was approved by the pope in 1741.

Saint Cornelius the Centurion

Cornelius was a Roman centurion who believed in the God of the Jews and lived in Caesarea (modern Turkey). When he received a vision in which an angel told him to send some of his men to find a man named Simon Peter, he obeyed. Saint Peter came to his house, and Cornelius and his household, though Gentiles, experienced the coming of the Holy Spirit. Peter baptized them,[32] and tradition says that Cornelius became the first bishop of Caesarea and that he suffered a great deal in his service of Christ and the Gospel.

Saint Andrew of Crete

Andrew was born on the island of Crete in the eighth century and became a hermit. The Byzantine emperor Constantine V was an iconoclast and prohibited the veneration of icons, with severe penalties for those who violated his orders. Andrew was righteously indignant that the emperor would prohibit prayer to God through his saints, so he left his hermitage and traveled to Constantinople to speak against this heresy. The emperor was not moved to conversion; he had Andrew tortured and flogged to death around the year 767.

Saint Bertilla (Anne Frances) Boscardin

Anne Frances (called Annetta) was born into a peasant family at Brendola, Italy, in 1888. She had a difficult childhood, in part because her father was a violent man who drank—as he himself testified later at his daughter's beatification. Annetta went only irregularly to school and had to work from an early age both at home and as a domestic servant. When a priest told her pastor that she might have a religious vocation, the pastor laughed, and a convent refused to accept her. However, the Sisters of Saint Dorothy at Vicenza decided to accept her when she was sixteen years old. She told the novice mistress, "I can't do anything.... I'm a poor thing, a goose. Teach me. I want to become a saint."[33] Taking the name Bertilla, she worked in the scullery (the kitchen of the convent), bakehouse, and laundry. Bertilla was sent to learn about nursing for a time, but she was kept working in the scullery until her profession in 1907. It was when she was sent to the children's diphtheria ward that she recognized her vocation in the service of the sick. In 1915, the convent hospital was taken over during World War I. Bertilla impressed the people around her with the way

---

[32] Acts 10:17–48.
[33] Walsh, *Butler's Lives of the Saints*, 347.

she remained calm, took care of the sick, and said her Rosary even during air raids. Her superior failed to understand her, thought she was too attached to her patients, and banished her to work in the laundry for four months, which she did without complaint. However, the mother general recognized Bertilla's abilities and then returned her to the hospital, where she was put in charge of the children's isolation ward. Bertilla lived in constant, severe pain from an internal sickness for the last twelve years of her life, and she died in 1922, three days after surgery was performed in hopes of helping her. Crowds flocked to her grave, and miracles of healing were attributed to her intercession.

> *Saint Paul, teach me how to meditate on the Passion of our Lord,*
> *that I might grow in love of Him.*
> *Saint Cornelius, help me to have faith in God, particularly when I don't*
> *understand what He's doing.*
> *Saint Andrew, help me to pray.*
> *Saint Bertilla, show me how to love and serve those who are sick or in pain.*

* * * * *

October 21

Saint Ursula and Companions of Cologne

According to tradition, Ursula was a British princess who traveled in the fourth century with her eleven companions to Rome. Apparently, a copyist changed that to eleven thousand companions at some point during the centuries, so the larger number is sometimes given. During their journey back to England, a pagan prince asked Ursula to marry him, and when she refused, she and all her companions were martyred together in Cologne, Germany.

Saint Hilarion of Cyprus

Hilarion was born in the year 291 in Tabatha near Gaza (Palestine), and his parents were pagans. He was sent to study in the great city of Alexandria, Egypt, which is where he learned about the Christian faith and was baptized when he was fifteen years old. He decided God was calling him to become a hermit, so he went to see the great Saint Anthony, hoping to learn from him how to live in solitude in the desert. However, Anthony's monastery was so overrun with visitors who also wanted to see him that Hilarion returned to his own country after only a few months. When he returned, he found that his parents had died and left everything to him. He gave everything that he had inherited to his brothers and to the poor and then settled in the desert. Hilarion's only clothes were sackcloth, a leather tunic that Anthony had given him, and a short cloak. He ate only fifteen figs a day, and he ate those only at sunset, though he later added vegetables, bread, and oil to his diet when he found that figs alone weren't enough to sustain him. He supported himself by farming and making baskets. At first, he lived in a shelter made of woven reeds, but later he built a small cell (which other people said looked like a tomb). After many years of this life, at the age of sixty-five, he had a revelation that Anthony had died. So he traveled to Anthony's mountain in honor of the holy man who had inspired him. When Hilarion returned and settled in a desert near Atfiah, he suffered from the same problem as Anthony—lots of visitors asking for advice and keeping him from living the life of silence he desired. So he left for Sicily. As he traveled there, miracles occurred along the way—people were healed from sicknesses, people were cured from snakebite, and rain came after a long drought—and people flocked to see him. He traveled to Cyprus, and there he managed to hide for a few years in an inaccessible place until he died at the age of eighty in the year 371.

> *Holy Martyrs, help me to refuse any worldly*
> *offers that go against the will of God.*
> *Saint Hilarion, show me how to remain hidden in Christ.*

* * * * *

October 22

Saints Philip and Hermes of Heraclea

Philip, the bishop of Heraclea (a city in modern Turkey), was arrested during the persecution of Christians under the Roman emperor Diocletian in the early fourth century, along with the deacon Hermes. The governor ordered Philip to be tortured and then forced him to watch as he burned Christian writings as well as the church building itself. A priest named Severus had gone into hiding during the persecution, but he surrendered himself to the authorities. All three men were left in prison for a time until a new governor replaced the previous one. After seven months of imprisonment, Philip was beaten to a pulp, and a few days later, Philip and Hermes were condemned to be burned at the stake. The men went joyfully to die for Christ, although Philip was badly injured and had to be carried to the stake. They praised God as long as they were able to speak during the burning, and their bodies, which were thrown in the river, were later recovered by the Christian faithful. Severus, left alone in prison, thanked God that the two men had given their lives for Christ, and he begged God for the same privilege. He was martyred the next day. It was the year 304.

Saint John Paul II

John Paul was born 1920 in Wadowice, Poland, to a noncommissioned officer in the army and given the name Karol Wojtyla. His mother died when he was nine years old, his elder brother died when he was twelve, and his father died when he was twenty-one. By that time, he was working in a quarry during the Nazi occupation of Poland during World War II, and he later worked in a chemical factory to avoid deportation to Germany. He felt called to the priesthood, but he and other future priests had to study clandestinely because of the war. He also helped organize a clandestine theater. When the war ended, he was able to study for the priesthood in the newly reopened seminary, receiving his ordination in 1946. He studied in Rome, attained a doctorate in theology, and then returned to Poland to serve in different parishes. He continued to study philosophy and theology and became a professor of moral theology and ethics. He was appointed auxiliary bishop of Cracow by Pope Pius XII in 1958, was named archbishop of Cracow by Pope Saint Paul VI in 1964, and was then made a cardinal. He participated in the Second Vatican Council, most notably influencing the document focused on the Church in the modern world, *Gaudium et Spes*. In 1978, he was elected pope—the first non-Italian pope since 1523. During his long pontificate, John Paul made 146 pastoral visits in Italy and 104 international apostolic journeys. He wrote fourteen encyclicals, dozens of other apostolic documents, and five books. Emphasizing the universal call to holiness for Christians, he proclaimed 1338 blesseds and 482 saints. To unify and educate the Church better, he promulgated the Codes of Canon Law and a new *Catechism of the Catholic Church*, as well as developing and explicating a new Theology of the Body to explain Catholic teaching about human relationships and sexuality from a personalist perspective. In 1981, an attempt was made on his life, and John Paul not only survived but personally forgave his attempted assassin. He died on Divine Mercy Sunday, a date that he had added to the Church's calendar. His holiness of life had inspired many to call him John Paul the Great, even before his death in 2005. He was canonized a saint in 2014.

> *Holy Martyrs, teach me to rejoice in my sufferings for the sake of Christ.*
> *Saint John Paul, show me how to give my life completely to Jesus, through Mary.*

* * * * *

October 23

Saint John of Capistrano, Optional Memorial

John was born in 1386. He was a talented young man, and after he studied law, he became the governor of Perugia in Italy and married a daughter of a city leader. However, he was captured and imprisoned during feuds between neighboring cities, and by the time he was released, he had decided to give up everything for religious life. It's not clear on what terms he and his wife separated, but one of his first acts was to ride through the city on a donkey, sitting backward and with his worst sins written on a huge paper hat on his head. He was covered with filth and had been pelted by children when he presented himself at the door of a Franciscan monastery and asked to enter the order. He was thirty years old. He was ordained a priest in 1420, and he lived an austere personal life: he walked barefoot, slept only three to four hours a day, and wore a hair shirt. His preaching brought many people to conversion, and he was also instrumental in changing the way he and his fellow friars lived the Franciscan Rule, placing themselves in greater conformity with Saint Francis' original rule. At one point, John was sent to Vienna with twelve Franciscans to serve in an Inquisition, as requested by the emperor Frederick III, to identify heretical Christians. Today, some people criticize the way he treated the followers of Jan Hus. John was merciful to those who repented of their involvement in the Hussites, a group that promoted violence as well as a religious heresy concerning the Eucharist, but, as described by *Butler's Lives of the Saints*, "his zeal was of the kind that scars and consumes."[34] When the Turks captured Constantinople, John wore himself out preaching a crusade to liberate the Holy Land and rallying the troops, which led to a great victory. However, many people became ill after the battle because the bodies of the dead were left lying in the fields, and John was one of them. He died peacefully in Villach, Hungary, on this date in 1456.

Saint Severinus Boethius

Boethius was born around the year 480 into a Christian family of Rome, and he married into the family of a senator. He became a Roman consul in the year 510 and was head of the civil service in the years 520 and 522. But the king, Theodoric, arrested him on trumped-up charges of conspiring against him and of being a magician, when Boethius' real crime was being a faithful Catholic while the king was a follower of the Arian heresy. Boethius was first imprisoned in Pavia, Italy, for nine months. During that time, he wrote *The Consolation of Philosophy*, a famous work of Christian philosophy in which he explains, among other things, that happiness can be found in God alone. Finally, the king ordered him to be tortured and put to death. Boethius died a martyr in the year 524 and is considered a Father of the Church.

Saint Allucius of Campuliano

Allucius (d. 1134) was a cowherd in Campuliano, Italy. After he survived a thunderstorm by standing under a large tree with his cattle—afraid the whole time that he would be killed by lightning—he dedicated his life to God. He began to care for hospital patients, and he eventually rebuilt an old hospital. His personal holiness and life of self-denial inspired many people to conversion. It was said that the power of Allucius' prayers restored sight to a man whose eyes had been gouged out, freed another man from demonic possession, and brought robbers to conversion.

Saint John, teach me humility.
Saint Boethius, help me understand that happiness is found in God alone.
Saint Allucius, show me how to live a life of service.

* * * * *

[34] Ibid., 352.

October 24

Saint Anthony Mary Claret, Optional Memorial

Anthony was born in Spain in 1807 and became a weaver like his father, but he later recognized God's call to become a priest. After learning Latin, he entered the seminary, was ordained, and seriously considered a vocation with the Jesuits in Rome. His health broke down while he was still a novice, so he returned to Spain. For about ten years, he gave retreats and missions as a diocesan priest. When other priests were inspired by his example and wanted to follow him, he founded the Missionary Sons of the Immaculate Heart of Mary in 1849, generally known as the Claretians. Anthony was later sent to faraway Cuba to serve as the local archbishop. While in Cuba, he instituted many reforms to encourage holiness and improve the moral behavior of his flock, but many people resented the changes. His life was in danger many times, as, for example, when a man tried to kill him because his mistress had left him and returned to an honest life because of Anthony's influence. In 1857, Anthony returned to Spain, became the private confessor to Queen Isabella II, and formally resigned as archbishop. He still devoted himself to missionary work and, an avid writer himself, encouraged good literature in Spain. During his lifetime, it's said that he preached ten thousand sermons and published two hundred books and pamphlets. Anthony also received amazing spiritual gifts: continual union with God, ecstasies, the gift of prophecy, and miraculous healings. During a political revolution in 1868, he was exiled from Spain along with the queen and went to live in Rome. While there, he promoted the doctrine of papal infallibility, which was being debated—and about to be defined. He died in France at a Cistercian monastery near Narbonne on this date in 1870.

Saint Senoch of Tours

Senoch (d. 576) was the abbot of a Benedictine monastery in Tours, France. He and his monks lived an austere life, fasting often on bread and water. Senoch's personal penances included spending most of his time alone in his cell and speaking very little. He visited his hometown on one occasion, and the people's admiration of him turned his head a bit. A good and holy friend who was a bishop, Saint Gregory of Tours, corrected him, telling him to spend more time with his fellow monks, which brought Senoch back to humility.

Saint Mark (Martin) of Vertou

Mark (527–601) lived in France and chose the life of a hermit. At first, he suffered from many temptations and found it a hard way of life, but in time he became detached and at peace in his solitude. Although he lived alone in a cave, word of his holiness eventually spread throughout the area. The men who came to be his disciples witnessed miracles that demonstrated Mark's holiness. For example, in his cave, there was a large boulder. His followers decided it might fall on him, so they decided to move it. As they worked to move it, Mark continued to kneel in prayer, even when it fell and only narrowly avoided crushing him. For three years, he was menaced by a mysterious serpent that stretched out in front of him while he prayed and slithered beside him when he slept. Mark ignored it. Finally the snake rushed out of the cave one day, set fire to bushes as it passed, and never returned, confirming Mark's belief that it had actually been a demon. On another occasion, Mark decided to chain himself to the ground as a penance, but his friend Saint Benedict of Nursia heard of it, wrote to him, and corrected him. Benedict told Mark that God's servants needed only the spiritual chains of Christ to bind them in place. Humbled, Mark removed the chain. When a young boy fell off the path leading to Mark's cave and was feared to be lost or dead, Mark prayed for him, and the boy was found safe.

Saint Joseph Le Dang Thi

Joseph was a Vietnamese layman and a captain in the army. He converted to the Catholic faith, though it was illegal at the time in Vietnam. When it was discovered that he was a Catholic, he was arrested and killed by strangulation, dying a martyr in 1860.

> Saint Anthony, help me discern God's call for my life and grow in holiness.
> Saint Senoch, protect me from pride.
> Saint Mark, teach me how to pray.
> Saint Joseph, help me choose faith in Christ over my culture's demands.

* * * * *

October 25

Saints Chrysanthus and Daria of Rome

During the persecution of the Church under the Roman emperor Carinus (or Numerian, the exact date isn't clear) around the year 283, the martyrs Chrysanthus and Daria were executed in the city of Rome. They were husband and wife, originally from Egypt, and were zealous in their desire to bring others to Christ.

Saints Crispin and Crispinian of Rome

Crispin and Crispinian were devout Christian brothers who lived in Rome in the third century. When a persecution of Christians began, the men moved to Gaul (France). During the day, they spoke to others about Jesus Christ and spread the Gospel, but in the evenings they worked as shoemakers. They asked people to pay them only what they were able to pay, and they lived in peace for several years until the Roman emperor Maximian visited their city of Soissons. Pagans of the city complained to the emperor about the presence of Christians, and the two men were arrested. Despite torture, they refused to give up their faith in Christ and were finally beheaded. It was the year 286.

Saint Gaudentius of Brescia

Philastrius was the bishop of Brescia, Italy, and a strong defender of the faith against the widespread Arian heresy. When he died, Gaudentius (d. ca. 410) succeeded him and was consecrated by the bishop of Milan, Saint Ambrose. Much of what we know about Gaudentius' faith is from a series of Easter sermons that he wrote down at the request of a noble, pious Christian of the town who was too sick to attend the sermons in person. When Saint John Chrysostom, patriarch of Constantinople, was falsely accused of heresy by Arians, Gaudentius was one of three bishops who were sent by the pope to Constantinople to support John at his trial. The emperor's men wouldn't even let them reach the city. When Gaudentius and the other two bishops asked for a fair hearing for John and refused to accept bribes, they were forcibly put on an unseaworthy ship and sent back to Rome. They almost died. Gaudentius died of natural causes a few years later.

> *Saints Chyrsanthus and Daria, help me bring my family to Christ.*
> *Saints Crispin and Crispinian, show me how to love God and my neighbor.*
> *Saint Gaudentius, beg the Lord to give me the grace to speak for those*
> *who suffer unjustly.*

* * * * *

October 26

Saints Lucian and Marcian of Nicomedia

Lucian lived in the third century of Nicomedia in modern Turkey. Far from being a Christian, he made his living as a sorcerer and worshipped evil spirits. One day, he cast a spell on a Christian woman, which she fended off by simply making the sign of the cross. Surprised, Lucian decided to learn more about this powerful Catholic faith—and converted. As often happens to converts, he spent the rest of his life zealously studying and explaining the true faith and exposing the errors of the false ones. Marcian was most probably a former pagan who had also converted to Christianity. During the persecution of Christians under the Roman emperor Decius around the year 250, both men were martyred for the faith.

Saint Cedd of Lastingham

Cedd (d. 664) was a brother of Chad, the bishop of York and also a future saint, and he had lived as a monk for many years in his native Northumbria when he was sent to preach the Gospel throughout the young Church in England. He built churches, ordained priests and deacons, founded monasteries, and served his people as bishop of the East Saxons until he died in the city of Lastingham during an epidemic.

> *Holy Martyrs, help me see through the lies of false worship.*
> *Saint Cedd, show me how to bring the faith to those around me.*

* * * * *

October 27

Saint Evaristus

Evaristus was pope from the year 97 to 105, and he succeeded Pope Saint Clement I. According to tradition, he was born into a Jewish family in Bethlehem. Christians enjoyed a relative peace during his reign, and he organized the Church in Rome into twenty-five parishes during this time. However, persecution of Christians broke out under the Roman emperor Trajan, and Evaristus died a martyr for the faith.

Saint Odrian (Oterano) of Waterford

Odrian was an abbot in Meath, Ireland, in the sixth century; he became the bishop of Waterford. When Saint Columba traveled to Scotland to evangelize the people there, Odrian went with him and became one of his monks at Iona Abbey in Scotland, where Odrian died.

> *Saint Evaristus, help me to face persecution with peace.*
> *Saint Odrian, help me find friends who will encourage me to share the faith with others.*

* * * * *

October 28

Saints Simon and Jude (Thaddeus) the Apostles, Feast

Simon is referred to as "the Cananaean"[35] or "the Zealot"[36] in the New Testament, and Jude is also called "Thaddeus"[37] and "the brother of James"[38], to distinguish him from Judas Iscariot. They were both chosen by Jesus Christ and became two of the Twelve Apostles. Jude's only words recorded in the Gospels were spoken during the Last Supper, when he asked Jesus, "Lord, how is it that

---

[35] Mt 10:4; Mk 3:18.
[36] Lk 6:15; Acts 1:13.
[37] Mt 10:3; Mk 3:18.
[38] Jude 1; note that whether the Apostle Jude wrote the Letter of Jude is debated.

you will manifest yourself to us, and not to the world?"[39] According to ancient tradition, the two men traveled together as missionaries to speak to people about Jesus Christ and died as martyrs in Persia (modern Iran).

Saints Francis Serrano, Joachim Royo, John Alcober, and Francis Diaz del Rincon

Joachim (1691–1748) was a Dominican priest from Valencia, Spain, who traveled as a missionary to the Philippines in 1712 and then to China in 1715. Because the Chinese government had forbidden Christianity, Joachim had to meet his parishioners at night and live in secret rooms during the day. He was found, arrested, and imprisoned for the crime of being a Christian in 1746. Francis Serrano (1695–1748) was a Spanish Dominican priest serving as a missionary to China; he was chosen to be the titular bishop of Tipasa while he was in prison for being a priest. John Alcober (1694–1748) was a Spanish Dominican priest and missionary serving in China. To escape detection, he pretended to be a water seller, was once smuggled into a home in a coffin to administer the sacraments to a dying Catholic, and once climbed a tree to hide from the authorities. When he began saying his evening prayers in the tree, his friend Father Francis Serrano, who was hiding in the tree nearby, surprised him by joining him. Francis Diaz del Rincon (1713–1748) was a Spanish Dominican priest to the Philippines before coming to China. He too was eventually arrested for being a Catholic priest. On this date in 1748, all these men were first tortured and then executed by strangulation in Fu-tsheu, China.

Holy Martyrs, give me the courage to speak publicly of Jesus Christ.

* * * * *

October 29

Saint Narcissus of Jerusalem

During Narcissus' long life (from roughly the year 99 to 215), the Catholic Church was underground and periodically persecuted by the Roman Empire. He was around one hundred years old when he became the bishop of Jerusalem, and he acted as a true father to the members of his flock. But he could also be a severe leader, and he made enemies. Because of the demands of his office, he yearned to spend more time in solitude and prayer, so when gossip began to spread in Jerusalem that he was guilty of a secret crime, he took that as an excuse to leave the city. He was gone for many years, and two temporary successors had served the people in his place when he finally returned to Jerusalem. Narcissus appointed a coadjutor, the first bishop to do so, to help him handle the demands of the office because of his great age. He was a decisive and strong

---

[39] Jn 14:22.

leader during difficult times, and he died at an even greater age—something between 116 and 122 years old.

Saint Zenobius of Sidon

During the persecution of the Church under the Roman emperor Diocletian, Christians were brought before the magistrate of Sidon, in modern Lebanon, and threatened with torture and death if they refused to give up their faith. Zenobius was a priest, and he encouraged his fellow Christians to remain steadfast and not renounce Christ. For doing so, he was killed in 310.

Saint Abraham Kidunaia of Edessa

Abraham was born near Edessa, Syria, around the year 296 and wanted to give his life to Christ. His family tried to force him into an arranged marriage instead, but he ran away during the wedding festivities and walled himself up in a building with only a small window for food and water. When his family discovered him, they relented and called off the wedding, and Abraham lived in this cell for ten years. The bishop of Edessa then came to visit him, ordered him to come out of his cell, ordained him against his wishes, and sent him as a missionary priest to a pagan village called Beth-Kiduna. After building a church there, Abraham smashed their pagan idols, endured their verbal and physical abuse with patience, and, through his holy example, converted the entire village. After a few years, he returned to the solitude of his cell. Because of his success at Kiduna, he was thereafter known as "Kidunaia". He spent the rest of his life in his cell, except for one trip in which he brought his niece from a wild life to conversion (the future Saint Mary of Edessa) by disguising himself as a soldier and talking to her over supper. When he died around the year 366, many came to mourn him, and his friend Ephraem (a deacon and now known as a saint) wrote his biography.

Saint Theuderius (Chef) of Vienna

Theuderius (d. 575) left Dauphine, France, to become a monk at the famous Lerins Abbey. Later he became a priest, and after many years, he returned to the abbey. In time, he left with several disciples and settled near Vienna, Austria, to establish a new monastery. Eventually, he was asked to live a penitential life as a hermit, in accordance with a local tradition in which a respected monk left the monastery to live alone. He spent the last twelve years of his life in this way, and the many miracles that resulted from his prayers made him famous throughout the countryside.

> *Saint Narcissus, help me recognize my weaknesses.*
> *Saint Zenobius, give me words of encouragement for*
> *Christians in danger of losing their faith.*
> *Saint Abraham, teach me your love of silence, that I might know the words*
> *that will bring others to repentance.*
> *Saint Theuderius, help me to pray.*

* * * * *

October 30

Saint Eutropia of Alexandria

During the persecution of the Church under the Roman emperor Valerian around the year 253, the martyr Eutropia died in the city of Alexandria, Egypt. According to tradition, she went to visit condemned Christians in prison to encourage them. The authorities recognized that she too was a Christian, so they arrested and tortured her to death.

Blessed Terrence Albert O'Brien

Terrence was born in Tower Hill, Ireland, in 1601. He became a Dominican priest and was the prior general for the Dominicans in Ireland, as well as bishop of Emly. When he was ordered to swear that the king of England was the head of the Church, he refused. He was executed on this date in 1651.

Saint Eutropia, help me find a way to encourage those who are in prison.
Blessed Terrence, help me always speak God's truth.

* * * * *

October 31

Saint Quentin

Quentin (d. 287) was the son of a Roman senator who converted to the Christian faith during the days of the early Church. He was sent as a missionary to Gaul (modern France) with Lucian of Beauvais, a priest who later died a martyr. Quentin's preaching and holy way of life brought many people to the faith. Because of his success, he was arrested by the prefect when the Roman emperor Maximus renewed the persecution of Christians in the empire. Quentin was tortured and beheaded. His relics have been in a church under his name for centuries in France—though it has been rebuilt multiple times.

Saint Wolfgang of Ratisbon

Wolfgang was born around the year 930 in Swabia, Germany, and was educated by Benedictine monks in Switzerland. He was a naturally talented and genuinely devout boy, and he rose to become the director of the abbey school. When his classmate and good friend Henry decided to move to Wurzburg, Wolfgang went with him. When Henry was made bishop of Trier, Wolfgang followed him there too. Wolfgang supported Henry's reforms of his diocese, and he became a lay teacher in the cathedral school there. After Henry died in the year 964, Wolfgang decided to become a Benedictine monk. He later became director of the monastery school and was ordained a priest. Wolfgang then became a missionary, preaching the Gospel to the Magyar people, with modest success.

However, he was soon given another important position: bishop of Ratisbon (now Regensburg, Germany). As bishop, Wolfgang lived a simple monastic life as much as possible, and he was a good administrator. He particularly encouraged charity toward the poor. He became ill while traveling down the Danube River, dying in the year 994.

Saint Alphonsus Rodriguez

Alphonsus was born around the year 1533 and was the third child of a well-to-do wool merchant living in Segovia, Spain. The preaching and example of a Jesuit priest, Saint Peter Faber, inspired him to want to live a holy life, and he and his brother studied under the Jesuits when Alphonsus was fourteen years old. But when his father died less than a year later, he had to leave school and take over the family business. At first, his mother assisted him, but when she retired, he managed the business on his own. He married when he was twenty-six years old, and the couple had a daughter and a son. But the daughter, his wife, and his mother all died within a span of a few years. Times were very difficult in Spain, and his personal tragedies led him to reconsider what God was calling him to do. He decided to sell his business and took his son to live with him and two maiden aunts. His aunts were pious women, and they taught him about mental prayer. When his son died, he asked to join the Jesuits. But he had poor health, he was almost forty years old, and he had a limited education. A friendly priest encouraged him to try to study Latin, so Alphonsus humbly learned Latin with little boys, worked as a servant, and even begged to support himself. In 1571, although some of the Jesuits opposed allowing Alphonsus to enter (probably because of his age and health), the Jesuit provincial overruled them. Alphonsus was made a temporal coadjutor (the Jesuit term for lay brother), became hall porter at the College of Montesione on Majorca, and served there until almost the end of his life. Everyone in the college came to love and respect Brother Alphonsus, who managed to balance the demands of constantly greeting visitors, students, and clergy while remaining habitually recollected and in a deep union with God. Alphonsus patiently endured both spiritual dry spells and ecstasies, and priests who knew him said they couldn't find a single fault in his words or actions in forty years. One of his most famous "pupils" was Saint Peter Claver, who became a famous missionary priest. In October 1617, Alphonsus knew his end was near. After he had received Holy Communion, his suffering ceased, and he spent two days in ecstasy, followed by a period of great agony. But his peace and composure returned at the end; he kissed his crucifix and called on the Holy Name of Jesus before he died.

> *Saint Quentin, show me how to suffer, that others might turn to Jesus Christ.*
> *Saint Wolfgang, help me to find holy friends who will lead me to Christ.*
> *Saint Alphonsus, teach me how to pray and be recollected at all times.*

November

November 1

All Saints' Day, Solemnity

From the fourth century, there have been various days commemorating groups of saints, celebrated in different regions. But in the year 835, Pope Gregory IV extended a solemnity to the entire Church on November 1 to celebrate the Church Triumphant in Heaven. Why? "Calling the saints to mind inspires, or rather arouses in us, above all else, a longing to join their company.... That we may rightly hope and strive for such blessedness, we must above all seek the prayers of the saints."[1]

Following are some saints who are specifically remembered by the Church, and who show the universality of the Church, on this date:

> **Saint Caesarius of Terracina** was a deacon who was imprisoned and then martyred because he publicly objected to the immorality of a pagan celebration of Apollo while he was traveling through Terracina, Italy, in the first few centuries after the death of Christ.
>
> **Saint Maturin** was born in France into a pagan family, converted to the faith when young, was ordained by Saint Polycarp (who died in the year 155), and became well known for his preaching, healing, and service as an exorcist, which is why he's now known as a patron for those who are mentally ill.
>
> **Saint Nuno de Santa Maria Alvares Pereira** was a career soldier and a hero for Portuguese independence; at his wife's death, he became a lay brother and was noted for his prayer, penance, devotion, and humility, dying in 1431.
>
> **Blessed Rupert Mayer** was a German priest who spoke out publicly against Nazism. He was arrested several times and spent almost two years in a concentration camp, but was released out of fear that his death would rally Catholics against the regime. He died in early 1945.
>
> **Blessed Theodore (Teodor) George Romzha** was a Greek rite Catholic priest in the Ukraine; he died a martyr by poisoning in 1947 for opposing Communist persecution of the Church.
>
> *All you saints, feed my zeal to become a saint.*

* * * * *

[1] *The Liturgy of the Hours*, vol. 4, from a sermon by Saint Bernard of Clairvaux (New York: Catholic Book Publishing, 1975), 1526–27.

November 2

All Souls' Day, Commemoration

In the year 988, on the initiative of the abbot of Cluny, Saint Odilo, a commemoration of all the faithful departed was celebrated on the day after All Saints' Day. This commemoration was officially adopted by the Church in the thirteenth century. In 1915, Pope Benedict XV gave all priests the privilege of offering three Masses on this day: one for the celebrant, one for the pope, and one for the faithful departed.

> *Eternal rest grant unto them, O Lord, / and let perpetual light shine upon them. / May they rest in peace. / Amen.*[2]

Saint Victorinus of Pettau

Victorinus was bishop of Pettau (modern Austria) and was martyred during the Roman emperor Diocletian's persecution of Christians in the year 303. Although he was the first Christian to write Latin expositions on the Scriptures and Saint Jerome admired his work, Victorinus also held an erroneous view that Christ would return and reign for a literal thousand years. Few of his writings have come down to us, perhaps because of concerns over his orthodoxy, but, by God's grace, he died a martyr.

Saint Marcian of Chalcedon

Marcian (d. 387) was born in Cyrrus of Syria, and his father was a member of the patrician class. Yet, Marcian left his well-born family to go live in the desert as a Christian hermit and built a cell for himself that was so narrow and low that he had to bend to stand or even lie in it. Even though he lived in the desert, his holiness was not hidden, and other men came to him for advice and to follow his example. He eventually became their abbot. When Marcian prayed, miracles happened, but he rejected all the attention he received as a wonder-worker. One day a man asked him to bless oil to be used to anoint his sick daughter, and Marcian refused—but the girl recovered at that same hour. Marcian lived to be very old, and several wealthy Christians built churches hoping to have his body as a relic when he died. He therefore asked a friend to bury him secretly when he died.

> *Saint Victorinus, help me stay rooted in God's truth and His Church.*
> *Saint Marcian, show me how to pray with faith*
> *in God's power to accomplish miracles.*

* * * * *

[2] Traditional Catholic prayer for the faithful departed.

November 3

Saint Martin de Porres, Optional Memorial

Martin was born in Lima, Peru, in 1579, and he was the illegitimate child of a freed black slave named Anna and a Spanish knight named John de Porres. De Porres acknowledged Martin and his sister as his children, but after a while, he essentially abandoned them, leaving them to the care of their mother. When Martin was twelve years old, he was apprenticed to a barber-surgeon and learned that trade. Three years later, he asked to be admitted as a Dominican tertiary, and he eventually became a professed Dominican lay brother. Martin personally cared for the sick, helped establish an orphanage and a foundling hospital, and cared for the slaves who had been brought to Peru from Africa. He was also an animal lover and kept a home for cats and dogs at his sister's house. Martin had an assistant, who later wrote about Martin and his acts of charity, describing his practicality in sowing herbs, his compassion in looking after those in need of material help, and his charity in begging for money for the poor. For example, he raised the money for his own niece's dowry in only three days by begging. Martin was a friend of the Dominican tertiary Saint Rose of Lima and the Dominican brother Blessed John Massias. He died on this date in 1639. Everyone had recognized his holiness even during his lifetime, and his body was carried to its grave by the most powerful men of Lima.

Saint Libertine of Agrigento

During the persecution of the Church in the Roman Empire in the third or fourth century, Libertine, the bishop of Agrigento, was executed. He was known for his excellent preaching, and a current cathedral is built on the same site as the one he built more than a millennium ago. In 1625, when a plague struck the town of Agrigento, the townspeople begged for his protection—and were heard by God.

Saint Joannicus of Mount Olympus

Born in Bithynia (modern Turkey) around the year 750, Joannicus was not a promising saint in his youth. He worked as a swineherd and then a professional soldier but was lazy and lived a wild life. But a friend became a monk, and that monk led him to conversion. Joannicus left everything behind when he was forty years old and became a hermit on Mount Olympus. His reputation for holiness spread, and he had to move a few times to escape men who wanted to be his disciples. At first, he had supported iconoclasm, but later he recognized the errors of prohibiting the use of icons in prayer, and he tried to make peace between those on both sides of the argument. He was friends with Saint Peter of Atroa, correctly predicted the end of the iconoclastic controversy, and worked miracles through his prayers. He died in the year 846 of natural causes.

My hope is the Father, my refuge is the Son, my shelter is the Holy Spirit.[3]

Saint Martin, teach me your compassion, humility, and wisdom.
Saint Libertine, show me how to build up the Body of Christ today.
Saint Joannicus, help me to be open to correction,
particularly in matters of faith and devotion.

* * * * *

November 4

Saint Charles Borromeo, Memorial

Charles was born in 1538. His father was Count Gilbert Borromeo, a noble, talented, and holy man; his mother, Margaret, was from the well-known and powerful Medici family. Charles was a serious and devout child, but he was also a slow student and suffered from a speech impediment. Soon after he earned a doctor's degree, both of his parents died, and his uncle was made pope. As Pope Pius IV's nephew, in keeping with papal tradition, Charles was named a cardinal and given many titles and positions within the Church, even though he was only twenty-two years old and had only received minor orders. Charles followed the practice of the times and maintained a large household in Rome, but he also did his best to reform the practice of the Catholic faith in the Archdiocese of Milan. When Pius IV reconvened the Council of Trent, Charles threw himself into the works of the council, and his diplomacy and support were pivotal in bringing the council to a successful end. At this point, one of Charles' relatives died, and he became the head of the family. Everyone assumed he would get married, but instead he resigned his family position, was ordained a priest, and was consecrated a bishop. Although he wasn't allowed to live in his diocese because he was needed in Rome, he was a true leader in the Catholic Counter-Reformation: he supervised the composition of the Catechism of the Council of Trent, reformed liturgical books and music, sent other people to work at the reform of his diocese, and implemented the decrees of the council as best he could. When Pius IV died, his successor, Pope Saint Pius V, offered to allow Charles to continue in his previous position, but Charles asked to serve the Church as Archbishop of Milan instead. After moving to Milan, Charles sold unnecessary goods of the archdiocese and gave the proceeds to the poor, implemented the council's decrees without favoring the rich and powerful, and established the Confraternity of Christian Doctrine for the education of children. A scandalous religious order called the Humiliati sent a priest to kill him,

---

[3] Prayer attributed to Saint Joannicus; see "Saint Joannicus of Mount Olympus", CatholicSaints.Info, June 13, 2018, https://catholicsaints.info/saint-joannicus-of-mount-olympus. For original prayer in Latin, see *Martyrologium Romanum*, Editio Altera (Libreria Editrice Vaticana, 2004).

but the assassin's bullet only shocked and bruised him. He corrected the practices of religious life in monasteries in the Alps and, during an outbreak of the plague, Charles even went into debt to provide help for those suffering from the sickness. Milan's leaders tried to make trouble for Charles with the pope, but the things they complained about were generally problems caused by their own inefficiency. Charles suffered from bad health, and the pope himself had warned him not to overdo his Lenten fasting. But in October 1584, having been bishop for eighteen years, he recognized that his end was near. He celebrated All Souls' Day Mass in Milan and died quietly in the night of November 3–4. He was forty-six years old.

Saints Vitalis and Agricola of Bologna

During the persecution of Christians under the Roman emperor Diocletian in the early fourth century, Agricola was a citizen of the city of Bologna, Italy, and Vitalis was his servant. But they were also great friends, and when Agricola became a Christian, Vitalis was baptized as well. Around the year 304, the two men were detected and arrested for being Christians. Some traditions say that Vitalis encouraged his friend and master while Agricola was being tortured; other traditions say that Vitalis was martyred first as part of the bloodthirsty Roman "games" and that Agricola was tortured afterward and then executed by crucifixion.

Saint Felix of Valois

Felix was born in 1127 into a noble family in Valois, France. When he was a young man, his parents divorced. Felix then decided to give up all his wealth and become a Cistercian monk. Later, he lived as a hermit and then a priest. He and his friend Saint John of Matha founded a religious order, called the Trinitarians, specifically to ransom those Christians who had been enslaved by Muslims in Spain and Africa. Within forty years, there were more than six hundred houses of Trinitarians in the world, seeking to serve those in chains. Felix died in 1212.

> *Saint Charles, show me how to put all the gifts God has given me*
> *completely at His service.*
> *Holy Martyrs, help me encourage my friends to be faithful to Christ.*
> *Saint Felix, show me how to help those who are enslaved today.*

* * * * *

November 5

Saint Bertilla

Bertilla was born during the seventh century in Soissons, France. She wanted to enter religious life from the time she was young. With the encouragement of Ouen, who was the bishop of Rouen and also known to us as a saint, Bertilla entered a monastery near Meaux and became a Benedictine nun. Later, she was sent by her abbess with several other nuns to establish an abbey at Chelles. The holy way of life she lived and taught to her nuns caused other holy, noble women to join her community, including Hereswitha, the widow of the king of the East Angles, and the widowed Queen Bathildis, who lived as a nun when she left the world behind. Bertilla lived a devout, penitential life into her old age, and when she died, she had governed her abbey for forty-six years. She died in 705.

Blessed Bernhard Lichtenberg

Bernhard (1875–1943) was a priest in Berlin, Germany, who served in the Berlin Cathedral. He was an outspoken critic of the Nazis, and he organized protests outside concentration camps, filed formal complaints against the racist views of the Nazi Party, and led public prayers for the Jews after Kristallnacht, a short, intense pogrom against Jews that destroyed lives and property. Bernhard was sent to prison for two years as a result of his protests, but he continued to oppose the Nazis after he was released. So the Nazis arrested him again and sent him to the Dachau concentration camp. He died in a cattle car on the way to the camp on this date.

Saint Bertilla, show me how to be holy in my vocation.
Blessed Bernhard, teach me how to be a voice for the voiceless.

* * * * *

November 6

Saint Paul of Constantinople

Paul (d. 350) was a priest and an assistant to the patriarch of Constantinople, Alexander. When Alexander died in the year 336, the city was split between Catholic and Arian sympathizers, each wanting a candidate who supported his position to be made the new patriarch. Eventually, Paul was chosen in the year 337. But when the Roman emperor Constantius II, who supported Arianism and had not been in the city during this time, returned to Constantinople, he angrily sent Paul into exile and forced his own Arian candidate, Eusebius of Nicomedia, into the position of patriarch. Paul took advantage of his time in exile to meet with Saint Athanasius of Alexandra, who had also been exiled from his archdiocese for opposing Arianism, as well as Pope Julius I. Paul repeatedly tried to return to Constantinople to regain his position and return the city to the true practice of the faith but was repeatedly sent into exile by the emperor. Finally, the emperor put him in prison, starved him, and then had him strangled, making him a martyr.

Saint Illtud (Illtyd) of Wales

Illtud (d. ca. 505) became a priest, a monk, and eventually the abbot at Llantwit in Glamorgan, Wales. Later traditions about his life tell us that before Illtud entered religious life he was both a married man and a knight. After being involved in a hunting accident that cost some of his friends their lives, he chose to leave the world behind. There were many pagans in Wales at the time, and he was persecuted by a local chieftain and had to hide in a cave. When there was a famine, he brought corn by ship to feed the hungry people, and he lived into old age. Illtud is one of the most beloved of all the Welsh saints.

Saint Leonard of Noblac

Leonard (d. 559) was a Frankish nobleman who was converted to the Catholic faith by the bishop of Rheims, Saint Remigius. When the king offered to make him a bishop, Leonard turned him down and instead went to live as a hermit in the forest near the city of Limoges in France. While the king and his pregnant queen were out hunting, the queen went into labor. They found Leonard's cell, and he prayed for her during her difficult labor. When both mother and baby were safe after childbirth, the king thanked him by giving him as much land as he could ride around on a donkey. Leonard rode all day to define the property lines of his gift from the king, and there he founded the Abbey of Noblac. Leonard and his monks preached the Gospel to the people all over the area. Leonard is now the heavenly patron both of women in labor and of prisoners of war because the king also promised that any prisoner Leonard converted to the faith would be released.

> *Saint Paul, help me to persevere when I face opposition.*
> *Saint Illtud, help me repent deeply.*
> *Saint Leonard, teach me how to win the favor of the King of Kings.*

* * * * *

November 7

Saint Herculanus of Perugia

Herculanus was the bishop of Perugia, Italy, when the pagan King Totila and his Goths captured the city in the year 549. By the king's orders, a thin slice of Herculanus' skin was pulled off of every part of his body. Thankfully, a pagan soldier pitied Herculanus and executed him by beheading before he died of this gruesome practice.

Saint Willibrord (Clement) of Echternach

At the age of seven, Willibrord (658–739) was sent to be educated at an English monastery directed by the bishop of York, Saint Wilfrid. When Willibrord was twenty years old, he went to Ireland and studied with Egbert and Wigbert (two monks who also became saints) for twelve years. After he was ordained to the priesthood, he was sent with eleven other English monks to evangelize northern Germany. In the year 690, they reached the city of Utrecht. The local leader, Pepin, gave them permission and encouragement to preach the Gospel in the region of Lower Friesland (modern Germany). Willibrord first went to

Rome to receive Pope Saint Sergius' permission to preach, and the optimistic pope also gave him relics to be used in the consecration of any churches he might establish. Willibrord and his companions brought many pagan people to faith in Jesus Christ, and he went to Rome in the year 695 to be ordained a bishop. Willibrord (though his name had been changed to Clement by the pope) returned as bishop of the diocese he had founded and built his cathedral in Utrecht. He tried to evangelize Upper Friesland and Denmark, but he was less successful with conversions there; one of his companions was killed and Willibrord himself narrowly escaped death in an attack. In the year 715, a political leader named Radbod took over regions of Friesland, and he destroyed churches, killed the Christian missionaries, and caused many to apostatize and return to paganism. Recognizing the dangers, Willibrord left the area, but when Radbod died in the year 719, he came back. By the time of his death at age eighty-one, Willibrord and his companions—including the man later named the Apostle of Germany, Saint Boniface—had brought the Gospel to Friesland, the Netherlands, and Holland.

Saint Engelbert of Cologne

Engelbert (d. 1225) was archbishop of Cologne, Germany, during violent times. Despite the constant political instability of the culture, he insisted that the priests and religious in his diocese follow clerical discipline and lead moral lives. He also led a crusade against the Albigensian heresy, which was common at the time. At one point, the pope excommunicated him because of false charges that he had threatened Emperor Otto IV with armed violence, but when that was disproven, the excommunication was lifted. Later, Engelbert publicly spoke out when Count Frederick of Isenberg, who happened to be his own cousin, was found to be stealing the land and goods of nuns in Essen. The count responded violently: fifty of his followers were sent to kill Engelbert. His martyred body was found covered with forty-seven wounds. He died on this date.

> *Saint Herculanus, show me how to suffer for Christ.*
> *Saint Willibrord, teach me to be patient in serving the Lord.*
> *Saint Engelbert, pray that the violence of this world*
> *will never deter me from speaking the truth.*

* * * * *

November 8

Saints Simpronian, Claudius, Nicostratus, Castorius, and Simplicius of Sirmium

These five brothers were Christian stone carvers in the early fourth century in Sirmium (modern Serbia) during the reign of the Roman emperor Diocletian. When they were ordered to carve a statue of Aesculapius, the Greek god of medicine, they refused. They were then ordered to make a sacrifice to the sun god, which they also refused to do. As a result, they were executed for the crime of being Christians by being tied up, fastened in lead boxes, and drowned in the river in the year 305. They are also known as the Holy Crowned Martyrs.[4]

Saint Deusdedit (Adeodatus I)

Deusdedit (d. 618) was the sixty-eighth pope; he reigned for almost three years. Because of the political instability in Rome at the time, his clergy were poor and in constant danger, but he supported them as best he could. He became widely respected for his heroic example in recovery efforts after a devastating earthquake and for his care for the sick during an outbreak of leprosy.

Saint Godfrey of Amiens

Godfrey was born in 1066 in Soissons, France, and was sent to the Benedictine abbey Mont Saint-Quentin to be educated when he was five years old. He later became a monk and priest. In time, his abbey sent him to repair the Abbey of Nogent—since both the abbey's buildings and the monks' practice of religious life needed to be fixed—and to serve as their abbot. Religious life at the monastery improved so dramatically that he was asked to take over as abbot of a larger monastery. Godfrey refused at first, saying, "God forbid I should ever desert a poor bride by preferring a rich one!"[5] When the king insisted he become bishop of Amiens, he resisted the honor but eventually gave in and was ordained a bishop, though he continued to live the simple, penitential life of a monk. For example, when he thought the cook was treating him too well, he gave away the best food to the poor. He was a just but severe shepherd, and he fought vigorously against the practice of simony and against those priests in his diocese who failed to practice clerical celibacy. His willingness to make hard decisions and enforce them made him very unpopular, and he considered resigning and becoming a simple Carthusian monk. He died during a journey to Soissons in 1115.

Blessed John Duns Scotus

John (1266–1308) was the son of a wealthy farmer, and he became a Franciscan Friar Minor at Dumfries, England, where his uncle happened to be the superior. He studied at Oxford and Paris and was ordained to the priesthood in 1291 when he was twenty-five years old. He was forced to leave France at one point because he took the pope's side in a disagreement between the pope and the French king over taxation of church property, but he was able to return in 1305 and receive his doctorate degree. John was a brilliant teacher and theologian: he brought together the best of the Augustinian and Franciscan theological traditions; the wisdom of Aristotle, Muslim philosophers, and Thomas Aquinas; and incorporated his own philosophical reflections. An entire school of scholastic

---

[4] Ancient traditions sometimes confuse these five brothers with four soldiers who were martyred together during Diocletian's reign, and they are sometimes called the Holy Four Crowned Martyrs.

[5] Michael Walsh, ed., *Butler's Lives of the Saints, Concise Edition, Revised and Updated* (San Francisco: HarperCollins Publishers, 1991), 368.

thought developed from his teachings and became known as Scotism. When Pope Pius IX solemnly defined the teaching of the Immaculate Conception of Mary six hundred years later, he used John Duns Scotus' arguments, in part, to do it.

> *Holy Martyrs, help me to recognize and reject the gods of my culture.*
> *Saint Deusdedit, help me to love and serve Christ and His Church.*
> *Saint Godfrey, show me how to confront immorality firmly but with charity.*
> *Blessed John, help me to understand and proclaim God's truth.*

* * * * *

November 9

The Dedication of the Lateran Basilica, Feast

The building of the world's first Catholic cathedral began in the year 315 under the Roman emperor Constantine, and it was consecrated by Pope Saint Sylvester I in the year 324 and dedicated to God in the name of our Savior. After surviving fires in Rome in the fourteenth century and being abandoned during the papal schism, when three men claimed to be pope and Rome was overcome by violent mobs, the church was rebuilt and dedicated to Saints John the Baptist and John the Evangelist in the sixteenth century. Saint John Lateran is the mother church of Rome, and it has hosted five ecumenical councils.

> *For we know that if the earthly tent we live in is destroyed, we have a building from God, a house not made with hands, eternal in the heavens.*[6]

Blessed George Napper

George was born in 1550 in Oxford, England. Because of the anti-Catholic laws of England at the time, he had to travel to France to be ordained a Catholic priest; when he returned to England in 1603, he wandered about the Oxfordshire countryside, ministering to Catholics secretly. His brother, William, put his own safety in jeopardy by letting George live with him. Eventually, he was suspected to be a priest and arrested while carrying items that made it clear that he was one: holy oils, a breviary, a reliquary, and a pyx containing consecrated Hosts. He was soon convicted, and when he served other Catholics in prison as a priest, he was treated as if he had committed yet another crime. He was offered exile rather than death if he would sign an oath of allegiance, but he refused. He was hanged, drawn, and quartered on this date in 1610.

Saint Elizabeth of the Trinity Catez

Elizabeth's father was a soldier, and she was born in a military camp in the Diocese of Bourges, France, in 1880. Her father died when she was only seven years

---

[6] 2 Cor 5:1.

old, and she and her sister were raised by their mother. Elizabeth was a popular girl and sometimes stubborn, but she was also reverent and attracted to private prayer. She became a gifted pianist, she taught the catechism to children, and she visited those who were sick. In 1901, despite her mother's opposition, she decided to enter the Discalced Carmelite monastery in Dijon, France. While in the monastery, her spiritual life deepened greatly, but she was also plagued by periods of darkness, and at one point her spiritual director even told her he doubted that she had a religious vocation at all. However, she prayed, persevered, and took final vows in 1903. She developed Addison's disease, a hormone disorder that caused her great pain and exhaustion. She died only a few years after becoming a nun in 1906. But the retreat guides and letters she wrote to those outside the monastery had made her an informal spiritual director to many people, who supported her cause for canonization after her death in 1906.

> *O my God, Trinity whom I adore, help me to forget myself entirely that I may be established in You as still and as peaceful as if my soul were already in eternity. May nothing trouble my peace or make me leave You, O my Unchanging One, but may each minute carry me further into the depths of Your Mystery.... O my Three, my All, my Beatitude, infinite Solitude, Immensity in which I lose myself, I surrender myself to You as Your prey. Bury Yourself in me that I may bury myself in You until I depart to contemplate in Your light the abyss of Your greatness.*[7]

> *Blessed George, show me how to live and die for Christ.*
> *Saint Elizabeth, help me to pray for a deeper understanding of the Holy Trinity.*

* * * * *

November 10

Saint Leo the Great (Leo I), Memorial

Leo was born around the year 400 in Rome. Although we know nothing of his early life, he clearly received a good education. He served as a deacon under two popes, Saints Celestine I and Sixtus III, and we know he was widely respected even at that point because (1) the archbishop of Alexandria, Saint Cyril, wrote directly to him and (2) the monk-saint John Cassian dedicated a treatise to him. In the year 440, Leo was sent to make peace between two feuding imperial generals. While he was away from Rome on this mission, the pope died, and Leo was elected pope to succeed him. After his consecration on September 29, 440, Leo preached systematically throughout the churches of Rome (we still have ninety-six of his sermons); wrote with obvious authority (we have 143 of his letters); and dealt with the heresy propagated by Eutyches, who rejected the

---

[7] Elizabeth of the Trinity, *The Complete Works*, vol. 1, trans. Sister Aletheia Kane, O.C.D. (Washington, D.C.: ICS Publications, 1984), 183–84.

teaching that Christ had both a human and divine nature. A group of bishops met together to show support for Eutyches, as well as his heretical teaching. This synod of bishops—known to history as the "Robber Synod" because it tried to steal the truth—acquitted Eutyches and condemned Flavian, the patriarch of Constantinople who opposed this false teaching about Christ. Their decision led to acts of violence, including the beating of Flavian, who died a martyr soon afterward. Pope Leo responded by sending his own delegates to a true council to settle the matter. Leo's letter to that council, called the *Tome of Leo*, so clearly explained the true teaching of the Church regarding the natures of Christ that the bishops accepted Leo's explanation and formally rejected the heresy. Just a few years later in 452, Attila the Hun invaded Italy and attacked many cities, but when he approached Rome, Leo and his clergy arranged a meeting. In a seemingly miraculous turn of events, the pagan Attila accepted a large payment from Rome instead of destroying the city. Three years later, another pagan army, the Vandals, came up to Rome to attack it, but this time Leo was only able to convince the Vandal chief to pillage the city and not kill all the inhabitants. After fifteen days of violence and destruction, the Vandals left, taking many people captive along with their booty. Leo organized people to repair the damage to Rome, sent priests and alms to help those who had been taken captive to Africa, and impressed everyone with his calm demeanor, despite the dangerous and difficult circumstances. Leo, having won the love and veneration of poor and rich, clergy and laity, Romans and barbarians, died in the year 461. The people proclaimed him "Leo the Great" almost immediately, and he's considered a Father of the Church. The Church proclaimed him a Doctor of the Church for his defense of the unity of Christ and protection of the unity of the Church.

> *[Speaking of the "field of the Lord":] With the grace of God "showering down from above," that field comes to be protected through faith, gets plowed through fasting, receives seed through almsgiving, and becomes fruitful through prayers. If we plant and water it in this manner, no bitter root will sprout, nor will any harmful shoots grow up. When every seed of vice has been wiped out, the blessed crop of virtues will become strong. Indeed, compassion encourages us to make this effort all the time.*[8]

Saint Andrew Avellino

Lancillotto (1521–1608) was born in Basilicata, Italy, was ordained a priest when he was twenty-six years old, studied law, and became an ecclesiastical lawyer. However, he told a lie during a heated argument in a trial for a friend. His repentance over that personal weakness and the holy example he saw in Jesuit priests that he knew led him to give up the practice of law. First, he began to live a penitential life as a priest. Then his archbishop sent him to reform a convent that was so undisciplined that it was creating a scandal. He succeeded in restoring celibacy and good order to the convent, but he was attacked and nearly killed at one point. On the night of the attack, he was taken to a house

---

[8] Leo the Great, *Sermons*, Sermon 14, trans. Jane Patricia Freeland, C.S.J.B., and Agnes Josephine Conway, S.S.J., Fathers of the Church Series, vol. 93 (Washington, D.C.: Catholic University of America Press, 1996), 55.

of the Theatine Clerks Regular, and he was so impressed with what he saw that he joined the order. He was then thirty-five years old, and he took the religious name of Andrew. In time, Andrew became master of novices and superior of the order, and he founded other Theatine houses in Italy. Through his eloquent preaching and spiritual direction, he brought many people back to the practice of their faith. He was also a writer and a friend of the holy cardinal, Saint Charles Borromeo. He suffered a stroke during Mass and died soon afterward.

Blessed Joaquin Pina Piazuelo

Joaquin was born at Caspes, Spain, in 1878 and became a member of the Hospitallers of Saint John of God. During the persecution of Catholics during the Spanish Civil War, he was executed. He died a martyr on this date in 1936 at the city of Barcelona.

Saint Leo, help me explain the faith to others.
Saint Andrew, teach me how to draw closer to God through repentance.
Blessed Joaquin, show me how to live and die for Christ.

* * * * *

November 11

Saint Martin of Tours, Memorial

Martin was born around the year 315 as the son of a pagan Roman army officer from the city of Sabaria (in modern Hungary), and, as the son of an officer, he was forced to enter the army when he was fifteen years old. Though he hadn't been baptized, he considered himself a Christian and lived a very simple life, more like a monk than a soldier. One day, while he was returning to town with his fellow soldiers on a winter day, he saw a poor man who was shivering and begging for alms. Everyone else ignored him, but Martin cut his cloak in two pieces and gave one piece to the man. That night, Martin dreamed that Jesus appeared to him and said, "Martin, yet a catechumen, has covered me with this garment."[9] Martin then "flew to be baptized",[10] as his disciple and biographer Sulpicius Severus wrote. Martin lived for five years as a soldier before he was ordered to fight. When he was ordered to participate in a battle against the barbarian invasion of Gaul, he refused. Though he was brought before the emperor himself, Martin continued to refuse to fight, although he offered to go before the enemy, but armed only with the name of Christ. He was imprisoned, but when an armistice was signed that ended the war, he was released. Martin went to Poitiers in France to study under the bishop of Poitiers, Saint Hilary, for a time, and then he returned to his home. He converted his mother to the faith

[9] Walsh, *Butler's Lives of the Saints*, 371.
[10] Ibid.

(but unfortunately not his father); he lived for ten years as a monk, and eventually became an abbot. Many people were converted by his words, and many people were healed by his prayers. The people of Tours loved him and wanted him to be their bishop. To trick him into accepting the office when their previous bishop died, they pretended a sick person was at church who needed Martin's help. When Martin showed up, they were able to convince him to accept. As bishop of Tours, Martin still lived the simple life of a monk, but he also preached throughout his diocese and attracted holy monks to the city. When the emperor decided that the appropriate punishment for heresy was execution, Martin spoke against it, preferring the relative leniency of excommunication. He died while traveling in a remote part of his diocese in the year 397, and he was the first person in the Church to be declared a saint who was not a martyr. He's also considered a Father of the Church.

Saint Mennas of Egypt

Mennas was born in 283 in Egypt to pious Christian parents, though Christianity was officially illegal at that time in the Roman Empire. Ancient traditions about his life vary, but they agree that he served as a soldier and then became a hermit, living his life alone with Christ. However, one day he boldly came to the brutal pagan games of the city and announced to everyone present that he was a Christian. He was quickly arrested, tortured, and beheaded for that crime in 309. Christians have called him a wonder-worker for centuries because of the miracles that have occurred as a result of his intercession.

Saint John the Almsgiver

John was born around the year 550 into a noble and rich family in Amathus, Cyprus. He married and had children, but after a time, they all died. He began to use his income to benefit the poor, and his reputation for personal holiness eventually caused him to be named the patriarch of Alexandria in Egypt. His first act was to ask for a list of his "masters". The poor, he said, were his masters because "they had such power in the court of Heaven to help those who had been good to them on earth."[11] He therefore gave away the gold found in the treasury when he was first consecrated to those in need, ordered the use of just weights and measures in Alexandria (protecting the poor from injustice), sat in front of his church twice a week to allow everyone to have access to him, and sent money, food, and workmen to rebuild Jerusalem after it had been plundered. He lived a very austere life himself, and when a wealthy friend learned that John had only one poor blanket, he gave John a very valuable one as a gift. John slept with it one night, but, reproaching himself all night for being in luxury while the poor had so little, he sold it the next day and gave the money to the poor. The friend found out, bought back the blanket, and gave it to him again. This happened three times, but John always replied with a smile. "We shall see who will get tired first."[12] When the governor proposed a tax,

[11] Ibid., 20.
[12] Ibid., 21.

John spoke against it in support of the poor. The governor was upset and left him in anger, but John sent him a letter in the afternoon that said, "The sun is going to set."[13] The biblical reminder that one should not "let the sun go down on your anger"[14] was effective, and the governor returned and apologized. At the end of his life, John traveled with the governor to Constantinople, but along the way John heard an interior warning from God that his end was near. He told the governor, "You invite me to the emperor of the earth; but the king of Heaven calls me to Himself."[15] He returned home and died at Amathus in the year 619.

Saint Marina of Omura

Marina was a Japanese woman who became a Dominican tertiary in 1626. She took the three vows of poverty, chastity, and obedience, and she risked her own life to shelter Catholic missionaries who were in hiding from a 1614 order banishing them from Japan. When she was found to be a Christian, she was arrested, fettered with chains, humiliated in a way designed to mock her chastity, and put to a slow death by fire at the stake in Nagasaki on this date in 1634.

Saint Martin, help me please Christ with acts of charity.
Saint Mennas, show me how to work wonders in a humble life lived for Christ.
Saint John, show me how I can serve the poor.
Saint Marina, help me be poor, chaste, and obedient.

* * * * *

November 12

Saint Josaphat (John) Kunsevich, Memorial

John was born around the year 1580 into a Catholic family in today's Ukraine. His father was a political leader (burgess) and wanted his son to become a merchant, but instead John spent his spare time learning the language spoken in church (Church Slavonic) so he could better participate in the liturgy. Jesuits encouraged him to consider religious life, and he became a monk in 1604, taking the name of Josaphat. He became a deacon and then a priest, always living an austere personal life. In that time and place, Orthodox Christians and Eastern rite Catholics lived side by side, and he yearned for reunion between the different Christian churches. When he became abbot in Vilna, he tried to

[13] Ibid.
[14] Eph 4:26.
[15] Walsh, *Butler's Lives of the Saints*, 21.

reform a nearby community of monks who were Orthodox (not Catholic) and who were living their monastic life in a very lax manner. Although the monks objected and even threatened his life, his attempt at reform ultimately increased good will between the Orthodox and Catholic believers in the area. He was made archbishop of Polotsk in 1617. The political situation between Orthodox and Catholics was turbulent, so this wasn't an easy job. He worked to improve the practice of religious life among priests and monks, though some of his priests had been married two or three times and even the monks were living decadent lives; he rebuilt churches that had been destroyed and preached the difficult truths of the Gospel to his people. In just a few years, the archdiocese was solidly Catholic again. However, at the same time, dissenting Christians attempted to set up their own church hierarchy, and the dissident "archbishop" sent to Polotsk spread lies that Josaphat wanted to turn Eastern rite Catholics into Roman rite Catholics. This led to violence, riots, and threats against Josaphat's life. In 1623, he traveled to the city of Vitebsk to respond to libelous claims made against him by a leader in that area, but a plot to trap him had already been set. As part of the plot, a priest named Elias insulted Josaphat and his Catholic faith to Josaphat's servants. After his servants had complained to Josaphat several times about the man's insults, Josaphat agreed to have the troublesome man arrested if he returned. When Elias returned, he was shut up in a room in the house. Josaphat's enemies seized this opportunity to call a mob together and demanded Elias' release. Josaphat released the man after he finished praying the Divine Office, but the mob broke into the house. When Josaphat approached them, they beat him with a halberd, shot him, and threw his body into the river.

Blessed John Cini

John (1353–1433) was a married man living in Pisa, Italy, when he underwent a profound conversion. Some say his conversion was a result of his repentance over participating in a sacrilegious attack on priests while serving as a soldier, while others say it was because he survived an incident as a soldier when most of his fellow soldiers were killed. Whatever the true cause, John became a Franciscan tertiary and gave his life over to prayer, penance, and works of mercy. He lived as a simple hermit near Pisa's Gate of Peace, so he's sometimes called John of Peace, receiving Holy Communion through a small window in his cell. He also founded the Franciscan Tertiary Hermits, a penitential confraternity of hermits, and a charitable institution that served the poor.

Saint Didacus of Alcala

Didacus was born in 1400 in Seville, Spain. He felt attracted to the solitary life when he was still young and became a hermit. He later became a Franciscan lay brother and was sent to be a missionary in the Canary Islands. He expected to die a martyr there, but instead he became the superior of his community, bringing about many conversions by his holy way of life and preaching. Didacus was sent to Rome in 1450, and during an epidemic, he healed many people through simple service as well as his prayers. After returning to his community in Alcala, he lived a prayerful, peaceful life. He died in 1463.

Blessed John, help me repent of my sins and amend my life.
Saint Didacus, show me how to live a prayerful life.
Saint Josaphat, teach me how to respond to hatred with peace.

* * * * *

November 13

Saint Nicholas I

As pope, Nicholas (d. 867) was noted for his generosity to the poor, his courage in confronting immorality and injustice regardless of rank, and his decisiveness in dealing with scandals within the Church. For example, he maintained a list of the blind and disabled to whom he sent food daily. He also deposed two French bishops and threatened others when they caved to the French king's demands that he be allowed to divorce his wife and marry his mistress. His response in the year 866 to the king of Bulgaria became a major document of papal teaching, in which he explained the doctrine of marriage as being effected solely by the mutual consent of the man and woman. He also condemned torture. Nicholas was also known to be humble, patient, and devoted to the liturgy and fasting.

Saint Abbo of Fleury

Abbo (945–1004) was a Benedictine monk from France who was educated in Paris, Rheims, and Orleans. He became a great scholar, writing about astronomy, grammar, philosophy, mathematics, canon law, and theology. He was also an administrator and teacher at an abbey school in England. He became abbot of Fleury in the year 988, and he brought the Cluniac observance of monastic life—that is, a greater emphasis on beautiful liturgies and monastic education—to his monks. When some disputed his election as abbot, the matter was settled by the bishop—a man who later became Pope Sylvester II. Abbo became an ambassador to the pope, a promoter of the rights of monks, and a peacemaker in the political disputes between Pope Gregory V and King Robert the Pious of France. He also reassured Christians of God's love when many were afraid that the end of the world was coming as the year changed to 1000. On November 13, 1004, while he was trying to restore discipline in a monastic community in Gascony, a riot broke out, and he was stabbed in the side with a lance. Since he was killed trying to bring peace, he's considered a martyr. Miracles were reported at his tomb.

Saint Frances (Mary Francesca) Xavier Cabrini, Memorial[16]

Mary Francesca was born in 1850, one of thirteen children in a farming family at Sant' Angelo Lodigiano in Italy. She was educated by her strict sister, and

---

[16] This saint is celebrated as a memorial in the *Liturgical Calendar for the Dioceses of the United States of America.*

she was a good student. She wanted to become a missionary, but her parents decided she should become a schoolteacher instead, and she duly passed her teaching exams. After her parents died in 1870, she lived for two years with her sister Rosa while she tried to enter two religious congregations. Both refused her, thinking her poor health would be an impediment to religious life. The priest in whose school she was teaching was so impressed with her, however, that he put her in charge of reforming a religious community that was running an orphanage. For several years, Frances faced personal abuse and many difficulties. The foundress of the orphanage resented her, was running the orphanage poorly, and appears to have been mentally unbalanced. But Frances persevered, and gradually women began to follow her example. In 1880, the bishop gave up his hope of reforming the community, and Sister Frances and her seven followers left and founded their own community. She wrote up the Rule for the Missionary Sisters of the Sacred Heart, and in it she explained their work of providing a Christian education for girls. Her community quickly grew to include many foundations in Italy. When it was first suggested that she and her nuns go to America to help the priests there with Italian immigrants, she refused. The archbishop of New York formally invited her, but it wasn't until the pope himself told her to go west, not east, that she and six sisters traveled to America. When they arrived in 1889, there was no place for them to stay because their living arrangements had fallen apart while the sisters were traveling to America. The archbishop told her to return to Italy, but Frances firmly told him that the pope had sent her to America, and there she would stay. Within just a few weeks, she reconciled the archbishop with the countess who had withdrawn her support and started a modest home for orphans. Mother Cabrini, over time, founded orphanages and schools all over the world. She had a difficult time understanding the faith of non-Catholic Christians (whom she encountered for the first time in America), and she refused to take illegitimate children in her fee-paying schools. But she was an excellent leader and a woman of great charity. Her initial eight nuns multiplied to over a thousand in more than fifty foundations by the time her congregation was approved in 1907. Her health failed in the last six years of her life, but she died suddenly, without anyone present, at her convent in Chicago on December 22, 1917. She was the first American citizen to be canonized.

> *Saint Nicholas, teach me your Christlike decisiveness.*
> *Saint Abbo, help me to be a peacemaker.*
> *Saint Frances, teach me to serve others with the charity of Christ.*

* * * * *

November 14

Saint Laurence O'Toole

Laurence (1128–1180) was the son of an Irish chieftain. He was captured during a raid by a neighboring tribe when he was ten years old, and after being treated poorly for two years, he was released when his father threatened to retaliate. At the age of twenty-five, he was made abbot of Glendalough. He escaped being made a bishop as well as abbot only because he pointed out the rules that required a bishop to be at least thirty years old. He governed his monastic community prudently, helped the people in the countryside during a famine, and patiently bore false accusations from other Christians. When he was made archbishop of Dublin in 1161, he immediately began to work to improve the discipline of his clergy. He continued to live like a monk, fed the poor at his own table, and preached often. When political tensions between the English king Henry II and the Irish kings flared up, Laurence served as peacemaker. During a trip to Rome, Pope Alexander III was pleased with Laurence's proposals to protect the Church in Ireland and remedy political disorders, and he gave Laurence greater authority and support. When Laurence began exercising this new power even before he had returned to Ireland, however, King Henry became nervous and refused to let him come back. After a few weeks, Laurence sought out the king, met with him, and received permission to return. But Laurence fell ill on his return journey, and he died on this date.

Saint Serapius of Africa

Serapius was born in 1179 and was the son of a captain in the court of King Henry II of England. He went on a Crusade, survived a shipwreck, and was taken hostage. But eventually he was able to return to England and became a courtier in the king's court. In 1221, he met Saint Peter Nolasco, the priest who founded the Order of Our Lady of Ransom, which sought to free Christians enslaved by Muslims. Serapius joined the order, and in 1240, when he was in Algeria trying to free slaves, he was captured, tortured, and then killed.

> *Saint Laurence, show me how to bring the peace of Christ to everyone I meet.*
> *Saint Serapius, show me how to free those in slavery around me.*

* * * * *

November 15

Saint Albert the Great, Optional Memorial

Albert was born in 1206 in Swabia (Germany) of the noble Bollstadt family. Though he was an ideal student during his studies at the University of Padua in Italy, he was also fascinated by the natural world, which he studied through hunting, fishing, and exploring. As a young man, he decided to become a Dominican. Though his uncle tried to discourage him and his father threatened to kidnap him if he tried, Albert entered anyway. His father apparently later cooled off. Albert received a master's degree, became a teacher at various schools of the Dominican order, and was regent at Cologne, where Thomas Aquinas became his student. He was always busy with his duties as a scholar, scientist, and teacher, but he was also devout in his duties as a Dominican priest. An excellent scientist who used reason and verified his conclusions through experimentation, Albert wrote extensively on many subjects, such as astronomy, geography, physics, chemistry, biology, mineralogy, and botany, and his works were used by scholars for centuries. But it was his use of Aristotle's philosophy to bring order to the study of theology that was his greatest contribution. The mendicant orders were controversial at the time, as well as daring to use the writings of the pagan Aristotle, and Albert was called on many times to defend both the Dominican order and his work. He was provincial general for his order at one point, and he served as the pope's personal theologian and canonist when he was in Rome. He was ordained bishop of Cologne, and although he resigned two years later, he continued to ordain priests and bless churches for the Dominican order. As all Dominicans are called to do, he preached the Gospel, and his sermons and writings on the Mass, the Eucharist, and the Blessed Virgin strongly influenced his own and later generations of priests. In his later years, he wrote and taught in relative peace until he was called to a general council in Lyons, France, in 1274. There he defended the teachings of his student Thomas Aquinas, who had recently died. In 1278, his memory failed while he was giving a lecture. His memory loss became serious, but he died two years later, sitting peacefully in his chair among his brothers in Cologne, who sang the Salve Regina for his soul when they recognized that the great Friar Albert had passed on. Some estimate that his writings total an incredible twenty million words. The only saint of the Church surnamed "the Great" because of his scholarly works,[17] Albert was also named a Doctor of the Church in 1931.

> *The procedure for someone teaching the things of God is to seek by prayer the gift of that truth about the things of God which is to be passed on to others, because any theological business has to begin with prayer.*[18]

Saint Leopold of Babenberg

Leopold (1073–1136) was from a noble family, and he succeeded his father as Margrave (military governor) of Austria when he was twenty-three years old. Ten years later, he married Agnes, who was the widowed daughter of the emperor Henry IV and the mother of two children. Leopold and Agnes had eighteen more children, although seven didn't survive childhood. He was a good leader and a good Christian man. He arranged an agreement that brought an end to the fight over royal versus ecclesiastical investiture (the conferring of ecclesiastical offices by political leaders, sometimes to unworthy candidates), and he defended his country against neighboring countries when it was needed. He humbly refused the offer to be made Holy Roman Emperor, and he founded monastic houses. Some say he died in a hunting accident, while others say he died of natural causes.

---

[17] Christopher Rengers, O.F.M. Cap., and Matthew E. Bunson, K.H.S., *The 35 Doctors of the Church*, rev. ed. (Charlotte, N.C.: TAN Books, 2014), 339.

[18] Albert the Great, "Dionysius' Mystical Theology", in *Albert and Thomas: Selected Writings*, trans. Simon Tugwell, O.P. (New York; Mahwah, N.J.: Paulist Press, 1988), 141.

Blesseds Hugh Faringdon, John Eynon, and John Rugg

Hugh Faringdon was abbot at Reading, a royal chaplain, a member of Parliament, and a friend of King Henry VIII of England (r. 1509–1547). John Eynon was a Benedictine monk and priest at Reading, England. John Rugg was a priest, a fellow at two colleges, and a Benedictine monk at Reading. Although all three men were condemned of other charges as well—Faringdon, for refusing to surrender his abbey to non-Catholic authorities; Eynon, for refusing to surrender his parish to the same; and Rugg, for refusing to give up a relic of Saint Anastasius—all three were ultimately condemned and martyred for the crime of denying Henry to be the head of the Church. The three men were brutally executed on this date in 1539.

Saint Raphael (Joseph) Kalinowski

Joseph (1835–1907) was the son of a prominent math professor in Vilna (modern Lithuania), and although he felt a call to the priesthood, he decided to pursue scientific studies instead. He became an officer in the Russian Military Engineering Corps, and in his duties, he planned and supervised the construction of a railway. He resigned from the Russian army to support the Polish uprising against the Russians; the Russians therefore arrested him and condemned him to death. But to avoid making him a political martyr, they changed his sentence to ten years of forced labor in the Siberian salt mines. When he survived and was released from this brutal punishment in 1873, they refused to let him return to his homeland. So he moved to Paris and worked as a tutor. At this point, he finally responded to God's call, joined the Carmelites, took the name Raphael, and was ordained a priest. As a priest, he worked to restore the Discalced Carmelite order to Poland, he encouraged unity between Christians, and he spent many, many hours serving his flock in the confessional.

> *Saint Albert, teach me God's wisdom.*
> *Saint Leopold, help me be holy in my vocation.*
> *Holy Martyrs, help me to be always faithful to Christ and His Church.*
> *Saint Raphael, show me how to unite my sufferings to Christ.*

* * * * *

November 16

Saint Margaret of Scotland, Optional Memorial

Margaret was born around the year 1046 and was the daughter of an English king. She and her family escaped from the dangers of the invasion of William the Conqueror by fleeing to the court of the king of Scotland, Malcolm. Margaret was both beautiful and good, and she and King Malcolm were married in 1070 when she was twenty-four years old. Margaret's influence not only improved her husband, who became one of the most virtuous Scottish kings ever to rule, but she improved the entire country by promoting the arts, education, and the faith. She and Malcolm were blessed with six sons and two daughters, and she personally taught them each about their Catholic faith. Despite being the queen, Margaret lived austerely—eating and sleeping very little—and she cared for the poor. In 1093, she was sick and confined to bed when she received the terrible news that her husband and her son Edward had been killed in battle. She died four days later on this date, and she was buried in the Abbey Church of Dunfermline, which she and Malcolm had founded.

Saint Gertrude the Great, Optional Memorial

Gertrude (1256–1302) was raised and educated in a Cistercian abbey in Saxony (Germany) from the time she was five years old. She heard God's call to religious life and became a Benedictine nun. One day, our Lord appeared to her in a vision and rebuked her for being more attached to philosophy than she was to Him. From that moment, she devoted herself to studying the Bible and Church Fathers. She wrote down her visions and experiences, and her writing about the importance of devotion to the Sacred Heart of Jesus is one of her more notable works. Her intelligence and deep piety earned her the title of Gertrude the Great.

> *O Sacred Heart of Jesus, fountain of eternal life, Your Heart is a glowing furnace of Love. You are my refuge and my sanctuary. O my adorable and loving Savior, consume my heart with the burning fire with which Yours is inflamed. Pour down on my soul those graces which flow from Your love. Let my heart be united with Yours. Let my will be conformed to Yours in all things. May Your Will be the rule of all my desires and actions. Amen.*[19]

Saints Augustinus and Felicitatis of Capua

During the persecution of the Church under the Roman emperor Decius around the year 250, the martyrs Augustinus and Felicitatis died in the city of Capua, Italy.

> *Saint Margaret, pray for me to be a living image of Christ to my family.*
> *Saint Gertrude, show me how to live in the Sacred Heart of Jesus.*
> *Saints Augustinus and Felicitatis, show me how to live and die for Christ.*

* * * * *

November 17

Saint Elizabeth of Hungary, Memorial

Elizabeth (1207–1231) was a princess of Hungary, and her parents, the king and queen, betrothed her to Ludwig, the future landgrave (ruler) of Thuringia (modern Germany), when she was four years old. She was sent to live in the

---

[19] Prayer to the Sacred Heart is widely attributed to Gertrude the Great.

Thuringian court, and she and Ludwig were married in 1221 when she was fourteen years old. Not only was she happy in her marriage and blessed with three children, but Ludwig supported her acts of charity, which included building a hospital and (on one occasion) putting a leper in her own bed to be cared for. When Ludwig was on his way to serve in a Crusade, he died of the plague. Elizabeth grieved so deeply that she said she felt the world had died to her, and she to the world. Her brother-in-law succeeded her husband as landgrave, and he soon decided to throw her and her three children out of the castle. Turned from queen into a beggar, forced to beg for food and shelter for herself and her children, she accepted the humiliation and poverty without resentment. She became a Third Order Franciscan and continued to care for people who were suffering. She died within two years of Ludwig's death.

Saint Gregory Thaumaturgus

Gregory was born into a wealthy pagan family living in Neocaesarea (a city now in Turkey) during the third century; he studied under the famous Christian teacher and Father of the Church Origen and later became the bishop of his hometown. Nicknamed "Thaumaturgas", or "Wonder-worker", because of the power of his prayers to work literal miracles, Gregory was also admired for the orthodoxy of his teaching and his effectiveness in explaining the faith to others. He served as bishop for thirty years, and, on his deathbed, he thanked God that though there had been only seventeen Christians in the whole town when he was made a bishop, there were only seventeen pagans left at his death. He died around the year 270.

Saint Gregory of Tours

Gregory was born into a noble French family around the year 538. He went on a pilgrimage to the city of Tours to pray for the healing of an illness, and the people there were so struck by his obvious piety that they chose him to be their bishop. He took the name Gregory, and he became well known for his intelligence as a historian and a writer. He also built many churches. He was respected by his contemporary, Pope Saint Gregory the Great, and died of natural causes in 594. He's considered a Father of the Church.

Saint Lazarus Zographos

Lazarus (d. 867) was a monk at Constantinople and a skilled painter. He opposed the heresy of iconoclasm and restored sacred images that iconoclasts had defaced. He was therefore arrested and tortured, but he was released when iconoclasts fell from power. Lazarus eventually became an ambassador to Rome and died of natural causes.

Saints Jordan (Hyacinth) Ansalone and Thomas Hioji Nishi Rokuzaemon

Jordan was born in 1598 in Italy, became a Dominican priest, and traveled to the Philippines and Japan to serve as a missionary. Thomas was born in Hirado,

Japan, in 1590. He became a Dominican priest and served as a missionary to his fellow countrymen, bringing the Gospel to Formosa and then Japan. When government persecution of Christianity intensified, they were both arrested for being Catholic priests, tortured, and martyred on this date in 1634.

Saint Elizabeth, teach me how to rejoice whether I have few comforts or many.
Saint Gregory Thaumaturgus, show me how to speak the truth and
pray with God's power.
Saint Gregory of Tours, help me to expect God in the unexpected.
Saint Lazarus, help me to draw closer to God through sacred art.
Holy Martyrs, show me how to live and die for Christ.

* * * * *

November 18

Dedication of the Basilicas of Saints Peter and Paul, Optional Memorial

Great basilicas in honor of Saint Peter and Saint Paul were built in the city of Rome during the time of the Roman emperor Constantine in the fourth century. Though these two basilicas have been rebuilt more than once, Christians have been praying before the relics of these two great apostles for centuries out of love for their love for Christ.

> *So then you are no longer strangers and sojourners, but you are fellow citizens with the saints and members of the household of God, built upon the foundation of the apostles and prophets, Christ Jesus himself being the cornerstone, in whom the whole structure is joined together and grows into a holy temple in the Lord; in whom you also are built into it for a dwelling place of God in the Spirit.*[20]

Saint Odo of Cluny

Odo was born around the year 879 and came from a noble family in France. He became a canon in Tours and studied music and theology in Paris. One day, he read the Rule of Saint Benedict and was so struck by his failure to live up to its demands that he left to become a monk at Cluny, taking his library of a hundred books with him. It was the year 909. When he was forty-eight years old, he became the abbot of Cluny, and it's said that he ruled his monks with great firmness. In time, his personal holiness and strong leadership in monastic discipline kindled a desire for monastic reform that swept all over Europe. The pope himself called on Odo to reform monastic houses, as well as negotiate peace between warring leaders. Odo died at a monastery at Tours while returning from Rome in 942.

---

[20] Eph 2:19–22.

Saint Rose Philippine Duchesne, Optional Memorial[21]

Rose was born in 1769 into a prosperous family in Grenoble, France, and was well educated. She joined the Visitation order of nuns when she was seventeen years old, but the outbreak of the anti-Catholic French Revolution and the resulting closing of convents caused her and the other nuns to be sent home. Rose quietly served the sick, children, and prisoners during this time, and she tried to reestablish her convent of Visitation nuns after the revolution had ended. But the remaining nuns were too old, so she considered founding a new order. Then she met Mother Madeleine-Sophie Barat, and, in 1804, she became a novice in Mother Barat's Society of the Sacred Heart. In 1818, she was sent to be the superior of a new community located in New Orleans in America. Rose had long desired to be a missionary, but the reality of life among the natives—and the difficulties of learning English—made this a difficult task for her and her nuns. The nuns were gradually able to expand their work, despite difficult journeys, illnesses, and other misunderstandings. (For example, her letters to Mother Barat were confiscated by a superior for two years without her knowledge.) Rose died on this date in 1852, known and loved by all for her holiness.

Blessed Karolina Kozkowna

Karolina was born in 1898, the fourth of eleven children in a family in Wal-Ruda, Poland. She was a pious girl who taught the catechism to other children and loved to pray the Rosary. In 1914, at the age of sixteen, she refused the advances of a Russian soldier, who then kidnapped her, dragged her into the forest, attempted to rape her, and stabbed her multiple times when she resisted. Her body was found on December 4, sixteen days later.

> *Saint Odo, help me be an example of holiness to others.*
> *Saint Rose, help me to persevere in my difficulties for the sake of Jesus Christ.*
> *Blessed Karolina, teach me purity and forgiveness.*

* * * * *

November 19

Prophet Obadiah

Obadiah lived and wrote after the conquest of Jerusalem by the Babylonian king Nebuchadnezzar II around the sixth century B.C. His short collection of writings predicts the coming of the Messiah and shows that he was familiar with the liturgy of the Jerusalem Temple, leading some people to think he was a Jewish priest. He was a prophet of hope in a time of disaster.

---

[21] This saint may be celebrated as an optional memorial in the *Liturgical Calendar for the Dioceses of the United States of America.*

The house of Jacob shall be a fire, and the house of Joseph a flame, and the house of Esau stubble.... Saviors shall go up to Mount Zion to rule Mount Esau; / and the kingdom shall be the LORD's.[22]

Saint Barlaam of Antioch

Barlaam was a simple, illiterate day laborer who lived near Antioch, a city in modern Turkey. During the persecution of Christians under the Roman emperor Diocletian in 304, he was brought before a judge and refused to renounce his Christian faith even when he was tortured. He endured being whipped and then being stretched on a rack until his bones were dislocated. When he still refused to renounce his faith in Christ, the judge tried to trick Barlaam. He thought Barlaam was uneducated and therefore unintelligent, so he brought him out from prison, had a fire to pagan gods lit on an altar, put incense in Barlaam's hand, and had Barlaam's hand placed in the flames. Rather than drop the incense into the fire and unintentionally offer sacrifice to the gods, Barlaam held his hand steady and left it in the flames until his hand was severely burned. He was then taken away and executed.

Saint Mechtilde of Helfta

Mechtilde was born around the year 1241 into a powerful but pious family of Thuringia (modern Germany). She was educated by nuns and later decided to become one herself. She first entered a monastery in Switzerland but then moved to the monastery in Helfta where her older sister was the abbess. By God's grace, she became a mystic and served her community by being novice mistress. One of her novices was the future saint Gertrude the Great, who wrote a book about Mechtilde's mystical teachings on grace. The nuns, laypeople, and even Dominican priests sought out her spiritual advice, and her prayers resulted in miracles, including the cure of a blind nun. She died on this date in 1298.

> *Prophet Obadiah, give me your hope in God.*
> *Saint Barlaam, help me be an unwavering witness to Christ.*
> *Saint Mechtilde, help me to pray deeply and draw close to God.*

* * * * *

November 20

Saint Edmund the Martyr

Edmund was born around the year 841 and was fourteen years old when he was crowned king of Norfolk (England) in the year 855. He became a successful ruler, but he was also a virtuous man who in his private life learned the

---

[22] Obad 18, 21.

Divine Office by heart so he could better participate in liturgical worship. In the year 866, the Danes invaded England, made peace with the East Angles, and began plundering and burning the countryside. In the year 870, Edmund's army fought against the Danes, and he was killed. Some say he was tortured and offered peace terms if he would renounce his Christian faith first.

Blessed Maria Fortunata (Anna Felicia) Viti

Anna Viti was born in Veroli, Italy, in 1827. Her father was a gambler and drinker, and her mother died when she was fourteen years old. She raised her eight siblings herself, working as a servant to support them. When she was twenty-four years old, she was able to leave them and join the Benedictines, taking the name Maria Fortunata. She couldn't read or write, so she never held a position of authority in the monastery and only performed simple tasks such as spinning, sewing, mending, and washing. However, the other nuns and the surrounding community knew and loved her for her humility, happy demeanor, and constant prayers. She spent seventy years living as a Benedictine nun and had a great devotion to the Blessed Sacrament. After her death in 1922, miracles resulted from prayers for her intercession.

Saint Edmund, show me how to lay down my life for my friends.
Blessed Maria, help me to accept the lowest chores in my family with cheerfulness.

* * * * *

November 21

The Presentation of Mary, Memorial

According to tradition, Mary was presented in the Temple in Jerusalem by her parents when she was three years old, following the tradition of the prophet Samuel.

And when [Hannah] had weaned [Samuel], she took him up with her, along with a three-year-old bull, an ephah of flour, and a skin of wine; and she brought him to the house of the LORD at Shiloh; and the child was young. Then they slew the bull, and they brought the child to Eli. And she said, "Oh, my lord! As you live, my lord, I am the woman who was standing here in your presence, praying to the LORD. For this child I prayed; and the LORD has granted me my petition which I made to him. Therefore I have lent him to the LORD; as long as he lives, he is lent to the LORD."[23]

Saint Agapius of Caesarea

During the persecution of the Church under the Roman emperor Diocletian in the year 306, the martyr Agapius died in Caesarea (in modern Israel). According

---

[23] 1 Sam 1:24–28.

to tradition, Agapius was arrested three times for being a Christian but was mercifully released. However, on the fourth arrest, he was left in prison for two years. He was then told he would be released if he renounced his faith in Christ; he refused and was martyred.

Saint Gelasius I

Gelasius (d. 496) was the son of an African immigrant. As a priest in Rome, he served as a secretary to two popes before being elected pope himself in the year 492; he reigned only four years. As pope, he compiled a list of saints and martyrs, created a compendium of important decrees from past Church synods, opposed the schismatic teachings of the patriarch Acacius and the heresies of Manichaeism, and wrote liturgical sacramentaries for use in the Church. He spoke out against the popular practice of Christians still celebrating pagan festivals, and he allowed Holy Communion to be received by the people under both species, the bread and the wine, in certain circumstances. He was also involved in a dispute with the patriarch of Constantinople over papal supremacy over the cities of Alexandria and Antioch.

Blessed Mother, present me to your Son.
Saint Agapius, help me bear crosses for the sake of Christ.
Saint Gelasius, give me your boldness in speaking the truth of the Good News.

* * * * *

November 22

Saint Cecilia (Cecily) of Rome, Memorial

Cecilia was born into a patrician (noble) family in Rome (probably in the third century) during the days of the underground Church. She was a devout Christian, and she lived a penitential life; for example, she fasted and wore coarse clothes rather than fancy ones. She also decided to remain a virgin for Christ, but her parents had other plans. They arranged for her to marry a young man, also from the patrician class, named Valerian. On their wedding night, Cecilia explained to Valerian about the vow of chastity she had made, told him that she saw angels around her, and told him the angels would protect her virginity. He asked to see the angels, and she told him that he would be able to see them if he was baptized. He agreed and was baptized by the pope. Then he saw the angels. Soon afterward he converted his brother to the Christian faith, and the two young men began performing other good works and burying the bodies of Christian martyrs. They were eventually arrested, died as martyrs, and were buried by Cecilia. When Cecilia herself was brought before the authorities and told to renounce her faith in Christ, she instead converted those who came to convince her, and Pope Urban is said to have baptized four hundred people she had converted when he visited her home. Cecilia was brought before the prefect a second time for the crime of being a Christian, and this time he condemned her to die (a noble death) by suffocation in her bath. However, although the room was heated as ordered, they found Cecilia was still alive seven days later. When a soldier was sent into the room to behead her, he was somehow only able to wound her. She was left on the floor of the bath, and there she bled to death, dying three days later. When her tomb was opened in the nineteenth century, witnesses found her body to be incorrupt after sixteen centuries. Cecilia is the patroness of music for various reasons: she sang a song in her heart as she prayed to God, and it's said that the pipes of her bath whistled.

Saint Philemon of Colossae

One of the shortest books of the Bible was written to Philemon; the Apostle Paul wrote to him to ask him to accept (and not punish) a runaway slave named Onesimus. Tradition says that Philemon was converted by Saint Paul himself, lived in Colossae (now in modern Turkey)—and that he freed Onesimus. Tradition also says that he was stoned to death for being a Christian in the first century.

Blessed Salvatore Lilli and Companions

Eight Franciscan friars were living in the Mujuk-Dersi region of Armenia (modern-day Turkey) in the late nineteenth century: Salvatore Lilli, Baldji Ohannès, Khodianin Kadir, Kouradji Tzeroum, Dimbalac Wartavar, Ieremias Boghos, David Oghlou, and Toros David. One of them, Salvatore, was born in Italy, became a Franciscan, and served as a missionary in Jerusalem and then Armenia. He preached the Gospel to the people in this region of Armenia, helped build schools and clinics for them, taught them about modern hygiene and sanitation methods to improve the health conditions of villagers living in remote areas, and cared for the sick during a cholera epidemic. When Islamic Turks invaded this area of Armenia in 1895, the eight men were captured and tortured. When the Muslims demanded that the men convert to Islam, they refused and were executed.

> *Saint Cecilia, show me how to praise God with my life.*
> *Saint Philemon, help me to forgive those who betray me.*
> *Holy Martyrs, give me your courage in suffering for Christ.*

* * * * *

November 23

Saint Clement I, Optional Memorial

Clement was the fourth pope (d. 97); he reigned for nine years. His letter to the Corinthians is said to have been written at about the same time as some books of the New Testament, and he's considered a Father of the Church. According to tradition, Clement was exiled and sent to work in the mines for the crime of being a Christian and the pope, and he was executed by being thrown from a ship with an anchor around his neck.

Lord, we entreat you to help us. Come to the aid of the afflicted, pity the lowly, raise up the fallen, show your face to the needy, heal the sick, convert the wayward, feed the hungry, deliver the captives, support the weak, encourage the fainthearted. Let all nations know that you alone are God; Jesus Christ is your Son and we are your people and the sheep of your pasture.[24]

Saint Columban of Ireland, Optional Memorial

Columban (d. 615) was an Irish monk and priest. Since paganism was present throughout Europe in the sixth and seventh centuries, Columban left his monastery when he was fifty years old to evangelize the pagan people living there. Despite great opposition, Columban established several monasteries in France, and these became great centers of learning. The pagans he encountered were deeply affected by the way he lived his life, particularly his practice of Irish penitential discipline and private confession. Local leaders resisted the strict moral teachings he taught, and he was eventually exiled from the area with his monks. But he simply moved to Germany and Italy to also evangelize those regions through the example of holy monastic life. Columban was a great preacher, poet, and teacher.

Saint Felicitas of Rome and Sons

Felicitas (d. 165) was a noble and wealthy widow living in Rome during the days of the underground Church. She was also a Christian and was known for her care for the poor. When she was arrested for being a Christian, she refused to apostatize. According to tradition, her seven sons—Alexander, Vitalis, Martial, Januarius, Felix, Philip, and Silvanus—were also arrested and refused to renounce their faith in Christ. After multiple unsuccessful attempts to change their minds, the Roman emperor Antoninus ordered them to be executed. Felicitas was forced to watch as each of her sons died. Then she too was martyred.

Blessed Miguel Agustin Pro, Optional Memorial[25]

Miguel was born in 1891 and grew up in a pious and well-to-do home in Guadalupe, Mexico, and his father was a mining engineer. He was known for his cheerfulness and spirited temperament, as well as his concern for the poor and the working classes. He became a Jesuit novice when he was twenty years old, but he was forced to leave Mexico during the anti-Catholic Mexican Revolution. He was ordained in Belgium at the age of thirty-six. Despite his bad health—he suffered from a recurrent stomach problem—he secretly returned to Mexico in 1926 to serve his people clandestinely as a priest. He had to disguise himself on many occasions to bring the sacraments to the faithful. In 1927, he was falsely blamed for a bombing attempt and was betrayed to the police. On September 23, 1927, he was condemned to death, although there hadn't even been a trial. As he was about to be shot, he forgave his executioners and

---

[24] *The Liturgy of the Hours*, vol. 3, from the letter to the Corinthians by Saint Clement I, pope (New York: Catholic Book Publishing, 1975), 55.

[25] This saint may be celebrated as an optional memorial in the *Liturgical Calendar for the Dioceses of the United States of America*.

refused a blindfold. He died shouting, "Viva Christo Rey! (Long live Christ the King!)"[26] Though a public funeral was forbidden by the government, faithful Catholics lined the streets as his body passed.

Saint Clement, help me to love Christ and His Church.
Saint Columban, teach me how to bring monastic simplicity to my life.
Saint Felicitas, give me your faith in God, even when I have to watch
my loved ones suffer.
Blessed Miguel, pray that Christ may always live as King of my heart.

* * * * *

November 24

Saint Andrew Dung Lac and Companions, Memorial

During the seventeenth, eighteenth, and nineteenth centuries, at least 130,000 Christians died for the faith in Vietnam. Of the many who were executed by decapitation and strangulation, 117 are recognized on this date. They include eleven Dominicans, ten members of the Society of Foreign Missions from Paris, and ninety-six Vietnamese Catholics (thirty-seven priests and fifty-nine laypersons). One of them, Andrew Dung, was born of pagan parents but was catechized about the Catholic faith at his parents' request. He grew up to become a catechist himself and then a priest. After he was arrested for being a Christian and released, he changed his last name to Lac, to protect his identity. But after another arrest and release, he was arrested with another priest, Peter Thi, and both were beheaded.

Saint Chrysogonus of Aquiliea

Chrysogonus (d. 304) was a Roman official who became a Christian and converted many people to the faith. It's said he was a friend of Saint Anastasia, a noblewoman who lived a devout life and also died a martyr for the faith. Chrysogonus was probably a bishop of Aquileia in Italy, and his evangelical activities caused him to be arrested, imprisoned for months, and then beheaded during the persecution of Christians under the Roman emperor Diocletian. His body was thrown into the sea but was rescued by a priest, and the church that's still in Rome and bears his name contains two of his relics: his head and his arm.

Saint Albert of Louvain

Albert was born around the year 1166 and was the son of the duke of Brabant (a city in modern Belgium). Due to his nobility, he was given the position of a canon when he was only twelve years old. For unknown reasons, he renounced his benefice as a canon when he was twenty-one years old and became a knight

---

[26] "Blessed Miguel Agustin Pro", CatholicSaints.Info, February 5, 2019, https://catholicsaints.info/blessed-miguel-agustin-pro.

for a count who had been a bitter enemy. But then, after hearing a papal legate preach in support of protecting the Christians of the Holy Land through a Crusade, he asked to receive back his position as a canon and serve the Church. In 1191, he and another man were named as candidates for bishop of Liege. Though Albert was supported by the clergy and officially appointed to the position, political intrigues with the emperor forced Albert to go to the pope and appeal to him in person for his support. To avoid being captured by the emperor, Albert even had to travel in disguise. The pope ruled in Albert's favor, but the emperor had already forced his own choice for bishop into the position, and that bishop kept Albert from taking possession of his office. Albert had to be ordained and consecrated by the bishop of Rheims, France, since the bishop of Cologne, Germany, was too afraid of the emperor to perform the ordination. Although Albert's noble relatives were ready to speak and fight on his behalf, he preferred to live in exile rather than start a war. So he stayed at Rheims, trying to bring peace to the situation. However, German knights apparently sent by the emperor attacked Albert on November 24, 1192, and killed him, making him a martyr. The city was horrified and buried him in the cathedral with honor.

Blessed Maria Anna Sala

Maria Anna was born in 1829 into a pious family in Brivio, Italy, and she was the fifth of eight children. She was educated at a convent school and wanted to join the sisters' order when she grew up, but she had to leave the convent to help her family instead. In 1848, after she had fulfilled all her obligations to her family, she joined the Sisters of Saint Marcellina in the city of Vimercate. She made her profession as a sister in 1852, and she taught for forty years at various schools of her order. In 1883, she was diagnosed with throat cancer, but she told no one. She worked for another eight years, and her quiet dignity and her unwavering devotion to Christ, despite the pain, impressed those who knew her. She died in 1891. Her body was found to be incorrupt when it was examined in 1920.

Holy Martyrs, help me bring others to Christ.
Saint Albert, show me how to live a life that speaks of faithfulness to Christ.
Blessed Maria Anna, teach me how to accept trials without complaints.

* * * * *

November 25

Saint Catherine of Alexandria, Optional Memorial

Catherine (d. 305) was a brilliant, wealthy, young Christian who lived in Alexandria, Egypt. Some traditions say the governor was so smitten with her beauty that he demanded that she marry him. Others say she protested against the persecution of Christians. Whatever the cause of her arrest, she refused to renounce her faith in Christ despite tortures that included being tied to a toothed wheel.

When the torture failed to break her, she was beheaded. Catherine is one of the Fourteen Holy Helpers, great saints who were called upon particularly for help during the bubonic plague in the fourteenth century.

Saint Moses of Rome

Moses was a priest in third-century Rome, perhaps a converted Jew, and he spoke and wrote against the heresy of Novatian, which divided Christians at the time. According to the bishop of Carthage, Saint Cyprian, he was one of the first Christians to confess his faith in Jesus Christ publicly during the persecution under the Roman emperor Decian, and after Moses had been in prison for eleven months and eleven days, he was executed on January 1, 251.

Saint Peter of Alexandria

Peter became bishop of Alexandria in Egypt in the year 300, when it was illegal to be a Christian in the Roman Empire. He was a good, merciful shepherd to his people. During a break in the persecution of Christians, he tried to reconcile those Christians who had betrayed their faith under the threat of torture or death and bring them back to the Church, though this caused some Christians to complain that he was being too lenient. At one point, Peter had to leave his city because the pagans living there were trying to assassinate him, and a man named Melitius was falsely appointed as his replacement. Peter's letter of excommunication against Melitius still exists, and in this letter, he told the Christians to refuse to be in communion with Melitius until Peter had met with him first. During a later persecution under the Roman emperor Maximinus Daia in the year 311, Peter was put to death.

Blesseds Luigi Beltrame Quattrocchi and Maria Corsini Beltrame Quattrocchi

Luigi (1880–1951) was from a large family but was informally adopted by a childless uncle and aunt and raised by them. He grew up to become a lawyer. Maria (1884–1965) was from a noble family, and they married in 1905. They had four children, but the pregnancy of the last child was very dangerous for Maria, and they were encouraged to have an abortion to save her life. They ignored the advice and had their baby, but the couple took a private vow to live as brother and sister, probably both for Maria's future safety and for spiritual reasons. Their home life was full of faith, friends, activities, and service. During World War II, they took refugees into their home to live with them. Luigi eventually held many important positions in government, including deputy general of Italy, and Maria became a professor and writer on education. Three of their children entered religious life. Luigi died of a heart attack at home, and Maria died fourteen years later in the arms of their youngest child.

Holy Martyrs, help me to remain faithful to Christ even in trying times. Blesseds Luigi and Maria, show me how to make my home into a domestic church.

* * * * *

Saint Siricius

Siricius (d. 399) was the thirty-eighth pope; he reigned for fourteen years. He was originally from Rome and was a lector and deacon before being elected to the papacy. His first act was to respond to a letter from a Spanish bishop (addressed to his predecessor, Pope Damasus, before his death) about fifteen different points. His response, on issues related to Baptism, penance, Church discipline, and clerical celibacy, is the oldest completely preserved papal edict that we have. Siricius was also very concerned about the maintenance of Church discipline. He took a strong stand against the teachings of heretical movements led by Jovinian, Bonosus, and Priscillian, as well as dealing with the controversial teachings of Bishop Meletius of Antioch. While Meletius opposed the Arian heresy, he also strongly promoted his own subtle and confusing interpretations of the faith, which led to a widespread and violent schism.

Saint Bellinus of Padua

Bellinus lived in the late eleventh century in Padua, Italy, and became a priest. Christendom was in turmoil at the time because of complex political situations involving the pope and an anti-pope; Bellinus showed his faithfulness to the Church by remaining loyal to the true pope. Perhaps as a result of that loyalty, he was named bishop of Padua. He undertook a serious reform to improve the lives of the clergy in his diocese and led a campaign to rebuild the cathedral after an earthquake. He also defended the rights of the Church against powerful nobles; one of those noble families resented that and sent assassins to kill him while he was on a trip to Rome in the year 1151, making him a martyr for justice.

Saint Silvester Gozzolini

Silvester was born in 1177 in Osimo, Italy. When he was a young man, he first studied law but then switched to theology. His father was so angry about this that he refused to speak to Silvester for ten years. In the meantime, Silvester became a canon, and he wasn't afraid to rebuke his own bishop, who was scandalizing many with his immoral way of life. In 1227, Silvester resigned his benefice and began to live a life of poverty, penance, and solitude. Disciples gradually gathered around him, and he established a monastery. He followed the Rule of Saint Benedict and governed his monks for thirty-six years. The group eventually became known as the Silvestrine Benedictines. He reformed and founded eleven monasteries before his death in 1267 at the age of ninety.

Saint Leonard of Port Maurice

Jerome (Leonard) was born in 1676 in Port Maurice, Italy. His father was a sea captain, and he was sent to live with an uncle when he was thirteen years old so that he could study medicine. When he decided against a career in medicine, however, the uncle disowned him. Jerome studied at the Jesuit College in Rome, but he eventually decided to join the Riformella, a branch of the Franciscans of the Strict Observance. He became a Franciscan friar, was ordained a priest, and took the name Leonard. He taught for a time, and he hoped to become a missionary to China, but he suffered from a bleeding ulcer and was therefore ordered to remain in Italy. Leonard became a great preacher; he encouraged Christians to practice their faith through devotions to the Blessed Sacrament, the Sacred Heart of Jesus, and the Immaculate Conception, and through the Stations of the Cross. The pope sent him to restore order to some religious orders with houses in Corsica. He was able to bring discipline back to the religious living there, but political upheaval in the area at the time made it difficult for him to preach and reach out to the laypeople. He returned to Rome, and there he lived for the rest of his life. He died in 1751.

Saint Siricius, help me to explain God's truth to those who are confused.
Saint Bellinus, show me how to stand up for justice with charity.
Saint Silvester, teach me about poverty, penance, and solitude.
Saint Leonard, remind me to practice my faith through everyday devotions.

* * * * *

November 27

Saint James Intercisus

James was a courtier in the court of King Yezdigerd of Persia (modern Iran) when the king began to persecute Christians in the year 420. James renounced his Christian faith in fear at the time, but later the king died. His Christian parents were heartbroken that he had given up his faith. They wrote to him, telling him that they wanted nothing more to do with him and that if he continued to reject God, God's justice would "reward" him with the same fate that the king had suffered. James was ashamed of himself, left the court, and returned to the practice of his Catholic faith. When the new king heard about this, he decreed that unless James denied his faith in Christ, he would be hung from a beam and slowly cut to pieces. Before the execution, his executioners tried to convince him to give in, but he replied that a painful death was a small price to pay for eternal life. As they cut pieces from his body—a total of twenty-eight by the time he was dead—he prayed and offered each piece to God. He was finally beheaded. It was the year 421.

Saint Fergus of Scotland

Fergus was born in seventh-century Ireland and became a priest. He traveled all over Ireland as bishop, and then he evangelized Scotland and established new churches there. He traveled to attend a church council in Rome called by Pope Gregory II in the year 721 and died around the year 730.

Saint James, help me to repent quickly when I sin and to face the consequences. Saint Fergus, show me how to bring the Gospel to people who haven't heard it before.

See also the Miraculous Medal of the Blessed Virgin Mary in the Calendar of Marian Dates.

* * * * *

November 28

Saint James of the Marches

James was born in 1391 in Monteprandone, Italy, and he entered the Friars Minor when he was twenty years old. He was a disciple of the priest Saint Bernardine of Siena. He preached all over Bosnia, Hungary, and Austria; spread devotion to the Holy Name of Jesus; and was known for his personal holiness. He's also known for founding an institution of holy pawnshops to protect the poor from usury and for providing them with low-interest loans. He died in 1476.

Blessed James Thompson

James was born in the sixteenth century in York, England, and was educated and ordained to the priesthood in France because of anti-Catholic laws in England at the time. He returned to York to minister to Catholics secretly, using the name James Hudson. But he was found and then imprisoned and hanged for the crime of being a priest in the year 1582.

Saint James, show me how God wants me to love and serve the poor. Blessed James, beg the Lord to give me the courage to serve Him at any cost.

* * * * *

November 29

Saint Sernin (Saturnius or Saturninus) of Toulouse

Sernin (d. 257) was from a noble Roman family in Patras, Greece. Despite the fact that Christianity was technically illegal in the Roman Empire at the time, he traveled to Toulouse, France, to bring the Gospel to the people there and became the first bishop of Toulouse around the year 250. He converted many people to the Christian faith until the large pagan community rose up against him. A mob grabbed him, dragged him into a pagan temple, and tied him by his feet to a bull that was about to be sacrificed. When the animal was driven down a hill, Sernin died a martyr.

Saint Radbod of Utrecht

Radbod (d. 918) was born in the line of Frisian (German) kings. Radbod's pagan great-grandfather had resisted the Christian faith and had even famously said that he "preferred to be in Hell with his ancestors rather than in Heaven without them".[27] Radbod, on the other hand, embraced the Christian faith and was educated in a school under the direction of the bishop of Cologne. He became a monk, was noted for his humility, and wrote poems and hymns. In the year 900, he was chosen to be bishop of Utrecht in the Netherlands. After he was ordained a bishop, Radbod gave himself difficult personal penances: he never tasted meat and fasted often. He was also known to the people for his kindness to the poor. He died peacefully.

Saint Francis Anthony (Giovanniello) Fasani of Lucera

Giovanniello (the Italian equivalent of Johnny) was born in Lucera, Italy, in 1681 in a family of farm workers. His father died when he was young, but his stepfather raised him and sent him to be educated by the Conventual Friars. He decided to enter the order when he was fifteen years old, was professed in 1696, and took the name Francis Anthony. He was ordained a priest in 1705 and later became a master of theology in Rome. Francis taught theology, became regent at the college, and served as guardian of the convent and novice master. But he was best known as a preacher, perhaps because he was careful to make his preaching easy for anyone, even the uneducated, to understand. Francis took care of the poor and suffering, as well as those in prison. Although the dogma of the Immaculate Conception hadn't been proclaimed during his lifetime, he was devoted to this teaching and told those who came to him to ask for help from our Blessed Mother under that title. He died on November 29, 1742, the first day of the (modern) novena to the Immaculate Conception.

> *Saint Sernin, help me suffer willingly for the sake of Christ.*
> *Saint Radbod, show me how to love penance.*
> *Saint Francis Anthony, teach me how to explain my faith to others.*

* * * * *

November 30

Saint Andrew the Apostle, Feast

Andrew (d. ca. 60), Simon Peter's brother, was a fisherman and a disciple of John the Baptist before he answered Jesus' call[28] and became his disciple. According to tradition, he spread the Gospel in Scythia (modern Eastern Europe

---

[27] Walsh, *Butler's Lives of the Saints*, 393.
[28] Jn 1:35–42.

and Central Asia) and Greece, and he died a martyr on an x-shaped cross in Patras, Greece.

> *One of the two who heard John speak, and followed him, was Andrew, Simon Peter's brother. He first found his brother Simon, and said to him, "We have found the Messiah" (which means Christ). He brought him to Jesus.*[29]

Saint Cuthbert Mayne

Cuthbert was born in 1544 at Youlston, England, and raised a Protestant by his uncle, who had been a Catholic priest before leaving the Church. Though Cuthbert wasn't particularly attracted to the life of a minister and wasn't educated to be one, he was ordained to the Church of England when he was eighteen or nineteen years old. However, he met the future martyr-saint Edmund Campion and Dr. Gregory Martin while he was studying at Oxford, and after those two men had gone to France to become priests, they wrote to encourage him to do the same. Cuthbert hesitated at first, uncertain about whether to leave Protestantism and afraid of the suffering that would be involved; but when one of their letters to him was intercepted and he narrowly escaped being arrested, he made up his mind. He left England for the city of Douai to become a Catholic priest, and three years later, he was sent back to England with John Payne (who later also died a martyr for the crime of being a priest). Cuthbert lived as a steward on an estate for a year until he was arrested simply because he was found to have an Agnus Dei (a circle of wax, impressed with the image of a lamb and blessed by the pope) around his neck and because a chalice and vestments were found in his possession. He was imprisoned in filthy cells, indicted on flimsy evidence, found guilty, and sentenced to death. The Catholic laymen who were tried with him were sentenced to life imprisonment. The day before his execution in 1577, Cuthbert was offered his freedom if he would swear to the queen's supremacy over the Church, which he refused to do. He was not allowed to address the crowd before his hanging, and he was probably (hopefully) unconscious before the torture of disembowelment was begun.

> *Saint Andrew, bring me close to Jesus.*
> *Saint Cuthbert, help me remain faithful when others oppose me.*

---

[29] Jn 1:40–42.

December

December 1

Prophet Nahum

Nahum is one of the twelve minor prophets. He lived around the fifth and sixth centuries B.C., and he wrote vividly of the coming of the Lord and the destruction of the Ninevites, who destroyed the sacred places of the Jews.

> The LORD is a jealous God and avenging.... The LORD is good, a stronghold in the day of trouble; he knows those who take refuge in him.[1]

Saint Eligius (Eloi) of Noyon

Eligius was born around the year 580 and became a blacksmith and goldworker in Limoges, France, directly serving the French kings Clotaire II and Dagobert. This work made him a very wealthy man. But he eventually decided to give his money to the poor and become a priest. He was ordained bishop of Noyon in the year 641, and, as bishop, he evangelized nearby pagans, freed slaves, and founded nunneries. He died in the year 660.

Saints Edmund Campion, Ralph Sherwin, and Alexander Briant

Edmund was born around the year 1540 and was the promising son of an English bookseller. He won a scholarship to Oxford University when he was only fifteen years old, became a junior fellow two years later, developed a reputation as an orator, and took the required Oath of Supremacy to Queen Elizabeth. But after he had become an Anglican deacon, his conscience began to trouble him, and he began to study Catholicism. He traveled to Ireland and lived in hiding when people became suspicious of his loyalties. He returned in disguise to England in 1571 to attend the trial of Blessed John Storey, a former member of Parliament who was arrested, tortured, and executed for his Catholic faith. Edmund then decided to become a priest and traveled to Douai, France, to study. After ordination, he went to Rome and entered the Jesuits. In 1579, he was sent secretly to England with Father Robert Persons to minister to Catholics. Edmund traveled all over England, converted many people to the Catholic faith, and narrowly escaped capture several times. On July 16, he was about to say Mass in a private house when he and two other priests were betrayed to the authorities. He was offered bribes at first but then was tortured and interrogated to try to make him betray himself and other Catholics. During

---

[1] Nahum 1:2, 7.

his trial, he was too weak to raise his own arm to be sworn in, so a companion had to do it for him. Campion defended himself and those accused with him against the false charge of inciting a rebellion; he stated their loyalty to the queen, discredited the evidence and witnesses, and demonstrated that their only crime was their Catholic faith. Although the jury found them guilty, it took them a long time, a whole hour, to do so. Blesseds Ralph Sherwin and Alexander Briant, who were Englishmen who had converted to Catholicism and became priests to serve English Catholics, just like Edmund, were executed with him on November 20, 1581, at Tyburn. Edmund publicly prayed for the queen before his death, and some of his blood splashed on the future martyr-saint Henry Walpole, who later became a Jesuit and was canonized as one of the Forty English Martyrs with Campion.

> Prophet Nahum, help me know the Lord.
> Saint Eligius, show me how to let go of worldly things for love of Jesus Christ.
> Holy Martyrs, help me to be always faithful to Christ and His Church.

* * * * *

December 2

Prophet Habakkuk

Habakkuk was an Old Testament prophet who lived during the time of Israel's captivity among the Chaldeans (Babylonians) in the seventh century B.C.

> Though the fig tree does not blossom, nor fruit be on the vines, the produce of the olive fail and the fields yield no food, the flock be cut off from the fold and there be no herd in the stalls, yet I will rejoice in the LORD, I will joy in the God of my salvation. GOD, the Lord, is my strength; he makes my feet like deer's feet, he makes me tread upon my high places.[2]

Saint Bibiana (Viviana) of Rome

Bibiana (d. 361) was the daughter of the powerful prefect of Rome. When the Roman emperor Julian the Apostate tried to return the empire to paganism and renewed the persecution of Christians, Bibiana's parents refused to renounce their faith and died as martyrs. Bibiana and her sister were left poor and on their own. Several months later, the governor of Rome came to visit them, certain that the experience of living in poverty would have caused them to give up their faith. But when he questioned them, the two women openly professed their belief in Jesus Christ, and Bibiana's sister fell down dead during the interrogation. Bibiana was sent to live with a pagan woman who was supposed to make her apostatize. But when Bibiana remained faithful, she was tortured, scourged, and then killed.

---

[2] Hab 3:17–19.

Saint Chromatius of Aquileia

Chromatius (d. 407) was raised in the city of Aquileia (Italy) by his widowed mother, whose Christian virtues were praised by Saint Jerome himself in a letter he wrote in the year 374. Chromatius grew up to become a priest, and he was made bishop of Aquileia after the city's bishop, Saint Valerian, died in the year 388. As bishop, he financially supported Jerome so he could complete his Latin translation of the Bible, corresponded with Jerome, and wrote his own commentaries on Scripture. During a controversy over the orthodoxy of the writings of the deceased Christian writer Origen, Chromatius tried to make peace between opposing (and vehement) factions of Christians. When the patriarch of Constantinople, Saint John Chrysostom, was persecuted for his faithfulness to Church teaching, Chromatius spoke in defense of John, though he wasn't able to stop John's martyrdom. Chromatius is considered a Father of the Church.

Saint Silverius

Silverius (d. 537) was only a subdeacon when he was raised to the papacy and its complicated politics. The king of Italy had forced Silverius to be named pope instead of a Byzantine candidate for political reasons, and after Silverius' election, the empress Theodora tried to convince Silverius to make two followers of the Monophysite heresy into the bishops of important sees. When Silverius responded to her with a polite refusal, he remarked to others that he was essentially signing his own death warrant. Unsurprisingly, the angry Theodora retaliated with forgery, kidnapping, and a conspiracy to get rid of Silverius, who was arrested and taken to a nearby island. There he died, apparently of poor treatment, a martyr for his faithfulness to the Church. Theodora then maneuvered to get her own candidate, Vigilius, chosen as the next pope, but she was deeply disappointed in the result. Pope Vigilius became a supporter of orthodoxy, which is all that is expected of a pope.

Blessed Maria Angela Astorch

Maria (1592–1665) was raised in a pious family, and she chose to become a Poor Clare Capuchin nun in a monastery in Barcelona, Spain. In time, she became novice mistress, spiritual director, and abbess. In her spare time, Maria Angela studied the Bible and great writers of the Church, and she bestowed on her sisters a profound understanding of the community's daily prayers. She was a mystic and a visionary, and she was blessed to be able to both see and communicate with her guardian angel.

> *Prophet Habakkuk, give me God's words of encouragement.*
> *Saint Bibiana, help me see all things as loss except for what leads to Jesus Christ.*
> *Saint Chromatius, show me how to support good Christian leaders today.*
> *Saint Silverius, help me to be faithful to my vocation.*
> *Blessed Maria Angela, help me to recognize God's blessings in my daily life.*

* * * * *

December 3

Saint Francis Xavier, Memorial

Francis was born in 1506 in the castle of Xavier in Spain and was the youngest member of a large family. When he was eighteen years old, he went to study at the University of Paris, where he met Ignatius, the future saint and founder of the Jesuit order. Although Francis didn't join Ignatius' order immediately, he eventually chose to follow him, and he became one of the first seven men who vowed themselves to serve God in the Society of Jesus in the year 1534. Three years later, Francis was ordained a priest, and in 1540, Ignatius sent him on the first missionary journey of the Jesuits to the East Indies. During the trip, Francis cared for sick sailors and helped reconcile their quarrels, and after a thirteen-month voyage (twice the usual time), he reached Goa (modern India). He was scandalized by the behavior of the Christians living in Goa and did his best to be a good example of Christian virtue to the native people. He taught them about the Christian faith, cared for those who were sick or in prison, offered Mass for lepers, and put the truths of the faith into songs, which rapidly spread the Gospel. After five months, Francis went to catechize the Paravas, a group of people who had been baptized by the Portuguese but who had no one to teach them about the faith. Francis lived in poverty alongside them, and his holy example caused so many people to come to be baptized by him that on one occasion his arms grew tired just from administering the sacrament so many times. Notorious European sinners as well as native people repented and amended their lives. After he had been in Goa for some time, he heard about the country of Japan from a fugitive Japanese man, and he sensed an openness to Christ in what he heard of the culture there. So he made his way to Japan, learned a simple translation of the Christian faith in Japanese, and recited it to the people he met in the city of Kagoshima. When he recognized that the example of evangelical poverty wasn't as effective in the Japanese culture, he improved his appearance and took small gifts to the local ruler. The Japanese leader was so delighted that he gave Francis an abandoned Buddhist monastery to use. When he began preaching in the area, many people asked to be baptized. However, Francis now wanted to bring the Gospel to China. He boarded a vessel with a few companions, although he knew it was forbidden for foreigners to enter China. But Francis became seriously ill on the voyage, and the sailors took him off the ship, laid him on the sand, and left him behind. A Portuguese merchant eventually had pity on Francis and took him into his simple shelter. Francis' Chinese friend Anthony cared for him until the end in 1552, watching Francis die with the name of Jesus on his lips. His body was originally packed in lime, but when it was removed from the coffin in Malacca, it was found to be incorrupt. And it still is.

Prophet Zephaniah

Zephaniah was an Old Testament prophet who lived during the reign of King Josiah of Judah (641–610 B.C.), the reformer king who sought to bring the

Jewish people back to true worship of the Lord. Zephaniah was a contemporary of the prophet Jeremiah.

> *Sing aloud, O daughter of Zion; shout, O Israel! Rejoice and exult with all your heart, O daughter of Jerusalem! The LORD has taken away the judgments against you, he has cast out your enemies. The King of Israel, the LORD, is in your midst; you shall fear evil no more.*[3]

Saint Cassian of Tangiers

A Roman centurion named Marcellus (d. 298) was brought to trial in Tangiers (modern Morocco) because he was a Christian. Cassian was the court stenographer at his trial, and when Marcellus was condemned to death for his faith, Cassian announced that he was a Christian too and spoke against condemning Marcellus. He was immediately arrested and martyred. Both men are acclaimed as saints.

> *Saint Francis, show me how to bring the Good News to those around me.*
> *Prophet Zephaniah, give me God's words of encouragement.*
> *Saint Cassian, give me your courage in defending the innocent.*

* * * * *

December 4

Saint John of Damascus (John Damascene), Optional Memorial

John was born around the year 676, and he and his adopted brother Cosmas were raised in Damascus in the Muslim country of Syria. Their father was an official in the caliph's court. John was baptized when he was a baby, received a good education, and was a humble, virtuous Christian official like his father. However, he and Cosmas eventually decided to leave the world behind and live in the monastery of Saint Sabas near Jerusalem. In their spare time, the two brothers wrote Christian books and hymns, but this was so innovative that it scandalized some of the other monks. The patriarch of Jerusalem recognized their abilities, however, and asked Cosmas to become a bishop. He also ordained John to be a priest for the city of Jerusalem. Cosmas served his people well as bishop, but John soon left the city to live in a monastery. At the time, the Byzantine emperor who ruled the area was an iconoclast, prohibiting the use of sacred images as offensive to God and violently persecuting those who had images in their possession. John wrote three works in defense of the use of icons, which were widely read by his contemporaries, and his arguments were so convincing—arguments based on reason, Church history, and Scripture— that no one has been able to improve upon them since. For example, he was

---

[3] Zeph 3:14–15.

one of the first Christians to note the distinction between worship, which is offered to God alone, and the veneration we offer to saints. Nevertheless, he was only safe from death at the hands of the emperor at any moment because he was careful not to cross into imperial territory. John wrote works of poetry, philosophy, and theology into his old age, and the Eastern Church holds John in as much regard as the Western Church respects Thomas Aquinas. He died around the year 749. He's now considered one of the Fathers of the Church and was formally proclaimed a Doctor of the Church in 1890.

> *Let everyone know, therefore, that anyone who attempts to destroy an image brought into being out of divine longing and zeal for the glory and memorial of Christ, or of his Mother the holy Theotokos, or of one of his saints, or for the disgrace of the devil and the defeat of him and his demons, and will not venerate or honor or greet it as a precious image and not as god, is an enemy of Christ and the holy Mother of God and the saints and a vindicator of the devil and his demons, and shows by his deed his sorrow that God and his saints are honored and glorified, and the devil put to shame. For the image is a triumph and manifestation and inscribed tablet in memory of the victory of the bravest and most eminent and of the shame of those worsted and overthrown.*[4]

Saint Barbara

Barbara (d. 235) lived in Heliopolis of Syria. When she became a Christian, her father, Dioscorus, who was a pagan, was so angry with her that he shut her up in a tower. When she refused to give up her faith in Christ, he reported her to the authorities as a Christian. She was tortured first, and then the judge ordered Dioscorus to execute his own daughter, which he did by taking her to the top of a mountain and killing her with a sword. On the way down the mountain, Dioscorus was struck by lightning and killed. Barbara is one of the Fourteen Holy Helpers, great saints who were called upon in Europe particularly during the bubonic plague in the fourteenth century.

Blesseds Francis Galvez, Jerome de Angelis, and Simon Yempo

Francis Galvez was born in Spain, joined the Franciscans in 1591, and became a missionary to the Philippines and then Japan. He returned to the Philippines for a time to escape detection, and he dyed his skin and took a disguise when he went back to Japan to evangelize the people. Jerome de Angelis was born in Italy in 1568, became a Jesuit priest, and was sent to Japan as a missionary, though it took him six years to arrive there because of difficulties along the way. Simon Yempo was born in Nozu, Japan, around the year 1580 and became a Buddhist monk. When he found out about the Christian faith, he converted and became a lay catechist and a Jesuit lay brother. Because of the renewed persecution of Christians by the Japanese government, which included the expulsion of all Christians in the year 1614, all three of these men had to practice their faith in secret and were in constant danger as they ministered to Catholics. They

---

[4] John of Damascus, *Three Treatises on the Divine Images*, Treatise II, no. 11, trans. Andrew Louth, Popular Patristic Series (Crestwood, N.Y.: St. Vladimir's Seminary Press, 2003), 68.

were eventually detected, arrested, and died as martyrs by being burned to death together on this date in the year 1623.

> *Saint John, help me to draw closer to God through sacred images.*
> *Saint Barbara, pray for me that I will never allow anyone to come*
> *between me and Jesus Christ.*
> *Holy Martyrs, show me how to live and die for Christ.*

* * * * *

December 5

Saint Crispina of Thagara

During Roman emperor Diocletian's persecution of the Church in the early fourth century, Crispina was arrested for being a Christian. She was a married woman with several children, and she was also a wealthy Roman citizen living in the city of Thagara (in modern Tunisia). During Crispina's trial, she was threatened and mistreated, but she responded by strongly defending her faith and refusing to renounce it. She was sentenced to death and was beheaded in the year 304.

Saint Sabas (Sabbas) of Mar Saba

Sabas was born in 439 in Cappadocia (modern Turkey) and was the son of an army officer. When his father was called away to serve in Alexandria, Egypt, he took his wife but left Sabas in the care of an uncle. That uncle treated Sabas so badly that he ran away to another uncle, and during the resulting lawsuits and animosity between the uncles, Sabas decided to run away again: this time to a monastery. After ten years, he sought out Saint Euthymius, an abbot who lived alone but with a monastery of his monks nearby, to ask him for spiritual guidance. Euthymius thought Sabas was too inexperienced for complete solitude, so he sent him to live at another monastery first. Later, he let Sabas live alone in a cave five days a week. Sabas spent his days praying and working by making fifty baskets a week, donating the baskets to the monastery. When Euthymius died, Sabas went to live in the desert, but four years later he moved to a cave. After some years, he unwillingly began accepting disciples of his own and founded a monastery that eventually housed 150 monks. When his monks complained that they didn't have a priest to say Mass for them, their bishop ordered Sabas to accept ordination so he could serve the monks as a priest. Sabas' reputation for holiness attracted many people, and his widowed mother eventually came to live under his spiritual direction and even gave him money to establish hospitals and a monastery. Sabas still lived mostly in solitude. At the age of seventy, Sabas was sent by his patriarch, along with some other abbots, to the emperor Anastasius in Constantinople in an attempt to stop the emperor's persecution of faithful bishops over debates about the Eutychian heresy. Although Sabas brought many people back to an orthodox understanding of the faith while visiting the great city, he apparently wasn't as successful with the emperor. When he was ninety-one years old, he was sent again by the patriarch to encourage the emperor Justinian to be merciful after a revolt in Samaria. The emperor treated him respectfully and offered to endow his monasteries financially, but Sabas replied that he didn't need financial support so long as the monks served God faithfully. However, Sabas did receive favors he requested, specifically a remission of taxes for Palestinians who had suffered during the revolt, a hospital for pilgrims, and a fortress to protect monks from marauders. Soon after returning to his monastery, Sabas became ill, appointed his successor, and lay alone in silence for four days to prepare to meet God. He died on this date in the year 532 at the age of ninety-three.

> *Saint Crispina, when challenged about my faith, help me find the best words to explain the truth to others.*
> *Saint Sabas, teach me how to live a life of solitude while remaining in the world.*

* * * * *

December 6

Saint Nicholas of Myra, Optional Memorial

Nicholas was born around the early fourth century at Patara in Asia Minor (modern Turkey). He became bishop of Myra, and he was well known for his personal piety, his zeal for the faith, and the miracles that resulted from his prayers. According to tradition, he secretly gave money to a poor family to prevent three daughters from being sold into slavery because they each lacked a dowry, one of his many acts of charity to the poor. This story was apparently embroidered into a story of him bringing three children, whose heads had been placed in a brine tub, back to life. He was imprisoned during the persecution of Christians under the Roman emperor Diocletian and confessed his faith in Christ. For whatever reason, however, he was imprisoned but not executed, and by God's grace, he survived. He attended the Council of Nicaea, where he condemned the heresy of Arianism. He died in 346 and was later buried in Myra.

Blessed Peter Paschal

Peter was born in Valencia, Spain, in 1227 and received a doctorate. He joined the Mercedarian order in 1250 and became a priest. He served as a tutor to the son of the king of Aragon before he became bishop of Jaen in 1289. The Muslims controlled this territory of Spain at the time, and he ransomed Christian captives back from slavery. He also spoke and wrote against Islamic teachings and their practice of taking hostages. In 1297, he was ambushed by Muslims and put in prison. A Muslim king ordered him to be beheaded. He died a martyr in 1300.

Saint Nicholas, help me give generously.
Blessed Peter, teach me how to speak the truth in love.

* * * * *

December 7

Saint Ambrose of Milan, Memorial

Ambrose's father was the Roman prefect of Gaul (modern France) when Ambrose was born around the year 340. After his father died, his widowed mother returned to Rome with her two young children, Ambrose and his sister, Marcellina, who later became a nun and was also named a saint by the Church. Ambrose became known as a talented poet, a great orator, and a lawyer, eventually being appointed the governor of the Italian regions of Liguria and Aemilia. When the bishop of Milan, who had been a follower of the Arian heresy, died, the whole city was divided over whether his replacement should be an Arian or a faithful Catholic. During an assembly to discuss the controversy, Ambrose spoke and encouraged the people to settle the matter peacefully, rather than with violence. The crowd was so impressed with his speech that people began spontaneously yelling for Ambrose to become the new bishop. Although Ambrose was a follower of Christ at the time, he hadn't even been baptized. So when their recommendation to make Ambrose the next bishop reached the emperor, Ambrose asked the emperor to excuse him from the honor. The emperor didn't let him off the hook, though, and, at the young age of thirty-five, Ambrose was ordained bishop of the great city of Milan. He studied Christian theology, lived a simple life, offered Mass daily, avoided being involved in political intrigues, and, most notably, made himself accessible to anyone in his flock who wanted to speak with him, for hours a day. His writings had great impact on the culture around him—for example, he wrote powerfully against the widespread heresy of Arianism, wrote against a pagan movement to reinstitute the goddess of Victory in the empire, wrote to encourage Christians to make the Blessed Virgin a pattern for living, and wrote in favor of the honor of virginity, which caused some people to complain hysterically that he was trying to depopulate the empire. One of those converted to the Catholic faith by the strength of his arguments and personal holiness was the man who later became the bishop of Hippo and a great saint, Augustine. Ambrose faced down the emperor and empress when they tried to take churches away from Catholics to give them to Arians, and when on one occasion the people had barricaded themselves inside a church to prevent its seizure by Arians, Ambrose joined them. He memorably summarized the key reason for his action during a sermon: "The emperor is in the Church, not over it."[5] When the Roman emperor Theodosius ordered a

---

[5] Michael Walsh, ed., *Butler's Lives of the Saints, Concise Edition, Revised and Updated* (San Francisco: HarperCollins Publishers, 1991), 409.

massacre of people in an amphitheater, Ambrose confronted him personally and refused to admit him to the sacraments until he had done penance—and the emperor obeyed. In 397 at the age of fifty-seven, sometime during the night of Good Friday and the morning of Holy Saturday, Ambrose died. For his powerful, lifelong example of holiness and his writings and sermons on many topics, he's not only considered a Father of the Church but also one of the four great Doctors of the Western Church.

> *The flower, even when cut, keeps its odor, and when bruised increases it, and when torn does not lose it; so, too, the Lord Jesus on that gibbet of the cross neither failed when bruised, nor fainted when torn; and when cut by the pricking of the lance, made more beautiful by the sacred color of the outpoured blood. He grew young again, Himself not knowing how to die and exhaling among the dead the gift of eternal life. On this flower, then, of the royal rod the Holy Spirit rested.*[6]

Saint Athenodorus of Mesopotamia

During the persecution of the Church under the Roman emperor Diocletian in the year 303, the martyr Athenodorus died in the region of Mesopotamia (modern Syria). According to tradition, he was arrested and condemned for refusing to give up his faith. When the soldiers tried to execute him by burning him at the stake, the fire wouldn't light. The sentence was changed to death by beheading, but the executioner dropped dead when he got close to Athenodorus. While the confused and superstitious pagans pondered what to try next, Athenodorus fell to his knees, began to pray, and died.

Saint John the Silent

John (454–558) came from a powerful family that included Armenian governors and generals. He was only eighteen years old when his parents died, and he decided to use his inheritance to build a monastery, moving into it to live as a monk with ten like-minded companions. Over time, his reputation for holiness led the archbishop of Sebaste to ordain him as the bishop of Colonia. John was a good, zealous bishop to his people, and he continued to live the austere life of a monk as much as he could, being particularly noted for his silence. However, there were certain widespread, evil practices among his people that he couldn't seem to eradicate. So after serving for only nine years as bishop, he quietly laid down his duties and went on a pilgrimage to Jerusalem. There he prayed and waited for God to show him what to do next. He received a vision in which he saw a cross and heard a voice, telling him to follow the light if he wished to be saved. He obeyed the voice and was led by a light to a large monastery ruled by a holy abbot, Saint Sabas of Mar Saba. Though John only served at the monastery as a lowly workman, not divulging his previous life as a monk and bishop, Abbot Sabas recognized that he was a holy man and decided to present John as a candidate for the priesthood to his superior, the patriarch Elias. John then

---

[6] Ambrose, "The Holy Spirit", in *Saint Ambrose: Theological and Dogmatic Works*, trans. Roy J. Deferrari, Fathers of the Church Series, vol. 44 (Washington, D.C.: Catholic University of America Press, 1963), 110.

privately told Elias that he had already been consecrated as a bishop, but that he had come to the desert because of his sins and to wait for the coming of the Lord. Elias told Abbot Sabas that he was unable to consecrate John as a priest, but he didn't tell him the reason. Somehow God eventually revealed the truth to Sabas, and he kept John's secret. Later, a quarrel arose among the monks, and Sabas was forced to leave his monastery. John left with him and only returned when Sabas was able to return. At the end of his life, John served as a spiritual advisor to many people who sought out his advice, and he spent the last days of his long life in uninterrupted praise of God.

Saint Mary Joseph (Benedetta) Rossello

Benedetta Rossello (1811–1888) was born into the poor family of a potter in Savona, Italy, and was one of nine children. She was pious even when she was young, but she had poor health and no dowry to offer, so the religious order she tried to join turned her down. For a while, she worked for a pious Christian couple. They could've afforded to give her the dowry money she needed, but they loved her too much to lose her from their family. She became a Franciscan tertiary when she was sixteen years old. When she was twenty-six years old, her bishop noticed her faith, and he gave her a house for her and three other young women to live with and educate girls. She placed the order that grew from that house, the Institute of the Daughters of Mercy, under the protection of Our Lady of Mercy and Saint Joseph, and she took the religious name of Mary Joseph. She accepted any deserving girl to join her order, whether she could afford the dowry or not; she governed it as superior for forty years.

Saint Ambrose, teach me humility.
Saint Athenodorus, show me how to live and die for Christ in peace.
Saint John, teach me to love silence.
Saint Mary Joseph, show me how to lead and teach others.

* * * * *

December 8

The Immaculate Conception of the Blessed Virgin Mary, Solemnity[7]

The dogma of Mary's Immaculate Conception wasn't proclaimed throughout the Church until 1854, but it had been debated and celebrated in local churches for centuries. In 1854, Pope Pius IX solemnly proclaimed in *Ineffabilius Deus*:

Wherefore, in humility and fasting, we unceasingly offered our private prayers as well as the public prayers of the Church to God the Father through his Son, that he would deign to direct and strengthen our mind by the power of the Holy

[7] Because the Immaculate Conception of the Blessed Virgin Mary is the patronal feast day of the United States, it is celebrated as a solemnity in the *Liturgical Calendar for the Dioceses of the United States of America*.

Spirit. In like manner did we implore the help of the entire heavenly host as we ardently invoked the Paraclete. Accordingly, by the inspiration of the Holy Spirit, for the honor of the Holy and undivided Trinity, for the glory and adornment of the Virgin Mother of God, for the exaltation of the Catholic Faith, and for the furtherance of the Catholic religion, by the authority of Jesus Christ our Lord, of the Blessed Apostles Peter and Paul, and by our own: "We declare, pronounce, and define that the doctrine which holds that the most Blessed Virgin Mary, in the first instance of her conception, by a singular grace and privilege granted by Almighty God, in view of the merits of Jesus Christ, the Savior of the human race, was preserved free from all stain of original sin, is a doctrine revealed by God and therefore to be believed firmly and constantly by all the faithful."[8]

And Heaven itself seemed to confirm this teaching when our Lady visited a peasant girl named Bernadette a few years later, saying, "I am the Immaculate Conception."

Saint Eutychian

Eutychian (d. 283) was the twenty-seventh pope; he reigned eight years. Because persecution of the Church was apparently dormant during this time period, it is unlikely that he died a martyr. However, being the pope during this time period was always dangerous because of the official Roman edict against Christianity, so some ancient Church traditions name him a martyr.

Saint Romaric of Remiremont

Romaric was born in the late sixth century in Austrasia, a large region now including France, Germany, the Netherlands, Luxembourg, and Belgium. His noble father was killed by Queen Brunhilda of Austrasia; Romaric himself became homeless when the queen took all of the family property as well. But Romaric was resourceful, and he eventually became a courtier of the king of the neighboring kingdom, King Clotaire II of Neustria (modern France), and became a wealthy man. However, after a conversation with the abbot of Remiremont, Saint Amatus, Romaric left everything behind and became a monk under Amatus' direction. Several of Romaric's serfs were so devoted to him that they entered religious life with him. Eventually Romaric became abbot himself. His last act was to visit the leader Grimoald, who happened to be the son of an old friend, and rebuke him for plotting against a prince. Grimoald and his nobles listened respectfully to the aged abbot and then sent him home, where he died three days later.

Saint Theobald of Marly

Theobald (d. 1247) was born into an illustrious French family in the castle of Marly. He was well educated, and everyone expected him to pursue a career in the French court. But Theobald loved to pray, and instead he decided to

---

[8] "Pius IX's *Ineffabilius Deus* (Defining the Immaculate Conception)", apostolic constitution issued December 8, 1854, EWTN.com, https://www.ewtn.com/catholicism/teachings/pius-ixs-ineffabilis-deus -defining-the-immaculate-conception-153.

become a Cistercian monk. In time, he became the abbot, and he lived humbly among his brothers in prayer, silence, and poverty. King Saint Louis IX knew Theobald and venerated him for his holiness.

Blessed Aloysius (Alojzy) Liguda

Aloysius was born in 1898 in Poland and became a priest and a member of the Society of the Divine Word. During World War II, he was arrested and sent to the Dachau concentration camp because he was a Catholic priest. He died a martyr on this date in 1942.

> *Mary, the Immaculate Conception, pray for my heart to be immaculate.*
> *Saint Eutychian, help me to love Christ and His Church.*
> *Saint Romaric, teach me how to put my talents at the service of Jesus Christ.*
> *Saint Theobald, teach me about prayer.*
> *Blessed Aloysius, help me remain faithful to Christ.*

* * * * *

December 9

Saint Juan Diego Cuauhtlatoatzin, Optional Memorial

Juan (1474–1548) and his wife were among the few natives of Mexico who converted to the Christian faith soon after missionaries came. He was a laborer, but neither poor nor rich, and he became a widower. One day while he was walking through the countryside to attend Mass, he encountered a beautiful woman on Tepeyac Hill. The woman told him to tell the bishop to build a chapel on that hill. He obediently went to the bishop, waited his turn to speak to him, and passed on the lady's message. The bishop listened to Juan but asked for time to pray about it. For a second time, Juan saw the lady, and she told him to go back to the bishop and ask again. But when Juan returned home after another unsuccessful meeting with the bishop, he found that his uncle had become seriously ill. He cared for his uncle all night, thinking he was near death, and then went to get medical help for him the next day. But though he tried to avoid the spot where he had seen the lady, she appeared to him again at another site but near the same hill. She told him not to worry about his uncle, and she arranged roses in Juan's tilma for him to take to the bishop as a sign. When Juan obeyed and opened the tilma in the presence of the bishop, people noticed not the miraculous flowers but the beautiful image of the lady, Our Lady of Guadalupe, which miraculously appeared on his tilma. Juan spent the rest of his life living near the church that housed the tilma and witnessing to others about the Virgin Mary's love for God's people, particularly those of Mexico.

Blessed Liborius Wagner

Liborius was born in 1593 in Muhlhausen, Germany, and raised in the Protestant faith. In 1621, after studying in a Jesuit school, he converted to

Catholicism, was ordained a priest, and served in a parish in a city that was predominantly Protestant. His holiness and personal witness brought many Protestants back to the Church. In 1631, he was forced to leave the city because of an approaching army of Protestant Swedes, so he hid in a city a few miles away. But the Swedes were informed of his location, captured him, dragged him behind a horse for miles, and imprisoned and tortured him for several days to try to make him renounce his faith. When that failed, they beat him to death on this date.

Saint Peter Fourier

Peter was born in 1565 in Mirecourt, Lorraine, in France, and his father sent him to be educated at a Jesuit university when he was fifteen years old. He recognized God's call to religious life and became an Augustinian Canon Regular when he was twenty years old. In 1589, he became a priest, but he refused to celebrate his first Mass for months because he felt he was so unworthy of the honor. His abbot sent him to study theology—where he surprised others with his amazing memory—and he earned his doctorate. Peter was called back to religious life in the monastery, served as procurator and vicar of a nearby parish, and attempted—despite ridicule from his fellow canons—to reform religious life at the monastery. He turned down opportunities to advance to higher offices, but he accepted the chance to become pastor at a particularly difficult parish in Mattaincourt in 1597. There he lived a simple, austere life, despite his own medical problems. He tried to start a school to educate boys from the area, but that plan failed. Finally, he found four female volunteers who supported his plan of educating girls and sent them to be trained at a house of female canons; he then set them to work teaching basic skills to girls, such as writing, composition, and proper diction, as well as practical skills. This became the order of the Canonesses Regular of Saint Augustine of the Congregation of Our Lady and was approved by the pope in 1616. In 1628, the rule of the order was changed, and the sisters were allowed to take an additional vow to provide free education to children. In 1622, Peter was asked by the bishop of Toul to unite and reform the Augustinian canons in his area. He was able to do that—though the canons resisted and didn't make it easy for him—and became their superior general in 1632. When France invaded the Duchy of Lorraine and French soldiers were ordered to fight alongside Protestants, he refused to take the oath of allegiance to King Louis XIII in support of violence against fellow Catholics and had to flee to eastern France. There he became the chaplain of a convent and taught in a free school he opened. He died four years later, in 1640.

> *Saint Juan, teach me how to love our Blessed Mother.*
> *Blessed Liborius, show me how to witness to my faith in Christ.*
> *Saint Peter, help me accept setbacks with God's grace.*

* * * * *

December 10

Saint Eulalia of Spain

Eulalia was only a twelve-year-old girl in Spain when a persecution of Christians broke out in the year 304. When she fearlessly confronted a local judge who had threatened Christians, he ordered her to be tortured. Executioners used metal hooks to rip apart her body and then set fire to her with torches. However, the flames caught her hair on fire, and she was mercifully smothered rather than burned to death.

Saint Gregory III

Gregory was a Syrian priest known for his holiness and intelligence. After the funeral of Pope Saint Gregory II in the year 731, the people spontaneously proclaimed him pope. Even from the early days in his pontificate, Gregory spoke against the violent iconoclastic policies of Emperor Leo III and supported the use of sacred images. When the angry emperor sent ships to forcibly bring Gregory to Constantinople, his ships were all lost in a storm. The emperor had to settle for punishing Gregory by seizing papal lands in Sicily and Calabria instead. Gregory rebuilt the churches that had been destroyed and set up images of our Lord and the saints with lamps around them, silently protesting the emperor's iconoclastic views. He sent missionaries to evangelize Germany (specifically, the priests and future saints Willibald and Boniface), and famously changed the balance of power in Europe by asking for help from Charles Martel (the de facto ruler of France at the time) when the Lombards threatened Rome, rather than the Byzantine emperor. He died on this date in the year 741.

Saints Polydore Plasden and Eustace White, and Blesseds Brian Lacey, John Mason, and Sidney Hodgson

All of the following saints and blesseds, who are commemorated today, lived in an England in which it was dangerous to be a Catholic and illegal to be a Catholic priest. Polydore Plasden was born in London in 1563, and his father was a horn maker. He went to France and Italy to study for the priesthood, returned to England as a priest to minister to Catholics secretly in 1586, and was arrested for the crime of celebrating Mass at a private home. Eustace White was rejected and cursed by his own father when he decided to become Catholic; he studied in France and Rome to become a priest and returned to minister to Catholics in 1588. Eustace was arrested for being a priest and was tortured repeatedly, but forgave the judges who condemned him. Brian Lacey, John Mason, and Sidney Hodgson were all Catholic laymen who were arrested for helping to hide Catholic priests from the authorities. They were all brutally interrogated and then tried and convicted on trumped-up charges. All these men were executed for their Catholic faith by being hanged, drawn, and quartered on this date in 1591.

Saint Eulalia, give me your courage in speaking the truth.
Saint Gregory, help me to draw closer to God through sacred art.
Holy Martyrs, show me how to help my priests.

* * * * *

December 11

Saint Damasus I

Damasus (d. 384) and his family are believed to be of Spanish origin, but he was born in Rome, and his father was a Catholic priest. Damasus was a deacon and unmarried when Pope Liberius died in the year 366, and he was proclaimed pope, but a small faction supported a different deacon. Their acts of violence caused civil unrest for a time, which unfortunately was only ended with even greater violence from civil leaders. After the chaos subsided, Damasus had the freedom to speak out and write against several heresies that were prevalent at the time and encourage Christians to remain faithful to true teaching. He also encouraged Saint Jerome to translate the entire Bible into Latin for the sake of the Church, and he ensured proper respect for the relics and resting places of the saints. He died when he was about eighty years old, and he was humbly laid to rest in a small church with his mother and sister since, as he had written at the papal crypt of Pope Saint Callistus' cemetery: "I, Damasus, wished to be buried here, but I feared to offend the ashes of these holy ones."[9]

Saint Daniel the Stylite

Daniel was born around the year 409 in Maratha, Syria, and was educated at a monastery at Samosata (modern Turkey). When he traveled as a pilgrim to see the famous Saint Simeon the Stylite in Syria, Simeon allowed Daniel to climb up on his pillar, and Simeon blessed him. Daniel returned and lived in a monastery until he was forty-two years old. Though the other monks asked him to become abbot when the previous abbot died, Daniel refused and eventually decided to live near an old temple outside Constantinople. When Simeon the Stylite died in the year 459, Daniel decided it was time to follow his example of penance, and for thirty-three years, Daniel lived on a pillar as a penance. The patriarch of Constantinople visited him once and ordained him a priest, though the patriarch had to climb the pillar himself to place his hands on Daniel's head for the ordination. He became so well known for his holiness that two emperors came to seek his advice. He left his pillar only one time, so that he could confront and correct an emperor. He died when he was more than eighty years old in 493.

---

[9] Walsh, *Butler's Lives of the Saints*, 414.

Blessed Arthur Bell

Arthur was born in Worcester, England, in 1590. When he decided to become a Catholic priest, he had to go to Spain to study for the priesthood due to the anti-Catholic laws in England at the time. After being ordained and joining the Franciscan order in 1618, he first served Catholics in France and Belgium. In 1634, he was sent to England to minister to covert Catholics. This he did until 1643, when the authorities found and arrested him. He was condemned to death for being a priest and was hanged, drawn, and quartered on this date in that year.

Saint Damasus, help me to be humble.
Saint Daniel, teach me how to live apart from the world.
Blessed Arthur, show me how to reach those who are far from Christ's Church.

* * * * *

December 12

Our Lady of Guadalupe, Feast[10]

In 1531, a peasant named Juan Diego was stopped by a beautiful woman who appeared to him on Tepeyac Hill outside Mexico City. During a series of apparitions, the lady identified herself as the Mother of God, spoke to the man with great affection, and arranged Castilian roses in his tilma for him to take back to the bishop as a sign that she wanted a church built on the spot. When Juan brought the roses to the bishop, however, all eyes were instead on the amazing image of the beautiful lady, which had been miraculously imprinted on the tilma. When the native people heard that the Mother of God had appeared to one of them, looking like them and asking them to worship her Son, they responded with great love and innumerable conversions.

Saints Epimachus, Alexander, Ammonaria, Mercuria, and Dionysia of Alexandria

Five individuals—Epimachus, Alexander, Ammonaria, Mercuria, and Dionysia—and one other unnamed Christian were martyred together during the persecution of Christians under the Roman emperor Decius in Alexandria, Egypt, in the year 250. The only other information we have about them is that they suffered greatly and with courage before being executed.

Our Lady, arrange and increase my meager virtues in a way that's pleasing to God.
Holy Martyrs, help me to suffer with patience for Christ.

* * * * *

[10] Because of the importance of Our Lady of Guadalupe in the Americas, it is celebrated as a feast in the *Liturgical Calendar for the Dioceses of the United States of America*, rather than an optional memorial.

December 13

Saint Lucy of Syracuse, Memorial

Lucy was born around 283 in Syracuse, Sicily. She was a Christian and was still a young woman when she decided to consecrate her life to Christ and never marry. A man who was angry that she refused to marry him took advantage of the current persecution of Christians under the Roman emperor Diocletian and informed the authorities that she was a Christian. Lucy was forcibly placed into a brothel, but she maintained her virginity. The authorities tried to kill her by setting fire to her, but failed. Tradition says that when a persecutor tore out her eyes, they were miraculously restored to her, which is why she's considered the patroness of the blind. They finally killed her with a sword. It was the year 304.

Saint Judoc (Josse)

Judoc was the son of Juthael, king of Armorica in Brittany (modern France). In the year 636, he withdrew from the world, was ordained a priest in Ponthieu, and went on a pilgrimage to Rome. When he returned to France, he lived a holy life as a hermit. After Judoc died in 668, his body was found to be incorrupt—so incorrupt that his hair, beard, and nails had to be trimmed from time to time.

Saint Lucy, help me to live a life of purity.
Saint Judoc, teach me how to withdraw from the world and live in Christ's presence.

* * * * *

December 14

Saint John of the Cross, Memorial

John (1542–1591) was born in Fontiveros, Spain. His father, Gonzalo, was from a well-to-do Spanish family, but his family disinherited him when he married a woman from a poor family out of love. When Gonzalo died, his mother, Catherine, was left alone, abandoned by her husband's family and destitute, to raise her three sons on her own. One son died in childhood, but John remained very close to his older brother, Francis, all his life. John attended a school for poor children and learned the basics of various trades. But instead of becoming a tradesman, he became a servant at a local hospital. While working as a servant and living a penitential life, he studied at a Jesuit college. At the age of twenty-one, he decided to enter a Carmelite friary and took the name in religious life of John of Saint Matthias. At the time, Carmelites were generally following a mitigated rule of life rather than the original Carmelite Rule, and John asked for (and was given) special permission to follow the stricter, original rule while he lived among the friars. Though out of humility he wanted to remain a lay brother, he had done so well in his studies that his superiors had him ordained to the priesthood. One day he met the Carmelite nun Saint Teresa of Avila, who was widely known at the time for her reformation of the Carmelite nuns. She recognized John as a kindred spirit and asked him to help her do the same for the male branch of the Carmelites. In 1568, he joyfully founded the first Discalced (meaning "shoeless") Carmelite monastery for friars and took the name John of the Cross. At the same time, he began to experience a great dryness in prayer, violent temptations from the devil, and persecution from other people. The fruit of this cross for him was one of his greatest writings, *The Dark Night of the Soul*, as well as the experience of great interior peace with God.

John became the spiritual director and confessor to Teresa's nuns, encouraging them in their spiritual lives, and his prayers even resulted in miracles, but the tensions between the Discalced and Mitigated Carmelite groups increased dramatically. Offended by the existence of the Discalced Carmelites and disregarding the official permission they had been given to reform the Carmelite order, the other Carmelites arrested John. They had armed men take him to their monastery in Toledo, locked him in a small, poorly lit cell that was only ten feet by six feet in size, and beat him daily in front of the other monks—as "discipline"—to try to force him to stop his "disobedience". He bore the marks of this torture for the rest of his life. He later told others: "Do not be surprised ... if I show a great love of suffering; God gave me a high idea of its value when I was in prison in Toledo."[11] He started writing poems during this time of great trial, and after nine months, he was able to escape from his prison cell, seemingly by a miracle. He returned to a Carmelite friary, served there as prior, became head of a college, and began his other great mystical writings. Though he held those under his care to a high standard of devotion and was quick to correct any lack of charity, he was affectionate by nature, quick to notice sadness or sickness in others, and encouraged others to place greater trust in God through personal renunciation. When Teresa died, a rift developed over whether to separate from the other Carmelite order completely. During this time, he founded new friaries, corrected abuses in the practices of some Carmelites, such as friars going to preach instead of living a contemplative life, and spoke in defense of moderation and in support of the Carmelite nuns. The vicar general, Father Nicholas Doria, was offended by John's support of the nuns, so he removed him from all his offices and sent him to a remote monastery. While John was there, two friars whom he had previously corrected now spread malicious gossip about him. When John became ill, he was given the choice of either going to a monastery where a friend of his was prior or going to a monastery in Ubeda where a friar he had corrected was

---

[11] Walsh, *Butler's Lives of the Saints*, 418.

prior. John chose Ubeda. He cheerfully submitted to painful operations and poor treatment from the prior himself at Ubeda. When the provincial found out what was happening, he rebuked the prior of Ubeda so sharply that the man repented. After three months of physical suffering, ignored by the order he had helped to found, and with false accusations still hanging over his head, John died on this date, imitating our Lord in His suffering to the very end. For his profound writings on mystical theology, which are still considered some of the deepest writings in all of Catholic mysticism, he was later named a Doctor of the Church.

> God desires the least degree of purity of conscience in you more than all the works you can perform.
>   God desires the least degree of obedience and submissiveness more than all those services you think of rendering Him. God values in you an inclination to aridity and suffering for love of Him more than all possible consolations, spiritual visions, and meditations.[12]

Saints Nicasius, Eutropia, Florentius, and Jucundus of Rheims

Nicasius (d. 451) was the bishop of Rheims, France, and the founder of its basilica. In a dream, he was warned in advance that barbarians were about to invade the city. During the invasion, he stood at the doorway of his church, trying to slow down the attackers so that his parishioners could escape. The invaders killed him, and his sister, Eutropia, was killed when she attacked her brother's murderer. The lector Jucundus and the deacon Florentius were also martyred with them.

> Saint John, help me to pray in my sufferings.
> Holy Martyrs, help me sacrifice myself for others.

* * * * *

December 15

Saint Valerian of Abbenza

During the fifth century, Vandal tribes invaded and plundered many regions around the Mediterranean Sea. The Vandals followed the Arian heresy and were bitterly opposed to faithful Catholics. Valerian was the bishop of Abbenza in North Africa. When Vandals invaded Abbenza, they ordered Valerian to turn over the church's sacred vessels—for the sake of the financial value of the

---

[12]John of the Cross, "Sayings of Light and Love", nos. 12–14, in *Collected Works of Saint John of the Cross*, trans. Kieran Kavanaugh, O.C.D., and Otilio Rodriguez, O.C.D. (Washington, D.C.: ICS Publications, 1979), 667.

items—but Valerian refused. They publicly ordered him to leave the city and prohibited anyone from providing him with shelter or assistance. Valerian was martyred by exposure to the elements in the year 457.

Saint Mary Victoria Fornari de Strata

Raised in the city of Genoa in Italy, Victoria (1562–1617) married Angelo Strata when she was seventeen years old, and the couple was happy and blessed with children. However, Angelo died after they had been married for only nine years. As a widow, Victoria was worried about being able to support her children and planned to marry again until our Blessed Mother appeared to her in a vision. In the vision, she told Victoria to be brave, to trust in the Mother of God's care for her, and to devote herself to the love of God. Victoria obeyed the vision. She gave away most of her wealth, and, by God's grace, she was able to raise her children without ever being in want. In 1604, when her children were older, she and some female friends gathered together to form a religious house of cloistered, contemplative nuns, and they became known as the Blue Nuns. Their society spread from Italy to France, and Victoria was the superior until her death at the age of fifty-five.

Saint Mary Crucifixa (Paula) di Rosa

In 1813, Mary was born the sixth of nine children to Clement di Rosa and the countess Camilla Albani in Brescia, Italy. Her mother died when she was eleven years old, and at the age of seventeen, she left school so that she could care for her father's household. He thought she should get married and even suggested a good husband for her. But Mary had already decided never to marry. For ten years, Mary lived at home and was involved in various good works despite her poor health. For example, she cared for the spiritual welfare of the young women working in her father's textile mill by creating a women's guild, and she arranged retreats and missions in their parish. During a cholera epidemic, she served the sick in the hospital, and that's when she met and worked with a widow with nursing experience, Gabriela Echenos-Bornati. After the epidemic ended, Mary was asked to take over the administration of a workhouse for girls who were poor or abandoned. But two years later, the project ended because the trustees wouldn't allow the girls they were helping to sleep in the house at night. Mary had shown herself to be courageous and quick-thinking; she once saved someone from a bolting horse and carriage. She was also practical and understanding. She decided to put her skills to work by opening a home for poor girls, as well as a home for deaf and dumb girls. In 1840, she was appointed superior of a religious society to care for people in hospitals, and with the help of Gabriela and the approval of her bishop, she founded the Handmaids of Charity of Brescia, an order of sisters that combined prayer and work. During wartime in northern Italy, she and her handmaids served in military hospitals years before Florence Nightingale and despite opposition from doctors who preferred secular nurses. In 1852, she took her vows with her first twenty-five sisters, taking the religious name Mother Mary of the Crucified. She became sick at Mantua within a few years and died peacefully three weeks later in 1855. She was forty-two years old.

> *Saint Valerian, help me to protect that which is sacred from the profane.*
> *Saint Victoria, help me to trust in our Blessed Mother's care for me.*
> *Saint Mary, show me how to care for those in need around me.*

* * * * *

December 16

Prophet Haggai

Haggai is one of the twelve minor prophets of the Old Testament. It's believed that he was born during the Babylonian Exile, returned with other Jews under the Jewish leader Zerubabbel, and encouraged Zerubbabel to reconstruct the Temple. Haggai's prophecies are dated around the year 520 B.C.

> *[Haggai said], "Yet now take courage, O Zerubbabel, says the Lord; take courage, O Joshua, son of Jehozadak, the high priest; take courage, all you people of the land, says the Lord; work, for I am with you, says the Lord of hosts, according to the promise that I made you when you came out of Egypt. My Spirit abides among you; fear not. For thus says the Lord of hosts: Once again, in a little while, I will shake the heavens and the earth and the sea and the dry land; and I will shake all nations, so that the treasures of all nations shall come in, and I will fill this house with splendor, says the Lord of hosts."*[13]

Martyred Women of Africa

In 482, Huneric, king of the Vandals, invaded Africa to conquer the lands and plunder its inhabitants. Huneric was also a follower of the Arian heresy, and he had little tolerance for faithful Catholics. In one region of northwest Africa, he ordered a large group of women to be executed—because they were faithful to the Son of God.

Saint Adelaide of Burgundy

Adelaide was born around the year 931 and was the daughter of King Rudolf II of Upper Burgundy (modern France). As a princess, her marriage was arranged for political reasons when she was two years old. At age sixteen, she married Lothair, who was king of Italy at the time, and they had a daughter named Emma, who later married King Lothaire II of France. But in the year 950, her husband, Lothair, died. Everyone knew that he had been poisoned by a powerful man, Berengarius of Ivrea (Italy), and Berengarius then demanded that Adelaide marry his son. When she refused to marry the son of her husband's murderer,

[13] Hag 2:4–7.

she was threatened and imprisoned in a castle. But King Otto the Great of Germany led an army into Italy, defeated Berengarius, and rescued Adelaide. She then married Otto, though she was twenty years younger than he was, and they had five children. She was a gracious, gentle queen and greatly loved by her people; in the year 962, Otto was crowned Holy Roman Emperor in Rome. However, this worldly success was balanced by troubles with her children: her stepson (Otto's child by a previous marriage) resented being passed over for the throne in favor of her son, and even her own son, Otto, was turned against her for a time by her daughter-in-law, Theophano. With the help of abbot Saint Majolus, Otto eventually repented and asked for his mother's forgiveness. When her son Otto died, Theophano took over as regent, and Adelaide left the court, but she returned to serve as regent for the country when Theophano died. As a ruler, she was generous and forgiving, she founded and restored monasteries, and she did what she could to encourage the Christian conversion of the nearby Slavic peoples. Although she had saintly abbots (Saints Adalbert, Majolus, and Odilo) to advise her, ruling an entire country was a heavy burden for the elderly, peace-loving woman. She died while she was in a monastery at Seltz, France, on this date in the year 999.

> *Prophet Haggai, show me how to trust in God always.*
> *Holy Martyrs, help me remain faithful to Christ.*
> *Saint Adelaide, help me be generous and forgiving.*

* * * * *

December 17

Martyrs of Eleutheropolis

In the year 638, the imperial Roman army of the emperor Heraclius was stationed in Eleutheropolis (now Beit Jibrin), Palestine. Invading Saracens (Muslim Arabs) killed sixty of the soldiers—specifically because they were Christians. We know the names of most of these men who gave up their lives rather than their faith.

Saint Sturmi of Fulda

Sturmi was born in the eighth century in Bavaria (Germany) to a Christian family. He was educated at an abbey under the direction of Saint Wigbert, became a priest, served as a missionary, and became the first German Benedictine monk. He and two companions decided to leave the monastery and live in solitude, and they eventually settled at a site that allowed them to evangelize the nearby Saxons. Sturmi became an abbot under the direction of the missionary bishop Saint Boniface. After Boniface's death, a privilege that Pope Saint Zachary had granted Sturmi's monastery—that it was subject directly to the Holy See, not a bishop—caused trouble with Boniface's successor, Saint Lull. There was a bitter struggle between these two saints, the civil authority, and the monks, but finally

Sturmi was allowed to remain abbot. The monks had only limited success in converting the Saxons, mostly because the many wars being fought between Christians at the time, as *Butler's Lives of the Saints* puts it, "were not calculated to recommend [the faith] to the heathen".[14] Sturmi and his monks had to leave the monastery for their own safety at one point. At the end of his life, Sturmi became ill, and despite the efforts of King Charlemagne's own doctor, he died on this date in the year 779.

Saint John de Matha of Rome

John was born in Provence, France, in 1155 and became a priest and theology professor in Paris. However, he gave up teaching after he received a vision in which he recognized God calling him to help free Christian slaves in Africa. John founded a religious order dedicated to the Holy Trinity called the Trinitarians. The order was devoted to acts of charity for those in need, particularly in ransoming slaves; it obtained papal approval in 1198. John died in Rome in 1213.

> *Holy Martyrs, show me how to live and die for Christ.*
> *Saint Sturmi, help me learn how to live in peace and solitude.*
> *Saint John, show me how to bring freedom to those in bondage to sin.*

* * * * *

December 18

Prophet Malachi

Malachi was one of the twelve minor prophets and the last of the Old Testament prophets, living in the fifth or sixth centuries B.C. He reproached the people of Jerusalem, particularly the priests, for their failure to offer worthy sacrifices to God and predicted the coming of the day of the Lord.

> *[The Lord said,] "Behold, I will send you Elijah the prophet before the great and awesome day of the LORD comes. And he will turn the hearts of fathers to their children and the hearts of children to their fathers, lest I come and strike the land with a curse."*[15]

Saint Flannan of Killaloe

Flannan was the son of a Celtic chieftain in seventh-century Ireland. According to tradition, he traveled (on a floating stone) on a pilgrimage to Rome and was consecrated by Pope John IV, becoming the first bishop of Killaloe. He talked his own father into becoming a monk in his old age, and when people suggested that Flannan succeed his father as chief, he prayed to be made ineligible. Soon afterward, his face broke out in unattractive rashes and scars, and he thankfully

---

[14] Walsh, *Butler's Lives of the Saints*, 423.
[15] Mal 4:5–6.

continued as a bishop. It's said that he, like some of the other Celtic monks of the time, recited his Divine Office while standing in icy water as a penance and also that he preached the Gospel to the people of the Western Isles, a series of islands that are now known by his name.

Saint Winebald of Heidenheim

Winebald was born around the year 701. He and his brother Willibald were sons of Richard the Saxon, a Saxon king and also now acclaimed a saint. Richard took his sons with him when he went on a pilgrimage from England to Rome, and while they were there, Willibald decided to complete his pilgrimage by going to the Holy Land. Winebald chose to stay in Rome, where he studied for seven years and became a monk. When he returned to England, he continued to go on pilgrimages to holy places. In the year 739, he met Saint Boniface, the missionary saint of Germany, who convinced him that he too could help with the evangelization of Germany. So Winebald went to Thuringia (modern-day central Germany); he was ordained a priest there, taught the Gospel to the people, and was eventually placed in charge of seven churches. Several years later, he felt God calling him to return to the life of the cloister, and he joined his brother Willibald, who was now bishop of Eichstatt but was living in a monastery. They asked their sister Walburga to join them, and she and Winebald governed a monastery for men and women in Willibald's diocese. Despite Winebald's continual health problems, he governed his monks wisely and bore all his illnesses patiently. He died in December 761, with his brother and sister at his side.

Saints Paul Nguyen Van My, Peter Truong Van Duong, and Peter Vu Van Truat

Paul My was a convert to the faith, and Peter Duong and Peter Truat were catechists. These three Vietnamese men spread the faith in their native country until they were arrested by the government for being Christians. They were executed by strangulation and died as martyrs on this date in 1838.

> *Prophet Malachi, help me to live a sacrificial life.*
> *Saint Flannan, help me pray and do penance for my sins.*
> *Saint Winebald, show me how to let my physical weakness lead me to Christ.*
> *Holy Martyrs, give me your zeal for spreading the Gospel.*

* * * * *

December 19

Saint Anastasius I

In the year 399, Anastasius succeeded Pope Saint Siricius as pope. Saints Jerome, Paulinus of Nola, and Augustine of Hippo all admired him. As *Butler's Lives of the Saints* puts it, "Jerome was as kind in speaking of his friends as he was merciless to his opponents,"[16] and Jerome said that Rome did not deserve such a good pope for fear that "the world's head be cut off"[17] as a result (a reference to the subsequent invasion of Rome by Alaric the Goth). As pope, Anastasius condemned certain writings of Origen that were causing disagreements among Christian leaders. He died in 401.

Saint Urban V

William de Grimoard was a Frenchman who became a priest, professor, abbot, and papal legate. While serving on a papal mission in 1362, he learned that Pope Innocent VI had died and that he himself had been elected pope to replace him. He took the name Urban V, and he dedicated his papacy to spreading the Gospel to foreign lands, reforming the lax moral life of Christians, and returning the seat of the papacy from Avignon to Rome. Despite great political opposition (and with the forceful encouragement of Saint Catherine of Siena), he was able to bring the papal court back to Rome. However, more political difficulties forced him to return to Avignon on September 5, 1370, and he died four months later.

Saints Francis Xavier Ha Trong Mau, Dominic Bui Van Uy, Thomas Nguyen Van De, Augustine Nguyen Van Moi, and Stephen Nguyen Van Vinh

All five of the men commemorated today were born in Vietnam and became Catholic. Most were laymen—farmers, tailors, peasants—who became Dominican tertiaries to grow in their faith and teach it to others. When the Vietnamese government cracked down on Christians, they were arrested for being Catholic, put in prison, tortured, and executed by strangling on this date in 1839.

> *Saint Anastasius, show me how to be a good leader.*
> *Saint Urban, help me trust in God, even when I seem to fail.*
> *Holy Martyrs, give me your zeal for sharing the faith with others.*

* * * * *

December 20

Saint Zephyrinus

Zephyrinus (d. 217) was a gentle but firm pope in the early days of the Church. His decision to allow repentant Christians who had apostatized during times of persecution to return to the Church was opposed by some, including Bishop

---

[16] Walsh, *Butler's Lives of the Saints*, 423–24.
[17] Ibid., 423.

Hippolytus, who set himself up as an anti-pope before later repenting. Zephyrinus is generally considered a martyr, since it appears his death was a result of the great difficulties he faced.

Saint Dominic of Silos

Dominic was born in 1000 in Navarre, Spain, and was from a peasant family. He tended his father's flocks when he was a young boy, and when he realized that he enjoyed solitude, he decided to enter the monastery of San Milan de la Cogolla. He became a Benedictine monk and later prior of the house. However, when the king demanded that he hand over certain possessions of the monastery, Dominic refused. He and two other monks were forced to leave the kingdom of Navarre. However, another king of Spain, King Ferdinand of Castile, welcomed the monks and gave them a remote (and run-down) monastery at Burgos. Under Dominic's leadership, the dying monastery came back to life and flourished spiritually, intellectually, and materially, becoming famous throughout Spain. Many miracles and healings were attributed to the power of his prayers. He died on this date in 1073.

> *Saint Zephyrinus, help me to be forgiving at all times.*
> *Saint Dominic, help me to love solitude.*

* * * * *

December 21

Saint Peter Canisius, Optional Memorial

Peter was born in Holland in 1521. His father had been made a member of the nobility because he served as a tutor to the nobility. Although Peter's mother died when he was young, his stepmother was a pious woman and a good, loving mother to him and his siblings. He accused himself later of many faults as a youngster, but he appears to have been a typical boy, though very intelligent and open to direction from others. Peter received his master of arts degree in Cologne, Germany, when he was only nineteen years old. He studied law at first to please his father, but when he recognized God was calling him to religious life, he took a vow of celibacy and began to study theology instead. He entered the Jesuits, became a priest, and became widely known for his effective preaching and writings about the faith. He personally served Saint Ignatius, the founder of the Jesuit order, until Ignatius sent him to teach in the first school started by the Jesuits. During this time of political and religious unrest due to the Protestant Revolt, Peter was sent throughout Germany—for example, to Bavaria, Vienna, Prague, Augsburg, and Dillingen. In each city, he became known as an excellent preacher and was tireless in serving those in need. He wrote thousands of letters—many of them essentially theological tracts—and his careful, exhaustive writings about the faith, particularly the popular catechism he wrote, refuted heretical teachings with equanimity but firmness. He reformed and established many Catholic schools and universities, earning them such a reputation for excellence that even Protestants sent their children to attend them. In all these efforts to bring people back to the Catholic faith from Protestantism, he was remarkably successful throughout Protestant Germany. However, Peter participated in public discussions between Catholics and Protestants out of obedience to his superiors only because he thought these were worse than useless due to the heated arguments that inevitably resulted. The pope wanted to make Peter the bishop of Vienna at one point, but Ignatius only allowed Peter to administer the diocese for one year. In 1591, Peter almost died when he suffered a paralytic seizure. He recovered, though, and with the help of a secretary, he continued writing until shortly before he died on this date in 1597. Peter was declared a Doctor of the Church in 1925.

So, after daring to approach your most loving heart and to plunge my thirst in it, I received a promise from you of a garment made of three parts: these were to cover my soul in its nakedness, and to belong especially to my religious profession. They were peace, love and forgiveness. Protected by this garment of salvation, I was confident that I would lack nothing but all would succeed and give you glory.[18]

Prophet Micah

Micah was an Old Testament prophet during the reigns of the kings Jotham, Ahaz, and Hezekiah (around 737–690 B.C.). He spoke God's words to His people, including a prediction of the coming Messiah.

But you, O Bethlehem Ephrathah, who are little to be among the clans of Judah, from you shall come forth for me one who is to be ruler in Israel, whose origin is from of old, from ancient days.[19]

Saint Themistocles of Lycia

During the persecution of the Church under the Roman emperor Valerian in the year 253, the martyr Themistocles died in the city of Myra (in modern Turkey). Themistocles was a shepherd, and he was arrested and killed because he wouldn't reveal the location of (future martyr-saint) Dioscorus, another Christian living in Myra.

Saint Peter, help me bring Christ to others.
Prophet Micah, teach me the peace of Christ.
Saint Themistocles, help me protect those in need.

* * * * *

[18] *The Liturgy of the Hours*, vol. 1, from the writings of Saint Peter Canisius, priest (New York: Catholic Book Publishing, 1975), 1249.
[19] Mic 5:2.

December 22

Saint Chaeremon of Nilopolis and Companions

During the persecution of Christians under the Roman emperor Decius in the year 250, many Egyptian Christians were driven into the desert. Most of them died of hunger or the harsh conditions of the desert, were killed by wild animals or bandits, or were captured and sold as slaves. We only know specific details about a few of these martyrs. Chaeremon was the elderly bishop of Nilopolis, and after fleeing into the desert with a companion, he was never seen again.

Blessed Thomas Holland

Thomas was born in 1600 in Sutton, England. When he decided to become a Catholic priest, he was forced to leave England in 1621 and study in France and Spain because of the anti-Catholic laws of the time. He was ordained a priest in Belgium and served as a priest in various places until he secretly returned to England in 1635. Because he was good at creating disguises and spoke many languages (Spanish, Flemish, and French, from his years spent abroad) he was able to move constantly from place to place and minister to Catholics covertly. But in 1642, he was arrested for the crime of being a priest, was convicted through the pretense of a trial, and sentenced to death. He was hanged, drawn, and quartered on December 12, 1642, in London.

> *Holy Martyrs, help me be faithful to Jesus Christ,*
> *particularly in my most severe trials.*

* * * * *

December 23

Saint John of Kanti (John Cantius), Optional Memorial

John was born in Kanti, Poland, in 1390. His parents recognized that he was an intelligent boy and sent him to the University of Cracow to be educated. He received his degree as a doctor of philosophy, was ordained a priest, and was given a teaching position at the university. When people warned John that his ascetic way of life would endanger his health, he pointed out that many of the Desert Fathers (who had lived strict lives too) often lived to be over one hundred years old. As often happens, some people were jealous of John's success, and they managed to get him removed from the university and sent to serve in a parish. Although his parishioners didn't like him at first, in the end he won over their hearts. In time, he was recalled to the University of Cracow and served there as a professor of Sacred Scripture for the rest of his life. John was kind and friendly to all, equally willing to speak with academics, nobility, or the poor. In penance, he never ate meat, he slept on the floor, and he traveled to Rome on foot carrying his own possessions. His prayers resulted in miracles, and during his last illness, the people of Cracow were terribly sad at the thought of losing him. He told them, "Never mind about this prison which is decaying,... but think of the soul that is going to leave it."[20] He died on Christmas Eve at the age of eighty-three in 1473.

Saint John Stone

John (d. 1539) was an Augustinian friar in Canterbury, England, before becoming a professor and a doctor of theology. When King Henry VIII declared himself the head of the Church in England, he tried to win the educated and respected Father Stone over to his side. But John publicly denounced Henry's claim of control over the Church. Later, the king demanded that every member of his friary sign an oath accepting his claim; all the brothers did except John, who carefully explained the reasons he could not sign. He was sent to prison, put on trial, convicted, and sentenced to death. He was hanged, drawn, and quartered in the month of December.

Saint Marie Marguerite d'Youville

Marguerite was born in 1701 in Canada, and her father died when she was seven years old. She was able to attend school only until she was thirteen years old, at which point she returned home to help care for and teach her five younger siblings. Her mother remarried, and the family moved to Montreal. There, at age twenty-one, she married Francois d'Youville, sharing a home with him and her mother-in-law. She bore her husband six children, though four died as infants. Just as painfully, her husband cheated on her, neglected her, and left her with nothing but debts when he died after seven years of marriage. Marguerite opened a small store to support herself and eventually founded an order of nuns called the Sisters of Charity of the General Hospital of Montreal (also known as the Grey Nuns), taking over the operation of a failing and rundown hospital in 1747. Serving the poor sick, Marguerite and her nuns suffered many difficulties. For example, lack of money repeatedly almost closed the hospital, and the armed conflicts between the French and English made life dangerous. Marguerite died at the age of seventy, exhausted from a lifetime of self-giving, in the year 1771.

> Saint John of Kanti, show me how to live a life of service for the love of Jesus Christ.
> Saint John Stone, help me to carefully and charitably explain God's truth to others.
> Saint Marguerite, teach me to see God's blessings in my sufferings.

* * * * *

---

[20] Walsh, *Butler's Lives of the Saints*, 427.

December 24

Saint Irmina of Trier

Irmina (d. 710) was the daughter of a king, Saint Dagobert II of Austrasia (a large region that includes the modern countries of the Netherlands, Belgium, France, Germany, and Luxembourg). When her promised husband was killed out of jealousy by an officer who wanted to marry Irmina himself, she decided to leave the world behind. She asked her father's permission to become a nun instead, and he agreed and even built a convent for her at Trier, Germany. She supported the missionary work of the priest Saint Willibrord, and after (she believed) his prayers had saved Irmina's nuns from an epidemic, she gave him land on which he built a monastery at Echternach.

Saint Paula Elizabeth (Constanza) Cerioli

Constanza was born into a noble family in Soncino, Italy, in 1816 and had poor health from birth, specifically a spinal deformity and a heart condition. When she was nineteen years old, her family arranged for her to marry fifty-nine-year-old Gaetano Busecchi. Gaetano had poor health and was a difficult man to deal with, but together they had three children. Two of them died very young, and the third died when he was sixteen years old, with her husband dying shortly afterward. Now that she was a widow, she began to use her wealth to care for the poor and for orphans, bringing them to her own home, and selling her jewelry, with such generosity that her friends thought she was unbalanced by her grief. After giving away her possessions, she gave herself to God: she took private vows of chastity, poverty, and obedience first, and she founded the Institute of the Sisters of the Holy Family in 1857. She took the name in religious life of Paula Elizabeth and founded an order for men, also to serve abandoned children and parents. She died on this date in 1865.

> Saints Irmina and Paula Elizabeth, help me renounce the
> things of this world for God's sake.

* * * * *

December 25

The Nativity of the Lord, Solemnity[21]

The Prologue of the Gospel of John: "In the beginning was the Word, and the Word was with God, and the Word was God. He was in the beginning with

---

[21] Saints have been included on this date for completeness, but the author recommends reading relevant Scripture passages instead or in addition: Mt 1:18–25; Lk 2:4–20.

God; all things were made through him, and without him was not anything made that was made. In him was life, and the life was the light of men. The light shines in the darkness, and the darkness has not overcome it."[22]

Saint Anastasia of Sirmium

During the persecution of the Church under the Roman emperor Diocletian in the year 304, the martyr Anastasia died in Sirmium, a city now in Serbia. Some traditions say that her husband was a pagan and turned her in to the authorities and that she learned about the faith from Saint Chrysogonus.

Blessed Peter the Venerable

Peter was born in 1092 into a noble family in France. He became a Benedictine monk and later abbot at the Abbey of Cluny. As the abbot of one of the most influential monasteries at the time, Peter's leadership affected all of Christendom as he encouraged the proper education of his monks; wrote poems, commentaries, sermons, and treatises; attended Church councils; and published a Latin translation of the Koran to help missionaries better understand Islamic teaching. He died of natural causes in 1156.

Blessed Michael Nakashima Saburoemon

Michael was born in 1582 in Michiai, Japan, became a Catholic when he was young, and lived a prayerful, penitential life. He also hid missionary priests from the Japanese authorities to protect them from certain death. He secretly entered the Jesuit order as a coadjutor brother in 1627, but he was arrested a year later when he refused to contribute to the wood being used to execute five priests by fire in his town. Even under torture, he refused to renounce his faith in Christ. He later wrote to others that he had called on the Blessed Virgin when the pain became too strong to bear, and it instantly ceased. In 1628, he was immersed in scalding water until it killed him.

Saint Albert (Adam) Chmielowski

After Adam (1845–1916) lost a leg fighting as a young soldier for his native Poland, he returned to his college studies. He became a successful artist; he tried to enter the Jesuits and later tried to become a Franciscan tertiary, but eventually gave up everything to care for the poor, taking the name Albert. In time, others began to follow his example, which became the orders of the Albertine Brothers and Albertine Sisters in Poland. Pope Saint John Paul II, who had written a play about Albert, canonized him.

> *All you holy saints, help me draw close to the Infant Jesus on His birthday.*

* * * * *

[22] Jn 1:1–5.

December 26

Saint Stephen the Deacon and Martyr, Feast

Stephen (d. ca. 34) was one of seven men selected by the apostles to be named deacons to assist them in their service of the early Church.[23] Stephen not only eloquently defended the Christian faith, but he also performed "wonders and signs among the people".[24] As an effective apologist, he was targeted by the Jewish religious leaders in Jerusalem, who instigated false charges of blasphemy against Stephen. Stephen's long speech before the Sanhedrin[25] shows his knowledge of the history of the Jews and the Old Testament, but also leads his listeners to see God's preparation for the Christ among His Chosen People. When Stephen confronted the people with their crime of executing an innocent man who was also their Messiah, they accused him of blasphemy, dragged him outside the city, and executed him by stoning. He died with words of forgiveness on his lips for his persecutors, the first martyr for Christ.

And as they were stoning Stephen, he prayed, "Lord Jesus, receive my spirit." And he knelt down and cried with a loud voice, "Lord, do not hold this sin against them." And when he had said this, he fell asleep.[26]

Saint Dionysius

Dionysius (d. 268) was the twenty-fifth pope; he reigned nine years. Before becoming pope, he had earned a reputation for his strength of character and learning during the Church controversy over the validity of Baptism when administered by heretical Christians. His predecessor had died a martyr, and the office of pope had been vacant for almost a year due to the prevalent persecution of Christians. After Dionysius became pope, however, the Roman emperor Gallienus temporarily halted the persecution. During this hiatus, Dionysius was able to recover some church buildings and improve the order and administration of the Church. He later issued documents explaining Church teaching against the heretical teachings of Sabellianism and Marcionism. He also sent funds to Christians in Cappadocia (modern Turkey) to redeem those who had been enslaved by the Goths. He died a martyr and is considered a Father of the Church.

Saint Zosimus

Zosimus (d. 418) was the forty-first pope; he reigned for less than two years. During his reign, he showed himself to be cautious and merciful in dealing with disputes over bishops' jurisdictions, as well as in his dealings with the heretical Pelagius and his followers. When the pope asked Pelagius for an explanation of

---

[23] Acts 6:3–5.
[24] Acts 6:8.
[25] Acts 7:2–53.
[26] Acts 7:59–60.

his teachings, for example, Pelagius' careful and shrewd explanations initially led Zosimus to defend him. But when the truth of Pelagius' character and teachings became obvious, Zosimus responded by condemning him and his teachings and articulating the traditional dogma of the Church about predestination and free will.

Saint Vincentia Maria Lopez Vicuna

Vincentia (1847–1896) was the daughter of a lawyer and was born in Spain. She refused an arranged marriage and instead lived with an aunt who had founded a home for domestic servants. She privately vowed to live a life of chastity, and she eventually created a group of women who ministered to working girls. This became the Daughters of Mary Immaculate for Domestic Service, and her order spread throughout Europe and Latin America during her own lifetime.

> *Saint Stephen, help me always remain faithful to Christ.*
> *Saints Dionysius and Zosimus, help me to love Christ and His Church.*
> *Saint Vincentia, show me how to sacrifice myself for those in need.*

* * * * *

December 27

Saint John the Apostle and Evangelist, Feast

John (d. ca. 100), son of Zebedee[27] and Mary Salome, the brother of James, was one of the first disciples who followed Christ.[28] John was also a fisherman,[29] knew the family of the high priest,[30] and was nicknamed a "son of thunder" by Christ.[31] John, James, and Peter alone were present when Jesus raised Jairus' daughter from death[32] and when he was transfigured before them on Mount Tabor.[33] Traditionally, the Gospel of John, three epistles, and the book of Revelation are attributed to him. Tradition also says that he escaped martyrdom through a miracle, cared for the Blessed Mother until her death, died at a great age himself, and was the last of the apostles to die.

> *For God so loved the world that he gave his only-begotten Son, that whoever believes in him should not perish but have eternal life.*[34]

[27] Mk 10:35.
[28] Mt 4:19.
[29] Mt 4:18.
[30] Jn 18:15.
[31] Mk 3:17.
[32] Lk 8:51.
[33] Mt 17:1.
[34] Jn 3:16.

Saints Theodore and Theophanes of Constantinople

The parents of these two brothers were originally from Kerak, the land of the ancient Moabite tribes and an area now in Jordan, before they moved to Jerusalem. Born in the late eighth century, Theodore and Theophanes were well educated, became monks at the monastery of Saint Sabas, and were known for their virtuous lives. The patriarch of Jerusalem ordained Theodore to the priesthood, and when Theodore wrote against the iconoclasm (opposition to sacred images) of the emperor Leo, both he and his brother were banished to an island of the Black Sea. There they suffered from hunger and cold, but when the emperor Leo died soon afterward, they were able to return to their monastery in Constantinople. However, the new emperor was also an iconoclast, and he ordered the two monks whipped before he banished them. Two years later, they were allowed to return, but when they still opposed iconoclasm, the emperor Theophilus ordered them to be tortured and humiliated by having twelve lines of iambic verse cut into their foreheads. This torture took more than a day, and they were then banished again, this time to Apamea in Bithynia (modern Turkey). Theodore died there in 841, but the emperor died soon too. In the year 842, Saint Methodius was made patriarch of Constantinople, and he allowed holy images to be restored to churches. Theophanes was honored for his faithfulness despite persecution and made bishop of Nicaea. He wrote hymns, including one about his brother Theodore, and died in 845. The two brothers are commonly called the "Graptoi", or "written on", because of the sufferings they were forced to endure.

Saint John, show me how to follow Christ, wherever He leads me.
Saints Theodore and Theophanes, help me to suffer patiently for the love of Christ.

* * * * *

December 28

The Holy Innocents, Feast

These children of Bethlehem—of unknown number—were killed under orders from King Herod the Great,[35] simply because they were boys and because one of them could possibly be the prophesied Messiah. As the first martyrs for Christ, the Church acclaims them saints, certain of their welcome into Heaven.

Saint Anthony of Lerins

Anthony (d. 520) was born in Valeria (modern Hungary) during the dangerous time of barbarian invasions. His father died when he was eight years old, and he was educated and raised in a monastery that had been founded by the hermit Saint Severinus. When Severinus died, the young Anthony was placed

---

[35] Mt 2:15–18.

under the care of his uncle Constantius, who happened to be the bishop of Lorch in Bavaria. In the year 488, at about the age of twenty, Anthony decided to become a monk. At first, he became a hermit and lived under the direction of a priest named Marius. Though Marius tried to convince him to become a priest, Anthony recognized that God was calling him to solitary life instead. So Anthony found a cave, where he lived, studied, prayed, and cultivated his garden. In time, Anthony's solitary life was no longer solitary because many people came to see him, talk to him, and ask for his advice. So he crossed the Alps and moved to Gaul (modern France), becoming a monk at the famous Lerins Abbey. There he became known for the miracles that resulted from his prayers and for his virtuous life until his death.

Saint Caspar (Gaspar) del Bufalo

As a young priest, Caspar (1786–1837) was exiled from his hometown of Rome when Napoleon's army invaded the city. When he was able to return to Rome, he began his life's work: spreading the Gospel. The Missioners of the Precious Blood, the community that Caspar founded, preached the Gospel all over Italy through parish missions. He insisted that his missioners be studious, devout, and humble, and they lived out that call, for example, by disciplining themselves publicly for their sins during their missions. Their humility led to many conversions. His missioners also served others in practical ways, and they served both the young and the old, male and female, rich and poor. Caspar died of cholera.

> Holy Innocents, show me how to offer my life for Christ today.
> Saint Anthony, show me how to live a simple life with God in my heart.
> Saint Caspar, help me to spread the Gospel.

* * * * *

December 29

King David of Israel

David was the youngest son of Jesse of Bethlehem and a humble shepherd when he killed the Philistine soldier Goliath.[36] Scholars postulate that he lived around the year 1000 B.C. He served King Saul until Saul's jealousy forced David to become an outlaw, but ultimately he became king of Judah and king of all twelve tribes. He was a soldier, reformer, father, sinner, penitent, and poet. The biblical books of 1 Kings and 2 Kings, 1 Samuel and 2 Samuel, 1 Chronicles and 2 Chronicles speak of David, and many of the psalms are attributed to him.

> I love you, O LORD, my strength. The LORD is my rock, and my fortress, and my deliverer, my God, my rock, in whom I take refuge, my shield, and the horn of my salvation, my stronghold. I call upon the LORD, who is worthy to be praised, and I am saved from my enemies.[37]

[36] 1 Sam 17:1–58.
[37] Ps 18:1–3.

Saint Thomas Becket, Optional Memorial

Thomas was born in London, England, in 1118, and his parents died when he was twenty-one years old. He was ordained a deacon in 1154, and a year later, his friend King Henry II appointed him his chancellor. Thomas lived a good Christian life, but temperamentally he struggled with pride, stubbornness, and a hot temper. When the bishop of Canterbury died, the king insisted on having Thomas replace him, though Thomas wasn't even ordained. With the pope's permission, Thomas was ordained a priest one day, and a bishop the next. Ordination seems to have affected Thomas; people began to notice that he wore a hair shirt, rose early to read the Bible every morning, doubled the alms he gave to the poor, and was less extravagant when entertaining. Initially, Thomas' relationship with the king seemed unchanged. But when in 1163 the king insisted that clergy who had committed a crime be turned over to civil authority for punishment, Thomas resisted this as an infringement on the Church's rights. The king responded angrily, and Thomas appeased him by accepting some of the king's demands. Soon, Thomas recognized that he had made a serious mistake in giving in to the king. He stopped celebrating Mass, then he wrote to the pope; he waited briefly for the pope to absolve him of his error and then impetuously left England to plead his case before the pope himself. Pope Alexander III strongly rebuked Thomas for giving in to King Henry, but after Thomas humbly resigned from his office as bishop, the pope relented and reinstated him. For six years, Thomas lived in France, first in a Cistercian monastery and then an abbey, because it was too dangerous for him to return to England. In the meantime, the king retaliated by persecuting Thomas' friends and associates in England. During heated negotiations between Thomas, the pope, and the kings of France and England, Thomas angrily excommunicated several of his enemies; the pope reversed some (but not all) of his actions. Finally, in July 1170, Henry and Thomas reconciled in person, with Thomas returning to England in December. However, the bishops who had given in to the king's demands—and who were therefore facing penalties from the pope—were not pleased to have Thomas back in England. Neither was King Henry, who, in a fit of rage, asked out loud one day whether someone would rid him of "this meddlesome priest".[38] Four of his knights saw this as a command to get rid of Thomas. They found Thomas, argued with him, followed him into a church, argued with him some more, and then killed him with an axe. Before he died, Thomas said, "Willingly I die for the name of Jesus and in defense of the Church."[39] The murder shocked everyone, and for a long time, Thomas' body lay in the church because no one was willing to touch it. Within two years, the pope had declared him a martyr, and within four years, the king—the most powerful ruler in Europe—did public penance for his role in the murder.

Blessed José Aparicio Sanz

During the Spanish Civil War from 1934 to 1939, thousands of Catholics were murdered during anti-Catholic persecution. José Aparicio Sanz (1893–1936)

---

[38] Matthew Bunson and Margaret Bunson, *Our Sunday Visitor's Encyclopedia of Saints*, 2nd ed. (Huntington, Ind.: Our Sunday Visitor Publishing Division, 2014), 808.

[39] Ibid.

was a parish priest and pastor known for his work with children and advocacy of Eucharistic Adoration and the Forty Hours' Devotion. He was arrested for the crime of being a priest and was executed on this date in 1936.

> *King David, show me how to keep my heart always open to God.*
> *Holy Martyrs, help me to be willing to live and die in Christ's service.*

* * * * *

December 30

Saint Felix I

Felix was from a Roman family, and he reigned as pope between the years 269 and 274. He was a strong leader: he opposed the heresy of Monarchianism (which misunderstood the Trinity, exaggerating the oneness between the Father and the Son and turning the distinctions between the three Divine Persons into three energies instead), dealt with a heretical patriarch of Antioch who refused to acknowledge the legitimate bishop, and provided for the celebration of Mass at the tombs of martyrs.

Saint Anysia of Thessalonica

Anysia (d. 304) was born into a wealthy and pious family in Thessaly, Greece, and she chose to live a life of chastity and service of the poor. One day, while on her way to Mass, a Roman soldier harassed her. The soldier recognized her as a Christian—perhaps she was afraid of him and made the sign of the cross—and threatened to take her to a temple and make her sacrifice. He tore off her veil, and she spit in his face. He then murdered her with his sword.

Saint Perpetuus of Tours

The acts for which Perpetuus (d. ca. 490) is best known as bishop of Tours, France, are: his decree requiring people in his diocese to fast on Wednesdays and Fridays (a practice that was followed for many years after his death); his devotion to his saintly predecessor, Saint Martin of Tours; his building of a basilica for the pilgrims who came to pray for Saint Martin's intercession; and his decision to leave everything—vineyards, gold, and houses—to the poor at his death.

Saint Egwin of Evesham

Egwin was born in the seventh century of the line of English Mercian kings, and from the time he was a young man, he recognized God's call to religious life. He became bishop of Worcester around the year 692, and he was both zealous in spreading the Christian faith and severe in correcting those who needed correction. When some of those he had rebuked accused him to the pope, he traveled to Rome to answer their accusations. When he returned, having vindicated himself from the charges, he founded the Abbey of Evesham. This monastery was supported by the pope, and it became a great Benedictine monastery in England for centuries, until it was completely destroyed during King Henry VIII's reign. Egwin died on this date in the year 717, and he was buried in the monastery.

Saint Felix, help me obey Christ and His Church.
Saint Anysia, help me to be always ready to face the Divine Judge.
Saint Perpetuus, show me how to pray, fast, and give alms today.
Saint Egwin, show me how to accept correction with humility.

* * * * *

December 31

Saint Sylvester I, Optional Memorial

Sylvester was a Roman who succeeded Pope Saint Miltiades in the year 314, less than a year after the Roman emperor Constantine's famous Edict of Milan, which granted freedom to the practice of Christianity. During his twenty-year pontificate, the Church flowered after being freed from centuries of imperial persecution. Sylvester sent representatives to the famous Council of Nicaea—where the Nicene Creed was developed and later approved by him—as well as to the Council of Arles to deal with heresies troubling the Church at the time. The emperor apparently gave Sylvester the Lateran Palace, which became the Saint John Lateran Archbasilica. After his death in 335, his holiness caused him to be one of the first nonmartyrs to be declared a saint.

Saint Columba of Sens

Columba was born around the year 257 in Spain into a noble family. When the persecution of Christians was renewed under the Roman emperor Aurelian, she and other Christians fled to Gaul (modern France). It wasn't long before the authorities in Gaul discovered them, and sixteen-year-old Columba and other Christians were put in prison. An old tradition says that when a jailor tried to rape her, a bear from the nearby amphitheater rescued her. Another ancient tradition says that a man named Aubertus was miraculously cured of blindness when he asked for Columba's intercession shortly after she was executed by beheading in 273.

Saint John Francis Regis

John (1597–1640) was born into the nobility and grew up in the area of Languedoc, France. He was a sensitive, devout, and serious child who accepted correction and persecution without complaint. His good example, patience, and Christ-centered words eventually won over many of his peers. And this pattern—of dedication to prayer, self-sacrifice, avoidance of all sin, kindness to everyone—was the pattern for his whole life. He became a Jesuit priest, completed additional studies, and brought a deeper devotion among those around him wherever he was sent. He lived an austere life and traveled to many places to offer missions and bring people to a greater love of Christ. Great crowds of people came to his funeral.

Saint Catherine Laboure

Zoe (Catherine) was born in 1806 into a large farming family at Fain-les-Moutiers in France. Her mother died when she was eight years old, and she stayed at home to care for the family instead of going to school. When she was fourteen years old, she recognized that God was calling her to religious life, and although an older sister had already left to become a Sister of Charity, her father resisted the idea of sending her away too. In 1830, he finally allowed her to enter the Sisters of Charity of Saint Vincent de Paul at Chatillon-sur-Seine. Taking the name of Catherine, she was sent to the sisters' house of Rue de Bac in Paris. On July 18, she was woken from sleep by a "shining child", who led her to the convent chapel. The Virgin Mary appeared to her there and spoke to her for over two hours, saying that Catherine would be given a difficult task. On November 27, the Blessed Mother appeared to Catherine again in the chapel, this time showing her two images, which Catherine heard a voice tell her to make into a medal. The voice also said that those who wore it with devotion would receive great graces through Mary's intercession. This vision was repeated several times until September 1831. She told her confessor about all that she had experienced, and he questioned her carefully about the visions. With his recommendation and the archbishop's permission, five hundred medals were made in June 1832. A canonical inquiry of her visions was made in 1836 by the archbishop, although she was too humble to appear in person and testify. However, her confessor was a prudent man, and his descriptions of Catherine along with the popularity of the Miraculous Medal (including the conversion of Alphonse Ratisbonne, a Jewish man who agreed to wear it in 1842 and became a Christian and then a priest) led to a favorable verdict from the Church about her visions. Catherine herself revealed nothing of what she had seen to the other sisters. Instead, she served her community as portress, took care of the poultry, served the aged in a hospice, and seemed insignificant to the other sisters. She revealed her visions to her superior only eight months before she died in 1876.

> *Saint Sylvester, teach me to love Christ and His Church.*
> *Saint Columba, show me how to live and die for Christ.*
> *Saint John, help me be patient and kind.*
> *Saint Catherine, help me trust in our Blessed Mother.*

Appendices

Appendix 1

Calendar of Marian Dates

The Catholic Church officially celebrates our Blessed Mother on many days throughout the liturgical year. The main calendar of this book includes all of the Marian dates that are present in the *Martyrologium Romanum* of 2004. But there are memorials that are widely celebrated that have been omitted from the *Martyrologium Romanum* and that are described here. Again, moveable dates are not included in this book.

April 26

Our Lady of Good Counsel

The Church of Santa Maria in Genazzano, Italy, was entrusted to Augustinian Canons in 1356. In the year 1467, a fresco painting of the Virgin Mary and the Christ Child on the wall of the church became the site of healings and a popular destination for pilgrims. The image became known as Our Lady of Good Counsel. Popes have visited the site, saints have prayed there, and many people have adopted our Blessed Mother as their patron, asking specifically for her counsel through their difficulties.

Our Lady of Good Counsel, pray for me to grow in wisdom.

June 27

Our Lady of Perpetual Help

A Byzantine-style icon with the comforting title of "Our Lady of Perpetual Help" is believed to date from the thirteenth century. This image shows the Mother of God holding the Christ Child, with the archangels Michael and Gabriel on each side and showing Him the instruments of His future Passion. Faithful Christians have been encouraged in their faith through praying before this image for centuries, with the support of various popes, despite changes in location and its disappearance and recovery forty years later. The icon has been enshrined in Rome since 1499.

Our Lady of Perpetual Help, help me trust in your intercession at all times.

August 21

Our Lady of Knock

On Thursday, August 21, 1879, at 8 P.M., fifteen people saw the Virgin Mary, Saint Joseph, and Saint John the Evangelist appear in a blaze of light on the south gable of Saint John the Baptist Church in Knock, Ireland. During the apparition, the Blessed Virgin was clothed in white with a crown on her head and prayed with her eyes lifted up to Heaven. Saint Joseph wore white and stood respectfully to her right. Saint John was also dressed in white, had a mitre like a bishop, and stood on her left, and he appeared to be preaching. An altar with a cross, a lamb, and an adoring angel appeared behind them. After the brief apparition ended, miraculous healings occurred.

> *Our Lady of Knock, Saint Joseph, Saint John, may your love for us bring healing to the world today.*

September 19

Our Lady of La Salette

On this date in 1846, two children, Maximin Giraud and Melanie Calvat, reported seeing a weeping woman whom they recognized as the Virgin Mary on Mount Sous-Les Baisses in France. The apparition spoke to them of her dismay that the people of France failed to respect the Sunday rest and used the name of God in vain; she called on them to repent and warned of punishments on France if they failed to change their ways. The apparition was declared authentic by the bishop of Grenoble five years later.

> *Our Lady of La Salette, help me to repent of my failures to respect the Lord and His commandments.*

September 24

Our Lady of Ransom

In the thirteenth century, Muslims captured Christians on the sea and in Spain and often tortured them for refusing to give up their Catholic faith. Peter Nolasco, a pious layman who later became a priest and saint, was inspired with the idea of ransoming these Christian prisoners from their Muslim captors and setting them free. In 1218, the Blessed Mother appeared to Peter, as well as to his confessor, the priest Saint Raymond of Penyafort, and King James I of Aragon, encouraging them in this effort. So the three men established the Mercedarians, a religious order devoted to the ransoming of captives. This date celebrates the Virgin Mary's intercession to liberate Christians from torture and death. Later, English Catholics prayed to the Blessed Mother as Our Lady of Ransom during times of anti-Catholic persecution, praying that England might become Our Lady's Dowry, a gift to God through her.

> *Our Lady of Ransom, help me free others from the bondage of sin.*

October 12

Our Lady of the Pillar

The Twelve Apostles did as Jesus commanded: they spent their lives spreading the Gospel to the ends of the earth.[1] According to tradition, the Apostle Saint

---

[1] Mt 28:16–20.

James the Greater traveled to Saragossa, Spain, around the year A.D. 40. At one point, he became discouraged in his mission, and the Blessed Mother appeared to him in a dream. She gave him a wooden statue of herself and a column of jasper stone for it to stand upon, and she commanded him to build a church in her honor to house it. James obediently built the shrine, and the people of Saragossa have been commemorating our Lady's love for them ever since. James returned to Jerusalem, and according to tradition, he was executed shortly afterward, as described in Acts 12:2.

Our Lady of the Pillar, draw me closer to Jesus.

November 27

Miraculous Medal of the Blessed Virgin Mary

In 1830, a sister living in Rue du Bac, Paris, received visions of the Blessed Mother, and a canonical inquiry into both the content of the alleged visions and the sister herself concluded that the visions were genuine. In the vision, the Mother of God appeared to Saint Catherine Laboure, showed her two faces of a medal, and told her that those who wore this medal with devotion would receive many graces. The symbolism of the medal illustrates the Blessed Mother's openness to interceding with her Son on behalf of those of us who are still on earth and need God's help. Interest in the medals spread rapidly among Catholics, particularly after a Jewish man reluctantly accepted a medal—and not only became Catholic but became a priest. Since then, the medals have poured out all over the world as a physical reminder to Catholics to ask Mary for graces in time of need.

Blessed Mother, remind me to ask for and expect help from God in my need.

December 10

Our Lady of Loreto

Some say that devout Christians moved our Lady's home in Nazareth to Loreto, Italy, in the fourth century. Some say that angels did it. Perhaps they shared the honor. Today's date commemorates the home of our Blessed Mother, which is currently housed inside a beautiful basilica in Loreto.

Our Lady of Loreto, show me how to make a home for Jesus Christ in my heart.

Appendix 2

Correspondence of the 1962 Roman Missal to the 2004 *Martyrologium Romanum*

In 2004, the Church issued an updated list of Catholic saints and blesseds. This book, *Martyrologium Romanum*,[1] is not exhaustive, and the Church continually recognizes more holy men and women as saints. In addition, each country may, with Vatican permission, make adjustments to the calendar to honor their own native saints.

For Catholics who wish to attend the Extraordinary Form (Latin) Mass there's one more complication: that Mass follows the Roman Missal of 1962, which has its own calendar of saints. There are plans to update that calendar of saints to include modern saints. But until that happens, the following table lists the saints in the Roman Missal of 1962 along with the corresponding date for each saint from the *Martyrologium Romanum* of 2004. Note that, for the sake of space, this table does not include celebrations not associated with a specific date (e.g., Easter) or show the different classes associated with those days (e.g., I, II, III) in the older calendar. Some minor changes have been made below to update to current common spelling, and vigils are omitted.

Saints' dates, as given in the Roman Missal of 1962	Corresponding saints' dates, as given in the *Martyrologium Romanum* of 2004
January 1: Octave of the Nativity of the Lord	January 1: Solemnity of Mary, Mother of God
January 2: The Most Holy Name of Jesus (or celebrated on the Sunday between the octave of the Nativity of the Lord and the Epiphany)	January 3
January 5: Saint Telesphorus, Pope and Martyr	January 2
January 6: Solemnity of the Epiphany of the Lord	January 6 or Sunday between January 2 and January 8
January 11: Saint Hyginus, Pope and Martyr	No change
January 13: The Baptism of Our Lord Jesus Christ	First Sunday after January 6
January 14: Saint Hilary, Bishop, Confessor, and Doctor of the Church; Saint Felix, Priest and Martyr	January 13: Saint Hilary January 14: Saint Felix

(continued)

[1] *Martyrologium Romanum*, Editio Altera (Libreria Editrice Vaticana, 2004).

Saints' dates, as given in the Roman Missal of 1962	Corresponding saints' dates, as given in the *Martyrologium Romanum* of 2004
January 15: Saint Paul the First Hermit, Confessor; Saint Maurus, Abbot	January 10: Saint Paul the Hermit No change: Saint Maurus
January 16: Saint Marcellus I, Pope and Martyr	No change
January 17: Saint Anthony, Abbot	No change
January 18: Saint Prisca, Virgin and Martyr	No change
January 19: Saints Marius, Martha, Audifax, and Abachum, Martyrs; Saint Canute, Martyr	No change: Saints Marius, Martha, Audifax, and Abachum January 7: Saint Canute
January 20: Saints Fabian, Pope, and Sebastian, Martyrs	No change
January 21: Saint Agnes, Virgin and Martyr	No change
January 22: Saints Vincent and Anastasius, Martyrs	Saint Vincent of Saragossa's memorial is changed to January 23 in the United States only No change: Saint Anastasius
January 23: Saint Raymund of Peñafort, Confessor; Saint Emerentiana, Virgin and Martyr	January 7: Saint Raymond of Penyafort No change: Saint Emerentiana
January 24: Saint Timothy, Bishop and Martyr	January 26
January 25: The Conversion of Saint Paul, Apostle	No change
January 26: Saint Polycarp, Bishop and Martyr	February 23
January 27: Saint John Chrysostom, Bishop, Confessor, and Doctor of the Church	September 13
January 28: Saint Peter Nolasco, Confessor; Saint Agnes, Virgin and Martyr	May 6: Saint Peter Nolasco January 21: Saint Agnes
January 29: Saint Francis de Sales, Bishop, Confessor, and Doctor of the Church	January 24
January 30: Saint Martina, Virgin and Martyr	No change
January 31: Saint John Bosco, Confessor	No change
February 1: Saint Ignatius of Antioch, Bishop and Martyr	October 17
February 2: The Purification of the Blessed Virgin Mary	The Presentation of the Infant Jesus in the Temple (change in title, not date)
February 3: Saint Blase, Bishop and Martyr	No change
February 4: Saint Andrew Corsini, Bishop and Confessor	January 6
February 5: Saint Agatha, Virgin and Martyr	No change
February 6: Saint Titus, Bishop and Confessor; Saint Dorothy, Virgin and Martyr	January 26: Saint Titus No change: Saint Dorothy

Saints' dates, as given in the Roman Missal of 1962	Corresponding saints' dates, as given in the *Martyrologium Romanum* of 2004
February 7: Saint Romuald, Abbot	June 19
February 8: Saint John of Matha, Confessor	December 17
February 9: Saint Cyril, Bishop of Alexandria, Confessor, and Doctor of the Church; Saint Apollonia, Virgin and Martyr	June 27: Saint Cyril of Alexandria No change: Saint Apollonia
February 10: Saint Scholastica, Virgin	No change
February 11: The Apparition of the Immaculate Virgin Mary (Lourdes)	No change
February 12: The Seven Holy Founders of the Servite Order, Confessors	February 17
February 14: Saint Valentine, Priest and Martyr	No change
February 15: Saints Faustinus and Jovita, Martyrs	No change
February 18: Saint Simeon, Bishop and Martyr	April 27
February 22: Chair of Saint Peter	No change
February 23: Saint Peter Damian, Bishop, Confessor, and Doctor of the Church	February 21
February 24: Saint Matthias, Apostle	May 14
February 27 or 28: Saint Gabriel of Our Lady of Sorrows	No change
March 4: Saint Casimir, Confessor; Saint Lucius I, Pope and Martyr	No change: Saint Casimir March 5: Saint Lucius I
March 6: Saints Perpetua and Felicity, Martyrs	March 7
March 7: Saint Thomas Aquinas, Confessor and Doctor of the Church	January 28
March 8: Saint John of God, Confessor	No change
March 9: Saint Frances of Rome, Widow	No change
March 10: The Forty Holy Martyrs	March 9
March 12: Saint Gregory I, Pope, Confessor, and Doctor of the Church	September 3
March 17: Saint Patrick, Bishop and Confessor	No change
March 18: Saint Cyril, Bishop of Jerusalem, Confessor, and Doctor of the Church	No change
March 19: Saint Joseph, Spouse of the Blessed Virgin Mary, Confessor, and Patron of the Universal Church	No change
March 21: Saint Benedict, Abbot	July 11
March 24: Saint Gabriel the Archangel	September 29

(continued)

Saints' dates, as given in the Roman Missal of 1962	Corresponding saints' dates, as given in the *Martyrologium Romanum* of 2004
March 25: Annunciation of the Blessed Virgin Mary	No change
March 27: Saint John Damascene, Confessor and Doctor of the Church	December 4
March 28: Saint John Capistran, Confessor	October 23
Friday after the First Sunday in Passiontide: The Seven Sorrows of the Blessed Virgin Mary	September 15 (now called Our Lady of Sorrows)
April 2: Saint Francis of Paula, Confessor	No change
April 4: Saint Isidore of Seville, Bishop, Confessor, and Doctor of the Church	No change
April 5: Saint Vincent Ferrer, Confessor	No change
April 11: Saint Leo I, Pope, Confessor, and Doctor of the Church	November 10
April 13: Saint Hermenegild, Martyr	No change
April 14: Saint Justin, Martyr; Saints Tiburtius, Valerian, and Maximus, Martyrs	June 1: Saint Justin No change: Saints Tiburtius, Valerian, and Maximus
April 17: Saint Anicetus, Pope and Martyr	April 20
April 21: Saint Anselm of Canterbury, Bishop, Confessor, and Doctor of the Church	No change
April 22: Saints Soter and Caius, Popes and Martyrs	No change
April 23: Saint George, Martyr	No change
April 24: Saint Fidelis of Sigmaringen, Martyr	No change
April 25: Saint Mark, Evangelist	No change
April 26: Saints Cletus and Marcellinus, Popes and Martyrs	No change: Saint Cletus Saint Marcellinus is not listed in *Martyrologium Romanum*, 2004 edition
April 27: Saint Peter Canisius, Confessor and Doctor of the Church	December 21
April 28: Saint Paul of the Cross, Confessor	October 20
April 29: Saint Peter of Verona, Martyr	April 6
April 30: Saint Catherine of Siena, Virgin, Doctor of the Church	April 29
May 1: Saint Joseph the Worker, Spouse of the Blessed Virgin Mary, Confessor	No change
May 2: Saint Athanasius, Bishop, Confessor, and Doctor of the Church	No change
May 3: Saints Alexander, Eventius, and Theodulus, Martyrs	No change

Saints' dates, as given in the Roman Missal of 1962	Corresponding saints' dates, as given in the *Martyrologium Romanum* of 2004
May 4: Saint Monica, Widow	August 27
May 5: Saint Pius V, Pope and Confessor	April 30
May 7: Saint Stanislaus, Bishop and Martyr	April 11
May 9: Saint Gregory Nazianzen, Bishop, Confessor, and Doctor of the Church	January 2
May 10: Saint Antoninus, Bishop and Confessor; Saints Gordian and Epimachus, Martyrs	May 2: Saint Antoninus of Florence No change: Saints Gordian and Epimachus
May 11: Saints Philip and James, Apostles	May 3
May 12: Saints Nereus, Achilleus, Domitilla, Virgin, and Pancras, Martyrs	No change: Saints Nereus, Achilleus, and Pancras May 7: Saint Domitilla
May 13: Saint Robert Bellarmine, Bishop, Confessor, and Doctor of the Church	September 17
May 14: Saint Boniface, Martyr	Not listed in *Martyrologium Romanum*, 2004 edition
May 15: Saint John Baptist de la Salle, Confessor	April 7
May 16: Saint Ubald, Bishop and Confessor	No change
May 17: Saint Paschal Baylon, Confessor	No change
May 18: Saint Venantius, Martyr	Not listed in *Martyrologium Romanum*, 2004 edition
May 19: Saint Peter Celestine, Pope and Confessor; Saint Pudentiana, Virgin	No change: Saint Peter Celestine Saint Pudentiana is not listed in *Martyrologium Romanum*, 2004 edition
May 20: Saint Bernardine of Siena, Confessor	No change
May 25: Saint Gregory VII, Pope and Confessor; Saint Urban I, Pope and Martyr	No change: Saint Gregory VII May 19: Saint Urban I
May 26: Saint Philip Neri, Confessor; Saint Eleutherius, Pope and Martyr	No change
May 27: Saint Bede the Venerable, Confessor and Doctor of the Church; Saint John I, Pope and Martyr	May 25: Saint Bede the Venerable May 18: Saint John I
May 28: Saint Augustine, Bishop and Confessor	August 28
May 29: Saint Mary Magdalen de Pazzi, Virgin	May 25
May 30: Saint Felix I, Pope and Martyr	December 30

(*continued*)

Saints' dates, as given in the Roman Missal of 1962	Corresponding saints' dates, as given in the *Martyrologium Romanum* of 2004
May 31: Our Lady Virgin and Queen; Saint Petronilla, Virgin	August 22: Queenship of Mary May 31: Saint Petronilla
June 1: Saint Angela Merici, Virgin	January 27
June 2: Saints Marcellinus, Peter, and Erasmus, Bishop, Martyrs	No change
June 4: Saint Francis Caracciolo, Confessor	No change
June 5: Saint Boniface, Bishop and Martyr	No change
June 6: Saint Norbert, Bishop and Confessor	No change
June 9: Saints Primus and Felician, Martyrs	No change
June 10: Saint Margaret, Queen and Widow	November 16
June 11: Saint Barnabas, Apostle	No change
June 12: Saint John of San Facundo, Confessor; Saints Basilides, Cyrinus, Nabor and Nazarius, Martyrs	June 11: Saint John of San Facundo No change: Saint Basilides Saints Cyrinus, Nabor, and Nazarius are not listed in *Martyrologium Romanum*, 2004 edition
June 13: Saint Anthony of Padua, Confessor and Doctor of the Church	No change
June 14: Saint Basil the Great, Bishop, Confessor, and Doctor of the Church	January 2
June 15: Saints Vitus, Modestus, and Crescentia, Martyrs	No change: Saint Vitus Saints Modestus and Crescentia are not listed in *Martyrologium Romanum*, 2004 edition
June 17: Saint Gregory Barbarigo, Bishop and Confessor	June 18
June 18: Saint Ephraem of Syria, Deacon, Confessor, and Doctor of the Church; Saints Mark and Marcellianus, Martyrs	June 9: Saint Ephraem No change: Saints Mark and Marcellian
June 19: Saint Juliana Falconieri, Virgin; Saints Gervase and Protase, Martyrs	No change
June 20: Saint Silverius, Pope and Martyr	December 2
June 21: Saint Aloysius Gonzaga, Confessor	No change
June 22: Saint Paulinus, Bishop and Confessor	No change
June 24: The Birthday of Saint John the Baptist	No change
June 25: Saint William of Vercelli, Bishop	No change
June 26: Saints John and Paul, Martyrs	No change
June 29: Saints Peter and Paul, Apostles	No change
June 30: Saint Paul, Apostle	Removed (Saint Paul has two other dates: January 25 and June 29)

Saints' dates, as given in the Roman Missal of 1962	Corresponding saints' dates, as given in the *Martyrologium Romanum* of 2004
July 1: The Most Precious Blood of our Lord Jesus Christ	Moveable solemnity in current calendar
July 2: The Visitation of the Blessed Virgin Mary; Saints Processus and Martinian, Martyrs	May 31: Visitation of the Blessed Virgin Mary No change: Saints Processus and Martinian
July 3: Saint Irenaeus of Lyons, Bishop and Martyr	June 28
July 5: Saint Anthony Mary Zaccaria, Confessor	No change
July 7: Saints Cyril and Methodius, Bishops and Confessors	February 14
July 8: Saint Elizabeth of Portugal, Queen and Widow	July 5
July 10: The Seven Holy Brothers, Martyrs; Saints Rufina and Secunda, Virgins and Martyrs	Seven Holy Brothers are not listed in *Martyrologium Romanum*, 2004 edition No change: Saints Rufina and Secunda
July 11: Saint Pius I, Pope and Martyr	No change
July 12: Saint John Gualbert, Abbot; Saints Nabor and Felix, Martyrs	No change
July 14: Saint Bonaventure, Bishop, Confessor, and Doctor of the Church	July 15
July 15: Saint Henry II, Emperor and Confessor	July 13
July 16: Our Lady of Mount Carmel	No change
July 17: Saint Alexius, Confessor	No change
July 18: Saint Camillus de Lellis, Confessor; Saint Symphorosa and Her Seven Sons, Martyrs	No change
July 19: Saint Vincent de Paul, Confessor	September 27
July 20: Saint Jerome Emiliani, Confessor; Saint Margaret, Virgin and Martyr	February 8: Saint Jerome Emiliani No change: Saint Margaret of Antioch
July 21: Saint Lawrence of Brindisi, Confessor and Doctor of the Church; Saint Praxedes, Virgin	No change
July 22: Saint Mary Magdalene, Penitent	No change
July 23: Saint Apollinaris, Bishop and Martyr; Saint Liborius, Bishop and Confessor	No change
July 24: Saint Christina of Bolsena, Virgin and Martyr	No change
July 25: Saint James, Apostle; Saint Christopher, Martyr	No change
July 26: Saint Anne, Mother of the Blessed Virgin Mary	No change

(*continued*)

Saints' dates, as given in the Roman Missal of 1962	Corresponding saints' dates, as given in the *Martyrologium Romanum* of 2004
July 27: Saint Pantaleon, Martyr	No change
July 28: Saints Nazarius and Celsus, Martyrs; Saint Victor I, Pope and Martyr; Saint Innocent I, Pope and Confessor	No change: Saints Nazarius, Celsus, and Victor I March 12: Saint Innocent I
July 29: Saint Martha, Virgin; Saints Felix, Simplicius, Faustinus, and Beatrice, Martyrs	No change: Saints Martha, Simplicius, Faustinus, and Beatrice December 30: Saint Felix I
July 30: Saints Abdon and Sennen, Martyrs	No change
July 31: Saint Ignatius of Loyola, Confessor	No change
August 1: The Holy Maccabees, Martyrs	No change
August 2: Saint Alphonsus Mary of Liguori, Bishop, Confessor, and Doctor of the Church; Saint Stephen I, Pope and Martyr	August 1: Saint Alphonsus Mary of Liguori No change: Saint Stephen I
August 4: Saint Dominic, Confessor	August 8
August 5: The Dedication of the Church of Saint Mary of the Snows	Change in title
August 6: The Transfiguration of Our Lord Jesus Christ; Saints Sixtus II, Pope, Felicissimus, and Agapitus, Martyrs	No change: Transfiguration of Our Lord August 7: Saint Sixtus II and Companions
August 7: Saint Cajetan, Confessor; Saint Donatus, Bishop and Martyr	No change
August 8: Saint John Mary Vianney, Confessor and Priest; Saints Cyriacus, Largus, and Smaragdus, Martyrs	August 4: Saint John Mary Vianney No change: Saints Cyriacus, Largus, and Smaragdus
August 9: Saint Romanus, Martyr	No change
August 10: Saint Laurence the Deacon, Martyr	No change
August 11: Saints Tiburtius and Susanna, Virgin, Martyrs	No change
August 12: Saint Clare, Virgin	August 11
August 13: Saints Hippolytus and Cassian, Martyrs	No change
August 14: Saint Eusebius, Confessor	No change
August 15: The Assumption of the Blessed Virgin Mary	No change
August 16: Saint Joachim, Father of the Blessed Virgin Mary, Confessor	July 26
August 17: Saint Hyacinth of Poland, Confessor	August 15
August 18: Saint Agapitus, Martyr	No change
August 19: Saint John Eudes, Confessor	No change
August 20: Saint Bernard of Clairvaux, Abbot and Doctor of the Church	No change

Saints' dates, as given in the Roman Missal of 1962	Corresponding saints' dates, as given in the *Martyrologium Romanum* of 2004
August 21: Saint Jane Frances de Chantal, Widow	August 12
August 22: The Immaculate Heart of the Blessed Virgin Mary; Saints Timothy and Companions, Martyrs	Queenship of the Blessed Virgin Mary (change in title) Saint Timothy: No change Saint Timothy's companions are not listed in *Martyrologium Romanum*, 2004 edition
August 23: Saint Philip Benizi, Confessor	August 22
August 24: Saint Bartholomew, Apostle	No change
August 25: Saint Louis, Confessor	No change
August 26: Saint Zephyrinus, Pope and Martyr	December 20
August 27: Saint Joseph Calasanctius, Confessor	August 25
August 28: Saint Augustine, Bishop, Confessor, and Doctor of the Church; Saint Hermes, Martyr	No change
August 29: The Beheading of Saint John the Baptist; Saint Sabina, Martyr	No change
August 30: Saint Rose of Lima, Virgin; Saints Felix and Adauctus, Martyrs	August 23: Saint Rose of Lima No change: Saints Felix and Adauctus
August 31: Saint Raymond Nonnatus, Confessor	No change
September 1: Saint Giles, Abbot; The Holy Twelve Brothers, Martyrs	No change: Saint Giles The Holy Twelve Brothers are not listed in *Martyrologium Romanum*, 2004 edition
September 2: Saint Stephen, Confessor	September 16
September 3: Saint Pius X, Pope and Confessor	August 21
September 5: Saint Laurence Justinian, Bishop and Confessor	January 8
September 8: The Nativity of the Blessed Virgin Mary; Saint Adrian, Martyr	No change
September 9: Saint Gorgonius, Martyr	No change
September 10: Saint Nicholas of Tolentino, Confessor	No change
September 11: Saints Protus and Hyacinth, Martyrs	No change
September 12: The Most Holy Name of Mary	No change
September 14: Exaltation of the Holy Cross	No change
September 15: The Seven Sorrows of the Blessed Virgin Mary; Saint Nicomedes, Martyr	No change (now called Our Lady of Sorrows)

(continued)

Saints' dates, as given in the Roman Missal of 1962	Corresponding saints' dates, as given in the *Martyrologium Romanum* of 2004
September 16: Saint Cornelius, Pope, and Saint Cyprian, Bishop, Martyrs; Saints Euphemia, Virgin, Lucy and Geminianus, Martyrs	No change: Saints Cornelius, Cyprian, and Euphemia Saints Lucy and Geminianus are not listed in *Martyrologium Romanum*, 2004 edition
September 17: The Impression of the Holy Stigmata of Saint Francis of Assisi, Confessor	Not listed in *Martyrologium Romanum*, 2004 edition
September 18: Saint Joseph of Cupertino, Confessor	No change
September 19: Saint Januarius, Bishop and Companions, Martyrs	No change
September 20: Saint Eustace and Companions, Martyrs	No change
September 21: Saint Matthew, Apostle and Evangelist	No change
September 22: Saint Thomas of Villanova, Bishop and Confessor; Saint Maurice and Companions, Martyrs	September 8: Saint Thomas of Villanova No change: Saint Maurice and Companions
September 23: Saint Linus, Pope and Martyr; Saint Thecla, Virgin and Martyr	No change: Saint Linus Saint Thecla is not listed in *Martyrologium Romanum*, 2004 edition
September 24: Our Lady of Ransom	Not listed in *Martyrologium Romanum*, 2004 edition
September 26: Saints Cyprian and Justina, Virgin, Martyrs	Not listed in *Martyrologium Romanum*, 2004 edition
September 27: Saints Cosmas and Damian, Martyrs	September 26
September 28: Saint Wenceslaus, Martyr	No change
September 29: The Dedication of Saint Michael the Archangel	No change
September 30: Saint Jerome, Confessor and Doctor of the Church	No change
October 1: Saint Remigius, Bishop and Confessor	January 13
October 2: The Holy Guardian Angels	No change
October 3: Saint Teresa of the Child Jesus, Virgin and Doctor of the Church	October 1
October 4: Saint Francis of Assisi, Confessor	No change
October 5: Saint Placid and Companions, Martyrs	No change
October 6: Saint Bruno, Confessor	No change
October 7: Our Lady of the Rosary; Saint Mark, Pope and Confessor	No change

Saints' dates, as given in the Roman Missal of 1962	Corresponding saints' dates, as given in the *Martyrologium Romanum* of 2004
October 8: Saint Bridget, Widow; Saints Sergius, Bacchus, Marcellus, and Apuleius, Martyrs	July 23: Saint Bridget October 7: Saints Sergius and Bacchus Saints Marcellus and Apuleius are not listed in *Martyrologium Romanum*, 2004 edition
October 9: Saint John Leonardi, Confessor; Saint Denis, Rusticus, and Eleutherius, Martyrs	No change
October 10: Saint Francis Borgia, Confessor	September 30
October 11: The Motherhood of the Blessed Virgin Mary	Not listed in *Martyrologium Romanum*, 2004 edition
October 13: Saint Edward, Confessor	January 5
October 14: Saint Callistus I, Pope and Martyr	No change
October 15: Saint Teresa of Avila, Virgin	No change
October 16: Saint Hedwig, Widow	No change
October 17: Saint Margaret Mary Alacoque, Virgin	October 16
October 18: Saint Luke, Evangelist	No change
October 19: Saint Peter of Alcantara, Confessor	October 18
October 20: Saint John Cantius, Confessor	December 23
October 21: Saint Hilarion, Abbot; Saint Ursula and Companions, Virgins and Martyrs	No change
October 23: Saint Anthony Mary Claret, Bishop and Confessor	October 24
October 24: Saint Raphael the Archangel	September 29
October 25: Saints Chrysanthus and Daria, Martyrs	October 7
October 26: Saint Evaristus, Pope and Martyr	October 27
October 28: Saints Simon and Jude, Apostles	No change
November 1: All Saints Day	No change
November 2: All Souls Day	No change
November 4: Saint Charles Borromeo, Bishop and Confessor; Saints Vitalis and Agricola, Martyrs	No change
November 8: The Holy Four Crowned Martyrs	No change
November 9: The Dedication of the Archbasilica of Our Most Holy Savior; Saint Theodore, Martyr	No change: Dedication of the Archbasilica of Saint John Lateran February 17: Saint Theodore

(continued)

Saints' dates, as given in the Roman Missal of 1962	Corresponding saints' dates, as given in the *Martyrologium Romanum* of 2004
November 10: Saint Andrew Avellino, Confessor; Saints Tryphon, Respicius, and Nympha, Martyrs	No change: Saint Andrew Avellino February 1: Saint Tryphon Saints Respicius and Nymphna are not listed in *Martyrologium Romanum*, 2004 edition
November 11: Saint Martin, Bishop and Confessor; Saint Mennas, Martyr	No change
November 12: Saint Martin I, Pope and Martyr	April 13
November 13: Saint Didacus, Confessor	November 12
November 14: Saint Josaphat, Bishop and Martyr	November 12
November 15: Saint Albert the Great, Bishop, Confessor, and Doctor of the Church	No change
November 16: Saint Gertrude, Virgin	No change
November 17: Saint Gregory Thaumaturgus, Bishop and Confessor	No change
November 18: The Dedication of the Basilicas of Saints Peter and Paul	No change
November 19: Saint Elisabeth of Hungary, Widow; Saint Pontianus, Pope and Martyr	November 17: Saint Elizabeth of Hungary August 13: Saint Pontian
November 20: Saint Felix of Valois, Confessor	November 4
November 21: The Presentation of the Blessed Virgin Mary	No change
November 22: Saint Cecilia, Virgin and Martyr	No change
November 23: Saint Clement I, Pope and Martyr; Saint Felicitas, Martyr	No change
November 24: Saint John of the Cross, Confessor and Doctor of the Church; Saint Chrysogonus, Martyr	December 14: Saint John of the Cross No change: Saint Chrysogonus
November 25: Saint Catherine of Alexandria, Virgin and Martyr	No change
November 26: Saint Sylvester, Abbot; Saint Peter of Alexandria, Bishop and Martyr	No change: Saint Silvester Gozzolini November 25: Saint Peter of Alexandria
November 29: Saint Saturninus, Bishop and Martyr	No change
November 30: Saint Andrew, Apostle	No change
December 2: Saint Bibiana, Virgin and Martyr	No change
December 3: Saint Francis Xavier, Confessor	No change
December 4: Saint Peter Chrysologus, Bishop, Confessor, and Doctor of the Church; Saint Barbara, Virgin and Martyr	July 30: Saint Peter Chrysologus No change: Saint Barbara

Saints' dates, as given in the Roman Missal of 1962	Corresponding saints' dates, as given in the *Martyrologium Romanum* of 2004
December 5: Saint Sabbas, Abbot	No change
December 6: Saint Nicholas, Bishop and Confessor	No change
December 7: Saint Ambrose, Bishop, Confessor, and Doctor of the Church	No change
December 8: The Immaculate Conception of the Blessed Virgin Mary	No change
December 10: Saint Melchiades, Pope and Martyr	January 10
December 11: Saint Damasus I, Pope and Confessor	No change
December 13: Saint Lucy, Virgin and Martyr	No change
December 16: Saint Eusebius, Bishop and Martyr	August 2
December 21: Saint Thomas, Apostle	July 3
December 25: On the Nativity of Our Lord Jesus Christ; Saint Anastasia, Martyr	No change
December 26: Octave of the Nativity of the Lord; Saint Stephen, Protomartyr	No change
December 27: Octave of the Nativity of the Lord; Saint John, Apostle and Evangelist	No change
December 28: Octave of the Nativity of the Lord; The Holy Innocents, Martyrs	No change
December 29: Octave of the Nativity of the Lord; Saint Thomas Becket, Bishop and Martyr	No change
December 30: Octave of the Nativity of the Lord	No change
December 31: Octave of the Nativity of the Lord; Saint Sylvester I, Pope and Confessor	No change

Appendix 3

Frequently Asked Questions

What are the meanings of the different titles regarding sainthood?

A saint, following the teaching of the Church,[1] is a pilgrim on a journey, just like us, but who lives a life of holiness, charity, and good example; the culmination of that journey is the beatific vision of God for all eternity. Because martyrdom became an unfortunately common experience in the first three centuries of the Church's existence, martyrs were the first Christians to be venerated as saints and acknowledged as residents of Heaven. Over the centuries, the Church has developed a process for acknowledging the extraordinary holiness of an individual Catholic, whether or not he died as a martyr.

1. According to the current practice of the Church, a candidate for sainthood may be called a *servant of God* if five years have elapsed since his death. The bishop of the candidate's diocese opens a cause for beatification.
2. If the Vatican Congregation for the Causes of Saints receives and examines the cause for beatification from the bishop and determines that the cause has merit, this congregation can confer the title of *venerable* on the candidate.
3. If a miracle, attributed to the candidate's intercession, is found, investigated, and approved, and if the pope approves, the candidate is given the title of *blessed*.
4. If another investigated and approved miracle occurs at the intercession of the candidate *after* the beatification ceremony, and if the pope approves, the candidate is given the title of *saint*. In individual cases, the pope can dispense with the qualifications of additional miracles.

What are the meanings of the different Church leadership positions?

Some of the saints in this collection were bishops, archbishops, patriarchs, and so forth, during their lifetimes. What do those mean?

Position	Description
Lector or reader	In most dioceses and parishes today, literacy is common, and just about anyone in the pews can read, making it easier to find someone who can read the readings aloud during a daily or Sunday Mass. But in ancient

(continued)

---

[1] See *Catechism of the Catholic Church* (United States Catholic Conference—Libreria Editrice Vaticana, 1994); English translation of the *Catechism of the Catholic Church: Modifications from the Editio Typica* (United States Conference of Catholic Bishops—Libreria Editrice Vaticana, 1997), nos. 954–62.

Position	Description
	times, being able to read was much less common. So from the earliest days of the Church, the position of lector (or reader) was an honored position. Even today, the term "lector" is generally used to describe a position that a man attains while in the process of becoming an ordained priest, although the title in some time periods has also implied that the man is a scholar. Saint Eusebius of Vercelli, for example, was ordained a lector and later became a bishop.
Priest	A Catholic priest places himself, by God's grace, at the service of all the Catholic faithful. His ministerial priesthood—as opposed to the common priesthood that all Catholics share through Christ—is a means by which Christ builds up his Church. The ministerial priesthood is transmitted by the Sacrament of Holy Orders.[2] The patron saint of priests is Saint John Vianney.
Subdeacon	Though some Christian churches, such as the Orthodox churches, still retain the order of subdeacon, Pope Paul VI ended the subdiaconate in the Catholic Church in 1972. The duties performed by the subdeacon are now performed by others. But prior to that date, a Catholic subdeacon served the deacon at Mass. It was considered the lowest of the major orders, though the exact requirements varied from age to age. Saint Gregory II was a subdeacon before becoming pope.
Rector	A rector is a priest who presides over a particular institution. Depending on the time and place, such institutions may include missions, universities, seminaries, colleges, and religious houses. In ancient times, the bishop was called the rector, and the pope could be called the rector of the world. Blessed Henryk Kaczorowski was a rector of a seminary.
Archdeacon	The archdeacon of a diocese has generally been responsible for the supervision of subordinate clergy and administration of church property. Originally, an archdeacon was selected from among deacons, but in later centuries, priests began to serve as archdeacons. Today, other officials, such as vicar general and auxiliary bishop, typically perform those duties.
Bishop	A bishop, as a successor to the apostles, has jurisdiction over his diocese, sometimes also called a "see". Saint John Nepomucene Neumann was a bishop.
Auxiliary bishop	A bishop may have auxiliary bishops to help him govern, particularly if he has a large diocese. Blessed Michael Kozal was an auxiliary bishop.
Coadjutor bishop	If a bishop names a coadjutor bishop, that man is an auxiliary bishop with the right to succeed him as bishop. Saint Francis de Sales was a coadjutor bishop before becoming bishop.
Suffragan bishop	A suffragan bishop is the bishop of a diocese that happens to be a part of a larger ecclesiastical province.
Archbishop	An archbishop is the leader of a principal archdiocese within an ecclesiastical province. Saint Antoninus was archbishop of Florence.
Metropolitan	An archbishop may also be called a metropolitan because of the importance of his diocesan city. As such, he may have other suffragan bishops (usually from neighboring dioceses) under him. Saint Caesarius of Arles was a metropolitan.

[2] See *Catechism of the Catholic Church*, no. 1547.

Position	Description
Patriarch	In centuries past, seven cities were so prominent that their bishop was given the title of patriarch to distinguish him among other bishops. There are currently seven bishops (plus the pope) who have the rank of patriarch. Catholic leaders who belong to rites other than the Latin rite (Eastern rites, for example) may also be called patriarchs. Saint John the Almsgiver was a patriarch.
Cardinal	A cardinal is an ordained man who has been given special responsibilities in the Church by the pope. Typically, cardinals are bishops (Saint Peter Damian) or archbishops, but priests (Saint Robert Bellarmine) have also been raised to this position. In addition to his responsibilities as a priest, bishop, or archbishop, each cardinal serves the pope and votes in papal elections.
Primate	Primate is an honorary title given to some bishops. In the past, though not according to canon law, a primate was a bishop with authority over a territory, not merely his own diocese. Saint Oliver Plunket was primate of All Ireland.
Curia	The papal Curia is the administrative body, ruled by the pope, that governs the entire Church. Every cardinal is a member of the pope's Curia.
Pope	The pope is the bishop of Rome, the successor of Saint Peter, and has many other titles, including Vicar of Jesus Christ, Supreme Pontiff of the Universal Church, Sovereign of the Vatican City State, and Servant of the Servants of God.

What are the terms used by the Church to describe "religious life"?

The Church explains the role of consecrated life in the *Catechism of the Catholic Church*.[3] The table below describes some of the common terms associated with religious life.

Term	Description
Abbot and Abbess	The abbot or abbess is the superior of a monastery or group of monasteries. The abbot is typically elected by secret ballot and, because of the territorial jurisdiction of that monastery, has a quasi-episcopal authority within the Church. Saint Hildegard of Bingen was an abbess.
Anchorite	An anchorite lives a more radical form of hermitic life, with only the essentials in food and living conditions. Saint Pachomius was an anchorite.
Brother	Brothers take solemn vows and live within a religious order or community. They are not priests and serve their order or community in other ways. Saint Gerard Majella, for example, was a brother who served as tailor and porter for his community.
Canon	A canon is a member of a chapter or a group of clerics living according to a specific rule of life, presided over by a leader. The Augustinian Canons Regular is one of the earliest and most common types of canons. Saint Peter Fourier was an Augustinian Canon.

(continued)

[3] See *Catechism of the Catholic Church*, nos. 914–33.

Term	Description
Cenobite	A cenobite is a monk or nun who lives in a religious community. Saint Theodosius (the Cenobiarch) was a cenobite before becoming a cenobiarch—that is, a leader of a group of cenobites.
Friar	The mendicant orders call their members "friars", which comes from the French and Latin words for brothers. A friar is distinct from a monk in that a friar has no fixed home and lives on the voluntary offerings of others. Saint John of the Cross was a friar.
Hermit	A hermit withdraws to a deserted place and lives in great simplicity, relying only on manual labor for support. Saint Anthony the Great is perhaps the most famous hermit.
Mendicant	A mendicant is a member of a religious order who is required to work or beg for his living. A mendicant is not bound by a vow of stability to remain at a specific monastery. Famous mendicants include Saint Francis of Assisi and Saint Dominic.
Monk	A monk is a man who has chosen to live a consecrated life through public profession of vows of poverty, chastity, and obedience. Monks also typically take vows of stability—that is, to live in one place alone. Saint Benedict of Nursia is a patron saint for monks.
Nuns and Sisters	Nuns take solemn vows and typically live in a cloistered community; sisters take simple vows and typically serve outside the convent. Saint Teresa of Avila was a nun; Saint Elizabeth Seton was a sister.
Prior and Prioress	A prior is a superior in a monastic order; the female form of the name is prioress. Depending on the order, there may be more than one prior, with slightly different titles, at a given monastery. Saint Anselm of Canterbury was prior at his monastery before becoming an archbishop.
Religious order	The members of a religious order traditionally take vows of stability, poverty, chastity, and obedience. Usually a religious community is not attached to a diocese. Although a religious order is technically different from a religious institute, the differences are relatively small and related to certain points of canon law. See the following table, which lists major religious orders.
Vows	Members of a religious order may take solemn vows after a period of temporary, simple vows. Solemn vows are absolute and irrevocable; ownership of property is prohibited and marriage is invalid. Simple vows can be taken temporarily or perpetually and allow ownership of personal property.

What are the differences between the major religious orders of the Church?

Below is a table showing the differences between various religious orders, but note that only orders with multiple saints in this book are included here.

Order	Founder	Type of Order	Characteristics
Augustinian Canons Regular	Saint Augustine and others	Religious order	In this order, priests live in community under the Rule of Saint Augustine, which emphasizes living the Gospel, interior life, study, and apostolic activities. Saint Sergius I

Order	Founder	Type of Order	Characteristics
			was an Augustinian Canon Regular before becoming pope.
Benedictines *Also called the Order of Saint Benedict*	Saint Benedict	Monastic religious order of men and women	This order of monks lives in community and is based on the Rule of Saint Benedict. Members balance daily prayer and daily manual labor, with emphasis on stability, fidelity, and obedience. There are many branches of this order. Saint Benedict is the most famous Benedictine, though many popes have also been Benedictines. Saint Hildegard of Bingen was a Benedictine.
Brothers of the Christian Schools *Also called the Institute of the Brothers of the Christian Schools*	Saint John Baptist de la Salle	Society of male religious	The goal of this institute is the sanctification of its members, who are male religious but not ordained, through providing Christian education, particularly for the poor.
Capuchin Franciscans *Also called the Order of Friars Minor Capuchin*	Mateo de Bascio, Bernardino Ochino	Mendicant religious order of friars	This branch of the Franciscan order was formed with the desire of practicing the most literal observance possible of the Rule of Saint Francis. Friars live in extreme austerity, poverty, and simplicity. Saint Laurence of Brindisi was a Capuchin; Saint Pio of Pieltrelcina, who lived and died in modern times, was a Capuchin as well.
Carmelites *Also called the Order of the Brothers of the Blessed Virgin Mary of Mount Carmel*	Uncertain, but began in the twelfth century with hermits living on Mount Carmel	Mendicant religious order	The charism of this order is contemplation, which encompasses prayer, community, and service. The order is inspired by the example of the Blessed Virgin Mary and the prophet Elijah, who lived on Mount Carmel. Saint Simon Stock is credited with the refounding of the Carmelite order in Europe.
Carthusians *Also called the Order of Saint Bruno*	Saint Bruno of Cologne	Monastic religious order of monks and nuns	In this enclosed monastic order, originally in the Chartreuse Mountains, hermits live in community, with a focus on contemplation of God, solitude, simplicity, and sobriety. Saint Anthelm was a Carthusian.
Cistercians *Also called the Order of Cistercians*	Saints Robert of Molesme, Alberic of Citeaux, Stephen Harding	Religious order of monks and nuns	Desiring a literal observance of the Rule of Saint Benedict, the order lives a monastic life with an emphasis on manual labor. Educational, architectural, and technological innovations have resulted over the centuries due to their focus on

(continued)

Order	Founder	Type of Order	Characteristics
			community self-sufficiency. Saint Bernard of Clairvaux is perhaps the most well known of all the Cistercian saints.
Conventual Franciscans *Also called the Order of Friars Minor Conventual*	Saint Francis	Mendicant religious order	This branch of the Franciscans particularly focuses on living together in friaries, working among the urban poor, disciplined austerity, generosity, harmonized prayer, and service to others. Saint Maximilian Kolbe was a Conventual Franciscan.
Discalced Carmelites *Also called the Barefoot Carmelites*	Saints Teresa of Avila and John of the Cross	Mendicant religious order and seculars	This branch of the Carmelites arose to reform the order and return it to its original practices, such as fasting, which had been modified to be less strict, and return the order's focus to contemplation of God. Saint Therese of Lisieux is a well-known Discalced Carmelite saint.
Dominicans *Also called the Order of Preachers*	Saint Dominic de Guzman	Mendicant religious order of friars, nuns, sisters, and seculars	Founded to preach the Gospel and oppose heresy, this order has a strong intellectual tradition. Saints Thomas Aquinas and Catherine of Siena were Dominicans.
Franciscans *Also called the Orders of Friars Minor*	Saint Francis of Assisi	Mendicant religious order and seculars	This order, founded by Saint Francis, focuses on his teaching and example, particularly through living the Gospel in poverty and fraternity. Saint Bonaventure was a Franciscan priest.
Jesuits *Also called the Society of Jesus*	Saint Ignatius of Loyola	Religious order of men	This society focuses on evangelization and apostolic ministry, particularly in education, research, and service. Saint Francis Xavier was a Jesuit priest.
Mercedarians *Also called the Royal, Celestial, and Military Order of Our Lady of Mercy and the Redemption of Captives*	Saint Peter Nolasco	Medicant religious order	This order was founded, along with many other associations in Europe in the Middle Ages, to ransom Christians who had been enslaved by Muslims. Members take an additional fourth vow to die for another person who is in danger of losing his faith. Saint Raymond Nonnatus was a Mercedarian.
Premonstratensians *Also called the Norbertines or Order of Canons Regular of Premontre*	Saint Norbert	Religious order of canons	This order of Canons Regular follows the Rule of Saint Augustine but was influenced by the Cistercians. It focuses on preaching and pastoral ministry. Blessed Hroznata of Bohemia was a Premonstratensian.

Order	Founder	Type of Order	Characteristics
Redemptorists *Also called the Congregation of the Holy Redeemer*	Saint Alphonsus Liguori	Congregation of priests and brothers	This congregation, dedicated to Our Mother of Perpetual Help, focuses on missionary work, preaching, and service, particularly among the rural poor. Saint Clement Hofbauer was a Redemptorist.
Salesians of Don Bosco *Also called the Society of Saint Francis de Sales*	Saint John Bosco	Clerical religious congregation	This religious institute focuses on spiritual and corporal works of charity toward the young, particularly the poor, and the education of boys to the priesthood. Blesseds Luigi Versiglia and Callisto Caravario were Salesians.
Servites *Also called the Servants of Mary*	Seven Holy Founders	Mendicant religious order of friars, nuns, sisters, and lay members	This order is dedicated to the sanctification of its members, preaching the Gospel, and the propagation of devotion, particularly to the Passion of Jesus and the Sorrows of the Virgin Mary. Saint Juliana Falconieri was a Servite nun.
Theatines *Also called the Congregation of Clerks Regular of the Divine Providence*	Saint Cajetan, Paolo Consiglieri, Bonifacio da Colle, Giovanni Pietro Carafa	Religious order	This order is dedicated to encouraging the pursuit of evangelical perfection among the clergy, particularly through preaching, virtuous living, and service. Saint Andrew Avellino was a Theatine priest.
Trappists *Also called the Order of the Cistercians of the Strict Observance*	Armand Jean le Bouthillier de Rance	Monastic religious order of monks and nuns	This branch of the Cistercians is a cloistered contemplative religious order formed in reaction to the previous relaxation of practices in the order. Members follow the Rule of Saint Benedict strictly, particularly through stability, fidelity to monastic life, and obedience. Saint Maria Gabriella Sagheddu was a Trappist nun.
Trinitarians *Also called the Order of the Most Holy Trinity and of the Captives*	Saint John de Matha	Religious order	This order was founded, along with many other associations in Europe in the Middle Ages, to ransom Christians who had been enslaved by Muslims. The order focuses on redemption, works of mercy, and devotion to the mystery of the Holy Trinity. Blessed Elizabeth Mora was a Trinitarian.

What is the General Roman Calendar?

The Roman Rite of the Catholic Church follows the General Roman Calendar, a liturgical calendar that includes celebrations on fixed and moveable dates throughout the year. The calendar changes from year to year and varies from nation to nation and sometimes even diocese to diocese. There are ranks for the types of celebration, from optional memorials to memorials to feasts to (the highest rank) solemnities. The most important celebrations are related to the mysteries of our Lord, with celebrations of the saints spread throughout the year around those dates.

In 1969, as part of the reforms of Vatican Council II, Pope Saint Paul VI promulgated a new General Roman Calendar for the Church. This revised calendar changed the dates of some saints' celebrations. For this reason, older calendars may list other dates than those listed here. The revised calendar also removed some saints' days from the calendar used by the entire Church, as part of the general desire of the council to bring the teachings of the Church to the modern world more effectively. Pope Saint John Paul II later amended that calendar, and local bishops can make further changes (with the permission of the Church) for regional reasons. For example, in North America, Saint Camillus de Lellis' date is transferred to July 18 since the American Saint Kateri Tekakwitha is celebrated on July 14.

An unfortunate consequence of these changes was that some people interpreted them to mean that certain saints, such as Saint Christopher or Saint Barbara, were no longer saints. While the physical evidence for some early Church martyrs' lives may not be as abundant as for modern saints' lives, the changes in the calendar reflect the Vatican Council's desire to achieve a better balance in our celebration of the liturgical year, not to ignore saints who have been inspirational to Catholics for centuries.

Controversies over important dates are nothing new to the Church. For example, during the first several centuries of the Church, great saints argued over the proper date to celebrate Easter (see Saints Adamnan of Iona, Anicetus, Cuthbert of Lindisfarne, Irenaeus of Lyons, Polycarp, Telesphorus, Victor I, and Wilfrid, for example). Should Easter be held on the fourteenth day of the month of Nisan according to the Jewish calendar, or should it be held on a Sunday after the spring equinox? Many people believe that on the very first Easter, when Jesus rose from the dead, the fourteenth day of Nisan *was* a Sunday, but that doesn't happen every year. Eventually, the Church decided that the day of the week (Sunday) was more important than following the Jewish calendar.

Appendix 4

Glossary of Catholic Terms

Anti-pope

No one ever said, "I'm an anti-pope!" But many men throughout history have claimed that they were the true pope and that the true pope was not the true pope. Usually, anti-popes make this claim for political reasons. The true pope of the Catholic Church is elected according to the canons of the Church; an anti-pope calls himself pope after collecting random admirers (often bishops, but not always) who are willing to repeat that fiction. Saint Hippolytus claims the distinction of being the only anti-pope to repent, be reconciled with the Church, and be recognized by the Church as a saint after his martyrdom.

Benefice

A benefice is a church office endowed with financial assets. Strictly speaking, a benefice indicates a right given permanently by the Church to a cleric to receive revenues for his performance of a spiritual service. Though benefices have been abused and misused many times over the centuries by those seeking power and money, the primary reason the Church has offered benefices has always been to put clerics in such a position that they can devote themselves to the service of the Gospel. See Saint John de Sahagun, for example.

Confessor

The term "confessor" can have one of two meanings in the Church. First, it can mean that the individual "confessed" to the faith during a time of persecution, was willing to die a martyr for the faith, but, for whatever reason, was not executed. Sometimes, for example, Christians in the early Church were imprisoned but a change in political winds or a more lenient local leader later resulted in those Christians being released from prison. Such people were called confessors; this category includes Pope Saint Caius and Saint Maximus the Confessor. The second and more recent meaning of "confessor" is as a reference to a priest who hears confessions. Some saintly priests have been particularly noted and loved for their ability to help Catholics repent and grow in holiness through this sacrament, including priests such as Saints John Vianney and Pio of Pietrelcina.

Confraternity

The terms "confraternity" and "sodality" mean virtually the same thing to Christians, though the former term is used more often these days. A group of Christians who voluntarily gather together to perform some work of Christian charity and piety may be called a confraternity. To Catholics, a confraternity must also have permission and guidance from the Church, usually from the diocese in which it resides. The type of work done by the group may vary; a confraternity may promote devotion to God, perform spiritual or corporal works of mercy, or support groups within or outside the Church. Some confraternities include only laypeople, some include only vowed religious or priests, and others include all of the above.

Divine Office

Our elder brothers, the Jews, have recited prayers at different hours of the day or night for thousands of years. Over the past two millennia, Catholics have similarly developed their own collection of prayers, which is called the Divine Office and is particularly prayed by priests and members of religious orders. The title of this collection of prayers indicates its purpose: it's something we offer to God as a duty—our "office"—to honor Him throughout the day. The number of separate hours of prayer has changed over time. Currently, the hours of the Divine Office, also called the Liturgy of the Hours or the breviary, are Office of Readings, Morning Prayer, Daytime Prayer, Evening Prayer, and Night Prayer. Religious orders may, with permission, follow their own calendar and offices.

Doctor of the Church

The Church has given the title of Doctor of the Church to (currently) thirty-six saints. In a way, these men and women serve as healers to the Body of Christ by effectively explaining both truth and falsehood in ways that outlast their lives on earth. To become a Doctor of the Church, one must:

- Be a saint. There have been many brilliant thinkers throughout history, but intelligence is no substitute for holiness.

- Write about the faith. The writings of the saint must both be important to the Catholic faithful and be faithful to the teachings of the Church.

- Be named a Doctor by the Church herself.

The following men and women have been named Doctors of the Church.

Name	Dates	Description
Saint Hilary of Poitiers	ca. 315–ca. 368	Bishop of Poitiers (France)
Saint Athanasius	ca. 297–373	Archbishop of Alexandria (Egypt)
Saint Ephraem	ca. 306–ca. 373	Deacon of Nisibus (Syria)
Saint Basil the Great	ca. 329–379	Founder of monastic order, bishop of Caesarea (Turkey)
Saint Cyril of Jerusalem	ca. 315–386	Bishop of Jerusalem (Israel)
Saint Gregory of Nazianzus	ca. 329–ca. 389	Bishop of Nazianzus (Turkey)

Name	Dates	Description
Saint Ambrose of Milan	ca. 340–397	Bishop of Milan (Italy)
Saint John Chrysostom	ca. 347–407	Patriarch of Constantinople (Turkey)
Saint Jerome	ca. 342–ca. 420	Priest, scholar, and hermit who died in Bethlehem (Israel)
Saint Augustine of Hippo	354–430	Bishop of Hippo (Algeria)
Saint Cyril of Alexandria	ca. 376–444	Patriarch of Alexandria (Egypt)
Saint Peter Chrysologus	ca. 406–ca. 450	Archbishop of Ravenna (Italy)
Saint Leo the Great	ca. 400–461	Benedictine monk and pope
Saint Gregory the Great	ca. 540–604	Pope
Saint Isidore of Seville	ca. 560–636	Bishop of Seville (Spain)
Saint Bede the Venerable	ca. 673–735	Benedictine monk and priest of Jarrow (England)
Saint John of Damascus	ca. 676–ca. 749	Priest and scholar of Damascus (Syria)
Saint Gregory of Narek	951–1003	Monk, priest, and theologian of Narek (Turkey)
Saint Peter Damian	ca. 1007–1072	Benedictine monk and cardinal bishop of Ostia (Italy)
Saint Anselm of Canterbury	1033–1109	Benedictine monk and archbishop of Canterbury (England)
Saint Bernard of Clairvaux	1090–1153	Priest and Cistercian abbot of Clairvaux (France)
Saint Hildegard of Bingen	1098–1179	Benedictine nun and abbess of Bingen (Germany)
Saint Anthony of Padua	1195–1231	Franciscan friar of Padua (Italy)
Saint Bonaventure	ca. 1221–1274	Franciscan priest and minister general, cardinal bishop of Albano (Italy)
Saint Thomas Aquinas	ca. 1225–1274	Dominican priest and theologian (Italy)
Saint Albert the Great	ca. 1206–1280	Dominican priest and bishop of Cologne (German)
Saint Catherine of Siena	1347–1380	Third Order Dominican of Siena (Italy)
Saint John of Avila	1499–1569	Priest (Spain)
Saint Teresa of Avila	1515–1582	Founder and nun of Discalced Carmelite order of Avila (Spain)
Saint John of the Cross	1542–1591	Founder and priest of Discalced Carmelite order (Spain)
Saint Peter Canisius	1521–1597	Jesuit priest (Holland, Germany)
Saint Lawrence of Brindisi	1559–1619	Capuchin priest (Italy)

(continued)

Name	Dates	Description
Saint Robert Bellarmine	1542–1621	Cardinal priest (Italy)
Saint Francis de Sales	1567–1622	Founder of the Order of the Visitation and bishop of Geneva (Switzerland)
Saint Alphonsus Liguori	1696–1787	Bishop of Saint Agata dei Gotti (Italy) and founder of order of Redemptorists
Saint Therese of Lisieux	1873–1897	Discalced Carmelite nun (France)

Father of the Church

Many Christian writers from the early days of the Church are now commonly called Fathers of the Church. Those who've earned that distinction include bishops, priests, and laymen, but all contributed, with the help of the Holy Spirit, to a better understanding and explanation of the fundamental doctrines of the Church. There are some Christians who are considered Fathers because they contributed to Church teaching but are not considered saints by the Church. This is sometimes because we lack more information about the individual, but also sometimes because of erroneous personal decisions that they made (e.g., Origen may have interpreted Matthew 5:29 too literally and had himself castrated[1]) or heretical positions that they held (e,g., Tertullian left the Church because he thought it was being too lenient with sinners). However, it has to be pointed out that the early Church lacked the terminology and historical experience that we take for granted today. Some heresies prove themselves most dangerous after people have tried to live them out, and development of doctrine takes time. The time period of the Fathers stretches from the time of the apostles until around the eighth century. The following saints are all Fathers of the Church and are all included in this book.

Name	Year of Death (approximate)	Description
Saint Barnabas	60	Missionary and martyr
Saint Dionysius the Aeropagite	95	Bishop of Athens (Greece)
Saint Clement I	97	Pope
Saint Polycarp	155	Bishop of Antioch (Turkey)
Saint Justin Martyr	165	Philosopher and martyr of Rome (Italy)
Saint Irenaeus of Lyons	203	Bishop of Lyons (France)
Saint Methodius of Olympus	311	Bishop of Olympus (Greece)
Saint Alexander of Alexandria	328	Bishop of Alexandria (Egypt)
Saint Pachomius	348	Anchorite and monk (Egypt)
Saint Hilary of Poitiers	368	Bishop of Poitiers (France)

---

[1] Mt 5:29 reads, "If your right eye causes you to sin, pluck it out and throw it away."

Name	Year of Death (approximate)	Description
Saint Eusebius of Vercelli	371	Bishop of Vercelli (Italy)
Saint Athanasius	373	Archbishop of Alexandria (Egypt)
Saint Ephraem the Deacon	373	Deacon of Nisibus (Syria)
Saint Basil the Great	379	Bishop of Caesarea (Turkey) and monastic founder
Saint Cyril of Jerusalem	386	Bishop of Jerusalem (Israel)
Saint Gregory of Nazianzus	389	Bishop of Nazianzus (Turkey)
Saint Ambrose of Milan	397	Bishop of Milan (Italy)
Saint Martin of Tours	397	Bishop of Tours (France)
Saint Chromatius	407	Bishop of Aquileia (Italy)
Saint John Chrysostom	407	Patriarch of Constantinople (Turkey)
Saint Nicetas of Remesiana	414	Bishop of Remesiana (Serbia)
Saint Jerome	420	Priest, scholar, and hermit who died in Bethlehem (Israel)
Saint Augustine of Hippo	430	Bishop of Hippo (Algeria)
Saint Paulinus of Nola	431	Bishop of Nola (Italy)
Saint Cyril of Alexandria	444	Archbishop of Alexandria (Egypt)
Saint Vincent of Lerins	445	Monk and priest of Lerins (France)
Saint Leo the Great	461	Pope
Saint Severinus Boethius	524	Philosopher and martyr of Rome (Italy)
Saint Caesarius of Arles	543	Bishop of Arles (France)
Saint Gregory of Tours	594	Bishop of Tours (France)
Saint Sophronius	639	Patriarch of Jerusalem (Israel)
Saint Braulio of Saragossa	651	Bishop of Saragossa (Spain)
Saint Maximus the Confessor	662	Monk and confessor
John of Damascus	749	Priest, monk and scholar (Syria)

Feast

In the liturgical calendar, a feast is a day of celebration that is of lesser importance than a solemnity but of greater importance than a memorial. For example, see the Feast of the Holy Innocents.

Memorial

In the Church's liturgical calendar, a memorial is a day of celebration that is less significant than a feast or a solemnity. So, for example, a memorial of a particular saint is generally trumped by the Sunday Mass celebration, because Sunday itself is of greater liturgical importance. Some memorials are optional, some are not, based on the decision of the local churches and with the agreement of the Vatican. Also, a particular memorial may be of greater importance to a given religious community or country. Notice what happens in communities with a long-standing Irish heritage if Saint Patrick's Day occurs on a Sunday in a given year.

Patron Saints and Petitions

In the ancient Roman world, men of greater power and wealth made themselves available each day, typically in the early morning, for men with lesser or no power and wealth to come to their homes and meet with them. Not unlike today's power lunches, funding applications, or even street begging, patrons heard the requests of those in need and decided whether or not to answer them. Sometimes a patron's intentions were primarily self-serving, such as a desire to increase his own power or avoid a riot (think Pontius Pilate), but having "help in high places" is not necessarily a bad thing.

As always, our prayer requests should be inspired by the Lord's Prayer, which reminds us to ask for our *daily* bread and for *God's* will to be done. But Catholics have invoked saints as heavenly patrons for their own personal needs for centuries precisely because *they* are in Heaven now, not us. They're literally in the presence of God for all eternity, so not only are they closer to God, but our reflections on their lives may help us put our own problems in perspective.

How is it that a saint will become known as a patron of a particular cause, illness, or group of people? Typically, that's due to the saint's words and actions during his earthly life. For example, Saint Thomas Aquinas (patron of students) was one of the most brilliant thinkers in the history of the Church: Wouldn't every student like his help when studying for a test? Sometimes a saint becomes known as a patron for reasons that are a bit more tenuous. For example, Saint Lucy is patroness of the blind—because torturers tore out her eyes to try to make her give up the faith. Sometimes a saint becomes known as a patron for miracles answered after the saint's death. For example, Saint Mary de la Cabeza is a patron of her native town because, after interceding for her help, the townspeople were saved from a devastating drought.

Rule of Life

Any person with any religious or philosophical beliefs can develop a rule of life—that is, a plan for living to ensure that those beliefs are lived out on a daily and monthly basis. Over the centuries, individual Catholics, particularly saints, have developed rules of life that they and others have found helpful in pursuing holiness. Each official rule has unique features, though all are based on fundamental Catholic ideals. For example, the Rule of Saint Benedict emphasizes the balance of Benedictines to both "pray and work", while Carmelites (members of a contemplative order) focus more on prayer and meditation. But all Catholic religious orders or organizations with a rule use that rule as a guide to help members strive for perfection in following Jesus Christ.

Sacristan

A sacristan is person who cares for the sacristy, the church, and all of its contents. Saint Andre Bessette, for example, served his community as sacristan, and many holy laymen, such as Saint Guy of Anderlecht, have served as sacristan for their parish church.

See

The Latin word *sedes* means "seat", and from earliest times, the bishop's seat or chair was a symbol of his authority. So a bishop's see is essentially the area over which he has jurisdiction, also called a diocese or archdiocese.

Simony

As described in Acts 8:9–24, a man named Simon lived in Samaria and enjoyed a considerable popular reputation as a magician. When Saints Peter and John came to the area to confirm converts to the faith, many Christians received the Holy Spirit. Apparently, their Confirmation experience was so visible and miraculous that Simon was impressed and offered to pay money so that he could receive the same gift too. Peter rebuked him for wanting to "buy" God's gifts, and Simon asked Peter to pray that God would forgive him.

In the history of the Church, people have tried to purchase all sorts of gifts that should be freely given, not bought and sold, which we might call a kick-back or bribe. One of these gifts is called material advantage, which involves physical property, money, and any other right that has a financial advantage. Another gift is called oral advantage. For example, an individual might pay a Church leader to speak publicly in his favor. The third gift is called homage, which involves paying for services that should be freely given.

This is more complicated than it might seem. On the surface, it's clear that no one should ever be deprived of the sacraments because he cannot pay, for example. But the faithful have an obligation to support their priests, out of charity and respect for the sacrifice that they make for us, and an excellent time to thank them would involve the celebration of sacraments such as marriage, Baptism, and Masses for our loved ones. This could be easily abused, on both sides.

Over the centuries, some of the greatest damage done to the Church has been the result of the buying and selling of ecclesiastical offices, rather than the selection of leaders based on fidelity to Christ's Church. When the position of priest, bishop, archbishop, cardinal, and even pope has been traded, negotiated, bought, and sold by secular or even leaders within the Church, the entire Church suffered. This problem was particularly widespread during the Middle Ages, when Church leadership was seen by some as a means of controlling politics, wealth, and personal power. Such leaders lived generally immoral lives, which scandalized the laity and resulted in lower standards for their own behavior. Regardless, the problem of men seeking Church leadership to advance political agendas rather than to emulate Jesus Christ, our humble and crucified Lord, will be with us until the Second Coming.

Solemnity

In the Church's liturgical calendar, a solemnity is a celebration of a belief, event, or person of the greatest importance and with universal significance to the Church. In the hierarchy of the Church, it is more important than a feast or a memorial. Christmas Day is, for example, a solemnity.

Third Orders or Tertiaries

When laymen are invited to join a religious order, they are referred to as Third Order members, tertiaries, or (more recently) Secular members. Third Order members usually don't live in community with other members of the order and usually do not wear religious garb. For example, Saint Catherine of Siena was a Third Order Dominican and lived at home, though she wore a modified habit that was common for tertiary members at the time.

Viaticum

The Latin word *viaticum* roughly means "food for the journey". When a person is in danger of death, a priest may give the person Viaticum (Holy Communion). This may also be accompanied by the Sacrament of the Anointing of the Sick, previously called the "last rites". Many of the saints in this collection received Viaticum and faced their deaths so peacefully that those in attendance remarked upon it. However, that's not a requirement for sanctity; Saint Ignatius of Loyola suddenly died in his sleep before he could receive Viaticum.

Appendix 5

Heresies or Theological Complexities

To our modern world, calling someone heretical sounds judgmental and intolerant. But there *is* objective truth, and to distort and falsify that truth and teach others to follow you is a truly evil thing. Therefore, the Church has tried both persuasion and outright condemnation in combatting heresies, particularly those that cause greater damage to individuals, families, and societies.

Albigensianism

See Catharism.

Arianism

Christian concepts that we take for granted now were considered controversial in the first few centuries of the Church's existence. In an attempt to rationalize away the distinction that Jesus is both the Son of God and the Son of Man—that is, both human and divine—the Catholic priest Arius (ca. 250–336) proposed a new teaching. He taught that Jesus Christ was the Son of Man, but was a second or inferior God, relative to God the Father. This distortion stripped away the mystery of the Incarnation, among other things, and it resulted in innumerable logical inconsistencies when compared to the clear teaching of Scripture itself. Though the Church opposed Arianism and condemned Arius' teachings, his heresy became widespread during his lifetime, particularly when emperors and even many bishops were captivated by it. It took decades—and many martyrs—for this heresy to be stamped out. Saint Athanasius of Alexandria was perhaps the most outspoken opponent of Arianism.

Catharism

A woman from Italy apparently brought the teachings of a neo-Manichaen sect (see Manichaeism) to the south of France in the eleventh century. Less a Christian heresy than a different religion with some Catholic trappings, it spread easily because of its simple principles, its appeal to those with wealth and leisure, and the scandalous example of some Christians who failed to live up to the demands of the Catholic faith. The Catharist movement and its many and varied branches boiled the universe down to two mutually opposed principles: one good and one evil. The spiritual world was believed to be good, but all matter was treated as evil. Therefore, being liberated from the captivity of a human body (through suicide or euthanasia) was a commendable goal. While many of the more devout Cathari lived penitential lives that appeared very similar to those of great Catholic ascetics, their motivation for fasting and penance was to tame their intrinsically evil bodies, rather than understanding the material world as a gift from God and part of our nature as human beings. Marriage and having children were also considered evil, although it was permitted for all but the "perfect". It took three centuries, many saints (Saint Dominic, for example), many Rosaries, and considerable effort (not always nonviolent) for the Church to rid herself of this evil, pernicious teaching, often spread by wealthy and high-placed leaders.

Eutychianism

See Monophysitism.

Gnosticism

The Greek word *gnostic* simply means "knowledge". From around the time of the birth of Christ until five centuries later, there were many Gnostic sects, each claiming to have their own special insights. The efforts of Saint Ephraem and Saint Irenaeus of Lyons helped expose the dangers of these heresies. The Gnostic sects borrowed from Jewish and Christian thought as it pleased them, but a distinguishing characteristic was their emphasis on their possession of superior (and often secret) knowledge of great mysteries. They generally glorified the spiritual world and disdained the physical world. This temptation to a desire for secret knowledge and a disdain for physical matter must be a great human temptation because similar heresies have come and gone for centuries to our own day—as we see in New Age groups and modern Christian cults.

Iconoclasm

The iconoclastic heresy was based on the false argument that Christians were committing sacrilege when they prayed and worshipped with images of Christ and the saints; it arose primarily in the Eastern Church during the eighth and ninth centuries. This heresy was fueled by political tensions between the East and the West, overzealous and undereducated Christian political leaders, and a growing Muslim presence in the region, since Muslims consider all representations of God as abominable. More than one Byzantine emperor in Constantinople ruthlessly persecuted and even executed all those who venerated images. Monks in particular were put to death, tortured, and banished. Catholic leaders, both in the East and the West but most notably Saint John of Damascus, tried to explain that venerating an image of our Lord or a saint as an expression of devotion was not an act of idolatry. This heresy caused great violence and destruction to Christians in the Byzantine Empire, and there were repeated separations between the Eastern churches and the Catholic Church in Rome as a result. Although this was not the ultimate cause of the schism between the Orthodox churches and the Catholic Church, arguments over iconoclasm fed the hostilities.

Jansenism

Cornelius Jansen, bishop of Ypres in France, died in 1638, leaving behind a manuscript he had written that contained the kernel of the teachings now known as Jansenism. His writing also contained the declaration that he was willing to accept the decision of the Church about the orthodoxy of these thoughts, and the Church later examined his teachings and condemned them. Unfortunately, too many people chose to follow Jansen's theology, rather than listen to the Church's condemnation. Jansen's teaching, which he based on Saint Augustine of Hippo's teaching about grace, took an extremely negative view about predestination. Catholics were discouraged from receiving Communion very often, for example, because of the false belief that God could already have predestined them to Hell, without them even being aware of it. Priests such as Saint Louis de Montfort and Saint Claude de la Colombiere preached strongly against this heresy. This depressing heretical belief became widespread, particularly in France, despite action from popes and the Church, until late in the eighteenth century.

Manichaeism

Not a Christian heresy but its own religion, Manichaeism was founded by a Persian in the third century. Claiming to be the true synthesis of all religions, it contained Buddhist ethics, Babylonian folklore, some Christian elements, and Zoroastrian Dualism, and it centered on two eternal principles of good and evil. But the key to the success of Manichaeism was probably its elaborate, mysterious, and seemingly mystical cosmogony. Mani (his title, not his name) claimed that his invented and complicated philosophical model described the origin, composition, and future of the entire universe. Using the age-old lure of "secret knowledge" that the follower can only understand as he spends more time (and money) to acquire, many people, including the young Saint Augustine of Hippo, were intrigued by this religion. Augustine eventually saw through Manichaeism's errors and, as a Christian, became an excellent voice against it. A flashy teaching that failed to lead its followers closer to God and the truth, it spread, declined, rose again (see Catharism), and finally died after about a thousand years.

Marcionism

Marcion was the son of a Catholic bishop and was born around the year 110 in Pontus (modern Turkey). He became a very wealthy ship owner and also a Catholic bishop. Believing that Christianity was defiled by its association with Judaism and wanting to eliminate the uncomfortable and "crude" Old Testament, he had to create a secondary deity to explain away the inconsistencies of his teachings. The idea of ignoring the theological complexity of Jewish teachings appealed to people for a time, but after Marcion's death, his followers led Marcionism into the direction of Gnosticism. This heresy lasted about three hundred years, longer in some places, before finally dying out.

Modernism

Pope Saint Pius X gathered together a number of dangerous and heretical teachings and tendencies that were threatening the Catholic faithful in the early twentieth century under the title of Modernism. This collection of ideas present in the Modern Age is hard to categorize because there were so many different threats. Three spirits found in these tendencies were (1) a spirit emphasizing movement and change, such as evolution, as an absolute good; (2) a spirit promoting emancipation of private conscience, of the State over the Church, of science over faith; and (3) a spirit promoting the authority of feelings and "peace" over religion and truth. Today's world is still widely infected with the heresies of Modernism.

Monarchianism

Also called Patripassianism, Sabellianism, and Modalism, this collection of heresies from the second and third centuries variously misunderstood the Trinity and Christ. It's hardly surprising that definitions of complex Christian doctrines took time for Christians to put into words; early teachings relied on pagan philosophical terms and ideas that sometimes obscured the truth rather than clarifying it. Monarchians exaggerated the oneness of the Father and the Son in such a way that they were referred to as one Person, making the three Persons of the Godhead into three modes instead. Sabellius taught that the Son was the Father and the Father was the Son. These heresies died out as the Church developed better terminology and a better understanding of God's revelation of the Holy Trinity.

Monophysitism

Having fought off the Nestorian heresy, a contrary heresy arose in the Church in the fifth century: Monophysitism, which was also called Eutychianism, after the man who started the controversy. Eutyches was an ascetic, more than seventy years old, and a leader of monks living in a monastery outside the walls of Constantinople. History indicates that he was generally a holy man but ignorant of the complexities involved. He was perhaps primarily trying to distance himself from the widespread errors of Nestorianism in his day when he taught and wrote that Jesus had two natures (human and divine) before the Incarnation but only one nature (divine) after he became a man. The controversy that arose over this teaching led to the "Robber Synod", a heretical synod of bishops that gathered together to exonerate Eutyches and condemn two faithful bishops, one of whom died of the injuries he sustained at the meeting. Although the battle to combat the heresy of Monophysitism unfortunately cost many lives and took a few centuries, in the end the Church was left with a more robust theological explanation of Christ's nature.

Monothelitism

The Monothelite heresy of the seventh century proposed that Christ had only a divine will, not a free and human will. This proposition, condemned by the Church, was suggested as a bridge to reconcile followers of Monophysitism to the Church. After a complicated and lengthy political battle, Monothelitism died in the early eighth century when the last heretical leader acknowledged his error.

Montanism

Montanus lived in the second century. Sometime after he converted to the Catholic faith, he claimed that the Spirit descended on him and his two female companions, Maximilla and Priscilla, and that all three experienced ecstasies, visions, and prophecies. Some of his prophetic utterances simply contained Christian beliefs, but those beliefs were taken to an extreme, and the manner in which they prophesied seemed closer to diabolical possession than Christian prayer. Within a decade, many Church leaders had taken severe steps against Montanus and his somewhat bizarre teachings. After the death of Montanus and his companions, Montanism endured for a time in its followers. Although it didn't have a specific doctrine, its most influential follower, Tertullian, took its more rigorous teachings to their natural conclusions: stating that all second marriages were wrong, that martyrdom is so good that one is forbidden to flee from it, and that some sins are unforgivable, for example. There are signs that remnants of Montanism, with its bizarre ecstasies and rigid conservatism, endured into the fourth century.

Nestorianism

Nestorius (d. 451) was a priest and monk with a reputation for eloquence when he was chosen by the emperor Theodosius II to be the patriarch of Constantinople. Though he swiftly acted against Arian and Novatian heretics and generally made a good impression with Christian leaders and the faithful at first, he soon began preaching that the Blessed Virgin should not be called the Mother of God, along with other heretical doctrines about Jesus' Incarnation. Attacked in homilies and writings by his own clergy and Saint Cyril of Alexandria in particular, Nestorius eventually retired with dignity to a monastery (but apparently without repentance for his heresy and its effects on the Church). A heretical sect following his teachings endured for several centuries in Persia.

Novatianism

Novatian was a Roman priest and a well-educated man who lived during the third century, when the Church was still officially illegal. He believed there were unpardonable sins—giving up the faith during threat of persecution, for example—and he declared himself a bishop and then a pope (though there happened to be a true pope at the time), creating a schism in the Church. Perhaps because some of Novatian's teachings were orthodox, some Christians were willing to accept the severe, merciless God that he preached. His sect became widespread, with followers throughout the empire, at least until the late sixth century, when we still find writings by Christian leaders against Novatian teachings.

Pelagianism

Though there are many things we don't know about Pelagius, we do know that he was a monk, that he lived in the late fourth and early fifth centuries, and that he lived for a long time in Rome. His writings about the role of the human will caused a firestorm of controversy, and although he wrote as a Christian, many of his ideas seem more rooted in Stoicism than in Christianity. Specifically, he denied the doctrine of Original Sin and said that the universality of sin was merely a result of Adam's bad example. He also taught that the attainment of virtue and perfection by a Christian could be accomplished through strength of personal will and a life of asceticism, not by God's grace. Our redemption was wrought in Christ, by his interpretation, merely through good teaching and good example. Pelagius' teachings ignited a great controversy among Christian theologians in the early fifth century; Saint Augustine of Hippo's heated defense of the role of grace, in opposition to Pelagius' emphasis on human will, was not only strongly influential at the time but also the reason Augustine is still referred to by the Church as the Doctor of Grace. After the Council of Ephesus (431) condemned Pelagius' teaching, it effectively died out among leaders in the Church, but some of its teachings rose again in different times and places over the centuries. See also Semi-Pelagianism.

Protestantism

In the early sixteenth century, Martin Luther, a monk from Germany, and Ulrich Zwingli, a pastor from Switzerland, "protested" against certain practices of the Catholic Church. Some of their propositions were later accepted by the Church as legitimate reforms to heal the Body of Christ. Three of their fundamental principles—*sola scriptura, sola fide,* and the priesthood of all believers— were not. This body of thought espoused by the Protestant leaders insisted (1) that the "Bible alone" (*sola scriptura*), not the teaching authority of the Church's Magisterium, was sufficient for every Christian believer to understand his faith; (2) that faith alone (*sola fide*)—not faith and good works—was sufficient to justify the believer in the sight of God; and (3) that all believers shared in a universal priesthood, making the ordained priesthood unnecessary. It is incontrovertible that these theological propositions were manipulated by secular leaders to promote national interests, pitting one Christian nation against another, leading to scandalous religious wars and making many martyrs. The Church called the Council of Trent to respond to the valid complaints that were raised by Protestantism and encourage Catholics to live and understand their faith better. Protestantism is with us still, splintering into more and more factions all the time, in part because of the reliance of their doctrines on the supremacy of individual freedom.

Sabellianism

See Monarchianism.

Semi-Pelagianism

Sometime after the Church condemned the teachings of Pelagius, monks of southern Gaul proposed a compromise between the extreme teachings of Pelagius and the bishop of Hippo, Saint Augustine of Hippo. They argued that Christian grace is indeed necessary for one to know and do what is good (with Augustine and against Pelagius), but they also said that perfect sinlessness is impossible during life on earth, even for those who have been justified by Christ (with Pelagius and against Augustine). Augustine replied by introducing the concept of the predestination of the elect into the discussion. The topics of predestination and grace created a debate about the balance between the roles of the human will and God's grace that lasted for at least another century, when the disagreement finally died out explicitly in the Roman Church. But finding the right balance in words to describe the relationship between man's free will and God's grace has been a difficult task for many Christian thinkers. Claims that certain teachings smack of Semi-Pelagianism have arisen many times over the centuries in discussions among Christians.

Appendix 6

Times of Anti-Catholic Persecution

It's too easy for us to read blithely over the statement that, say, a group of saints died during the reign of the Roman emperor Diocletian, as if being fed to the lions was as commonplace for them as going to the mall is for us. When we take the time to think about the time and place in which they lived, we will have greater respect for their sacrifices and be more inspired to emulate their example.

Many of the saints listed in this book did not die as martyrs. But once you begin to study the saints, the example of the martyrs—and the recurrent widespread violence against Catholics at different times in history—is striking. The following table lists only some of the largest and most dangerous occurrences of persecution, and some of the periods involved violence against Catholic peoples or nations, not the Catholic Church as an institution. Nevertheless, such persecutions occurred precisely because Catholics refused to capitulate over their Catholic beliefs and way of life. All dates listed are approximate.

Century	Location	Cause of Persecution
1st	Holy Land	The early Jewish rejection of Christianity led to Jewish persecution of the Church. Saint James the Greater was executed for this reason.
1st–3rd	Roman Empire	Nero's imperial edict against Christianity in the year 64—intermittently ignored but always on the books until the time of the Roman emperor Constantine in the year 313—declared all Christians to be traitors to the state and subject to execution. Saints Peter and Paul, along with all the early Church martyrs, died because of this persecution.
4th	Roman Empire	Various Roman emperors persecuted Christians during this century after the death of Emperor Constantine. Emperor Julian the Apostate explicitly rejected Christianity; other Roman emperors demanded adherence to various Christian heresies (such as Arianism), leading to death and persecution for those who remained faithful to the Catholic Church. Saint Bibiana was executed for this reason.
5th	Europe	When Barbarian tribes (Goths, Huns) invaded Europe, they killed Catholics from many nations, before they settled down in Europe and eventually became Christians themselves. See Saint Herculanus.

(continued)

Century	Location	Cause of Persecution
8th–15th	Spain	During the Muslim conquest of Spain, which was intended to be an invasion of all of Europe, Christians were persecuted and often killed for their refusal to convert to Islam. See Saint Leocritia of Cordoba.
8th–9th	East	The iconoclast heresy, generally promulgated by Byzantine emperors, resulted in the death and persecution of many faithful Catholics. Saint John of Damascus avoided death from this persecution, for example, only by avoiding entering lands controlled by the Byzantine emperor.
9th	Europe	The pagan Vikings invaded Europe in order to conquer Catholic nations, which resulted in the death of many Christians who attempted to defend themselves and their land. See Saint Gohardus of Nantes for an example.
11th–13th	Holy Land	When Muslim forces invaded the Holy Land and prevented Catholics from safely coming on pilgrimage to the holy sites, Christians of Europe raised armies in multiple Crusades to regain the access of Christian pilgrims to those sites. Saint Bernard of Clairvaux preached to encourage men to protect the faith by joining a Crusade; King Saint Louis IX of France personally joined two Crusades.
15th–19th	Japan	When the Japanese government cut the nation off from almost all contact with the outside (particularly Western) world, it also began persecuting and executing Catholic missionaries, as well as Japanese converts to Catholicism. Saint Paul Miki, for example, was the first native Japanese martyr.
16th–17th	Europe	With the eruption of Protestantism, multiple Wars of Religion between Christian nations led to death and persecution for many faithful Christians, including Catholics. The Martyrs of Gorkum, for example, died from anti-Catholic violence.
16th–19th	England and Ireland	Faithful Catholics in England and Ireland suffered centuries of persecution and death for their refusal to convert to the official English (Anglican) church. Saint Oliver Plunket was among them.
17th–19th	Vietnam	Vietnamese leaders concluded that Christianity was incompatible with prevalent Confucian beliefs, particularly ancestor worship, and periodically persecuted and executed Catholic missionaries and Vietnamese converts to the faith. Saint Andrew Dung Lac was a native Vietnamese martyr, for example.
18th	France	The French Revolution was, at its heart, not just an attack on the established monarchy, but also an attack on the Catholic Church. See the Martyrs of September for a particularly brutal example.
18th–21st	China	Persecution of Westerners in general and Christians in particular has erupted many times and led to death for both Catholic missionaries (such as Saint Jean Gabriel Taurin Dufresse) and Chinese converts to the faith (such as Saint Augustine Zhao Rong). Though the persecution abated under some regimes, persecution of Christians in China continues under the Communist government today.

Century	Location	Cause of Persecution
19th	Korea	Anti–Christian Korean authorities persecuted and executed both Western missionaries and their native converts to the Catholic faith. For example, Saint Andrew Kim Tae-gon was a Korean convert to the faith who was martyred.
19th	Uganda	Northern Africa had been evangelized for centuries before the Good News reached sub-Saharan Africa. When both Catholic and Protestant missionaries brought the Gospel throughout the African continent, some African tribal leaders resented the intrusion of Christianity on their native (animist) beliefs. Saint Charles Lwanga, for example, was one of many native Africans martyred during anti-Christian persecution.
20th	Mexico	During decades of violent armed conflict during the Mexican Revolution and its aftermath, Catholic institutions were attacked and outlawed, and faithful Catholic clergy, such as Blessed Miguel Pro, as well as laity were killed.
20th	Spain	During the Spanish Civil War, leftist and rightist factions struggled for control of the country; both sides committed atrocities, and faithful Catholics and Catholic institutions, among others, were persecuted and killed. See Blessed José Aparicio Sanz, for example.
20th	Russia and other Slavic countries	Communism explicitly rejects God and religion; when Communists took control of Russia, they did their best to persecute, destroy, and control all people of faith, including Catholics. See Blessed Aloysius Stepanic.
20th	Global	The racist and pagan beliefs of Nazism were opposed by the Church even before the advent of World War II. Millions of Jews died at the hands of the Nazis in camps, but so did many Catholic priests (see Blessed Joseph Kowalski) and others who opposed them (see Blessed Mary Restituta Kafka).

ACKNOWLEDGMENTS

The Bible tells us seventy-one times to, "Give thanks!"

I wish to thank the editors and staff of Ignatius Press for all their patience and professionalism in bringing this book to completion.

I also wish to thank the many publishers who have generously allowed me to use excerpts from their books so that everyone can become better acquainted with the saints in this book: Harper Collins, Baronius Press, Bloomsbury Publishing, Catholic Book Publishing, Catholic University of America Press, Cistercian Publications, Franciscan Institute Publications, Hachette Book Group, Hackett Publishing, ICS Publications, Libreria Editrice Vaticana, Marian Press, New City Press, Our Sunday Visitor Publishing, Paulist Press, Penguin Books, Penguin Random House, Princeton University Press, St. Vladimir's Seminary Press, TAN Books, as well as CatholicSaints.info and NewAdvent.org.

Most particularly, I wish to thank my family, friends, parish, and diocesan community for their support, and I want to thank my children for encouraging me to believe that this collection could help other Christians grow daily in their love of the Lord.

* * * * *

Permissions granted for excerpts from the following titles:

Ambrose of Milan. *Saint Ambrose: Theological and Dogmatic Works*. Translated by Roy J. Deferrari. Fathers of the Church Series. Vol. 44. Washington, D.C.: Catholic University of America Press, 1963. Republished with permission of Catholic University of America Press. Permission conveyed through Copyright Clearance Center, Inc.

Augustine. *Sermon* 199. In *Essential Sermons*. Hyde Park, N.Y.: New City Press, 2007. Used by permission.

Benedict. *The Rule of Saint Benedict*. Translated by Anthony C. Meisel and M. L. del Mastro. New York: Image Books, Doubleday, 1975. Used by permission of Doubleday, an imprint of the Knopf Doubleday Publishing Group, a division of Penguin Random House LLC. All rights reserved.

Bernard of Clairvaux. *On the Song of Songs*. Translated by Irene Edmonds. Vol. 4. Kalamazoo: Cistercian Publications, 1980. Copyright © 2008 by Order of Saint Benedict (Collegeville, Minn.). Used with permission.

Bunson, Matthew, and Margaret Bunson. *Our Sunday Visitor's Encyclopedia of Saints*. 2nd ed. Huntington, Ind.: Our Sunday Visitor Publishing, 2014. www .osv.com. Used by permission. No other use of this material is authorized.

Chrysologus, Peter. *Selected Sermons*. Fathers of the Church Series. Vol. 109. Translated by William B. Palardy. Washington, D.C.: Catholic University of America Press, 2004. Republished with permission of Catholic University of America Press. Permission conveyed through Copyright Clearance Center, Inc.

Chrysostom, Saint John. *On Marriage and Family Life*. Translated by Catherine P. Roth and David Anderson. Popular Patristics Series. Crestwood, N.Y.: St. Vladimir's Seminary Press, 1986. Used by permission.

Damian, Peter. *Letters*. Fathers of the Church Series. Vol. 2. Translated by Owen Blum, O.F.M. Washington, D.C.: Catholic University of America Press, 1990. Republished with permission of Catholic University of America Press. Permission conveyed through Copyright Clearance Center, Inc.

Elizabeth of the Trinity. *The Complete Works*. Vol. 1. Translated by Sister Aletheia Kane, O.C.D.: Washington, D.C.: ICS Publications, 1984. www.ics publications.org. Used by permission.

Gregory the Great. *Dialogues*. Translated by Odo John Zimmerman, O.S.B. Fathers of the Church Series. Vol. 39. Washington, D.C.: Catholic University of America Press, 1959. Republished with permission of Catholic University of America Press. Permission conveyed through Copyright Clearance Center, Inc.

Gregory of Nazianzus. *On God and Man: The Theological Poetry of St. Gregory of Nazianzus*. Translated by Peter Gilbert. Crestwood, N.Y.: St. Vladimir's Seminary Press, 2001. Used by permission.

Hilary of Poitiers. *The Trinity*. Translated by Stephen McKenna, C.Ss.R. Fathers of the Church Series. Vol. 25. Washington, D.C.: Catholic University of America Press, 1954. Republished with permission of Catholic University of America Press. Permission conveyed through Copyright Clearance Center, Inc.

John of the Cross. *The Collected Works of Saint John of the Cross*. Translated by Kieran Kavanaugh, O.C.D., and Otilio Rodriguez, O.C.D. Washington, D.C.: ICS Publications, 1964, 1979, 1991. www.icspublications.org.

John of Damascus. *Three Treatises on the Divine Images*. Translated by Andrew Louth. Popular Patristic Series. Crestwood, N.Y.: St. Vladimir's Seminary Press, 2003. Used by permission.

Leo the Great. *Sermons*. Translated by Jane Patricia Freeland, C.S.J.B., and Agnes Josephine Conway, S.S.J. Fathers of the Church Series. Vol. 93. Washington,

D.C.: Catholic University of America Press, 1996. Republished with permission of Catholic University of America Press. Permission conveyed through Copyright Clearance Center, Inc.

The Liturgy of the Hours. The English translation of nonbiblical readings, copyright © 1973, 1974, 1975 by International Commission on English in the Liturgy Corporation. All rights reserved.

Patrick. *The Confession of Saint Patrick: The Classic Text in New Translation*. Translated by John Skinner. New York: Image Books, Doubleday, 1998. Used by permission of Image Books, an imprint of Random House, a division of Penguin Random House LLC. All rights reserved.

Teresa of Avila. *Teresa of Avila: The Book of Her Life*. Translated by Kieran Kavanaugh, O.C.D., and Otilio Rodriguez, O.C.D. Washington, D.C.: ICS Publications, 1995. www.icspublications.org. Reprinted in 2008 by Hackett Publishing Company (Indianapolis, Cambridge).

Thérèse of Lisieux. *The Autobiography of Saint Thérèse of Lisieux: The Story of a Soul*. Translated by John Beevers. Translation copyright © 1957 by Doubleday (New York), a division of Random House. Copyright renewed © 1985 by Mrs. John Beevers. Used by permission of Image Books (New York), an imprint of Random House, a division of Penguin Random House LLC. All rights reserved.

Walsh, Michael J. *Butler's Lives of the Saints: Concise Edition*. Copyright © 1956, 1985 by Burnes and Oates (Tunbridge Wells, Kent). Reprinted by permission of HarperCollins Publishers (San Francisco).

Walsh, Michael J. *Butler's Lives of the Saints: Concise Edition, Revised and Updated*. San Francisco: HarperCollins Publishers, 1991. Copyright © 1956 by Burns and Oates. Used by kind permission of Bloomsbury Publishing Plc.

SELECT BIBLIOGRAPHY

The saints are wonderful friends, and, hopefully, this collection of the saints will inspire you to want to know more about them. The following resources were most useful in developing this collection. The resources with an asterisk (*) are highly recommended.

Books

Benedict XVI, Pope. *Doctors of the Church.* Huntington, Ind.: Our Sunday Visitor Publishing Division, 2011. [A collection of catecheses about thirty-two Doctors of the Church, given by Pope Benedict XVI during weekday general audiences.]

Bentley, James. *A Calendar of Saints.* London: Time Warner Books, 2005. [A beautiful collection of saints with biographies and artwork.]

Cruz, Joan Carroll. *Saintly Women of Modern Times.* Huntington, Ind.: Our Sunday Visitor Publishing Division, 2004. [Short but detailed biographies of lesser-known women saints from the modern day.]

Daily Roman Missal: According to the Roman Missal, Third Edition. 7th ed. Edited by Rev. James Socias. Downers Grove, Ill.: Midwest Theological Forum, 2011. [This book includes Sunday and weekday Mass readings, including Mass readings and prayers for the saints.]

Klein, Peter, ed. *The Catholic Source Book.* 4th. ed. Huntington, Ind.: Our Sunday Visitor, 2008. [This book contains helpful definitions and information about general Catholic terms.]

Martyrologium Romanum, Editio Altera. Libreria Editrice Vaticana, 2004. [Note that this book is currently available only in Latin.]

Rengers, Christopher, O.F.M. Cap., and Matthew E. Bunson, K.H.S. *The 35 Doctors of the Church.* Rev. ed. Charlotte, N.C.: Tan Books, 2014. [Contains detailed biographies of all the thirty-five Doctors of the Church declared at the time of its publication.]

Walsh, Michael, ed. *Butler's Lives of the Saints, Concise Edition Revised and Updated.* San Francisco: HarperCollins Publishers, 1991.* [An excellent collection of saints, one for every day of the year.]

Websites

CatholicSaints.Info.* [Excellent site that contains brief biographies of many saints, a detailed calendar of saints, and other information.]

CauseSanti.va. [Contains information about holy men and women who have recently been named saints and blesseds. Note that the text of this site is in Italian.]

NewAdvent.org. [Contains many saints' biographies from the *Catholic Encyclopedia* (originally published in 1917).]

Us.Magnificat.net. [*Magnificat* magazine contains daily Mass readings, daily prayers, saints' biographies, and gorgeous artwork; a subscription is required.]

Vatican.va. [Vatican-issued biographies of those who have recently been canonized and beatified.]

Wikipedia.com. [While there is valid and widespread concern about the accuracy and impartiality of Wikipedia, with some cautious interpretation, basic information about many, many saints can be found at that site.]

Zenit.org. [Contains news articles about canonizations and beatifications by the Vatican, and other recent information about saints.]

NAME INDEX

Cagnoald, Saint, 334
Caius, Saint, 167
Cajetan the Theatine, Saint, 298
Calafato, Saint Eustochia (Smeralda), 60
Calasanz (Calasanctius), Saint Joseph, 319
Callistus I (Calixtus), Saint, 381
Callo, Blessed Marcel, 131
Calungsod, Saint Pedro (Peter), 146
Campion, Saint Edmund, 441
Canefro, Blessed Hugh, of Genoa, 375
Canh, Saint Joseph Hoang Luong, 333
Cantalupe, Saint Thomas, 320
Cantianella of Rome, Saint, 215
Cantianus of Rome, Saint, 215
Cantius of Rome, Saint, 215
Camillus de Lellis, Saint, 265, 269
Canisius, Saint Peter, 467
Capitainio, Saint Bartholomea, 281
Caracciolo, Saint Francis, 219
Caradoc of Wales, Saint, 158
Caravario, Blessed Callisto, 103
Carvalho, Blessed Diego (Didacus), 101
Casilda of Toledo, Saint, 155
Casimir of Poland, Saint, 112
Cassian, Saint John, 277
Cassian of Imola, Saint, 305
Cassian of Tangiers, Saint, 445
Cassius of Clermont, Saint, 195
Castorius of Sirmium, Saint, 410
Catanoso, Saint Gaetano, 149
Catherine of Alexandria, Saint, 434
Catherine of Bologna, Saint, 119
Catherine Fieschi of Genoa, Saint, 346
Catherine of Siena, Saint, 174
Catherine of Sweden, Saint, 136
Cecilia (Cecily) of Rome, Saint, 430
Cedd of Lastingham, Saint, 397
Celestine I, Saint, 283
Celestine V (Pietro), Saint, 200
Celsus of Milan, Saint, 284
Cerioli, Saint Paula Elizabeth (Constanza), 471
Chad (Ceadda) of Mercia, Saint, 109
Chaeremon of Nilopolis, Saint, and Companions, 469
Chair of Saint Peter, 100
Chaminade, Blessed William (Joseph), 62
Chanel, Saint Peter Mary, 172
Chapdelaine, Saint Auguste, 107
Charles the Good, Blessed, 109
Chmielowski, Saint Albert (Adam), 472
Christina the Astonishing, Saint, 279
Christina of Bolsena, Saint, 278
Christopher, Saint, 280
Chrodegang of Metz, Saint, 114

Chromatius of Aquileia, Saint, 443
Chrysanthus of Rome, Saint, 396
Chrysogonus of Aquiliea, Saint, 433
Chrysologus, Saint Peter, 287
Chrysostom, Saint John, 342
Cini, Blessed John, 418
Clare of Assisi, Saint, 303
Clare of Montefalco, Saint, 310
Claret, Saint Anthony Mary, 395
Claudius of Sirmium, Saint, 410
Claver, Saint Peter, 338
Clement of Okhrida, Saint, and Companions, 283
Clement I, Saint, 431
Cleophas, Saint, 358
Climacus, Saint John, 141
Clitherow, Saint Margaret, 137
Clodoald (Cloud) of France, Saint, 335
Clotilda of France, Saint, 218
Colette Boylet of Corbie, Saint, 115
Colman of Stockerau, Saint, 268
Columba of Cordoba, Saint, 349
Columba of Iona, Saint, 224
Columba of Sens, Saint, 479
Columban of Ireland, Saint, 432
Cono the Gardener, Saint, 112
Conrad of Piacenza, Blessed, 97
Cope, Saint Marianne, 64
Corbinian, Saint, 336
Cordero, Saint Michael Febres, 85
Cornelius, Saint, 346
Cornelius the Centurion, Saint, 390
Corsini, Saint Andrew, 44
Cosmas, Saint, 359
Couderc, Saint Teresa (Maria Victoria), 359
Crispin of Rome, Saint, 396
Crispina of Thagara, 447
Crispinian of Rome, Saint, 396
Crispino of Viterbo, Saint, 200
Cuauhtlatoatzin, Saint Juan Diego, 453
Cunegund, Saint, 110
Cuthbert of Lindisfarne, Saint, 131
Cyprian of Carthage, Saint, 346
Cyricus, Saint, 233
Cyriacus, Saint, and Companions, 300
Cyriacus of Attalia, Saint, 180
Cyril of Alexandria, Saint, 245
Cyril of Jerusalem, Saint, 129
Cyril, Saint, Apostle of the Slavs, 90

Da, Saint Peter (Phero), 234
da Costa, Blessed Alexandrina Maria, 380
Dalby, Blessed Robert, 128
d'Alleman, Blessed John-Marie du Lau, and Companions, 330